THE PAPERS OF

THOMAS JEFFERSON

BARBARA B. OBERG
GENERAL EDITOR

THE PAPERS OF
Thomas Jefferson

Volume 33
17 February to 30 April 1801

BARBARA B. OBERG, EDITOR

JAMES P. McCLURE AND ELAINE WEBER PASCU,

SENIOR ASSOCIATE EDITORS

MARTHA J. KING, ASSOCIATE EDITOR

TOM DOWNEY AND AMY SPECKART,

ASSISTANT EDITORS

LINDA MONACO, EDITORIAL ASSISTANT

JOHN E. LITTLE, RESEARCH ASSOCIATE

PRINCETON AND OXFORD

PRINCETON UNIVERSITY PRESS

2006

As INDICATED in the first volume, this edition was made possible by a grant of $200,000 from The New York Times Company to Princeton University. Since this initial subvention, its continuance has been assured by additional contributions from The New York Times Company Foundation; by grants of the Ford Foundation, the National Historical Publications and Records Commission, and the National Endowment for the Humanities; by grants of the Andrew W. Mellon Foundation, the Packard Humanities Institute, the Pew Charitable Trusts, the John Ben Snow Memorial Trust, and the L. J. Skaggs and Mary C. Skaggs Foundation to Founding Fathers Papers, Inc.; by benefactions from the Barkley Fund and the Lyn and Norman Lear Foundation through the National Trust for the Humanities, the Florence Gould Foundation, the Charlotte Palmer Phillips Foundation, Time Inc., the Dyson Foundation, and the Lucius N. Littauer Foundation; and by gifts and support from Sara and James Adler, Ruth and Sidney Lapidus, Sara Lee and Axel Schupf, Diane and John Cooke, Robert C. Baron, James Russell Wiggins, David K. E. Bruce, and B. Batmanghelidj. In common with other editions of historical documents, THE PAPERS OF THOMAS JEFFERSON is a beneficiary of the good offices of the National Historical Publications and Records Commission, tendered in many forms through its dedicated staff. We offer our gratitude to William G. Bowen, Robert F. Goheen, Drew R. McCoy, Merrill D. Peterson, and Harold T. Shapiro, who now become honorary members of our Advisory Committee.

FOREWORD

U NDER normal circumstances, Thomas Jefferson would have had more than two months—from December 1800, when the results of the states' electoral ballots became evident, until inauguration day on 4 March 1801—to prepare for the commencement of his presidential administration. But the election of 1800 could not be resolved by the usual means, and for much of the winter Jefferson did not know if he, Aaron Burr, or someone else would be the third president of the United States. It was only on 17 February 1801, when the House of Representatives finally settled the tied electoral vote, that he could really begin to prepare, and with only two weeks until the inauguration, he could not immediately collect his cabinet. Levi Lincoln, the Massachusetts congressman he selected as attorney general and who played an important role assisting him over the next few weeks, was in Washington. So was Albert Gallatin, his intended secretary of the Treasury, but Jefferson waited until the Senate recessed before appointing him. Henry Dearborn was at his home in Maine when Jefferson wrote him on 18 February asking him to be secretary of war. James Madison, the obvious and expected choice as secretary of state, was in Virginia recovering from an illness and tending to affairs of his ailing father, who died late in February. In order to provide sea letters for American ships, Jefferson quietly asked John Marshall—who in the closing days of John Adams's administration was both the new chief justice of the Supreme Court and the acting secretary of state—to remain in the latter capacity through the inauguration. Then on 5 March, the day the Senate confirmed Lincoln as attorney general, Jefferson also made him the acting head of the State Department. The navy clearly required careful attention, given the restructuring of that service that was called for by the recently passed Peace Establishment Act, the still somewhat uncertain relationship with France at sea, and an unsettled situation in the Mediterranean, where Tripoli threatened war on the United States. Jefferson, however, had been unable to convince Robert R. Livingston to take on the superintendence of the Navy Department. Benjamin Stoddert, the secretary of the navy under Adams, agreed to remain in that position until the end of March, when Jefferson authorized Dearborn to be acting secretary of the navy and persuaded Samuel Smith of Baltimore to manage the department on an interim basis. Jefferson also retained, for the moment, Joseph Habersham as postmaster general and Samuel Dexter as secretary of the Treasury, but did not involve them or Stoddert in cabinet discussions.

On 28 February he bade farewell to the Senate, over which he had presided for four years as vice president. He had "no doubt" that he had made mistakes, yet "for honest errors however indulgence may be hoped." He had no time to confer with Madison, or any of his other close political confidants in Virginia, about his inaugural address. We can reconstruct the sequence of the surviving stages of the text, but apparently he left no evidence of when he wrote the address or how long the process took him (there is no indication that he began before 17 February). The earliest extant draft, a later stage of the composition, and the version published in Samuel Harrison Smith's *National Intelligencer* on inauguration day are all printed in this volume. As he penned the address to his "fellow citizens," he had Samuel Adams in mind, as he later informed that elder statesman of the revolutionary cause. On Wednesday, 4 March, Jefferson made his famous walk from his boarding house to the Senate Chamber—the completed portion of the Capitol—to read his speech before a packed audience and, at midday, take the oath of office. He felt, as he wrote to Joseph Priestley, that the country had survived a time of "barbarians." The new president's allies and opponents alike examined the inaugural address as a declaration of his principles and intentions.

In the address he invoked the policy of "peace, commerce & honest friendship with all nations, entangling alliances with none." He had already taken steps to shape his foreign policy, writing to Livingston on 24 February to ask the New Yorker to be minister plenipotentiary to France, where there had been no resident U.S. minister since George Washington's recall of James Monroe. In the fall of 1800, representatives of the two republics had signed a convention that would allow a return to normal commercial and diplomatic relations. The Senate consented to the pact, with modifications, in February. Jefferson almost certainly wrote the instructions that went to Oliver Ellsworth and William Vans Murray over Lincoln's signature as acting secretary of state on 18 March, asking them to return to Paris to negotiate the final ratification. That letter looked forward to a time when "we shall be free from compact with every nation." Jefferson also revitalized his personal ties with Europe. When Congressman John Dawson of Virginia boarded the sloop *Maryland* in March to convey the convention to Paris, he carried several letters from Jefferson to old friends in France, some of whom had not received any word directly from him for several years. He also entrusted Dawson to speak confidentially to comrades in France—among them Lafayette, Paine, and Kosciuszko—to bring them up to date about affairs in America. That news, Jefferson assured the Comte de Volney, "will astonish you." Jefferson did nothing, for the moment, about Rufus King, the staunchly Federalist U.S. minister in London, but he asked Charles Pinckney to succeed David Humphreys, who had been minister to Spain since 1796. On 12 March, Pinckney, who was in Washington, agreed, and five days later Lincoln sent Humphreys a letter of recall written by Jefferson.

Many people who saw the new president's speech in newspapers were anxious to discover what the call for unity—his condemnation of "political intolerance" and his assertion that "we are all republicans: we are all federalists"—would mean for Federalists holding appointive positions in the government. He privately avowed that the great majority of Federalists had acceded to his election and that they had found repugnant the actions of a small cadre of their party's leaders, who would never reach accommodation with Jefferson and had attempted to exploit the deadlock in the House of Representatives. The new president's intention, as he wrote to William Short on 17 March and to French diplomat Philippe de Létombe on the 19th, was "to reunite the nation in harmony and in interest," "to re-harmonize my countrymen, without abandoning republican principles." But he had to contend with the political legacy of the "desperados"— the "incurables," as he called his most intransigent opponents. The challenge of coming together "with one heart & one mind" (as he phrased it in his address) had been made more formidable by the Judiciary Act approved on 13 February, under which Adams had appointed several new federal judges, and by other appointments made as Adams's administration and the Sixth Congress had both drawn to a close. Jefferson characterized as "midnight" appointments any nominations made after 12 December 1800, the date on which it became clear in Washington that Adams had lost the election. He began—tentatively, as he informed Giles on 23 March—to sort out criteria for retentions and replacements. Faced with a flood of job requests, recommendations, and advice concerning dozens of prospective nominees, he began organizing the information himself, creating and maintaining tables and lists to help him keep track of positions, incumbents who might be removed for cause or whose terms would expire, prospective appointees, and the people who recommended them (see the compilation of his data in Appendix I). As he informed Horatio Gates on 8 March, "geographical equilibrium" was a factor. Also, to avoid the appearance of cronyism, he was reluctant to appoint anyone who was too closely tied to him by blood or association, and he was leery of nominating Virginians. It could seem as if every letter-writer, after offering congratulations, went on to mention his own availability, need, and preferences for employment or recommended a friend or relative for some job. Even Rembrandt Peale, writing in regard to a copy of his oil portrait of Jefferson, took care to note that an undemanding foreign posting would provide the means for him to study the art of Europe. Catherine Church remarked that only women, excluded as they were from political favor or government employment, could be free of "ignorant affectation" and address the president honestly. She could therefore write to Jefferson "in the language of the heart that will at least have the merit of sincerity." The political privilege of women, Elizabeth House Trist echoed, was "that of freely communicating our sentiments."

Monroe and Giles cautioned him against allowing a desire for harmony with the other party to go too far. The Republicans' enemies were not dead, Giles warned: "They only sleep." Giles and Monroe also reminded him that political loyalty needed reinforcement in the form of government jobs. For a state like Pennsylvania, where Governor Thomas McKean had already established a system of partisan patronage, the process would be different from what was required for places such as New England or South Carolina, where the judicious distribution of federal positions could help to consolidate the Republican party. On 5 March Jefferson sent the nominations of Madison, Lincoln, Dearborn, and Livingston to the Senate, which approved them before adjourning until the Seventh Congress convened in December. The appointments that Jefferson made after 5 March—including Gallatin's, in May, as secretary of the Treasury—were all recess appointments, many of which went before the Senate in January 1802, when its control by Republicans was assured.

With Congress out of session, public business requiring the attention of the executive was limited. The senators from Tennessee and a senator and a congressman from Georgia wrote to Jefferson at an early opportunity to urge new negotiations with Indian tribes over lands and roads. Gallatin, although not yet secretary of the Treasury, penned on 14 March "some rough sketches relative to our financial situation," projecting the means by which a curtailment of expenditures might allow for an abolishment of internal taxes. Jefferson met with Gallatin, Lincoln, and Dearborn on 8 March, but the leading topic on that occasion was appointments. Some requests for pardons did require the president's early attention. On 12 March he gave clemency to Massachusetts political protester David Brown, who lacked the means to pay his fine and obtain release from jail, and on the 16th Jefferson pardoned the gadfly journalist James Thomson Callender. Both Brown and Callender had been convicted under the

Sedition Act, which expired on 3 March, but Jefferson also dealt with less politically charged cases of clemency.

John and Abigail Adams left Washington before daylight on Jefferson's inaugural morning. On 8 March Jefferson forwarded some private papers that had come for Adams, covering the packet with a brief note, and on the 24th Adams replied, reporting "a State of perfect Tranquility" in Massachusetts. The former president wished his successor "a quiet and prosperous Administration." They would not correspond again for almost eleven years. It was not until about two weeks after the inauguration that the new president changed his residence from Conrad & McMunn's hotel on Capitol Hill to the President's House on Pennsylvania Avenue. He had begun well before that, however, to plan the presidential household, expecting "as great difficulty" in assembling the staff for the residence, as he told Létombe on 22 February, as he would "probably find in composing an administration for the government." He required both a good chef and a proper steward, or maître d'hôtel, to run the household. He enlisted the help of failed speculator Robert Morris and foreign diplomats in Philadelphia, Létombe of France and Carlos Martínez de Irujo of Spain, who understood the requirements of a fine official household on the European model. This process located in Philadelphia two skilled Frenchmen, Honoré Julien and Joseph Rapin, who became the chef and steward, respectively, of the President's House. Also resident in the household after the first of April was a young army officer from Virginia, Meriwether Lewis, whom Jefferson, before his inauguration, had summoned from the frontier to serve as his private secretary.

Jefferson had been in Washington since late November. Both of his daughters, Martha Randolph and Maria Eppes, were pregnant. As vice president he had only lived in the capital city when the Senate was in session, often not arriving until the session had started and departing a few days before the session closed. As president he would need to be at the seat of government much more of the year. Having put the first essential arrangements for his presidency into place, he determined to make a quick visit home to Monticello. Before he left he asked Dr. Enoch Edwards to obtain for him in Philadelphia a "handsome chariot for both city & country use," relying on Edwards's—and Mrs. Edwards's—judgment regarding any questions of "taste & convenience" pertaining to the vehicle. Before his departure, also, he saw that preparations were begun for a long cruise by a squadron of American warships, with an expectation that their destination would probably be the Barbary Coast of the Mediterranean Sea. Then on the first morning of April he crossed the Potomac and headed for home. At Monticello he occupied himself with putting his affairs into order in anticipation of another absence and received some reports from Washington. By the end of the month he was back in the capital to "begin our work systematically," as he phrased it to his younger daughter on 11 April.

This new phase of Jefferson's life has required some practical measures on the part of his editors. We have included, in this volume, the very interesting congratulatory addresses that the new president received from citizens' groups, churches, and Republican associations, and his replies. (We omit any addresses or letters to him that appeared in newspapers but which we cannot verify that he received.) Some of the considerable correspondence relating to job-seekers' applications we have not printed in full but have treated in summary form in our annotation. In general we will not print or list routine procedural papers signed by the president such as commissions or ships' passports. Jefferson did not note such documents in his record of letters (called by us SJL) and did not think of them as part of his correspondence. When he endorsed letters he received, he often noted the applicant's name and some identification of the desired position. He made similar notations in SJL. In our descriptions of the documents we will report the information from those endorsements and notations.

The volume contains four appendices. The first contains Jefferson's own tables and lists, from early in his presidency, of appointments and removals, supplemented by our annotation and an explanatory editorial note. Appendix II, which lists Senate documents that bear markings in Jefferson's hand, concludes a series of appendices that have appeared in the volumes from the vice-presidential period (beginning with Volume 29). Another appendix, which is new to our volumes, lists letters from the period of the volume that were addressed to or written by Jefferson but which for reasons of space we will not be printing in full. The fourth appendix, listing correspondence that Jefferson recorded in SJL but which has not been located, is also new to the edition.

ACKNOWLEDGMENTS

M ANY individuals have given the Editors the benefit of their aid in the preparation of this volume, and we offer them our thanks. Those who helped us use manuscript collections, answered research queries, assisted with translations, or advised in other ways are John S. Dyson, William C. Jordan, Robert A. Kaster, and Volker Schröder, Princeton University; in the libraries at Princeton, Karin A. Trainer, University Librarian, and Elizabeth Z. Bennett, Mary George, Sooni K. Johnson, Daniel J. Linke, and Ben Primer; Timothy Connelly, Dane Hartgrove, and Michael Meier of the NHPRC; James H. Hutson and the staff at the Manuscript Division of the Library of Congress, especially Ernest Emrich, Jeffrey Flannery, Gerard W. Gawalt, Joseph Jackson, Patrick Kerwin, and Bruce Kirby; Peter Drummey and the library staff of the Masachusetts Historical Society and especially Nancy Heywood, the coordinator of digital projects; Robert C. Ritchie, John Rhodehamel, and others at the Huntington Library; Lucia C. Stanton and Susan R. Stein of the Thomas Jefferson Foundation at Monticello; Michael Plunkett, Regina Rush, and the staff of Special Collections at the University of Virginia Library; John D. Haskell, Jr., and Susan A. Riggs, Swem Library, the College of William and Mary; the staff of the Missouri Historical Society; Robert M. Peck and the library staff of the Academy of Natural Sciences; Martin Levitt and Roy Goodman of the American Philosophical Society; Elaine Bunn of Drew University; George L. Vogt, Marge McNinch, and Barbara Hall, Hagley Museum and Library; Brent Tarter at the Library of Virginia; Charles T. Cullen at the Newberry Library; the staff of the New York Public Library; the Gilder Lehrman Institute of American History and the New-York Historical Society; Richard Nicoll of the Colonial Williamsburg Foundation; Peter Harbison of the Royal Irish Academy; Charles M. Harris of the Papers of William Thornton, and our fellow editors at the Thomas Jefferson Retirement Series at Monticello, the Adams Papers at the Massachusetts Historical Society, the Papers of George Washington and the Papers of James Madison at the University of Virginia, and the Papers of Benjamin Franklin at Yale University. Alfred L. Bush of Princeton, Lisa Kathleen Grady and Bonnie Lilienfeld of the National Museum of American History, Smithsonian Institution, and Yvonne Brooks of the Library of Congress assisted with the illustrations. Scott McClure and Kate McClure have contributed to the creation of the documents database that will be the foundation of the presidential volumes. We thank Alice Calaprice for careful reading and Jan Lilly for her unparalleled mastery of what a Jefferson volume must be. We thank those at Princeton University Press who never fail to give these volumes the benefit of their expertise: Chuck Creesy, Dimitri Karetnikov, Neil Litt, Elizabeth Litz, Linny Schenck, and Brigitta van Rheinberg.

EDITORIAL METHOD AND APPARATUS

1. RENDERING THE TEXT

Julian P. Boyd eloquently set forth a comprehensive editorial policy in Volume 1 of *The Papers of Thomas Jefferson*. Adopting what he described as a "middle course" for rendering eighteenth-century handwritten materials into print, Boyd set the standards for modern historical editing. His successors, Charles T. Cullen and John Catanzariti, reaffirmed Boyd's high standards. At the same time, they made changes in textual policy and editorial apparatus as they deemed appropriate. For Boyd's policy and subsequent modifications to it, readers are encouraged to consult Vol. 1: xxix-xxxviii; Vol. 22: vii-xi; and Vol. 24: vii-viii.

The revised, more literal textual method, which appeared for the first time in Volume 30, adheres to the following guidelines: Abbreviations will be retained as written. Where the meaning is sufficiently unclear to require editorial intervention, the expansion will be given in the explanatory annotation. Capitalization will follow the usage of the writer. Because the line between uppercase and lowercase letters can be a very fine and fluctuating one, when it is impossible to make an absolute determination of the author's intention, we will adopt modern usage. Jefferson rarely began his sentences with an uppercase letter, and we conform to his usage. Punctuation will be retained as written and double marks of punctuation, such as a period followed by a dash, will be allowed to stand. Misspellings or so-called slips of the pen will be allowed to stand or will be recorded in a subjoined textual note.

English translations or translation summaries will be supplied for foreign-language documents. In some instances, when documents are lengthy and not especially pertinent to Jefferson's concerns or if our edition's typography cannot adequately represent the script of a language, we will provide only a summary in English. In most cases we will print in full the text in its original language and also provide a full English translation. If a contemporary translation that Jefferson made or would have used is extant, we may print it in lieu of a modern translation. Our own translations are designed to provide a basic readable English text for the modern user rather than to preserve all aspects of the original diction and language.

2. *TEXTUAL DEVICES*

The following devices are employed throughout the work to clarify the presentation of the text.

[. . .]	Text missing and not conjecturable.
[ ]	Number or part of a number missing or illegible.
[roman]	Conjectural reading for missing or illegible matter. A question mark follows when the reading is doubtful.
[*italic*]	Editorial comment inserted in the text.
<*italic*>	Matter deleted in the MS but restored in our text.

3. *DESCRIPTIVE SYMBOLS*

The following symbols are employed throughout the work to describe the various kinds of manuscript originals. When a series of versions is recorded, the first to be recorded is the version used for the printed text.

Dft	draft (usually a composition or rough draft; later drafts, when identifiable as such, are designated "2d Dft," &c.)
Dupl	duplicate
MS	manuscript (arbitrarily applied to most documents other than letters)
N	note, notes (memoranda, fragments, &c.)
PoC	polygraph copy
PrC	press copy
RC	recipient's copy
SC	stylograph copy
Tripl	triplicate

All manuscripts of the above types are assumed to be in the hand of the author of the document to which the descriptive symbol pertains. If not, that *fact is stated*. On the other hand, the following types of manuscripts are assumed *not* to be in the hand of the author, and exceptions will be noted:

FC	file copy (applied to all contemporary copies retained by the author or his agents)
Lb	letterbook (ordinarily used with FC and Tr to denote texts copied into bound volumes)
Tr	transcript (applied to all contemporary and later copies except file copies; period of transcription, unless clear by implication, will be given when known)

4. LOCATION SYMBOLS

The locations of documents printed in this edition from originals in private hands and from printed sources are recorded in self-explanatory form in the descriptive note following each document. The locations of documents printed from originals held by public and private institutions in the United States are recorded by means of the symbols used in the National Union Catalog in the Library of Congress; an explanation of how these symbols are formed is given in Vol. 1: xl. The symbols DLC and MHi by themselves stand for the collections of Jefferson Papers proper in these repositories; when texts are drawn from other collections held by these two institutions, the names of those collections will be added. Location symbols for documents held by institutions outside the United States are given in a subjoined list. The lists of symbols are limited to the institutions represented by documents printed or referred to in this volume.

CSmH   The Huntington Library, San Marino, California
CtHi   Connecticut Historical Society, Hartford
CtY   Yale University, New Haven
DLC   Library of Congress
DNA   The National Archives, with identifications of series
        (preceded by record group number) as follows:
        RG 28   Records of the Post Office Department
                LPG   Letters Sent by the Postmaster
                        General
        RG 42   Records of the Office of Public Buildings and
                Public Parks of the National Capital
                DCLB   District of Columbia Letterbook
                PC   Proceedings of the Board of Commis-
                        sioners of the District of Columbia
        RG 45   Naval Records Collection of the Office of
                Naval Records and Library
                MLR   Misc. Letters Received
                MLS   Misc. Letters Sent
                LSO   Letters Sent to Officers
                LSP   Letters Sent to the President
        RG 46   Records of the United States Senate
                PMEN   President's Messages, Executive
                        Nominations
        RG 59   General Records of the Department of State
                CD   Consular Dispatches

DCI   Diplomatic and Consular Instructions
DD   Diplomatic Dispatches
GPR   General Pardon Records
LAR   Letters of Application and
          Recommendation
MCL   Misc. Commissions and Lists
MLR   Misc. Letters Received
MPTPC Misc. Permanent and Temporary
          Presidential Commissions
NL   Notes from Legations
PTCC   Permanent and Temporary Consular
          Commissions
RD   Resignations and Declinations
SDR   State Department Reports
RG 107 Records of the Office of the Secretary of War
MLS   Misc. Letters Sent
RLRMS Register of Letters Received, Main
          Series
RG 217 Records of the Accounting Officers of the
      Department of the Treasury
MTA   Misc. Treasury Accounts
RG 233 Records of the United States House of
      Representatives
DNCD   National Society of the Colonial Dames of America,
        Washington, D.C.
DNT   National Trust for Historic Preservation, Washington,
        D.C.
DeGH   Hagley Museum and Library, Greenville, Delaware
ICN   Newberry Library, Chicago
InU   Indiana University, Bloomington
KyLo   Louisville Free Public Library, Kentucky
MH   Harvard University, Cambridge, Massachusetts
MHi   Massachusetts Historical Society, Boston
MeB   Bowdoin College, Brunswick, Maine
MiU-C   William L. Clements Library, University of Michigan,
        Ann Arbor
MoSHi   Missouri Historical Society, St. Louis
N   New York State Library, Albany
NHC   Colgate University, Hamilton, New York
NHi   New-York Historical Society, New York City
NIC   Cornell University, Ithaca, New York
NN   New York Public Library

NNFoM   Forbes Magazine, Inc., New York City
NNMus   Museum of the City of New York
NNPM   Pierpont Morgan Library, New York City
NhD   Dartmouth College, Hanover, New Hampshire
NhHi   New Hampshire Historical Society, Concord
PHi   Historical Society of Pennsylvania, Philadelphia
PPAmP   American Philosophical Society, Philadelphia
PPRF   Rosenbach Foundation, Philadelphia
T   Tennessee State Library and Archives, Nashville
TxU   University of Texas, Austin
ViHi   Virginia Historical Society, Richmond
ViU   University of Virginia, Charlottesville
ViW   College of William and Mary, Williamsburg, Virginia
VtU-W   University of Vermont, Wilbur Collection, Burlington

The following symbols represent repositories located outside of the United States:

AHN   Archivo Histórico Nacional, Madrid

5. OTHER SYMBOLS AND ABBREVIATIONS

The following symbols and abbreviations are commonly employed in the annotation throughout the work.

Second Series   The topical series to be published as part of this edition, comprising those materials which are best suited to a topical rather than a chronological arrangement (see Vol. 1: xv-xvi)

TJ   Thomas Jefferson

TJ Editorial Files   Photoduplicates and other editorial materials in the office of The Papers of Thomas Jefferson, Princeton University Library

TJ Papers   Jefferson Papers (applied to a collection of manuscripts when the precise location of an undated, misdated, or otherwise problematic document must be furnished, and always preceded by the symbol for the institutional repository; thus "DLC: TJ Papers, 4:628-9" represents a document in the Library of Congress, Jefferson Papers, volume 4, pages 628 and 629. Citations to volumes and folio numbers of the Jefferson Papers at the Library of Congress refer to the collection as it was arranged at the time the first microfilm edition was made in 1944-45. Access to the microfilm edition of the collection as it was rearranged under the Library's Presidential

Papers Program is provided by the Index to the Thomas Jefferson Papers [Washington, D.C., 1976])

RG   Record Group (used in designating the location of documents in the National Archives)

SJL   Jefferson's "Summary Journal of Letters" written and received for the period 11 Nov. 1783 to 25 June 1826 (in DLC: TJ Papers). This register, kept in Jefferson's hand, has been checked against the TJ Editorial Files. It is to be assumed that all outgoing letters are recorded in SJL unless there is a note to the contrary. When the date of receipt of an incoming letter is recorded in SJL, it is incorporated in the notes. Information and discrepancies revealed in SJL but not found in the letter itself are also noted. Missing letters recorded in SJL are, where possible, accounted for in the notes to documents mentioning them or in related documents. A more detailed discussion of this register and its use in this edition appears in Vol. 6: vii-x

SJPL   "Summary Journal of Public Letters," an incomplete list of letters and documents written by TJ from 16 Apr. 1784 to 31 Dec. 1793, with brief summaries, in an amanuensis's hand. This is supplemented by six pages in TJ's hand, compiled at a later date, listing private and confidential memorandums and notes as well as official reports and communications by and to him as Secretary of State, 11 Oct. 1789 to 31 Dec. 1793 (in DLC: TJ Papers, Epistolary Record, 514-59 and 209-11, respectively; see Vol. 22: ix-x). Since nearly all documents in the amanuensis's list are registered in SJL, while few in TJ's list are so recorded, it is to be assumed that all references to SJPL are to the list in TJ's hand unless there is a statement to the contrary

V   Ecu

f   Florin

£   Pound sterling or livre, depending upon context (in doubtful cases, a clarifying note will be given)

s   Shilling or sou (also expressed as /)

d   Penny or denier

tt   Livre Tournois

₱   Per (occasionally used for pro, pre)

6. SHORT TITLES

The following list includes short titles of works cited frequently in this edition. Since it is impossible to anticipate all the works to be cited in abbreviated form, the list is revised from volume to volume.

Adams, *Diary*   L. H. Butterfield and others, eds., *Diary and Autobiography of John Adams*, Cambridge, Mass., 1961, 4 vols.

Adams, *Works*   Charles Francis Adams, ed., *The Works of John Adams*, Boston, 1850-56, 10 vols.

Ammon, *Monroe*   Harry Ammon, *James Monroe: The Quest for National Identity*, New York, 1971

ANB   John A. Garraty and Mark C. Carnes, eds., *American National Biography*, New York and Oxford, 1999, 24 vols.

Annals   *Annals of the Congress of the United States: The Debates and Proceedings in the Congress of the United States . . . Compiled from Authentic Materials*, Washington, D.C., Gales & Seaton, 1834-56, 42 vols. All editions are undependable and pagination varies from one printing to another. The first two volumes of the set cited here have "Compiled . . . by Joseph Gales, Senior" on the title page and bear the caption "Gales & Seatons History" on verso and "of Debates in Congress" on recto pages. The remaining volumes bear the caption "History of Congress" on both recto and verso pages. Those using the first two volumes with the latter caption will need to employ the date of the debate or the indexes of debates and speakers.

APS   American Philosophical Society

ASP   *American State Papers: Documents, Legislative and Executive, of the Congress of the United States*, Washington, D.C., 1832-61, 38 vols.

Bear, *Family Letters*   Edwin M. Betts and James A. Bear, Jr., eds., *Family Letters of Thomas Jefferson*, Columbia, Mo., 1966

Betts, *Farm Book*   Edwin M. Betts, ed., *Thomas Jefferson's Farm Book*, Princeton, 1953

Betts, *Garden Book*   Edwin M. Betts, ed., *Thomas Jefferson's Garden Book, 1766-1824*, Philadelphia, 1944

Biog. Dir. Cong.   *Biographical Directory of the United States Congress, 1774-1989*, Washington, D.C., 1989

Brant, *Madison*   Irving Brant, *James Madison*, Indianapolis, 1941-61, 6 vols.

Brigham, *American Newspapers*   Clarence S. Brigham, *History and Bibliography of American Newspapers, 1690-1820*, Worcester, Mass., 1947, 2 vols.

Bryan, *National Capital*   Wilhelmus B. Bryan, *A History of the National Capital From Its Foundation Through the Period of the Adoption of the Organic Act*, New York, 1914-16, 2 vols.

Bush, *Life Portraits*   Alfred L. Bush, *The Life Portraits of Thomas Jefferson*, rev. ed., Charlottesville, 1987

Conway, *Omitted Chapters*   Moncure Daniel Conway, *Omitted Chapters of History Disclosed in the Life and Papers of Edmund Randolph, Governor of Virginia; First Attorney-General United States, Secretary of State*, New York, 1888

Cooke, *Coxe*   Jacob E. Cooke, *Tench Coxe and the Early Republic*, Chapel Hill, 1978

Cunningham, *Jeffersonian Republicans in Power*   Noble E. Cunningham, Jr., *The Jeffersonian Republicans in Power, Party Operations, 1801-1809*, Chapel Hill, 1963

Cunningham, *Process of Government*   Nobel E. Cunningham, Jr., *The Process of Government Under Jefferson*, Princeton, 1978

CVSP   William P. Palmer and others, eds., *Calendar of Virginia State Papers . . . Preserved in the Capitol at Richmond*, Richmond, 1875-93, 11 vols.

DAB   Allen Johnson and Dumas Malone, eds., *Dictionary of American Biography*, New York, 1928-36, 20 vols.

Daniels, *Randolphs of Virginia*   Jonathan Daniels, *The Randolphs of Virginia*, Garden City, N.Y., 1972

Dauer, *Adams Federalists*   Manning J. Dauer, *The Adams Federalists*, Baltimore, 1953

Dexter, *Yale*   Franklin Bowditch Dexter, *Biographical Sketches of the Graduates of Yale College with Annals of the College History*, New York, 1885-1912, 6 vols.

DHRC   Merrill Jensen, John P. Kaminski, Gaspare J. Saladino, and others, eds., *The Documentary History of the Ratification of the Constitution*, Madison, Wis., 1976-   , 20 vols.

DHSC   Maeva Marcus and others, eds., *The Documentary History of the Supreme Court of the United States, 1789-1800*, New York, 1985-   , 7 vols.

Dictionnaire   *Dictionnaire de biographie française*, Paris, 1933-   , 19 vols.

DNB   H. C. G. Matthew and Brian Harrison, eds., *Oxford Dictionary of National Biography, In Association with The British Academy, From the earliest times to the year 2000*, Oxford, 2004, 60 vols.

DSB   Charles C. Gillispie, ed., *Dictionary of Scientific Biography*, New York, 1970-80, 16 vols.

Duvergier, *Lois*   Jean B. Duvergier and others, eds., *Collection Complète des Lois, Décrets, Ordonnances, Réglemens, avis du Conseil-d'État*, Paris, 1834-1908, 108 vols.

EG   Dickinson W. Adams and Ruth W. Lester, eds., *Jefferson's Extracts from the Gospels*, Princeton, 1983, *The Papers of Thomas Jefferson*, Second Series

Ehrman, *Pitt*   John Ehrman, *The Younger Pitt: The Consuming Struggle*, London, 1996

Evans   Charles Evans, Clifford K. Shipton, and Roger P. Bristol, comps., *American Bibliography: A Chronological Dictionary of all Books, Pamphlets and Periodical Publications Printed in the United States of America from . . . 1639 . . . to . . . 1820*, Chicago and Worcester, Mass., 1903-59, 14 vols.

Ford   Paul Leicester Ford, ed., *The Writings of Thomas Jefferson*, Letterpress Edition, New York, 1892-99, 10 vols.

Gallatin, *Papers*   Carl E. Prince and Helene E. Fineman, eds., *The Papers of Albert Gallatin*, microfilm edition in 46 reels, Philadelphia, 1969, and Supplement, Barbara B. Oberg, ed., reels 47-51, Wilmington, Del., 1985

Gilpatrick, *Jeffersonian Democracy in North Carolina*   Delbert Harold Gilpatrick, *Jeffersonian Democracy in North Carolina, 1789-1816*, New York, 1931

Harris, *Thornton*,   C. M. Harris, ed., *Papers of William Thornton: Volume One, 1781-1802*, Charlottesville, 1995

Harrison, *Princetonians, 1769-1775*   Richard A. Harrison, *Princetonians, 1769-1775: A Biographical Dictionary*, Princeton, 1980

HAW   Henry A. Washington, ed., *The Writings of Thomas Jefferson*, New York, 1853-54, 9 vols.

Heitman, *Dictionary*   Francis B. Heitman, comp., *Historical Register and Dictionary of the United States Army*, Washington, D.C., 1903, 2 vols.

Heitman, *Register*   Francis B. Heitman, *Historical Register of Officers of the Continental Army during the War of the Revolution, April, 1775, to December, 1793*, new ed., Washington, D.C., 1914

JAH   *Journal of American History*, 1964-

JEP   *Journal of the Executive Proceedings of the Senate of the United States . . . to the Termination of the Nineteenth Congress*, Washington, D.C., 1828, 3 vols.

JHD   *Journal of the House of Delegates of the Commonwealth of Virginia* (cited by session and date of publication)

JHR   *Journal of the House of Representatives of the United States*, Washington, D.C., 1826, 9 vols.

JS   *Journal of the Senate of the United States*, Washington, D.C., 1820-21, 5 vols.

King, *Life*   Charles R. King, ed., *The Life and Correspondence of Rufus King: Comprising His Letters, Private and Official, His Public Documents and His Speeches*, New York, 1894-1900, 6 vols.

Kline, *Burr* Mary-Jo Kline, ed., *Political Correspondence and Public Papers of Aaron Burr*, Princeton, 1983, 2 vols.

L & B Andrew A. Lipscomb and Albert E. Bergh, eds., *The Writings of Thomas Jefferson*, Washington, D.C., 1903-04, 20 vols.

LCB Douglas L. Wilson, ed., *Jefferson's Literary Commonplace Book*, Princeton, 1989, *The Papers of Thomas Jefferson*, Second Series

Leonard, *General Assembly* Cynthia Miller Leonard, comp., *The General Assembly of Virginia, July 30, 1619-January 11, 1978: A Bicentennial Register of Members*, Richmond, 1978

List of Alumni *A Provisional List of Alumni, Grammar School Students, Members of the Faculty, and Members of the Board of Visitors of the College of William and Mary in Virginia, from 1693 to 1888*, Richmond, 1941

List of Patents *A List of Patents granted by the United States from April 10, 1792, to December 31, 1836*, Washington, D.C., 1872

Madison, *Letters* William C. Rives and Philip R. Fendall, eds., *Letters and Other Writings of James Madison . . . Published by Order of Congress*, Philadelphia, 1865, 4 vols.

Madison, *Papers* William T. Hutchinson, Robert A. Rutland, J. C. A. Stagg, and others, eds., *The Papers of James Madison*, Chicago and Charlottesville, 1962- , 29 vols.
  Sec. of State Ser., 1986- , 7 vols.
  Pres. Ser., 1984- , 5 vols.

Malone, *Jefferson* Dumas Malone, *Jefferson and His Time*, Boston, 1948-81, 6 vols.

Marshall, *Papers* Herbert A. Johnson, Charles T. Cullen, Charles F. Hobson, and others, eds., *The Papers of John Marshall*, Chapel Hill, 1974- , 11 vols.

Martin's Bench and Bar John H. Martin, *Martin's Bench and Bar of Philadelphia*, Philadelphia, 1883

MB James A. Bear, Jr., and Lucia C. Stanton, eds., *Jefferson's Memorandum Books: Accounts, with Legal Records and Miscellany, 1767-1826*, Princeton, 1997, *The Papers of Thomas Jefferson*, Second Series

Merrill, *Jefferson's Nephews* Boynton Merrill, Jr., *Jefferson's Nephews: A Frontier Tragedy*, Princeton, 1976

Miller, *Alexandria Artisans* T. Michael Miller, comp., *Artisans and Merchants of Alexandria, Virginia, 1780-1820*, Bowie, Md., 1991-92, 2 vols.

Miller, *Treaties* Hunter Miller, ed., *Treaties and other International Acts of the United States of America*, Washington, D.C., 1931-48, 8 vols.

Monroe, *Writings*   Stanislaus Murray Hamilton, ed., *The Writings of James Monroe*, New York, 1898-1903, 7 vols.

NDBW   Dudley W. Knox, ed., *Naval Documents Related to the United States Wars with the Barbary Powers*, Washington, D.C., 1939-44, 6 vols. and *Register of Officer Personnel and Ships' Data, 1801-1807*, Washington, D.C., 1945

NDQW   Dudley W. Knox, ed., *Naval Documents Related to the Quasi-War between the United States and France, Naval Operations*, Washington, D.C., 1935-38, 7 vols. (cited by years)

Niemcewicz, *Under Their Vine*   Julian Ursin Niemcewicz, *Under Their Vine and Fig Tree: Travels through America in 1797-1799, 1805, with some Further Account of Life in New Jersey*, trans. and ed., Metchie J. E. Budka, Elizabeth, N.J., 1965

Notes, ed. Peden   Thomas Jefferson, *Notes on the State of Virginia*, ed. William Peden, Chapel Hill, 1955

OED   J. A. Simpson and E. S. C. Weiner, eds., *The Oxford English Dictionary*, Oxford, 1989, 20 vols.

Pa. Arch.   Samuel Hazard and others, eds., *Pennsylvania Archives. Selected and Arranged from Original Documents in the Office of the Secretary of the Commonwealth*, Harrisburg, 1852-1935, 119 vols.

Papenfuse, *Maryland Legislature*   Edward C. Papenfuse, Alan F. Day, David W. Jordan, Gregory A. Stiverson, eds., *A Biographical Dictionary of the Maryland Legislature, 1635-1789*, Baltimore, 1979-85, 2 vols.

Parliamentary Manual, 1801   Thomas Jefferson, *A Manual of Parliamentary Practice. For the Use of the Senate of the United States*, Washington, D.C., 1801

Parry, *Consolidated Treaty Series*   Clive Parry, ed., *The Consolidated Treaty Series*, Dobbs Ferry, N.Y., 1969-81, 231 vols.

Pasley, *Tyranny of Printers*   Jeffrey L. Pasley, *"The Tyranny of Printers": Newspaper Politics in the Early American Republic*, Charlottesville, 2001

Peale, *Papers*   Lillian B. Miller and others, eds., *The Selected Papers of Charles Willson Peale and His Family*, New Haven, 1983-2000, 5 vols. in 6

Perkins, *First Rapprochement*   Bradford Perkins, *The First Rapprochement: England and the United States, 1795-1805*, Philadelphia, 1955; Berkeley, 1967

PMHB   *Pennsylvania Magazine of History and Biography*, 1877-

Preston, *Catalogue*   Daniel Preston, *A Comprehensive Catalogue of the Correspondence and Papers of James Monroe*, Westport, Conn., 2001, 2 vols.

Prince, *Federalists*   Carl E. Prince, *The Federalists and the Origins of the U.S. Civil Service*, New York, 1977

PW   Wilbur S. Howell, ed., *Jefferson's Parliamentary Writings*, Princeton, 1988, *The Papers of Thomas Jefferson*, Second Series

Randolph, *Domestic Life*   Sarah N. Randolph, *The Domestic Life of Thomas Jefferson, Compiled from Family Letters and Reminiscences by His Great-Granddaughter*, 3d ed., Cambridge, Mass., 1939

RCHS   *Records of the Columbia Historical Society*, 1895-1989

Rowe, *McKean*   G. S. Rowe, *Thomas McKean, The Shaping of an American Republicanism*, Boulder, Colo., 1978

RS   J. Jefferson Looney and others, eds., *The Papers of Thomas Jefferson: Retirement Series*, Princeton, 2004-   , 2 vols.

Saricks, *Du Pont*   Ambrose Saricks, *Pierre Samuel Du Pont de Nemours*, Lawrence, Kans., 1965

S.C. Biographical Directory, House of Representatives   J. S. R. Faunt, Walter B. Edgar, N. Louise Bailey, and others, eds., *Biographical Directory of the South Carolina House of Representatives*, Columbia, S.C., 1974-92, 5 vols.

S.C. Biographical Directory, Senate   N. Louise Bailey and others, eds., *Biographical Directory of the South Carolina Senate, 1776-1985*, Columbia, S.C., 1986, 3 vols.

Shackelford, *Jefferson's Adoptive Son*   George Green Shackelford, *Jefferson's Adoptive Son: The Life of William Short, 1759-1848*, Lexington, Ky., 1993

Shaw-Shoemaker   Ralph R. Shaw and Richard H. Shoemaker, comps., *American Bibliography: A Preliminary Checklist for 1801-1819*, New York, 1958-63, 22 vols.

Shepherd, *Statutes*   Samuel Shepherd, ed., *The Statutes at Large of Virginia, from October Session 1792, to December Session 1806*, Richmond, 1835-36, 3 vols.

Sibley   John L. Sibley and Clifford K. Shipton, *Sibley's Harvard Graduates: Biographical Sketches of Those Who Attended Harvard College*, Cambridge, Mass., 1873-1975, 17 vols.

Smith, *Freedom's Fetters*   James Morton Smith, *Freedom's Fetters: The Alien and Sedition Laws and American Civil Liberties*, Ithaca, N.Y., 1956

Smith, *Napoleonic Wars*   Digby G. Smith, *The Greenhill Napoleonic Wars Data Book*, London, 1998

Sowerby   E. Millicent Sowerby, comp., *Catalogue of the Library of Thomas Jefferson*, Washington, D.C., 1952-59, 5 vols.

Sprague, *American Pulpit*   William B. Sprague, *Annals of the American Pulpit, or, Commemorative Notices of Distinguished*

American Clergymen of Various Denominations, New York, 1857-69, 9 vols.

Stafford, *Baltimore Directory, for 1802*   Cornelius William Stafford, *The Baltimore Directory, for 1802*, Baltimore, 1802

Stafford, *Philadelphia Directory, for 1800*   Cornelius William Stafford, *The Philadelphia Directory, for 1800*, Philadelphia, 1800

Stafford, *Philadelphia Directory, for 1801*   Cornelius William Stafford, *The Philadelphia Directory, for 1801*, Philadelphia, 1801

Stanton, *Free Some Day*   Lucia Stanton, *Free Some Day*, Thomas Jefferson Foundation, Inc., 2000

Stets, *Postmasters*   Robert J. Stets, *Postmasters & Postoffices of the United States, 1782-1811*, Lake Oswego, Oregon, 1994

Stewart, *French Revolution*   John H. Stewart, *A Documentary Survey of the French Revolution*, New York, 1951

Syrett, *Hamilton*   Harold C. Syrett and others, eds., *The Papers of Alexander Hamilton*, New York, 1961-87, 27 vols.

Terr. Papers   Clarence E. Carter and John Porter Bloom, eds., *The Territorial Papers of the United States*, Washington, D.C., 1934-75, 28 vols.

TJR   Thomas Jefferson Randolph, ed., *Memoir, Correspondence, and Miscellanies, from the Papers of Thomas Jefferson*, Charlottesville, 1829, 4 vols.

Toussaint, *Mauritius*   A. Toussaint, ed., *Early American Trade with Mauritius*, Port Louis, Mauritius, 1954

Tulard, *Dictionnaire Napoléon*   Jean Tulard, *Dictionnaire Napoléon*, Paris, 1987

U.S. Statutes at Large   Richard Peters, ed., *The Public Statutes at Large of the United States . . . 1789 to March 3, 1845*, Boston, 1855-56, 8 vols.

VMHB   *Virginia Magazine of History and Biography*, 1893-

Washington, *Diaries*   Donald Jackson and Dorothy Twohig, eds., *The Diaries of George Washington*, Charlottesville, 1976-79, 6 vols.

Washington, *Papers*   W. W. Abbot, Dorothy Twohig, Philander D. Chase, and others, eds., *The Papers of George Washington*, Charlottesville, 1983- , 46 vols.

   Pres. Ser, 1987- , 12 vols.

   Ret. Ser, 1998-99, 4 vols.

WMQ   *William and Mary Quarterly*, 1892-

Woods, *Albemarle*   Edgar Woods, *Albemarle County in Virginia*, Charlottesville, 1901

CONTENTS

CONTENTS

CONTENTS

CONTENTS

CONTENTS

CONTENTS

CONTENTS

CONTENTS

CONTENTS

CONTENTS

CONTENTS

[xxxix]

CONTENTS

CONTENTS

CONTENTS

CONTENTS

APPENDICES

ILLUSTRATIONS

Following page 406

BROADSIDE

This broadside, measuring 13 by 9 inches, printed on 17 Feb. 1801 at "two o'clock," announced the result of the thirty-sixth ballot in the House of Representatives for the presidential election of 1800. For six days the House was deadlocked between Jefferson and Aaron Burr. The handbill illustrated here was printed in Alexandria, Virginia, by the office of the Alexandria *Times*.
Courtesy of The Newberry Library.

REVISED DRAFT OF JEFFERSON'S FIRST INAUGURAL ADDRESS

Designated Jefferson's "Revised Draft" in this edition, the manuscript illustrated here is believed to be the copy of his First Inaugural Address that Jefferson gave to Samuel Harrison Smith, editor of the *National Intelligencer*, hours before he delivered the speech to Congress. Smith had imprints of the speech available for sale on inauguration day. Clues to the use of this copy by Smith's printing office include the consecutive numbers on the right margin of each of the three pages, written in a different hand, and the numbers' alignment with lines drawn across the pages. The manuscript was thus divided into sections, which would have been distributed among typesetters at the printer's office (Jefferson Papers, Editorial Files). This copy was also the draft from which Jefferson made his reading copy for the delivery of the speech.

The illustration is printed as the first page of the First Inaugural Address, Document II. The first five textual notes describe Jefferson's emendations to the illustrated page.

The page measures approximately $7\frac{3}{4}$ by $9\frac{1}{2}$ inches.
Courtesy of the Library of Congress.

CREAMWARE PITCHER

Featuring a likeness of the president and a phrase from the First Inaugural Address, this imported creamware pitcher was an affordable memento of Jefferson's inauguration for ordinary Americans. The image of Jefferson that is the centerpiece of the pitcher was based on engravings of Rembrandt Peale's portrait of 1800 (Vol. 31:xli). The garland framing the portrait bears the names of fifteen states (omitting Tennessee). At top are the familiar words echoing Jefferson's inaugural address, "We are all Republicans—all Federalists," and below, "THOMAS JEFFERSON PRESIDENT of the United States of AMERICA 1801." On the opposite side of the pitcher is a coat of arms representing the United States. Measuring $7\frac{3}{4}$ inches in height and $7\frac{1}{2}$ inches in width, the pitcher has a black transfer print on a cream-colored body and is attributed to the Herculaneaum pottery outside Liverpool.

In its shape, coloring, and decoration, the object is typical of the inexpensive, transfer-printed earthenware that was exported from Liverpool between 1760 and 1820, often decorated with images that commemorated American historical events and people. Several Liverpool transfer-print designs on varying ceramic forms honored Jefferson as president of the United States. Another extant pitcher, for example, dated 1802, features a different excerpt from Jefferson's Inaugural Address: "Peace, Commerce and honest Friendship with all Nations, Entangling Alliances with none" (David and Linda Arman, *Anglo-American Ceramics,* Vol. 1, *Transfer Printed Creamware and Pearlware for the American Market, 1760-1860* [Portsmouth, R.I., 1998], 11, 13, 114-19; Noble E. Cunningham, *The Image of Thomas Jefferson in the Public Eye* [Charlottesville, 1981], 98).

Courtesy of the National Museum of American History, Smithsonian Institution.

VIEW OF THE CAPITOL

William Russell Birch's watercolor of the north wing of the Capitol in a pastoral setting, painted around 1800, illustrates the physical surroundings of two major events covered by this volume, the balloting in the House of Representatives for the presidential election of 1800 and Jefferson's delivery of his First Inaugural Address. Construction of the Capitol began in 1793, but when Congress moved from Philadelphia to Washington in November 1800, only the north wing was completed. The House of Representatives met in the Senate Chamber for a year, until a temporary building was constructed on the foundations of the south wing. In 1801, the north wing also housed the Supreme Court, the circuit court for the District of Columbia, and a collection of books that was the precursor to the Library of Congress. Birch's placement of the north wing at the far left of the frame allowed him to hide from view the construction of the other portions of the Capitol.

Birch, an English-born miniature painter and stipple engraver, is best known for his series of engravings, *The City of Philadelphia, in the State of Pennsylvania North America; as it appeared in the Year 1800* (Philadelphia, 1800). The image shown here measures approximately $8\frac{1}{2}$ by 11 inches (Bryan, *National Capital,* 1:213, 377, 420, 426; Vol. 31:xlii).

Courtesy of the Library of Congress.

JEFFERSON BANNER

This banner of hand-painted linen is believed to have been made in 1801 to celebrate Jefferson's election to the presidency. The now faded red words read "T. Jefferson/President of the United States of America/John Adams is No More." The flag seems to be a rare survival of material culture from one of the many public events around the country that celebrated Jefferson's inauguration on and just after 4 Mch. Newspapers described processions, orations, and banquets accompanied by patriotic music, organized by local Republican committees. Images of Jefferson were prominent in these events. The highlight of a "Republican Entertainment" in Charleston, South Carolina, for example, was the illumination of a transparent painting of Jefferson, which elicited "a spontaneous burst of applause."

Jefferson's image on this banner, showing him with a blue coat and hair that appears black, is based on one of several engravings of Rembrandt Peale's portrait of Jefferson of 1800. Atop an oval frame decorated with sixteen red and blue stars, one for each state, sits an eagle, a symbol of the American republic, holding the streamers that bear the written message. The flag measures 30 by 37 inches.

The banner was donated to the Smithsonian Institution as part of the Ralph E. Becker Collection of Political Americana. Becker acquired the object near Mansfield, Massachusetts, around 1964 (Charleston *City Gazette and Daily Advertiser*, 14 Mch. 1801; Herbert Ridgeway Collins, *Threads of History: Americana Recorded on Cloth: 1775 to the Present* [Washington, D.C., 1979], 60; Cunningham, *Image of Thomas Jefferson*, 137).

Courtesy of the National Museum of American History, Smithsonian Institution.

"PIECES TO BE SUNG AT THE GERMAN REFORMED CHURCH"

Jefferson's supporters in Philadelphia celebrated his inauguration day with a procession that included military units, bands, political societies, Pennsylvania officials, and a boat on wheels that was escorted through the streets by the city's shipbuilders. The parade culminated in a ceremony at the German Reformed Church, on Race Street near Fourth Street, where John Beckley delivered an oration. The handbill illustrated here, "Pieces To be sung at the German Reformed Church, on Wednesday, the 4th of March, 1801," provided lyrics for the four songs performed: a "Solemn Invocation"; "The People's Friend"; a "Chorus"; and four lines to be sung "After the Oration." Charles Willson Peale sent this copy of the songsheet to Jefferson with marginal notations identifying Peter S. Du Ponceau as the author of the invocation, Rembrandt Peale as the lyricist of "The People's Friend," and Georg Friedrich Händel as the source of the lines sung after Beckley's oration. The words from Händel, beginning "'Tis Liberty, dear Liberty alone," come from the first act of the oratorio *Judas Maccabaeus*. Philadelphia's German Reformed Church, built in 1747, was also the site of a ceremony held on Washington's birthday in 1800 (*Aurora*, 6 Mch. 1801; *Philadelphia Gazette*, 5 Mch. 1801; J. Thomas Scharf and Thompson Westcott, *History of Philadelphia, 1609-1884*, 3 vols. [Philadelphia, 1884], 1:503-4; 2:856; Georg Friedrich Händel, music, Thomas Morell, libretto, *Judas Maccabäus*, ed. Arthur D. Walker [Adliswil-Zurich, Switzerland, 1971], 50-2; DNB; Charles Willson Peale to TJ, 8 Mch. 1801).

The songsheet is approximately $8\frac{1}{4}$ by 10 inches.

Courtesy of the Library of Congress.

"THE PEOPLE'S FRIEND"

The inauguration day celebration in Philadelphia featured music composed for the occasion. "Jefferson's March," possibly the work of Du Ponceau, enjoyed great popularity in the city around the time of the inauguration. Both that piece and "The People's Friend" were performed at the ceremony in the German Reformed Church. Philadelphia music master and instrument maker

John Isaac Hawkins, from whom Jefferson had purchased a portable piano for his daughter Maria, composed the melody of "The People's Friend." Hawkins also wrote to mark the inauguration "The People's March" and "Election, the People's Right." He arranged for George Willig, who sold music at 185 Market Street in Philadelphia, to have "The People's Friend" available for sale by the morning of the inauguration festivities. Willig published a two-sided sheet, with "The People's Friend" on one side (see illustration) and the anonymous "Chorus," which was also performed at the church, on the other side. The sheet, which measures 9½ by 14 inches, credits Hawkins with the music of "The People's Friend," but attributes the song's words to "a Citizen" (Rembrandt Peale, see above). The four verses that conclude "The People's Friend" read:

> What joyful prospects rise before!
> Peace, Arts and Science hail our Shore,
> And thro' the Country spread—
> Long may these blessings be preserv'd
> And by a virtuous Land deserv'd,
> With JEFFERSON our head.

An unnamed "favorite Air" was the source of the melody of the "Chorus" on the reverse side of Willig's publication. The *Aurora*, in its recounting of the inaugural events in Philadelphia, printed the lyrics of both songs (Philadelphia *Aurora*, 3, 4, 6 Mch. 1801; Richard J. Wolfe, *Secular Music in America, 1801-1825*, 3 vols. [New York, 1964], 1:350; H. Glenn Brown and Maude O. Brown, *A Directory of the Book-Arts and Book Trade in Philadelphia to 1820, Including Painters and Engravers* [New York, 1950], 125; Philippe de Létombe to TJ, 28 Feb.; Charles Willson Peale to TJ, 8 Mch. 1801).

Courtesy of the Music Division, Library of Congress.

LIST OF CANDIDATES

Working on a single piece of paper, primarily between December 1800 and March 1801, Jefferson created this list of more than 60 candidates for office. The list represents an early effort by him to organize and record the requests and recommendations for office that he received in writing and conversation. To create the list, Jefferson divided a page, which measures approximately 7½ by 9½ inches, into five columns with the following headings: "Candidates," "Residence," "Office," "by whom recommended," and "Date." Checkmarks appear beside the names of seven men who received commissions for consulships in June 1801. Jefferson appears to have been especially careful to record recommendations by his regular correspondents and Republican congressmen.

The list is printed as Appendix I, List 1.

Courtesy of the Library of Congress.

Volume 33

17 February to 30 April 1801

JEFFERSON CHRONOLOGY

1743 · 1826

1743	Born at Shadwell, 13 Apr. (New Style).
1760	Entered the College of William and Mary.
1762	"quitted college."
1762-1767	Self-education and preparation for law.
1769-1774	Albemarle delegate to House of Burgesses.
1772	Married Martha Wayles Skelton, 1 Jan.
1775-1776	In Continental Congress.
1776	Drafted Declaration of Independence.
1776-1779	In Virginia House of Delegates.
1779	Submitted Bill for Establishing Religious Freedom.
1779-1781	Governor of Virginia.
1782	His wife died, 6 Sep.
1783-1784	In Continental Congress.
1784-1789	In France as Minister Plenipotentiary to negotiate commercial treaties and as Minister Plenipotentiary resident at Versailles.
1790-1793	Secretary of State of the United States.
1797-1801	Vice President of the United States.
1801-1809	President of the United States.
1814-1826	Established the University of Virginia.
1826	Died at Monticello, 4 July.

VOLUME 33

17 February 1801 to 30 April 1801

17	Feb.	Elected president by the House of Representatives on the 36th ballot.
18	Feb.	Offers Henry Dearborn secretaryship of the War Department.
20	Feb.	Engraving of TJ by Cornelius Tiebout advertised for sale.
21	Feb.	Letter of thanks read to the House of Representatives.
23	Feb.	Offers Meriwether Lewis appointment as private secretary.
27	Feb.	*Manual of Parliamentary Practice* advertised for sale in the *National Intelligencer*.
28	Feb.	Presents farewell address to the Senate as vice president.
3	Mch.	Peace Establishment Act to reduce the navy passed by Congress.
4	Mch.	Inaugurated in Senate chamber as third president of the U.S.
5	Mch.	Presents first nominations to the Senate; Congress adjourns.
8	Mch.	Holds first cabinet meeting; Gallatin, Dearborn, and Lincoln attend.
14	Mch.	Attends public dinner in Alexandria at Gadsby's Hotel; Gallatin sends proposal for reducing the federal budget.
16	Mch.	Issues presidential pardon for James Thomson Callender.
18	Mch.	Hires Joseph Rapin as steward of the President's House.
ca. 19 Mch.		Takes up residence in the President's House.
21	Mch.	Treaty of Aranjuez formally acknowledges Spanish cession of Louisiana to France.
22	Mch.	John Dawson sails for Paris with amended convention with France.
24	Mch.	Hires James Oldham as house joiner at Monticello.
30	Mch.	Instructs Enoch Edwards on purchase of a carriage at Philadelphia.
1	Apr.	Leaves Washington for Monticello, arriving on 4 Apr.
20	Apr.	Calculates tobacco crop for 1800 at Monticello to be 10,028 lbs.; receives four carriage horses purchased for $1,600.
26	Apr.	Leaves Monticello for Washington, arriving on 29 Apr.

THE PAPERS OF
THOMAS JEFFERSON

·《 ━━━━━━━━ 》·

Announcement of Election Results

[17 Feb. 1801]

By Express from the City of Washington ! !

To the EDITORS of the TIMES.

THIS moment the election is decided. Morris, from Vermont, absented himself, so that Vermont was for Jefferson. The four members from Maryland, who had voted for Burr, put in blank tickets. The result was then ten for Jefferson.

I hope you will have the cannon out to announce the news.

Yours,

N.B. This was the second ballot to-day. Bayard is appointed ambassador to France.

Tuesday, two o'clock.

Printed (ICN).

(Alexandria *Times*, 18 Feb. 1801; Madison, *Papers*, 17:471).

THE TIMES: *The Times; and District of Columbia Daily Advertiser*, which was published in Alexandria, Virginia. TJ perhaps did not see the handbill above, which was made up in the newspaper's office on 17 Feb. and provided many Virginians with their first confirmation of his election. In Fredericksburg on the evening of the 19th, Fontaine Maury saw a copy that was on its way by express messenger to Governor James Monroe in Richmond. The editors of the *Times* reprinted the announcement in their columns on 18 Feb., omitting the sentence about the CANNON salute. By then cannonades had already taken place in Alexandria, where celebrants fired 16 rounds from an artillery piece brought to the courthouse square on the 17th, and they repeated the tribute from a wharf on the Potomac that evening. Cannon shots also announced the news in Fredericksburg

BAYARD IS APPOINTED AMBASSADOR: in a letter dated 13 Feb., but presented to the Senate on Tuesday, the 17th, John Adams nominated James A. Bayard as minister plenipotentiary to France. The Senate debated the appointment on 18 Feb. and consented to it the next day. On 2 Mch., Adams notified the Senate that the Delaware congressman had declined the appointment "for reasons equally applicable to every other person suitable for the service." The president concluded that he would leave the appointment of a minister and the conveyance of the Convention of 1800 to France to his successor, that he "may proceed with them according to his wisdom" (JEP, 1:380, 382-3, 388).

As the single Delaware vote, Bayard had played a pivotal role in breaking the tie between TJ and Burr in the House. On 17 Feb., after the decisive ballot, Bayard wrote Allen McLane, the avowedly

[3]

Federalist collector at Wilmington: "Mr Jefferson is our President. Our opposition was continued till it was demonstrated that Burr could not be brought in, and even if he could he meant to come in as a Democrat. In such case to evidence his sincerity he must have swept every officer in the U. States. I have direct information that Mr Jefferson will not pursue that plan." Bayard noted that the New England congressmen had been ready "to go without a constitution and take the risk of a Civil War." In the end, "Mr J. did not get a Foederal vote. Vermont gave a vote by means of Morris withdrawing—the same thing happened with Maryland. The Votes of S. Carolina and Delaware were blank." Bayard concluded: "I have taken good care of you, and think if prudent, you are safe." At some point, TJ received a copy of this letter from Thomas Mann Randolph and noted: "Bayard James A. of Delaware. a copy of a letter from him to Colo. Mc.lane of Delaware, written pending the election between Th:J and A. Burr the original was put by Colo Mc.lane in to the hands of TMR. who made this copy from it" (Tr in DLC, in Randolph's

hand, with TJ's notation on verso; RC in ViU, addressed: "Allen MClane Esqr Wilmington Delaware," franked and postmarked; Tr in same, reportedly in the hand of Judge Allen McLane—a descendant—summarized and incomplete, lacks final sentence that concludes "if prudent you are safe"; for the second Tr, see Elizabeth Donnan, ed., *Papers of James A. Bayard, 1796-1815* [Washington, D.C., 1915; repr. New York, 1971], 127-8).

TJ may have received the transcript of this letter from his son-in-law in 1806, when depositions were taken regarding the charge that TJ had bargained with Bayard for the presidency, through the offices of Samuel Smith. Randolph was serving as a Virginia congressman at the time. For a discussion of the controversy, see Malone, *Jefferson*, 4:487-93; Joanne B. Freeman, *Affairs of Honor: National Politics in the New Republic* (New Haven, 2001), 250-3; and Kline, *Burr*, 2:962-8. TJ was accused of agreeing not to dismiss certain government officers on political grounds alone, specifically McLane and George Latimer, collector at Philadelphia (Malone, *Jefferson*, 4:489).

From Hugh Henry Brackenridge

SIR,   Pittsburg February 17th: 1801.

Just about to leave this place to which I will not return until the first of June next. In the mean time shall be in Philadelphia and on the circuit.

The event of your Presidency has most probably by this time taken place, at least designation of taking place on the fourth of March next. I think it morally impossible that the vote of Congress could ultimately be contrary to the voice of the nation known in fact, though not organically expressed; or that the terrific consequences of a suspension, or usurpation of the federal government would be dared. Thinking of you then as the President designate, and on the fourth of March next about to assume the extensive trust, I wish to intrude upon you for a moment with an observation on the removal of quondam officers which may be necessary, and to a certain extent take place. This, the more, because an answer to a question of yours made to me in Philadelphia, and what was said by me in a letter addressed to you some time ago may mislead as to my opinion correctly stated on this subject.

[4]

The question was, what the effect of the decision and proscription as it was called, of Governor McKean's Administration in the removal of officers. My answer was that having not acted with that rigor he would not have been Governor a second time, and that in a memoir to him I had strongly enforced that rigor with regard to the Western Country.

In my letter to you I have said to this effect if my memory serves me that in the change of our elections in favor of the republican interest, experience has shewn that the advice was salutary. But meaning now to explain, I have to say that the removal of officers by Governor McKean was not indiscriminate, but guided by nice discernment judgment and discretion. Policy was consulted, and where the officer was not bad, and had not been an outrageous adversary he was not[1] removed unless indeed in some instance where the office was absolutely wanted to compensate an active friend, perhaps more in need of it than the officer who had possessed it. General hostility and war must be moderated by a skillful man in order to support himself for the use of his friends. Hitting the exact medium in this most delicate part of administration must depend on the most intimate knowledge of characters and standing. Your removals will doubtless be confined chiefly to the higher state officers for some time but will extend ultimately and gradually through the whole organization of the system. It may be of use to you therefore to have the information of the most inconsiderable. It will be of the less consequence for me because there will be representatives in Congress from the districts can inform. Our officers in the Western Country in the Revenue have chiefly been under the appointment of Ross or Addison, I mean Assessors &ca.

It strikes me to say something on the official arrangement of the War Office which occurs to me from the attention I have paid to it from my residence in this Country which has been with short intervals the scene of war for a long time. The errors of military men, or of arrangements in the Army department have been obvious. The present administration appears to be at a loss for a War officer the succeeding will be at a loss for some time also. The War department has long labored under disorders which menaced its destruction—founded on false principles, it has grown in errors and increased in deformities; and now having reached a state of utter chaos, it is to be consigned with all its odium to a new administrator, without records to instruct, guide, guard or govern Him. In this state of things it occurs, that the Senior military officer may be usefully employed in removing the embarrassments and perplexities which encompass this department—Because he has had the chief command of the established troops for more than four years, and has preserved his official correspondence since the year ninety.

It is presumable that he possesses a perfect knowledge of the troops in being, as well their moral energies as their physical capacities.

He understands perfectly the disposition of these troops, & the motives which directed it; and commanding an intimate knowledge of the geography of his country, of the Indian occupancies and force within its limits, and of the fortifications of foreign Powers which border thereon, their strength and objects; he can best determine the expediency of maintaining our present posts, of demolishing them or of erecting new ones.

The obligations of duty which have pointed his attentions to the several departments of the Army, their provisions and expenditures enable him to explain the total destitution of responsibility, of order, discrimation and œconomy throughout, and will assist him to suggest the necessary remedies, to correct the follies and abuses which pervade every branch of service.

At the same time his knowledge of individual merits and pretentions, and of the proper functions of the host of dependents attached to the Military, will enable him to select and to recommend the honest, the able and the deserving.

Being in possession of the immediate projects as well as the ultimate views of the late administration (for the present is without plan principle or design) he may derive much utility from this source.

Give him then the charge of the department to retrench and systematize it—being a western man and popular in the most remote settlements, this avocation may flatter, oblige and give confidence to the people of that portion of the Union. While a minister, competent to the able discharge of the important duties of the station, may be sought for at leisure.

I am Sir With solicitude for your official honor and personal happiness, Your Most Obedient Humble Servant

H H BRACKENRIDGE

RC (DLC); in a clerk's hand, signed by Brackenridge; endorsed by TJ as received 28 Feb. and so recorded in SJL.

The earlier LETTER from Brackenridge was that of 30 Jan.

SENIOR MILITARY OFFICER: James Wilkinson.

[1] Preceding three words repeated in MS.

From Thomas Leiper

DEAR SIR   Philada. Febry. 17th. 1801—

I have this day examined nine Hogsheads of your Tobacco and find
none of them have been Wet & Dried again—It is true one of them is
a little wet but when it received this damage none can tell it might
have been in comming down your River or it might have received it
on its way to Philadelphia but it is so extremely little that I think
there is nothing due on the Score of Damage. Six of the Hhds of
Tobo. were inspected at SPR Two at NNS and One at Lynch. Jackson & Wharton are extremely sorry for the information they give me
the other day that one of your Hhds fell short in weight 234 lb. this
Hhd they find on examination to be none of yours. J & Wharton
shewed me an invoice of Tobacco purchased at the same time of yours
which they say the quality was supperiour to yours—Ten Hhds at
31/6 and Fourteen Hhds at 33/ pr Ct. V. Currency—J & Wharton informs their orders at Richmond was not to exceed for the very best
Tobacco Five Dollars Fifty Cents—their friends from the character of
your Tobacco give six and ship't it them informing them at the same
time if they would give them the first Cost and Commission they
might have it which they agreed to do. It was not convenient to see
any more of the Tobacco to day but I give them to understand I
should attend when the others were opened and if there was any
damage I had full powers from you to make the Allowence They informed me I ought to make an allowence of half a Dollar pr Ct. as the
quality was not so good as formerly I was obliged to acknowledge it
was the worst crop of yours I ever saw—I asked them their price for
the whole Crop they said $7\frac{1}{2}$ Dollars—I told them that was half a
Dollar more than any sale that had been made in Town and I told
them that about the time they made a Purchase of your Tobacco they
had sold Twenty Hhds to be picked from 40 for six Dollars and a half
at 60 and 90 days being in possission of these facts they had nothing
to say but still I must inform you if the Crop of Tobacco I purchased
of you last year and the Crop of yours in the hands of J & Wharton
were both for sale. I certainly would give some $\frac{75}{100}$ or One Dollar pr
Ct. more for what I had than what J & Wharton have got for sale—
The prices of Tobacco at Richmond on the 10th. New 30/ Old 34/
Cash—& 36/ at 90 days—and as the Virginians expect great things
from their intercourse with France I still hope that J & W will get
clear of their Tobo. without much loss—I was beged to take it at Cost
and charges but as the Tobacco was sound I did not see any claim
they had upon you unless your friends engaged it as good as what

I purchased of you last year. in that case they would. I still see the appearance as if the Tobacco had been hung up from hands taken from the heart of the Hhds but nothing like as if they had been Wet—I observe you have said nothing to Clark or Gibson & Jefferson respectg. the Tobacco. to the later I think you should say nothing but Clark you may give my compliment to him and inform it is my opinion if he handles your Tobacco as bad as he has done it this last year you will soon lose your Character of raising fine Tobacco—I am Dear Sir
Your most Obedient St.   THOMAS LEIPER

RC (MHi); at foot of text: "Hon: Thomas Jefferson Vice President of the U States"; endorsed by TJ as received 20 Feb. and so recorded in SJL.

INFORMATION THEY GIVE ME THE OTHER DAY: See Leiper to TJ, 11 Feb. 1801, Vol. 32:572-4.

THEIR FRIENDS: McMurdo & Fisher.

From George Meade

MY DEAR SIR   Philadelphia 17th. February 1801

Interested as I am & every man in America must & ought to be, you must no doubt suppose I am exceedingly Concernd & very desirous of knowing the result of the Election for President of the United States. you may remember that I informd You, how much I was hurt by Mr Adams behaviour respecting the Oration deliverd at our Chappel, nevertheless I am free to declare I wishd him from his long Services (tho' many of them, not approved of by me, as well as others) that he might have been the Successful Candidate at the present Election; but when I came to know he would not be so, & certain, that neither Mr Burr or his friends, could ever entertain an Idea, that he would be the Man, I confess I have felt exceedingly hurt & Mortifyd, that my worthy Mr Jefferson, has not had an unanimous Vote, to make him President. it is a disgrace to the Proceedings of Congress, & will hurt us exceedingly, in the Eyes of all Europe. I have been almost led to curse Party Proceedings, to which only this measure, can be attributed. I yet hope that those unthinking & deluded States, will recover their Senses, & do what is right, by Electing you, & which I am pleased to find, many of the other Side of the Question, wish may be the Case. may you I most sincerely wish be the man, & may you so Conduct Yourself as to put an end to Party Spirit, & gain Immortal honor & be revered as much as our late father of his Country Washington was, by America at large. it is Impossible to Please all Parties, let a man only act, what he deems most beneficial for the good of his Country, & merit must & will have its reward. I wait most anxiously for the decision, & hope in the Course of the week at furthest, to have

Confirmd what I wish for that my friend Mr Jefferson may be announcd to his Country, as our President.   I would sooner have addressd you, but that I have been very unwell & am but just recovering from my Indisposition. with every good wish, & with Sincere Esteem, & regard, believe me to be My Dr. Sir

  Your afft. friend, obliged, & most Obedt. hble Servant

GEO: MEADE

I am apprehensive I shall be too late for to days Post

RC (DLC); addressed: "Honble Thomas Jefferson Esqr President of the Senate, & Vice President of the United States Washington City Mail"; franked and postmarked; endorsed by TJ as received 20 Feb. and so recorded in SJL.

From Nicholas J. Roosevelt

SIR!   New York Feby. 17th. 1801—

I understand sir! that the bill to incorporate a company to work mines and manufacture Metals in the United States is now before your house

I hope you will pardon the liberty I have taken of addressing you on the subject of the Bill when I inform you that I have for several years past been struglling with all the means I could command to make this business successful and find after committing my all, to the event of its success, that few, if any, individual fortunes are equal to the necessary expence of the establishments I have commenced. I must therefore sir! entreat you as the friend of useful manufactures to afford your kind aid and influence with the members of the Senate.—I would have written to you on this subject before had I not expected Chancellor Livingston at my house every day, from whom I intended getting a letter to you on the subject—This Gentleman has regularly visited the works (I have erected) every few months since their commencement and you will see by his subscription to the Mine & Metal Company that he has no doubt of the success of this business provided the Act passes—The Genn. (G Morris) who so warmly opposed the bill the last session is I am informed still opposed, and I fear many others of his party, who would I am convinced rather see me derive that aid from Great Britain which I now solicite from the goverment of the United States. I cannot otherwise see on what grounds Mr. M can oppose the Bill—he cannot possibly oppose it on the grounds of it being unconstitutional when he reflects that the US Bank dailey does business under the Charter granted by Congress:—nor can he oppose it on the principle of monopoly, when he sees that the capital is limitted to a sum, barely sufficient for the objects contemplated, and confined solely to those objects.—

To intrude any longer on your patience would be taking a liberty which I am not entitld to till I obtain a proper introduction—I will therefore close by assuring you that I am sir!

with the greatest respect Your Obedient & Humble St.

NICHS. J. ROOSEVELT

RC (MH); at head of text: "The Honl. Thos. Jefferson Esqr."; endorsed by TJ as received 23 Feb. and so recorded in SJL.

Nicholas J. Roosevelt (1767-1854) established the Soho metal works in New Jersey, operated a rolling mill near Philadelphia, and had a contract to supply the U.S. Navy with copper. He also designed and built steam engines, including one for Robert R. Livingston's experimental steam-powered boat, the *Polacca*. Roosevelt later joined Livingston and Robert Fulton in developing steam navigation on western rivers. In 1808 he married Benjamin Latrobe's daughter Lydia (ANB; Vol. 31:548).

A BILL for the incorporation of Roosevelt's copper mining enterprise had passed the House of Representatives on 30 Jan. and was, when Roosevelt wrote the letter above, in the hands of a Senate committee. On 2 Mch. the Senate declined to advance the bill to a third reading (JHR, 3:740, 766, 778-9; JS, 3:120, 136, 138). A similar measure had failed in the previous session of Congress. For Livingston's involvement in the company and TJ's comments on the incorporation attempt, see Vol. 31:547-50.

Notes on a Letter of William Pinkney

[after 17 Feb. 1801]

a letter from mr Pinckney to mr Thompson   the brother in law of mr Mercer, communicated to mr Rodney,[1] by mr Duval who had seen it, and to Colo. Mercer by Thompson.

'that nothing had raised the credit of America in the eyes of Europe, & even of England itself, as the late election; & that had he been here himself he would have supported it with all his might.'

MS (DLC: TJ Papers, 232:42032); undated; entirely in TJ's hand.

William Pinkney was serving as one of the U.S. commissioners in London appointed to settle claims under Article 7 of the Jay Treaty when the letter described above was written. Upon learning how the letter was being interpreted, he wrote his brother Ninian on 21 July 1801: "Report has certainly taken great liberties with my letter to Mr. Thompson. Undoubtedly I have never written to any person sentiments that go the length you state."

Pinkney noted that when the contest was reduced to TJ and Burr, he decidedly preferred TJ and, when the result of the election in the House of Representatives was known, he may have noted to some of his friends that he was "highly pleased" with the outcome. He also admitted that he had earlier observed that, unlike some Federalists, he was not alarmed at the prospect of a change in administration. Pinkney concluded: "I never could persuade myself to tremble, lest the United States should find, in the presidency of Mr. Jefferson, the evils which might be expected to flow from a weak or a wicked government. I am, on the contrary, satisfied that he has talents, knowledge, integrity, and stake in the country sufficient to give us well-founded confidence, that our affairs will be well administered so far as shall depend on him." But in the summer of 1800, Pinkney had also expressed confidence in Adams's administration and noted to his brother Ninian that he had "done nothing to deserve to be discarded." He continued: "Slight errors should be overlooked in a man who means well, and who has acted essentially right in situations peculiarly arduous and embarrassing" (ANB; Henry Wheaton, *Some*

Account of the Life, Writings, and Speeches of William Pinkney [Philadelphia, 1826], 36-7; William Pinkney, *The Life of William Pinkney* [New York, 1853], 369-73).

Hugh THOMPSON was married to Elizabeth Sprigg and John F. MERCER to Sophia Sprigg, daughters of Richard and Margaret Caile Sprigg (Papenfuse, *Maryland Legislature*, 2:594).

[1] TJ first wrote "the brother in law of mr Duval who communicated it to mr Rodney" before altering the passage to read as above and adding the remainder of the sentence.

Notes on New York Patronage

[after 17 Feb. 1801]

David Gelston of N.Y. Collector of revenue vice Sands. recommdd. by Genl. John Smith.

estimable, popular, a merchant formerly.—but Armstrong says not estimated

devoted to Burr. at any rate this is to lie for further information.[1]

Willett is not popular, not esteemd

liv'd. in ad—y &c—a tool &c—

not approvd. by Clinton. devotd to B.

—————

Rogers the naval officer is an Englishman, come over not long since.

—————

Harrison & Giles ought to go out.

H. a revolutry. tory

G. was an officer. most violent party man.

packs grand juries[2]

—————

Willett was a sheriff many years and a very good one. he might do for that. still not popular.

MS (DNA: RG 59, LAR, 4:0549); undated; entirely in TJ's hand, written on a scrap of paper, probably at several sittings as indicated by interlineations and horizontal rules.

On 9 July TJ appointed David GELSTON to replace Joshua Sands as collector

of New York. JOHN SMITH and Senator John ARMSTRONG were in Washington serving as members of the Sixth Congress from New York and thus were available to offer their opinions on Gelston's candidacy immediately following TJ's election in the House. Noting that he did not know TJ personally, Gelston, on 13 Mch., requested that Madison intervene with the president in his favor. Madison forwarded Gelston's letter to TJ; the president endorsed it and kept it with his papers on appointments (RC in DNA: RG 59, LAR; *Biog. Dir. Cong.*; JEP, 1:403; Madison, *Papers, Sec. of State Ser.*, 1:16-17; Appendix I, List 3).

LIV'D. IN AD—Y: lived in adultery. In 1799 Marinus Willett divorced Susannah Vardle, whom he had married in 1793 immediately after the death of his first wife. Shortly after the divorce he married Margaret Bancker, a much younger woman than he. Willett also had an illegitimate son who was born in 1783 while he was married to his first wife (ANB; Kline, *Burr*, 1:524n). See also Willett to TJ, 24 Feb. 1801.

Although a Federalist with a Loyalist background, Richard ROGERS retained his lucrative position as naval officer at the customs office until 1803 because the Republicans could not agree upon an acceptable replacement for him (Kline, *Burr*, 1:537-8; JEP, 1:453).

In late March, TJ removed Richard Harison, the U.S. district attorney for New York nominated by Washington in 1789, and Aquila GILES, the U.S. marshal in New York since 1792. In one of his lists, TJ noted that Giles was "delinquent in money largely." TJ appointed Edward Livingston and John Swartwout to serve, respectively, in those positions (JEP, 1:32-3, 121-2, 217, 362-3; Appendix I, Lists 3 and 4). That TJ does not list the candidates for these offices indicates that he wrote this note early in his consideration of New York appointments.

[1] Preceding passage, beginning at "but Armstrong," interlined.

[2] Preceding three words interlined above "party man."

To John Adams

SIR,   In Senate, February the 18th. 1801.

I do myself the honor to enclose to you a Resolution of the Senate of this day.

I have the honor to be, Sir, Your most obedient and very humble servant   TH: JEFFERSON

RC (DNA: RG 59, MLR); at foot of text: "The President of the United States"; in hand of Samuel A. Otis, signed by TJ. Not recorded in SJL. Enclosure: Senate resolution of 18 Feb. (same, in Otis's hand; see below).

The Senate on 18 Feb., after receiving official notification from the House of Representatives that the presidential election had been completed, passed a RESOLUTION requesting the president of the U.S. to send Aaron Burr notification of his election to the vice presidency. In accordance with the resolution, TJ as president of the Senate signed a certificate that confirmed the opening and counting of the electoral votes on the second Wednesday in February and the subsequent breaking of the electoral tie by the House, "by all of which it appears, that Aaron Burr Esquire, of New York, is duly elected, agreeably to the Constitution, Vice President of the United States of America." The resolution called for TJ to transmit the certificate to Adams (MS in PHi, certificate dated 18 Feb., in a clerk's hand, signed by TJ, sealed; JS, 3:127-8).

To Henry Dearborn

DEAR SIR   Washington Feb. 18. 1801.

The House of Representatives having yesterday concluded their choice of a person for the chair of the US. and called me to that office, it now becomes necessary to provide an administration composed of persons whose qualifications and standing have possessed them of the public confidence, and whose wisdom may ensure to our fellow citizens the advantages they sanguinely expect. on a review of the characters in the different states proper for the different departments, I have had no hesitation in considering you as the person to whom it would be most advantageous to the public to confide the Department of war. may I therefore hope, Sir, that you will give your country the aid of your talents as Secretary of war? the delay which has attended the election has very much abridged our time and rendered the call more sudden & pressing than I could have wished. I am in hopes our administration may be assembled during the first week of March, except yourself, and that you can be with us a few days after. indeed it is probable we shall be but a few days together (perhaps to the middle of the month) to make some general & pressing arrangements & then go home for a short time to make our final removal hither. I mention these circumstances that you may see the urgency of setting out for this place with the shortest delay possible, which may be the shorter as you can return again to your family, as we shall, to make your final arrangements for removal. I hope I shall not be disappointed in counting on your aid, and that you will favor me with an answer by return of post. accept assurances of sincere esteem & high respect from Dear Sir Your most obedt. & most humble servt   TH: JEFFERSON

RC (NNFoM); at foot of text: "Genl. Dearborn"; at head of text, probably in Levi Lincoln's hand: "No. 4"; addressed by Lincoln: "Honble. Henry Dearborn Esq Pittston District of Maine—Mass"; franked by Lincoln; endorsed by Dearborn. PrC (DLC).

Henry Dearborn (1751-1829) had served two terms in the U.S. House of Representatives, 1793-97, where he favored reductions in the military establishment and drew Madison's notice as an opponent of the Jay Treaty. He was also on TJ's list, drawn up probably in the spring of 1800, of people who were to receive copies of the new appendix to the *Notes on the State of Virginia*. With a common-school education and some practical medical training, Dearborn had set out to be a physician in his native state of New Hampshire, but at the commencement of the war with Britain in 1775 he began military service as a captain. He remained in the army until 1783, attaining the rank of lieutenant colonel and also serving briefly as deputy quartermaster general. After the war he lived in Maine, which was still part of Massachusetts. Prior to his election to Congress he held local office, was a shipowner and government contractor, and served as U.S. marshal. He held the militia rank of major general (ANB; Richard Alton Erney, *The Public Life of Henry Dearborn* [New York, 1979; orig. Ph.D. diss., Columbia University, 1957], 22-5, 29-31; *Biog. Dir. Cong.*, 888; Vol. 29:94-5; Vol. 31:551).

To William Jackson

Washington Feb. 18. 1801.

Your favor of the 3d. inst. has been duly recieved. I percieve in it that friendship which I ever found in your character, & which honors every character in which it is found. I feel myself indebted also for the justice you do me as to opinions which others, with less candour, have imputed to me. I have recieved many letters stating to me, in the spirit of prophecy, caricatures which the writers, it seems, know are to be the principles of my administration. to these no answer has been given, because the prejudiced spirit in which they have been written proved the writers not in a state of mind to yield to truth or reason. to the friendly stile of your letter I would gladly answer in detail, were it in my power. but I have thought that I ought not to permit myself to form opinions in detail until I can have the counsel of those, of whose services I wish to avail the public in the administration of their affairs. till this can be done, you have justly resorted to the only proper ground, that of estimating my future, by my past conduct. upwards of [30.] years passed on the stage of public life & under the public eye, may surely enable them to judge whether my future course is likely to be marked with those departures from reason & moderation, which the passions of [some] have been willing to foresee. one imputation in particular has been repeated till it seems as if some at least believed it: that I am an enemy to commerce. they admit me a friend to agriculture, and suppose me an enemy to the only means of disposing of it's produce. I might appeal too to evidences of my attention to the commerce & navigation of our country in different stations connected with them. but this would lead to details not to be expected. I have deferred answering your letter till this day lest the motives for these explanations should be mistaken you will be so good as to consider the communication so far confidential as not to put it in the power of any person [to commit] it to the press.

I am with great esteem Dear Sir Your most obedt. servt

Th: Jefferson

PrC (DLC); faint; at foot of text: "Majr. William Jackson."

List of John Adams's Judicial Appointments

qu. Lowell (now district judge) to be Chief judge
+   Benj. Bourne (R.I.) ⎫
+   Jer. Smith. (N.H.) ⎬ judges of 1st. circuit
                        ⎭
qu   John Davis. (now district atty) judge vice Lowell
—   H. G. Otis distr. atty vice Davis.
qu. Ray Greene distr. judge vice Bourne
—   E. St. L. Livermore. N.H. distr. atty vice Smith.

———————

2d. circuit
+   Benson. chief judge
+   Ol. Wolcott   ⎫
+   Saml. Hitchcock Verm. ⎬ judges circuit
                          ⎭

———————

3d. Circuit
Ingersoll. Ch. judge[1]
+   Basset   ⎫
+   Wm. Griffith. N.J ⎬ judges circ.
                      ⎭
—   Kittera distr. atty vice Ingersol

———————

4th. circ.
Chas. Lee Ch. judge[2]
⊕   Phil. B. Key. Maryld. ⎫
+   G. Keith Taylor Va.   ⎬ judges.
                          ⎭
—   Theoph. Parsons Atty Gen. vice Lee

MS (DNA: RG 59, MCL); undated; entirely in TJ's hand, with symbols and "qu." added in margin and cancellations (see notes below) made at a later date; endorsed by TJ on verso: "appointmts. by mr Adams."

On 18 Feb. John Adams sent the above judicial nominations to the Senate. TJ probably made this list as he presided and heard the names read. The appointments were approved two days later. The Senate learned shortly afterwards that Jared Ingersoll and Charles Lee had declined appointment, and TJ accordingly canceled their names. Adams's nomination of Philip B. Key in the place of Lee accounts for the special symbol by Key's name (JEP, 1:381, 383, 385-6).

On a separate scrap of paper dated 24 Feb., TJ noted the name of "Elijah Paine. judge," Adams's nominee for the Vermont district judgeship vacated by Samuel Hitchcock's appointment as circuit judge. On the same paper, with a date of 25 Feb., TJ wrote "Philip B. Key. chief judge vice Lee" and "Magill judge of W. distr. Virga." He added plus signs, probably in pencil, in front of the three names, which were approved by the Senate on the 25th and 26th (MS in DNA: RG 59, MCL, entirely in TJ's hand; JEP, 1:384-6).

[1] Entry canceled.
[2] Entry canceled.

To James Madison

Notwithstanding the suspected infidelity of the post, I must hazard this communication. The Minority in the H. of R. after seeing the impossibility of electing B. the certainty that a legislative usurpation would be resisted by arms, and a recourse to a Convention to reorganise & amend the government, held a consultation on this dilemma. Whether it would be better for them to come over in a body, and go with the tide of the times, or by a negative conduct suffer the election to be made by a bare majority, keeping their body entire & unbroken, to act in phalanx on such ground of opposition as circumstances shall offer? we knew their determination on this question only by their vote of yesterday. Morris of V. withdrew, which made Lyon's vote that of his state. the 4 Maryland Federalists put in 4. blanks which made the positive tickets of the collegues the vote of the state. S. Carolina & Delaware put in blanks. so there were 10. states for one candidate. 4. for another & 2. blanks. we consider this therefore as a declaration of war, on the part of this band. but their conduct appears to have brought over to us the whole body of Federalists, who being alarmed with the danger of a dissolution of the government, had been made most anxiously to wish the very administration they had opposed, & to view it when obtained as a child of their own. they see too their quondam leaders separated fairly from them & themselves aggregated under other banners. even Hamilton & Higginson have been zealous partisans for us. this circumstance, with the unbounded confidence which will attach to the new ministry as soon as known, will start us on high ground. mr A. embarrasses us. He keeps the offices of State & War vacant, has named Bayard M.P. to France, and has called an unorganized Senate on the 4th. of March. as you do not like to be here on that day, I wish you could come within a day or two after. I think that between that & the middle of the month we can so far put things under way, as that we may go home to make arrangements for our final removal. come to Conrad's where I will bespeak lodgings for you.—yesterday mr A. nominated Bayard to be M.P. of the US. to the French republic: to-day Theophilus Parsons Atty Genl of the US. in the room of C. Lee, who with Keith Taylor cum multis aliis are appointed judges under the new system. H. G. Otis is nominated a district attorney. a vessel has been waiting for some time in readiness to carry the new minister to France. my affectionate salutations to mrs Madison & yourself. Adieu.

RC (DLC: Madison Papers, Rives Collection); addressed: "James Madison junr. near Orange court house"; franked; postmarked 19 Feb. PrC (DLC).

The votes of Lewis R. MORRIS and Matthew Lyon canceled each other out until the last ballot on 17 Feb., in which Morris withdrew from the chamber giving Lyon control of Vermont's vote in favor of TJ. John C. Thomas, William Craik, John Dennis, and George Baer as the four MARYLAND FEDERALISTS cast blank votes, thereby allowing the vote of colleagues Samuel Smith, George Dent, Joseph H. Nicholson, and Gabriel Christie to become THE VOTE OF THE STATE (*Annals*, 10:1032-3).

HAMILTON & HIGGINSON: Alexander Hamilton and Stephen Higginson, Sr., a Federalist and Boston merchant.

COME TO CONRAD'S: Conrad & McMunn's boarding house.

CUM MULTIS ALIIS: with many others.

From Benjamin Perkins

SIR   Washington City February 18th 1801

Inclosed you will find a Plan for a Capitol for a Column or Pilaster upon a new Principle

the Stripes is an Emblem of the United States Supported by two Cornucopia's Emblems of Plenty   the Oak Leafes & acorns are an Emblem of Freedom an Extinguished Torch an Emblem of Death the Drooping willow Emblem of Mourning—

I have Made Some Progress in Drawing a Mausoleum Connected with a Semenary of Education the Room Designed for Commencment & Publick Speaking to have a Concave Ceiling Supported with Dime Pilasters upon this Plan which Should be Called the Washington Order

If it is not too much Trouble Pleas to give me your Opinion of this Idea—if it is not Proper for me to Expects it of you Give yourself no Trouble

    I am with Respect your Hbl Svt   BENJN. PERKINS

a Post

    NB I am a Scholar of Mr Daniel Trump of Philadelphia

RC (ViW); addressed: "Thomas Jefferson Vice President of the United States Washington City"; postmarked 19 Feb.; endorsed by TJ as received 20 Feb. and so recorded in SJL. Enclosure: drawing of the capital of a column as described in the letter above (MS in same; signed by Perkins and dated by him 15 Dec. 1801).

Perkins was apparently the brother of Thomas Perkins and may have come originally from Delaware. Benjamin Perkins lodged in Washington on New York Avenue near the Octagon, John Tayloe's town house designed by William Thornton. Perkins was still in Washington in 1805, when he joined a subscription to establish a school (RCHS, 33-4 [1932], 289; C. M. Harris, ed., *Papers of William Thornton: Volume One, 1781-1802* [Charlottesville, 1995], 584-6; Thomas Perkins to TJ, 24 Mch. 1801, and Benjamin Perkins's letter of 15 May noted there).

To Craven Peyton

DEAR SIR   Washington Feb. 18. 1801.

I find myself very much indebted for your kind agency in the purchase of the lands for me from the Henderson's, and shall be still more so if you will take for me also Tucker Woodson's part at the price of 500. D. proposed by him, putting off paiment till the month of June, within the course of which all the shares shall be paid for. you mention having bought mr Kerr's part. I do not know whether I am to conclude from your letter that you would be willing to let that go with the others. I should willingly give you the same price as to Tucker Woodson, as it is interesting to me to get as much of the tract as I can. I still think it would be better that it should be kept quite out of sight that I am concerned in this: if the division could be put off till immediately after our April court I may attend to it, or at least be in the way to advise concerning it. should you procure Woodson's or propose to part with your own share, I will thank you for a line.

Yesterday the election was concluded, which fixes me here. I shall nevertheless pay a visit to Monticello somewhere between the middle of March & our April court. accept assurances of the esteem of Dear Sir

Your friend & servt   TH: JEFFERSON

PrC (ViU); at foot of text: "Craven Peyton esq."; endorsed by TJ in ink on verso.

For TJ's PURCHASE OF THE LANDS from the Henderson estate, see Craven Peyton to TJ, 6 Feb., and Vol. 31:199n.

From Benjamin Stoddert

SIR   February 18. 1801.

My health & my private affairs have for sometime required more of my attention than the duties of my office would permit me to give to them; and I have therefore been anxious to relinquish my official situation, which would have been done before this time, had Mr Adams been re-elected, for in that event he could have found no difficulty in supplying my vacancy.

Thus circumstanced, I hope you will attribute to the true motives, this early expression of my wish, that it may be consistent with your arrangements to provide a successor for me, in the Department of the Navy, so that I may be relieved from its duties in the course of the next month—the sooner in the month, the more convenient it will be to me.

Permit me to add, that though I am not among the number of those who desired your elevation to the important station you are about to fill; none will more sincerely pray that your administration may realize the most sanguine expectations which have been formed of it—nor, in the Walks of private life, more zealously support the Just measures of the Government.

I have the honor to be with due Respect sir Yr. most Obed. Servt.

BEN STODDERT

RC (DLC); endorsed by TJ as received 20 Feb. and so recorded in SJL.

Benjamin Stoddert (1751-1813) had been secretary of the navy since the spring of 1798. TJ had also had some contact with him in the early 1790s, when Stoddert, a Georgetown tobacco merchant and business partner of Uriah Forrest, was involved in land transactions in the Federal District (ANB; Vol. 20:78-9; Vol. 22:41n; Vol. 23:323).

From Caspar Wistar

DR SIR   Philada Feby. 18th 1801.

I should have replied sooner to your favour of Feby. 3d. but I did not wish to intrude upon you at a period so awfully important to our Country—the accounts we have received this day (from Washington on Sunday) are such as give us great reason to hope that some of the Gentlemen to whom accident has given the power to decide will have obeyed the dictates of reason & finished the dispute before this reaches you—Upon this subject I think it right to state to you the strong conviction of my mind, that the great bulk of the people here who are of the federal party, as it is improperly called, do not approve of the late proceedings of that party in Congress, but consider them as contrary to the spirit & principles of our Constitution. The spirit of party is much stronger among some Gentlemen in public life, than it is among the people at large who if left to themselves would reciprocally tolerate with good humour the diversity of political sentiment which seems inevitable in our present situation—

It seems very reasonable to hope that under the approaching Administration many angry passions will subside, & social intercourse will be greatly improved, as the people cannot but see that the late proceedings have originated in the wish to retain power & influence—with this pleasing hope I leave the subject for the present—

Your extracts from Chanceller Livingston's letter do not afford as strong reasons for hoping that we shall soon complete our Skeleton at Philada & I feel the propriety of the suggestion to fix upon a few of the most important parts & confine the request to them, but I find myself in the situation of a country man who was asked what he would be helped to at a large entertainment, &, after surveying the table with great attention, replied I should like a little of all—as all cannot be had, I will beg to be helped to the head & feet & shoulder blade if they are to spare. From the description which I have the pleasure to inclose, you will see that the Specimens are remarkably large, it is therefore to be wished that the curious People of[1] may take good care of them, especially of the head—You probably have been informed ere this of the election of Chancellor Livingsto[n,] it is remarkable that it should be left to so late a Period—Mr Ellicott who was engaged in writing to you at the time of the election charged himself with the care of the Diploma—Having made this letter too long I will only add that

with sentiments of most sincere esteem I am your obliged friend

C. WISTAR JUNR.

RC (DLC); margin frayed; at foot of text: "Honble T. Jefferson"; endorsed by TJ as received 21 Feb. and so recorded in SJL. Enclosure: very likely Sylvanus Miller's letter of 20 Sep. 1800 to Samuel L. Mitchill on the recently discovered fossil bones; a clipping of the first two pages of Miller's letter, as printed in Mitchill's *Medical Repository*, 4 [1801], 211-12, and with what appears to be Wistar's note at the foot summarizing the remainder of the account, is in TJ's papers (DLC: TJ Papers, 107:18373).

TJ's letter to Wistar on 3 Feb. contained EXTRACTS of Robert R. Livingston's communication of 7 Jan. about the prospects of acquiring some portion of the SKELETON of the "mammoth" (mastodon) that had been discovered west of Newburgh, New York (see also Wistar to TJ, 19 Oct., 8 Dec. 1800; TJ to Livingston, 14 Dec.). For Livingston's ELECTION to the American Philosophical Society, see TJ's letter to him of 16 Feb. 1801. Andrew ELLICOTT wrote TJ on 18 Jan., two days after Livingston's election to membership.

[1] Wistar omitted a word at the turn of a page in MS.

To Thomas Mann Randolph

TH: J. TO TMR.   Washington Feb. 19. 1801.

After exactly a week's balloting there at length appeared 10. states for me, 4. for Burr & 2. voted blanks. this was done without a single vote coming over. Morris of Vermont withdrew, so that Lyon's vote became that of the state. the 4. Maryland federalists put in blanks, so that the vote of the 4. Republicans became that of their state. mr Huger of S. Carolina (who had constantly voted for me) withdrew by agreement, his collegues agreeing in that case to put in blanks. Bayard the sole member of Delaware voted blank. they had before deliberated whether they would come over in a body, when they saw they could not force

Burr on the republicans, or keep their body entire & unbroken to act in phalanx on such ground of opposition as they shall hereafter be able to conjure up. their vote shewed what they had decided on, and is considered as a declaration of perpetual war. but their conduct has completely left them without support. our information from all quarters is that the whole body of federalists concurred with the Republicans in the last election, & with equal anxiety. they had been made to interest themselves so warmly for the very choice, which while before the people they opposed, that when obtained it came as a thing of their own wishes, and they find themselves embodied with the republicans, & their quondam leaders separated from them. and I verily believe they will remain embodied with us: so that this conduct of the minority has done in one week what very probably could hardly have been effected by years of mild and impartial administration. a letter from mr Eppes informs me that Maria is in a situation which induces them not to risk a journey to Monticello, so we shall not have the pleasure of meeting them there. I begin to hope I may be able to leave this place by the Middle of March. my tenderest love to my ever dear Martha & kisses to the little ones. accept yourself sincere & affectionate salutations. Adieu.

RC (DLC); endorsed by Randolph as received on the 26th. PrC (same).

For the LETTER FROM John Wayles EPPES, see TJ to Eppes, 22 Feb.

From Stephen Thorn

HONOURED SIR   George Town Feby 19th: 1801

Some time in December last, I had the honour of sending you by post, a large packet of Letters from Mr Paine at Paris, particularly entrusted to my care by the writer, which with the books[1] accompanying the same, I hope you have received.—Permit me to congratulate you on your late appointment to the Office of President of the United States—It will greatly add to the triumph of Republican principles in Europe as well as in the Country where fair freedom rose

Having been several years in Europe, nay throughout the greatest part thereof, and during a long residence in paris, have followed up the history of the French Revolution, being assisted by several literary characters there of great respectability in some observations thereon; to complete which, as well as to arange some private concerns in that Country, where I have a landed property, makes me desirous to return there—therefore as the treaty is adopted and we have no consular agent at Havre, I could wish for that appointment, and to return by the first public occasion—The enclosed papers are submitted for your consideration, besides my friend Col Lyon, and who has known me from a boy, will give you any information respecting me—

Salut et respect   STEPN. THORN

RC (DNA: RG 59, LAR); at foot of text: "Mr. Jefferson"; endorsed by TJ as received 20 Feb. and so recorded in SJL; also endorsed by TJ: "to be consul at Havre." Enclosures not found.

THE TREATY IS ADOPTED: on 3 Feb. the Senate agreed to the Convention of 1800 with France, but only if Article 2 were excised and an eight-year limit imposed on the duration of the pact. The convention's second article would have postponed the settlement of indemnities for private shipping that had been captured at sea during the period of hostility between the two nations, and it made the treaties of 1778 and the consular convention of 1788 inoperative until the indemnities were resolved. During the negotiations in 1800, indemnification was a paramount issue for the American envoys (Oliver Ellsworth, William Vans Murray, and William R. Davie). However, the United States had abrogated the treaties of 1778, which contained articles that conflicted with privileges granted to Britain by the Jay Treaty. The French, who hoped to avoid responsibility for payment of indemnities, would

not discuss the settlement of spoliation claims without receiving in return either an affirmation of the terms of the earlier alliance or a new treaty that would give France status equal, at least, to that enjoyed by Great Britain. In order to break the impasse and allow the two nations to come to terms on other matters, the Americans suggested a deferment of the problem issues. Article 2—and the designation of the pact as a convention rather than a treaty—was the result of that compromise. The Senate, by refusing to approve the article, indicated that restoration of the treaty of amity and commerce of 1778 was not a possibility, although the excision of Article 2 also meant that the convention would contain no provision for the settlement of spoliation claims (JEP, 1:377; Miller, *Treaties*, 2:458-9; E. Wilson Lyon, "The Franco-American Convention of 1800," *Journal of Modern History*, 12 [1940], 305-33; TJ to Oliver Ellsworth and William Vans Murray, [18] Mch. 1801; Vol. 32:159n, 504, 539-40n).

[1] MS: "books books."

To Thomas Whitlaw

SIR   Washington Feb 19. 1801.

As it is now settled that I am to [remain here] I can no longer [. . .] to build myself the nailshop at Monticello which I proposed to you to undertake. I must therefore engage you to do it yourself out & out, and will give you the price you then stated to be the lowest you could take. what that was I do not now recollect with certainty, but I have a note of it at home, made at the time as I [suppose] you have also.[1] I shall be at home about the 19th. or 20th. of March, at which time I should be glad [if] you could make it convenient to be ready to begin [the shop]. the [. . .] ought to be got into place by that time. my reason for wishing to be at home when it is begun is in order to [. . .] on the plan & some other particulars. it is probable my waggon could be hired to you by the day [for] a part of the [loading]. I know not what sort of work [. . .] do [. . .] team of mules; but I should expect only a proportion [. . .]. I will thank you to drop me a line directed to this place immediately, that I may know whether I may consider the matter as [set]. I am Sir

Your very humble servt   TH: JEFFERSON

PrC (MoSHi: Jefferson Papers); faint and blurred; frayed at margin; at foot of text: "Mr. Thomas Whately"; endorsed by TJ in ink on verso.

Thomas Whitlaw, whom TJ addressed and recorded in SJL as "Whately," is probably the brickmason recorded by Nicholas Lewis as "Thomas Whitlough," who earlier had built a kitchen oven at Monticello. Whitlaw hired TJ's slave Jupiter while TJ was in France. In June 1801, Whitlaw was preparing to build the walls of the public tobacco warehouse in Richmond. He was described as "a stone mason celebrated for faithful execution of his work" (Jack McLaughlin, *Jefferson and Monticello: The Biography of a Builder* [New York, 1988], 247, 425; CVSP, 9:234, 258).

On 28 Feb., the day after receiving the letter above, Whitlaw responded from "Albemarle" that he was "exceedingly sorry" but previous engagements prevented him from being at Monticello on the date TJ requested. He closed by noting that as soon as the "business on hand" was completed he would be happy to come if TJ still wanted him (RC in MoSHi: Jefferson Papers; endorsed by TJ as received 6 Mch. and so recorded in SJL). TJ paid Whitlaw for stone in 1799 but he does not appear again in TJ's financial records (MB, 2:1009).

A letter from Whitlaw to TJ of 13 Feb. 1794, recorded in SJL as received the following day, has not been found.

[1] Preceding six words interlined.

From John Adams

SIR   Washington Feb. 20. 1801

In order to save you the trouble and Expence of purchasing Horses and Carriages, which will not be necessary, I have to inform you that I shall leave in the stables of the United States seven Horses and two Carriages with Harness the Property of the United States. These may not be suitable for you: but they will certainly save you a considerable Expence as they belong to the studd of the Presidents Household.

I have the Honor to be with great respect, Sir your most obedient and humble Servant   JOHN ADAMS

RC (Amor Hollingsworth, Boston, 1951); at foot of text: "Thomas Jefferson Esqr Vice President of the United States and President Elect for four years from the 4 of March next"; endorsed by TJ as received 21 Feb. and so recorded in SJL. FC (Lb in MHi: Adams Papers).

When the House of Representatives discussed appropriations for the president's household on 2 Mch., Joseph Varnum and Samuel Smith expressed dismay that Adams had bought the HORSES and vehicles with funds approved for furnishings. Congress, by an act approved the next day, determined that all items in the president's household other than furniture should be sold, along with any furniture not fit for use, and the proceeds combined with appropriations to purchase additional furniture (*Annals*, 10:1070-1; U.S. Statutes at Large, 2:121-2; Malone, *Jefferson*, 4:41).

To Samuel Dexter

DEAR SIR   Washington Feb. 20. 1801.

The liberality of the conversation you honored me with yesterday evening has given me great satisfaction, & demands my sincere thanks. it is certain that those of the cabinet council of the President should be of his bosom-confidence. our geographical position has been an impediment to that, while I can with candor declare that the imperfect opportunities I have had of acquaintance with you have inspired an entire esteem for your character, and that you will carry with you that esteem and sincere wish to be useful to you. the accomodation you have been so kind as to offer as to the particular date of retiring from[1] office is thankfully accepted, and shall be the subject of a particular letter to you as soon as circumstances shall enable me to speak with certainty. in the mean time accept assurances of my high respect & consideration.   TH: JEFFERSON

RC (DLC); at foot of text: "The honble Samuel Dexter Secretary of the Treasury."

DATE OF RETIRING: Dexter continued in office until 6 May (*Biog. Dir. Cong.*).

[1] TJ here canceled "your."

From Pierre Samuel Du Pont de Nemours

MONSIEUR,   New York 20 Fevrier 1801.

Vous n'avez jamais eu qu' *un Vice*. Je fais mon compliment à votre Patrie et aux deux Mondes de ce qu'enfin vous l'avez perdu.

Salut et respect.   DU PONT (DE NEMOURS)

EDITORS' TRANSLATION

SIR,   New York, 20 February 1801

You have never had but *one vice*. I compliment your fatherland and both worlds on the fact that you have finally lost it.

Greetings and respect.   DU PONT (DE NEMOURS)

RC (MHi); at head of text in English: "To greatest Man in greatest Place of the United States"; endorsed by TJ as received 25 Feb. and so recorded in SJL.

To the House of Representatives

Feb. 20. 1801.

I recieve Gentlemen[1] with profound thankfulness, this testimony of   confidence from the great representative council of our nation. it fills up the measure of that grateful satisfaction which had already been derived from the suffrages of my fellow citizens themselves, designating me as one of those to whom they were willing to commit this charge, the most important of all others to them. In deciding between the candidates, whom their equal vote presented to your choice,[2] I am sensible that age has been respected, rather than more active & useful qualifications. I know the difficulties of the station to which I am called, and feel and acknolege[3] my incompetence to them.   but whatsoever of understanding, whatsoever of diligence, whatsoever of justice, or of affectionate concern for the happiness of man, it has pleased providence to place within the compass of my faculties, shall be called forth for the discharge of the duties confided to me, & for procuring to my fellow citizens all the benefits which our constitution has placed under the guardianship of the general government.   Guided by the wisdom and patriotism of those to whom it belongs to express the legislative will of the nation, I will give to that will a faithful execution.   I pray you, Gent. to convey to the honorable body from which you are deputed the homage of my humble acknolegements, & the sentiments of zeal & fidelity, by which I shall endeavor to merit these proofs of confidence from the nation and it's representatives.[4]

Accept yourselves, gentlemen,[5] my particular thanks for the obliging terms in which you have been pleased to communicate their will.

TH: JEFFERSON

Dft (DLC); at foot of text: "Messrs. Pinckney, Tazewell & Bayard"; general appearance and use of erasure for several changes suggest that TJ may have initially intended this manuscript to be the RC or a fair copy. Printed in JHR, 3:815, with variations in punctuation, spelling, capitalization, and paragraphing. Not recorded in SJL.

THE GREAT REPRESENTATIVE COUNCIL OF OUR NATION: the House of Representatives. Immediately after completing the balloting for president on 17 Feb. the House appointed Thomas Pinckney, Littleton W. Tazewell, and James A. Bayard to wait on Adams and inform him of TJ's election. Two days later the House ordered the same committee to notify the president-elect. TJ received a copy of the House's order, extracted from the journal and signed by the clerk, John H. Oswald (MS in DLC). Pinckney informed the House that the committee also made a brief address to TJ: "The committee beg leave to express their wishes for the prosperity of your administration; and their sincere desire that it may promote your own happiness and the welfare of our country." The House received TJ's reply on the 21st (JHR, 3:803, 808, 815).

[1] Word interlined.

[2] TJ here interlined, then erased, "of the H. of R."

[3] Preceding two words interlined.

[4] JHR continues here with a semicolon, the word "and," and no paragraph break.

[5] Word lacking in JHR.

From Josef Ignacio de Viar

SIR   Philadelphia 20th. Febry. 1801

The agreeable News, which Reached us yesterday Morning of your Election to the Presidential Chair, have afforded me singular satisfaction, and Now beg, you will accept of my most sincere congratulation on the Occassion.

I have the honor to be with great esteem, and Respect Sir Your most obt and humble Servt   JOSEPH IGNAT VIAR

RC (DLC); at foot of text: "Thoms. Jefferson Esqr. Vice-President of the United States. &c"; endorsed by TJ as received 23 Feb. and so recorded in SJL.

From George Logan

RESPECTED CITIZEN   Lancaster Feby: 20: 1801

I congratulate you & our Country on the determination of the important question in which every real friend to his Country found himself deeply interested. I received a Letter last evening from our friend John Dickinson of Wilmington, no man is more anxious for the republican cause. The Legislature of this State have continued in Session to this time, in order to take measures in case of an usurpation. We shall now adjourn in two or three days—

I am with sentiments of respect Your friend   GEO LOGAN

RC (DLC); endorsed by TJ as received 23 Feb. and so recorded in SJL.

MEASURES IN CASE OF AN USURPATION: see Thomas McKean to TJ, 20 Feb. and 21 Mch.

From James Lyon

SIR   GeoTown. Feb. 20th. 1801

The important contest in which the friends of Liberty have been so long and so arduously engaged, having been so happily decided, I cannot refrain from congratulating you, and through you, Mankind, not one of whom but must, more or less, sooner or later, participate in the benefits immediately or remotely resulting from the present triumph of republican Principles.—

As the period will very shortly arrive when you are to take the management of the executive business of the nation, and when important affairs must so croud your attention, that you cannot be expected to have leisure to attend to the individual concerns of your friends, without being in some way informed of their wishes; and being convinced that no change in your situation can subvert that urbanity and frankness of manners ever characteristic of honest republicans, I prefer addressing you without formality, in a manner altogether in my power, to the more ceremonious and troublesome channel of friends.

Wishing not to be two early in my application and fearing lest the object of it might be secured to some other person, I have been halting between two opinions, but have chose to make my application direct, relying upon your liberality to pardon any impropriety in point time, manner, &c. The favor which I am about to ask from you, I am sensible does not derive immediately from yourself, but I am confident it will be none the less at your command.

I understand that the Secretary of State is authorised to contract for printing the necessary quantity of the Laws of Congress, which, together with other printing attached to his office, would be a very valuable acquisition to my business. If the printing of the laws of the present session of Congress will fall under the direction of the new Secretary of State, it will, perhaps, be easy for you to assist me to that business.

What pretentions it is necessary to prefer, to command success in this application, I know not, neither do I know what competitors I have or whether any—but since the patriotic Bache, Greenleaf, and Adams are no more, there can be *none*, of my profession, *older* in the service of the republican cause, than myself. Altho' I disclaim the idea of asking, or considering a preference of this kind as a compensation for extraordinary exertions and sufferings in that cause, yet if those things have any weight in the scale of preferment, it is but fair for me to claim the merit of those exertions, and even to boast of having been for eight years past a victim of opposition, to a system of policy, and measures, which in the cradle of their infancy, few were discerning enough to foresee the gigantic stature to which they have since arrived. Yes, I claim the honor of having established the first republican press in Vermont; of having for six years, at the expence of my time and patrimony, combatted those destructive measures; and of having by my exertions contributed to keep *one district*, even in the verge of the N. England vortex, correct in their politicks from the first until oppression, and persecution for those principles, which are now triumphant, drove me out. My pursuits for the last two years you have a sufficient knowledge of, to Judge of the advantages, if any, derived therefrom. I have often regretted my want of capital, and in some instances, want of support, to enable me to proceed in that pride of pursuits, the establishment of Republican presses: there are yet many circles where the noxious vapours of aristocracy, require to be dispelled by the rays of republican presses, and should any future situation enable me to do it, I should, with pride, renew that goodly work.

If you feel at liberty to communicate with me upon the subject of this letter, I shall be happy to receive a line from you.

Sir with perfect Esteem, your obedient Servt.   J LYON

RC (DNA: RG 59, LAR); addressed: "Thomas Jefferson, Esquire, President elect, of the U.S."; endorsed by TJ as received 20 Feb. and so recorded in SJL.

Lyon's deceased fellow republican printers were Benjamin Franklin BACHE of the Philadelphia *Aurora*, Thomas GREENLEAF of the New York *Argus*, and Thomas ADAMS of the Boston *Independent Chronicle*.

From Thomas McKean

DEAR SIR,   Lancaster Febry. 20th. 1801.

Your favor of the 2d. instant did not come to hand until last Saturday night; I had written a long answer, and detailed my intended operations in case of a certain unfortunate event in the decision of the House of Representatives of the U.S. Engaged in this work a little before eleven this forenoon our Express arrived from Washington with letters from my friends, announcing the glorious intelligence of your election as President; on which permit me to congratulate you and my country. In consequence of this news my long letter has been committed to the flames. The Bells in this Borough have been ringing ever since until Sundown—The two Houses of our Legislature were electrified, and in a few minutes adjourned 'till tomorrow: my Republican friends had agreed to continue in Session till after the 4th. of March, to aid my projected Plan, which the Federalists would call, "a bold stroke."

I have had a daily communication of what has passed in your city since the 9th. and must charge the days that have passed since to the account of anxiety & distress. However every thing is now as it should be, a new æra has commenced, and I fear not for the future, tho' from experience, I know, you will have for a time to wade thro' a sea of troubles.

On Wednesday General Muhlenberg was elected by *a joint vote* of the two Houses of this State a Senator in the Senate of the U.S.; he had 46 votes, Doctor Geo. Logan 45—the choice was a surprize on the Republicans, for all the federalists to a man (34) voted for the former: both of the candidates are good Republicans & worthy men, but the Republicans knew that General Mulenberg was not only elected for the next two years in the House of Representatives, but would be so in future as long as he chose, and that the vacating his seat would put his place to hazard, and therefore they preferred the latter. An Express has been just sent to General Muhlenberg to acquaint him with these particulars; if he declines serving as a Senator, which I hope, I shall receive his resignation after our Legislature shall have adjourned, and will forthwith appoint Doctor Logan until their next meeting in December; so that at all or any event you may depend on having a Republican Senator in the Senate of the U.S. on the 4th. of March. I have had a summons for a Senator for this State to attend on that day at ten o'clock A.M. &c signed by President Adams, which I shall detain until I learn General Muhlenberg's determination.

I can add no more, as the mail will presently close for tonight, but that I am, with great sincerity & truth anxious for your health and happiness,   Your   THOS M:KEAN

P.S. excuse haste &c.

RC (DLC); at head of text: "Private"; endorsed by TJ as received 25 Feb. and so recorded in SJL.

PROJECTED PLAN: see McKean to TJ, 21 Mch. 1801.

John Peter Gabriel MUHLENBERG, elected to the U.S. Senate on 18 Feb., accepted the appointment and attended the special session of Congress on 4-5 Mch. He resigned the seat on 30 June and McKean appointed George LOGAN, who served the remainder of the term (*Biog. Dir. Cong.*; JS, 3:147).

In Washington on 20 Feb. the Republican congressmen from Pennsylvania, Michael Leib, Robert Brown, Joseph Hiester, John Smilie, John A. Hanna, and Andrew Gregg, addressed and signed a communication to "the President of the United States" recommending Muhlenberg for the position of supervisor of the revenue for the state. They explained: "the merits of General Muhlenberg fully entitle him to this office, he having served his Country with fidelity & success as a General officer during the Revolutionary war, & having, since the establishment of the present government been an uniform & able supporter of the Republican cause" (MS in DNA: RG 59, LAR; endorsed by TJ: "Muhlenburg Genl."). TJ did not record this document in SJL but he entered Muhlenberg's name on his list of candidates and noted he was recommended by "delegates of Pensva." on 20 Feb. On 27 June, TJ appointed Muhlenberg to the position as recommended by his congressional colleagues (See Appendix I, Lists 1 and 3).

From Stephen Sayre

Sɪʀ   Philaa. 20th. Feb: 1801—

I am honor'd with your answer, so far as it was, then in your power to reply—and I am truly sensible of your kindness.

We have now the grateful sound of bells & cannon, on the happy event, of your election.—to us, who have risque'd our future hopes, on the issue, who deem'd our country lost, or saved, by the result, you must suppose it was music to the soul—to others, the news was like the pangs of death. May you long enjoy those delicious feelings, which must fill your mind, & delate your heart, to be, thus, the object of your native country's confidence, & love. You have enemies, but they are the enemies of the state.

Don't suppose this flattery—I have never yet practised the means by which I might have found my advantage, & where it was necessary—& I shall not begin with Mr Jefferson, who must hold the language of adulation in contempt—on the contrary, I now take the liberty, to remark—that the conflict has not been personal—you are the depository of our confidence to secure the blessings, which we expect under the forms & principles of a republican government—we trust you will not only act upon those principles, yourself, but employ none of those who have, dared to oppose them. to say this, I am, impel'd by duty—because I hear my fellow citizens, every hour, express their fears, that you will forgive their political sins

If you will take the trouble of looking over my letter again—you will find no Idea, express'd, or imply'd, as to our geting entangled in the affairs of Europe—I most cordially detest our policy, respecting our foreign relations, for many years past—but when an opportunity presents itself, such as at this moment, in which we should act as mediators, on the great scale of universal peace, & happiness, surely; some benefit may be secured—no injury provoked—

We must have a Minister in France, to settle the accounts of our seven years delerium, hypocricy, & folly—and why not lend his aid, in perfecting a system, to unite the world, in brotherly love—one of the great blessings of commerce is that of creating & preserving a friendly intercourse.

Who can read the letter book of a merchant, trading to various ports, without sensibly feeling the force of its influence—they write in the language of love, & are interested in all their family disasters, or happiness—You allow, that commerce is desirable—but is it not desirable to place it upon the basis of security, & universal protection—can this be expected while the British, are the pirates of Europe, & the Algierines, of Asia—

I need not inform Mr Jefferson, that if the powers of all Europe were now represented at Paris, for the express purpose of emancipating commerce, from depredation, & piracy—that the assembly would be like many others, composed of men, ignorant, selfish, & deceitful, with a few, very few, honest, & well inform'd. The councils of your Minister, his information, his honest policy, and perseverance, might finally privail.

You will, of necessity send an agent to France—If you can find any other citizen, in the union, better qualified to conciliate, or to act, in this station, I shall forever be silent. I will not trouble you farther at this moment, when you must take upon you the great & solemn charge of your high appointment

I am most respectfully your obt   STEPHEN SAYRE

RC (DNA: RG 59, LAR); addressed: "Thomas Jefferson Esqr Vice President of the United States Washington"; franked and postmarked; endorsed by TJ as received 25 Feb. and so recorded in SJL.

YOUR ANSWER: TJ to Sayre, 14 Feb.

From John Wright

SIR   Philadelphia Febry 20 1801

Having lately arrived in this City with the view of erecting sundry patent Machines to facilitate the business of agriculture, I take the liberty of addressing you for the purpose of knowing, whether you will be pleased to accept of one, to cut straw upon a principle different from Any now in use—. If this offir should be accepted, I will with pleasure forward the machine to any place you direct—

I am Sir with great respect Your humble Servt

JOHN WRIGHT

RC (MHi); at foot of text: "Thos. Jefferson Washington"; endorsed by TJ as received 25 Feb. and so recorded in SJL.

From John Dickinson

MY DEAR FRIEND,   Wilmington the 21st of the 2d. Month 1801

Amidst the many and important Affairs that must engage thy Attention at this Time, my Heart impells Me to congratulate our Country and of Course thyself, on thy Promotion to the high Office of presiding over her Wellfare.

What I have felt for several Years, and what I now hope, it is needless and would be difficult to express.

As to the past, as far as I am enabled to form a Judgment, I believe, that our Minds have been in perfect Unison.

As to the future, thou art to be the principal Actor, and among Millions of deeply interested Free men willing ready and expecting to give merited Applauses, I, if I live, am to be a Spectator.

Nor, probably, is the Influence of our Transactions to be confined within the Limits of our own Land.

Perhaps, We are the selected People upon Earth, from whom large Portions of Mankind are to learn, that Liberty is really a transcendent Blessing, as capable by its enlightened Energies of calmly dissipating its internal Enemies, as of triumphantly repelling its foreign Foes.

May Events be propitious; and I trust, they will be.

The adorable Creator of the world is infinitely benevolent, tho it is impossible for our finite Capacities to comprehend all his Dispensations. However, We know enough to excite our warmest Gratitude and firmest Confidence.

My Belief is unhesitating, that by his superintending Providence a Period greatly favorable is commencing in the Destinies of the Human Race.

That he may be pleased to honour thee, as an Instrument for advancing his gracious Purposes, and that he may be thy Guide and Protector, is the ardent Wish, the fervent Prayer of thy truely affectionate Friend   JOHN DICKINSON

RC (DLC); endorsed by TJ as received 26 Feb. and so recorded in SJL. Dft (PHi). FC (same); in Dickinson's hand.

From Joseph Fay

SIR   New York 21t. Feby. 1801

I can not let so fair an opportunity pass for renewing my former acquaintance with you, and of offering my Warmest Congratulations upon your being placed at the Head of our Government, an event which fills the hearts of all true Republicans with joy! the more so (if possible) from the unwarrantable opposition which has been made. This last act of Fœderalism went far towards filling up the measures of a corrupt administration, & to shew the desperate resort to which Wicked men were driven, in support of measures which have proved so destructive to this Country, and which had nearly annihilated our

Government!—Heaven be praised that our prospects once more brighten!—I hope your Administration will afford a new & lasting evidence of the support of a Republican System.—Your task will no doubt be an arduous one, but be assured my Dear Sir, that you possess the Love and affection, & may rely on the constant support of the Great body of the People, and of all honest men!

Since I had the honor & the happiness of your acquaintance, I have removed my Family from Vermont to this city, where I have resided for the last seven years in private life; it will always afford me pleasure to serve you should occasion offer. My best regards also await Mr Maddison who I presume will be near you, as a friend & Counseller in the many important Scenes before you.

The late *degrading* conduct, will at least have the Good effect of uniting the parties, in avoiding so Hazardous an expedient on any future occasion. The alarm had become General, and altho' the Fœderals felt great mortifications on yielding their favorite object, yet they universally express their satisfaction that our Government was relieved from the imminent danger to which it had been exposed.— That Heaven may continue to bless you with Wisdom, & fortitude, and incline the hearts of Good men to aid your administration, and may the Good effects go far to relieve the Wretchedness of Mankind universally, is the sincere wish of your friend & Very Humble Servant

JOSEPH FAY

RC (DLC); at head of text: "Honl. Thomas Jefferson Esqe."; at foot of text: "No 57 Pearl St. N. York"; endorsed by TJ as received 26 Feb. and so recorded in SJL.

FORMER ACQUAINTANCE: TJ and Fay had corresponded about maple seeds, politics, and other subjects since 1791, when

TJ and Madison visited Bennington, Vermont, Fay's residence at the time. The last previous correspondence between them consisted of unanswered letters from Fay in May 1793 and November 1795 (Vol. 20:440-4; Vol. 22:18, 102-3, 150-1, 351-2; Vol. 25:672-3).

To George Jefferson

DEAR SIR   Washington Feb. 21. 1801.

I inclose you another letter from mr Lieper, written after a further examination of the tobo. you will find it turns out that the tobacco has [never] been wet, nor otherwise injured, except one hhd, & whether that was [wet] between Richmd & Philadelphia is uncertain; that the [pretended?]¹ great deficiencies in weight are entirely retracted: that the tobacco is not as good in quality by about $\frac{3}{4}$ Doll. pr. Cwt. as that of the preceding year, which you [knew was] the finest tobacco [yet ever known] in Virginia; and when I sold that [crop] to mr Lieper I told him he would probably never get such another from me. he says that Clarke's tobo. has been badly handled. on this subject I [shall] write to Clarke. it seems that messrs. J. & W. had happened to recieve [some] good crops of some other persons, which *they say* (but Lieper has not [seen proof]) are superior to mine, at $5\frac{1}{4}$ & $5\frac{1}{2}$ Dollars. on this ground they have thought proper to hazard the insinuation of fraud in myself personally.—be so good as to return me this & the former letter, and take no trouble [about] further enquiry as to the duckings of the tobacco which never happened. I am Dear Sir

Your's affectionately   TH: JEFFERSON

P.S. I wrote the above under the impression that I had already inclosed you mr Leiper's first letter of Feb. 11. I find I had not done it, & therefore now do it

PrC (MHi); faint and blurred; at foot of text: "Mr G Jefferson"; endorsed by TJ in ink on verso. Enclosures: Thomas Leiper to TJ, 11 and 17 Feb. 1801.

I INCLOSE YOU ANOTHER LETTER: on 19 Feb. TJ wrote George Jefferson with the intention of enclosing the 11 Feb. letter he had received from Thomas Leiper. In his letter of the 19th, TJ requested that George Jefferson question the watermen to find out how many hogsheads of tobacco had accidentally gotten wet in transit. TJ also noted that he would write Bowling Clark about the matter. TJ feared that his

tobacco had been purchased by "very illiberal men in Philadelphia," as indicated by the letter from Jackson & Wharton to McMurdo & Fisher, which George Jefferson had transmitted to TJ on 29 Jan. Leiper's letter of 11 Feb. confirmed this (PrC in MHi; faint and blurred; at foot of text in ink: "Mr. George Jefferson"; endorsed by TJ in ink on verso).

According to SJL, TJ wrote Bowling Clark (CLARKE) on 24 Feb. but the letter has not been found.

J. & W.: Jackson & Wharton.

[1] Word interlined.

To Charles Willson Peale

DEAR SIR   Washington Feb. 21. 1801.

I have to thank you for a copy of your introductory lecture recieved some time since, & not before acknoleged for want of time. I have read it with great pleasure, and lament that while I have been so near to your valuable collection, occupations much less pleasing to me have always put it out of my power to avail myself of it. may I ask the favor of you to present my request to your son that he would be so good as to[1] make a copy of the portrait he took of me, and of the same size? it is intended for a friend who has expressed a wish for it; and when ready I will give directions to whom it shall be delivered if he

will be so good as to drop me a line mentioning it & the price. I am
with great and affectionate esteem Dear Sir

Your friend & servt.   TH: JEFFERSON

P.S. only the inner frame will be necessary.

RC (TxU); at foot of text: "C. W.
Peale." PrC (DLC); endorsed by TJ in
ink on verso.

INTRODUCTORY LECTURE: Peale's *Discourse Introductory to a Course of Lectures
on the Science of Nature; with Original
Music, Composed For, and Sung On, the*

Occasion (Philadelphia, 1800), presented
at the University of Pennsylvania on 8
Nov. 1800; Evans, No. 38203. For Rembrandt Peale's PORTRAIT of TJ, probably
painted in the winter or spring of 1800,
see Vol. 31:xli, 368 (illus.).

[1] Preceding 14 words interlined.

To Benjamin Stoddert

SIR   Washington Feb. 21. 1801.

Your favor of the 18th. did not get to my hand till yesterday. I
thank you for the accomodation in point of time therein offered; circumstances may render it a convenience, in which case I will avail myself
of it, without too far encroaching on your wishes. at this [moment] it is
not in my power to say any thing certain on the subject of time. the declarations of support to the administration of our government are such as
were to be expected from your character and attachment to our constitution. I wish support from no quarter longer than my actions candidly
scanned, shall merit it, & especially not longer than I shall rigorously ad-
here to the constitution. I am with respect Sir

Your most obedt. humble servt   TH: JEFFERSON

PrC (DLC); faint; at foot of text: "The honble Benj. Stoddart Secretary of the navy."

To Daniel Trump

DEAR SIR   Washington Feb. 21. 1801.

You have no doubt heard of the unfortunate fate of poor mr
Holmes. he happened to be alone on his scaffold at the time; so no one
knows what occasioned his fall. he was a valuable young man, and his
loss has given great concern to me, as it must doubtless his friends.
the object of the present is to see if you can procure one to supply his
place. good humor & sobriety are the two indispensable qualities.
skill in his business is now become more important, as I shall be little
at home myself. still I shall give the principal directions & make

myself the most important drawings. whoever goes will find a valuable friend & companion in James Dinsmore whom mr Carstairs procured for me in Philadelphia about 3. or 4. years ago. I had agreed to give Holmes either 180. or 200. D. a year, I do not remember which, tho' I have a note of it at home. I will give the person you shall engage the same, with board & lodging. he will have a black man under him to rough out his work. it would be well he should carry his tools, as they are not to be had there. he should go by water to Richmond, and thence take his passage in a boat or by a waggon, both of which conveyances are always to be had. it is 70. miles from Richmond to my house. if he could arrive there the first week in April he would be sure to find me there, and it would be considerably for his advantage as well as my own.

I wrote you last year for a pair of glass doors. I imagine they have not been made; & if not, they need not be made till further orders. but I shall be obliged to you to make & send me immediately 6. circular, & 2. semicircular mahogany sashes, radius 26. I. clear, consequently 4. f. 4. I. diameter. the latter are to be exact semicircles, including the bottom rail. the circulars had better be in the form in the margin, because should a pane get broke we can cut one of the center panes from one of 12. I. square, and one of the outer ones from a pane of 12. by 18. I. these being the two sizes of which I must always keep a stock. the circulars will open on pivots horizontally as at a.b. the semicirculars will be fixed. they must come ready glazed, and securely packed, addressed to messrs. Gibson & Jefferson. Richmond. I wish they could be at my house by the first week of April as I shall then be at home. I shall be glad to hear from you on both the subjects of this letter.—a friend of mine has desired me to have such sashes as mine made for a house he has built. he is to send me the particulars soon, or perhaps will give them to me when I go home. I shall forward you the order, which will be considerable. I am Dear Sir

Your most obedt. servt   TH: JEFFERSON

PrC (MHi); at foot of first page: "Mr Trump"; endorsed by TJ in ink on verso.

I WROTE YOU LAST YEAR: for the missing correspondence, see TJ to John Barnes, 19 July 1800. For TJ's previous order, see Trump to TJ, 4 Aug. 1800.

To John Wayles Eppes

Dear Sir   Washington Feb. 22. 1801.

I wrote to Maria on the 15th. inst. yours of the 12th. was recieved on the 18th. mr Tyler who was the bearer of my letter to Maria, set out so instantly after the event of the election that I could not write, but as he had promised to send Maria's letter, he would probably notify that event at the same time.   I cannot regret entirely the disappointment of meeting Maria & yourself at Monticello because of the cause, which must be a subject of pleasure to us all. but I think this circumstance might well lead to quite a different conclusion. would it not be better that you should go at an early stage and take up your residence at Monticello? the house & every thing in it & about it with the servants are at your disposal, and your own farm near enough to furnish you necessaries. it would make me happy to find & leave you there, and I think a journey would then be safer for Maria than at the season you propose. I earnestly recommend this subject to your consideration. there is a tolerable stock of bacon (45. hogs) coming on from Bedford. the stock of soap and 5 casks of butter (415. lb) are already sent. this with the supplies of your own farm would probably carry you through the year, as you would hardly have as much company as were I at home.

The purchase of horses, if shortly made, can only be with bills on Gibson & Jefferson at 90. days date. I would desire them to accept them, that the seller might have no want of confidence, and I should furnish the drawees in time for their satisfaction. in this way I should be glad to have Doctr. Walker's horse purchased immediately, and also the match which mr Bell speaks of, or any other you approve. we must not stand on moderate demands above their value. I shall still want another capital pair, but as I can do a while longer without them, and the preparatory expences of my new office are very heavy, it would not be safe for me to undertake paiment even at 90. days. the same as to mr Haxhall's horse. I must have him. but a purchase made from Colo. Hoomes, tho' not finally sufficient, will enable me to do some two or three months longer. Dr Walker's & his match I should wish to recieve while at Monticello, and would send for them if I have notice they are ready. in the mean time you can be trying Haxhall to see what the price must be.

The conduct of the minority in the election, and that on the last vote has been so universally condemned by the Federalists in all quarters, & during the crisis they were made generally so uneasy & anxious for the event, that when it happened, it came as the thing of their strongest wish. I verily believe that week of unwise conduct has brought over more to us than two or three years of wise & conciliating administration would have done. the great body of federalists throughout the US. are by this means consolidated with us, and with a conciliatory conduct may be firmly cemented, & the party division be obliterated so far as it had affected the people. their late leaders can never come over; but they are now left alone, & will fall into oblivion. the only danger now ahead of us is that the Senate, imperfect as it will be on the 4th. of March, may reject my nominations. this to be sure would dismast our ship, before leaving port.—we have no news from Europe. my tenderest love to my beloved Maria, and sincere affections to yourself. Adieu.

Th: Jefferson

RC (Florence P. Kennedy, Washington, D.C., 1962); at foot of first page: "J. W. Eppes." PrC (CSmH); endorsed by TJ in ink on verso.

SUBJECT OF PLEASURE TO US ALL: Eppes's letter of 12 Feb., recorded in SJL as received from Bermuda Hundred on the 18th, but now missing, evidently included the news that Maria was pregnant.

To William Evans

DEAR SIR   Washington Feb. 22. 1801.

You mentioned to me in conversation here that you sometimes saw my former servant James, & that he made his engagements such as to keep himself always free to come to me. could I get the favor of you to send for him & to tell him I shall be glad to recieve him as soon as he can come to me?   Francis Sayes who also lived with me formerly and, since that, with you, came here some time ago to offer himself to me. he had begun to drink a little before he left me, & I fear he continues it. he moreover says that his wife has good custom in Baltimore as a washer, & particularly your [custom]. I represented to him the inexpediency of removing from an established [house] of business & running the risk of business for her here: for tho' I might possibly give him a birth, yet I could not employ or take in his family, and I endeavored to throw cold water on his proposition. he seemed however so desirous, that I told him if I should be able to employ him, I would write to him: & he returned to Baltimore on this ground. in truth I would rather he would decline it. should he be with you, or fall into your way, I would thank you to discourage him from the idea. he was an affectionate & honest servant to me, which makes me unwilling to reject him absolutely; and yet the fear of his

drinking and of his getting his family into distress by removing them, induces me to wish rather that he would decline the thought.—I owe you many apologies for troubling you with these small things: but the truth is that I am so much embarrassed in composing a good houshold for myself, as in providing a good administration for our country.—accept assurances of the esteem with which I am Dear Sir
Your most obedt. servt   TH: JEFFERSON

PrC (MHi); faint; at foot of text: "Mr. Evans"; endorsed by TJ in ink on verso.

William Evans conducted the inn at the sign of the Indian Queen located at 187 Baltimore Street—commonly called Market—the principal street in Baltimore. It was the site of Evans's tav-

ern and the starting point for both the Philadelphia and southern mail stages (*The New Baltimore Directory, and Annual Register; For 1800 and 1801* [Baltimore, 1801], 6, 12, 37).

MY FORMER SERVANT: James Hemings, who had served as TJ's chef from 1787 until 1796, when he was freed (see Vol. 27:119-20).

From Robert Gourlay

No. 54 Spring Garden Cockspur Street London—
SIR.—   Feby. 22d. 1801—
Entreating you will pardon the liberty I now take, not having the honor of being known to Your Excellency.—& complying with Mr. Jenings request, by the accompanying letter, I have the pleasure to enclose, the suppos'd necessary papers, for your acceptance, of what we are willing to persuade ourselves, (from your very kind Correspondence with Mrs. Randolph,) your Excellency will be so obliging as favor us with; the Guardianship of the Grandchildren of my late esteem'd friend.—I beg to refer to Mr Jenings letter, for the melancholly particulars of her death.

Respecting the paragraph in Mr Jenings letter, with regard to, "the Construction of the words of the Will," we beg to leave it entirely to your Excellencys determination.—If what has formerly been written your Excellency, is not sufficient, we hope this Power, will be so,—& enable you to accommodate Mr. Edmd. Randolph; his worthy Mother, never having meant, any payment on his part, if inconvenient.—if however, any further papers are necessary, your Excellencys request to Mr. Jenings or me, shall be without delay, & with great pleasure complied with.—   Altho' the good Lady thought proper to appoint me Executor, I have consulted Mr. Jenings, in every step that has been taken, & have had his approbation.—We have thought it proper, for the present, to make your Excellency a remittance of £100 Sterling, as Windham & Sisters may want mourning &ca. & particularly, that they may not be pressing in future, upon the—pocket of their kind Uncle.—When the debts here are paid, it is probable, a Balance may remain with me, of about £240 Sterling.—It being a favor, to procure a Bill here upon America, allow me the liberty to request, that your Excellency will be so good as draw on me, by return of Ships, for £200 Sterling, which is the best mode of remitting, & for whatever balance may remain with me, I will endeavour to procure a Bill.—Mr. Jenings & I, have by this opportunity written Windham & Sister.—

Persuading ourselves we shall have the honor of an answer as soon as convenient.—

I remain—Most respectfully—Your Excellencys—Very obedient humble Servant   ROBERT GOURLAY

Please direct for me—"Virginia Coffee House—Cornhill London—"

RC (U.S. District Court for the Eastern District of Virginia, Richmond); addressed: "His Excellency Thomas Jefferson Esqr."; endorsed by TJ as received 6 May and so recorded in SJL. Dupl (DLC); at head of text: "Copy ⅌ Captn. Curran"; endorsed by TJ as received 15 May and so recorded in SJL with minor variations of punctuation, capitalization, and spelling. Enclosures: see below.

The NECESSARY PAPERS, which have not been found, were a power of attorney, a copy of the will of Ariana Jenings Randolph, and a letter from Edmund Jenings to TJ, 21 Feb. 1801, which is recorded in SJL as received from London on 6 May 1801. Gourlay also sent a bill of exchange. See TJ to Charles W. Grymes, 7 May 1801.

WINDHAM & SISTERS: Charles Wyndham Grymes and his sisters Mary and Ariana, the children of Ariana Jenings Randolph's daughter Susanna (or Susan) Beverley Randolph and her husband John Randolph Grymes (Robert Isham Randolph, *The Randolphs of Virginia* [Chicago?, 1936?], 201; TJ to Robert Gourlay, 30 Mch. 1802; Vol. 32:63-4).

THEIR KIND UNCLE: Philip Ludwell Grymes.

From Elijah Griffiths

DEAR SIR   Alms-Hous February 22d. 1801

The United States have now time to contemplate the late astonishing political Scenery. That incongruous aggregation; the high toned federal faction, the staunch old tories, the whole tribe of English renegadoes & apostate Americans, with views widely distinct from each other. Again the Lancasten & Spartan band, the conflagration of public offices and the last expiring struggle in congress; will combine to form a lasting monument for posterity to point to, of unpresidented foreign influence, and domestic obduracy. Meantime the republicans

have little to regret (Save the depravity of some, and credulity of others, of their countrymen) while their open, steady & manly persevereance has been crowned with success: how far the same condition of mind may be applied to the antirepublicans is best expressed by a retrospect of their late conduct. Permit me now Sir a long anticipated pleasure, that of congratulating you President of the United States Elect; at the same time let me wish you every happiness so extensive a stage of action will admit of. Will Pitt now commence a system of depredation, negociation & intrigue, or will he commit Hostilities against this country; by the former he will save his friends, keep his plunderers busy and still profit by our commerce; by the latter, he will compleatly dismantle the British faction here, which will be unloosing englands firmest hold of us: however the knowledge of being able to command the persons & fortunes of englishmen far beyond any thing the American goverment can attempt; may prompt to a hope by open Hostilities to render unpopular & odious, a republican administration, if nothing more: I however firmly believe the American goverment by a judicious line of conduct, will at all times be able to command the wills & resources of their constituents to any necessary extent. Permit me to recommend John Smith of this city to your notice, as a gentleman that has made considerable sacrafices in the republican cause; previous to the electoral election of 1796 he made an extensive tour through the interior of this state, at his private expence, which doubless had its share in promoting the Success of the republican ticket. I have represented the impropriety of Mr Smith's being thus prematurely thrust into view; but I need say little to you of the eagerness with which expectants urge their pretentions. There is no doubt at this time many waiting for a general dislodgment of the Feds, similar to what took place in this State about 12 month ago: how far such mens patriotism extends beyond their expectations, and how far such a step would be consistent with sound policy; an extensive political experience must have made you a competent judge.—
Early last September I sustain'd a Smart attack of fever & pleurisy which was soon succeeded by the dysentery, this last held me till cold weather and was only just gone off when a succession of violent colds brong on a return of fever with a determination to the breast, which has obliged me to keep house Since the 9 of last December, am now in a convalesent state but still very irritable, my indisposition is to be refered to a weak constitution & being much among the sick in the confin'd air of wards containing from 20 to 40 patients & these the most foul of all the human race: I have some thoughts of an eastindia voyage as a restorative, in preference to country practice, which is

unhealthy & laborious, at the same time it deprives a man of society & study.—I feel some anxiety lest a letter I sent you early[1] in July last may have miscarried, as I suspect a strong inclination in the federal post officers to peep into letters address'd to noted republican characters.—If the present hurry of public affairs will permit you to drop me a few lines it will gratify your Sincere friend & humble servant

ELIJAH GRIFFITHS

RC (DLC); at foot of text: "Thomas Jefferson Esqre. Vice President of the United States"; endorsed by TJ as received 26 Feb. and so recorded in SJL.

LETTER I SENT YOU: Griffiths to TJ, 8 July 1800.

[1] MS: "eary."

From Israel Israel

HONORED & MUCH ESTEEMED SIR   Philada. 22nd February 1801

Permit me to offer at this time my congratulations on the triumph of the principles of republicanism over the deep laid plans of monarchy and despotism, You Sir under the will of heaven is placed in a situation to be enabled to give new life and vigor to the drooping Cause of Liberty and the rights of Man in America, and to you do the People look up to for the opperation and true effects that is to be derived from the constitution—for as yet we have had no fair trial of that Instrument—

To you Sir doth the groaning republicans over the World look up to for relief, now do we expect under your administration that this Country will be an asylum for the oppressed of all nations, and to your adminstration we have a right to look for a stop being put to the venal system of speculation that has disgraced our Country and destroyed the Virtue of our Citizens;

but in obtaining those grand Objects I feel for you, knowing as I well do the power of our Political enemies, but trusting in that god that has brought us thus far through, I with confidence recommend you Dr Sir to his keeping and his direction, and pray that you may be supported through the ardious undertaking and preserved to the People,—

Trusting I shall be excused for thus troubling you I remain

Dear Sir, your sincere friend & huml Servt   ISRAEL ISRAEL

RC (MoSHi: Jefferson Papers); at foot of text: "Thomas Jefferson Esqr. Washington"; endorsed by TJ as received 25 Feb. and so recorded in SJL.

Israel Israel (1744?-1822), a Philadelphian of Jewish heritage, was an innkeeper, livery stabler, and member of the Democratic Society, who ran repeatedly and unsuccessfully for public office in the 1790s before his election as Republican sheriff in October 1800. His short-lived Pennsylvania senatorial victory over Benjamin Morgan in 1797 had been declared void and resulted in a special election and reversal in February 1798 (James Hardie, *Philadelphia Directory and Register* [Philadelphia, 1793], 71; Stafford, *Philadelphia Directory for 1800*, 67; Richard G. Miller, *Philadelphia—The Federalist City: A Study of Urban Politics, 1789-1801* [Port Washington, N.Y., 1976], 94-95, 97-102; PMHB, 126 [2002], 400-1; Vol. 30:127n; Vol. 32:221-2).

To Philippe de Létombe

DEAR SIR   Washington Feb. 22. 1801.

I fear you will consider me as taking much too great a liberty in what I am now about to ask of you; and yet I have had such experience of the friendliness of your disposition, and feel such a consciousness of a reciprocal disposition to serve you, that I am emboldened to go on. being now obliged to fix myself here, I find as great difficulty in composing my houshold, as I shall probably find in composing an administration for the government. you know the importance of a good maitre d'hotel, in a large house, & the impossibility of finding one among the natives of our country. I have imagined that such a person might be found perhaps among the French in Philadelphia, that no one would be more likely to know it than yourself, & that no one would be a better judge of his qualifications. honesty & skill in making the dessert are indispen[sable] qualifications. that he should be good humored & of a discreet, steady disposition is also important. if there be such a one within the compass of your knolege, will you have the goodness to engage him to come to me immediately? and to drop me a line of information whether I stand a chance to get one? if you could, by saying a word about price, fix him to some reasonable demand, it would add to the obligation: as he might on arriving here & seeing my distress take advantage from it to extort what would be unreasonable. you have sometimes given me apprehensions you meant to leave us soon. I should sincerely regret it, as I know the comfort of doing business with a person so rational & accomodating as yourself. it is a blessing to both nations to have such a person placed between them. should however any circumstances lead you to persist in this purpose, I should be happy if you would leave me the legacy of your Maitre d'hotel on your departure, if you think he has the necessary qualifications. I have a good cook: but it is pour l'office, & to take charge of the family that I am distressed. accept assurances of my great & cordial esteem and respect.

TH: JEFFERSON

PrC (MHi); damaged; at foot of text: "M. LaTombe"; endorsed by TJ in ink on verso.

I HAVE A GOOD COOK: TJ hoped to employ James Hemings as his chef in Washington; see TJ to William Evans, 22 Feb.

POUR L'OFFICE: that is, for the domestic staff.

From James Martin

SIR   Jamaica Long Island February 22, 1801—

I am somewhat in the Situation (upon being asked for a Letter of introduction to you) of the French Captain described by Sterne, who first introduces his friend and then himself. Capt. Lewis who has the honour to deliver this held an Office under the late Administration which he is desirous, I believe, to renew under yours—. His Testimonials I understand are ample and I am incompent to add to them— I should not have taken the liberty of introducing him if I had not been anxious for the opportunity it affords me of thanking you for the condescending manner in which you Noticed the Oration I transmitted to you—the pen you are good enough to say should be more Employed is, as it ever has been, devoted to you and the Cause of which you have been the Support—I wish it was adequate to express the gratitude I owe you as an American individual and the Sentiments of respect with which I have the honor to be

your faithful and Obedient Servant   JAMES MARTIN

RC (ViW); endorsed by TJ as received 19 Mch. and so recorded in SJL.

Laurence STERNE uses a debonair French captain to depict the art of making introductions in an early chapter of *A Sentimental Journey Through France and Italy* entitled "In the Street. Calais." For TJ's 1770 edition of the work, see Sowerby, No. 4335.

YOU NOTICED THE ORATION: see TJ to Martin, 23 Feb. 1798, for TJ's receipt of a copy of the 4th of July address the New York Republican delivered at Jamaica, Long Island, in 1796.

From William Munson

SIR   City of New Haven February 22. 1801

I Congratulate you and Myself on your Election as President of the United States, the News of which arrived here Last Evening

You No doubt remember, that at the time that I delivered to you the Votes of the Electors of the State of Connecticut, that I informed you that I was the Surveyor of the District of New Haven, and that there was a probability that the office of the Collector would Soon become Vacant, and that in Case it should happen, that I would wish to be Considered as a Candidate for that office

My Very perticular friend Pierpont Edwards Esquire, in his Letter to you of the 5th instant, informed you that the Event which I then Expected has taken place

It is Needless for me to go into a perticular detail of my pretentions to that office; it is probable that my Letters and papers on that Subject, which I have Sent to President Adams, will of Coarse fall into your hands, provided an appointment should not be made before you have full power to act as the Supreme Majistrate of the United States; I however in a few words inform you, that I have faithfully Served my Country, as a Commisiond officer, from the begining, to the End of the Late American war, and that I have Served in the office of Surveyor and Inspector of the Revenue in this District from the tenth day of February 1793 and have once during a Vacancy of a Collector, performed that Duty more than two months

You are no doubt personally acquainted with Mr Eliza Goodrich, a Member of Congress, who I Conceive to be the most powerful Candidate for the office now in question; all my other Competitors for this office as farr as has Come to my knowledge, have Exerted their whole power and force against your Election, and in Case their papers should Come into your hands you will probably be acquainted with Some of the Most Influencial Chareacters that Support them

I have not Since the death of the Collector taken any pains to procure any recommendations other than those I had procured on former Occasions, all which have been forwarded to the President of the United States, I therefore Now Submit the business to those that have the appointment, and Not without hope that I may Succed in my application

I have the honor to be Sir your most Obedient and Very humble Servant   WILLIAM MUNSON

RC (DNA: RG 59, LAR); at foot of text: "Thomas Jefferson Esquire"; endorsed by TJ as received 2 Mch. and so recorded in SJL.

William Munson (1747-1826), a Republican merchant in New Haven, continued to serve as surveyor of customs for the port until his death (Kline, *Burr*, 1:543-4; JEP, 1:129-30).

When Munson delivered the VOTES OF THE ELECTORS for the state of Connecticut in December 1800, he brought along a letter of introduction from PIERPONT EDWARDS (Edwards to TJ, 16 Dec. 1800). On 6 Feb. Edwards informed TJ of the death of the New Haven collector and recommended Munson, "a meritorious officer, and a very worthy republican," for the office. Edwards observed: "it is the wish of the republicans here, and, I believe, of the major part of the Federalists that he shou'd be appointed collector; for which office I deem him well qualified in every respect" (RC in DLC; at foot of text: "Honorable Thomas Jefferson"; endorsed by TJ as received 12 Feb. and so recorded in SJL).

MY LETTERS AND PAPERS: on 5 Feb. 1801 Munson wrote Adams informing him of the vacancy in the collector's office and applying for the position. He enclosed copies of his previous applications in 1793 and 1799 and the references he had obtained, including those from town officials and those signed by numerous merchants from New Haven and the separate districts of Derby and Milford (MHi: Adams Papers).

VACANCY OF A COLLECTOR: Jonathan Fitch, appointed collector at New Haven in 1789, died in September 1793, several months after Munson became surveyor. Munson assumed the collector's duties and submitted reports to the Treasury Department until the appointment of David Austin, Sr., who was confirmed by the Senate on 30 Dec. 1793 (Syrett, *Hamilton*, 14:92; 15:340, 352, 360-1, 396; JEP, 1:10, 143-4).

On 18 Feb. Adams nominated Elizur GOODRICH to serve as collector at New Haven in place of Austin. Goodrich resigned his congressional seat to accept the appointment (JEP, 1:382; *Biog. Dir. Cong.*).

From James Thomson Callender

SIR   Richmond Jail Febry. 23d 1801

I am to get out of this place in ten days, upon my having paid a fine of two hundred dollars. The money is ready; but if I am to pay it, I shall be so much reduced in my finances, as hardly to be able to go up to Philadelphia. Mr. Jones has advised me to state the matter to you, with reference to a remission. I thought it my duty to do so; and under the supposition of that, I shall wait here for a few days after the expiration of the term. Indeed there is nobody here to whom I can pay the cash, or who can tell me in what manner the security is to be given, as Marshall, the man who should take it, has gone up to the federal city.

I should not have been so bare of money, but that I paid for the print and paper of the two pamphlets you have seen; and could not get the last of them ready till the assembly had broke up; so that, for the present, they must remain almost entirely upon hand. I printed them in the genuine spirit of contradiction, as I may perhaps never have another opportunity of letting the world see how I can write in a jail. If I am to hear upon the subject of remission, you will perceive the expediency of its being done as early as possible.

We had a very pretty illumination upon the news of the Republicans having finally landed upon *Terra firma*. There has been a prodigious change in the mind of the people, within the last twelve months; and even always increasing. The burning of the war office and treasury, and the attempt to disappoint the choice of the people, have disgusted many of their best friends. The singular accuracy of my prediction, as to the *second* fire, produced such a roar of laughter, and such a pang of indignation in Richmond, as I would not have lost the Satisfaction of for an hundred dollars. I would not, for the price of an estate, be divested of the self-congratulation that I feel, in having been able to go so straightly through this great national crisis, without having to look back upon one moment of trimming, or flinching. I would have begun to write, as soon as I came in, but the Newspapers were so crammed with stuff about my trial, that I thought it useless.

I expect that, in Tuesday's Examiner, you will see three columns of mine crouded with new facts, as well as a defence of your letter of Septr. 4th., with a very outré postscript to his excellency, Mr Adams. This relates to his letter to John Marshall, about the *hanging of tories*. I always say, with Job, *Oh that mine Adversary would write a book*! I have now got John into a corner, from which he *Shall* not escape, without iredeemable disgrace. I sent Mr Adams and you, each a copy of the *Petersburg Republican*, containing *his* character in five columns. It is probable, Sir, that many of the newspapers, from various presses, which I have sent you, were destroyed by the *Post office* criminals; for surely, a more detestable sink of infamy never did exist, than a *federal* Post office. I speak with some exceptions. They have stopt several letters of mine; and have by that means, put me to the most racking inconvenience, and to uneasiness about my children.[1]

I had been called out in the middle of writing a Sentence, and the length of the letter warns me of stopping. I cannot express how much I have been indebted to the kindness of Mr. Rose, and his little family of friendship.

I am Sir Your most obliged & obedt. Servant

JAS. T. CALLENDER

P.S. David M. Randolph's windows were *not* illuminated and his lady quarrelled with one of her neighbours for doing so.

RC (DLC); above postscript: "Mr Jefferson"; endorsed by TJ as received 27 Feb. and so recorded in SJL.

MARSHALL, THE MAN WHO SHOULD TAKE IT: probably William Marshall, clerk of the U.S. circuit and district courts for Virginia and John Marshall's brother. Callender paid the fine to the U.S. mar-

shal, David Meade Randolph (DHSC, 5:319; Marshall, *Papers*, 2:117; TJ to George Jefferson, 4 Mch. 1801).

TWO PAMPHLETS: Callender published the second volume of *The Prospect Before Us* in two parts. The first was available 1 Nov. 1800 but the second part was not ready for distribution until 1801. YOUR LETTER: TJ to John Vanmetre of 4 Sep.

1800, published in the Richmond *Examiner* on 27 Jan. 1801 (see Vanmetre to TJ, 28 Feb. 1801). On 10 Feb. John Adams wrote JOHN MARSHALL to certify that the letter attributed to him dated 15 Dec. 1780 to Thomas Cushing, lieutenant governor of Massachusetts, which was again being reprinted, was a forgery (Marshall, *Papers*, 6:76-7; see Vol. 29:505-6, for an earlier reference to the forged letter). Adams closed his letter to Marshall: "This declaration I pray you to file in your office and you have my consent to publish it if you think fit." On 16 Feb. the *Washington Federalist* printed Adams's letter to Marshall and an extract of the 1780 letter to Cushing.

[1] Callender here canceled: "I shall now, from personal pride, send."

From Catherine Church

N. York Febry. 23d

At a moment when called by the voice of a nation to its highest station congratulations flow to you from all quarters shall an insignificant individual of it presume to offer you her's. Yes my good Sir I flatter myself you will permit it, when I reflect on the many proofs of your good will towards me & persuaded that the effusions of a grateful remembrance can never want a welcome from the goodness & sensibility which have given rise to them—& in the pleasure arising from the elevation of those whom we value recognize the interest I have in this event; Did either my situation in life, my age, or (perhaps more properly) my sex, render me fit or *adequate* to be a Politician the basis of my satisfaction might be in *public good* but as I am nothing less than that, I will only address you in the language of the heart that will at least have the merit of sincerity while the other would be only an ignorant affectation and since you my dear Sir can never have any reason to quarrel with truths I may offer them to you in all their simplicity; May you after having satisfied the ambition of your Friends realize the Wishes of affection & in the cares of government never know a diminution of happiness, & if to the empire over hearts, can be connected one equally fascinating let this addition prove such to you; the latter may perhaps boast of one charm, than the former can have in your eyes, the attraction of novelty—

I wrote to my dear Maria last summer, It is very long since I have heard from her & hope my letter found her as well & as happy as I ever wish her to be—since that I have had a long & dangerous illness, which has exiled me a little from my friends in interrupting our correspondence—pray do me the favor to mention me affectionately to her & Mrs. Randolph—

You will see *en passant* a charming little friend of whom Carolina robs us; I wish for her sake & that of your Daughters that she left us to be near them, as their goodness & amicability render them worthy of each other—Her father & our Vice President has the complaisance to take charge of this letter—Remember Sir that you are now to make no *jaloux* & that the state of N. York will expect a visit from its President—& I am well disposed to urge their claim very strongly—

Adieu Sir accept with your usual *bienviellance* the assurances of my respectful attachment   CATHERINE CHURCH

RC (MHi); addressed: "To his Excellency Thomas Jefferson Favored by Coll. Burr"; endorsed by TJ as received 2 Mch. 1801 and so recorded in SJL.

Theodosia Burr, the CHARMING LITTLE FRIEND OF WHOM CAROLINA ROBS US, was Aaron Burr's only child. She married the wealthy South Carolina planter, Joseph Alston, on 2 Feb. 1801, much to the amazement of her New York friends (ANB).

MAKE NO JALOUX: excite no jealousy. BIENVIELLANCE: kindness.

From Thomas T. Davis

SIR   Washington Feby. 23rd 1801

I ask leave to lay before you the inclosed Letter from Tho. Green Senr. about ninety-one Years of age to M. Clay of Virga. It will shew to you the State of things in the Mississippi Territory, which is shortly to be under your care, other written evidences are here but the age & Respectability of the writer of this Letter entitles him to attention. Mr Claiboun of Tinnessee would be pleased with an opportunity of Residing in that Territory.

I am with Respect yr most obt Servt   THO. T. DAVIS

RC (DLC); endorsed by TJ as received 24 Feb. and so recorded in SJL. Enclosure: Thomas Green, Sr., to Matthew Clay, 22 Dec. 1800, from Natchez, decrying a "Junto of Villains" attempting to block the advancement of the Mississippi Territory to a second stage of territorial organization that would include a more representative government; Green, who had settled near Natchez in the early 1780s, also declaring that Winthrop Sargent, governor of the territory and center of the faction that promoted its own private interests instead of republican principles, was more of an arbitrary tyrant than his predecessors under Spanish rule had been (same, endorsed by TJ; Dunbar Rowland, ed., *Encyclopedia of Mississippi History*, 2 vols. [Madison, Wis., 1907], 1:796-7; Vol. 31:337n, 549n).

Thomas Terry Davis (d. 1807), an attorney, represented Kentucky in the U.S. House of Representatives for three terms beginning in March 1797. He received a judicial appointment in Indiana Territory in February 1803 (*Biog. Dir. Cong.*, 883).

To Thomas Leiper

I am much indebted to you for the trouble you have been so good as to take with messrs. Jackson & Wharton, on the subject of my tobo. for tho' I am under no obligation to have any thing to do with them, my tobo. having been sold to Mc.Murdo & Fisher of Richmond, yet had there been any fraud in the package of the tobo. I should have no hesitation to relieve them from it. but from your favors of Feb. 11. & 17. the suggestion of it's having been wet before it was packed, of having laid in the water till near rotten, of deficiency of two or three hundred weight to the hogshead, seem to have vanished, & the fact to be only that they had bought one or two crops for a half or $\frac{3}{4}$ dollar less which *they think* of better quality. but this I presume happens to every man in every purchase. you observe it is $\frac{3}{4}$ of a dollar per Cwt. inferior to my crop of the preceding year. I never doubted that. the preceding year is understood to have been the best year for the quality of tobo. which any planter ever remembers to have seen. when I sold you that crop I told you that my information was that I had never made one of equal quality, & probably should never be able to offer you such another. Mc.Murdo & Fisher gave me more than was given currently at Richmond at the time for other good crops. if they had desired, it should have been reinspected, as there is always a risk of some injury in the batteau. they chose to take that risk, rather than give an extra price for the privilege of reinspection. you mention that Clarke has not handled it as neatly as usual. I shall give him a lesson on that subject, and if you think it so grossly mis-handled as to be a fraud on the purchaser & merit an allowance, I hope you will make it, & do whatever you think I ought in conscience to do, which I will confirm. observe that I have no knolege of this matter myself. I never saw a leaf of my tobo. packed in my life. when this sale was made to Mc.M. & F. I had not been at the place where the tobo. grew (the Bedford) for 20. years.—I thank you for your congratulations, & the sound principles you recommend. they are worthy of an upright mind & perfectly consonant with my own. accept assurances of the high esteem & respect of Dear Sir

Your friend & servt   Th: Jefferson

PrC (MHi); at foot of text: "Thomas Leiper esq."; endorsed by TJ in ink on verso.

To Meriwether Lewis

DEAR SIR   Washington Feb. 23. 1801.

The appointment to the Presidency of the US. has rendered it necessary for me to have a private secretary, and in selecting one I have thought it important to respect not only his capacity to aid in the private concerns of the houshold, but also to contribute to the mass of information which it is interesting for the administration to acquire. your knolege of the Western country, of the army and of all it's interests & relations has rendered it desireable for public as well as private purposes that you should be engaged in that office. in point of profit it has little to offer: the salary being only 500. D. which would scarcely be more than an equivalent for your pay & rations, which you would be obliged to relinquish while withdrawn from active service, but retaining your rank & right to rise. but it would be an easier office, would make you know & be known to characters of influence in the affairs of our country, and give you the advantage of their [. . .] you would of course save also the expence of subsistence & lodging as you would be one of my family. if these or any other views which your own reflections may suggest should present the office of my private secretary as worthy of acceptance you will make me happy in accepting it. it has been sollicited by several, who will have no answer till I hear from you. should you accept, it would be necessary that you should wind up whatever affairs you are engaged in as expeditiously as your own & the public interest will admit, & repair to this place: and that immediately on reciept of this you inform me by letter of your determinations. it would also be necessary that you wait on Genl Wilkinson & obtain his approbation, & his aid in making such arrangements as may render your absence as little injurious to the service as may be. I write to him on this subject.

Accept assurances of the esteem of Dear Sir Your friend & servt.

TH: JEFFERSON

PrC (DLC); at foot of text: "Lt. Meriwether Lewis"; blurred; endorsed by TJ in ink on verso. Enclosed in TJ to Tarleton Bates, printed at 28 Feb.

Meriwether Lewis (1774-1809) was a native of Albemarle County. When he was five his father, William Lewis, died, and the boy spent some time in Georgia following the remarriage of his mother, Lucy Meriwether Lewis. As a youth he attended Latin school in Albemarle County. He inherited his father's plantation, "Locust Hill," but volunteered for military service during the Whiskey Rebellion and obtained an ensign's commission in the regular army in 1795. Serving at various frontier posts, he was also in Charlottesville, 1798-99, on recruiting service. He became a lieutenant in March 1799 and a captain late in 1800. He was the president's private secretary from 1801 to 1803, when TJ named him to lead—with William Clark, Lewis's choice as co-commander—the expedition that traversed the continent to the Pacific Ocean. Named governor of the territory of Upper Louisiana, Lewis took up residence in

St. Louis in 1808. His death in Tennessee while en route to Washington was considered a suicide: in a biographical sketch, TJ wrote that he had perceived "depressions of mind" in Lewis, that other members of that branch of Lewis's family had been subject to similar "hypocondriac affections," and that Lewis reportedly showed symptoms of a mental "paroxysm" at the time of his death. Some writers have suggested, however, that Lewis's death by gunshot may not have been by his own hand. Writing later of the selection of Lewis for the western expedition, TJ credited him with "a firmness & perseverance of purpose which nothing but impossibilities could divert from it's direction." He was, TJ declared, "of courage undaunted" (ANB; TJ to Paul Allen, 18 Aug. 1813, MS in DNT, also printed in Allen's *History of the Expedition Under the Command of Captains Lewis and Clark, to the Sources of the Missouri, Thence Across the Rocky Mountains and Down the River Columbia to the Pacific Ocean*, 2 vols. [Philadelphia, 1814], 1:vii-xxiii).

List of John Adams's Appointments

Feb. 23

qu.	Thos. Bee. chief judge	
qu.	John Sitgreaves of N.C. distr. judge	5th Circ.
+	Joseph Clay. of Georgia	

+ Wm. Mc.lung: Kentuky. to be circuit judge of 6th.
qu. Jacob Read. judge of distr. of S.C. vice Bee
qu. Wm. H. Hill. distr. judge of N.C. vice Sitgreaves
— Saml. Blackburn. Atty for Western distr. Virga
— Rob. Grattan. of Staunton. marshall of W. distr. Virga
+ Thos Gray. atty E. distr. Tennessee
+ Chas J. Porter. to be marsh. of E. distr. Tennessee
— Wm. Pitt Beers. of Albany Atty distr. Albany
— James Dole. marsh. distr. Alby.
— J. C. Mountflorence. of N.C. commerl agent Paris.

MS (DNA: RG 59, MCL); entirely in TJ's hand, with symbols and "qu." added at a later date, in pencil.

In a letter dated 21 Feb., President Adams sent the nominations on the list above to the Senate. They were presented and read on Monday, 23 Feb., and approved the next day. Both Thomas BEE and JOHN SITGREAVES declined their appointments, leaving Senator JACOB READ and Congressman William H. HILL without judicial positions (JEP, 1:383-5, 401).

Adams's nominees of 28 Feb. were listed by TJ on a scrap of paper torn from an address sheet with a partial postmark. The president appointed Thomas Johnson, James M. Marshall, and William Cranch—TJ wrote simply "Cranch"—as judges of the District of Columbia, "Swan of Alexa—Atty" and "Lingan of G. Town—marshal." They were confirmed on 3 Mch., but TJ did not add marks beside the names as he had done on his other lists (MS in DNA: RG 59, MCL, entirely in TJ's hand; JEP, 1:386-7, 389).

From John Moody

DEAR SIR   23d Feby. 1801.

on Some Momentuos Occasions heretofore I have taken the liberty to
Addres you I Must now Once more Transgress on your Patience to
Congratulate your Election and particularly So after Such an Obstinate
Party Resistance The Happines here among Republicans are Beyond
Expresion and I Believe the Gloom is as much So with the Opposite &
obstinate The Milder ones appear well Satisfyed. The Matter in Dis-
pute is So amicably Desided and it is to [hope?] peace and Tranquilty
will Reign in our Happy land.—Hail Columbia—from the year 76
I was a strong friend to the American Cause and Never will abandon it
and May your Administration be the will of the people.
Misfortunes unavoidable in the Merchantile line have Overtaken me.
But Nothing Shall Shake my faith a little Countenance from friends
would be of Infinite Service. one line from you would be Gratification
for Every thing asking pardon for this

   I am with Sincerity your Most Obt.   JOHN MOODY

RC (ViW); torn at seal; addressed:
"Thomas Jefferson Esqr Vice President of
the united States Federal City"; franked;
postmarked at Richmond; endorsed by
TJ as received 27 Feb. and so recorded
in SJL.

For the OCCASIONS HERETOFORE on
which Moody addressed TJ, see Vol.
29:428-9.

From Francis Say

SIR   Baltimor Febuary 23 1801

I have spoke to James according to your Desire he has made mention
again as he did before that he was willing to serve you before any
other man   in the Union but sence he understands that he
would have to be among strange servants he would be very much
obliged to you if you would send him a few lines of engagement and
on what conditions and what wages you would please to give him
with your own hand wreiting—
and I myself should be very much obliged to you if you let me know
How soon you would want me I should myself wish to serve you before
any other man   I have already refused some good employment
on acount of yours since Mr. Randolph has made mention to me when
he came from Philadelphia. you know very well that I am a poor man

   I remain with due respest your Humble Servant

                                                    FRANCIS SAY

RC (MHi); endorsed by TJ as received 25 Feb. and so recorded in SJL.

Francis Say was a laborer living on Hanover Street in Baltimore (*The New Baltimore Directory, and Annual Register; For 1800 and 1801* [Baltimore, 1801], 83).

To Samuel Harrison Smith

TH:J. TO MR SMITH.   Monday morn. [23 Feb. 1801]

The bookbinder promises me 40. copies of the Manual on Thursday morning. your's therefore might be offered for sale on Saturday.

A commee of the H. of R. communicated to me the record of their having elected me &c. I took that occasion to make my acknolegements to the House & to the nation. their communication & my answer are entered on the Journals of the house, & I wish them published. I could give you a copy of my answer, but not of so much of their communication as was verbal, because I had it not in writing. you could probably get it from their clerk.

RC (DLC: J. Henley Smith Papers); partially dated; addressed: "Mr. Saml. H. Smith"; endorsed by Smith.

OFFERED FOR SALE: the advertisement for TJ's *Manual of Parliamentary Practice* first appeared in the *National Intelligencer* on Friday, 27 Feb.

Smith immediately published the COMMUNICATION of the House committee to the president-elect and TJ's ANSWER of 20 Feb. (*National Intelligencer*, 23 Feb. 1801).

To James Wilkinson

DEAR GENERAL   Washington Feb. 23. 1801.

I take the liberty of asking the protection of your cover for a letter to Lieutt. Meriwether Lewis, not knowing where he may be. in selecting a private secretary, I have thought it would be advantageous to take one who possessing a knolege of the Western country, of the army & it's situation, might sometimes aid us with informations of detail, which we may not otherwise possess. a personal acquaintance with him, arising from his being of my neighborhood, has induced me to select him, if his presence can be dispensed with, without injury to the service: for tho' the public ought justly to be relieved from the charge of pay and rations while absent from his post, yet I should propose that he might retain his rank & right to rise. I have [desired] him to wait on you and to recieve your pleasure on this subject, and I would sollicit such arrangements from you as might enable him to wind up whatever affairs he is engaged in as speedily as the public, & his own, interest would permit, without injury to either. should he not be with you, I will ask the favor of you to avail your[self] of the best conveyance of this which may occur.

I pray you to accept assurances of high consideration & regard [from] Dear Genl.

Your most obedt. & most humble servt   TH: JEFFERSON

PrC (DLC); faint and blurred; at foot of text: "Genl. Wilkinson"; endorsed by TJ in ink on verso. Enclosed in TJ to Tarleton Bates, printed at 28 Feb.

From James Bowdoin

SIR   Boston feba. 24th. 1801.

Although I am personally unknown to you, it is not with the less pleasure, that I congratulate you upon the events of the late election, which introduce you to the chair of the United States. The contest has been an arduous one, & the triumph, which has succeeded it, I trust, will prove not less beneficial to our common country, than honourable to you.   Be assured Sir, that neither my wishes, nor my influence, *such as it has been*) have been wanting, to resist the politics, which have prevailed in this state, for some time past: but I trust, that the soundness of your political principles, & the just consideration due to your character, will soon dispel the deceptions, the calumnies, & the mis-representations, wch. have been but too artfully diffused. Wearied as you must necessarily be, with the opposition & abuse, wch have assailed you, it becomes those, who wish well to your administration, to inspire your confidence, to tender their Services and to offer you the consolation of a ready Support.

If Sir, my feeble aid can in any way, contribute to the success of your administration, confiding as I fully do, in the rectitude & purity of your intentions, I have no hesitance in tendering to you my Services, without being able to point out in what, they can be particularly useful.

I recollect wth pleasure your acquaintance with my late father, & the respect he bore to you; and it was a mortification to me, when you visited Boston, on taking passage for France, that I happened to be at a distance from home.

Be assured Sir, of the consideration & respect, with which I have the honour to subscribe myself.

Sir, your most obedt Servt.   JAMES BOWDOIN

RC (DLC); at foot of text: "His Excelcy. Thos. Jefferson Esqr."; endorsed by TJ as received 6 Mch. and so recorded in SJL. FC (Lb in MeB: James Bowdoin Letterbook).

James Bowdoin (1752-1811) was the son of Elizabeth Erving and James Bowdoin, a Massachusetts merchant and governor, who had corresponded with TJ

and died in 1790. Educated at Harvard, the younger Bowdoin held several seats in the Massachusetts legislature in the 1780s and 1790s and was named by TJ as minister plenipotentiary to Spain in November 1804 (ANB; DAB; Robert L. Volz, *Governor Bowdoin & His Family: A Guide to an Exhibition and a Catalogue* [Brunswick, Me., 1969], 28-9).

From Elbridge Gerry

MY DEAR SIR,   Cambridge 24th Feby. 1801

At nine oClock last evening, Mr Lee, a [sincere?] friend of yours & mine, came up from Boston to inform me of your election.

The precarious state, in which by the [wiles] of party, the federal executive was suspended, the irritation which would have resulted from your non-election, even if Mr Burr had obtained the vote, the great danger of a collision of parties, whose *habits* of animosity, established by their duration, would have made them equally [violent] in their Support of & opposition to a President pro tempore, the triumph which such a disgraceful event would have given to the enemies of our revolution & republican government, & the disrepute it would have entailed on free governments in general, whose principles, it would have been urged, however clearly delineated, will be always defeated by the factions which they naturally generate all conspired to produce in my mind an extreme anxiety for the issue, with which it has pleased the supreme disposer of events to favor the U States.

Under existing circumstances, your office is not enviable; your task is arduous. Wisdom, moderation, & firmness, are indispensable, so to administer the government as to temper the resentment of the injured, to enlighten & quiet the deluded & [. . .], to confirm the wavering, & by seperating the chaff from the wheat, as far as filtration is necessary, to prevent in future a political fermentation.—that you may be duly supported & be able to attain these important objects, & their natural concometant the welfare of the nation, is my ardent wish, hope, & prayer.

By Judge Lincoln I wrote you two fugitive[1] letters, which a want of leisure prevented me from correcting, digesting, or compressing. if they indicated too much feeling, it was naturally roused by the wanton, & the unprovoked aggressions of the feudal oligarchy.

I have mentioned Mr Lee, as our mutual friend, but this is a consideration which has no weight in regard to my subsequent observations relative to him. my first acquaintance with him was at Paris, where his character was well established, both with Americans & frenchmen, as a man of integrity, honor, morality, social vertue & pleasing manners, & of good information in the line of his commercial profession. that this was the opinion of all the envoys, was evident, from the honorable mention which they made of him to the President, & their letter of recommendation of him, for the office of Consul. he unfortunately arrived here at the critical period of the federal mania, & being charged in the federal papers with being the bearer of private letters to yourself Mr Monroe & others, he was in great danger, for this unpardonable crime, of being the victim of popular resentment. from that time to this, he has been considered by the oligarchists, as a Jacobin: a reproachful term, without a definite meaning, but uniformly applied, to brand with infamy, every man who has refused to abandon his rights & reason, & to become the tool of an unprincipled party. the unmerited attacks on his character, engaged in his behalf a number of respectable moderate men, & produced to the [. . .] additional recommendations of him for the office mentioned. if the President should make any such nominations, I think it probable that his name will be on the list; but as the former event is problematical, or if it should take place, it may be defeated in the Senate as it is now composed, I feel an obligation of Justice to present to your view, this upright, honest republican, who has been persecuted, because he was suspected of fidelity to his honorable engagements. perhaps it may be said, he is not a native of the U States; but his parents were, his father was imprisoned at halifax during the revolutionary war for advocating their cause, he has more relations in this state, than any candidate for office, & was himself educated in it, & has made it his constant residence. he married moreover a daughter of Colo. Palfrey's, who was paymaster General of the American, & this lady, who is amiable & accomplished, has none but american connections. indeed the assurances which Mr Lee has received from Government, has led him to wait the event of the pending negotiation, & to refuse several lucrative offers of business, notwithstanding the indispensable calls of his amiable & encreasing family; a circumstance which perhaps merits attention. either of the Consulates of Bourdeaux, Marseilles, Havre & Rouen, Cape Francois, or the general consulate of² Gaudaloupe, would answer his purpose.—altho in regard to yourself, I think it unnecessary to bring into view that upright man & true American Mr Skipwith, yet the persecution he has suffered, because a republican, has interested my feelings in his behalf, & prompts me to express them.

And now, my dear Sir, permit me with the most sincere, respectful & affectionate attachments, to bid you adeiu & to assure you that I remain Your real friend, & obedt Servt.   E GERRY

RC (DLC); with indistinct text; at foot of text: "His Excellency Mr Jefferson"; at top of fifth page of MS: "2d sheet"; endorsed by TJ as received 6 Mch. and so recorded in SJL.

For the controversy sparked by William Lee's arrival in the United States in June 1798 with several PRIVATE LETTERS from France, see Vol. 30:175, 183, 186-7n, 499.

TWO FUGITIVE LETTERS: Gerry to TJ, 15 and 20 Jan. 1801.

[1] Word interlined.
[2] Preceding four words interlined.

From William Jackson

SIR,   Philadelphia February 24th: 1801

I was yesterday honored by the receipt of your letter of the 18th instant. I shall punctually obey your injunction as to the degree of confidence, in which you request it should be considered—This does not, I trust, extend to forbid the communication, in a private manner, of those sentiments, so honorable to him who has expressed them, and so consolatory to all good men.

You could not mean, I am persuaded, to withhold from the virtuous citizen, whose property and kindred give him the most anxious interest in the happiness of his country, the pleasure to know that her prosperity, far from suffering interruption or decline, will be cherished and increased.

Under this construction of your request, I have ventured to impart the general tenor of your letter to some of our most respectable citizens—Words would fail me to represent the satisfaction, which it has diffused—and I must refer to the future evidences of their conduct as the best illustration of their feelings.

For myself, Sir, looking forward to the benefit of a wise and dignified administration of our government—to an administration, which shall heal dissension, give encouragement to science, protection to property, and tranquillity to the virtuous man, I hesitate not to declare that if my agency can, in any degree, contribute to the furtherance of such magnanimous policy, it shall be rendered with zeal and fidelity—and if my personal services, in this quarter, can in any way promote your private convenience, I pray that many occasions may be afforded me to attest the truth of that respectful attachment, with which I have the honor to be

Sir, your much obliged and faithful Servant   W Jackson

RC (DLC); at foot of text: "Thomas Jefferson Esquire Vice-President of the United States"; endorsed by TJ as received 27 Feb. and so recorded in SJL.

From Thomas Lewis, Jr.

DEAR SIR   Boston Feby 24th, 1801

The subscriber a Native Citizen of Boston, but Strainger to you, prays you will Excuse the freedom in Expressing the warmest Congratulations of his Heart, that beats with Unutterable Joy, Occasioned by the Glorous News this nights mail unfolds to us,

That your Excellency is President of the United States the ensueing four years, Notwithstanding the Late Scene that has bin acted,— which Surpasses the power of Language to discribe, or even of the imagination to conceive

A Faction in its last struggle, appear'd determined to Hazzard the peace of the Union, & even the Permanance of the Constitution itself: and to poison the delight of the Republicans, not a man in America ever doubted, that your Excellency was designed by the great body of the People, to be President of the United States of America, (By the Vote of their Electors)

But if the Republicans continue firm, everey measure the Anglo Faction can devise, will be terminated in their own confusion & disgrace,

I have flatterd & pointed out to myself for years past, of seeing this Happy Period,—

Thanks be to God, for not raising my Expectations in Vain, this is an Eve of Jubilee, to the Republicans of this Town, that for years past have bin Crush'd by a Party that Triumphant over them with Insults & abuses, unto everey one who have dared to Speak as they thought,—

Thank Heaven those times are past, and may that divine Providence which has heretoo protected your Valuable Life, unto this Important Crisis, smile with Continuance of his Bountyfull Bendictions, in still Preserveing your Health, which is so Precious to the rights & Liberty of this Great Nation, (as Mankind in General)

May everey greatfull Heart from Georgea, to main, on the fourth of the Ensueing month, which gives new Birth to American Liberty, and a mortal Wound to Tyranny—Burst with Thanksgiveing & Praise, that our Posterity are Freed from the Iorn Yoke of Despots, &c—

the Inducement for droping those few Hasty & ungarded Expressions of the Heart, from an unlearnt Pen,—I hope will be Pardonable: if at your Leasure you Should cast an Eye over them, It comes from one, (who with his Father that is Co: Partnership in Trade with Him,—

Are for their Uniformity, of Republican principle, Branded, (by those of Opsit Politics) with Jacobinism, or—for we think freely, & always Express our thoughts in, The intrests of Republicanism, which we have ever Supported,

And ever Shall Contribute our part to maintain its Principles, & Support its Libertys, with those of our Distinguishd Patriotic Townsmen, whose names I cannot forbare to mention, Vizt. late Gov Adams, Dr Eustis, Dr Jarvis & Bn Austin Jr. Esqr. whose Talent's are well Known, with Hundreds of others that I forbare to mention, but well deserving—

Pray God those Principles may not dye with us nor our Posterity, but live forever—forever.—

Accept assurances of the Greatest Respect, which fills the Breast of your verey Humble Servant   THOMAS LEWIS JR.

of the House of

Thomas Lewis & Son

P.S.

as I have taken the liberty to address your Excellency as aforesaid, with a few weak, but Sincere Expressions,—

and heareing a French Commissioner's arrival at Washington, but Ignorant of the measures to take in Application for Redress, of such a Loss as is mentioned in a Paragraph of one of our Late News Papers, which I have taken the Liberty to Enclose, this Vessell & Cargo was worth to us $25,000—Two others we had taken by the French, befor the Treaty worth $32,000—without Insurance, (feel Consious it is not Pardonable in Troubleing you on such Business)

RC (MoSHi: Jefferson Papers); addressed: "Hon. Thomas Jefferson Esqr at Present Vice President of United States but President of US on & after 4 March 1801"; endorsed by TJ as received 7 Mch. and so recorded in SJL. Enclosure: unidentified newspaper clipping noting that the ship *Hope*, loaded with provisions and bound for Barbados, was captured on 21 Dec. by the schooner *Patriot* and taken to Guadeloupe, where it was condemned six days later (same).

Thomas Lewis & Son, merchants at Lewis's wharf in Boston, were in the West Indies trade (*Boston Directory* [Boston, 1800], 71; Boston *Columbian Centinel*, 25 Feb. 1801).

To Robert R. Livingston

DEAR SIR   Washington Feb. 24. 1801.

It has occurred to me that possibly you might be willing to undertake the mission as Minister Plenipotentiary to France. if so I shall most gladly avail the public of your services in that office. though I am sensible of the advantage derived from your talents to your particular state, yet I cannot suppress the desire of adding them to the mass to be employed on the broader scale of the nation at large. I will ask the favor of an immediate answer, that I may give in the nomination to the Senate, observing at the same time that the period of your departure cannot be settled till we get our administration together, and may perhaps be delayed till we recieve the ratification of the treaty which would probably be 4. months. consequently the commission would not be made out till then. this will give you ample time to make your departure convenient. in hopes of hearing from you as speedily as you can form your resolution & hoping it will be favorable I tender you my respectful & affectionate salutations.

TH: JEFFERSON

RC (NNMus); addressed: "The honble Robert R. Livingston Chancellor of New York"; franked and postmarked 1 Mch.; "New York" in address canceled, "Clermont" being substituted in an unidentified hand, that word also canceled and replaced in another hand by "Albany"; endorsed by Livingston. PrC (DLC).

TJ had no reply until 23 Mch., but sent Livingston's NOMINATION TO THE SENATE at the close of the Sixth Congress on 5 Mch. The Senate immediately approved the appointment. Livingston did not recieve the letter above until a week after his confirmation (Livingston to TJ, 12 Mch.; JEP, 1:395-6).

From Jonathan H. Nichols

REVERED SIR,   Boston, Feb. 24. 1801.

As your Countrymen have been taught to look up to you as the friend of human Nature, rational freedom, and the patron of Arts, Sciences &c. A humble Citizen, from whose industry alone his Subsistence is obtained, with diffidence & respect Solicits, a favor of you, Sir, in permitting him to Dedicate to your Name, a volume of Elegant literature, which he proposes to publish, entitled The Miscellaneous Dictionary, Compiled from the writing of the most eminent and esteemed athors, ancient & modern. An alphabetical arrangement of Literary, moral, philosophical and humorous essays in prose & poesy.

If Sir, you do not object to its dedication to you Sir, I shall have the honor of transmitting the Copy to you for your examination; Your Name will have great weight in procuring the Sale & reputation of the work, as your literary talents, and excellencis of intellect & heart are printed on the memory of your grateful fellow Citizens. The favor will add individual, to general obligations.

Yours with esteem & respect   JON. H. NICHOLS

RC (CSmH); at foot of text: "Hon. T. Jefferson Esq."; endorsed by TJ as received 7 Mch. and so recorded in SJL.

From Joseph Nourse

SIR!   City of Washington 24 feb: 1801

Having devoted about twenty one Years of my past Life in the Service of the United States in the Treasury Department; I beg leave to offer the continuance thereof under the Executive of the Government, to which Sir! you have been elected in an accordance with the wishes of the People; and on which occasion, I wou'd beg the acceptance of my best Congratulations, and to assure you of my high personal Respects and attachment to your Administration

I have the honor to be Sir! Your most obed. & most humble Servant   JOSEPH NOURSE

RC (DNA: RG 59, LAR); at foot of text: "Thomas Jefferson Esqr President of the United States Elect"; endorsed by TJ as received 24 Feb. and so recorded in SJL.

Nourse continued as register of the Treasury in the TREASURY DEPARTMENT until his removal by Andrew Jackson in May 1829 (Washington, *Papers, Pres. Ser.*, 3:32).

From Marinus Willett

SIR.   New York February 24th 1801

The very slender personal acquaintance I have with you may require an apology for this address—I do not recollect having the honor of being in your company except at the Introduction of President Washington on my arrival at this City with Mr McGillivray (the Creek Chief) and once at Dinner with President Washington—No person however can be more compleatly happy on account of your Election to the Chief Magestracy of the United States than I am—

The design of this address is to offer myself to your consideration for an appointment under the Federal Goverment—It will not I presume be deemed unreasonable in the Republicans of these States to hope that they will be delivered from the state of reprobation under which they have laboured for some time past and be suffered to participate in the offices of honor and profit of their Country—For tho no one spurns the Idea of Immitating those practices of prosecuting and persecuting people for opinions (such as have been exhibited) more than I do, Yet after witnesing the ungenerous and cruel conduct which has been manifested on account of opinions I trust it will not be conceived unreasonable to hope that while such unmanly practices are avoided measures will be adopted for placing offices in the hands of those republicans who have had to encounter such large portions of Calumny and Illnature—In this Expectation Sir, I beg leave to offer myself if new appointments should take place in this city in either the Offices of Supervisor for Collecting duties on Spirits, the Commissioner of loans or Marshal of this District—

When I returned from the Commission to the Creek Nation, the President was pleased to express his particular satisfaction on the execution of that business and gave me expectation to hope for something as reward for that Service—Not long after through General Knox he made me the offer of Marshal for this District, The emoluments of the office at that time were small, and an assurance of a more valuable office under this State caused me to decline that offer—No offer from the General Goverment has been made since except the appointment of Brigadier General at the time General Wain was appointed to command. That appointment for very cogent reasons I could not accept—An appointment under the General Goverment is at this time particularly desirable to me—For Information respecting me I beg leave to refer you to Colonel Burr, to the Republican, And Indeed to every member of Congress from this State—fully satisfied that in all public trusts I have demeaned myself so as to compel even my political enemies to confess their approbation of the attention and fidelity of my department—

I shall trespass no longer on your time than to assure you that if I shall be favoured agreeable to my wishes, I will be very careful that those who confide in me shall never have cause to regret their Confidence—

With Sentiments of the most exalted esteem and respect I have the honor to be Sir, Your very Obedient humble servant

MARINUS WILLETT

[63]

RC (DNA: RG 59, LAR); addressed: "Thomas Jefferson Vice president of the United States"; endorsed by TJ as received 2 Mch. and so recorded in SJL.

Marinus Willett (1740-1830) joined the militia during the French and Indian War, was a leader of the Sons of Liberty in New York City, and served as an officer in the Continental Army until the end of the War for Independence. He reached the rank of colonel in that service and in 1792 declined a commission as brigadier general under Anthony Wayne. Sent by George Washington as an envoy to the Cherokees and Creeks in 1790, Willett brought Alexander McGillivray and other Creek leaders to New York City to negotiate a treaty. At the end of the Revolution, George Clinton, then governor, gave Willett and another officer the supervision of confiscated Loyalist property in the city, and Willett, who was originally a cabinetmaker, acquired forfeited estates for himself at low prices. He also had a mercantile business and was one of Aaron Burr's creditors. Willett served two terms as sheriff between 1784 and 1796 and was prominent among those Republicans who affiliated themselves with Clinton (ANB; Kline, *Burr*, 1:292; 2:740n; Vol. 17:288-91; Vol. 23:244n, 408, 492).

From John Gardiner

City of Washington—Little Hotel

SIR   feby 25th. 1801

The Writer hereof left Dublin last Summer with a Cargo of Goods & Passengers *bound to this City*, & in Novemr. last was unfortunately stranded on Sandy Hook near New York, where he has left his Family & part of the Cargo saved—Apprehensive that he has not sufficient left to make a livelihood by keeping a store in this City, without some other means, & hearing that some of the Clerks in Public Offices were resigning he takes the liberty of solliciting as an unfortunate Stranger, from your Benevolence, a Clerkship, for the duties of which he has been fitted by a Mercantile Education—his introductory letters were to Messrs. Danl Stone & Co. Norfolk—I have the honor to be

Sir Your obedt hu Servt   JOHN GARDINER

RC (DNA: RG 59, LAR); endorsed by TJ as received 26 Feb. and so recorded in SJL.

John Gardiner (d. 1839) claimed to have been the superintendent of a cotton manufactory in Ireland for several years before being shipwrecked in a transatlantic passage and settling in Washington, where he sought employment, advertising as a furniture auctioneer and keeper of a boarding and day school on Pennsylvania Avenue. By 1807, he was employed as a clerk in the land office under the Treasury Department (Allen C. Clark, "The Mayoralty of Robert Brent," RCHS, 33-34 [1932], 273-5; Cunningham, *Process of Government*, 328).

Among the other correspondents who wrote TJ soliciting a clerkship or offering their services were: (1) John Fleming to TJ, Washington Inn, 11 Mch. 1801, requesting TJ's interference on his behalf for a public office "which may secure a moderate competency to a tolerable penman and accountant" (RC in DLC; endorsed by TJ as received 11 Mch. and so recorded in SJL). (2) Nathaniel W. Price to TJ, Columbia, Virginia, 12 Mch. 1801, referencing TJ's acquaintance with his late father, Meredith Price, and brother, Alexander P. Price, formerly of the firm of Moody & Price of Milton, and noting the dissolution of Moody & Price of Richmond, of which he was copartner, asking to be placed in "a station as a clerk in some office attached to the Government" (RC in DNA: RG 59, LAR; endorsed by TJ as received 18 Mch. and so recorded in SJL). (3) Samuel Bootes to TJ, 1 Apr.

1801, "Near Rhodes's Hotel," applying for "a Clerk's place in some one of the public Offices" (same; endorsed by TJ as received 9 Apr. and so recorded in SJL). (4) Francis Hoskins to TJ, Baltimore, 6 Apr. 1801, requesting a place "as a clerk in any of the Offices" (same; endorsed by TJ as received 16 Apr. and so recorded in SJL). (5) John H. Stone, former governor of Maryland, to TJ, George Town, 10 May 1801, offering his services and talents "exercised with honesty delegence & attention, for the good of the public and devoted to your administration" (same; endorsed by TJ as received 16 May and so recorded in SJL).

From William Heath

SIR,   Massachusetts Roxbury (near Boston) Febry. 25th 1801

Although I have not the honour of an intimate acquaintance with you,—I am too well acquainted with your true character, and ardent love for the best interests of our Common Country, and of mankind, not to felicitate my fellow Citizens on your elevation, or refrain from expressing to you, those feelings of satisfaction, and that confidence which is inspired in my breast on the present occasion, and to intreat you, to be pleased to accept, my most sincere congratulations on your advancment to the Presidency of the Union.

You are called Sir, to this important and high station, at a moment on some accounts, difficult and embarrassing, but no One knows better than you do, the present tone of the public pulse, in all its members, or that line of true policy, wisdom and Justice, which will lead to your own honour, and satisfaction, as well as the prosperity and happiness of your Country.—Your own enlightned understanding and calm deliberation, will be an inexhaustable source *at hand* on every emergence.

The arduous struggle for the Liberties and Independence of our Country, cost me, the prime of my life, hence you will readily conceive, how important, and dear, their defence and preservation are held in my estimation, and how pleasing the reflection when *assured*, that their sacred portals are guarded, by *faithful*, and *friendy* centinels.

I am now growing an Old man, and my glass is nearly run; but permit me to assure you Sir, that my remaining small abilities, and influence, shall be exerted in *this quarter*, to aid and support your administration.

Wishing you a Continuation of health, and an administration honorable and satisfactory to yourself, advantageous, and acceptable to your Country.

I have the honor to be with the most profound respect Sir Your very humble Servant   W. HEATH

RC (DLC); at foot of text: "Honorable Thomas Jefferson Vice President of the United States, & President Elect"; endorsed by TJ as received 7 Mch. 1801 and so recorded in SJL.

William Heath (1737-1814), a farmer and native of Roxbury, Massachusetts, was commissioned in the Massachusetts militia and served as a brigadier and major general in the Continental Army during the Revolutionary War and as a state senator in the 1790s. He became a Jefferson supporter in large part because of his views on the federal government's power to tax. Heath was defeated for Congress in 1798 by Harrison Gray Otis and was elected lieutenant governor in 1806, but refused to serve (ANB, DAB).

TJ replied on 8 Mch. 1801: "I was honoured with your favor of Feb. 26. and return you my thanks for the friendly congratulations, and the expressions of personal regard contained in it. it is indeed a subject of mutual congratulation that the spirit of our revolution, which for a time appeared to be extinguishing, has at length rekindled under circumstances which promise to continue. ... we are to rejoice in the triumph of old principles. ... if we succeed, we shall be a shining example for imitat[ion]" (PrC in DLC; faint and blurred; at foot of text: "Genl. Heath").

To Thomas Lomax

DEAR SIR   Washington Feb. 25. 1801.

Your favor of the 5th. came to hand on the 20th. and I have but time to acknolege it under the present pressure of business. I recognise in it those sentiments of virtue & patriotism which you have ever manifested. the suspension of public opinion from the 11th. to the 17th. the alarm into which it throws all the patriotic part of the federalists, the danger of the dissolution of our union & unknown consequences of that, brought over the great body of them to wish with anxiety & sollicitude for a choice to which they had before been strenuously opposed. in this state of mind, they separated from their Congressional leaders, and came over to us; and the manner in which the last ballot was given has drawn a fixed line of separation between them and their leaders. when the election took effect, it was as the most desireable of events to them. this made it a thing of their choice, and finding themselves aggregated with us accidentally, they are in a state of mind to be consolidated with us, if no intemperate measures on our part revolt them again. I am persuaded that week of ill-judged conduct here, has strengthened us more than years of prudent & conciliatory administration could have done. if we can once more get social intercourse restored to it's pristine harmony, I shall believe we have not lived in vain. and that it may, by rallying them to true republican principles, which few of them had thrown off, I sanguinely hope. accept assurances of the high esteem & respect of Dear Sir

    Your friend & servt   TH: JEFFERSON

PrC (DLC); at foot of text: "Thomas Lomax esq."

To Richard Richardson

SIR   Washington Feb. 25. 1801.

Your's of the 16th. has been duly recieved. it has not been in my power to enquire the price of journeymen here, as I have been very closely confined by business, and the buildings are so scattered here, that one does not know where to go for enquiry. I believe there will be a good deal of work done the ensuing season at this place, and am told workmen are more in demand here than at Philadelphia, where the demand is said to be very dull: I suppose therefore they will flock from there to this place.

As I am to be fixed in this place, I give up all idea of carrying on any more stone or brick work myself. I have therefore accepted Whately's proposal to undertake my shop &c himself, out & out, he to do the quarrying, hauling & every thing. of course I have nothing in which I could engage you. Lilly succeeded in getting as many hands as I wanted, and after finishing the clearing for mr Craven, will be employed this summer on the canal—I believe there will be little public work done here this summer: it will be chiefly private. I am Dear Sir

    Your friend & servt   TH: JEFFERSON

RC (ViU: photostat); clipped below signature. PrC (MHi); at foot of text: "Mr. Richard Richardson"; endorsed by TJ in ink on verso.

WHATELY'S PROPOSAL: see TJ to Thomas Whitlaw, 19 Feb. 1801.

From Benjamin Stoddert

SIR,   Nav Dep 25 Feb 1801

By direction of the President, I have the honor to enclose, for your information, a letter addressed to me by Mr Fitzsimmons, on behalf of the Chamber of Commerce of Philadelphia—and a copy of my answer.

I have the honor to be, with great respect, Sir, Your most obt Servt.

BEN STODDERT

RC (DLC); at foot of text: "Thomas Jefferson Esqr. President elect"; endorsed by TJ as received 25 Feb. and so recorded in SJL. FC (Lb in DNA: RG 45, LSP). Enclosures: see below.

On 17 Feb. Thomas FitzSimons, as president of the Philadelphia CHAMBER OF COMMERCE, had written to Stoddert complaining about British privateers' captures of American vessels trading with Spanish colonies in the West Indies. John Marshall forwarded the complaint to British chargé Edward Thornton and also wrote to Rufus King in London. In his answer to FitzSimons on 23 Feb., Stoddert said that the United States had means of protection "in our own hands" and need not depend entirely on the British government. Noting the "impropriety" of undertaking significant initiatives in the closing days of a presidential administration, Stoddert did not dispatch the *Portsmouth* from Norfolk but did order the ship to be made ready (Tr in DLC; NDQW, Dec. 1800-Dec. 1801, 120, 128; Marshall, *Papers*, 6:80-5; Philadelphia *Aurora*, 2 Mch. 1801).

From Isaac Weaver, Jr.

SIR   Lancaster feby. 25th. 1801.

Altho' acquainted only with your publick character, I gratify feelings which appear to be in unison with those of this State, in congratulating you on the happy issue of the momentous struggle of America to continue advantages gaind'd by the price of revolutionary blood, in preserving the right of electing to the highest office in the United States, the man in whom the publick choice centers, free and without contamination—Impress'd with those feelings I freely declare, however democratic I may be consider'd by my friends, or anarchic by others, that I am of that class of citizens who wish a government and laws sufficiently nervous to enforce order at home, and to protect the citizen from invasion from abroad; yet always considering power deriv'd from the people, which is greater than this, unnecessarily surrender'd, and uselessly if not unjustly exercis'd by those who in a free government ought never to be arm'd, but for the *general* good—

By a long course of services you have justly attracted the attention of your fellow citizens, and by submitting your political opinions to their investigation, they are long since convinced, that with candor was united in you, abilities competent to the rendering essential services to our common country—Under this view, you have had my feeble support, which cannot be withdrawn from your administration, while you continue to act under principles which are correct; and which I have no doubt are establish'd in your mind—. But whenever I discover a defection, I must lose sight of the politician, and lament the loss my country has sustain'd, not by the *Death* but *desertion* of a *once* valuable citizen

I have the Honour to be With sentiments of esteem Your fellow Citizen   ISAAC WEAVER JUNR.

RC (DLC); at foot of text: "Thos. Jefferson Esquire President (Elect) of the United States"; endorsed by TJ as received 5 Mch. and so recorded in SJL.

Isaac Weaver, Jr. (1756-1830) represented Greene County in the Pennsylvania House of Representatives. During the 1798 session he was one of 22 representatives who voted against sending a letter to President Adams in support of his policies. The group explained its action in *The Dissent of the Minority, of the House of Representatives of the Commonwealth of Pennsylvania, From the Address to the President of the United States, Adopted by Said House, December, 1798* (Philadelphia, 1799). When Republicans gained control of the House in 1799, Weaver was elected speaker, a position he held until 1803, when he became state treasurer. In 1808, Weaver began serving in the state senate. He is credited with writing *Experience the Test of Government: In Eighteen Essays. Written During the Years 1805 and 1806. To Aid the Investigation of Principles, and Operation of the Existing Constitution and Laws of Pennsylvania,* published by William Duane in Philadelphia in 1807. The advertisement published in the volume called attention to the "enormous abuses" that flowed from the "exorbitant power vested in the executive" (*Pa. Arch.*, 9th ser., 3:1908-9, 2218; PMHB, 62 [1938], 219-21; *Journal of the First Session of the Tenth House of Representatives of the Commonwealth of Pennsylvania,* Dec. 1799-Mch. 1800 [Lancaster, 1800], 5; *Journal of the Senate of the Commonwealth of Pennsylvania,* Dec. 1808-Apr. 1809 [Lancaster, 1809], 4; Weaver to Albert Gallatin, 14 Dec. 1799, in NHi: Gallatin Papers).

From Joseph Anderson and William Cocke

SIR   Feby 26th 1801

In bringing, thus early, to your View, a Subject deeply interesting to the Citizens of Tennessee, we hope we Shall not be considered, as tresspassing upon the rules of propriety—If however it Shou'd be thought, in any degree improper, thus to Obtrude, upon the first Majistrate of the Union, previous to his Official inauguration—we trust that the Consideration of the Short time, the Senate may probably be continued together (after the close of the Session) will plead our apology—

At the last Session of Congress, a law was pass'd Authoriseing the President of the United States to hold a treaty with the Indians, South of the River Ohio—and the Sum of fifteen thousand dollars, was appropriated for that purpose—The *late* President, hath never yet, thought proper to take any Step, to Carry the law into operation—The Object of this law, was to Obtain, from the Cherokee Indians, all the Tract of land (claim'd by them) north of the Tennessee River—or so much thereof, as they cou'd be prevail'd upon, to part with—The Tract of Country in Tennessee called the Wilderness (and which divides the Holston, from the Cumberland Settlements) is about One hundred Miles in length and perhaps fifty, in breadth—The Indian claim to this Tract, never haveing been regularly extinguish'd (by the United States) proves a Source of Very great inconvenience to the Communication, between the Eastern, and Western parts of the State—and Matter of great greviance to those Citizens, who honestly possess'd themselves of titles *therein*, under the State of North Carolina,—Previous to the Treaty of Holston—

If however the Indians Shou'd not be disposed to Make Sale of the Whole Tract, or even of any part thereof—it wou'd prove a Very great accomodation, to Obtain from them, the Previlege of Establishing Stations or houses, along the road, at proper distances for the *Shelter* and *protection*, of our Citizens who are repeatedly Necessitated, to pass the Wilderness—

We are Sir With Sentiments of the highest Consideration—most respectfully your Very Obt Servts   JOS: ANDERSON
                                                                           WM COCKE

RC (DLC); in Anderson's hand, signed by him and Cocke; at foot of text: "The President Elect"; endorsed by TJ as received 27 Feb. and so recorded in SJL. FC (T); with some variations in wording.

Anderson and Cocke were the U.S. senators from Tennessee; for their political careers, see Vol. 19:381-408 and Vol. 29:169-70n, respectively. The LAW appropriating funds for a treaty with Indians south of the Ohio River was approved 13 May 1800. The United States had negotiated the TREATY OF HOLSTON with the Cherokees in 1791. In June 1801 TJ's administration initiated negotiations for new land cessions from the Cherokees and other Indians in the Southwest. TJ and Dearborn instructed the government's commissioners, James Wilkinson, Benjamin Hawkins, and Andrew Pickens, to obtain, among other objects, right of way for a ROAD from the Tennessee settlements to Natchez (U.S. Statutes at Large, 2:82; ASP, *Indian Affairs*, 1:648-50; Anthony F. C. Wallace, *Jefferson and the Indians: The Tragic Fate of the First Americans* [Cambridge, Mass., 1999], 218-19, 286).

From Samuel Bryan

S<small>IR</small>, [ca. 26 Feb. 1801]

Altho' personally an entire stranger to you, I am encouraged by a knowledge of your public principles and conduct to address you on the subject of an appointment under the new administration of the Federal Government—

Aware that you will be oppressed with the number and length of statements of the pretensions of Candidates for Office, I shall be as brief in the exhibition of mine as the nature of the case will admit of.—

I was the first person who under the signature of "Centinel" pointed out the defects of the federal Constitution when laid before the United States for consideration, and under various signatures supported the opposition to its *unqualified* adoption.

Among the numerous productions of mine on that highly important subject, I beg leave to refer particularly to the reasons of Dissent of the minority of the Convention of this State who adopted this frame of federal Government,—republished in Careys Museum.—

I have uniformly since advocated the principles of republicanism.

When the State Government was removed from Philadelphia to Lancaster, the State Officers were nearly all aristocratic, and the truly important eventful[1] Election of Governor was rapidly approaching. On this great occasion I dared every consequence in support of a republican Governor, altho' I principally depended on my salary for support and Mr. Ross was a warm tried personal friend of mine.—

The County of Lancaster had been for 20 years dictated to by the highest toned aristocracy in the Union, and what gave a peculiar edge to the virulence of party spirit against me was my prosecution of the late Receiver-General a very influential aristocrat and a favourite family connection of James Ross—

My exertions on the late all-important Election have of course added to the mass of enmity against me on the part of the aristocracy.

As a specimen of the zeal & spirit manifested by me I enclose a copy of my "Sketch of an Address" which was published in the English & German Languages and several thousand copies thereof circulated in this & the neighbouring States, also a copy of a vindication and attack upon my political enemies for the torrents of abuse poured on me.—

Having rendered myself peculiarly obnoxious by my exertions to maintain as I apprehend just principles at a great Crisis in our national affairs, and this place being otherwise a very unpleasant residence from the habits which govern its Society, I should feel highly gratified and obligated to you to be enabled by an adequate appointment from you to remove to some other place—

With the freedom & plainess of a republican I submit to your consideration my wish & pretensions for official notice and am

With the sincerest esteem and regard, Your friend & well-wisher

SAML BRYAN

NB I dare say you were acquainted with my Father Judge Bryan.

NB. I should greatly prefer an appointment in this State, and am averse to one at Washington, having a very weakly Constitution & of a bilious habit.

P.S. 27th. Feby 1801 The Legislature rising this day prevents Governer Mc.Kean having his letter of recommendation ready in time for the present conveyance, but it shall be sent by next opportunity—it will be found I have no doubt to confirm the sentiments expressed a long time since by his private Secretary Mr. Hastings, see his letter

S. BRYAN

RC (DNA: RG 59, LAR); undated, but see postscript; addressed: "His Excellency Thomas Jefferson President"; endorsed by TJ as received 7 Mch. and so recorded in SJL with a brace connecting this letter and those by McClay and Reed (Nos. 3 and 4 below), all delivered to TJ by John Woodward (see note to Woodward to TJ, 7 Mch.). Enclosures: (1) John Hastings to Samuel Bryan, Philadelphia, 14 July 1800, noting that Governor Thomas McKean "will at all times, be happy to receive any communications you may be pleased to make" as he considers Bryan "a sincere friend, a zealous advocate of his administration, and a determined, upright and faithful public Officer, possessed of a thorough knowledge of Men and Measures" (RC in same; with notation by Bryan: "Note. Mr. Hastings is private Secretary to the Governor of Penna."). (2) Certificate of Jacob Carpenter, Lancaster, 24 Feb. 1801, testifying to the political conduct of Bryan, whom he has known for only a short time, but who became the "object of the obliquy & slander of the federal partizens" in 1799, served as an advocate of the Republican candidate in the Pennsylvania gubernatorial election, and has used his zeal and talents to the best effect "in promoting the Election of Thomas Jefferson" (MS in same; with notation by Bryan:

"NB. Mr. Carpenter is State Treasurer appointed by Legislative vote. He was Chairman of all the republican meetings in the Borough of Lancaster for promoting the election of Mr. Jefferson & by his talents as a writer was very useful. He was also 1 of 5 appointed by the County of Lancaster to address the State"). (3) Samuel Maclay to TJ, Lancaster, 24 Feb. 1801, noting that although unknown personally to TJ, he seeks to recommend his long-time friend as a man of talent and integrity, who would be gratified with his current state appointment "were it not for some unpleasant circumstances that have been Brought on him by his uncommon Exertions in the Republican cause" (RC in same; torn; with notation by Bryan: "Note. Mr. Maclay is held in high estimation, being justly considered as the most able, intelligent and judicious member of the Legislature. He took a distinguished part in Congress in the opposition given to the British Treaty"; endorsed by TJ as received 7 Mch. and so recorded in SJL). (4) William Reed to TJ, Lancaster, 26 Feb. 1801, congratulating TJ, although they are strangers, on his election and "on the revival of the republican energy," noting that Bryan labored "earnestly and incessantly" for the republican cause during the election and crediting his prompt and plain statements which were circulated in Adams County, Pennsylvania, and the neighboring counties with "the great change of Political opinions and conduct which has taken place there" (RC in same; at foot of text: "Thomas Jefferson Esqr—Presidt. Elect"; with notation by Bryan: "Mr. Reed says he has a full conviction that the 'Sketch of Address' carried the Election in Frederick County Maryland for the State Legislature in favor of the republicans" and "NB. Mr. Reed is a Brigade Inspector of the Militia and a senator in our Legislature from York and Adams Counties"; endorsed by TJ as received 7 Mch. and so recorded in SJL). (5) Samuel Bryan, "Sketch of an Address," has not been found. For the other enclosed pamphlet, see below.

Samuel Bryan (1759-1821) was the eldest son of Irish Presbyterian immigrant George Bryan and Elizabeth Smith Bryan, daughter of the prominent Presbyterian merchant Samuel Smith. Following his father into politics, Samuel Bryan was elected clerk of the Pennsylvania General Assembly from 1784 to 1786. He served as register-general of Pennsylvania for six years before becoming the state's comptroller general in 1801, a position he held until late 1805 when he was replaced after opposing the reelection of Governor McKean. In 1809 he became register of wills for Philadelphia, a position he held until 1821. As a member of the Lancaster Republican committee, which included Tench Coxe, Timothy Matlack, Frederick A. Muhlenberg, and Jacob Carpenter, Bryan devoted himself to the Republican cause in the election of 1800 (Rowe, *McKean*, 363-6; Joseph S. Foster, *In Pursuit of Equal Liberty: George Bryan and the Revolution in Pennsylvania* [University Park, Pa., 1994], 2-3, 10, 140, 163; Cooke, *Coxe*, 377-8; DHRC, 13:326).

Using the SIGNATURE OF "CENTINEL" Bryan wrote 18 essays, printed first in the *Independent Gazetteer*, a leading Antifederalist newspaper in Philadelphia, between 5 Oct. 1787 and 9 Apr. 1788. The letters warned that the newly formed Constitution, unless modified, posed a threat to civil liberties and the sovereignty of the states. DISSENT OF THE MINORITY: this is apparently Bryan's first acknowledgment

that he penned this document signed by 21 of the 23 Antifederalists who voted against ratification of the Constitution. It was published in the *Pennsylvania Packet and Daily Advertiser*, 18 Dec. 1787, as "The Address and Reasons of Dissent of the Minority of the Convention of the State of Pennsylvania to their Constituents." Bryan was not a delegate to the Pennsylvania ratification convention and did not sign "The Address and Reasons." This address and "Centinel" essays have been described as "two of the most widely circulated and influential Antifederalist attacks on the Constitution" (PMHB, 112 [1988], 107-8, 123; DHRC, 2:128-9, 617-18, 639; 13:326-8).

Bryan's charges that Francis Johnston, former RECEIVER-GENERAL of the land office, had used public monies for private purposes resulted in Johnston's resignation. In late 1799 Bryan charged that Johnston still owed the state more than $8,000 ([Samuel Bryan], *Proceedings in the Case of Francis Johnston, Esq. Late Receiver-General of the Land-Office, Prosecuted for Delinquencies in the Said Office* [Lancaster, Pa., 1799], iii-iv, 19; Evans, No. 36065). Bryan's publication of documents in the case against Johnston prompted criticism by members of the Pennsylvania House. When Bryan wrote a letter in defense of his actions dated 14 Jan. 1800 to Speaker of the House Isaac Weaver, an unsuccessful attempt was made to have him arrested, brought before the House to apologize, and then removed from office. Weaver cast the tie-breaking vote, which kept Bryan from being seized. In response Bryan published A VINDICATION, under the pseudonym "Centinel," entitled *A Statement of the Measures Contemplated Against Samuel Bryan, Esquire, Register-General of the Commonwealth of Pennsylvania, Unparalleled in the United States, and Without a Precedent Even in the Corrupt Parliament of Great-Britain ...* (Philadelphia, 1800), 5-11, 18-24; Evans, No. 38557.

MY FATHER JUDGE BRYAN: a strong supporter of Pennsylvania's radical state constitution of 1776, George Bryan served as a judge in the state supreme court from 1780 until his death in 1791 (ANB).

---

[1] Word interlined.

From Pierce Butler

near Charleston Feby. the 26th 1801

I come, said Arius Antonius to the Emperor Nerva, with others, to Congrat[ulate] not Your good fortune, but that of the Roman Empire.—

Not in the habit of aiming at a Correspondence with any person in an elevated situation; as You are at present; yet I am prompted by a wish to see Your Administration easy and honorable to Yourself; and still more, by Attachment to the honor and interests of the Union, to intrude this letter on You—That You are equal to meet the nice situation in which Your acceptance of the Office of Chief Magistrate will place You, I have no doubt—that your Ability to extricate the Union from it's present embarrassment, is Commensurate with the arduousness of the undertaking is unquestionable; but You will I trust excuse me for being apprehensive lest the uprightness of Your own intentions, aided by a Philanthropic feeling, may induce an indecisive Commencement, which must ever after be irretrieveable; and not only embitter Your Administration, but frustrate Your good intentions towards the Union—Of the motives and views of the two existing Parties in America, You are well acquainted; but of the means by which one Party wishes to establish it's Doctrine, and with it a preeminence, pardon me if I question Your being as well acquainted as Men of less perception, who mix more in active scenes than You do, or rather have done—That the Party, which H— considers himself the head of, will make a violent run at You in the commencement of Your Administration, with a hope of intimidating, and thus drawing from You halfway measures, cannot be doubted—have they not playd the same part with Mr. A— finding they could not lead him in strings, they became Bullies, with a hope intimidating—Pickering was instructed to commence the bullying system, which was follow'd up by H— P. in manners and disposition a Savage, used no address—his attack was so gross that it justly rous'd the indignant feelings of A— and frustrated at the time, the expectations of the party—W— the creature of H— next Advances, but the Clumsiness of P— open'd the eyes of A— H. advances again, but with no better success—H. well knowing that Your principles are too well fix'd for him to hope for any success from the servile parts he too successfully Acted with Gen. W.— will at once commence his opposition to You by a Storm—the whole Phalanx will attack You at the same time, in every part of the Union. if they find that they gain one Inch, they will be encouraged to more rude attacks, with a hope of distroying the general Confidence in Your Administration—Supported as You will be, while true to Yourself, in the most decided manner, by those who aided in placing You in the Chair, Excuse me if I say You have but one line of Conduct to observe; that is, a most decisive One towards the Enemies of the Principles You embrace, and which placed you at the head of the Government—Without a mark'd decision, Your friends will despond and drop off—the Government get into disorder, for the very object of these Men will be to disorder it, and Yourself be made unhappy—

I have now to apologise for the freedom I have taken; and to pray You to be assured that it proceeds from Correct motives—It is the first time I have offer'd my opinion to a President of the United States—the whole time of Gen. Washington's Administration, when to my knowledge, other Senators made a practice of offering him their individual opinions in private, I confined myself to the publick duty of a Senator—If I depart from that rule now, I am encouraged thereto, by the different opinion I indulge of Your mind and disposition, from what a close observation forced me to form, of the mind of Mr. W—

Accept the Assurances of my high Esteem   P. BUTLER

RC (DLC); torn; at foot of text: "T. Jefferson"; endorsed by TJ as received 13 Mch. and so recorded in SJL.

I COME ... TO CONGRATULATE NOT YOUR GOOD FORTUNE, BUT THAT OF THE ROMAN EMPIRE: *Epitome de Caesaribus*, 12:2-3; see John D. Grainger, *Nerva and the Roman Succession Crisis of AD 96-99* (London, 2003), 38, 134n.

H—: Alexander Hamilton. MR. A—: John Adams. P.: Timothy Pickering. W—: Oliver Wolcott, Jr. GEN. W.: George Washington.

From Nicolas Gouin Dufief

MONSIEUR,   Philadelphie. 26 de Fevrier. 1801

Il m'a fallu attendre l'arrivée de plusieurs caisses de livres qui m'étoient expédiées d'Hambourg avant de pouvoir vous adresser ceux que vous me demandez, par votre lettre du 9. Janvier dernier

Je ne dois pas passer sous silence que j'ai reçu aussi un ouvrage entrepris au Commencement de la Revolution & qui vient d'être terminé.

Il a pour titre, *Encyclopédie des Voyages; contenant l'abregé historique des mœurs, usages, habitudes domestiques &ca. de tous les peuples, & la collection complète des Costumes civils, militaires, re-ligieux, dignitaires de tous les peuples, dessinés d'après nature, gravés avec soin & Coloriés, par Grasset de St Sauveur, ci devant Vice Consul de France en Hongrie.*

On voit par le programme en tête du 1er. numéro qu'il s'est publié par Souscription à 6 livres la livraison; il y en 48, chacune contient l'histoire de plusieurs peuples avec six planches superbement coloriés

J'ai fait relier magnifiquement ces 48 livraisons en 3 Vs. 4o.

Si vous desirez faire l'acquisition de ce bel ouvrage je vous le passerai a 50 Dollars; prix au dessous de celui de la souscription, & qui devroit être fort au dessus si l'on considere les droits le frêt &ca. la reliure & le profit auquel un libraire doit s'attendre pour le fruit de ses peines & l'hemploi de ses fonds. Ce qui me permet de le vendre à ce prix, c'est que j'ai acheté a assez bon marché une collection nombreuse de livres Francais, parmi lesquels etoient 2 exemplaires de cet ouvrage—

Un livre qui sera toujours très curieux, & qui est autentique se trouve parmi ceux qu'on m'a envoyés. C'est *le rapport fait au nom de la Commission Chargée de l'examen des papiers trouvés chez Robespierre & Ses Complices, par Courtois*

Je ne Grossis pas davantage ma liste, crainte de ne plus vous intéresser, & de vous dérober des momens précieux—

Agréez, Je vous prie, ma profonde estime & mon respectueux devouement N. GOUIN DUFIEF

EDITORS' TRANSLATION

SIR, Philadelphia, 26 February, 1801
I had to await the arrival of several chests of books that were shipped to me from Hamburg before being able to direct to you those that you asked for in your letter of last January 9.

I must not omit saying that I also received a work undertaken at the beginning of the Revolution and which has just been finished.

Its title is *Encyclopedia of the Travels; containing an abridged history of the customs, uses, domestic habits, etc. of all the peoples, and the complete collection of the civil, military, and dignitary costumes of all the peoples, drawn from nature, engraved with care and colored, by Grasset de St. Sauveur, formerly Vice-Consul of France in Hungary.*

One sees by the program at the head of the first volume that it was published by subscription at 6 livres per issue; there are 48 of them, each one containing the history of several peoples with six plates superbly colored.

I have had these 48 issues magnificently bound in three quarto volumes.

If you wish to acquire this fine work, I can let you have it for 50 dollars; a price below the subscription, and which should be much above it if one takes into account the duties, the freight, etc., the binding, and the profit that a bookseller should expect as the fruit of his trouble and the return on his funds. What allows me to sell it at this price is that I bought at quite a good price a large collection of French books, among which were two copies of this work.

A book that will always be very curious and which is authentic is also among those that were sent to me. It is *The report made in the name of the commission charged to examine the papers found in the house of Robespierre and his accomplices, by Courtois.*

I will not expand my list any further for fear of losing your interest and stealing precious moments from you.

Accept, I beg of you, my profound esteem and my respectful devotion

N. GOUIN DUFIEF

RC (DLC); at foot of text: "Ts. Jefferson. Esqre."; endorsed by TJ as received 3 Mch. and so recorded in SJL.

Jacques Grasset de Saint-Sauveur's work appeared in installments printed in

Bordeaux, 1792-93, and in Paris in 1796. Edme Bonaventure Courtois's *Rapport* was published in Paris in 1794 and 1795.

From William Findley

SIR   Lancaster Feby 26. 1801

While I make free to call your attention to a few Subjects which I conceive to be of importance, I will not detain you with Congratulations, nor those expressions of satisffaction which I feel with greater force than I can utter on the account of the final happy result of the presidential election and the flattering prospect of our affairs, my Joy however is mingled with as Sincere Sympathy. I am sensible of the difficulties of the important station which you are called by your Country to occupy and in the calling you to which the voice of the people was much more general than the Constitutional expressions of it which they were permitted to make

The purging of the public offices will be perhaps the most invidious part of the task, not so much on the account of the clamour that will be raised on the account of removals which from both Moral and political causes will be necessary, but also on the Account of the difficulty of Supplying their place to advantage.

Perhaps all the Departments will require changes, but it is the postoffice to which I make free particularly to call your attention. it must be purged[1] The abuses in that department have been general and scandalous, at least in pennsylvania. The suppresion or mislaying of the votes for Electors in 1796 was an Attrocious and public instance of abuse and all the changes made since within my knowledge have been for the worse. Indeed I am not aquainted with any unexceptionable postmasters, except probably Mr peters of the City and Mr Moore of Lancaster, there may be more. Before a crooked policy dictated a change of those officers, the officers in that department had been selected for their fittness and conducted with propriety.

The postmaster general expressed the highest approbation of the postmaster of Greensburgh near where I live to me and before the Session was over he was removed and a character the most exeptionable in every point of view put in his place. He had nothing to recommend him but a talent for low invictive which he unceasingly exercised against the Republicans, the Revenue of the office has sunk under his hand. I complained of him to the postmaster genl. some years Since who acknowledged he had seen my own Letters returned and burned in the office, during one Session of Congress every letter of mine sent by that office was lost except that to my wife and to a Federal friend. I wrote last year to the postmaster genl. what I thought sufficient causes for his removal without being attended to except in the case of some unjust charges of fees against myself. The postmaster in Carlisle and in most if not all the Western Counties of the state are highly exceptionable. There are exceptionable officers in other departments respecting whom our Members of Congress can give more correct information, therefore I shall only mention the Supervisor of the Excise, He never was qualified for it nor worthy of the trust and his removal would not encrease the number of our enemies and would be gratefull to our friends and I think promote the public interest. He has been active against us to the last degree

It is not my design Sir, to trouble you with applications for my friends. I feel indeed for the uneasiness you will be made to suffer by numerous solicitations for office, though being the means of introducing a worthy person to office has its merit, I shall therefore make free to Mention one Samuel Bryan Esqr now Register General for the state of pennsylvania, I think would be a valuable appointment for an office that would require the Superintendance of Revenue and Compelling the settlement of accounts[2] In this way he has been the most indefatigable faithfull and Correct officer that ever the state has employed. And his deetecting the numerous Mistakes of former officers, and the abuses in various departments and especially with Landofficers and Contractors under the very relaxed administration of the late governor has occasioned him many enemies. his detecting the enormous and long Continued frauds against the public last year, committed by Col Johnson receiver genl. of the land office Subjected him to the enmity of the Federal party and his able and very usefull writings in favour of the Republican cause, especially before the two last elections has strengthened that enmity. However he is happy in this, that no stain has ever attached itself to his Moral or official character, nor any charge of partiallity. His father the late Judge Bryan did honour to the Republican cause and was long its principle support in this state and was never forgiven for refusing to pardon the Traitors Roberts and Carlisle. He died poor and governor Mifflin Voluntarily promised to provide for his family, but first delayed and then failed in making the provision he had promised. It was his the governors[3] fortune to be supported by the Whigs while his favours were chiefly bestowed on the torys. The effects of this are severely felt in the state. Mr Bryan has a wish to be indebted to you Sir for an appointment but is too modest to Urge. He is well known to Mr Gregg and most of our other Members of Congress. Be pleased Sir to excuse my freedom and believe to be with the most unfeigned esteem and the most Sincere wishes for the success of your administration

Your most obedt and very humble servt   WM FINDLEY

SIR
After Writing the enclosed I received a Letter from Genl. Wm. Irwin of Carlisle, of the substance of which he seemd, to wish You to be informed. He says that whilst, the Feds with them held out the language of Conciliation they at the same time behave with the greatest rancour, he informs me of some stricking instances of this even within this few days, though he is the most respectable Citizen in the place, they have excluded him and Mr Hamilton the Republican Lawyer from their Society. He thinks and so does most other of our friends with whom I converse that there ought to be a general change of public officers. In this however I am tender in advising but official influence and insolence has gone to a great height in pennsylvania. I am convinced Numerous removals would make more friends than enemies, but from the intimate experience I have had of numerous changes in our own State for a year past, I am convinced that notwithstanding the loud Clamour that was made about the Numerous removals, some and indeed too many mistaken appointments has done more harm as well some not being removed who ought to have There are no Men more to be guarded against then

[79]

confident office hunters, recommendations can be procured with too much facility. The rapid encrease in wealth of the Collectors of Excise affords ground of suspicion but I am unaquainted with their Conduct. I crave indulgence for the freedom of these hints, they are well intended.

RC (DNA: RG 59, LAR); at foot of third page: "The honorable Thomas Jefferson"; endorsed by TJ as received 3 Mch. and so recorded in SJL; TJ later canceled "Findley Wm." and added "Boyer Samuel" to the endorsement.

William Findley (1742-1821) migrated to Cumberland County, Pennsylvania, from the north of Ireland with other Scotch Irish Presbyterians in 1763. He served as a militia captain in 1776 and 1777. In 1782 Findley moved to Westmoreland County, where he resided the rest of his life. A leading spokesman for the Antifederalists, Findley voted against the ratification of the Constitution in 1787. He regularly held elective political office, including that of congressman from 1791 to 1799 and again from 1803 to 1817. During the years he was not in Congress, he served in the state senate. Findley's publications include *History of the Insurrection, in the Four Western Counties of Pennsylvania*, a history of the Whiskey Rebellion (Philadelphia, 1796; see Sowerby, No. 532). He also wrote numerous newspaper articles for the western Pennsylvania press, often in opposition to Hugh Henry Brackenridge (ANB; DHRC, 2:728; Callista Schramm, "William Findley in Pennsylvania Politics," *Western Pennsylvania Historical Magazine*, 20 [1937], 31-40).

MR PETERS OF THE CITY: Findley probably referred to Robert Patton who had served as the postmaster at Philadelphia since 1789. GREENSBURGH: David McKeehan was appointed postmaster at Greensburg, in Westmoreland County, in April 1798 in place of John Morrison. When McKeehan resigned in April 1801, Joseph Habersham requested that Findley select a suitable successor but noted that it should not be Morrison because he had been "removed for not rendering his accounts regularly." Findley recommended Thomas McGuire, who was said to possess "many good qualities for a Postmaster" even by those who differed with him on "political subjects." He served as postmaster until 1804. John P. Thomson was POSTMASTER IN CARLISLE from February 1800 to January 1802 (Habersham to Findley, 10 Apr. and 11 May 1801, Habersham to McKeehan, 11 May 1801, all FCs in Lb in DNA: RG 28, LPG; Stets, *Postmasters*, 218, 220, 224).

SUPERVISOR OF THE EXCISE: Henry Miller (JEP, 1:164).

In 1778 George Bryan refused to pardon John ROBERTS and Abraham CARLISLE although more than 7,000 petitioners pleaded for the lives of the two men convicted of treason (Joseph S. Foster, *In Pursuit of Equal Liberty: George Bryan and the Revolution in Pennsylvania* [University Park, Pa., 1994], 154).

[1] Preceding four words interlined.

[2] Findley added in the margin, without indicating where it was to be inserted: "He has been Several years Register General in the office of Accounts for the state after having been long first Clerk."

[3] Preceding two words interlined.

From Philippe de Létombe

Philadelphie, 8 ventose an 9
de la République française.

MONSIEUR,   (26 fevrier 1801. v. st.)

J'ai vu naître les Etats-unis; je Vous suis attaché depuis seize ans; voila mes titres pour Vous offrir mon Compliment sur votre nomination à la Présidence.

Aimé et estimé dans ces Etats et dans l'Europe, Vous justifierez le choix de vos concitoyens; Vous gagnerez tous les cœurs; Vous rendrez votre nation l'exemple du monde; la Philosophie Vous placera au rang des Bienfaiteurs de l'humanité et la Postérité au nombre des grands hommes.

Daignez agreer, Monsieur, l'hommage d'un Cœur pénétré de vos anciennes bontés et d'admiration pour votre Gloire.

LÉTOMBE

EDITORS' TRANSLATION

Philadelphia, 8 Ventôse Year 9
of the French Republic.

SIR,   (26 February 1801 old style)

I saw the birth of the United States; I have been devoted to you for sixteen years; those are my qualifications for offering you my compliments on your nomination to the presidency.

Loved and esteemed in the United States and in Europe, you will justify the choice of your fellow-citizens; you will win every heart; you will make your nation the example for the world; philosophy will place you among the benefactors of humanity, and posterity among the number of great men.

Be pleased to accept, Sir, the homage of a heart imbued with your former kindnesses and with admiration for your glory.   LÉTOMBE

RC (DLC); 8 Ventose, Year 9, was 27, not 26, Feb. 1801; at foot of text: "Thomas Jefferson, Président élu des Etats-unis"; endorsed by TJ as a letter of 26 Feb. received 2 Mch. and so recorded in SJL.

To Robert Morris

DEAR SIR   Washington Feb. 26. 1801.

Being in want of a Steward or Maitre d'Hotel, a person [by the] name of Tate has been recommended to me, with information that he had [served] you some years in that capacity. as it is highly important to a house that that officer be honest and skilful, I have flattered myself you would be so kind as to give me his character with as much detail as would be interesting to me. I shall consider it as a great favor, as I find it very difficult to get a person fit for that service in the establishment I must make. I hope you will excuse the freedom I take in giving you this trouble and accept assurances of the constant esteem of Dear Sir

Your most obedt. servt   TH: JEFFERSON

P.S. early information will be thankfully recieved.
I forgot to ask about his wife who it has been said might be advantageously employed also in the house.

PrC (MHi); faint and torn; at foot of text: "Robert Morris esq."; endorsed by TJ in ink on verso.

From Patrick Sim

SIR   Feby. 26th. 1801.

I hope you will excuse the maner in which I take the liberty to offer myself to you a Stuard of your Famely it will be needless for me to say more at present then that. I shall be satisfyed with very Moderate Wagers. that my recomendations shall be from the best people—Mrs. Sim who you can soon be satisfyed has been in that line of life which has qualifyed her to mannage a Genteel Famely will have no objections to take derections of yr. Houshold affars. added to us we have One of the best Cooks this part of the Cuntrey affords. wich you can also have if you chuse—should it not be perfectly convenent for you to see me on this business today a Note derected to me at Mr. Stills Tavern Signafying when you chuse I should wait on shall be attended to any time after Tuesday next. till that time I shall be ingaged Out of Town after that I shall be at liberty to enter on any business If you have not supplyed yourself I flater myself I could Conduct myself in a manner that would be satisfactorey to you—and hearing my pretentions you would give me the preference to many others who may apply.—With Sincere wishes for your helth. I have the honour to be with profound Respect—

Yr. Mt. Obdt. Hub Sevt.   PATRICK SIM

RC (MHi); endorsed by TJ as received 26 Feb. and so recorded in SJL.

From John Strode

WORTHY SIR   Culpeper 26 febry. 1801

Imprest with respectfull Awe and the most profound esteem, I presume to approach your hand; not that I conceive your friendship for an individual however small or remote, in any degree lessen'd; but because the business of your elevated Station, will continually require your attention to matters of transcendantly more importance; I beg leave to introduce to you my friend & Neighbour Robert B Voss esquire, with whom if I remember right, you said you Once had a small acquaintance in Europe; He understands there is some public Serv[ice] by commissioners to be perform'd to the southwd. in delineating the boundarys of some Indian Tribe or Nation; the pecuniary reward attach'd to that Service can be no object with a Man of Mr. Vosses Estate practice & abillitys, but that [he] has a strong desire to see that country, perhaps there are but few, if any better qualified on acct. of Mathematical and Legal knowledge, and in point of general p[erspi]casity, industry and perseverance, He is not I believe, [. . .] to any. In my humble situation, I have small [. . .]sions to recommend, but were I ever so worthy of At[. . .] One Syllable should not on that head escape me; did I not concieve, I was serving my country through the Man prop[osed] to its Service.

For some time an awful and portentous silence pervaded this country; the solemn and determined countenance of each individual bespoke the labouring Movements of His Mind; but at last, and we humbly thank God for it, the late election in Congress concluded to General satisfaction—the gloom is dispersed—and transports of Joy appear in every countenance, and that without one single disenting Voice. Gracious Heaven preserve you long very long, [in]deed preserve your precious Life, for sake of your family, your friend, and your country. So pray, many, & many a Thousand this day, but none more fervently, than, Sir, Your most Obdt hble servt

JOHN STRODE

RC (DLC); frayed at edge; at foot of text: "[Th]omas Jefferson Esqr. [Pre]sident of the United States"; endorsed by TJ as received 11 Mch. and so recorded in SJL, where TJ noted that he received it and James Monroe's letter of 5 Mch. from Voss.

TJ had encountered a Virginian named VOSS in Europe in the mid-

1780s, when Voss, perhaps for reasons of trade, traveled to Paris, Amsterdam, and London, where he also called on John Adams. Robert B. Voss lived on a Culpeper County estate called Mountain Prospect. The only correspondence between him and TJ would appear to have been an undated letter from Voss that is recorded in SJL as received from Culpeper on 26 May 1808 in support of

Mordecai Barbour for the Richmond postmastership (Raleigh Travers Green, comp., *Genealogical and Historical Notes on Culpeper County, Virginia. Embracing a Revised and Enlarged Edition of Dr. Philip Slaughter's History of St. Mark's Parish* [Culpeper, Va., 1900], pt. 2:55-6; Mordecai Barbour to Madison, 12 Oct. 1808, in DNA: RG 59, LAR; Vol. 9:183-4, 364n; Vol. 10:256, 302, 305).

From John Beckley

DEAR SIR,   Philadelphia, 27th: February 1801.

So inseparable, are the feelings of my mind, from a deep concern, in the welfare and happiness of our common Country, and for the success and honorable reputation, of that administration of its affairs, which you are about to commence, that I cannot permit myself to withhold the present communication. If it may in any degree conduce to aid the purposes of your own mind, Or that view of things which occasion and reflection have led you to take, my wish and object will be fully answered.

In taking the helm of government at this tempestuous moment of party violence and collision, I perceive the delicacy and difficulty you will experience at the outset, from the opposite claims of firmness and decision on the one side, and of conciliation and compromise on the other. Truly to appreciate the considerations which may lead to a right decision it would seem necessary to regard,

1st: the respective Character of the republican & fœderal party.
2d: the views and policy of the late fœderal administration.
3d: the real interest and true policy of the United States, and the best means to promote it.

On the first and second points, few reflections can be offered which the superior information you possess will not have embraced. In point of fact however, I think it may be safely assumed,

1st: That in the proportion of numbers thro' the U:S. the republicans constitute five eighths of the whole.
2d: That in like proportion is the relative degree of property and talents between the parties.
3d: That the fœderal party are, *strictly* speaking, Monarchical in their principles, views and wishes.
4th: That it was the policy of Mr: *A's* administration to approach that object; by close and intimate connection with Monarchical

Governmts. and by repellant or hostile measures towards those of a republican character.

On the last point, which essentially involves the conclusion to a right decision, I think it may be equally assumed on the ground of real interest and true policy,

1st: That all political relation, by treaty, with foreign nations should be avoided.

2d: That simple Commercial connections on a basis of perfect reciprocity and the most conducive to the principles of free commerce should be pursued.

3d: That the defensive system of protecting commerce by a limited Navy, Embargo, Suspension of intercourse, and fortified ports and harbors, is the most sure, safe, cheap, and effectual.

4th: That protecting duties for the encouragement of Manufactures ought to be imposed as far as revenue considerations will admit, and the Alien laws repealed.

5th: That the Agricultural interest be promoted, by repeal of Excises and Land tax, to effect which rigid œconomy should be enforced in all the departments of Government, all unnecessary Establishments put down, sine cure offices abolished, and all speculation on the public wants, by jobs and contracts done away.

6th: That a new organization of the executive departments of Government be made,

1st: by a revision and amendment of the Constitution of each.
2d: by new, simple, and effectual interior regulations.
3d: by changes of men in office and new appointments so as *gradually*, but certainly & effectually, to place the executive administration in the hands of decided republicans, distinguished for talents & integrity.

The last proposition I regard as the pivot of the whole, and that on which the late happy change of the Executive was effected. So far as my opportunities of information go, and they have been considerable with men of calm, cool, reflecting minds from almost every State, there is but one opinion, and that is, that a change thorough and complete, but gradual should be made: that as no confidence can be placed in fœderal views or principles, so is there no safety in the admission or appointment of doubtful political character: that such an admission would implant jealousy, disunion and discord both in and out of the administration: that the public mind now aroused to a complete union of action in every State, to republicanize the whole, would be damped & paralized by a temporizing policy: that considering the character and conduct of the fœderal party they merit no respect, and from their numbers; wealth, or talents compared with the republicans should excite no fears of their future efforts: that future measures of Amelioration in our foreign and domestic concerns, will, aided by the present universal republican impulse, if that impulse be not unwisely counteracted, speedily put an end to the *present* views and wishes, and even to the very name of a fœderal party:—And lastly, Sir, that a temporizing policy founded on any principle of conciliation or compromise will essentially injure your reputation and the success of your administration, since it would be difficult to remove the impression from the public mind that the reiterated charge of your supposed want of political firmness was not well grounded—an impression which would be the more indelible from the general persuasion that no principles of policy, prudence, propriety, safety, or justice, will *at this time* warrant any concessions to your and our political opponents.

I might add, that so far as respects the general principle of a change of men, the experience of pennsylvania, has proved the wisdom of the policy, since, except in a few instances of intemperance and indiscretion in the execution of that principle, nothing has so much conduced, to the stability and success of republicanism in this state, and to the reputation of its government among the mass of Citizens.

There is however one modification or exception to the general rule, that merits respect, it is the case of revolutionary Whigs and Soldiers of the late Army, whose politics have not been marked by active or party exertion, and whose adherence to the fœderal side has been merely passive.

Besides the general motives which have induced this letter I beg leave to offer those of my highest personal Esteem & attachment— and remain, dear Sir,

Your obedt: Servt. and sincere friend   JOHN BECKLEY.

RC (DLC); addressed: "Thomas Jefferson, Esqre."; probably delivered by "Genl: Dearborn," whose name also appears in Beckley's hand; endorsed by TJ as received 3 Mch. 1801 and so recorded in SJL.

From Delamotte

havre 27. fevrier 1801.

J'apprends á l'instant d'une maniere á peû prés certaine que vous etes élû président des Etats unis d'Amérique, comme je l'esperois depuis quelques mois. C'est un évenement tel qu'il n'y en a guere qui puisse m'interesser davantage. j'aime á vous voir promû á cette dignité, parceque je Sçais combien vous etes digne d'elle et elle digne de vous. puissiés vous, Monsieur, y trouver, par vos succés á Avancer la prospérité de votre pays, la recompense de vos travaux. C'est, á coup sûr, celle que vous desirés—& c'est aussi celle que je ne doute pas que vous obtiendrés. permettés que je vous félicite sur votre promotion; Si vous connoissiés tout mon Attachement, vous sauriés que j'ai besoin d'etre félicité aussi á cette occasion, comme de chose qui m'est personnelle. permettés aussi que je me rejouisse Avec vous des Auspices heureux sous lesquels j'espere que vous passerés toute votre présidence. la paix va rendre á toute l'Europe, que dis-je? á toute la terre, la tranquilité, la prosperité & le bonheur dont on est privé depuis Si longtems. l'Amerique est appellée á faire des progrés bien considerables et ce sera vous, Monsieur, qui les dirigerés. je ne vois rien á vous Souhaitter qu'une bonne Santé, je vous la souhaitte de tout mon cœur.

Vous connoissés Sans doute dejà notre traité de paix avec l'Empereur, tant en son nom qu'au nom de l'empire, qui nous assure la possession de la Belgique et nous donne le bord du Rhin pour limite sans lacune. la Coalition des puissances du Nord nous amenera aussi la paix avec l'Angleterre. le changement de tout son ministere annonce assés ses dispositions pour esperer que cette paix aura lieu incessament. elle vous sauvera l'embarras d'avoir á vous déclarer participans á la Coalition, comme on vous auroit infailliblement invités á le faire. les droits des puissances neutres seront établis et ils seront respectés, je crois, dans les guerres á venir. l'Egypte restera probablement á la france et Malthe á la Russie; l'une et l'autre puissances sont en situation á obtenir ces deux points sans grandes difficultés. Il est pré[sumable] aussi que le Commerce de la Russie eprouvera des changemens plus favorables à toutes les nations, au prejudice de l'Angleterre.

Quelle Issûe pour la france d'une révolution aussi dégoutante dans bien des points! que d'horreurs, que de gloire cette fermentation revolutionnaire a fait éclore! mais nous en sommes heureusement venûs á dire avec Shakespear "all is well, that ends well" nous avons notre Washington (en verité, notre bon Buonaparte, notre [heros ayant pris] le votre pour modèle) C'est á lui que nous devons tout le bien qui s'est operé depuis quinze mois, comme par enchantement. Autant notre gouvernement inspiroit de crainte & repoussoit la Confiance, autant il est respecté aujourdhuy et par la nation & par l'etranger. la Seule chose qui nous reste á Craindre, C'est que notre force ne fasse naitre l'inquiétude des autres puissances et il nous faudra bien de la sagesse et de la moderation pour éviter cet écueïl, Cependant, aprés avoir eû un Washington, il [faut] esperer que nous Aurons aussi d'autres hommes Sages, pour nous gouverner aprés lui.

J'ai ecrit au secretaire d'Etat pour solliciter d'etre nommé de nouveau Consul ou Vice-Consul des E.U. au Havre. trois ans d'une interruption absoluë de tout Commerce au Havre, me laissent le besoin d'appeller cette place á mon Secours. C'est á vous, Monsieur, que je la devois, C'est encore á vous que je la demande et je vous supplie de vouloir bien m'etre favorable. Si le nouveau Consul general de france a été chargé de vous inviter á ne nommer que des Americains, j'abandonne mes Sollicitations, mais s'il ne l'a pas fait, c'est une preuve que notre gouvernement entend l'article de notre Constitution relatif á cet objet dans son sens naturel, C'est á dire, qu'il ne fait pas une loi aux françois de ne pas accepter des fonctions etrangeres, mais que ceux qui les acceptent perdent [leurs] droits politiques de Citoyens françois & restent assimilés aux étrangers residans en france, chose à laquelle je me soumettrai si je dois appartenir aux E.U. d'Amerique.

Il me reste á vous prier, Monsieur, de trouver bon que je vous écrive quelquefois. mes lettres ne vous obligent pas á des reponses et il me seroit pénible d'etre privé du plaisir de vous écrire. Je ne vous demande plus de m'adresser vos Commissions, Mr. Short m'en sauroit mauvais gre, mais je m'estimerai heur[eu]x toutes les fois qu'il m'arrivera d'avoir quelqu'ordre de vous á remplir.

J'ai l'honneur d'etre avec le respect le plus [sincere] Monsieur Votre trés humble & trés obeissant Serviteur.   DELAMOTTE

SIR   Le Havre, 27 February 1801
I have learned this minute from an almost certain source that you have been elected president of the United States of America, as I had been hoping for some months. Hardly any event could interest me more. I like to see you promoted to that dignity, because I know how worthy of it you are and it worthy of you. May you, Sir, find therein, through your successes in advancing the prosperity of your country, the reward of your labors. That is certainly the one that you desire and it is certainly the one that you doubtless will obtain. Allow me to congratulate you on your promotion; if you knew

all my affection, you would know that I too need to be congratulated on this occasion, as something that is personal to me. Allow me also to rejoice with you for the fortunate auspices under which I hope you will spend your entire presidency. Peace is going to give back to Europe—what am I saying?—to the entire earth, the tranquility, the prosperity, and the happiness of which we have been deprived for such a long time. America is called to make considerable progress, and it will be you, Sir, who will direct it. I see nothing more to wish you but good health, and I wish it with all my heart.

You probably already know of our treaty of peace with the emperor, as much in his name as in the name of the empire, which assures to us the possession of Belgium and gives us the banks of the Rhine as our uninterrupted limit. The coalition of the northern powers will also bring us peace with England. The changing of its entire ministry announces quite well enough her dispositions to hope for a peace that will take place immediately. That will save you from the difficulty of having to declare yourselves participants in the coalition, as you would inevitably be invited to do. The rights of neutral powers will be established and will be respected, I believe, in the wars to come. Egypt will probably remain France's, and Malta, Russia's; both powers are in condition to obtain those two points without great difficulties. It is also to be presumed that Russia's commerce will undergo changes more favorable to all nations, to the detriment of England.

What an outcome for France from a revolution so disgusting in so many respects! How many horrors, how much glory this revolutionary ferment has brought about! But we have fortunately come to say with Shakespeare, "All's well that ends well." We have our Washington (in truth, our good Bonaparte, our hero, having taken yours as a model). It is to him that we owe all the good that has taken place for fifteen months, as if by enchantment. As much as our government inspired fear and rebuffed confidence, by so much it is today respected both by the nation and abroad. The only thing that remains for us to fear is that our strength may cause uneasiness in the other powers, and we will need much wisdom and moderation to avoid that reef. Nevertheless, after having had one Washington, it must be hoped that we also will have other wise men to govern us after him.

I wrote to the secretary of state to solicit an appointment again as consul or vice consul of the U.S. at Le Havre. Three years of total interruption of all commerce at Le Havre have left me in need of that position. It is to you, Sir, that I owed it; and once again, it is of you that I request it and beg you kindly to be favorable to me. If the new consul general of France has been ordered to invite you to name only Americans, I abandon my solicitations, but if he has not done so, that is a proof that our government understands the article of our constitution that relates to this matter in its natural sense, that is to say, that it does not make a law that Frenchmen may not accept foreign functions, but that those who accept them lose their political rights as French citizens and remain on the same footing as foreigners residing in France, something to which I shall submit if I am to belong to the United States of America.

It remains for me to beg you, Sir, to find it acceptable that I write to you sometimes. My letters do not require answers, and it would be painful to me to be deprived of the pleasure of writing to you. I no longer ask you to address your errands to me; Mr. Short would hold it against me, but I shall consider myself fortunate every time it happens to me to have some order from you to carry out.

I have the honor to be with the most sincere respect, Sir, your very humble and very obedient servant.   DELAMOTTE

RC (DLC); damaged; at foot of first page: "Monsieur Jefferson Président des E.U. d'Am."; endorsed by TJ as received 27 Aug. and so recorded in SJL.

NOTRE TRAITÉ DE PAIX AVEC L'EM-PEREUR: the treaty between France and Emperor Francis II of Austria, agreed to at Lunéville on 9 Feb.; see Thomas Newton to TJ, 29 Dec. 1800.

LE CHANGEMENT DE TOUT SON MIN-ISTERE: George III's dissatisfaction with William Pitt's policies toward Ireland precipitated the resignation of Pitt, Grenville, and the rest of the British cabinet early in February. Henry Addington, speaker of the House of Commons, became the new prime minister. His government, delayed by illness of the king, took office in mid-March (John D. Grainger, *The Amiens Truce: Britain and Bonaparte, 1801-1803* [Rochester, N.Y., 2004], 23-4; Clive Emsley, *British Society and the French Wars, 1793-1815* [London, 1979], 90).

From Johann Eckstein

SIR,   Philadelphia Febr 27th. 1801

On the occasion of the prospect that a Mausoleum or monument will be erected in commemoration of the illistrous Washington I feel that solicitude which is common with every artist, when an occasion so important presents itself.

Sir, I am emboldned to take upon me the honor of adressing You and to solicit Your interest in my behalf, knowing from Your public Character that it gives You delight to encourage the Arts and Sciences, and beg leave to say that I shall do all in my power to approve myself worthy of Your patronage.

Sir, permit me to enumerate shortly those incidents of my career as Artist upon which my Ambition in coming forward on this occasion is founded. After having visited the principal Academies of Europe the last of which was that of London, I had the satisfaction of being presented by that academy with the first premium as Statuary; I was then called to the Court of Berlin and there promoted kings statuary by the late king Frederick the 2d. in which capacity I was employed untill I came to this Country, and here I enjoy the satisfaction of seeing myself honored with Sentiments of the first artists, which they have done me the favor to subjoin to this, and to which, I beg leave to refer.

Not being acquainted with any of the most influential Characters I was at a loss how to make application with success, the method

I adopted of procuring which, was first to present to congress a Modell, not intended as a final proposal as to its Idea, but only to show how far I am able to execute any design government might have in contemplation, this I did last Iear, I allso addressed some time since the speaker of the house of representatives in order to bring into notice that any statuary work which may be attached to the monument or mausoleum might perhaps be as well done in this Country as in any part of Europe.

I have the honor to subscribe myself of Your Excellency's most Obedient humble Servant   JOH: ECKSTEIN

RC (DLC); in an unidentified hand, signed by Eckstein; below signature: "No. 211 Market"; addressed: "To his Excellency Thomas Jefferson Washington City"; with subjoined testimonial in hand of Charles Willson Peale, signed by Peale, Rembrandt Peale, and the sculptor William Rush: "We the Subscribers, having seen of Mr. Eckstein's drawings, models & Sculptures, are of opinion that his merit entitles him to encouragement from the Public, in executing a Monument to the Memory of our late illustrious chief"; stamped; postmarked at Philadelphia 26 Feb.; endorsed by TJ as received 2 Mch. and so recorded in SJL.

Johann Eckstein (c. 1736-1817) had made a death mask and bust of Frederick the Great while employed by the Prussian court. In 1794 he crossed the Atlantic and took up residence in Philadelphia. His son Frederick, also an artist, accompanied him to the United States. The elder Eckstein worked in sculpture, painting, and engraving during his career. His design for a monument to George Washington, which he promoted for several years, depicted Washington in Roman attire on horseback (George C. Groce and David H. Wallace, *The New-York Historical Society's Dictionary of Artists in America, 1564-1860* [New Haven, 1957], 205; DAB).

For the debate in Congress over the erection of a MAUSOLEUM in memory of George Washington, see Vol. 32: 385-6.

From William Evans

HONORED SIR/   Baltimore Feby. 27th. 1801

Your favour of the 22d instant came Duly to hand. that part of the contents of which relative to your former Servant James I Immediately communicated to him, he told that he was under an engagement with Mr Peck, a Tavern Keeper, of this place, which he said was out of his power to relinquish for a few days, I requested him to be particular In mentioning the time he could be in readiness to go you, he gave me for answer that he would make up his mind in the course of the evening and let me Know his determinations, but on finding that he did not call agreeable to promise I sent for him a second time, the answer he returned me, was, that he would not go untill you should write to himself—

I will endeavour to persuade Francis from the idea of getting into your employ as I am rather inclined to believe that, he would not answer your purposes from his being overly fond of liquor, permit me Honored Sir to congratulate you on being promoted to the Chief Majestry of America, and believe me with every Sentiment of respect your obedient

Servant   WILLIAM EVANS

RC (MHi); at foot of text: "Thos Jefferson Esqr."; endorsed by TJ as received 28 Feb. and so recorded in SJL.

An inn run by Henry PECK was at 237 Baltimore Street, not far from the one run by Evans (Stafford, *Baltimore Directory, for 1802*, 83).

From George Jefferson

DEAR SIR   Richmond 27th. February 1801

I return you inclosed herein Mr. Leiper's two letters.   I am glad to find that the Tobacco has turned out to be sound, and not to have been wet—as J. & W. cannot possibly now have any legal, or just claim on you.   As to their demand of a deduction on account of *the quality* of the Tobo., I think I may venture to affirm that a more unreasonable expectation was never entertained by Man.   In order to silence them entirely however, I think I would propose that if they can point out a single instance of a deduction ever having been made *in this place* for such a reason, I would make the allowance they claim. indeed I should think myself *perfectly safe* to agree to make it, if even such *a demand* was ever made before. As well might you, had the Tobacco turned out better than was expected, (and it might have done so altho' we supposed it was *very* good) have made an additional claim on them! and I should like very much to know, what they, as rational men, (if indeed they are so) would have said to such a claim? why surely I would suppose, the most absurd, that ever entered into the head of the most absurd being on Earth.

Seven Hhds of your last crop have come down from Milton—they were forwarded by a Mr. Garrett there, who desired us to pay the carriage—we however did not wish to do it, and informed the waterman that you chose to pay it yourself—but upon his representing to us, that he was informed he should have the money here—and that the overseer had directed it, we concluded it could make no difference with you, and paid him 2/. ℔ C. We should not however have done it, but he said that if he did not get it, he should be much at a loss for money, & must be put to a very serious inconvenience. The Molasses is forwarded

I am Dear Sir Your Very humble servt.   GEO. JEFFERSON

RC (MHi); at foot of text: "Thos. Jefferson esqr."; endorsed by TJ as received 4 Mch. and so recorded in SJL. Enclosures: Thomas Leiper to TJ, 11 and 17 Feb. 1801.

J. & W.: Jackson & Wharton.

From George Logan

MY DEAR FRIEND   Lancaster Feby 27: 1801—

This Letter will be delivered to you by Mr: P: C: Lane of Virginia; but who has for several years resided in Pennsylvania, he is a Representative in our Legislature from the County of Fayette. I beg leave to refer you to him for information respecting the situation of parties in this State. he is well acquainted with the Governor, and in some degree with his opinions respecting public affairs

Your election has relieved my mind from great anxiety, respecting my Country. You have an arduous task before you. I pray to God that you may be enabled to select Men of the *strictest honor* & *probity* to assist you—

Permit me to suggest to your consideration, two objects; which I consider of National importance & which merits the earliest attention in your administration

The first: To take prompt & decided measures to countenance & promote the Useful Arts, and Manufactures in the United States. As long as we are dependent on Great Britain for our cloathing and other necessaries; we must be influenced by her baneful politics—

The second object, is, to pay attention to the Northern Powers of Europe. It is of immense importance to the small Governments or States of Europe, & not less to our own Country, that the Sea, as the great high way of all Nations, should be perfectly free. No period was ever more favorable to accomplish this great object than the present. The monopolising spirit, and the outrages of the English, has awakened the jealousy of the Emperor of Russia, he is a perfect Russ, considering no Country or People equal to his own. The King of Denmark is said to have virtuous & enlightened Ministers. The young king of Sweden is influenced by his Uncle, the Duke De Surdimania, who conducted the affairs of that kingdom with considerable prudence during the minority of the king. I had the pleasure of being frequently in his company at Rome in the Winter of 1780; he is not a Man of eminent abilities, but of an honest heart & a sound understanding. The king of Prussia is perfectly alive to every thing useful or honorable to his Country. The Batavian Republic will find it their interest to unite in any general measure to effect the perfect freedom of Commerce. Whether it may be thought proper for the United States to join an armed neutrality of the Northern Powers; it is undoubtedly the interest of this Country to promote it, as the most effectual measure to destroy the present domineering power of England; & by engaging France in the measure commit her honor to support it, when she hereafter may become more powerful at Sea than any other Nation: This is to be looked for—

I am informed Mr Short has been appointed by the President to negociate with France; he is by no means in as high estimation in France as Mr: Barlow—the latter is a Man of talents, & undoubted integrity.

I return to Stenton tomorrow. the Legislature will adjourn this day I am with Sentiments of the highest Respect Your Friend

GEO. LOGAN

RC (DLC); endorsed by TJ as received 5 Mch. 1801 and so recorded in SJL.

Until Gustav IV Adolf, the KING OF SWEDEN, came of age in 1796, his uncle Karl, the duke of Södermanland (and later King Karl XIII), ruled as regent (H. Arnold Barton, *Scandinavia in the Revolutionary Era, 1760-1815* [Minneapolis, 1986], 136, 202, 204, 231; Irene Scobbie, *Historical Dictionary of Sweden* [Metuchen, N.J., 1995], 85-6, 108-9).

The rumor that William SHORT would be minister to France, Bayard having declined the post, was false (Shackelford, *Jefferson's Adoptive Son*, 131).

To Tarleton Bates

SIR   Washington Feb. [. . .] 1801.

Not knowing where the persons to whom the [enclosed are?] directed, may be at this time, and believing that this knoledge may [be] acquired at Pittsburg, I have taken the liberty of putting them under cover to you, and of adding a sollicitation that you would be so good as to address and forward them by any conveyance which may occur to the persons for whom they are, wheresoever they may happen to be. the importance of their getting speedily & safely to their [destinations will] I hope plead my excuse for the liberty I take. I am with [esteem] Sir

Your most obedt. servt   TH: JEFFERSON

PrC (DLC); faint; recorded in SJL under 28 Feb., but in his endorsement TJ may have intended a date of 23 Feb. and Bates acknowledged this as a letter of the 26th (see below); at foot of text: "Mr. Bates"; endorsed by TJ in ink on verso. Enclosures: (1) TJ to Meriwether Lewis, 23 Feb. (2) TJ to James Wilkinson, 23 Feb.

Born in Goochland County, Virginia, Tarleton Bates (1775-1806) moved to Pittsburgh in 1793. He worked in the quartermaster's department of the army, then in 1801 became a clerk in the office of the county prothonotary. Allying himself in business and politics with influential local attorneys, he was an energetic advocate of Republican candidates, including TJ. He knew both Wilkinson and Lewis and had further contacts in the Northwest Territory through his brother Frederick, who had established himself as a merchant at Detroit. Tarleton Bates, who was prothonotary at the time of his death, died in a duel that resulted from political disputes among Pennsylvania Republicans (Russell J. Ferguson, *Early*

Western Pennsylvania Politics [Pittsburgh, 1938], 144, 165-6, 170, 188-9, 191; Mrs. Elvert M. Davis, ed., "The Letters of Tarleton Bates, 1795-1805," *Western Pennsylvania Historical Magazine*, 12 [1929], 32-53; T. L. Rodgers, "The Last Duel in Pennsylvania," same, 54-7; PMHB, 13 [1889], 13, 19; 32 [1908], 254-5; DAB, 2:49-50).

ADDRESS AND FORWARD THEM: on 6 Mch. Bates wrote TJ to say that on that day he had received TJ's communication, which he identified as a letter of the 26th. Lewis had arrived in Pittsburgh from Detroit late on 5 Mch. and received TJ's letter directly from Bates on the 6th. Wilkinson left Pittsburgh for Washington on 1 Mch., so Bates put TJ's letter to him into the care of Campbell Smith, an army officer and friend of the general. In his brief letter Bates also congratulated TJ and the country "upon the ascendency which the principles of '76 have regained" (RC in DLC, endorsed by TJ as received on 13 Mch. and so recorded in SJL; Heitman, *Dictionary*, 1:894-5; Lewis to TJ, 10 Mch.).

From Joseph Hardy

SIR,   New York 28h, February 1801

It is publickly asserted here, as an event highly probable, that the Office of Surveyor of this port will become vacant the 4h, next month—In which case, having been a Candidate for the same previous to the present nomination, I would take the liberty of renewing my application that may be found on the files of the President under date of the 7h, March last. This was accompanied with a number of Letters from respectable characters here to the President—Secretary of the Treasury, Senators, and Representatives—to all which I would humbly sollicit your reference. If these documents should authorize Your Excellency to give me a preference, I can only say my whole time and attention shall be devoted to the faithful execution of the duties of Office.

I will just add that I have the honor of being known to the Vice President—and that I am with the highest consideration and respect, Your Excellency's most Obt. & Hble Servt.   J: HARDY

RC (DNA: RG 59, LAR); endorsed by TJ as received 6 Mch. 1801 and so recorded in SJL.

Joseph Hardy appeared in the *New-York City Directory for 1801* as a merchant with a residence at 88 Broad and a store at 220 Front Street. He was a member of the New York State Society of the Cincinnati and served as its assistant treasurer in 1803 (*Longworth's American Almanac, New-York Register, and City Directory, for the Twenty-Sixth Year of American Independence* [New York, 1801], 186; Kline, *Burr*, 2:775). For Hardy's previous government service and applications for positions in the Washington administration, see Washington, *Papers, Pres. Ser.*, 2:438-9.

From Philippe de Létombe

MONSIEUR LE PRÉSIDENT,

Philadelphie, 9 ventose an 9
de la Republique francaise
(28 fevrier 1801)

Rien n'a pu retarder mon empressement de répondre à la confiance dont vous m'honorez. Aussitot après avoir reçu votre lettre, je me suis mis à la recherche de ce que vous desirez et je viens de trouver précisément ce qui vous convient.

Ç'est un homme de 42 ans; probe; sédentaire; d'une humeur toujours égale; parlant le francais et l'anglais; uniquement attaché à ses devoirs; s'occupant sans cesse; adroit à tous les petits ouvrages; entendant parfaitement l'office et fort instruit de son état de Maître d'Hotel; toujours attentif à l'économie dans la maison; en état enfin de surveiller un domestique nombreux. Mais il est marié et ne veut pas quitter sa femme qui a 44 ans et point d'enfans. Elle seroit une excellente Femme de charge, en état de prendre le plus grand soin du linge de table et de corps, de l'argenterie, des meubles, et de tenir une maison dans le plus grand ordre.—Leur ayant demandé le prix de leur service, ils ont répondu qu'ils ne vouloient plus servir, que dieu avoit béni leurs travaux et qu'ils avoient de quoi vivre honnêtement. Mais à votre nom, Monsieur, ils ont consenti à tout et ils vous demandent Cent guinées de gage (annuellement pour eux deux): c'est à dire Rien en comparaison de l'utilité dont ils vous seront. Le mari a dit, avec enthousiasme, qu'il avoit eu l'honneur de Vous servir plusieurs fois chez le chevalier de Freire dont il etoit le Maître d'Hotel.—Le chevalier d'Yrujo, Monsieur de Ternant, Monsieur Flamand Vous certifieront le compte que J'ai l'honneur de vous rendre de ces bonnes gens.—Ainsi, honorez moi de vos ordres: le mari partira, sur le champ, pour Washington et sa femme s'y rendra aussitot après avoir disposé de la maison qu'ils occupent et qui leur appartient.—Vous voyez, Monsieur, qu'il n'y a plus de difficultés à composer votre maison. Cette composition ne vous donnera aucun embarras. Tout l'art consiste à donner à chacun la tâche qu'il sait faire. Et quoi que votre modestie (qui est celle d'un grand homme) ait bien voulu m'en dire, Vous n'en trouverez pas plus à composer l'Administration de votre Gouvernement et à confirmer cette maxime d'un ancien: que pour former un bon Gouvernement il faut que les Philosophes soient souverains ou les souverains Philosophes.

Votre lettre, Monsieur, m'a ému, attendri; je me suis mis à pleurer après l'avoir lue. Votre suffrage est la récompense la plus flatteuse de mes longs travaux. C'est l'honneur de ma vieillesse. Assurément Vous me faites regretter de n'être pas le témoin des prodiges que Vous allez opérer. J'ai un sucçesseur. Mais j'entendrai de ma retraite les acclamations de l'Amérique et j'y mêlerai ma voix foible et cassée.

Je vous supplie, Monsieur, de vouloir bien agréér mon profond Respect. LÉTOMBE

P.S. Protecteur des beaux Arts,

J'ouvre ma lettre pour y joindre une Marche que mon Chancelier, partageant l'enthousiasme public, a composé, qu'il met à vos pieds et qu'il vous supplie de vouloir bien agréér. Elle vient d'être éxécutée à grand chœur. Elle a eu le plus grand sucçès. Ses partitions et le chant seront gravés pour mercredi prochain, jour des rejouissances ici pour votre installation à la Présidence. L

EDITORS' TRANSLATION

Philadelphia, 9 Ventose Year 9
of the French Republic
MR. PRESIDENT,   (28 February 1801)

Nothing could restrain my haste in answering the confidence with which you honor me. Immediately after receiving your letter, I set out to seek what you desire, and I have just found exactly what suits you.

He is a man, 42 years old, of integrity, settled, of a constantly even disposition, speaking French and English, attached solely to his duties, always keeping busy, skilled in all the minor chores; understanding perfectly the pantry, and very knowledgeable about his position as maîtred'; always attentive to the household economy; able, in sum, to watch over numerous servants. But he is married and does not wish to leave his wife, who is 44 years old with no children. She would be an excellent housekeeper, able to take the greatest care of the personal and table linen, the silverware, the furniture, and to keep the house in the strictest order.—Having asked them the price of their service, they answered that they did not wish to serve any longer, that God had blessed their labor and that they had enough to live decently. But at your name, Sir, they agreed to everything, and they ask you for one hundred guineas wages (annually for both of them): that is to say, nothing in comparison to how useful they will be to you. The husband said enthusiastically that he had had the honor to serve you several times in the home of the Chevalier de Freire, whose maître d' he was. The Chevalier de Irujo, Monsieur de Ternant, and Monsieur Flamand will vouch for the account I have the honor to render you concerning these fine people.—So, honor me with your orders: the husband will depart immediately for Washington, and his wife will go there as soon as she has disposed of the house they occupy, and which belongs to them.—You see, Sir, there are no more difficulties in forming your household. This arrangement will be no burden to you. The whole art is in giving to each person the task that he or she knows how to do. And whatever your modesty (which is that of a great man) may have wished to tell me about it, you will not find it any more burdensome to form the administration of your government and confirm this maxim of an ancient: that to form a good government the philosophers must be sovereigns or the sovereigns, philosophers.

Your letter, Sir, moved me, affected me; I began to weep after reading it. Your approval is the most flattering reward of my long labors. It is the honor of my old age. Definitely, you make me regret not to witness the miracles that you are going to bring to pass. I have a successor. But I shall hear from my retreat America's applause and I shall mingle with it my weak and broken voice.

I beg you, Sir, please to accept my deep respect. LÉTOMBE

P.S. Protector of the fine arts,

I am opening my letter to include a march that my chancellor, sharing the public enthusiasm, has composed, which he lays at your feet and begs you to accept. It has just been performed with a great choir. It has had the greatest success. Its score and lyrics will be engraved for next Wednesday, the day of rejoicing here for your installation in the presidency. L

RC (DLC); at foot of first page: "Thomas Jefferson, Président des Etatsunis d'amérique"; endorsed by TJ as received 4 Mch. and so recorded in SJL. Enclosure: see below.

Joseph Rapin was the MAÎTRE D'HOTEL suggested by Létombe in reply to TJ's request of 22 Feb.; see Rapin to TJ, 3 Apr. 1801.

MONSIEUR FLAMAND may have been Philadelphia grocer James Flamand (Stafford, *Philadelphia Directory, for 1801*, 140).

MAXIME D'UN ANCIEN: in *The Republic*, Plato expounded Socrates' argument that ideal government could be attained only if kings became philosophers or philosophers became kings (Plato, *The Republic*, Paul Shorey,

trans., 2 vols. [London, 1930-35], 1:xvii, 508-9).

UNE MARCHE: likely "Jefferson's March," called by the *Aurora* "an original composition . . . by a French gentleman of great musical talents." Neither the newspaper nor published arrangements of the score named the composer, who may have been Peter S. Du Ponceau. On a handbill that Charles Willson Peale sent to TJ, Peale identified Du Ponceau as the author of a "Solemn Invocation" sung at the Philadelphia ceremony that commemorated TJ's inauguration on 4 Mch. (see Peale to TJ, 8 Mch., and illustration). Du Ponceau also matched Létombe's characterization of the composer of the march as MON CHANCELIER—"my chancellor." A native of France, long established in

Philadelphia as an attorney with expertise in international law, Du Ponceau was the French legation's lawyer and represented the French government in a variety of legal matters during Létombe's service as minister to the United States. The organizers of Philadelphia's inaugural tribute on 4 Mch. used "Jefferson's March" to open and close the primary celebration at the German Reformed Church, and a band played the tune at a subscription dinner that afternoon. Enthusiasts quickly asked to hear it at the Chestnut Street (or New) Theatre, where the musical director, Alexander Reinagle, had written a "new President's March" to mark the political transition. The theater had been a showcase for some Federalist songs, and the *Philadelphia Gazette*, attempting to warn the proprietors against any change in partisan inflection, claimed that the new works were "offensive" to three-fourths of the people who regularly attended the theater's performances. There was at least one other piece of music called "Jefferson's March," issued by a New York music teacher and publisher, James Hewitt, in March 1801. It was apparently Hewitt's own composition, unrelated to the Philadelphia melody. To compound the confusion of titles, a few months later Michael Fortune put new words to the Philadelphia score of "Jefferson's March" and called it "Jefferson and Liberty." The latter title was also used for at least one other set of lyrics in 1801, sung to an existing tune at the time of the inauguration (*Aurora*, 4, 6 Mch. 1801; *Philadelphia Gazette*, 6 Mch.; Alexandria *Times*, 19 Feb. 1801; Frances Sergeant Childs, *French Refugee Life in the United States, 1790-1800: An American Chapter of the French Revolution* [Baltimore, 1940], 100-1; Du Ponceau to Louis André Pichon, 1 July 1801, Lb in Du Ponceau Papers, PHi; Richard J. Wolfe, *Secular Music in America, 1801-1825*, 3 vols. [New York, 1964], 1:371-2, 376, 448; 2:449; Michael Fortune, *Jefferson and Liberty. A New Song* [Philadelphia, 1801; Shaw-Shoemaker, No. 734]; ANB, s.v. "Reinagle, Alexander"; Vol. 30:325n; Fortune to TJ, 23 June 1801).

From James Madison

DEAR SIR   Feby. 28. 1801

Your favor of the 1st. instant was to have been acknowledged a week ago, but the irregularity of the post occasioned by high waters has delayed it to the present opportunity. I have now to acknowledge your two subsequent ones of the 12th. & 19th. In compliance with the last, I had proposed to leave home in a few days, so as to be with you shortly after the 4th. of March. A melancholy occurrence has arrested this intention. My father's health for several weeks latterly seemed to revive, and we had hopes that the approach of milder seasons would still further contribute to keep him with us. A few days past how ever he became sensibly worse, and yesterday morning rather suddenly, tho' very gently the flame of life went out. It is impossible for me now to speak of any movements with precision. Altho' the exact degree of agency devolving on me remains to be known, a crowd of indispensible attentions must necessarily be due from me. In this posture of things I can only say that I shall wait the return of the post after this reaches, by which I hope to learn whether your intended continuance at Washington will admit, and the state of things will require, my being there before you leave it. By this information I shall be governed, unless imperiously controuled by circumstances here.

The conduct of Mr. A. is not such as was to have been wished or perhaps expected. Instead of smoothing the path for his successor, he plays into the hands of those who are endeavoring to strew it with as many difficulties as possible; and with this view does not manifest a very squeamish regard to the Constn. Will not his appts. to offices, not vacant actually at the time, even if afterwards vacated by acceptances of the translations, be null?

The result of the contest in the H. of R. was generally looked for in this quarter. It was thought not probable that the phalanx would hold out agst. the general revolt of its partizans out of doors & without any military force to abet usurpation. How fortunate that the latter has been witheld; and what a lesson to America & the world, is given by the efficacy of the public will when there is no army to be turned agst. it!

I observe that a Come. is appd. to enquire into the effects of the late fires. This is no doubt proper; but does not I think promise much. More is to be expected from the scrutinies of the honest heads of depts. aided by the documents & other evidences which they will have time & the best means of examining. I take for granted one of the first steps of the new admn. will be to institute returns, particularly in the Navy & war depts. of the precise state in which every circumstance involved in them, comes into the new hands. This will answer the double purpose of enabling the public to do justice both to the authors of past errors & abuses, and the authors of future reforms.

I recd. a few days ago the inclosed letter from Mr. Page. Altho' there are parts of it, which might well be omitted in the transmission to you, yet the length of the proper extracts tempts me to spare the trouble of makg them. In justice to Docr. Tucker, I say with pleasure, that I have always regarded him as a man of the greatest moral & political probity, truly attached to republican principles, of a very ingenious mind, extensive information, & great exactitude in his ideas & habits of business; and consequently well fitted for public service.—The letter from Callendar, seems from its contents to have been meant for you, tho' superscribed to me.

Most affectionately I am Dr. Sir Yrs.   Js MADISON JR.

RC (DLC: Madison Papers); endorsed by TJ as received 7 Mch. 1801 and so recorded in SJL. Enclosure not found.

The letter of the 19TH was postmarked on this date but written and recorded in SJL on 18 Feb.

For the committee formed to investigate the LATE FIRES in the War Department and Treasury Department, see Thomas McKean to TJ, 10 Jan. 1801.

John PAGE apparently wrote to both Madison and TJ seeking positions in the Mint for himself and Thomas Tudor TUCKER of South Carolina; see Page to TJ, 5 Mch., and TJ to Page, 23 Mch.

LETTER FROM CALLENDAR: for the 23 Jan. 1801 letter from James Callender to Madison, see TJ to Madison, 1 Feb. 1801.

To the Senate

GENTLEMEN OF THE SENATE   Feb. 28. 1801.

To give the usual opportunity of appointing a President pro tempore, I now propose to retire from the chair of the Senate: and as the time is near at hand,[1] when the relations will cease, which have for some time subsisted between this honorable house & myself, I beg leave before I withdraw, to return them my grateful thanks for all the instances of attention & respect with which they have been pleased to honor me. in the discharge of my functions here it has been my conscientious[2] endeavor to observe impartial justice, without regard to persons or subjects:[3] and if I have failed of impressing this on the mind of the Senate, it will be to me a circumstance of the deepest regret. I may have erred at times. no doubt I have erred. this is the law of human nature. for honest errors however indulgence may be hoped.

I owe to truth &[4] justice at the same time to declare that the habits of order & decorum which so strongly characterize the proceedings of the Senate, have rendered the umpirage of their President an office of little difficulty: that in times, & on questions which have severely tried the sensibilities of the house, calm and temperate discussion has rarely been disturbed by departures from order.

Should the support which I have recieved from the Senate, in the performance of my duties here, attend me into the new station to which the public will has transferred me, I shall consider it as commencing under the happiest auspices.

With these expressions of my dutiful regard to the Senate as a body, I ask leave to mingle my particular wishes for the health & happiness of the individuals who compose it; and to tender them my cordial and respectful Adieux.   TH: JEFFERSON

RC (DNA: RG 46, 6th Cong., 2d sess.). Dft (DLC).

TJ's final act as president of the Senate was to deliver this address. The senators immediately elected James Hillhouse to serve as PRESIDENT PRO TEMPORE, and formed a committee consisting of Gouverneur Morris, Jonathan Mason, and Jonathan Dayton "with instruction to prepare and report the draft of an address in answer" to the vice president (MS in DLC, being an order of the Senate dated 28 Feb., in Samuel A. Otis's hand and signed by him; JS, 3:134-5).

[1] In Dft preceding three words are written over partially erased "fast approaching."

[2] Word interlined in Dft.

[3] In RC TJ first wrote "to the persons or subjects to which they related" before altering the passage to read as above, entering dashes in place of the erased words. TJ then altered the Dft to reflect the changes made in the RC.

[4] Preceding word and ampersand interlined in Dft.

From John Vanmetre

SIR   Berkeley County, Feby. 28th 1801

I have to acknowledge the receipt of your friendly letter Addressed to me dated monticello September the 4th 1800, and Also to Apoligise for its publication—The fact was that though it was particularly gratifying to me as An Individual yet I could not deny myself the pleasure Of Communicating its Contents to some of my friends Whom I also conceived to be the friends (in common) of the great Cause in which we were all engaged, they took Copies of it And it was their Opinion it should not be published untill the Temper of the times, or the exigency of the Case would justify Its publication. Under these impressions I had no hesitation in Suffering a few confidential freinds to take Copies, from one Of which the publication was made, And I observe that it is Now generally Copied in the republican Newspapers throughout The United States. but if I may be so bold as to give my Opinion, I think it does equal honor to the Writer, as well as the Cause. The great question which divided our fellow Citizens, Was truly as you say "Whether a preponderance of power should be lodged with the Monarchial or the republican branch of our Government" The truth is, we had felt so much of the Insolence of men in Office that the present is a desirable change for us all, And we hope will produce the most beneficial Effects to the people in general. And that this Change will produce that Uniformity of Sentiment Which is the Ardent wish of good men of all parties. The Character and the Views of Thomas Jefferson was much Vilified and abused. This was a temporary panic, but time and reflection has cured the

Mania Which then Seized the whole body of Federalism, And all things Will soon come right. The labouring Citizen can not be supposed To long Advocate Opinions Which (to say what they Isue in) doom The labouring poor, to sweat and toil for the support of a set of useless pagents—the Caterpillars of a Nation!

Such Sir have we had amongst us! But to General Darke (who does me the honor of delivering this Letter) I refer you. He will be able to direct the *Necessary* Changes which Ought, And is expected to take place in this department of your government—My Ardent wish is that the consoling thought of your being considered by the republican portion of Your fellow citizens as the safe depository of their rights, may Always be continued to you, We feel pleased to find it is the first wish of your heart, And Anxiously hope it will continue Through out the remainder of your days to be a pleasing theme of Consolation. To you Sir republicans look as to a common Father. Their wishes, And their prayers are for your happiness And Welfare—And that you may long continue A blessing To these United States is sir the Ardent desire of Your Sincer freind And Obedient Humble Servant JOHN VANMETRE

N.B

Should it be found necessary to make any Change in the Officers Of the general Government here, you will give me leave to mention William Brown & William Sommerville, Who would meet the Wishes of the people, And who have both the highest claim from their Exertions, to fill any Office which may become Vacant, should Any change take place in this part of the Country—but Genl. Darke will give you full information on that subject.

JOHN VANMETRE

RC (MoSHi: Jefferson Papers); at foot of second page: "Thomas Jefferson Esquire"; endorsed by TJ as received 3 Mch. and so recorded in SJL.

Meriwether Jones obtained one of the COPIES of TJ's letter to Vanmetre of 4 Sep. and published it in the Richmond *Examiner* on 27 Jan. 1801. Other REPUB-LICAN NEWSPAPERS, including the *National Intelligencer* on 2 Feb., quickly reprinted it. Jones introduced the letter as one from TJ to a friend in Berkeley County, noting it did "equal honor" to TJ's "head and heart" and manifested "much benevolence and forbearance" toward those who had slandered him.

From Burgess Allison

RESPECTED SIR/   Frankford March 1. 1801

Knowing the Pleasure which evry improvement in the Arts and Sciences afford you, and especially those mechanical Arts which promise to become useful to Society; I have taken the liberty of communicating to you one, made by Mr. Hawkins upon Saddles, which appears to answer the purpose design'd exceedingly well. It is the application of spiral brass wire Springs to the Seat and Stirrups of Saddles, which renders them so elastic as to ride perfectly easy. You will in the course of a day or two have an oppertunity of trying their goodness, as Mr. Stephen Burrowes Sadler in Philadelphia, who has purchased the Patent-right from Mr. Hawkins, is about to forward one to the address of your Agent at the City of Washington; of which he desires me in his name, to beg your acceptance, he not having the honour of a personal acquaintance with you himself—

Mr. Hawkins also proposes to apply a Combination of those Springs to the Swings of Carriages, which will doubtless permit the Carriage to ride much more easy than when hung with stiff leathern straps in the ordinary way.

As it is probable that Artists of the first Abilities will be sought after to execute the Monument in Memory of General Washington, I feel a pleasure in mentioning one Gentleman, who ranks amongst the highest in his profession as a Sculptor or Modeller. It is a Mr. Extine a Prussian Artist, whose republican Principles have induced him to take up his residence in this Country. I have seen several elegant Pieces of his execution in the small way, which bear handsome Testimony of his Talents—

With evry Sentiment of Esteem, I remain Dr. Sir, your very Hbe. Svt.   B ALLISON

RC (DLC); endorsed by TJ as received 3 Mch. and so recorded in SJL.

A native of Bordentown, New Jersey, Burgess Allison (1753-1827) studied at Rhode Island College and became pastor of a Baptist congregation and founder of a classical boarding school in his hometown. After he retired from his school in 1796, he devoted his energies to invention and the improvement of machines, among them the polygraph, physiognotrace, and paper ruling machine. John

Isaac Hawkins shared with Allison a passion for scientific experiment and together they patented an improved method for making paper from cornstalks. When his financial resources plummeted, Allison resumed his Bordentown boarding school post in October 1801 and accepted the local pulpit. In 1816 he became chaplain of the U.S. House of Representatives and was thereafter appointed chaplain at the Navy Yard in Washington, a post he held until his death. An elected member and once secretary of the American Philosophical Society, he was also a member of the Society for Promoting Agriculture and Home Manufactures, and a founding member of the Columbianum (APS, *Transactions*, 5 [1802], xii, 82-9; Peale, *Papers*, v. 2, pt. 1:108n; Charles Coleman Sellers, *Charles Willson Peale*, 2 vols. [Philadelphia, 1947], 2:157-8; Sprague, *American Pulpit*, 6:121-4; *List of Patents*, 31).

From Joseph Anderson

SIR   March 1st 1801

Although I do not feel myself Authorisd to interfere, in the Smallest degree, with any thing, that may in the least appertain to your Administration,—Yet feeling Very much interested, in the welfare of the Family of Mr. John Hall—Marshall of Pennsylvania,—I hope you will pardon my presumeing to request, that he may be Continued in his present office—I have had, a Very early and *long* acquaintance with Mr. Hall and his lady (who is a daughter of the Reverd. Doctr. Ewing of Philadelphia)—Mr. Hall at an early period of his life, engaged in the Service of his Country, and hath Uniformly been (in my Opinion) a Real Republican—He acted for many years, as Secretary of the land office of Pennsylvania,—with Reputation—and had (I am well informd) the Confidence of Governor Mifflin—In the late *Contest* for Chief Majistrate of Pennsylvania—Mr. Hall from personal—(not political) dislike to Mr. MKean, Voted against him—(as did to my knowledge many other good Republicans for the same reasons)—The Consequence was, that Mr. Hall was *Oblig'd* to Relinquish his Office—and on that account, he was appointed Marshall—(I contributed all in my power, to Obtain him the appointment) and as it *respected him*, political opinion was not called in question—his Vote against Mr. MKean, having been considered a Sufficient Criterion—which I *well know* to have been *badly* founded—Mr. Halls Conduct in his present appointment, (from Observations I had an Oppertunity of makeing in Philadelphia, and other Correct information), hath been as *impartial*, and mild in every Respect—as the *rage* of the late administration, wou'd possibly admit—Although Sir, I feel Unwilling, to Speak to your feelings—I cannot help observeing, that Mr. Hall, has an Amiable, Sensible Wife (who is a good Republican) a family of Seven Children, and no other means of provideing for *their* Support, but the Emoluments, ariseing from his present office—Shou'd you Under all Considerations, think proper to Continue him—it will be a most grateful thing to me,—as I feel Confident, that his *real principles*, and *practice*, will prove Such—that you will have no Cause for regret—

I am with Sentiments of Very great personal and political Respect Yr. Mo Ob Sev   JOS: ANDERSON

[PS] the inclosed letter tho adressed to me was meant for your View—I therefore take the liberty of presenting it—

PS had I not been informed that an attempt will be made to Remove Mr. Hall—I Shou'd not have presum'd to trouble you.

J A

RC (DNA: RG 59, LAR); addressed: "Thomas Jefferson President of the United States"; endorsed by TJ as received 2 Mch. and so recorded in SJL; TJ later canceled "Anderson" and added "Hall" to the endorsement. Enclosure not found.

In the aftermath of the LATE CONTEST for the governorship of Pennsylvania, Thomas McKean dismissed most of the Federalist officeholders and made 166 appointments in 1800 (James Hedley Peeling, "Governor McKean and the Pennsylvania Jacobins [1799-1808]," PMHB, 54 [1930], 322-4).

From Elijah Boardman

SIR   New Milford (Connecticut) March 1—1801

In the course of the last year it was found that some desining men in New England had conceived and were attempting to bring forth a new machine of terror for the more effectually to *subjugate* and *govern* the people of the United States—namely that Religion and State policy Should be connected and by that coalition, together with the encreased power and patronage of the President would enable the Executive branch of our government to bear down all oposition— I call this *new* because as a system in this Country it is so—altho in Europe it is old, and its fatal effects on civil liberty hath[1] long been felt in that quarter of the globe—

Feeling as I did that if a measure of this kind should be adopted it would eventually prove fatal to the Civil & Religious liberties of my[2] country, and expressing these ideas to a Clergiman living in the Town to which I belong, it was found that he entertained ideas similar to my own, and in October last he delivd a discourse a copy of which his friends requested for the Press and, Sir, I have taken the liberty of Sending to Your Excellency one of those Sermons.

—I am sensible this may appear improper not having the honor of any acquaintance with you and to the people in New England (if known) would appear still more improper to Send for parusal, a Sermon, to a person who, as many of them have attempted to insenuate, is totally destitute of *any* Religion, and hath treated (in certain conversation) contumusly the very author of our Religion—

But Sir, be your *ideas* what they may respecting an other moad of existance—they are doubtless correct, respecting the State of existance, of which we are *Sure*—And give me leave farther to observe that about half the people in New England congratulate each other on the issue of the interesting, and all important event, of the late election of President of the United States and that a great proportion of the other half will embrace simelar ideas should they be convinced that the measures of the Executive are conformable to, and in support of, the Constitution of the United States, and *real Republicanism* and more espetially if his actions are dictated by the *council of his own mind*—

Pardon for this once, the bold intrusion of an unknown friend while he remains with impressions of profound respect, and esteem
Sincearly Yours ELIJAH BOARDMAN

RC (DLC); at foot of text: "Mr. Jefferson"; endorsed by TJ as received 13 Mch. and so recorded in SJL. Dupl (same); at foot of text: "His Excellency Thomas Jefferson Esqr City of Washington"; endorsed by TJ as received 27 June and so recorded in SJL. Enclosure: Stanley Griswold, *Truth its own test and God its only judge. Or, an inquiry,—how far men may claim authority over each other's religious opinions?* (Bridgeport, Conn., 1800); Sowerby, No. 3236. Dupl enclosed in Boardman to TJ, 18 June 1801.

Elijah Boardman (1760-1823), a Connecticut merchant and trader, served in the Revolution under the command of Colonel Charles Webb. In 1779 he moved to New Haven to clerk for the well-established merchants Elijah and Archibald Austin before opening a dry goods store of his own two years later in New Milford. He and his brothers joined the Connecticut Land Company in 1794 and bought a large tract in the Ohio Territory. They invested in the first two Western Reserve towns, Palmyra and Boardman, and later in Medina. For most of 1799 and 1800, Boardman and six employees surveyed the land holdings in Boardman Township. In 1800 Boardman was part of a Republican minority in Federalist Litchfield County, Connecticut, but he became increasingly involved in politics and remained outspoken against what he termed the NEW MACHINE OF TERROR or the coalition of church and state especially active in New England. From 1821 to 1823 he served as U.S. senator (*Biog. Dir. Cong.*; Rachel D. Carley, ed., *Voices from the Past: A History as Told by the New Milford Historical Society's Portraits and Paintings* [West Kennebunk, Maine, 2000], 44-8).

[1] MS: "thath."
[2] Dupl: "our."

From William Duane

SIR   Washington, March 1. 1801

The papers accompanying were given me for communication to you, they originated in the following manner. Prior to my setting out for Lancaster in the month of October last, Mr. Lee, the person whom they concern, called on me and stated that he had been dismissed from his situation for discovering the removal of papers from the Department of State by means of a false key, and wished me to publish the facts. I objected to publish unless he would commit the matters to writing and depose to them before a magistrate, which he offered to do. Thereupon I wrote a note to Mr. Gardner, requesting him to attend to the matter while I was absent, which he did and the matters stated in the accompanying papers were given in the presence of Mr. Gardner and Mr. James Ker, of Philadelphia. I did not think the facts so strongly stated as he at first represented them to me, & therefore did not publish them.

The receipt of a letter from Mr. Gardner induces me to lay the papers now before you. The poor man appears to have been sacrificed for his fidelity, and to be reduced to the extremest wretchedness. Perhaps in any arrangements that may be hereafter made, some situation of equal value with what he held before might be found in the Custom house or elsewhere.

I have no other knowlege of the man than what arises from the occurrences in this case—and am impelled only by duty to present the papers and state what I know on the subject—submitting the case with deference to your consideration

I am with respect Your obed Sert   WM DUANE

RC (DLC); at foot of text: "Thos Jefferson. Esqr"; endorsed by TJ as received 2 Mch. and so recorded in SJL. Enclosures not found.

MR. LEE: John Lee was an office-keeper and messenger in the Department of State who claimed that he was "left behind" when the office moved from Philadelphia to Washington for being "a true & Faithfull Servant to the Goverment of the United States." On 4 Apr., Lee wrote James Madison requesting that he be reinstated or placed in a new position. If Madison needed more information, Lee referred him to TJ, "in whose posession are full proofs of what I herein Justify" (Lee to Madison, 4 Apr.

1801, in DNA: RG 59, LAR; Madison, *Papers, Sec. of State Ser.*, 1:166-7, 483-4).

MR. GARDNER: William P. Gardner of Philadelphia was a former clerk in the Auditor's Office of the Treasury Department. A devout Republican, around May or June 1800 Gardner and fellow clerk Anthony Campbell clandestinely forwarded Treasury records to Duane and Philadelphia innkeeper Israel Israel that documented alleged misuse of public monies by Timothy Pickering and Senator Jonathan Dayton, with the complicity of Oliver Wolcott. Duane used the information in a series of scathing articles that appeared in the *Aurora* in June and July 1800. Gardner resigned from the Auditor's Office before his role in the affair became public (Jay C. Heinlein, "Albert Gallatin: A Pioneer in Public Administration," WMQ, 3d ser., 7 [1950], 92-3; Kline, *Burr*, 1:528-30; Syrett, *Hamilton*, 25:54-6, 423-7; *Aurora*, 17, 18, 20, 21, 23, 24, 25, 30 June; 2, 3, 4, 8, 9 July 1800).

From Benjamin Hawkins

Took,au,bat,che 1st. march 1801.

I now send you My dear Sir, the seperate communication promised you; It would have been sent somewhat sooner, but I have moved from the Lower to the upper creeks, to be more in the center of the nation, and to have a more commanding influence among them; and of course to be in a situation where my exertions will have the best effect in carrying the benevolent views of our government into operation. This had seperated me from my papers for a while, and untill I got into a house, which I have but lately done, I was not in a situation to write.

In the course of the spring I am to visit all the upper towns and shall amend the sketch now sent up to the time present; and will send you the amendment.

I wrote you on the 12th July and sent the creek and chickasaw, for your short vocabulary, and since then I wrote you and sent the Choctaw. This now sent will not fill up the measure of my promise as I have in forwardness a vocabulary of the Creek tongue, as well as a map of this country the courses taken by a pocket compass and the distance taken in minutes from creek to creek, on the routs I have traveled.

Do me the favour I pray you to state to me such queries as when answered will throw that light on the state of our indians as philosophy may require. This request is not made to the Vice president or as expect to the president of the United states but to the man placed as the first in science and philosophy in our country.

Accept of my sincere wishes for your present and future welfare and believe me with the truest exteem and regard

My dear Sir, your most obedient Servt.

BENJAMIN HAWKINS

RC (DLC); at foot of text: "The Honble Mr. Jefferson"; endorsed by TJ as received 1 May and so recorded in SJL. Enclosure: "A sketch of the present state of the objects under the charge of the principal agent for Indian affairs, south of the Ohio," a discussion of Creek Indian society with particular emphasis on the progress of Hawkins's efforts to alter the Creeks' economy and governance; Document No. 1 in *Message and Communication from the President of the United*

States to the Senate and House of Representatives, Delivered on the Commencement of the First Session of the Seventh Congress, The 8th of December, 1801. With the Accompanying Documents (Washington, D.C., 1801); also printed in ASP, Indian Affairs, 1:646-8.

For TJ's request for a COMMUNICATION about the Creeks, see Hawkins to TJ, 23 Jan. 1800, and TJ to Hawkins, 14 Mch. 1800. Hawkins enclosed a CHOCTAW vocabulary list in his letter of 6 Nov. 1800, in which he also mentioned the relocation of his agency to Tuckabatchee.

Hawkins called his travel record, in which he recorded such information as the DISTANCE from stream to stream along each day's route, his "viatory" (Thomas Foster, ed., The Collected Works of Benjamin Hawkins, 1796-1810 [Tuscaloosa, Ala., 2003], viii-xxiv, 1j-89j).

From John Garland Jefferson

DEAR SIR   Amelia Mar. 1st. 1801.

Your favor of Feby. 1st. has come safe to hand, and I acknoledge myself highly gratified with the receipt, since it has enabled me to explain your vote for Johnson in a satisfactory manner to most who have heard your reasons. The news of your election to the presidential chair, has been the source of great, and general joy. The people have now the satisfaction of seing the man of their choice raised to the first in the Government, and are at the same time freed from the fears of civil war. This was an event for which the minds of most of us was prepared. I will now my dear Sir open to you a subject upon which I enter with a great degree of hesitation, and reluctance. The nomination to most of the offices under government will now devolve upon you, and if you shoud deem it proper I shoud be pleased with some appointment. I have never once applied to one of your predecessors, nor woud I have accepted an office under a man who might have exacted from me any thing inconsistent with the principles of the strictest honor, nor with my ideas of the most rigid integrity. I am confident that my interest and wishes in an affair of this nature will be laid entirely out of the question. The interest of the community will be alone consulted: nor woud you on the contrary appoint one less fit in consequence of the influence or extent of his connexions. I expect however, that in your appointments, you will for your own sake, as well as that of the community, appoint persons in whose Zeal for your honor, and the honor of your administration, you have the most absolute reliance. How coud you expect that your administration woud be prosperous and happy, when offices shoud be entrusted to men who woud rejoice at your removal or disgrace? And who my dear Sir coud feel a more lively interest in the success and happiness of your administration than one who owes you as many obligations as I do. But I forbear to enlarge upon this subject least I shoud incur the imputation of presumption. I have been led into these remarks from a fear that my application may have the appearance of indelicacy or impropriety, altho I am not conscious that it has the shades of either: and I know that scarcely you yourself can feel more anxiety about the prosperity of the government as it relates to your management, than I do. If you shoud think that it woud be any way expedient I suppose I coud procure a number of letters on the subject of my application from gentlemen of the first respectability. Whatever may be your opinion, it will be received with the same deference, and carry with it the same weight as the opinion of a father in whose judgment I had the utmost confidence, and in whose affection I had the most positive reliance. The practice of the law is on many accounts disagreeable to me, too much crouded to be very profitable, and I have a growing family for whose interest it is necessary I shoud provide. I am dear Sir with sentiments of the most grateful esteem

Your most obt. servant   JNO G JEFFERSON

RC (ViU: Carr-Cary Papers); at foot of first page: "The Honourable Thomas Jefferson"; endorsed by TJ as received 9 Mch. and so recorded in SJL. Enclosed in George Jefferson to TJ, 4 Mch. 1801.

From Matthew Lyon

SIR—   Washington March 1st. 1801

Being sensible that Jabez Fitch Marshal of Vermont has no title to the good opinion of any honest man I cannot suppose he will be sufferd to remain one day in office to disgrace the Administration of the Man he has so often Cursed and defamed—

Three Candidates have applied to me to be recomended to that appointment either of whom are Qualified to perform the duties of the Office, I think it proper to name them all and give their Charracters—

The first who applied to me is Doctor John Willard of Adison County he is somewhat eminent in his profession & practices in Middlebury where he lives & several adjacent Townships, his ocupation has given him great opportunity to defend the republican cause which he has done with much Skill, Zeal, & fidelity for many years and has been a great means of holding a Majority in that Quarter on the republican side, he has Served the town of Middlebury which contains A large number of Aristocratic Lawyers as a member of Convention and Assembly & the year before last he was choosen by the People of the State as one of the Council of Censors.

The next person who has applied is General Isaac Clark an active Veteran more famed for Valour & Bravery than an other man in Vermont he is one of the first Settlers of that Country, his father served as President of the Convention at and before the formation of the Constitution & filled many Important stations after to his death. General Clark rose from a private Soldier step by step to the rank of a Brigadier General haveing earned every promotion by some distinguished Act of Bravery, his last promotion was in Consequence of his Zeal, prudence, & sound discretion in suppressing a ramification of Shays's insurection which reached into Vermont—

On the Admission of Vermont into the Union General Clark would have been more universally approved of for Marshal than any other man, but a kind of Modesty which N England people are seldom guilty of possessing prevented Governor Chittenden from recomending him because he was his Son in Law and Clark would not Ask of him the favor.

Every effort of the Anglo Fedreal party to disceminate their poison in Vermont has met with General Clarks opposition & his popularity in their early attempts was a strong barrier against them, consequently that popularity must be destroyed by them. he has for the greater part of the time been a member of the Legislature since 1778 in Sepr 1798 when it was decreed that I should be imprisoned he was to be expelled, and as soon as he was chosen it was rumor'd among the Feds that he was to be expelled but no one could tell for what, When the Legislature met Clark was as usual appointed one of the Committee to sort & Count the votes for Governor & Council. while that bussness was doing a Young knaveish lawyer by the name of Jacob Smith who represented Royaltown in the County of Windsor contrary to the usual rotine of the bussness left his County Collegues and intruded himself upon General Clark to join him in counting Votes, Smith took down the Number on a peice of paper as Clark counted them, the agragate of the whole votes were sorted & decleration made, the next day an accusation was brought forward against General Clark & Jacob Smith was brought to prove that he had given off wrong numbers of Votes which were added to the sum total of the Votes, an other person (who was undoubtedly in the secret) picked up the Original papers which had been thrown away those Smith indentified, on this evidence Clark was expelled the house, altho the Alteration made in the

Votes were palpably improbable for him to make and every body knew that if Clark had been guilty of a thing of the kind he would have secured the original papers instead of throwing them on the floor with the rest, Clark had at least as good a right to Charge Smith with Setting down the Votes different from what he gave them off as Smith had to charge him with the error—the republican Members 44 in number opposed the vote of expulsion and believed Clark to be innocent & Smith the Villian, the people of the Town of Castelton concurred in the opinion & immediately elected & - returned him to the same assembly, but in the face of the Constitution which forbids a second expulsion for the same offence they refused him a seat. in Sepr 1799 he was again elected & served in the Assembly.

When I was last in Vermont I avoided saying any thing to him on the subject of the Marshalship knowing that if he should be favord with a nomination Chipman & Payne would oppose & Villifie him in the Senate & possibly defeat his appointment, but he has writen to me in such terms that I cannot avoid makeing the Application, he recounts his services & sufferings which I am well acquainted with, he says (and I know it to be true) that he never before solicited an office, that he is growing old & unable to push his domestic bussness as he formerly did, that he is well able to perform the duties of that Office, that had he solicited the Marshalship on our admission into the Union it could not have been denied him.

Altho Sir I consider General Clark to be a Man of Strict Honour & probity capable of fulfilling the duties of the Office with honour to the Goverment as he possesses a peculiar adroitness which in distinguished Stations never fails to render him popular, I would not mention him without intimateing what his enimies will say against him, nor would I wish to risque the weight of a single hair of the popularity of your Administration for to serve any friend or even myself In the present case I am too much in General Clark's Intrest to be a judge of the effects of such an appointment on the popularity of the Administration on an extensive scale. but I am certain every republican in Vermont would approve of the measure exept those who may themselves be disappointed

The other Candidate is Doctor James Witherill of Fairhaven he has been my successor in the Legislature of Vermont & Stands on equal Ground with Doctor Willard in point of Merrit & Qualification. They are all my intimate friends—with great respect I am Sir

   your hble Servt   M Lyon

RC (DNA: RG 59, LAR); at foot of text: "Mr Jefferson"; incongruously endorsed by TJ as a letter of 1 Mch. but received 28 Feb. and so recorded in SJL; also endorsed by TJ: "Dr. John Willard Genl. Isaac Clarke Doctr. James Wither-ill," with names connected by a brace and labeled, "candidates for Marshalsy vice Jabel Fitch to be removed."

Noted as a "very zealous" Republican, GENERAL ISAAC CLARK was married to Hannah Chittenden, daughter of Governor Thomas Chittenden (E. P. Walton, ed., *Records of the Governor and Council of the State of Vermont*, 8 vols. [Montpelier, Vt., 1873-80], 1:121-2).

Lyon's THREE CANDIDATES and a reference to this letter are recorded in Appendix I, List 1.

From Rembrandt Peale

SIR   Philadelphia March 1st: 1801.

To your flattering Communication, an immediate answer was unavoidably prevented. I shall feel happy in being able to furnish you with an accurate Copy of your Portrait, at my usual price 30 Dollars—which shall be immediately begun and finished as soon as possible. It has met with general approbation, but from the difficulty of the front face, I am afraid the marks of *Copy* may not be so much hid as I could wish.

While on this subject, I must say that I was much mortified at the abominable abuse of this Picture in the Print first made from it; and was in hopes a Second (just finished) would have been, under my inspection, sufficiently accurate—But the Engraver does not possess the necessary delicacy of hand & eye, & altho' it is much better, am still disappointed. The same cause exists among us for the imperfection of Engraving as of Painting—yet the want of Encouragement cannot repress my fondness for the Art, nor my wish to become eminent in it. We fondly hope for better times—much will be done by Example.

I remain your much obliged Friend & Servant

REMBRANDT PEALE.

RC (ViW); endorsed by TJ as received 5 Mch. and so recorded in SJL.

FLATTERING COMMUNICATION: see TJ's 21 Feb. letter to Peale's father.

David Edwin made the first PRINT of Peale's portrait of TJ in 1800. The SECOND engraving was by Cornelius Tiebout (Vol. 31:xli).

From Elizabeth House Trist

As an old friend I cannot resist the impulse of my heart, in expressing to you its exultation on the Triumph of Republicanism—No event of a publick nature ever afforded me half the *pleasure* proportinate to the depression occasion'd by those base Men in Congress, who were labouring to subvert the intentions of the majority of their Country and the apprehension of an unconstitutinal Election which wou'd have plunged us into the dreadful calamity of a Civil War) great was our joy hearing you pronounced President—After felicitateing my Country on its choice believeing that we shall now have a fair experiment of What a Republican Administration can effect as to the happiness of the people, I have only to regret that the task which devolves upon you, will be attended with difficulties, especially as your Predecessor seems disposed to trammel you all *he* can but I hope and trust that you will rise superior to all their machinations. it has mortified many of your friends that you have express'd such favorable sentiments of Mr. Adams none of whom think him deserving of any elogium from you—Your minds are not congenial his being too contracted to contain a generous or disinterested sentiment and his conduct towards you has evinced it—he has done all he cou'd to injure you and he hates you on that account—and I hope you will not Compliment him in your Inaugeration address, it will be sufficiently generous not to retort a little of his own abuse upon him—Your known abilities as a Statesman and Philosopher your virtues as a politician and friend to the Rights of Man, and not your age believe me, gave you the preimminence for a thousand old fellows cou'd have been found equal to your Predecessor to have taken his place I need not appologize for the freedom I take in thus addressing you. The only privilege our sex injoy is that of freely communicating our sentiments. We are generally thought of little consiquence in the Political World. but if we are incompetent to decide properly on these subjects, we certainly can revibrate the opinion of others—and I have often thought that those placed at the head of the Nation have been led to do unpopular things for want of a Friend that wou'd candidly inform them of the real sentiments of the people. that you will ever commit any act prejudicial to your Country I can never contemplate—but a generous nature may some times by praising their enemies commit their best friends When are we to have the pleasure of seeing you in Albemarle I hope your new appointment will not deprive us of your society during the recess of Congress. I am very anxious to get home altho Richmond is a charming place I wou'd not exchange the Mountain for this situation expect to leave this some time next Month when I shall joyfully turn my attention to rural economy being heartily tired of being Idle

Mrs Monroe Eliza and Polly Unite with me in wishing every happiness and believe me truly Your Friend   E. TRIST

RC (MHi); addressed: "Thomas Jefferson President of the United States City of Washington"; franked; postmarked 2 Mch.; endorsed by TJ as received 6 Mch. and so recorded in SJL.

TJ's reply to Elizabeth Trist, presumably that enclosed in TJ to James Monroe of 7 Mch. and recorded in SJL as written on that date, has not been found.

From Stephen Burrowes

SIR/   Philadelphia 2d. March 1801

As a tribute of respect to your merits as a Friend of the People, & a promoter of the useful arts, I beg your acceptance of a Patent Saddle the construction of which I hope you will be pleased with, it is sent on by the stage this day directed to the care of Mr. Barnes.

I am Sir Respectfully yours.   STEPHEN BURROWES

RC (DLC); addressed: "Thomas Jefferson vice President of the United States Washington"; franked and postmarked; endorsed by TJ as received 4 Mch. and so recorded in SJL. Enclosure: 1801 advertisement of elastic patent saddles, along with "a general assortment of *Saddles, Bridles, Portmanteaus, Trunks, Whips*," for sale at Burrowes's Philadelphia manufactory (printed broadside in same).

From Joseph Eggleston

SIR,   Washington 2nd. March 1801

From the conversation you were pleased to hold with me last evening on the subject of the possible vacancy of the Office of Marsshall for the State of Virginia, I am induced to give you the trouble of reading the following remarks respecting Major Joseph Scott a resident of the County of Amelia.   This gentleman served as an Officer in the revolutionary war with a reputation equal to that of any man of his rank. In the battle of German town he acted as a brigade Major, & was dangerously wounded & taken prisoner whilst bravely pressing on to Philadelphia with the 9th. Virginia Regiment. The Wound he then received has been troublesome & inconvenient ever since, & at intervals it has been dangerous.   Just before the close of the War, he lost his Wife, who left him five children whom he has raised, married off, & placed in different professions, through many pressures & difficulties arising from narrow circumstances. Though thus confined & straitened, he has found time to read many books, & aided by a strong, penetrating mind, & considerable knowlege of men, he may justly be considered as a firm, enlightened Republican. In addition to these qualities, he is remarkable for sobriety, discretion, punctuality, good morals & pleasing manners. I speak from personal knowlege, having known him for 24 years, & having lived as his neighbour for seventeen years, unconnected except as a friend. He has a competent knowlege of the duties of the ministerial Offices of the State Courts, & is far from being unacquainted with the principles of Law; he is a good Accountant, has a manly person, & a fluent commanding mode of expression. Indeed I think him in every respect fitted to discharge the duties of a Marshall, & could readily venture to pledge myself for his Ability & Fidelity. When I present to my View his qualifications, his former services, & his personal respectability, I cannot but think his appointment to the Office, if it should become vacant, would be honorable to the Government, & satisfactory to the State.

With every Sentiment of the highest Respect, I am, Sir, yr. obedt. Servt. JOS: EGGLESTON

RC (DNA: RG 59, LAR); endorsed by TJ as received 2 Mch. and so recorded in SJL; also endorsed by TJ: "Scott to be Marshal."

Joseph Eggleston (1754-1811), son of a Virginia planter, resided near Amelia Court House. A 1776 graduate of the College of William and Mary, Eggleston joined Henry Lee's Lighthorse Cavalry during the Revolution, advancing from captain to major. He served in the Virginia House of Delegates from 1785 to 1788 and from 1791 to 1799. He was elected to Congress to fill the vacancy

caused by the resignation of William B. Giles in October 1798. He continued as Virginia's congressman from the ninth district until March 1801, voting consistently as a Republican (*Biog. Dir. Cong.*; Dauer, *Adams Federalists*, 309, 314, 320, 325).

A VACANCY occurred in the office of marshal for the eastern district of Virginia when David Meade Randolph was dismissed for packing juries and withholding money. On 24 Mch. MAJOR JOSEPH SCOTT was appointed to the position (see Appendix I, Lists 3 and 4).

To James Hillhouse

SIR Washington Mar. 2. 1801.

I beg leave through you to inform the honorable the Senate of the US. that I propose to take the oath which the Constitution prescribes to the President of the US. before he enters on the execution of his office, on Wednesday the 4th. inst. at twelve aclock in the Senate chamber.

I have the honor to be with the greatest respect Sir Your most obedient and most humble servant   TH: JEFFERSON

RC (Charles N. Lowrie, New York City, 1950); at foot of text: "The President pro tempore of the Senate." PrC (DLC).

The Senate read the letter above on 2 Mch. and appointed Gouverneur Morris, Jonathan Dayton, and James Ross to report on it (JS, 3:137). For that response, see Samuel A. Otis to TJ at 3 Mch. and enclosure.

TJ addressed a similar letter to Speaker of the House Theodore Sedgwick, which was read on 2 Mch. shortly after the House came to order (PrC in DLC, at foot of text: "The Speaker of the H. of Representatives"; FC in DNA: RG 59, SDR; JHR, 3:837).

From James Hillhouse

SIR,   [2 Mch. 1801]

While we congratulate you on those expressions of the public will which called you to the first Office in the United States, we cannot but lament the loss of that intelligence, attention and impartiality with which you have presided over our deliberations. The Senate feel themselves much gratified by the sense you have been pleased to express of their support in the performance of your late duties. Be persuaded that it will never be withheld from a Chief Magistrate, who in the exercise of his Office shall be influenced by a due regard to the honor and interest of our Country. In the confidence that your official conduct will be directed to these great objects, a confidence derived from past events, we repeat to you, Sir, the assurance of our constitutional support in your future administration.

                                                    JAMES HILLHOUSE

RC (DLC); undated; in clerk's hand, signed by Hillhouse, with "President of the Senate pro Tempore" added below signature in another hand. FC (same); in same clerk's hand; lacks signature; in TJ's hand at foot of text: "James Hillhouse Presidt of the Senate pro tempore."

As chair of the committee appointed to respond to TJ's address upon retiring from the Senate on 28 Feb., Gouverneur Morris reported on 2 Mch. with the answer above

under the signature of the Senate president pro tempore. A CONFIDENCE DERIVED FROM PAST EVENTS: a motion to strike out this phrase was defeated 19 to 9. The Senate then accepted the report and ordered Morris and the other two committee members, Jonathan Mason and Jonathan Dayton, to present it to the vice president (MS in DLC, being an order of the Senate of 2 Mch., in clerk's hand, attested by Otis, on verso of order of the Senate of 28 Feb. 1801; JS, 3:136-7).

To John Marshall

SIR   Washington Mar. 2. 1801.

I was desired two or three days ago to sign some sea letters to be dated on or after the 4th. of Mar. but in the mean time to be forwarded to the different ports; and I understood you would countersign them as the person appointed to perform the duties of Secretary of state, but that you thought a reappointment to be dated the 4th. of March would be necessary. I shall with pleasure sign such a reappointment nunc pro tunc, if you can direct it to be made out, not being able to do it myself for want of a knowledge of the form.

I propose to take the oath or oaths of office as President of the US on Wednesday the 4th. inst. at 12. aclock in the Senate chamber. may I hope the favor of your attendance to administer the oath? as the two houses have notice of the hour, I presume a precise punctuality to it will be expected from me. I would pray you in the mean time to consider whether the oath prescribed in the constitution be not the only one necessary to take? it seems to comprehend the substance of that prescribed by the act of Congress to all officers, and it may be questionable whether the legislature can require any new oath from the President. I do not know what has been done in this heretofore; but I presume the oaths administered to my predecessors are recorded in the Secretary of state's office.

Not being yet provided with a private Secretary, & needing some person on Wednesday to be the bearer of a message or messages to the Senate, I presume the chief clerk of the department of state might be employed with propriety. permit me through you to ask the favor of his attendance on me to my lodgings on Wednesday after I shall have been qualified. I have the honor to be with great respect Sir

Your most obedt. humble sert   TH: JEFFERSON

PrC (DLC); at foot of text: "The honble John Marshall"; in SJL TJ noted Marshall as "C.J. US."

Marshall was performing the DUTIES OF SECRETARY OF STATE but was also chief justice of the Supreme Court. Adams named him chief justice on 20 Jan., the Senate confirmed the appointment seven days later, and Adams signed the commission on the 31st. On 4 Feb., when Marshall assumed his new function, Adams appointed him to continue handling the responsibilities of secretary of state until that office could be filled. The legal princi-ple NUNC PRO TUNC, literally "now for then," allows an oversight in the record to be overcome by giving effect to an action that should have occurred on another date (Marshall, *Papers*, 6:61-2, 73-4; Bryan A. Garner, ed., *A Dictionary of Modern Legal Usage*, 2d ed. [New York, 1995], 607; Bryan A. Garner, ed. in chief, *Black's Law Dictionary*, 8th ed. [St. Paul, Minn., 2004], 1100).

It was in Marshall's capacity as chief justice that he would administer the presidential OATH to TJ. An ACT OF CONGRESS "to regulate the Time and Manner of administering certain Oaths," approved

1 June 1789, was the first act passed by the First Congress (U.S. Statutes at Large, 1:23-4).

The CHIEF CLERK was Jacob Wagner, who had held the job since Timothy Pickering's administration of the department.

TJ had no private secretary until Meriwether Lewis arrived in Washington to assume that role, so for a while after the inauguration TJ continued to use Wagner as his clerk or messenger (Kline, *Burr*, 2:804; Marshall, *Papers*, 6:90).

From John Marshall

SIR   Washington March 2d. 1801

I am this instant honord with yours of to day.

Not being the Secretary of State, & only performing the duties of that office at the request of the President, the request becomes indispensably necessary to give validity to any act which purports to be done on the 4th. of March.

In the confidence that it will be receivd I shall immediately proceed to sign the sea letters. No form is prescribd. Any letter desiring me to do the duties of the office generally on the 4th. of March will be sufficient.

I shall with much pleasure attend to administer the oath of office on the 4th. & shall make a point of being punctual. The records of the office of the department of state furnish no information respecting the oaths which have been heretofore taken. That prescribd in the constitution seems to me to be the only which is to be administerd. I will however enquire what has been the practice.

The chief clerk of this department will attend you at the time requested.

     I have the honor to be with great respect Sir Your most obedt. hble Servt   J MARSHALL

RC (DLC); endorsed by TJ as received 3 Mch. and so recorded in SJL.

TJ wrote Marshall a brief letter appointing him to the DUTIES of the office: "In pursuance of the act of Congress providing that in case of vacancy in the office of Secretary of state the President of the US. may authorize a person to perform the duties of the same, I am to ask the favor of you, & hereby authorize you to perform the duties of the Secretary of state until a successor to that office shall be appointed. I have the honor to be Sir Your most obedt. sert." Although TJ dated the letter 4 Mch. and recorded it in SJL under that date, he actually wrote it no later than the 3d, when he received a response from Marshall. An act of 13 Feb. 1795 allowed the president to appoint someone to perform the duties of the secretary of state, the secretary of the treasury, or the secretary of war in the event of a vacancy, placing a six-month limit on any such appointment (RC in DNA: RG 59, MLR, signed, at foot of text: "The honble John Marshall"; PrC in DLC; U.S. Statutes at Large, 1:415). Marshall's reply, also dated 4 Mch. but recorded in SJL as received 3 Mch., said: "I have receivd your letter requesting me to perform the duties of Secretary of State until a successor be appointed. I shall with great pleasure obey this request & beg leave to assure you that I am with high & respectful consideration Your obedt. Humble Servt." (RC in DLC; dated 4 Mch. 1781; endorsed by TJ as a letter of 4 Mch. 1801 received in March).

From Robert Morris

DEAR SIR   Philada. March 2d. 1801

I was this day honoured with the receipt of your letter of the 26th. ulto. and immediately sent in quest of James Tate the person of whose Character You enquire, he came, and I communicated to him your intentions, he told me that he is now employed in the Custom House & that he thought it a duty he owed to the Collector Mr Latimer to consult him previous to any determination on his own part, altho his inclination would lead him to engage in your service because he conceived himself to be capable of performing the duties of the Station, I then gave him your letter to shew to Mr Latimer, and he has just returned with a line from that Gentleman to me which for your satisfaction is enclosed herein. James Tate served me in the Capacity of Steward or upper Servant for three or four years; I always considered him as Capable faithfull, attentive, sober & honest; my misfortunes dismissed him from my service, there was no other cause that I know of, It is however proper to observe that he is a man of *Temper* this to me was no inconvenience but on the contrary as I put up with some things, his Spirit saved me the trouble with subordinate Servants in many instances and in a smaller degree required the interference of *The Master*, (Mrs Morris who returns her esteem for you) desires me to tell you, as a thing she deems highly important, that he is very cleanly, which I mention perhaps with more pleasure from a selfish motive as I expect (notwithstanding my present situation and age)[1] some day or other to partake of your hospitality. I think it proper however to tell you that in my days of affluence I was generally well Served by my domesticks, and that I attributed to Mrs. Morris the merit of an attentive superintendance which caused the performance of domestick duty. The Eye of a Master or Mistress is ever usefull in this respect. We had here a plentifull Market Tate knew the people that brought good things he knew how to buy & how they ought to be cooked & Served. I reposed in him a confidence of which he was proud & for which I thought him gratefull it is some years since we parted, he has since kept a Tavern & I cannot answer for the habits or manners he may since that time have acquired but Mr. Latimer's letter is much in his favour He has a Wife & three Children, his Wife is as he tells me very capable of taking the charge of the linen &c of any family and if he engages with you one at least of his children will remain behind with its Grandmother. He will attend you immediately if your answer to this letter requires it, and I have told him that if his Conduct in your service meets & Merits your approbation that your liberality will induce you to place him at parting in some situation that will enable him to provide for a growing family. permit me to assure you that my esteem & Respect for your personal Character has never abated from party considerations as many of your friends & foes well know, for I have invariably averred that your administration if you came into the chief Magistracy, would be governed by good sense and strict integrity, pardon me if you think I should have been silent on this head & believe that I am very truly dear Sir

Your most obedt Servt   ROBT MORRIS

RC (DLC); addressed: "The Honorable Thos. Jefferson Esqr Washington"; franked; postmarked 3 Mch.; endorsed by TJ as received 5 Mch. and so recorded in SJL. Enclosure: George Latimer to Robert Morris, Philadelphia, 2 Mch. 1801, noting that James Tate, employed as a messenger and keeper of the stores at the Custom House for the previous 18 months, was "an attentive diligent and very honest Man" who "conducted himself in all respects with the greatest propriety" (RC in same).

MY MISFORTUNES: Morris was imprisoned for debt in February 1798 after the failure of speculative land ventures in collaboration with John Nicholson and James Greenleaf. He was released in 1801 (ANB; Bruce H. Mann, *Republic of Debtors: Bankruptcy in the Age of American Independence* [Cambridge, Mass., 2002], 199-202, 253).

[1] Closing parenthesis supplied by Editors.

From Anonymous

[before 3 Mch. 1801]

· ⠂ · As the subject of this letter is delicate, I rely on your knowledge of the hand writing.

In this moment when so many personal and official vexations are brought to bear on persons in every grade of public station I consider it as a duty to inform you that casual circumstances have given me reason to expect, that · ⠂ · will make an application to you at sometime after the 3d. of March. I presume it will be made personal, but whether in writing or otherwise, I have no ground for an opinion. A person, who is wrong, is not always the less urgent for answers, which will exculpate him. A person, who is right as to intentions but who has been deceived, is often urgent for such answers. In every case of such applications, it is a duty of a goodman, citizen and officer to enable those who have been long engaged in the most arduous duties and trying times to meet calmly and with preparation such persons. It is a sense of this duty which occasions me trouble you with this communication. Papers, Memories, and other circumstances necessary in such a case are now at your hand, and may not be so then.

MS (DLC: TJ Papers, 232:42167); extract in unidentified hand; undated.

From David Jones

DEAR SIR/   George Town March 3d. 1801

As I know a multitude of business will necessarily croud on, it is with reluctance, I would now call your attention to several Subjects, some of which are of importance to the publick.

The first, I wish to mention is the Salt springs. within our present Purchase in the N.w. Territory, I am well acquainted with their Situations, and hope I can perform the Duty as well as any other person. I wish to be appointed to examine the strength of the water, &c. & report the same, in order to enable Congress to act on the Subject next Session.

This, I suppose, will be included in your Duty in preparing Business for next Session; but of this you are the best Judge.

Another subject respects the Changes, which will take Place in heads of Departments. My youngest Daughter is married to Archibald McClean in alexandria. his Character is without exception. Not having a fortune, & having received a liberal education, he kept an academy cheifly english in alexandria for some years past, & continues in that Station.

he has been among the most active Democrates, which proved some Disadvantage in his School, the Scotch being his enemies. He wishes to be appointed Collector of the revenue at alexandria in the Place of Sims, who is now provided for by his *Master*.

he expects Mr. Page, who is clerk to Sims to be recommended by the aristocratic Scotch Merchants. Page is an aristocrate himself; but has been more prudent than Sims. he has reason to suppose that Col.

Peaton, who is a good republican, will also apply; but as Mr. Peaton is a man of fortune he has no need of an office, and Mr. McCleans appointment will meet his approbation, he expects no Difficulty from that Quarter.

If my application meets your approbation, it will be most gratefully acknowledged by me, & I am fully perswaded that you will never have cause to repent the appointment of my Son in Law as he is a man of Integrity and immoveable in his Principles.

You will find chringing aristocrates applying for appointments, one of which I will mention that you may be gaurded against him, and you may depend on it, he cannot be your Friend, nor has he one good Qualification, nor does he merit any favor of the Publick, yet he has got some Senecure either from Pennsylvania or the united States for many years. I mean Francis Mintgis. I know not what is his object, but I saw him spaking with one of the Senate, & I am perswaded some office is his object, but he is worthy of none.

Most Sincerely, I pray that God may bless your administration, & give that Degree of wisdom, which may enable you to triumph in the Cause of Liberty. I Subscribe myself your unchchangeable Friend

DAVID JONES

RC (DNA: RG 59, LAR); at foot of text: "Thomas Jefferson President Elect"; endorsed by TJ as received 3 Mch. and so recorded in SJL.

Born in New Castle County, Delaware, David Jones (1736-1820) joined the Welsh Tract Baptist Church before moving to New Jersey, where he attended Hopewell Academy and was ordained a Baptist pastor in Freehold in 1766. He served as an army chaplain under General Anthony Wayne during the Revolution. On 28 Feb. 1800, Congress received Jones's memorial regarding the salt springs in the Northwest Territory and his desire "to work one of the said springs rising near Walnut Creek, on such terms as Congress shall think reasonable and just" (DAB; JHR, 3:608; Sprague, *American Pulpit*, 6:85-9; *Pa. Arch.*, 2d ser., 8:754).

Jones wrote again on behalf of McClean on 2 July 1801 (RC in DLC). McClean, upon learning of his father-in-law's correspondence twice on his behalf, wrote TJ on 22 Feb. 1802, apologizing for his family's interference and justifying his initial application. McClean explained that prior to TJ's inauguration it was widely believed that Charles Simms, COLLECTOR OF THE REVENUE AT ALEXANDRIA as of 9 Aug. 1799 and later mayor of the city, would receive one of Adams's judicial appointments, thus creating a vacancy in the Alexandria collectorship. Upon Jones's urging, McClean inquired about the position but when neither Simms's resignation nor removal occurred, McClean dropped the matter. He explained that his father-in-law did not mean to displace an officer and that his own motives were "national interest, not private emolument." He did not seek "publick remuneration" but if "a post to which profit is attached be presented to my option, the increasing expenses of a growing family would probably admonish me to accept the offer, were my qualifications deemed competent to the discharge of its duties." McClean enclosed with his letter a slip of paper stating: "Should Mr Jeferson wish to write to me, he may direct to Revd David Jones Chester County Pennsylvania, To the Care of Dr Rogers at the university Philadelphia" (RC in DNA: RG 59, LAR, endorsed by TJ as received 25 Feb. 1802 and so recorded in SJL; Mary G. Powell,

The History of Old Alexandria, Virginia, from July 13, 1749 to May 24, 1861 [Richmond, 1928], 259-60; JEP, 1:326).

The ARISTOCRATIC SCOTCH MERCHANTS were probably members of the St.

Andrews Society of Alexandria (Powell, *History of Old Alexandria*, 237-40). COL PEATON: probably Francis Peyton who became mayor of Alexandria (Miller, *Alexandria Artisans*, 1:xxvii).

From Matthew Lyon

SIR   Washington March 3d. 1801

Both the last times I had the pleasure of speaking with you on the Subject of appointments in Vermont it sliped my mind to Mention the US Attorney in that District, the present Attorney is Charles Marsh a Violent Federalist. I have no particular cause of complaint against him, but several friends have wrote me wishing him to be displaced. we have but two Respectable Republican Lawyers in the State one is Jonathan Robinson brother to the Governor & the other is David Fay a Nephew of his, The latter is recomended to me by the former the Change is univesally expected & wished, by the Repub [licans.] Fay is a man of very Respectable Tallents & quite deserveing the place, he lives in Bennington—

The Supervisor of the District lives in Bennington also he is a Violent Federalist but his daughter is married to a Son of Governor Robinson or there is such family Connections that he will not be complained of, he is however a very honest man—

The officer of the Customs at Burlington Vt is a petulant, Vain, busy Aristocrat by the name of Russel, he ought to be displaced but I have no one on my mind to recomend at present—   I am Sir with great respect

your humble Servt   M LYON

RC (DNA: RG 59, LAR); torn; at foot of text: "Mr Jefferson"; endorsed by TJ as received 3 Mch. and so recorded in SJL; also endorsed by TJ: "Charles Marsh. Atty to be removed. Jonathan Robinson David Fay."

On 5 Mch. TJ appointed David Fay to replace Charles Marsh as U.S. ATTORNEY for Vermont. Fay was the NEPHEW of Moses Robinson who in 1762 had married Mary Fay, daughter of Stephen Fay and sister of Joseph Fay (Abby Maria Hemenway and others, eds., *Vermont Historical Gazetteer*, 5 vols. [Burlington, Vt., 1868-91], 1:171-2; Appendix I, List 3). Nathaniel Brush, appointed SUPERVISOR of the revenue for the Vermont district in late 1794, continued in the position during TJ's presidency. Brush's DAUGHTER was married to Moses Robinson's third SON Samuel (Hemenway, ed., *Vermont Historical Gazetteer*, 1:169; JEP, 1:163-4; Gallatin, *Papers*, 22:256-8).

In February 1803 Jabez Penniman became collector of CUSTOMS for Vermont on Lake Champlain in place of David Russell who was removed (JEP, 1:441).

From James Monroe

Dear Sir   Richmond 3. March 1801.

Yours of the 15th. (last) was left here by Mr. Tyler while I was on a trip to Albemarle. The necessity I was under of remaining here while the affr. at Georgetown was depending had delayed some arrangements on my plantation of importance to me. as soon as that affr. was settled I went up for a few days and was sorry to find on my return that Mr. Tyler had passed in my absence. I lose the details he wod. have given me, but only details, for knowing the men & the dilemma they were in, I presume I am not much at a loss for the spirit wh. animated them. A compromise of any kind wod. have ruined the republican interest of our country. It wod. have confounded parties, & principles, thereby bewildered the understanding & checked the ardor of the people. It wod. have covered in part the past enormities & propped the declining fortunes of the tory faction. There is no political error more to be avoided, than a step wh. gives cause to suspect, an accomodation with that party, or coloring to an opinion it is feared or respected. Such a step wod. shake the republican ranks, & prove the foundation of a growing interest to its antagonist. The royalist faction has lost deservedly the publick confidence. It will sink under its own weight if we leave it to itself. I hint this to remark that in the course I took, I wod. never consider, what was likely to pass the Senate, but what in itself was just & right, pursuing it with decision, & risking the consequences with the people. By such a course the Senate will be driven before the wind. By a spirit of accomodation it will daily gain ground, be called a spartan band, & the republican cause be overwhelmed. Be assured, with the leaders of the royalist party you will never have a friend. with principles so opposit, it is impossible you shod. The way is, to draw off the mass of the people by a wise, firm, yet moderate course, from those leaders, and leave them to the ignominy they merit. The spirit of the republican party must be supported and preserved, which can only be done by a bold and magnanimous policy. When you came into the admn. of this State the firmness and decision which you shewed in the case of Hamilton, at a time when Washington suffered our people to perish in the jails & prison ships of N. York, by a pusilanimous and temporising policy, advanc'd yr. fame & served the cause. The publick opinion expects some tone to be given yr. admn. immediately, & it will not long balance before it is formed, or the subject of what they are to expect from it. There is a conflict of principle & either democracy, that is the govt. of the people, or royalty must prevail. The opposing parties can never be united,

I mean the leaders of them, because their views are as opposit as light & darkness. You always had the people and now have the govt. on yr. side, so that the prospect is as favorable as cod. be wished. At the same time it must be admitted you have much trouble, and difficulty to encounter. many friends may grow cool from disappointment; the violent who have their passions too much excited, will experience mortification, in not finding them fully gratified: in addition to which it is to be observed, that the discomfited tory party, profiting of past divisions & follies wh. have contributed much to overwhelm them, will reunite thier scattered force agnst us. This party has retired into the judiciary, in a strong body where it lives on the treasury, & therefore cannot be starved out. While in possession of that ground it can check the popular current which runs against them, & seize the favorable occasion to promote reaction, wh. it does not despair of. It is a desperate party because it knows it has lost the publick confidence. It will intrigue with foreign powers & therefore ought to be watched. Your difficulties will indeed be great, yet I trust and believe you will surmount them, if you will pursue the dictates of yr. excellent judgment rather than the benevolent suggestions of yr. heart. I have written you in haste for the post, and have rather sought to throw intelligibly my ideas before you, than to give them form, being perfectly satisfied you will properly appreciate the motive wh. has led me into the freedom of this communication. most sincerely & affectionately yours.

JAS. MONROE

you see that Adams has done every thing in his power to embarrass yr. admn. In some of his appointments too he has nominated his enemies to strengthen his party. This shews that personal hatreds are sacrificd to the good of the cause.

RC (DLC); endorsed by TJ as received 7 Mch. and so recorded in SJL. Dft (DLC: Monroe Papers); dated 2 Mch.

For the rumored scheme to give the SENATE power to select the president, see Monroe to TJ, 6 Jan. 1801, and see Monroe's letters of 18 and 27 Jan. for action contemplated by Virginia leaders. Monroe apparently associated the schemers' caucuses with Georgetown, where some members of Congress boarded (TJ to Thomas Mann Randolph, 5 Dec. 1800).

Immediately on taking office as governor in June 1779, TJ confronted the case of the British officer Henry HAMILTON, who had surrendered to George Rogers Clark at Vincennes. As governor of Detroit, Hamilton had gained notoriety in Virginia for inciting attacks by Indians against the state's frontier settlements—the "indiscriminate murther of men, Women and children," as TJ expressed it. TJ and the Virginia Council ordered that Hamilton be kept in irons at Williamsburg without access to writing materials or visitors. In response to protests by the British, who refused to exchange any captured officers of the Virginia line until Hamilton received better treatment, TJ noted the deplorable conditions endured by Americans held prisoner by the British. Congress and George WASHINGTON left the matter to the discretion of the state government, although Washington pointed out that it was not customary to confine under such harsh conditions an officer who had agreed to terms of capitulation. The council and TJ released Hamilton from irons and expected to arrange a partial parole, but the prisoner refused to sign terms that prohibited him from saying anything against the United States. He remained in jail, and TJ feared retaliation against captured Virginia officers confined by the British at New York. Sentiment against Hamilton in Virginia remained strong, and the state held him even after giving Congress custody of most other British prisoners. In October 1780 Hamilton agreed to parole terms that allowed him to go to New York, subject to recall (Vol. 2:286-7, 292-5, 299; Vol. 3:25-8, 31-2, 40-2, 44-9, 58-9, 61, 86-7, 94-104, 113, 198-9, 205-6, 245-6, 333, 488, 605-6, 665; Vol. 4:24-5, 566-7).

From Samuel A. Otis

Office of the Secretary of the Senate of the
Sir,   United States, March the 3d. 1801.
    I do myself the honor to enclose a copy of the Order of Senate on the Letter you was yesterday pleased to lay before them, and
    Have the honor to be, Sir, Your most humble servant
SAM: A. OTIS

I notified to Spanish Minister & to Mr Thornton that seats would be provided for them.

RC (DLC); in clerk's hand, except for signature and postscript in Otis's hand; at foot of text: "To The President Elect of the United States."

For TJ's LETTER to the Senate, see TJ to James Hillhouse, 2 Mch.

ENCLOSURE

Orders on the Inauguration

Congress of the United States
In Senate, March the 2nd. 1801.
    Ordered, that the Letter received from the President, elect, of the United States be referred to Mr. Morris, Mr. Dayton and Mr. Ross, to report thereon
    Ordered, that the Committee who were appointed to take into consideration the Letter from the President, elect, of the United States, of this day, be discharged.
    A motion was made as follows.
    The President, elect, of the United States having informed the Senate that he proposes to take the oath which the Constitution prescribes to the President of the United States before he enters on the execution of his office, on Wednesday the 4th. instant, at twelve o'clock in the Senate Chamber:
    Ordered, that the Secretary communicate that information to the House of Representatives that seats be provided for such members of the House of

Representatives and such of the public Ministers, as may think proper to attend; and that the Gallery be opened to the Citizens of the United States.

And the motion was agreed to and the Secretary notified the House of Representatives accordingly.

Attest, SAM: A. OTIS Secretary

MS (DLC); in clerk's hand, attested by Otis.

From Theodore Peters

SIR   Washington 3d. March 1801.

Encouraged by a Number of respectable Citizens of the United States and particularly by Some of the Members of Congress, I take the liberty to lay before You a short but true and Sincere Statement of my Situation and the relations I stand in with the American Merchants; if the merits of it may be deemed worth Your Attention, I beg leave to produce the unquestionable Vouchers in Support of my assertions: Your moments being taken up with more Important Matters I rely on Your goodness and Indulgence in forgiving me for Intruding upon them.

From the bottom of my heart I Join the good people of the United States in their Joy on your Election to the Presidential Chair, Your talents, Virtues and Ardent Zeal for the happyness of this Extensive Country have placed you there, may your exertions be crowned with Success and the people of This Country under Your administration arrive to a Degree of happyness hitherto Unknown Among Nations!

Accept the homages of my Sincere respect and high esteem and believe me truly

Sir Your humble and most Obed Servant

THEODORE PETERS

RC (DNA: RG 59 LAR); endorsed by TJ as received 4 Mch. and so recorded in SJL. Enclosure: Statement in Peters's hand giving an account of his life and extensive knowledge of commerce and European languages, which, in the judgment of American merchants who knew the services he had rendered them at Bordeaux, qualified him for a consulship there, even though he was not a native born American (MS in same).

In July TJ named Peters vice commercial agent at Bordeaux (JEP, 1:402; Appendix I, Lists 1 and 4).

From Moses Robinson

DEAR SIR,   Bennington March 3d 1801

Permit me to Express the feelings of My heart in Congratulating you on your Election to the important office of President of the

United States be assured Sir that it gives me (and I trust every true Republican) great Joy and Satisfaction not merely on your account but a more important one the happiness of the people over whom you may have the Honor to Preside. I have no doubt they ever had their Eye on your Self as the Successor of Washington, in that they faild— to Say no more, the late Administration gave them Greater Evidence of the importance of Placing one in the Executive branch of Government whom they were Perswaided Possessed the Same Sentiments that Generally prevaild in 1776 as Contain in the declaration of Independence who believe that a Republican form of Government is best Calculated to promote the happiness of man kind—to Such a person and to Such only Should the people of the United States Commit the Administration of the Government, as the Safe Guardian of their Constitutional Rights and privaledges—I hope however that the time may arive when the Safty of our Civil and Religious Rights will not so much depend on the disposition of the person administring the Executive branch of Government, as at present it does— Should the people Continue to See the importance of improving the Right of Elections I trust the Federal Ligislature would not betray their trust and Give up their own and the peoples Rights at the pleasure of the Executive— —

This State have ever Since the X Y and Z business, been deceivd Especially the Eastern part of it adjacent to the State of New hampshire and Massachusetts, they begin to have their Eyes opend. but at the last session of the Legislature there was but a mere majority I believe it will not Continue long in the Same Sentiments as in other parts of the union So in this State every Republican were Represented as Enemies to their Country and friends to France and many honest men truly beleiv'd it to be the Case—it has in a measure Subsided—and the Republicans appear to be gaining Ground at least they are bolder and the Federalist appear more down—Tomorrow is a day to be Celebrated by the Republicans in this town for the Victory obtaind in the late Election of President & Vice president. it is Esteemd by the most Sober men of the Republicans in this place as an auspicious Event in the Course of divine Providence which ought to be duly notic'd—

I perceive by the papers that the French have obtain'd a Signal Victory over the Austrians in a General action which you have before this doubtless Seen it is Grevious to think of the Great Carnage and Sheding of human blood in Europe but there will doubtless Come good from this partial Evil I Rejoice to See the Republican Interest prevail in any Place or Country but more Especially in our native land— —

That you may Sir be Guided by the Spirit of unerring wisdom to Execute the important trust Reposd in you by the people of the united States is the hearty desire of your most Obedient Servant

MOSES ROBINSON

RC (DLC); addressed: "Thomas Jefferson Esquire President of the U.S. the City of Washington or at his seat Virginia"; endorsed by TJ as received 16 Mch. and so recorded in SJL.

As a young man, Moses Robinson (1742-1813) joined a Separatist congregation established under his father's leadership in Bennington, Vermont. He served as colonel in the state militia during the American Revolution. He received an honorary M.A. degree from Yale in 1789 and Dartmouth the following year. During their "Northern Journey" in 1791, TJ and Madison visited Robinson, former governor of Vermont, at his home in Bennington, where they also socialized with Anthony Haswell and Joseph Fay. Serving in the U.S.

Senate from 1791 to 1796, Robinson followed TJ and Madison's leadership on issues and voted against the Jay Treaty. After retiring from the Senate he continued to support Jeffersonian policies, including the embargo (ANB; Vol. 20: 440, 444).

SIGNAL VICTORY: fought in Bavaria east of Munich on 3 Dec. 1800, the battle of Hohenlinden was a dramatic clash during the brief renewal of fighting late in the year. News of the battle, in which 76,000 soldiers under Jean Victor Moreau defeated an Austro-Bavarian force of 58,000, reached New York on 20 Feb. 1801 (Smith, *Napoleonic Wars*, 188-90; Philadelphia *Aurora*, 24, 25 Feb. 1801; Joseph Barnes to TJ, 22 Dec. 1800).

To the Senate

GENTLEMEN   Mar. 3. 1801.

I recieve with due sensibility the congratulations of the Senate on being called to the first Executive office of our government,[1] and I accept with great satisfaction their assurances of support in whatever regards the honor & interest of our country.   knowing no other object in the discharge of my public duties, their confidence in my future conduct derived from past events, shall not be disappointed, so far as my judgment may enable me to discern those objects.

The approbation they are so good as to express of my conduct in the chair of the Senate, is highly gratifying to me; and I pray them to accept my humble thanks for these declarations of it.

TH: JEFFERSON

RC (DNA: RG 46, 6th Cong., 2d sess.); endorsed by clerk: "Reply of the President Elect of the United States to the address of the Senate in answer to his speech to them on leaving the Chair of the Senate. March 3d. 1801." PrC (DLC).

Gouverneur Morris presented the CONGRATULATIONS OF THE SENATE to TJ on 3 Mch. (see James Hillhouse to TJ, printed at 2 Mch.) and brought TJ's reply with him when he returned (JS, 3:140).

¹ In RC, TJ wrote the preceding eight words over the partially erased passage "by the government to the first Executive office." PrC emended by TJ in ink to reflect alteration.

From Benjamin Stoddert

SIR   Navy Department. 3d March 1801.

I have the honor, by permission of the President, to enclose for your information & consideration, letters Just recd. from the West Indies.—Also a copy of the Instructions given to Capt Barry, the Commanding officer on the Windward Station—at a time when it was not known whether the Treaty with France would, or would not be ratified.

All our other Public Vessels have recd. similar Instructions.

I have the honor to be With great respect sir Yr. Most Obed. servt.

BEN STODDERT

RC (InU: M. A. I. Blair Papers); at foot of text: "Thomas Jefferson Esqr. President Elect." FC (Lb in DNA: RG 45, LSP). Enclosures: see below.

Captain Thomas Truxtun and the *President* had recently arrived in Norfolk from the WEST INDIES. Commanders of ships in that squadron had written reports in January and early February (NDQW, Dec. 1800-Dec. 1801, 69-70, 72, 86-90, 112-14, 119, 129).

Captain John BARRY had been dispatched to St. Kitts with the frigate *United States* to take command of the navy's squadron on the Guadeloupe Station and to convoy merchant ships to the Windward Islands. His initial orders from Stoddert were dated 6 Dec., when rumors of a TREATY with France were circulating. In those instructions Adams and Stoddert asked the captain to avoid encounters with French naval vessels unless they continued to capture American ships. Barry was not to hold back against privateers, however, until he received definitive word of a peace and could ascertain that the privateers no longer molested American shipping. On 30 Dec. Stoddert sent additional instructions based on the arrival of the Convention of 1800 in Washington. The convention contained a provision for the return of any shipping captured by either side since 1 Oct., but had not yet been ratified. The secretary instructed Barry in the meantime to treat all armed French vessels, whether privateers or ships of the line, "exactly as you find they treat our Trading vessels" (same, 14-15, 55-6).

From Stephen Thorn

HONOURED SIR   George Town March 3rd: 1801—

I beg you to excuse the liberty I take in addressing You—It is not an account of myself further than as a member of the Republican community, but in behalf of an old acquaintance Col Lyon, and this without his or any other persons knowledge, and be Assured that whether my solicitations are of avail or no, (and I do not expect an answer) secrecy, will be most inviolably observed by me—   Col Lyon's patriotism is undoubted, his abilities are very decent, and above all his probity unquestionable; therefore as he has left Vermont (to which state he has renderd more real services in respect to her Agricultural and Manufactorial Interests, independant of his political exertions, than any other individual whatsoever) and sought an asylum in the western part of the United States, and whether he cannot expect to be brought forward by the People until after a residence among them.—

I know his delicacy, his aversion to apply for any office which respects immediately himself; his mind is taken up in a great manner on the further prospects of his son here, therefore will not I am apprehensive request one for himself, altho eminently qualified for the one I am going only to suggest, the Governorship of the Natchez—I once proposed to him to make the application, to which he refused, however acknowledged such an appointment would be most acceptable, but that he was tenacious of making the application, had he even a prospect of succeeding—

I am sensible he would add more to the population and prosperity of that Country (the political consequence of which you have a much better idea of than myself) than almost any other individual in the United States, and the Natchez would rise under his care, far more rapidly than Vermont did under his worthy father in law, Governer Chittenden, and emigration from Vermont, New York, Connecticut, Massachusetts &c would become in a surprizing degree the happy consequence—   At any rate I hope Sir you will have him in mind, not alone because he is a Republican, but because he is worthy and capable, and will be useful in almost any public station.—

I am Sir with great respect your very huml. Sert.

STEPN. THORN

RC (DNA: RG 59, LAR); at foot of text: "Mr. Jefferson"; below signature: "Spread Eagle, Rogers's Inn. Geo. Town"; endorsed by TJ as received 4 Mch. and so recorded in SJL; TJ later canceled endorsement and added: "Lyon Matthew. office Natchez."

HIS SON: Matthew Lyon's son, James, the Georgetown printer (James Lyon to TJ, 29 Nov. 1800).

First Inaugural Address

I. FIRST DRAFT [BEFORE 4 MCH. 1801]
II. REVISED DRAFT [BEFORE 4 MCH. 1801]
III. FIRST INAUGURAL ADDRESS, 4 MCH. 1801

EDITORIAL NOTE

At noon on 4 Mch. 1801 in the Senate chamber of the Capitol, fifty-seven-year-old Thomas Jefferson took the oath of office as the nation's third president. The occasion was, in Margaret Bayard Smith's often quoted words, "one of the most interesting scenes, a free people can ever witness." According to Aaron Burr, the "Day was serene & temperate—The Concourse of people immense—all passed off handsomely—great joy but no riot—no accident," and these scenes are reported in an account of the day that appeared in the *National Intelligencer* on 6 Mch. (Gaillard Hunt, ed., *The First Forty Years of Washington Society* [New York, 1906], 25-6; Kline, *Burr*, 1:518).

The morning began with a discharge of cannon from the company of Washington artillery, and at 10:00 the Alexandria company of riflemen joined them to parade in front of Conrad and McMunn's boardinghouse, on New Jersey Avenue near the Capitol, where Jefferson was residing. At noon, dressed as "a plain citizen, without any distinctive badge of office," the president-elect walked up Capitol Hill for the ceremony. Unlike his predecessors, he wore no ceremonial sword. Joined by a number of his fellow citizens and members of Congress, Jefferson was preceded by a detachment of Alexandria militia officers, swords drawn, and by the marshal and deputy marshals of the district of Maryland. When Jefferson arrived at his destination, the officers opened ranks and saluted. Another discharge of the artillery was sounded, and he entered the Capitol. Members of the House and Senate rose to their feet in the Senate Chamber, a large semi-circular room with an arched roof and spacious gallery. Senators sat on one side of the chamber, and the other was given over by the members of the House to the women who were in attendance. Aaron Burr rose to relinquish the chair of the presiding officer of the Senate, which he had temporarily occupied, to Jefferson. After a short pause, Jefferson stood to deliver his speech in a room that was, Margaret Bayard Smith claimed, "so crowded that I believe not another creature could enter," and that according to newspaper reports held the "largest concourse of citizens ever assembled here." The *Aurora* reported an audience of 1,140 (of whom about 154 were women) in addition to members of Congress. After delivering his address in "so low a tone that few heard it," Jefferson seated himself for a short time and then proceeded to the clerk's desk to take the oath of office, which Chief Justice John Marshall administered. The artillery salutes resumed, with 16 rounds fired by the Alexandria artillery company from two field pieces brought specially from their town for that purpose. The citizens responded with 16 discharges from a 6-pounder that was positioned just below the town. Jefferson and the procession returned to Conrad and McMunn's, where he was again saluted. Foreign ministers, members of

Congress, and residents of the District of Columbia who had come to pay their respects awaited him. Other inhabitants of the nation's capital assembled to call upon Vice President Aaron Burr, who also received a 16-gun salute. A final display of firepower ended the evening, and the Alexandria artillery company crossed the Potomac to return home (Malone, *Jefferson*, 4:17-18; Merrill D. Peterson, *Thomas Jefferson and the New Nation* [New York, 1970], 654-5; Noble E. Cunningham, Jr., *The Inaugural Addresses of President Thomas Jefferson, 1801 and 1805* [Columbia, Mo., 2001], 1-4; Cunningham, *Process of Government*, 10; *National Intelligencer*, 6 Mch. 1801; Alexandria *Times*, 6 Mch.; Philadelphia *Aurora*, 18 Mch.).

If Jefferson waited to write his address until he was voted president by the House of Representatives on 17 Feb., he had only two weeks for the task. His surviving papers give no indication that he began to draft it in advance or that he consulted with James Madison or other trusted Virginians (unlike the draft of his Second Inaugural, which he circulated to members of his Cabinet in advance). On the other hand, formulating his political beliefs and putting into eloquent language what he believed to be the commonly held sentiments of his fellow citizens was no new exercise for him. In public documents like the Declaration of Independence and the Kentucky Resolutions of 1798 and in private correspondence, most notably his letter of 26 Jan. 1799 to Elbridge Gerry, he had gained experience in formulating phrases that became embedded in American culture (see Vol. 30:529-49, 645-53). The nation's most prestigious crafter of elegant and lasting fundamental language for the nation and one of its few living statesmen from the Revolutionary generation used this address to set forth, in its fullest form yet, a statement of his "political faith," the phrase he had earlier used to Gerry, and his "political creed," as he described the speech to John Page on 23 Mch. Jefferson's first message to the nation's citizens as their president is a well-developed statement of his republican principles that echoed the simplicity of the inaugural ceremony itself.

Three texts of the message in Jefferson's hand survive in his papers at the Library of Congress: Document I, which appears to be his earliest draft, with substantial emendations; Document II, his revised text, still with numerous revisions and reworkings; and a third (DLC: TJ Papers, 110:18836-7, undated, on four sides of two sheets of paper, completely in TJ's hand, with a significant number of abbreviations and a few slight variations, not reproduced here). Paul Leicester Ford mistook this third text for Jefferson's first draft, probably because he assumed the manuscript was so filled with abbreviations that Jefferson must have intended to get his thoughts on paper quickly and return later to expand the contractions and make any revisions. The numerous abbreviations with superscripts, which are not characteristic of Jefferson, and the use of relatively short lines of text variously indented from the left margin so as to approximate an outline indicate that this was probably a text from which to read. It would be small enough ($6\frac{1}{2}$ by $5\frac{1}{8}$ inches) to carry with him to the Senate chamber and simple to follow when delivering the address orally. This "reading text" corresponds, with only minor variations, to the wording of Document II (Ford, 8:1-6; Cunningham, *Process of Government*, 8).

Document II has incorporated a substantial number of the changes Jefferson had marked on Document I. He made additional revisions as he worked on II, canceling some sections and rewriting others. He had so heavily emended one portion of text that he cut a small rectangular piece of paper to fit over it, made a fair copy of his revised wording, and affixed the small piece along the left margin of the page. This, we surmise, was to render what he was delivering to Samuel Harrison Smith for publication in the *National Intelligencer* more legible for setting in type. Margaret Bayard Smith indicated that Jefferson gave her husband the address early in the morning on 4 Mch., "so that on coming out of the house, the paper was distributed immediately. Since then there has been a constant succession of persons coming for the papers" (Hunt, *First Forty Years*, 26).

Smith's imprint, reproduced here as Document III, is the earliest published text of the First Inaugural Address and the version that served as the basis for the newspaper, pamphlet, and broadside printings that followed over the next two to three weeks. By 5 Mch., the Alexandria *Times*, the *Washington Federalist*, and the Baltimore *American* had obtained copies of the speech (the *American*'s having been delivered by express "at one o'clock this morning") and published it. Two days later the address had reached Philadelphia and appeared in the *Aurora* and the *Gazette of the United States*. By 9 Mch., it had been printed in broadside in New York and as an "Extra" by the Norfolk *Herald*. The Boston *Independent Chronicle* advertised on 19 Mch. that its version would be "executed with neatness, and in a form calculated to adorn the Parlours of all true FEDERAL REPUBLICANS." Mathew Carey had elegant prints on superfine wove paper with a miniature likeness of Jefferson at the top for sale at a quarter apiece and satin ones at prices of $1.25 to $1.75. Carey sent Jefferson one of each (Cunningham, *Inaugural Addresses*, 17-20; Carey to TJ, 17, 31 Mch. 1801).

Jefferson revised a number of passages, ranging in length from a single word to an entire sentence, to emphasize the republican character of his message, beginning with the first sentence, where he moved from the term "first executive magistrate" in the first draft to "first Executive office" in his final wording. His choice of words was never casual or unintentional, and not only did he reject the more formal and overbearing "magistrate," but he shifted the emphasis from the individual person to the office itself. His wording became more republican over the course of his revisions, moving from "first executive magistrate" to "first executive," to "first executive office" (see Document I and Document II, note 1). His letter to the Senate of 3 Mch. accepting their congratulations repeated the formulaic statement, "being called to the first Executive office of our government."

In creating his text, Jefferson struggled in his second paragraph to achieve just the right expression for the relationship between the will of the majority and the rights of the minority as he analyzed the impact of the electoral contest that he defined as having been "decided by the voice of the nation." Between Document I and Document II he revised his original wording to elevate the importance of the will of the majority by insisting that it was a "sacred principle." The phrase does not appear in Document I. In both versions Jefferson argued that the will of the majority must be "reasonable" and that members of the minority "possess" (he first wrote "retain") their "equal rights." Violating those rights of the minority, which are to be protected by the law, would be "oppression" (he first wrote "tyranny"). Other changes pointed to an avoidance of language that might alarm or raise the hackles of the Federalists. In his first draft, for example, Jefferson mentioned being "entangled" in commerce, but when he revised the draft he used the more neutral "engaged."

Perhaps the phrase that has received the most attention over the last two hundred years is the unifying and conciliatory exhortation that "we are all republicans: we are all federalists." Jefferson had long been grappling with what it meant to be a "federalist" or a "republican," and he had paired the two words as early as 1792. After the elections that year he wrote that "those who felt themselves republicans and federalists too" would not be duped by the alarmists who wanted to equate republicanism with "the ghost of anti-federalism" and French Jacobinism (Jefferson to Thomas Pinckney, 3 Dec. 1792). In 1798 he made the same point, noting that "both parties claim to be Federalists and Republicans, & I believe with truth" (Vol. 24:697; Vol. 30:98). The way he used the words was not new for him, but to others the vocabulary quickly became the iconic shorthand for the moderate sentiments of the address. In many newspaper printings after the first and in the special broadside publications, the words were transformed by capitalization, italics, block printing, or bold typeface, seemingly highlighting their importance in the speech. For Jefferson the expression was the culmination of the way he had come to think about American politics over the decade of the 1790s. For Americans at the time who read and considered the words, Jefferson's presidency would embody moderation, conciliation, and the true spirit of 1776. Commentary in newspapers after 1801 on occasion capitalized the nouns and reversed their order: "we are all Federalists; we are all Republicans" (see, for example, *The Republican or, Anti-Democrat*, 31 May 1802, and the *New-York Evening Post*, 18 Aug. 1802).

In general, the Federalists praised the caution and wisdom of Jefferson's words, which expressed sentiments far less dangerous and "Jacobin" than they had feared. Although Gouverneur Morris called the speech "Too long by Half," James A. Bayard wrote to Alexander Hamilton on 8 Mch. that it was "in political substance better than *we* expected; and not answerable to the expectations of the Partizans of the other side." George Cabot informed Rufus King on 20 Mch. that while it contained "*some foolish & some pernicious*" ideas, on the whole "its temper entitles it to respect." In fact, Cabot wrote in another letter of the same day, Jefferson's speech was liked better by the Federalists than by members of his own party. John Marshall, at four o'clock in the afternoon of Inauguration Day, called the speech "well judgd & conciliatory," though "strongly characteristic of the general cast" of Jefferson's political theory (Cunningham, *Inaugural Addresses*, 39; Hamilton, *Papers*, 25:344; King, *Life*, 3:407-8; Marshall, *Papers*, 6:89-90). Federalists also waited to see how he would implement the bipartisan sentiments expressed.

Republicans welcomed the address and Jefferson's presidency. Jefferson was portrayed as having soothed ("softened down") his critics by using language that showed him fit for his station as president (John R. Livingston to Robert R. Livingston, 13 Mch. 1801, in NHi: Livingston Papers). James Monroe wrote Madison that the speech "gave general satisfaction," commanding the "unqualified approbation of the republicans" and conciliating the "opposite party" (Madison, *Papers, Sec. of State Ser.*, 1:11). Republicans could read into his words an affirmation of liberties they felt had been undercut by the Adams administration's Sedition Act and the possibility as well that they would once again find a place in government. Within a few months, as his supporters sought to find those places in government, Jefferson would be proceeding too slowly for some who wanted offices immediately.

Jefferson's speech soon was widely printed abroad. The London *Times*, using Baltimore's *Federal Gazette* as its source, published the speech in full on 14 Apr. Translations of the address appeared in European newspapers and pamphlets over the next several months. Joel Barlow sent to Jefferson from Paris in October a "polyglotte" edition of the address in the English, French, Italian, and German languages, "printed here & distributed to all the ambassadors & other persons from foreign countries." Barlow remarked that his speech "has had a general run in Europe & will have a good effect." In London, the *Monthly Magazine* described the words as "animated, but cautious" and the author of a preface to an English pamphlet edition of it took the opportunity to offer praise for the American Constitution, calling it a model "for statesmen to work by" and "the most free we know of." Jefferson was said to be "the new Trans-Atlantic President," associated with liberty and just government. In Pisa, Philip Mazzei printed a translation of the address into Italian, but handled it "clandestinely" (London *Times*, 14 Apr. 1801; Cunningham, *Inaugural Addresses*, 49-70; *Monthly Magazine* [London], 1 May 1801; *The speech of Thomas Jefferson . . . By an Englishman* [London, 1801]; Sowerby, Nos. 3260-2; Joel Barlow to TJ, 4 Oct. 1801; Philip Mazzei to TJ, 15 Nov. 1801, 10 Apr. 1802).

Departing significantly in form and substance from those of his two predecessors, Jefferson's First Inaugural Address established the formula that was used by all American presidents until Lincoln. The nation's third president avoided specific mention of issues of policy or reference to the partisan nature of the election and emphasized abstract political concepts that all could embrace (Jeffrey K. Tulis, *The Rhetorical Presidency* [Princeton, 1987], 50). While his interpretation of fundamental republican principles in fact meshed nicely with the policies of the Republican party, his conciliatory rhetoric brilliantly embraced both parties by describing a single nation, one that the heroes of the Revolutionary generation would recognize and approve. In his revised draft, in fact, he made a pointed allusion to George Washington, the "first and greatest revolutionary character, whose preeminent services had entitled him to the first place in his country's love." In delivering his first public message to the country as president, Jefferson sought the mantle of the father of the country to lend legitimacy. But as he drafted the address, Jefferson also asked himself, "is this exactly in the spirit of the patriarch of liberty, Samuel Adams? is it as he would express it? will he approve of it?" (TJ to Samuel Adams, 29 Mch.). Jefferson's brilliance lay in being able to encompass in his Inaugural Address the ideals of Samuel Adams and George Washington, finding room for both within the political spectrum of the republicanism of the Revolution.

I. First Draft

Friends & fellow-citizens

Called by the voice of our country to undertake the duties of it's first executive magistrate I avail myself of the presence of that portion of my fellow citizens which is here assembled to express my grateful thanks for the favor with which they have been pleased to look towards me, to declare a sincere consciousness that the task is above my talents, and that I approach it with those anxious & awful presentiments, which the greatness of the charge, & the weakness of my powers, so justly inspire.[1] a rising nation, spread over a wide and fruitful land,[2] traversing all the seas with the rich productions of their industry, entangled in commerce with nations who feel power and forget right, advancing rapidly to destinies beyond the reach of mortal eye, when I contemplate these transcendent objects, and see the honour, the happiness & the hopes of this beloved country committed to the issue & the auspices of this day, I shrink from the contemplation, and humble myself before the magnitude of the undertaking. utterly indeed should I despair, did not the presence of many, whom I here see, remind me, that in the other high authorities provided by our constitution I shall[3] find resources of wisdom, of virtue, and of zeal, on which to rely under all difficulties. to you then gentlemen, who are[4] charged with the sovereign functions of legislation, & to those associated with you, I look with encouragement for that guidance & support which may enable us to steer with safety the vessel in which we are all embarked, among the conflicting elements of a troubled world.

During the contest of opinion and of choice[5] through which we have passed, the animation of discussions & exertions has sometimes worn an aspect which might impose on strangers, unused to think freely, & to speak & to write what they think. but this being now decided by the voice of the nation, enounced according to the rules of the constitution, all will of course arrange themselves under the will of the law, and unite in the common efforts for the public good. the succesful majority too will keep in mind that tho' their will is to prevail,[6] that will, to be rightful, must be reasonable; that the minority retain their equal rights, which equal law must protect, and to violate would be tyranny. let us then, fellow citizens unite with one heart & one mind; let us restore to social intercourse that harmony & affection, without which liberty, and life itself, are but dreary things: and let us reflect that having banished from our land that religious intolerance, under which mankind so long bled and suffered,[7] we have yet gained little[8] if we countenance a political intolerance as despotic, as wicked, and capable of as bitter and bloody persecution.   during the throes & convulsions of the antient world, during the agonising spasms of infuriated man, seeking through blood & slaughter his long lost liberty, it was not wonderful that the agitation of the billows should reach even this distant and peaceful[9] shore: that this should be more felt & feared by some, & less by others and should divide opinions as to measures of safety.[10]—but let it not be imagined that every difference of opinion or of[11] feeling is a difference of principle. we have called by different names modificns of the same principle. we are all republicans: we are all federalists. I do not believe there is one native citizen in the US. who wishes to dissolve this union. I am confident there are few native citizens who wish to change it's republican features. I know indeed that some honest men have feared that a republican government cannot be strong: that this government is not strong enough. I believe exactly the contrary. I believe this the strongest govmt on earth. I believe it the only one where every man, at the call of the law, would fly to the standard of the law. his only previous question would be Is this standard erected to support or to suppress the law? and were it possible that the standard of the law should be in one place, & he who is charged with it in another, the American citizen knows where his station should be. the law is his sovereign. we are but the servants of the law. in attempting to be more, we become nothing.   Some times it is said that man can not be trusted with the government of himself. can he then be trusted with the government of others? or have we found angels in the form of kings to govern him?   Let history—answer this question.

Let us then with courage and confidence pursue our principles of federal republicanism, or republicn. federalism. kindly separated by nature & a wide ocean from the exterminating havoc of one quarter of the globe, too high minded to endure the degradations of the others, possessing a chosen country with room enough for our descendants to the thousandth generation, enjoying the most favorable temperatures of climate, entertaining[12] a due sense of our equal right[13] to the use of our own faculties[14] to the acquisitions of our own industry, to honour & confidence from our fellow citizens resulting not from birth but[15] our own good actions, enlightened by a benign religion, professed indeed and practised in various forms, yet all of them inculcating honesty, truth, temperance, gratitude & the love of man, acknoleging & adoring an over-ruling providence which, by all it's dispensations, proves that it delights in the happiness of man here, and his greater happiness hereafter; with all these blessings, what more is necessary to make us a happy & a prosperous people? still one thing more, fellow citizens,[16] a wise & frugal government[17] which shall restrain men from injuring one another, shall leave them otherwise free to regulate their own pursuits of industry or improvement, and shall not take from the mouth of labour[18] the bread it has earned. this is the sum of good government,[19] and this is necessary to close the circle of our felicities.

About to enter, fellow citizens, on the exercise of duties which comprehend every thing dear & valuable to you, it is proper you should understand what I deem the essential principles of our government, and consequently those which are to shape[20] it's administration. I will compress them within the shortest compass they will bear, stating only the general principle, without it's limitations.

equal and exact justice to all men of whatever state or persuasion, religious or political.

peace, commerce and honest friendship[21] with all nations, alliance with none.[22]

the support of the state governments in their constitutional rights, as the most competent administration of our domestic concerns, and[23] our surest bulwarks against antirepublican tendencies.

the preservation of the general government[24] as the sheet anchor of our peace[25] at home, and safety abroad.

free & frequent elections by the people in person, & the more[26] frequent within the limits of their convenience, and the more extensive the right of suffrage, the more perfect within the definition of a genuine republic:

absolute acquiescence in the decisions of the majority, the vital principle of republics, from which is no appeal but to force the vital principle and the parent[27] of despotism:

economy in public expence, that labour may enjoy it's earnings:

a well disciplined militia, our best reliance in peace, & for the first moments of war, till regulars may relieve them:

the honest paiment of debts:

encouragement of agriculture; and of Commerce as it's handmaid:[28]

the diffusion of information, & arraignment of all abuses at the tribunal of public reason:[29]

freedom of religion: freedom of the press:

freedom of person, under the never-ceasing protection of the Hab. corp. And trial by juries impartially selected.

These principles form the bright constellation, which has gone before us & guided our steps thro' an age of revoln & reformn.[30] the wisdom of our sages, & blood of our heroes has been devoted to their attainment:

they should be the creed of our political faith: the text of public instruction:

the touchstone by which to try the services of those we trust:

and should we wander from them in moments of error or of alarm, let us hasten to retrace our steps, & to regain the road which alone leads to peace, liberty and safety.

I repair then, fellow citizens, to the post you have assigned me.[31] with experience enough in subordinate offices to have seen the difficulties of this, the greatest of all, I have learnt to expect that it will rarely fall to the lot of imperfect man to retire from this station with the reputation & the favor which bring him into it. Without pretensions to that high confidence you reposed in the great revolutionary characters who have preceded me, whose preeminent services had entitled them to the first place in the affections of their country, and destined for them the fairest pages in the volume of faithful history, I ask so much confidence only as may give firmness and effect to the legal administration of your affairs. I shall often go wrong thro' defect of judgment. when right, I shall often be thought wrong by those whose positions will not command a view of the whole ground. I ask your indulgence for my own errors, which will never be intentional; & your support against the errors of others, who may condemn what they would not, if seen in all it's parts. the approbation implied by your suffrage is a great consolation to me for the past, and all I ambition for the future is[32] to retain the good opinion of those who have bestowed it in advance, to conciliate that of others by doing them all the good in my power and to be instrumental to the happiness and freedom of all.

Relying then on the protection of your good will, I advance with obedience to the work, ready to retire from it whenever you become sensible how much better choices it is in your power to make: and may that infinite power which rules the destinies of the universe, lead our councils to what is best, and give them a favorable issue for your peace and prosperity.

MS (DLC: TJ Papers, 110:18838); undated, but apparently the earliest surviving Dft and composed before 4 Mch.; entirely in TJ's hand, on recto and verso of a single sheet of heavyweight paper, $9\frac{1}{2}$ by $15\frac{3}{4}$ inches; TJ made numerous erasures resulting in occasional extra space between words (which has silently been closed) and at times entered abbreviations and interlinations in a minuscule hand.

[1] TJ here canceled "with experience enough in subordinate offices to have seen the difficulties of this, the greatest of all, I have learned to expect that it will rarely

fall to the lot of imperfect man to retire from this station with the reputation and the favor which bring him into it." He transferred the passage to the second paragraph from the end. See note 31.

[2] TJ here canceled "enjoying the most favorable temperatures of climate" and moved the phrase to the third paragraph. See note 12.

[3] Word reworked from "should."

[4] Preceding two words interlined.

[5] Preceding six words interlined in place of "animation of all discussions and exertions," which he used later in the sentence.

[6] TJ here canceled "the law."

[7] Preceding eight words interlined in place of "which no longer finds a single advocate."

[8] TJ first wrote "have gained little indeed" before revising the phrase to read as above.

[9] Preceding two words interlined.

[10] Preceding nine words interlined.

[11] Preceding three words interlined.

[12] Preceding eight words interlined.

[13] TJ first wrote "rights" and then deleted the "s."

[14] TJ here canceled "for our own purposes."

[15] Preceding four words interlined.

[16] Preceding six words and commas interlined.

[17] TJ here interlined the next eleven words and "other—" and from this point through "improvement" reworked the sentence, writing over an erasure.

[18] Preceding two words interlined.

[19] TJ reworked the remainder of the sentence, writing over an erasure and interlining "is necessary to" and "circle of our felicities." He may originally have ended the sentence with "government."

[20] TJ first wrote "to give shape to," before altering the phrase to read as above.

[21] Preceding three words interlined.

[22] TJ here canceled an entire line of text: "that hospitality to the fugitives from oppression, which the savages of the wilderness extended to our fathers, & transmitted as a duty of inheritance to us."

[23] Preceding nine words and comma interlined.

[24] Word interlined.

[25] TJ here canceled "and administration of it's government on the principles of those who advocated it's adoption, not of those who opposed it" and interlined the concluding five words and punctuation in the sentence.

[26] TJ originally wrote "the more perfect" before revising the phrase to read as above.

[27] Preceding three words interlined.

[28] TJ first wrote "Commerce as it's handmaid" on a separate line below this one, with an additional three or four words. He then canceled the entire line, changed the colon after "agriculture" to a semicolon, and appended the phrase on commerce.

[29] Preceding word written over partially erased "opinion." TJ interlined "bar" above "tribunal" and "the" before "public reason" without indicating that "tribunal" should be canceled.

[30] Preceding nine words and ampersand added at end of line in smaller hand.

[31] TJ here wrote over erased text, interlined the sentence he had removed from the opening paragraph of his address (see note 1), and added the sentence ending "of your affairs."

[32] TJ here canceled "to be instrumental to your happiness & freedom, and," then reworked the remainder of the sentence, adding several phrases over erasures and interlining the final eleven words and closing period in order to have the sentence read as above.

II. Revised Draft

Friends & fellow citizens

    Called upon to undertake the duties of the first Executive office of our country,[1] I avail myself of the presence of that portion of my fellow citizens which is here assembled, to express my grateful thanks for the favor with which they have been pleased to look towards me, to declare a sincere consciousness that the task is above my talents, & that I approach it with those anxious &[2] awful presentiments which the greatness of the charge & the weakness of my powers so justly inspire. a rising nation, spread over a wide & fruitful land, traversing all the seas with the rich productions of their industry, engaged in commerce with nations who feel power & forget right, advancing rapidly to destinies beyond the reach of mortal eye; when I contemplate these transcendent objects, & see the honour, the happiness, & the hopes of this beloved country committed to the issue & the auspices of this day, I shrink from the contemplation, & humble myself before the magnitude of the undertaking. utterly indeed should I despair, did not the presence of many, whom I here see, remind me, that, in the other high authorities provided by our constitution, I shall find resources of wisdom, of virtue, & of zeal, on which to rely under all difficulties. to you then, gentlemen, who are charged with the sovereign functions of legislation, & to those associated with you, I look with encouragement for that guidance & support which may enable us to steer with safety the vessel in which we are all embarked, amidst the conflicting elements of a troubled world.

During the contest of opinion[3] through which we have past, the animation of discussions & of exertions has sometimes worn an aspect which might impose on strangers unused to think freely, & to speak & to write what they think. but this being now decided by the voice of the nation, enounced according to the rules of the constitution, all will of course arrange themselves under the will of the law, & unite in common efforts for the common good. all too will bear in mind this sacred principle that tho the will of the majority is in all cases to prevail,[4] that will, to be rightful, must be reasonable; that the minority possess their equal rights, which equal laws must protect, & to violate would be oppression.[5] let us then, fellow citizens, unite with one heart & one mind, let us restore to social intercourse that harmony & affection without which liberty, & even life itself, are but dreary things. and let us reflect that having banished from our land that religious intolerance under which mankind so long bled & suffered, we have yet gained little if we countenance a political intolerance, as despotic, as wicked, & capable of as bitter & bloody persecutions. during the throes & convulsions of the antient world, during the agonising spasms of infuriated man, seeking thro' blood & slaughter his long-lost liberty, it was not wonderful that the agitation of the billows should reach even this distant & peaceful shore; that this should be more felt & feared by some & less by others; & should divide opinions as to measures of safety—but every difference of opinion, is not a difference of principle. we have called by different names brethren of the same principle. we are all republicans: we[6] are all federalists. if there be any among us who would wish to dissolve this Union, or to change it's republican form, let them stand undisturbed as monuments of the safety with which error of opinion may be tolerated, where reason is left free to combat it.[7] I know indeed that some honest men fear that a republican government cannot be strong; that this government is not strong enough.[8] but would the honest patriot, in the full tide of succesful experiment, abandon a government which has so far kept us free and firm, on the theoretic & visionary fear, that this government, the world's best hope, may, by possibility, want energy to preserve itself? I trust not. I believe this, on the contrary the strongest government on earth. I believe it the only one where every man, at the call of the law, would fly to the standard of the law,[9] and would meet invasions of the public order, as his own personal concern.— sometimes it is said that man can not be trusted with the government of himself. can he then be trusted with the government of others? or have we found angels, in the forms of kings, to govern him? Let history answer this question.

Let us then, with courage & confidence, pursue our own[10] federal & republican principles; our attachment to union & representative government. kindly separated by nature & a wide ocean from the exterminating havoc of one quarter of the globe; too high-minded to endure the degradations of the others, possessing a chosen country, with room enough for our descendants to the thousandth & thousandth generation,[11] entertaining a due sense of our equal right to the use of our own faculties, to the acquisitions of our own industry, to honour & confidence from our fellow citizens, resulting not from birth, but from our actions & their sense of them, enlightened by a benign religion, professed indeed & practised in various forms, yet all of them inculcating Honesty, truth, temperance, gratitude & the love of man, acknoleging and adoring an overruling providence, which by all it's dispensations proves that it delights in the happiness of man here, & his greater happiness hereafter: with all these blessings, what more is necessary to make us a happy & a prosperous people? still one thing more, fellow citizens. a wise & frugal government, which shall restrain men from injuring one another, shall leave them otherwise free to regulate their own pursuits of industry & improvement, & shall not take from the mouth of labor, the bread it has earned. this is the sum of good government; & this is necessary to close the circle of our felicities.

About to enter, fellow citizens, on the exercise of duties which comprehend every thing dear & valuable to you, it is proper you should understand what I deem the essential principles of our government, &

consequently those which ought to shape it's administration. I will compress them within the narrowest compass they will bear, stating the general principle, but not all it's limitations.—Equal & exact justice to all men, of whatever state or persuasion, religious or political:—Peace, commerce & honest friendship with all nations, entangling[12] alliances with none:—the support of the state governments in all their rights. as the most competent administrations for our domestic concerns, & the surest bulwarks against anti-republican tendencies:—the preservation of the General government in it's whole[13] constitutional vigour, as the sheet anchor of our peace at home, & safety abroad:—[14] a jealous care of the right of election by the people, a mild and safe corrective of abuses which are lopped by the sword of revolution where peaceable remedies are unprovided:—

—absolute acquiescence in the decisions of the majority, the vital principle of republics, from which is no appeal but to force, the vital principle & immediate parent of despotism:—a well disciplined militia, our best reliance in peace, & for the first moments of war, till regulars may relieve them: the supremacy of the civil over the military authority:—[15] economy in the Public expence, that labor may be lightly burthened:—[16] the honest paiment of our debts and sacred preservation of the public faith:—[17] encouragement of agriculture; and of Commerce as it's handmaid:—the diffusion of information, & arraignment of all abuses at the bar of the public reason:—freedom of religion; freedom of the press; & freedom of person, under the[18] protection of the Habeas corpus:—and trial by juries impartially selected. these principles form the bright constellation, which has gone before us, & guided our steps through an age of revolution & reformation. the wisdom of our sages, & blood of our heroes have been devoted to their attainment: they should be the creed of our political faith; the text of civic[19] instruction, the touchstone by which to try the services of those we trust; and should we wander from them in moments of error or of alarm, let us hasten to retrace our steps, & to regain the road, which alone leads to Peace, liberty & safety.

I repair then, fellow citizens, to the post you have assigned me. with experience enough in subordinate offices to have seen the difficulties of this the greatest of all, I have learnt to expect that it will rarely fall to the lot of imperfect man to retire from this station with the reputation, & the favor which bring him into it. without pretensions to that high confidence you reposed[20] in our first and greatest revolutionary character, whose preeminent services had entitled him to the first place in his country's love and destined for him the fairest page in the volume of faithful history, I ask so much

confidence only as may give firmness & effect to the legal administration of your affairs. I shall often go wrong through defect of
judgment. when right, I shall often be thought wrong by those
whose positions will not command a view of the whole ground. I
ask your indulgence for my own errors, which will never be intentional; and your support against the errors of others, who may condemn what they would not, if seen in all it's parts. the approbation
implied by your suffrage, is a great consolation to me for the past;
and my future sollicitude will be,[21] to retain the good opinion of
those who have bestowed it in advance, to conciliate that of others
by doing them all the good in my power, and to be instrumental to
the happiness & freedom of all.

Relying then on the patronage of your good will, I advance with
obedience to the work, ready to retire from it whenever you become
sensible how much better choices it is in your power to make: and
may that infinite power which rules the destinies of the universe, lead
our councils to what is best, & give them a favorable issue for your
peace and prosperity.

MS (DLC: TJ Papers, 110: lacking
folio numbers but follows 18835);
undated, but after Document 1; entirely in
TJ's hand, but with numbers 1 through
11, one set of brackets, and other markings added by Samuel Harrison Smith,
not shown here, indicating this was the
text TJ sent to the press; written on both
sides of two sheets, with a slip of paper
containing revised text attached to first
sheet (see notes 6, 7, 8); and flourishes or
long dashes inserted to fill space left by
erasures.

[1] Preceding passage beginning after
"Called" written over "by the voice of our
country to undertake the duties of it's first
executive," erased, and "magistrate," canceled, being text from Document 1 above.

[2] Word interlined.

[3] TJ here erased "and of choice" and
filled the space with a flourish.

[4] Passage from beginning of sentence
to this point interlined in place of "the
successful majority too will keep in mind,
that tho' their will is to prevail."

[5] Word written over "tyranny," erased.

[6] TJ here attached a small slip of paper
with revised text to fit exactly over heavily
emended text extending from this point to
the line ending on the main sheet with a

hyphenated "sometimes," with "some-"
being the final word on the attached slip
of paper.

[7] TJ first wrote "I do not believe there
is one native citizen of the US. who
wishes to dissolve this union: I am
confident there are few native citizens
who wish to change it's republican features" before altering the sentence to read
"if there be any among us who wish to
dissolve this union, or to change it's republican form, let them <*remain?*> stand
undisturbed, as <*standing*> monuments
of the safety with which error of opinion
may be tolerated while reason is left free
to combat it."

[8] TJ here canceled: "I believe exactly
contrary" and then interlined "but should
the honest patriot, in the full tide of successful experiment, abandon a govmt
which has so far kept us free & firm <*for
one which has bound men in chains in
every country and thru' all time*> on the
theoretical & visionary fear that this
govmt the world's best hope, may, by possibility, want energy to preserve itself?
I trust not. I believe this."

[9] Remainder of sentence interlined in
place of "his only previous question
would be, is this standard erected to support or to suppress the law? and were

it possible that the standard of the law should be in one place, & he who is charged with it in another, the American citizen knows where his station should be. the law is his sovereign. we are but the servants of the law. in attempting to be <*come*> more we become nothing."

[10] Word interlined.

[11] TJ here canceled "enjoying the most favourable temperatures of climate."

[12] Word interlined.

[13] Word interlined.

[14] Remainder of paragraph interlined in place of "free & frequent elections by the people in person, & the more frequent within the limits of their convenience, & the more extensive the right of suffrage, the more perfectly within the definition of a genuine republic."

[15] Preceding nine words and punctuation interlined.

[16] Preceding three words written over "enjoy it's earnings," erased.

[17] Preceding seven words and colon interlined.

[18] TJ here canceled "never ceasing."

[19] Word written over "public," erased.

[20] With this word, TJ began to rework the following passage, writing over portions of erased text, inserting "and greatest," and deleting "who have preceded me." He had first written "the great revolutionary characters who have preceded me, whose preeminent services had entitled them to the first place in the affection of their country, and destined for them the fairest pages" before altering the passage to read as above, inserting a flourish after "love" to fill space left by erased text.

[21] Preceding five words written over erased "all I ambition for the future is."

III. First Inaugural Address

Friends & Fellow Citizens,

Called upon to undertake the duties of the first Executive office of our country, I avail myself of the presence of that portion of my fellow citizens which is here assembled to express my grateful thanks for the favor with which they have been pleased to look towards me, to declare a sincere consciousness that the task is above my talents, and that I approach it with those anxious and awful presentiments which the greatness of the charge, and the weakness of my powers so justly inspire. A rising nation, spread over a wide and fruitful land, traversing all the seas with the rich productions of their industry, engaged in commerce with nations who feel power and forget right, advancing rapidly to destinies beyond the reach of mortal eye; when I contemplate these transcendent objects, and see the honour, the happiness, and the hopes of this beloved country committed to the issue and the auspices of this day, I shrink from the contemplation & humble myself before the magnitude of the undertaking. Utterly indeed should I despair, did not the presence of many, whom I here see, remind me, that, in the other high authorities provided by our constitution, I shall find resources of wisdom, of virtue, and of zeal, on which to rely under all difficulties. To you, then, gentlemen, who are charged with the sovereign functions of legislation, and to those associated with you, I look with encouragement for that guidance and support which may enable us to steer with safety the vessel in which we are all embarked, amidst the conflicting elements of a troubled world.

During the contest of opinion through which we have past, the animation of discusions and of exertions has sometimes worn an aspect which might impose on strangers unused to think freely, and to speak and to write what they think; but this being now decided by the voice of the nation, announced according to the rules of the constitution all will of course arrange themselves under the will of the law, and unite in common efforts for the common good.   All too will bear in mind this sacred principle, that though the will of the majority is in all cases to prevail, that will, to be rightful, must be reasonable; that the minority possess their equal rights, which equal laws must protect, and to violate would be oppression. Let us then, fellow citizens, unite with one heart and one mind, let us restore to social intercourse that harmony and affection without which liberty, and even life itself, are but dreary things. And let us reflect that having banished from our land that religious intolerance under which mankind so long bled and suffered, we have yet gained little if we countenance a political intolerance, as despotic, as wicked, and capable of as bitter and bloody persecutions. During the throes and convulsions of the ancient world, during the agonising spasms of infuriated man, seeking through blood and slaughter his long lost liberty, it was not wonderful that the agitation of the billows should reach even this distant and peaceful shore; that this should be more felt and feared by some and less by others; and should divide opinions as to measures of safety; but every difference of opinion is not a difference of principle. We have called by different names brethren of the same principle. We are all republicans: we are all federalists. If there be any among us who would wish to dissolve this Union, or to change its republican form, let them stand undisturbed as monuments of the safety with which error of opinion may be tolerated, where reason is left free to combat it. I know indeed that some honest men fear that a republican government cannot be strong; that this government is not strong enough. But would the honest patriot, in the full tide of successful experiment, abandon a government which has so far kept us free and firm, on the theoretic and visionary fear, that this government, the world's best hope, may, by possibility, want energy to preserve itself? I trust not. I believe this, on the contrary, the strongest government on earth. I believe it the only one, where every man, at the call of the law, would fly to the standard of the law, and would meet invasions of the public order as his own personal concern. — Sometimes it is said that man cannot be trusted with the government of himself. Can he then be trusted with the government of others? Or have we found angels, in the form of kings, to govern him? Let history answer this question.

Let us then, with courage and confidence, pursue our own federal and republican principles; our attachment to union and representative government. Kindly separated by nature and a wide ocean from the exterminating havoc of one quarter of the globe; too high minded to endure the degradations of the others, possessing a chosen country, with room enough for our descendants to the thousandth and thousandth generation, entertaining a due sense of our equal right to the use of our own faculties, to the acquisitions of our own industry, to honor and confidence from our fellow citizens, resulting not from birth, but from our actions and their sense of them, enlightened by a benign religion, professed indeed and practised in various forms, yet all of them inculcating honesty, truth, temperance, gratitude and the love of man, acknowledging and adoring an overruling providence, which by all its dispensations proves that it delights in the happiness of man here, and his greater happiness hereafter; with all these blessings, what more is necessary to make us a happy and a prosperous people? Still one thing more, fellow citizens, a wise and frugal government, which shall restrain men from injuring one another, shall leave them otherwise free to regulate their own pursuits of industry and improvement, and shall not take from the mouth of labor the bread it has earned. This is the sum of good government; and this is necessary to close the circle of our felicities.

About to enter, fellow citizens, on the exercise of duties which comprehend every thing dear and valuable to you, it is proper you should understand what I deem the essential principles of our government, and consequently those which ought to shape its administration. I will compress them within the narrowest compass they will bear, stating the general principle, but not all its limitations. — Equal and exact justice to all men, of whatever state or persuasion, religious or political: — peace, commerce, and honest friendship with all nations, entangling alliances with none: — the support of the state governments in all their rights, as the most competent administrations for our domestic concerns, and the surest bulwarks against anti-republican tendencies: — the preservation of the General government in its whole constitutional vigor, as the sheet anchor of our peace at home, and safety abroad: a jealous care of the right of election by the people, a mild and safe corrective of abuses which are lopped by the sword of revolution where peaceable remedies are unprovided:—absolute acquiescence in the decisions of the majority, the vital principle of republics, from which is no appeal but to force, the vital principle and immediate parent of the despotism:—a well disciplined militia, our best reliance in peace, and for the first moments of war, till regulars may relieve them:—the supremacy of the civil over the military authority:—economy in the public expence, that labor may be lightly burthened:—the honest payment of our debts and sacred preservation of the public faith:—encouragement of agriculture, and of commerce as its handmaid:—the diffusion of information, and arraignment of all abuses at the bar of the public reason:—freedom of religion; freedom of the press; and freedom of person, under the protection of the Habeas Corpus:—and trial by juries impartially selected. These principles form the bright constellation, which has gone before us and guided our steps through an age of revolution and reformation. The wisdom of our sages, and blood of our heroes have been devoted to their attainment:—they should be the creed of our political faith; the text of civic instruction, the touchstone by which to try the services of those we trust; and should we wander from them in moments of error or of alarm, let us hasten to retrace our steps, and to regain the road which alone leads to peace, liberty and safety.

I repair then, fellow citizens, to the post you have assigned me. With experience enough in subordinate offices to have seen the difficulties of this the greatest of all, I have learnt to expect that it will rarely fall to the lot of imperfect man to retire from this station with the reputation, and the favor, which bring him into it. Without pretensions to that high confidence you reposed in our first and greatest revolutionary character, whose pre-eminent services had entitled him to the first place in his country's love, and destined for him the fairest page in the volume of faithful history, I ask so much confidence only as may give firmness and effect to the legal administration of your affairs. I shall often go wrong through defect of judgment. When right, I shall often be thought wrong by those whose positions will not command a view of the whole ground. I ask your indulgence for my own errors, which will never be intentional; and your support against the errors of others, who may condemn what they would not if seen in all its parts. The approbation implied by your suffrage, is a great consolation to me for the past; and my future solicitude will be, to retain the good opinion of those who have bestowed it in advance, to conciliate that of others by doing them all the good in my power, and to be instrumental to the happiness and freedom of all.

Relying then on the patronage of your good will, I advance with obedience to the work, ready to retire from it whenever you become sensible how much better choices it is in your power to make. And may that infinite power, which rules the destinies of the universe, lead our councils to what is best, and give them a favorable issue for your peace and prosperity.

Printed in the *National Intelligencer*, 4 Mch. 1801; at head of text: "President's Speech this day At 12 o'clock, THOMAS JEFFERSON, President of the United States, Took the oath of office required by the Constitution, in the Senate Chamber, in the presence of the Senate, the members of the House of Representatives, the public officers, and a large concourse of citizens. Previously to which he delivered the following Address:" (this version in DLC: TJ Papers, 110:18838).

From Arthur Campbell

SIR   Washington March 4. 1801

Of all your old Friends, none can more sincerely rejoice than I, on your elevation to preside in the Councils of the American People. Not so much from personal feelings, or a local attachment; but from a confidence, that you will *restore* the administration of their government, to the original principles of the Revolution: to the dignity of the Rights of Man.

Minute Philosophers, and narrow-minded Statesmen, may labour to depreciate this grand idea; or by despotism, hush a murmuring World: But America some years since, in a very audible Voice, announced its birth; other Nations are now claiming the honor of fostering the Infant. It will soon have many Parents, very many Friends.

Federalism is an honorable appellation, if by the expression is meant perpetual union, but the greatest zealots, for that order of Things, will find themselves mistaken, if strong traits of democracy, are not interwoven, to compleat the character.

It would be presumption in me, to offer you advice, how you may conduct yourself with success, in your present station. You have an excellent education, in the School of experience; and I know the goodness of your heart. My best Wishes, and prayers, will not be wanting.

Being now arrived at that time of life, that it becomes me to prepare for another state of existence: on this subject, I may once and again, trouble you, for you may rest assured, I fervently wish you a much greater reward, for your patriotic labours, than the temporary praise of good Men, or even the blame of the Wicked.—Thus far I trust, I will be made welcome; thus far I will be an officious Friend, and an affectionate fellow Citizen.

Accept Sir, this token of my veneration and Respect.

ARTHUR CAMPBELL

RC (DLC); endorsed by TJ as received from Washington, Virginia, on 9 Apr. and so recorded in SJL.

From Thomas Claxton

HONORED SIR   President's House 4th March, 1801

I have thought it my duty to inform you, that at four oClock this morning the late president left this house, which, by order of the Secretary of the Treasury, I took possession of immediately—

I have the honor to be with the most sincere Respect & esteem, Your most obt. Hble. Svt.   THOS CLAXTON

RC (MHi); endorsed by TJ as received 4 Mch. and so recorded in SJL.

Thomas Claxton (d. 1821), the door-keeper of the U.S. House of Representatives for the Fourth through Sixteenth Congresses, was also the "Agent for furnishing the President's House" for John Adams and TJ. An undated account that Claxton submitted to the president, probably sometime in 1801, recorded $17,702, composed of $15,000 "Cash Appropriated by Act of Congress for furnishing the President's house," $1,102 as the balance of an appropriation for John Adams, and $1,600 from the "Sale of Horses, Carriages &c. in the possession of the late President." Expenditures appeared in the amount of $9,089.38, consisting of $5,959.38 drawn by Claxton "at sundry times," $800 "drawn by Gen Lee for a picture of Gen Washington," $2,050 for "accounts not yet satisfied," and $280 "compensation to myself for Superintendance &c. not yet called for" (MS in MHi; in Claxton's hand). On 2 Mch., Congress voted approval for Claxton and two other congressional door-keepers, James Mathers and Thomas Dunn, to occupy, rent free, government-owned houses on the Capitol square with ground contiguous to each for a garden (Biog. Dir. Cong.; U.S. Statutes at Large, 2:55, 127; JHR, 15:80; MB, 2:1046n).

According to legislation approved on 3 Mch., THE SECRETARY OF THE TREASURY was to appoint an individual to receive and take an inventory of the outgoing president's public property. Any furniture that was deemed "decayed, out of repair, or unfit for use" and property other than furniture would be sold under the direction of the heads of the departments of state, treasury, war, and navy, with the proceeds of the sale to provide furniture for the "house erected for the accommodation of the President of the United States." Although Adams vacated the President's House on 4 Mch., TJ did not occupy it until 15 days later, remaining instead at Conrad & McMunn's (U.S. Statutes at Large, 2:121-2; William Searle, The President's House: A History, 2 vols. [Washington, D.C., 1986], 1:89).

From the District of Columbia Commissioners

S<small>IR</small>   Commissioners' Office 4th March 1801.

The enclosed Writing sufficiently explains it's object, and we presume, the utility of the Measure proposed, must be apparent, especially to those who have seen the number of wooden Houses lately erected by the Description of people whose accommodation is more immediately contemplated.

We however, respectfully submit the Subject to Your Consideration; and if the Measure be approved, we request the writing may be returned with your Signature, that those inclined to erect Wooden Houses in the City, may have early Notice of the suspension of the prohibitory Articles.—We are, with sentiments of the highest Respect, Sir, Yr. Mo: Obt. Servants.   W<small>ILLIAM</small> T<small>HORNTON</small>
A<small>LEXR</small> W<small>HITE</small>

RC (MHi); in hand of William Brent, signed by Thornton and White; at foot of text: "President of the United-States"; endorsed by TJ as received on the same day as written and so recorded in SJL. FC (DNA: RG 42, DCLB).

E N C L O S U R E

Suspension of Certain Building Regulations

By the President of the United States

Whereas by the first Article of the Terms and conditions declared by the President of the United States on the 17th. day of October 1791, for regulating the Materials and manner of Buildings and Improvements on the Lots in the City of Washington it is provided, "that the outer and party Walls of all Houses in the said City, shall be built of Brick or Stone," and by the third Article of the same Terms and Conditions, it is declared, "that the Wall of no House Shall be higher than forty feet to the Roof, in any part of the City, nor shall any be lower than thirty five feet on any of the Avenues" And whereas the above recited Articles were found to impede the Settlement in the City of Mechanics and others whose Circumstances did not admit of erecting Houses authorised by the said Regulations for which cause the President of the United States, by a writing under his Hand, bearing date the twenty fifth Day of June 1796 Suspended the operation of the said Articles until the first Monday of December 1800, And the beneficial effects arising from such Suspension having been experienced, it is deemed proper to revive the same Wherefore I Thomas Jefferson, president[1] of the United States do declare, that the operation of the first and third Articles above recited shall be, and the Same is hereby Suspended until the first Day of January 1802 and that all the Houses which shall be erected in the said City of Washington previous to the said first day of January 1802 conformable in other respects to the regulations aforesaid Shall be considered as lawfully Erected except that no Wooden House shall be erected within twenty four feet of any brick or Stone House

Given under my Hand this *11th.* Day of *March 1801.*

TH: JEFFERSON

MS (DLC: District of Columbia Papers); in William Thornton's hand; signed by TJ, who supplied date in blanks (reproduced in italics).

Authority to regulate construction in the capital city remained with the president until James Monroe's first term. Building regulations issued by George Washington in 1791 required that outer walls be made of BRICK OR STONE, allowing frame construction only for temporary structures. Washington's 1796 suspension of the rules on construction materials and heights of buildings was renewed by successive administrations until 1818. As secretary of state TJ had advised the president about the initial regulations, and from the earliest consideration of the subject he advocated a limit on the height of buildings. He believed that such a

policy worked well in Paris and had multiple advantages. The earliest rules for the district also specified the minimum height for buildings along the AVENUES. Following TJ's preferences, the regulations controlled building height but said nothing about the distance between the front of a building and the edge of the street. Naming Philadelphia as an example, TJ asserted in 1790 that placing buildings a uniform distance from the street produced "a disgusting monotony" (Bryan, *National Capital*, 1:162-3, 278; Samuel Burch, comp., *A Digest of the Laws of the Corporation of the City of Washington, to the First of June, 1823* [Washington, D.C., 1823], 326-30; Vol. 17:454, 461; Vol. 20:38; Vol. 22:89-91, 136).

[1] MS: "presid."

From William Falkener

SIR! Warrenton No. Cara. March 4th 1801

As Secretary to the Committee, appointed by the Inhabitants of Warren County, to prepare an Address to the President of the United States, I have the Honour to forward the enclosed—

Accept my Sincere Wishes for your personal Happiness and beleive me to be

With great Respect Your mot. obt. Servt.

W. A. K. FALKENER,

RC (DLC); endorsed by TJ as received 16 Mch. and so recorded in SJL.

William Falkener (d. 1819) came to the United States from London sometime after

1790 and settled in Warrenton, where he established a school for girls (*North Carolina Historical Review*, 12 [1935], 268).

On 4 Mch. the citizens of Warren fired 16 platoons of small arms, gathered at noon for mutual congratulations, and sat down for a substantial dinner at McKeen's tavern. Falkener delivered a congratulatory ADDRESS TO THE PRESIDENT OF THE UNITED STATES from the inhabitants of Warren County (see below). The address was followed by a reading of the Declaration of Independence. Sixteen official toasts and another firing of 16 platoons concluded the day's celebration, which was succeeded by a ball two days later (*Raleigh Register and North-Carolina State Gazette*, 10 Mch. 1801).

ENCLOSURE

From Warren County Inhabitants

The Inhabitants of Warren County in the State of North Carolina duly impressed with the awful Check the Will of the People of the United States met with by the House of Representatives, do now feel themselves in the highest of Exultation from the public Will being at last explicitly expressed; we do in the utmost Joyfulness of our Hearts congratulate you Sir on your Election to the cheif Magistracy of our Country. our undissenting Voice has long proclaimed our wishes and our highest Gratification is now satisfied by your Appointment in the Manner pointed out by our excellent Constitution. That you may long live to fill the cheif Magistracy of your Country and by your Wisdom keep us clear of foreign Influence as well as domestic Faction, which from your Publick as well as private Character we have no Doubt will be the Case, and that after this Life you may finally join the almighty Ruler of Worlds in Company with the Heroes and Patriots of your Country is our sincere Wish.

Signed by Order of the Citizens convened at Warrenton on the fourth Day of March One Thousand eight Hundred and one.

W. K. FALKENER Secretary

RC (DLC); at head of text: "To Thomas Jefferson, President, of the United States."

From Fayetteville Republican Citizens

SIR   Fayetteville, North Carolina March the 4th 1801

You have long been ranked among the number of distinguished Patriots, whose transcendent virtues claim the Plaudits of United America.

In chusing you to fill the arduous office of First Magistrate of the Union, the Nations of the Earth shall behold another signal Instance evincing decided Worth alone, deserves the Suffrages of Freemen!

Whatever diversity of opinion may have recently prevailed, we dare hazard the prediction, it will be found in the Event to have been substantially that salutary Jealousy of Rights inseparable from the Nature of Man in society.

We respectfully felicitate you Sir; and heartily congratulate our Fellow Citizens in general, on the auspicious Issue of the late Election; which has so conspicuously proved the excellence of the system we have adopted, and prefer to all others.

Contemplating the extensive powers delegated to the Supreme Executive, we feel our Confidence animated by the reflection, that the Trust is reposed in the Sage, who dictated and penned the ever Memorable Instrument of 1776.

May the Almighty Ruler inspire, and direct your Councils; and prolong your useful Life!

Signed on behalf of the Republican Citizens of the Town and Vicinity of Fayetteville ROBERT COCHRAN MICHAEL MOLTON

RC (DLC); in unidentified hand, signed by Cochran and Molton; at head of text: "To Thomas Jefferson, President of the United States"; endorsed by TJ as received 13 Mch. and so recorded in SJL.

On 4 Mch. the REPUBLICAN CITIZENS OF Fayetteville, North Carolina, held a dinner in honor of TJ's election followed by 16 toasts, patriotic songs, and an illumination displaying the name of "our illustrious Chief" (Gilpatrick, *Jeffersonian Democracy in North Carolina*, 124; *Raleigh Register and North-Carolina State Gazette*, 10 Mch. 1801).

From Cyrus Griffin

DEAR SIR   Wmsburg March 4th. 1801.

Permit me to offer the most sincere congratulations upon your election to the Office of President.

We anticipate with heartfelt pleasure that your wise Administration will reconcile the contending Parties of our common Country.

From early and long attachment, & with the most perfect respect and esteem, I have the honour to be, dear Sir, your faithful & obedient Servant and friend,   CYRUS GRIFFIN.

RC (DLC); endorsed by TJ as received 9 Mch. and so recorded in SJL.

To George Jefferson

DEAR SIR   Washington Mar. 4. 1801.

I must ask the favor of you to call on mr Callender & to inform him that I have recieved his letter; that his fine will be remitted, but that as it requires the presence of the head of the department, it cannot be done till his arrival, which will be in a very few days. the moment he is here & qualified, it shall be dispatched.

A cask of clover seed marked TMR. is gone to the address of messrs. Pollard, Picket & Johnson. it is for T. M. Randolph & I will pray you to have it called for & sent by the first conveyance as the season is [. . .]. I am Dear Sir

Yours affectionately · · · · · · · · · · · · · · · · · · TH: JEFFERSON

PrC (MHi); blurred; at foot of text: "Mr. George Jefferson"; endorsed by TJ in ink on verso.

According to David Meade Randolph's accounts, James T. CALLENDER paid his $200 fine to the marshal on 4 Mch. Legal obstructions imposed by Randolph prevented Callender from recovering his fine until 20 June (Malone, *Jefferson*, 4:208-9; Madison, *Papers, Sec. of State Ser.*, 1:117-21, 236-7).

From George Jefferson

MY DEAR SIR · · · · · · · · · · · · · · · · · · Richmond 4th March 1801

I am now about to address you on a subject which I am very apprehensive may be deemed obtrusive and impertinent; for it certainly does not become me to advise you what your conduct should be—as my acquaintance with you does not justify such a liberty, and *much* less am I justified, from ability to give counsel: but being by my Brother placed under the disagreeable necessity of forwarding the inclosed letter, which he sent open for my perusal, I cannot forbear making a few remarks on it.

I am extremely grieved to attempt in any way to thwart the wishes of a friend and Brother—but *much more* am I grieved, that that Brother should be so extremely solicitous in seeking an Office—and particularly that he should be so entirely destitute of reflection and of delicacy, as to ask any thing of you—when he surely should conclude from what you have already done for him, that if there were any Office in your gift to the duties of which you considered him competent, and there were no other objection to his filling it, that you would undoubtedly recollect him without any solicitation—but taking for granted his capacity to fill some Office—which probably would not stand the test of investigation—inasmuch as a person would perhaps be nearly as well qualified to commence the practice of the law without any previous study, as he would be to engage in any business, which I suppose he can contemplate—yet, for a moment laying that objection aside, there is another which with you I think should be insurmountable and *unalterable*.

There was no part of Genl. Washington's character which met with such universal approbation as his disinterestedness in uniformly refusing to appoint any relation to Office—and there was no part of Mr. Adams's, on the contrary, which so much contributed to lower him in my estimation as conduct directly the reverse.—The objection to which I allude certainly does not hold good in the present case, except in a very remote degree—but the relationship could not generally be known to be so distant—and from the small number of the name, it would probably be thought to be nearer.—If my Brother would be willing to run the smallest risk of hearing you blamed for appointing a relation (however distant) to Office—he must possess feelings very different indeed from mine.   The danger of incurring such censure would be increased from the necessity you would find yourself under of displacing some from Office who have acted improperly—and with what avidity they would catch at the smallest opening to charge you with turning others out of Office in order to make room for your relation, you may form but too correct a judgment from your experience of their enmity on former occasions.   indeed I have *already* heard insinuations of family influence—I have heard it said by Federalists (as they stile themselves) that although many will lose their Offices, yet, *that one*, who has acted with the greatest impropriety in the opinion of every republican I ever heard speak upon the subject, will continue to hold his, on account of the family connexion.

Thus it is that wretches speak, who, judging others from the depravity of their own souls, can have no idea of any motive of action, unless it springs from interest, or family aggrandisement—and who cannot conceive that a good Man in such a case can feel entirely free of all sort of influence, except that which prompts him to be more rigid with family connexions than with others—and especially if he had any hand in bestowing the Office they hold.

I hope My Dear Sir you will excuse me for having taken up so much of your time at this juncture, when the whole of it must be required in more important concerns—nothing would have induced me to have done it, but the distressing situation in which I am placed by my Brother.

I would have delayed forwarding his letter in the hope of dissuading him from his purpose—but I have on a former occasion, something similar to the present, experienced the total inefficasy of any such attempt.

My unwillingness to interrupt you at this time is increased by the fear that your table will be but too much crouded with petitions for Office—and unwelcome (when uninteresting) letters of advice. for my part however I promise you, that however indulgent a view you may take of this, I will never be tempted to repeat the impropriety.

I am Dear Sir Your Very humble servt.   Geo. Jefferson

My Brother having ask'd my opinion of his application I shall send him a copy of this—silence from you will be therefore understood.

G. J.

RC (MHi); at foot of text: "Thomas Jefferson esqr."; endorsed by TJ as received 9 Mch. and so recorded in SJL. Enclosure: John Garland Jefferson to TJ, 1 Mch. 1801.

THAT ONE, WHO HAS ACTED WITH THE GREATEST IMPROPRIETY: probably David Meade Randolph (see TJ to Thomas Mann Randolph, 12 Mch. 1801).

From Peter Legaux

Monsieur   Springmill, Mont Gomery County ce 4 Mars 1801.

Le moment de La naissance des Arts, de La régénération de La Liberté en Amérique et de L'Encouragement que son Agriculture sollicite depuis Longtemps est Enfin arrivé aujourdhuy; je m'en félicite infiniment ainsi que Ces Contrées qui L'attendoient avec la derniere impatience. La Crainte de Blesser une des moindres qualités du phylosophe qui doit opérer ces heureux pronostics; sa modestie naturele, dis je, impose des bornes à ce que je pourrois et voudrois dire de plus, mais Elle n'en peut mettre aucune, aux Sentiments Les plus Respecteux avec Les quels j'ai L'honneur d'être trés parfaitement

De son Excellence Le trés humble et trés dévoué Serviteur

P. Legaux

P.S. ma vigne desirant que je prie un de ses plus zêlés protecteur d'accepter de sa part quelques milliers de ses Enfants pour Etre *Éduqués* et propagés En Virginie, Votre Excellence, voudroit elle bien Lui indiquer La voie la plus sûre pour Les Lui faire parvenir Le plus Convenablement possible et Leur accorder un Emplacement sur ses terres. Le 26 mars de L'année derniere, Lorsque je prie la Liberté de faire hommage à votre Excellence, d'un très petit Essai des vins et Eau-de-vie que j'avois faits ici, je profitai en même temps de L'offre qu'elle avoit bien voulu me faire, de remettre elle même Le Duplicata de ma premiere Lettre à Mr. Monroue; sans doute que mes Lettres sur La seconde branche de L'Agriculture Lui auront déplues, ou ne méritérent aucune reponse, ou qu'il est peut être, ce que j'ignore, de L'Etiquet ou usage des Gouverneurs de L'Etat de Virginie de ne répondre qu'aux Lettres qui traitent d'affaires de Gouvernement, je souhaiterois que ce fut cette raison et qu'aù moins je ne Lui Eusse pas été importun.

EDITORS' TRANSLATION

SIR   Spring Mill, Montgomery County, this 4 March 1801

The moment of the birth of the arts, the regeneration of liberty in America, and the encouragement of its agriculture, urged for so long a time, has finally arrived this day; I rejoice boundlessly in it, as do those regions that were awaiting it with infinite impatience. The fear of wounding one of the slightest qualities of the philosopher who is going to accomplish these happy forecasts, his natural modesty, I mean, imposes limits to what I could and would wish to say besides, but it can set none to the most respectful sentiments with which I have the honor to be perfectly

His excellency's very humble and very devoted servant

P. LEGAUX

P.S. My vineyard, desiring that I beseech one of its most zealous protectors to accept on its behalf some thousands of its children to be *brought up* and propagated in Virginia, would Your Excellency kindly indicate the safest way to send them to him in the most proper way and to grant them a site on his lands. March 26th of last year, when I took the liberty of paying homage to Your Excellency with a very small sample of the wines and the brandy that I had made here, I took advantage at the same time of the offer he had kindly made me of delivering himself the duplicate of my first letter to Mr. Monroe; my letters on the second branch of agriculture must have displeased him or were worthy of no reply, or perhaps it is—I do not know—part of the protocol or custom of governors of the State of Virginia to reply only to letters concerning governmental affairs; I should hope that that was the reason and that at least I had not importuned him.

RC (DLC); at head of text: "À son Excellence Thomas jefferson Esqr. Président des Etats unis de L'Amérique"; endorsed by TJ. Enclosures: five tables of meteorological data containing detailed observations from 1789 and composite information for the years 1787-1800; with a report in the form of a letter from Legaux to the American Philosophical Society, 25 Feb. 1801, explaining the contents of the tables and the instruments used for the observations; the APS having requested, in November 1800, duplicates of tables sent earlier that had been mislaid (MS in PPAmP, addressed: "À son Excellence Thomas Jéfferson Esqr. Président des Etats unix de l'Amérique et Président de La société Phylosophique Américaine," the letter consisting of 24 numbered pages in French, entirely in Legaux's hand, a subsequent English translation being in an unidentified hand, the tables in French and English, some portions printed, with Legaux's notations distinguishing the duplicates sent to TJ in 1801 from other versions of the tables at PPAmP; APS, *Proceedings*, 22, pt. 3 [1884], 172, 305; see also TJ to Legaux, 24 Mch.).

26 MARS DE L'ANNÉE DERNIERE: Legaux wrote TJ on 26 Mch. 1800 and again on the 29th of that month, but the letters have not been found; see Vol. 30:42n.

From Francis Mentges

SIR   Washington 4t. March 1801

I trust that my Official conduct from the 20t. july 1790, when I was honored with the Appointment as Inspector of the troops in the service of the United States, has been such, as to merit approbation, and to prove in the best manner the sense entertained of the favors and attention towards me during the continuance of service to the present time—

Permit me then Sir to solicit your Attention for the Claim of one who, through the course of the late war uniformly exerted himself in a Military Character and whose hopes rest entirely in being still engaged in the service of his Country, I am informed that the Office of Inspector of Fortifications is still vacant, in this, or in any station you may deem me qualified I shall be happy to evince my gratitude and Respect, with high considr

I am Sir your Ob hb Servt.   F MENTGES

RC (DNA: RG 59, LAR); at head of text: "The President of the United States"; endorsed by TJ as received 2 Mch. and so recorded in SJL.

Francis Mentges (d. 1805) was a native of the duchy of Zweibrücken. During the Revolutionary War he served as an officer in several Pennsylvania regiments. Nathanael Greene made him inspector of the Southern Army in November 1782. He served as inspector general of the Pennsylvania state militia, and then as an unofficial inspector for U.S. troops. Since 1797 Mentges served as procurement agent for the reconstruction of Fort Mifflin on Mud Island in the Delaware River, charged with acquiring construction materials, paying laborers, and disbursing funds. The agency ceased in May 1801 by the order of Secretary of War Henry Dearborn. In March 1805 Dearborn hired Mentges to help oversee construction of a federal armory at Rocky Mount, South Carolina (*South Carolina Historical Magazine*, 29 [1928], 158-9; 81 [1980], 219, 221; PMHB, 45 [1921], 385; Richard K. Showman and others, eds., *The Papers of General Nathanael Greene*, 13 vols. [Chapel Hill, 1976-2005], 12:147-8; *Pennsylvania Gazette*, 4 Oct. 1786; *Report, from the Committee of Claims, to whom was Referred . . . the Petition of Francis Mentges . . . 16th February, 1805* [Washington, 1805]; Francis Mentges to Henry Dearborn, 19 Dec. 1801, RC in DLC).

From the New Jerusalem Church of Baltimore

SIR,   Baltimore 4th: March 1801.

It is with singular pleasure and profound respect, that WE the Minister and Acting Committe of the *New Jerusalem Church*, in the City of Baltimore, beg leave to congratulate you, on your accession to the chief Magistracy of our beloved Country—A Country hitherto eminently favor'd by the *Divine Providence* with a peculiar degree of Civil and religious liberty.

The present sanguinary & turbulent aspect of the Eastern continent, is doubtless truly painful to every philantropic and disinterested lover of Mankind; But still, The Heavenly Doctrines of the *"New Church"* confirm us in the belief, that, *"God rides on the Whirlwind, and directs the storm"*! — and encourage us to anticipate, with indescribable sensations, an approaching period — "a *consumation devoutly to be wish'd for,"* when genuine charity, liberallity, and brotherly kindness, towards all who differ from us in mere *opinions,* shall become *"The order of the day;"* — When Theology, Philosophy, & Politics, shall, like *"Gold seven times tried in the fire,"* loose all their *"dross and tin";* — and when *Reason* and *Religion* shall fully unite their sacred & all powerful influence, in promoting *"Peace on Earth, & Goodwill among all men."*

With the most sincere & fervent prayers, That the LORD GOD of HOSTS may long preserve & keep you — & the nation over whom you now preside, from all EVIL; — and richly replenish your *Will & Understanding* with such divine *affections* & *perceptions,* as may eminently qualify you for the exalted & important station you are now call'd unto,

We remain Sir, with due respect Your's &c. &c. in all duty —

JOHN HARGROVE, MINISTER
New Jerusalem Church
City of Baltimore

Sign'd per Order

George Higson ⎫
John Boyer ⎬ Acting Committe
John Kerr ⎭ of the New Church

RC (DLC); in Hargrove's hand and signed by him; at head of text: "To Thomas Jefferson Esqr. President of the United States of America"; endorsed by TJ as received 5 Mch. and so recorded in SJL.

Ordained as a Methodist clergyman in 1795, John Hargrove (1750-1839) became a Swedenborgian minister three years later. For many years he served as pastor of the New Jerusalem Church in Baltimore and presided over the opening of the first Swedenborgian temple in the United States in January 1800. In August 1801 he began publishing *The Temple of Truth: or A Vindication of Various Passages and Doctrines of the Holy Scriptures* to refute the deistic arguments published in *The Temple of Reason.* Thirteen numbers of his periodical were published

before it went out of existence in October 1801. During his first trip to Washington in December 1802, Hargrove delivered a sermon at the Capitol attended by the president. Two years later he again delivered a sermon before Congress. TJ had both sermons in his library (see Sowerby, Nos. 1671-2). Since Swedenborgian ministers were not compensated, Hargrove had to seek other employment to support his wife and eight children. In 1801 and 1802 Arthur Campbell wrote Madison seeking a clerical position for him in one of the executive departments. By 1809 he was serving as registrar for the city of Baltimore (Hargrove, *A Sermon, on the True Object and Nature of Christian Worship; Delivered at the Opening of the New Jerusalem Temple, in the City of Baltimore* [Baltimore, 1800]; Hargrove, *The Substance of a Sermon, on the Leading Doctrines of the New Jerusalem Church; Delivered the 26th December, 1802, before the President of the United States and Several Members of Congress* [Baltimore, 1803], i-ii; Baltimore, Md., *Summary of All the Monies Received and Paid by the Register, from February 1, 1809, to January 31, 1810, Inclusive* [Baltimore, 1810], see Shaw-Shoemaker, No. 19411; Madison, *Papers, Sec. of State Ser.*, 1:34-5, 2:419-20; Marguerite Beck Block, *The New Church in the New World: A Study of Swedenborgianism in America* [New York, 1932], 90-93; Ednah C. Silver, *Sketches of the New Church in America* [Boston, 1920], 40-46).

From Richard Dobbs Spaight

SIR,   Washington City 4 March 1801.

When Congress first began to fortify the ports & Harbours of the United States in 1794, among others a fort was directed to be erected on Beacon Island near Ocracock bar, to defend that Inlet. An Engineer was sent forward, who laid off the fort and the works were commenced, & carried on untill November following.

In 1795. From the neglect of the then Secretary of War (Genl. Knox) nothing was done. In 1796 when the subject again came before Congress, My Predecessor in the House of Representatives, who at that time, had never been at Ocracock bar, who was totally destitute of Commercial information, and knew not the importance of a fort there, for the protection of the trade of No. Carolina, told Genl. Knox that a fort at that place would be useless, he accordingly made a report to that effect, to Congress, and the works were discontinued & remained so untill I took my seat in Congress in Decr. 1798.

Being fully impressed with the advantages that would be derived from a fort being built there as a protection to our commerce in time of War, and to the revenue of the United States at all times: (for there is no place on earth where smuggling can be carried on with more advantage, & with less probability of Detection, it being seventy miles from any Collectors office), On my arrival at Philadelphia in 1798, I endeavoured to make both the Secretary of War, and of the Treasury, sensible of these facts; and pointed out to the latter, the necessity there was for a Surveyor being established at that place, in order to secure the revenue.

From my representations those Gentlemen acceded to the Measure, & Mr. McHenry gave the necessary orders for the fort to be completed; and Mr. Wolcott in a law passed that Session established a port and a Surveyor at that place: and Capt. James Taylor was soon after made Surveyor of the port & Captain of the fort. Things were in this situation & measures taking to have the fort finished, when the works were put a stop to by Mr. Dexter, who in a letter to Capt. Taylor gave orders to discontinue them in Novemr. last, under a pretence that the monies appropriated for that purpose was exhausted. Which was not a fact as Mr. Wolcott at the first of the Session, reported a balance of that fund, remaining unexpended of between 57 & 58,000 Dollars—And on an enquiry which I made at the Treasury Department in Jany. after I had heard from Capt. Taylor, I was informed that on the 1st. Jany. last there remained unexpended of those appropriations the Sum of $57,241. Dolls.—

All the trade of No. Carolina except what is carried on at Wilmington, and a little at Beaufort & Swannsborough, passes over Ocracock bar: and the fort at Beacon Island command both Harbours, or, roads, where the shipping bound either in, or out come too in order to lighten, to enable them to pass the swash. It likewise commands both the passages that lead from the harbours or roads, up into the Country.

I could venture to say to a Certainty that the revenue saved to the United States, in consequence of a fort being built, and a surveyor established there will fully eaqual the Annual expenditure, occasioned by the Establishment, and in my Opinion, will in the course of ten or a Dozen years repay the United States the monies which the works will cost.

I have thus agreeably to your desire thrown my Ideas on this subject in a hasty manner on paper, and I make no doubt but that an Object of such magnitude, will receive due attention from The administration.

With Sentiments of Consideration & Respect I am Sir, Your most Obt. Sevt.   RICHD. DOBBS SPAIGHT

RC (PHi); at foot of text: "Thomas Jefferson Esqr. President of the United States"; endorsed by TJ as received 4 Mch. and so recorded in SJL; also endorsed by TJ: "refd to the Secretary at War for his opinion Th:J."

Richard Dobbs Spaight (1758-1802) of New Bern was a member of the Continental Congress from 1783 to 1785, a delegate to the federal Constitutional Convention in 1787, and governor of North Carolina from 1792 to 1795. In 1798 he won a special election to fill the congressional seat vacated by the death of his PREDECESSOR, Nathan Bryan. A Republican, Spaight remained in Congress until 3 Mch. 1801. Subsequently elected to the North Carolina Senate, he became involved in a

political controversy with his successor in Congress, John Stanly, a Federalist. The rivalry culminated in a duel between the two men on 5 Sep. 1802, in which Spaight was mortally wounded (William S. Powell, ed., *Dictionary of North Carolina Biography*, 6 vols. [Chapel Hill, 1979-96], 5:403-4; *Biog. Dir. Cong.*).

John Adams appointed JAMES TAYLOR inspector and surveyor for the port of Beacon Island, N.C., on 14 June 1799. Congress abolished the post in April 1806, replacing it with the newly created collection district of "Ocracocke" (Ocracoke). TJ appointed Taylor collector and inspector of the district in 1806 (JEP, 1:325, 2:44; U.S. Statutes at Large, 2:399-400).

Work on the FORT AT BEACON ISLAND was not resumed during TJ's administration. In 1806 Henry Dearborn reported that no practical work could be erected at that place and that gunboats could more effectively protect Ocracoke harbor than a fixed fortification (ASP, *Military Affairs*, 1:195).

From John Cleves Symmes

SIR,   Northbend, Miami, 4th. March 1801.

Samuel Heighway esquire, and Mr. John Poole, both of the Miami purchase, have lately invented a Machine on the principle of steam, that I am inclined to believe will excel any thing of the kind that the world has yet been favored with.   From several years acquaintance with Mr. Heighway, and prepossession in favor of his integrity and judgment, I am inclined to hope that the gentlemen are not mistaken in their calculations, nor too sanguine in their expectations from the powers of their projected Mechanism.

Great indeed, will be the Usefulness of such a performance to every part of the United States, and to none more, than to the Inhabitants of this country whose prosperity depends on Inland navigation, and Manufactures of various kinds, which will be greatly promoted by their Machine.

Permit me Sir, to commend these gentlemen (one or both of whom will have the honor to wait on you with this address) to your patronage and countenance.—Their wish is to avail themselves of the advantages of the best artizans in Philadelphia, and proper Materials for compassing the work, and to obtain, if found worthy, a patent from Congress, that they may in a moderate degree secure to themselves some pecuniary emoluments from their long studied and expensive invention, which the same must necessarily prove to them, by the time the work is perfected.

I have the honor to be, Sir, with the highest consideration and respect, Your most Obedient humble Servant.

JOHN CLEVES SYMMES.

RC (CSmH); at head of text: "To Thomas Jefferson Esquire, President of the philosophical society of arts and sciences at Philadelphia"; endorsed by TJ as received 9 Oct. and so recorded in SJL with notation "by mr John Poole."

Englishman SAMUEL HEIGHWAY and two partners purchased a large portion of Symmes's Miami lands in 1796, within which they laid out the town of Waynes- ville. JOHN POOLE received a PATENT on 13 Oct. 1801 for a "syphonic steam machine." In 1801 Heighway and Poole advertised for subscribers to invest in their "mechanical project" that would propel a boat upstream "by the power of steam or elastic vapor." In 1803 they sold their unfinished invention to the Miami Exporting Company of Cincinnati, which converted the craft into a conventional flatboat (Emily Foster, ed., *The Ohio*

Frontier: An Anthology of Early Writings [Lexington, Ky., 1996], 96; *List of Patents*, 26; Emilius O. Randall and Daniel J. Ryan, *History of Ohio: The Rise and Progress of an American State*, 5 vols. [New York, 1912], 4:490; 5:269-70; Henry A. Ford and Kate B. Ford, *History of Cincinnati, Ohio, with Illustrations and Biographical Sketches* [Cleveland, 1881], 53, 349).

From James Warren

SIR,   Plymouth, Mass: March 4th. 1801

Having seldom been in the habit of Addressing Men in high Stations, and in no instance of flattering them, the feelings of my own heart, on an Occasion so Congenial to its sentiments, must be my Apology for troubling You with this Letter. I sincerely congratulate my Country on the happy result of their Change of Opinion, and I as sincerely congratulate You, on your Elevation to the first Magistracy of the Union, and the triumph of Virtue over the most malignant, virulent, and slanderous party, that perhaps ever existed in any Country.—

Driven myself from active Scenes of political Life into neglect and obscurity, by the malice of persecution, I have sat like a Man under the Shade of a tree, unnoticed himself, contemplating the progress, and exploring the Springs of publick Affairs.—In this situation for many Years past, I have seen much to reprobate and little to approve.—I have seen principle sacrificed to Ambition, and Consistency of sentiment to the interest of the Moment.—The glare of Etiquet and imitation of splendid and expensive Systems, preferred to fundamental principles and the happiness of the people.—

An old Man who can recollect the process of three periods, may enjoy the present with a satisfaction unknown to those, who know very little of the first.—I sincerely wish your Administration may be pleasant to yourself, and happy to your Country, notwithstanding the many sources of existing Embarrassments the preceding Administration have left on Yours, and perhaps some it has created.—A virulent party exists here with an extensive influence and connexion, called the Essex Junto; violent and incorrigible, because unprincipled, their drooping Spirits are revived by a long List of Nominations which has appeared in our papers, which is not marked with delicacy on the winding up of an Administration, and appears suspicious in its views.—

But I will not longer detain you from Your own Contemplations, much more important than mine.—I will flatter myself that your wisdom, and the firm support of your numerous friends, will defeat the

Intrigues, the Virulence, and Malice of your Enemies, and am with Sentiments of the greatest Esteem & Respect Your Obedient & Huml: Servant   JAMES WARREN

RC (DLC); in unidentified hand, signed by Warren; addressed: "Thomas Jefferson Esqre. President of the United States Washington"; endorsed by TJ as received 18 Mch. and so recorded in SJL.

James Warren (1726-1808), outspoken Massachusetts political leader and a member of the governor's council from 1792 to 1794, became an ardent Jeffersonian in later life. Although defeated in elections for lieutenant governor and twice for a seat in Congress, he was chosen, at the age of seventy-eight, as a presidential elector for Massachusetts in 1804. An infrequent correspondent with TJ, he last wrote him on behalf of his son in October 1785 (DAB; Vol. 8:599-600).

For the ESSEX JUNTO, see Vol. 32:385-6.

From "Your Unknown Friend"

SIR/   Phila. Mar 4. 1801—
    Permit a natural born Citizen of the United States independent as to pecuniary concerns of expecting or wishing any post of profit under or in the gift of any department in the United States,—to sugest to you what in his opinion will contribute to your honour and the happiness of the people who you will preside over—

1. Never to displace any officer because he has differ'd in political sentiments from you.
2. Never to appoint any whoes abilities and integrity does not qualify him for the place.
3. Appoint no violent party man whoes judgement & descretion is under such prejudices as to endanger his duty to the United states & create jealousies of his impartial & upright conduct.
4. To fulfill all the ingagements of the Government so far as it can be done with propriety & to inculate the principles of individuals doing the same in all there Contract & concerns, To promote American Manufactories to practice frugality & economy—
5. To support Agriculture & Commerce the two principle pursuits of the people of these States—The Eastern States from habit is so attach'd to commerce that the evident neglect of it by Goverment wou'd endanger the Union by a seperation of those states from the southern—the evils that wou'd arise from that event is more to be deprecated than every thing else which cou'd happen.
6. To weigh well all the important measure of Goverment let prejudice & passion have no influence, the smooth paths of honour, Candour, & Justice pursue & leave the events to an alwise providence—That

your administration may be crown'd with success & tranquility is the ardent wish of—   Your unknown friend.

N.B. Since writing the above I have had the pleasure of reading your Publick declaration on points mention'd in my letter, they are approv'd by all—I now only fear your being led to make appointments on recriminations which too often prefer persons the most unfit when political prejudices influence the mind—

RC (DLC); addressed: "Thomas Jefferson Esqr President of the United States Washington"; franked; postmarked 18 Mch.; endorsed by TJ as received 21 Mch. from "Anonymous" and so recorded in SJL.

From Joseph Yznardi, Sr.

Exmo. Señor   Philadelphia 4 de Marzo del 1801

Muy Señor, mio, y de todo mi Respecto confiado, en la Rectitud de su Justicia me tomo la Livertad de Molestar por este Momento su Atension, en el Idioma Castellano por qe V.E lo entiende, y me es mas fasil produsirme, en el con la Claridad que desseo, y respecto qe devo

en el Año de 93 fui mi Hijo ℔ Influxo de mis Amigos Nombrado Consul de Cadiz por este Govierno, y quando V.E Administró la Secretaria de estado en Cuya Epoca es Escusado presentar Merito Alguno á favor Mio pues le Consta por los documentos dirigidos a su oficina

en la Administrassion de su Subsesor Mr. Pickering las dos Copias de sus Cartas qe con No 3 aconpaño á V.E manifiestan mi prosedimiento, y con no Menos Satisfaccion he Meresido la aprovasion de la Ultima Administrasion de Mr. Marshal como lo Acredito con Copa de su Carta No 4 de Manera qe desde el principio eñ qe recayó el enpleo en mi Familia en lugar de Correciones he Meresido Aplausos como dichos documentos lo Manifiestan.

á pesar de la Confiansa qe poseía Justamente me veo Insultado en el Consepto publico por Averseme removido del Empleo sin mas Antesedente qe el de Aves Nonbrado Subsesor hecho, a la Verdad Inesperado de una persona á quien venerava como Caveza de la Soberania de este Govierno, y sin saver el Motibo qe produsgo un Movimiento tan Infusto Acudy al Dho Mr Marshal, y preguntadole la Causa me respondio Ignorarla, paresiondo Admirado, y ofresiondome Indagarla, como en efecto lo verificó al día Siguiente dandome por satisfaccion, que el Unico Motibo en qe fundó, la remossion, el Cavallero Mr Adams fui el Allarce

empeñado á favor del Subsesor, y por qe desseava recayesen los
Consulados, en Natibos Americanos (u a lo Menos qe fuesen Ciu-
dadanos) por Maxima Adoctada en este Govierno tomando princi-
pio en el desposo de una Meresida, y Justa posesion hecho á mi ver
fuera de principios de umanidad por qe sus resultas son las de
Obscureser el Merito de un hombre bueno, y premiarle con un
Castigo, digolo assy por quanto si Ubiese Admitido el empleo de
Consul con renumcia del fuero Español me Allaria defraudado del
Dro de mis Leyes, y de las de America por no ser Ciudadano, despues de Aver Servidole por 7 Años con toda mi Eficasia personal,
Intelectual, y propiedad pecunaria pues Antes de Saver quien
pagaria mis Adelantos adelante Sumas Cresidas en el Socorro de
Infinitos Ciudadanos destituidos del Auxilio de su Govierno
permanesiendo en en desenbolso 4 Años Como lo Acreditarán los
documentos Infinitos Actualmente en la Secretaria de Estado en la
qe Assy Mismo pareseran aver sido la Causa de livertar de la Injusticia de Corsarios 122 Buques que abrian sido Condenados
como otros, en los varios puertos de Europa.

543 Marineros por mis Auxilios han sido restuidos á este Conte-
nente los qe al Contrario abrian Ocupadose al Servisio de Otras
Nasiones quando sus Indigencias en la Guerra presente no le
Ubiezan Obligado á pelear contra sus Mismos conciudadanos

yo no he renunciado mi enpleo, ni debo Asserlo al presente pues á de
mas de estar en desembolso de Serca de 5000 ps fuertes en Socorros,
y otros gastos nasionales hechos en los 3 Años Ultimos se hallan a mi
Cargo varias defensas de Buques, y Cargamentos Cuyas Causas
apeladas me son deudoras de Sumas de entidad qe no podría recobrar-
las fuera del Oficio, y por lo tanto me veo en la Nessesidad de reclamar
se me debuelba la posesion a lo Menos hasta Concluir los Asuntos pen-
dientes quando desde luego Resignaré con voluntad, para qe recaiga en
la persona qe V.E tenga á bien

no tan Solamente Exmo. Señor, fundo mi Justicia en las aprova-
seones qe dirigo de mi conducta por este Govo si no es Assy Mismo en
la qe he Meresido del de España acreditadas por las Certificasiones de
Xefes Militiras, Navales, y Siviles qe con el No. 5 Incluigo como tanbien de los prinsipales Honbres de Negosios de Comercio de Cadiz con
el No. 6 con el fin dl qe V.E tenga la vondad de Examinarlas, y de Man-
dar se me debuelvan para la Satisfaccion de mi Familia, y Amigos, qe
Mirarán con Dolor mi Suerte Considerandome Ansiano Emigrado de
mi Patria desposcido de la reunion de mi Esposa é Hijos Victimas en
la enfermedad de Cadiz de Cuyo peligro podria (como otros) averlos
livertado si me Ubiese allado presente

si residen facultades en V.E (como lo Considero) espero en la Notoría rectitud de su Justicia me restituira a la posesion de mi enpleo pues con ello Satisfará en Consepto que Justa Mente merese su mas Obediente Servidor

Exmo. Señor con el Respecto qe devó   JOSEF YZNARDY

EDITORS' TRANSLATION

MOST EXCELLENT SIR   Philadelphia 4 Mch. 1801

My dear Sir and with all my respect, confident in the rightness of your justice, I am taking the liberty of intruding on your attention at this time in the Castilian language because Your Excellency understands it, and it is easier for me to compose in it with the desired clarity and due respect.

In the year '93 by the influence of my friends, my son was named consul at Cadiz by this government, and since Your Excellency administered the secretaryship of state during that term, I am justified in presenting some merit favorable to myself, as is made clear by the documents sent to your office.

During the administration of your successor, Mr. Pickering, the two copies of his letters, which with No. 3 I send to Your Excellency, show my procedure, and with no less satisfaction I merited the approval of the last administration, of Mr. Marshall, as I show by means of a copy of his letter, No. 4. So, right from the beginning, when the post fell to my family, instead of corrections I have merited applause, as the aforementioned documents show.

In spite of the trust that I had, I see myself actually insulted in the public arena for having been discharged from employment without warning other than the naming of a successor, something genuinely unexpected from a person whom I venerated as the sovereign head of this government, and without knowing the motive that produced such an unjust action, I appealed to the said Mr. Marshall and asked of him the cause. He answered me saying he did not know, appearing surprised and offering to investigate it for me, which indeed he carried out the next day, giving me as satisfaction that the only motive on which it was founded—the discharge—was that the cavalier Mr. Adams, finding himself in favor of the successor, and because he wanted the consulates to be given to native Americans (or at least to those who were citizens) since they are most indoctrinated in this government, taking the principal part in stripping away a worthy and fair possession—an act that, in my opinion, exceeds the principles of humanity because it results in diminishing the merit of a good man, and rewarding him with a punishment. I put it this way, for if the post of consul had required renouncing Spanish laws, I would find myself defrauded of the rights of my laws and of those of America for not being a citizen after having served for seven years with all my personal, intellectual, and monetary efficacy—since before knowing who would repay my outlay, I advanced increasing sums to help infinite numbers of citizens bereft of help from their government; covering expenses for four years as attested to in the infinite number of documents presently in the secretary of state's office, where they will appear to have been the cause of freeing from the injustice of corsairs 122 ships that would been condemned like others in the various ports of Europe.

Because of my help, 543 sailors have been restored to this continent who otherwise would have gone into service to other nations, since they were not obliged by their indigence to fight against their fellow citizens during the present war.

I have not renounced my post nor should I at present, since not only am I in outlay of nearly 5000 pesetas in aid and other national expenses made in the last three years; my responsibility includes various defenses of ships and cargo whose legal appeals are owed to me in such sums that I could not collect if I were not in office, and, therefore, I find myself with the need to request that my post be restored, at least in order to conclude outstanding matters—at which time, of course, I will resign voluntarily so that it may be given to the person whom Your Excellency deems fit.

Not only, most excellent Sir, do I base my justice on the approvals that I derive from my conduct on behalf of this government but also as much as that I have merited from Spain—accredited by the certifications of military, naval, and civil leaders whom I include with No. 5, as well as those of principal men of business and commerce of Cadiz with No. 6, for the purpose of Your Excellency being so good as to examine them, and to send them back to me for the satisfaction of my family and friends who look with pain at my luck, considering me an old emigrant from my country dispossessed of the reunion with my wife and children, victims of the sickness of Cadiz, from whose danger I might have (as others did) freed them if I could have been present.

If the power and authority reside in Your Excellency (as I do believe) I have hope in the well-known rightness of your justice; that you restore to me the possession of my employment, since with it you will satisfy the opinion that your most obedient servant justly deserves.

Most Excellent Sir with due respect   JOSEF YZNARDY

RC (DNA: RG 59, LAR); at foot of text: "Exmo. Sor. Dn. Thomas Jefferson como Presidente de los E U de america"; endorsed by TJ as received 10 Mch. and so recorded in SJL. Enclosures not found.

The Adams administration had named Henry Preble as U.S. consul at CADIZ, Spain, to replace Yznardi's son; see David Humphreys to TJ, 23 Sep. 1800. For the controversy that had brought Yznardi to the United States to defend his actions while serving as consul under his son's authority, see Yznardi's letter to TJ of 4 Jan. 1801.

LA INJUSTICIA DE CORSARIOS: privateers with French commissions had captured a number of American merchant vessels and taken them to Spanish ports for condemnation as prizes by French consular tribunals (Marshall, Papers, 4:265-73, 301-2; Madison, Papers, Sec. of State Ser., 1:52, 220; Humphreys to the secretary of state, 13 Jan., 24 Feb. 1801, in DNA: RG 59, DD).

LA ENFERMEDAD: plague, yellow fever, or possibly both diseases devastated southern Spain in the fall of 1800, causing thousands of deaths (Douglas Hilt, The Troubled Trinity: Godoy and the Spanish Monarchs [Tuscaloosa, Ala., 1987], 114; Humphreys to the secretary of state, 28 Oct., 7 Nov. 1800, in DNA: RG 59, DD).

Circular Letter to Midnight Appointees

SIR   [after 4 Mch. 1801]

The late president, mr Adams, having not long before his retirement from office, made several appointments to *civil* offices holden *during the will* of the President, when so restricted in time as not to admit sufficient enquiry & consideration, the present President deems it proper that those appointments should be a subject of reconsideration & further enquiry. he considers it as of palpable justice that the officers who are to begin their course as agents of his administration should be persons on whom he has personal reliance[1] for a faithful execution of his views. you will therefore be pleased to consider the appointment you have recieved[2] as if never made, of which this early notice is given to prevent any derangements which that appointment might produce.

Dft (DNA: RG 59, LAR, 6:0085); undated; entirely in TJ's hand.

It is not known to whom this letter was sent, but TJ may have given it to Jacob Wagner to send to those civil officers appointed by Adams NOT LONG BEFORE HIS RETIREMENT FROM OFFICE. Probably shortly after TJ took office, and at his request, Wagner sent TJ a one-page, undated memorandum with two headings. The list of names under the first, "Commissions not in the office," included William H. Dorsey, as judge of the Orphans Court for Washington County; William Thornton, Thomas Peter, and Dorsey, justices of the peace for Washington County; Charles Alexander, George Gilpin, Jonah Thompson, John Herbert, Cuthbert Powell, and Jacob Houghman, justices of the peace for Alexandria County; Thomas Johnson, James Marshall, and William Cranch, judges of the circuit court; and Thomas Swan, U.S. attorney for the district. Under the second heading, "Commissions not made out," appeared the names of Richard Forrest, Cornelius Coningham, Lewis Deblois, George Taylor, Dennis Ramsay, Jonathan Swift, Abraham Faw, and Cleon Moore, justices of the peace for the county of Alexandria; and Samuel Hanson and Henry Moore, appointed notaries for the county. All were nominated by President Adams on 28 Feb. and 2 Mch. and approved by the Senate 3 Mch. (MS in DNA: RG 59, MCL, in Wagner's hand, endorsed by TJ: "Commissions, issued & not issued"; JEP, 1:387-90).

Wagner sent TJ another undated memorandum consisting of "An additional list of commissions remaining in the Office of the department of State." The list included James C. Mountflorence, Isaac Cox Barnet, William Lee, John J. Waldo, Thomas W. Griffith, William Foster, Jr., John Mitchell, George Rundle, James H. Hooe, Turell Tufts, and John M. Forbes, nominated as commercial agents in France; George Stacey, as commercial agent for the Île de France and Bourbon (Réunion) Island; Thomas Aborn, as the commerical agent for Cayenne; and Henry Preble, as consul at Cadiz. Jacob Read, appointed judge of the district of South Carolina, headed the list and was the only judicial appointment. Eleven of the names were put forward by Adams on 18 Feb. and confirmed by the Senate six days later. When TJ named replacements for eight of these appointees he noted "nominated February 18, but not appointed." The three other posts were left vacant. Of the remaining four, Read and Mountflorence were nominated on 21 Feb. and Tufts and Aborn on the 24th. They were promptly confirmed. TJ replaced Mountflorence and Tufts but confirmed Aborn in his appointment (MS in DNA: RG 59, MCL, in Wagner's hand, endorsed by TJ: "Mr. Adams's last appointments"; ASP, *Miscellaneous*, 1:307-8; JEP, 1:381-6, 402-3). For the outcome of Read's judicial appointment, see List of John Adams's Appointments, 23 Feb.

On 17 Apr. the *National Intelligencer* printed a list of those appointed by Adams during the last session of Congress, along with the dates of their commissions. The same list, but from another newspaper, is in DNA: RG 59, MCL.

[1] Preceding three words interlined in place of "can rely."

[2] TJ first wrote "the recent appointment you recieved" before altering the passage to read as above.

From Joseph Anderson
and William Cocke

SIR   Washington March 5th 1801

In order to exhibit a mere commensurate Veiw, of the ground, upon which we conceive a treaty with the Cherokee Indians Ought to be held—we beg leave to Submit the following Statement

It is well known to you Sir, that at the time of forming the Old Confederation, the States respectively reserved to themselves—exclusive Jurisdiction and right of Domain, to all the lands, which lay within their Charterd limits—This Soveriegnty enabled the States to parcel out their lands, in Such manner as the Legislatures thereof—might from time to time direct—In pursueance of this power, the State of North Carolina, pass'd Several laws—Opening land offices for the Sale of her Vacant and unappropriated lands, and in Consequence thereof, Sold that Tract of Country *called* the Wilderness, and Issued Patents, to the Several purchasers for the Same—Some of the Citizens who had purchased, took possession of their lands, and others were about so to do—when the Treaty of Holston was made with the Cherokee Indians—whereby all the *above* Tract, was guaranteed to *them* for their hunting grounds— and those Citizens who had Setled were removed, and others who were about to Settle were prevented—Thus the property of a Very considerable number of good Citizens—(many of whom had Ventured their all in the purchase) was taken from them for the Use of the United States— and they have ever Since been deprived thereof, without any Compensation haveing ever been made—Petitions have Several times been presented to Congress, by the Claimants of those lands—and Several reports have been made in their favor—and in no instance (as we have been inform'd) hath the Justice of their claim been questiond by Congress—we are Authorisd to Say, that many Original holders of *Certificates*, who became purchasers, in expectation of Obtaining immediate possession of their lands—and being peaceably continued therein; have by the treaty of Holston been reduced to extreme indigence—

We anxiously hope that the foregoing Considerations in adition to those heretofore exhibited to the President will induce him, to direct the treaty to be holden—

With Sentiments of the highest Consideration we are Sir most respectfully your Obt Servts   JOS: ANDERSON
                                                          WM COCKE

The Citizens of North Carolina, being also much interested in the extinguishment of the Indian Claims to the lands lying in the wilderness—The Senators from that State, wish one of their Citizens may be appointed a Commissioner—They have accordingly requested us to Mention—Willie Jones—and William Richardson Divie—either of whom—they will be Satisfyd with—we wish Colonel Alexander Outlaw of the County of Jefferson in East Tennessee, and General James Robertson of Nashville in West Tennessee—to be appointed—in the event of holding the Treaty—Those gentlemen we believe, wou'd give as entire Satisfaction to all those interested, and also to the United States—as perhaps, any other Characters that we cou'd name— JOS: ANDERSON

WM COCKE

RC (DLC); in Anderson's hand, signed by him and Cocke; addressed: "The President of the United States"; endorsed by TJ as received on the same day as written and so recorded in SJL.

In June TJ named William R. Davie a COMMISSIONER for the new negotiation with the Cherokees, but Davie declined and Andrew Pickens took his place (ASP, *Indian Affairs*, 1:649-50).

From Abraham Baldwin and Benjamin Taliaferro

SIR, Washington March 5th. 1801

By the treaty between the United States and the Creek Indians at New York in the year 1790 the County of Tallisee, on the frontier of the State of Georgia, was ceded to the Creek Indians, as the only condition on which a treaty could be effected; this measure occasioned great uneasiness and alarm to the citizens of that State, both on account of the principle on which it was founded, and the special injuries which attended its application to that case.

The present settlements of Georgia are, a stripe up and down the Savannah river, which divides it from South Carolina, from its mouth to its source; and at right angles with it, another stripe, along the Sea coast to Florida, from 30 to 40 Miles wide, to the mouth of St. Mary's river, which divides it from Florida, as the line was run before the revolution, in some measure in shape of a Carpenters work square, the hollow of the square being all Indian County.

Since the Treaty concluded with the Indians, at the close of the revolution, the only land which that State has attempted to purchase of the Indians, is this hollow square, by which the frontier line of the State would be considerably shortened, and the Indians thrown back from Savannah and the first settled parts of the State. This purchase was effected in the year 1786, at the Treaty of Shoulderbone, and laid out into a County called Tallassee. There was as little complaint respecting that purchase as of any purchase made of Indians, and it was afterwards fully approved by General Lincoln Colo. Humphreys & Judge Griffin Commissioners of the United States, who with much labour and diligence examined into those transactions on the spot, at a meeting with the Indians on that frontier, as will be seen by their report (see Vol. 1st. of Confidential communications from the department of War to the House of Representatives).

When the County was given back to the Indians, and they let down again into that hollow square, by which the whole State was once more made a frontier line, it was scarcely possible to prevent outrageous tumult and disorder, and this was principally effected by the strongest assurances from the general Government that these evils should very soon be removed, that the most effective negotiations should be immediately commenced, which should avail themselves of the first moment of tranquility among the Indians, when there should be any prospect of success, in forming another treaty with them. Applications to the president were repeated and assurances given, till, nothing being done, and the people worn out with their disappointment the Legislature of the State at their Session in January 1797 addressed a memorial and remonstrance on the subject to the president and to Congress. This was referred to a Committee consisting of Thomas Pinkney Abraham Venable & Nathl Smith who made a favourable report, stating all the facts which are above mentioned. this report has been inclosed to the president seven or eight times, the last of them on the 4th of December last, we would now inclose another but we are not able to find one: the resolution of the house, confirming that report, is in the journals of the third Session of the fifth Congress page 136. and the Law for carrying it into effect is in the fourth Volume of Laws Page 256. Since the passage of this law, the subject has been pursued unremittingly by those who have represented the State in Congress, and to this time it has never been in their power to obtain a single line in writing to return to the Legislature of that State, to let them know whether any thing has been done, or is in contemplation, to carry into effect the law founded on their memorial and remonstrance. we have been deeply sensible of the disrespect to the Legislature of a State on a subject vastly interesting to its citizens, which we should not have expected would have been shewn to the common application of an individual.

In our repeated calls at the War Office we have been shewn letters said to have been sent to Colo Hawkins, the agent of the United States among the Creeks, but we have never been able to obtain copies of any of them to send to the Legislature, we have observed with regreat that there has been from the first a studied system of evasion on this subject.

Not long before we left home we were repeatedly assured by persons who had lately seen Colo Hawkins, that he had never received any letter or instruction from the president on that subject, that should he receive such instructions he believed there would be no difficulty in accomplishing that object, that since the establishment of public stores there the Indians had become greatly indebted, and were much alarmed for fear no more goods would be sent till they had made payment, that they said they had no other way of making payment unless they did it in land and he had no doubt they would be willing to give up the Tallasee and the fork adjoining it called Oakmulgee fork; this fork is become of no importance to the Indians for hunting ground, it has long since ceased to be a range for game; it will be very desirable to obtain it as some gratification to the people on that frontier for their long disappointment respecting Tallasee County.

Should Colo Hawkins be made fully acquainted with all the foregoing circumstances, and the interest which the general Government should take in getting possession of Tallasee County and the Oakmulgee fork, we can entertain no doubt but he would be able to accomplish it in the course of the summer, and nothing would be more gratifying to the people of that State in general. Where there is so great an extent of Indian Country, and the settlement of the whites along the line has been thickening for twenty years, and rendered much more inconvenient by the disappointment of the prospects of those who had removed to settle themselves in Tallassee County, the experience of no part of the frontier Country will warrant an expectation, that they can without great difficulty, be much longer kept in a state of tranquility.

With great respect we are Sir. Your Obt Servts.

ABR BALDWIN
BEN. TALIAFERRO

RC (DLC); in Taliaferro's hand, signed by him and Baldwin; closing parenthesis supplied; endorsed by TJ as received 7 Mch. and so recorded in SJL.

Benjamin Taliaferro (1750-1821), who was born and grew up in Virginia, settled in Georgia in 1785. He represented his adoptive state in Congress, 1799-1802. Baldwin was one of the state's U.S. senators (*Biog. Dir. Cong.*).

The treaty at NEW YORK in 1790 between the United States and Creek chiefs led by Alexander McGillivray is printed in ASP, *Indian Affairs*, 1:81-2. The treaty made at the CLOSE OF THE REVOLUTION was a November 1783 agreement between the Creeks and the state of Georgia. Three years later McGillivray influenced most of the tribe to stay away from talks with state commissioners at SHOULDERBONE Creek. Information gathered by Benjamin Lincoln, David Humphreys, and Cyrus Griffin as COMMISSIONERS OF THE UNITED STATES to the southern tribes was part of a CONFIDENTIAL communication of documents to Congress by George Washington in January 1790 (same, 15, 23-4, 59, 65-80; John Walton Caughey, *McGillivray of the Creeks* [Norman, Okla., 1938], 31-2, 129-30, 138-9).

Congress received the MEMORIAL AND REMONSTRANCE of the Georgia legislature late in November 1797. The plea asked for revision of existing U.S. treaties with the Creeks and of an act of 19 May 1796 that specified the boundary of Indian territory on the frontier, restricted access to that territory, and prohibited the acquisition of land from Indian tribes except in conjunction with treaties made under the authority of the U.S. The Georgia memorial also requested confirmation of a tract of land

and payment of losses. On 3 May 1798 the committee of the House of Representatives made its report, which was not considered by the whole House until the end of the year. On 1 Feb. 1799, rejecting a proposal to compensate the state for damages related to the cession of land to the Creeks under the 1790 treaty, the House resolved to fund a new treaty that would give Georgia possession of land in the county of Tallassee or an equivalent tract. A LAW approved on 19 Feb. 1799 appropriated up to $25,000 for the expense of a treaty, "*Provided*, nothing in this act contained shall be construed to admit an obligation on the part of the United States to extinguish, for the benefit of any state or individual citizen, Indian claims to any lands lying within the limits of the United States" (JHR, 3:95, 285, 418, 423, 460-1, 467, 475-6, 480, 484; JS, 2:412; U.S. Statutes at Large, 1:469-74, 618).

From William Findley

SIR   Greencastle March 5th 1801

After the freedom I have used in writing to you under cover to Mr Gregg a few days Since, the present attempt might Justly require an apology. The confidence I have of your good nature and of your favourable[1] opinion of my intentions, is however the only apollogy I shall make free to offer

Since the State Legislature adjourned I have travailed through several of the most oppulent Counties of pennsylvania and conversed with a Number of the best Informed, Influential and stedfast republican characters and all of them are not only convinced of the Necessity of a thorough change in the postoffice department, but also in all the offices of the internal revenue. They all agree with me in opinion that the opposition to the Excise Law chiefly if not solely originated from the contempt in which the character of the persons appointed to fill these offices has always been held and from their indiscretion in office. For the truth of this were it necessary to make an appeal, I might appeal to Mr Ross of the Senate. He applied to me when he came into Senate to assist in procuring a general change. I declined the proposal untill we had time to know and procure more suitable characters, before that could be done an insurrection was Artfully promoted, when the opposition ceased the president thought it improper to change the officers who had been insulted untill they would for a time enjoy their offices in quietness

It was a Serious misfortune that the prejudices against the Excise Law detered good Men from soliciting or even accepting of appointments under it and encouraged the most obnoxious and improper Characters to push themselves into office. That no change should have been urged during the late Administration is easeily accounted for. The expectation of a Revision now however is general and I believe necessary. The great risk is of not supplying vacancys with persons Sufficiently capable and respectable. On this head my experience has made me perhaps too anxious.

The most respectable citizens are now however willing to accept of Such offices and Solicitous to obtain them,

probably at present it is necessary to mention or think of a person to fill the highest place under the Excise Laws. There is no difference of opinion among any sensible Man of any party with[2] whom I have ever conversed with respect to the unfitness and I might add unworthiness of Mr Miller for that trust. perhaps there may however be many Applicants for the place and those may be all good Men and yet not equally fit for the duties of that office.

proposing a proper Candidate is a delicate thing and the attempt perhaps too assuming, but in doing it probably my long and extensive acquaintance in this state may be admitted as an Excuse. Genl. Wm. Irwine of Carlisle is believed by all with whom I have conversed on the Subject to be a[3] proper character for the office of Supervisor: his temperance and integrity are examplery. He having been long considered by a large proportion of the Citizens as a Suitable Candidate for the government would certainly present him in a respectable point of view for this office. I can assure you Sir, that it was the difference of Opinion or perhaps the difference of interests between him and Mr P. Muhlenberg a Citizen of great respectability that made way for the Election of Govr Mc.Kean. Genl Irwins turn of mind and habits of Life seem to quallify him for the office and his very extensive Aquaintance through the whole State aquired by the prominent public trusts which he has discharged with unimpeached fidelity will render his appointment popular, and his having become obnoxious to a Certain Class of Citizens on the account of his Republican principles and his perservering endeavors to promote the Election of an Anti-Anglo president Merits some Consideration.

Untill the first officer in this department be determined it is not necessary to Mention Candidates for the Subordinate offices. private business and visiting friends having took me of my usual rout to my family and enlarged my opportunity of information I have made free to write this in haste and not without Confession: I am with the most unfeigned esteem and the most Sincere wishes for your personal and official prosperity,

Your most obedient and very humble servt,   WM FINDLEY

RC (DNA: RG 59, LAR); addressed: "Thomas Jefferson, president of the United States"; franked; postmarked 7 Mch.; endorsed by TJ as received 14 Mch. and so recorded in SJL; TJ later canceled "Findley Wm." and added "Irwine Genl." to the endorsement.

TJ appointed William Irvine superintendent of military stores in Philadelphia (see Thomas McKean to TJ, 10 Jan. 1801).

[1] Word interlined.
[2] MS: "with with."
[3] Word interlined in place of "the most."

From Nicholas King and Others

SIR,   March 5. 1801

Among the Magistrates to be appointed for this District, of Columbia, it would be pleasing to many of our fellow Citizens in Washington to see the name of Benjamin More.—A man whose industry, talent, and integrity, we are persuaded will enable him to discharge the duties of that station with honor to himself, and advantage to society.

We are sir with respect Yours &ca.   NICHS. KING
                                          W M DUNCANSON
                                          BENJ GRAYSON ORR
                                          CORNS CONNINGHAM
                                          JOHN OAKLEY
                                          WM BRENT

RC (DNA: RG 59, LAR); in King's hand, signed by all; at head of text: "The President of the U.S."; endorsed by TJ as received 6 Mch. but recorded in SJL at the 7th; TJ later canceled "King Nichs. & others" and added "More Benjamin to be justice" to the endorsement.

BENJAMIN MORE, the founding editor of the short-lived *Washington Gazette* from 1796 to 1798, was included in a 5 Mch. entry on TJ's list of appointments along with 14 others as justice of the peace for Washington County (Appendix I, List 4; Brigham, *American Newspapers*, 1:102; JEP, 1:404, 417).

To Philippe de Létombe

DEAR SIR   Washington Mar. 5. 1801.

The kindness and effect with which you have been so good as to exert yourself in procuring me a Maitre d'Hotel require and recieve my friendly thanks to you. I accede to the proposition to recieve the man you speak of and his wife at the annual wages of one hundred guineas. I should be glad to recieve him as soon as possible. his wife may come at her leisure, as I shall probably leave this place in a fortnight to be absent 3. or 4. weeks, & it would be only on my return that I should wish to find every thing prepared for regular housekeeping.

I recieve with great sensibility your congratulations on my election to the Presidency. I feel a great load of public favor & of public expectation. more confidence is placed in me than my qualifications merit, and I dread the disappointment of my friends who have suffered themselves to [count?] on me for too much. I am sorry that in the moment of my coming into place, we are to lose the benefit of your friendly agency in preserving harmony & friendship between the two nations. it is a disposition equally precious to the country employing you as to that in which you are employed. may your return to your own country be prosperous, and your future days be filled with honour, health, & happiness. accept assurances of my high consideration & esteem, and that they will attend you wherever you go.

                                                    TH: JEFFERSON

PrC (MHi); blurred; at foot of text: "Citizen Le Tombe"; endorsed by TJ in ink on verso.

To Levi Lincoln

SIR   Washington Mar. 5. 1801.

in pursuance of the act of Congress providing that in case of vacancy in the office of Secretary of state the President of the US. may authorize a person to perform the duties of the same, I am to ask the favor of you & hereby authorize you to perform the duties of the Secretary of state until a successor to the office shall be appointed. I have the honor to be Sir

your most obedt. servt   TH: JEFFERSON

PrC (DLC); at foot of text: "Levi Lincoln esq."

Levi Lincoln (1749-1820), a Massachusetts lawyer, Harvard graduate, and veteran of the Revolutionary War, became increasingly active in state and national politics and won a congressional seat in 1800 after a bitter contest to replace Dwight Foster. Lincoln resigned this seat when TJ appointed him attorney general and ad interim secretary of state because of the delayed arrival of James Madison to the Federal City. Lincoln attacked the political activities of the clergy in his *Letters to the People. By a Farmer* (Salem, 1802; Sowerby, No. 3442). He resigned as attorney general at the end of TJ's first term and returned to Massachusetts politics, where he was elected to the Governor's Council, served as lieutenant governor, and became governor in 1808. Upon refusing a nomination by President Madison to the U.S. Supreme Court in 1812, he spent his final years on his Worcester farm (ANB; DAB; Malone, *Jefferson*, 4:34; *Biog. Dir. Cong.*).

ACT OF CONGRESS: see John Marshall to TJ, 2 Mch.

Receipt from John Minchin

March 5th 1801   Bot. of John Minchin

One pair of Shoes	3.
One ditto Silk Strings	.25
One ditto Bootees	6. $9. $\frac{25}{166}$
Received payment infull	

JOHN MINCHIN

MS (MHi); in Minchin's hand and signed by him; at head of text: "His Excellency Thos. Jefferson, President of the United States"; with order in TJ's hand at foot of text: "Mr. Barnes will be pleased to pay the above. Th: Jefferson."

John Minchin, a boot and shoe manufacturer in Philadelphia in the late 1790s, moved to New Jersey Avenue near the Capitol in Washington in 1801, and TJ continued to place orders with him (*National Intelligencer*, 7 Jan. 1801; MB, 2:984; Vol. 31:77).

RECEIVED PAYMENT INFULL: in his financial accounts, TJ noted that on 5 Mch. he gave Minchin an order on John Barnes for $9.25 (MB, 2:1035).

On 27 Mch. 1801, Minchin gave TJ another receipt for payment in full for one pair of shoes at $3, a pair of silk strings for 25 cents, and "To Straping a pr. Boot tops ommitted" an additional 25 cents, for a total charge of $3.50. In his financial records, TJ noted that on 25 Mch. he paid Minchin $3.50 for a pair of shoes (MS in MHi, in Minchin's hand and signed by him, endorsed by TJ on verso as paid on 26 Mch.; MB, 2:1036). Three days later Minchin gave TJ another receipt for the payment in full of $2 for the purchase of "One pair of Boot tops with side and back Straps." TJ recorded the transaction in his financial records at 31 Mch. (MS in same, in Minchin's hand and signed by him, endorsed by TJ on verso as paid; MB, 2:1036). On 19 Nov., Minchin gave TJ a receipt for the payment of $1.50 for six pairs of silk shoe strings (MS in same, in Minchin's hand and signed by him, endorsed by TJ on verso; MB, 2:1059).

From James Monroe

DEAR SIR   Richmond 5. March 1801.

Permit me to present to yr. acquaintance the bearer Mr. Voss of Culpepper county, a young man of merit, who has expressd a wish of being personally known to you. He is a lawyer by profession, of respectable standing at the bar, and a fair prospect of becoming eminent if he pursues his profession. He intends making a visit this spring to the south, and hearing that it is proposed to adjust the boundary line between the UStates and Georgia, wishes to be employed in that service. I am not acquainted with Mr. Voss's proficiency in the mathematicks, but am persuaded he wod. not accept the trust if he did not think himself competent to the discharge of its duties. with great respect & esteem I am Dear Sir yr. obt. servt.   JAS. MONROE

RC (DLC); endorsed by TJ as received 11 Mch. and so recorded in SJL, where TJ noted that he received it from Robert B. Voss along with John Strode's letter of 26 Feb.

Voss apparently anticipated either the potential negotiations with Indian tribes on the southwestern frontier or the adjustment of territorial claims between GEORGIA and the United States under an act of Congress of 10 May 1800 (U.S. Statutes at Large, 1:549-50; 2:69-70; Vol. 31:547, 549n).

Notes on New Jersey Patronage

[ca. 5 Mch.-before June 1801]

George Maxwell Atty for N. Jersey vice Stockdon resd & Frelinghuysen.
Oliver Barnet vice Lowry who is expected to resign for Marshall recommdd. by mr Linn, who says Condit and Kitchell concurred

---

John Hurd (a Brigadr. genl of militia horse) of Middlesex county to be collector (qu.) of the port of Amboy, vice
    Bell a refugee officer who was aid to Genl Carlton, fought agt us during the whole war.
    Judge Patterson's first wife was Bell's sister.
Hurd was a capt of horse with us during the whole war, good officer, much respected, a good republican.

Dunham, supervisor, a very immoral profligate man, complained of in mr Adams's time, & would have been removed if they could have agreed on a successor. it is believed he is delinquent in his accounts; & that there are papers in the Treasury office against him.

MS (DNA: RG 59, LAR, 1:0665); undated; entirely in TJ's hand, probably written at three sittings, as indicated by the horizontal rules, the first entries dating from early March; endorsed by TJ: "New Jersey Attorney Marshall."

Before he left Washington in early March, James Linn recommended GEORGE MAXWELL as district attorney and Dr. OLIVER BARNET as marshal for New Jersey. In April, Linn wrote Peter Muhlenberg that at the urging of New Jersey Representatives John CONDIT and Aaron KITCHELL, he had mentioned the two candidates to the president, and Republicans in the state were anxiously awaiting the appointments (*Biog. Dir. Cong.*; Linn to Muhlenberg, 20 Apr. 1801, in DNA: RG 59, LAR; Linn to TJ, 1 May). Maxwell received his appointment on 26 June, but Barnet did not receive his for another year as it became intertwined with the appointment of John Heard (HURD). According to his lists of appointments and removals, TJ named Heard marshal of New Jersey in place of Thomas Lowry, "removed for high federalism," on 28 Mch. At a 17 May Cabinet meeting, however, Heard was designated to be COLLECTOR at Perth Amboy in place of Andrew Bell, and the next day Gallatin requested, but did not receive, a commission for him. This did not hinder Daniel Marsh, a member of the state executive council, from traveling to Washington in June and returning with the commission as collector of the New Jersey port, although Gallatin reminded the president that Heard had been recommended for the position. In the confusion Heard had not received his commission as marshal either. In August Burr and others became concerned that without the commission Heard would be unable "to discharge the duties at the approaching Court." For the president's uncertainty about Heard's appointment and deliberate delays in sending the commission, see TJ to Gallatin, 21 Aug. 1801. Heard finally replaced Lowry after the meeting of the court and served as marshal until Marsh's death in April 1802. Heard then became collector and Barnet became marshal as originally proposed in the document above (Carl E. Prince, *New Jersey's Jeffersonian Republicans: The Genesis of an Early Party Machine, 1789-1817* [Chapel Hill, 1964], 237-8; Madison, *Papers, Sec. of State Ser.*, 1:193-4, 362; Kline, *Burr*, 2:613-14; JEP, 1:403, 432; Appendix I, Lists 3 and 4; Gallatin to TJ, 3 June 1801; TJ to Madison, 28 Aug. 1801; Heard to TJ, 29 Apr. 1802).

Andrew BELL'S SISTER Cornelia married William Paterson in 1779 (ANB, 17:120).

In a letter to Burr dated 8 Apr., Joseph Bloomfield noted that Oliver Wolcott, Jr., proposed to remove Aaron DUNHAM for intemperance. He remained in office because Wolcott and Adams could not agree upon a successor. Bloomfield also noted that "Dunham threatned his Deputys with removal, if they presumed to favor the Democratic interest." Burr forwarded Bloomfield's letter to TJ and the president endorsed it as received 29 Apr. On 6 June TJ removed Dunham "for habitual drunkeness" (Kline, *Burr*, 1:555-8; Appendix I, List 4). For the appointment of Linn as supervisor in place of Dunham, see Linn to TJ, 24 Mch.

From John Page

Rosewell March 5th. 1801

I received, my dear Jefferson, yours of the 12th. Ultimo after its circuitous Rout through the Post Roads to Richmond, & thence by the Weekly Post-cross-Road to Gloucester Court House, where I suppose it arrived eight days later than it would have arrived had it not reached Richmond after the Gloucester weekly mail had been closed, or sent off. I mention these Circumstances as an Explanation of the Delay of my Acknowledgment of the Receipt of your Favor.

I am much pleased with Paine's Compact maritime which as happily exposes to the Abhorrence of the World "*the Jacobinism of the English, at Sea*," as his Common Sense did to the United Colonies, the Absurdity of submitting to the british Government, or of ever living under a monarchical form of Government; & which I trust will go as far towards establishing "the *Association of Nations*" proposed therein as his Common Sense did, to establish the Confederation of the *Ud. Ss.* And I am as much displeased, with the Conduct of the insolent Faction in the House of Representatives—They have now given the last & damning Proof of their base & perfidious Designs— They have now demonstrated to the World, their deep rooted Aversion to republican Principles; their utter Contempt of the Opinions & Wishes of the People, & their Eagerness to prove this to the Tools of that detestable Government, for a shamefully intimate Connexion with which, they have long impatiently sighed. But their Friends in Britain will despise them for the contemptible manner in which they attempted to accomplish their Wishes; & for their Folly, in so fruitless a manner exposing to the Republican World the Influence of Britain, which, at this time above all others, unless sure of success, ought to be concealed from Republicans, & even from the Monarchies which have been induced by her Treachery Intrigues & Insolence to hate her Cordially. Their Tools in the *Ud. Ss.* are astonished at their Rashness, & many of their best Friends give them up to the Censure they deserve; whilst nothing but the calm & dispassionate Spirit of the American People, & the benign Influence of pure republican Principles, have saved them from the severest Chastisement, & even utter Destruction, amidst the Tumults & Confusion which *they* seemed anxious to excite, that they might at least prove in some sort the Truth of a favorite Assertion of the Enemies of representative Governments; I mean, that interesting Elections can not be fairly conducted; or ever decided against the wish of a Party, without Violence, & outrages dangerous to the Existence of Government. And sure I am that the Friends of Man throughout the World will hate them, & Posterity will execrate their Memory. They, in their eagerness to grasp at the Shadow have lost the Substance. Their Power & Influence is gone forever—a divine Infatuation seems to have seized on them & on all the Enemies of Man at the same time & will lead them to their merited Destruction. Some of my Friends however, fear that *they* will say with Milton's fallen Angels
"We neither repent nor change
  What though the Field be lost
All is not lost; th'unconquerable will,

And Study of Revenge, immortal hate,
And Courage never to submit or yield."
    But happily, I think, we may say, that they can not proceed, & say with those congenial Spirits,
    "And what is else, not to be overcome;
     That glory never shall success, or might
     Extort from us."
But you have had enough of these Devils.
You will probably see in an Examiner next Week, an account of our rejoycings at Gloucester Court House yesterday, as the day of your Inauguration; as the Commencement of a new Æra, or the day of the Revival of Republicanism, & of the Death of the Sedition Act, that detestable Act which converted the Heads of Departments, Supervisors, Marshals Collectors, Postmasters & God knows how many more of a long Train into State Inquisitors, & made the federal Judges in fact Licensers of the American Press.
In my last, I presented my hearty Congratulations, & added what I am ashamed to allude to, & what as I suppose it reached you, I need not recapitulate.
I will trouble you no longer at present, but conclude like a Republican—
    Health & Fraternity—   JOHN PAGE

RC (DLC); extraneous quotation marks omitted; addressed: "Thos. Jefferson President of the United States at the City of Washington"; endorsed by TJ as received 14 Mch. and so recorded in SJL.

YOURS OF THE 12TH. ULTIMO: see TJ's letters reporting on the balloting in the House of Representatives, printed as a group at 12 Feb. 1801. The one sent to Page has not been found. With each of those letters TJ sent a copy of Thomas PAINE's recent essays on neutrality, published together in the United States as a tract called *Compact Maritime*. Paine titled one of the pieces "On the Jacobinism of the English at Sea" (Paine to TJ, 1 Oct. 1800).

SAY WITH MILTON'S FALLEN ANGELS: Page quoted with some modification lines 96 and 105-111 of the first book of *Paradise Lost*. He gave Satan's expressions, which in the poem are singular, plural form and substituted "success" for "his wrath."

Page's last letter, dated 1 Feb. but now missing, contained CONGRATULATIONS and recommended Page and Thomas Tudor Tucker for positions in the U.S. Mint; see TJ's entry in Appendix I, List 1, and TJ to Page, 23 Mch.

From Charles Pinckney

DEAR SIR   March 5: 1801—George Town
    I recollect before I left Carolina I requested you by letter not to make any arrangements or take any step respecting that State until I had seen you as I had some opinions & information to communicate on that subject—

On reflection since, I have been induced to suppose that this request on my part was an improper one, & that I ought not to presume so far as to wish to intrude on you my opinions on state arrangements, or any other subjects, even as they respect South Carolina.—I therefore intreat, You *will not recollect such* a request has ever been made *by me.*—motives of delicacy & unfeigned respect for you make this request proper on my part before I leave Georgetown.—

From the difficulty of obtaining such a conveyance either by land or water from hence as is convenient I am afraid I shall be detained some days—if in the interim Mr Madison for whom I have had unchangeable respect & friendship should arrive I will be particularly obliged to you to ask him to inform me of it that I may have an opportunity of seeing him before I go—

If you remain here as long as I do I will do myself the honour of paying my respects to You before I set out & with my most sincere wishes for Your health & honour & success in the administration I remain with respect & regard

Dear Sir Your's truly · · · · · · · · · · · · · · CHARLES PINCKNEY

RC (DLC); endorsed by TJ as received 6 Mch. and so recorded in SJL.

In a postscript to his letter printed at 3 Dec. 1800 Pinckney noted that he was collecting "a Body of information" for TJ's use and REQUESTED that ARRANGEMENTS for appointments in South Carolina be postponed until he arrived in Washington. Pinckney repeated the request in letters to TJ of 20 Dec. and 8 Jan. 1801. In the former he noted that he had information important to the Republican interest in his state, which he did not "choose to commit to Paper."

From Providence Citizens

SIR · Providence (RI) 5th March 1801

Permit us in behalf of a number of respectable Citizens of this Town to offer to you our sincere congratulations on your elevation to the first magistracy of the United States—

Persuaded as we are that a government *entirely* elective is alone consistent with the dignity of man—best calculated to promote his happiness & exclusively adapted to the genius—habits & situation of the People of the United States, it is with no common joy we behold at the head of the american administration a man whose uniform political integrity—whose correct & extensive information & affectionate concern for the happiness of the human race will add to the splendour & secure the stability of our favorite system—

Friends to the great leading principles of our constitution we expect with confidence that during your administration there will be given to that constitution the safe & honest meaning only which was contemplated by the plain understanding of the People of the United States at the time of its adoption—

From the humane & magnanimous policy, which Your conduct & character through life authorize us to beleive you will pursue, we have no apprehension of war from narrow or party policy; but delight in looking forward to the cultivation of universal peace—& liberal intercourse with all the nations of the world—

Thus reposing with equal security on the strength of your abilities & the goodness of your heart—we doubt not that your administration will dispel all artificial terror—revive mutual confidence & affection among our fellow citizens—promote the prosperity of our Country & advance the general felicity & perfection of man—

Accept our warmest wishes for your health & personal happiness & beleive us to be

With sentiments of the most profound respect, Sir, Your Friends & Affectionate Fellow Citizens
    SAMUEL EDDY
    JONA. RUSSELL
    SAML. THURBER JUNR.
    LEVI WHEATON
    HENRY SMITH

RC (DCL); in Russell's hand, signed by all; at foot of text: "Thomas Jefferson President of the United States"; endorsed by TJ as received 25 Mch. and so recorded in SJL. Enclosed in Samuel L. Mitchill to TJ, 21 Mch. 1801 (see note below).

Being unable to deliver this address to TJ in person as expected by the signer who had sent it to him, New York City Congressman Samuel L. Mitchill enclosed it in a letter to TJ on 21 Mch. Mitchill identified Samuel Eddy as the secretary of state of Rhode Island, Levi Wheaton as the former clerk of Hudson, New York, and the other three signers as reputable merchants in Providence (RC in DLC; addressed: "Thomas Jefferson President of the United States Washington—City; franked and postmarked; endorsed by TJ as received 25 Mch. and so recorded in SJL).

To the Senate

GENTLEMEN OF THE SENATE   March 5. 1801.

The offices of Secretary of state, Secretary of war, Attorney general of the United States, and Minister plenipotentiary to the republic of France being vacant, I nominate the following persons to them
James Madison junr. of Virginia, to be Secretary of State:
Henry Dearborn of Massachusets to be Secretary of War:

Levi Lincoln of Massachusets to be Attorney General of the United States:

Robert R. Livingston, of New York to be Minister Plenipotentiary for the United States to the republic of France.

TH: JEFFERSON

MS (DNA: RG 46, PMEN); entirely in TJ's hand, with date emended from "4" to "5" Mch. by TJ; endorsed. PrC (DLC).

I NOMINATE: Jacob Wagner carried TJ's first executive message on nomina-

tions to the Senate on 5 Mch. The Senate immediately consented to the appointments and, upon finding that the president had no other communications for them, adjourned (JEP, 1:395-6).

From John R. Smith

SIR   Philada. March 5th. 1801.

It being more agreeable to the feelings of Mr. Caldwell, to whom the enclosed papers relate, to present them in person than through the usual official channels, I have at his request Sir, taken the liberty of introducing his name to you.

The lapse of time & the consequent alterations produced by it in the person, would otherwise perhaps prevent your recollecting in him Sir the adopted son of the Marquis De la Fayette, under whose protection he had sometimes the honor of meeting you during your residence in France.

Be pleased Sir to excuse the liberty here taken, which would not indeed have been assumed had not the writer from his professional concerns with Mr. Caldwell had the most satisfactory proofs of that personal worth & capacity set forth in the respectable testimonials accompanying his present application.

With sentiments of the highest deference & respect I have the honor to be Sir your very obed: Servt: JNO: R: SMITH

RC (DNA: RG 59, LAR); at foot of text: "Thomas Jefferson Esquire"; endorsed by TJ as received 11 Mch. and so recorded in SJL. Enclosures: possibly a memorial or other papers from Elias Boudinot and Benjamin Rush, 21 Feb., not found, not listed in SJL, recommending John Edwards Caldwell for a consulship in the West Indies; see entries for Caldwell in Appendix I, List 1.

John R. Smith was a Philadelphia attorney and a brother of Samuel Harri-

son Smith (Stafford, *Philadelphia Directory, for 1801*, 29; *Martin's Bench and Bar*, 312; William E. Ames, *A History of the National Intelligencer* [Chapel Hill, 1972], 16-17).

When Lafayette returned to France from a visit to the United States in 1784, at the request of former Continental Army officers he took with him John Edwards CALDWELL, the fourteen-year-old orphan of a Revolutionary War chaplain. In Paris, Lafayette enrolled Caldwell, a Protestant, in a Benedictine school attended by Crèvecoeur's sons, and with some effort the marquis obtained the youth's release from the school's Catholic religious services. Caldwell returned to the United States about 1787. In June 1801 TJ named Caldwell, whose residence was then in New Jersey, commer- cial agent for the city of Santo Domingo. The following January the Senate confirmed that recess appointment (Harlow Giles Unger, *Lafayette* [Hoboken, N.J., 2002], 203, 207-8, 226; Madison, *Papers, Sec. of State Ser.*, 1:346-7, 434; JEP, 1:401, 405).

From Edward Thornton

SIR,   Washington 5 March. 1801.

The voluntary expression of those sentiments of just and enlarged policy, which you were pleased to make me the organ of conveying to His Majesty's Government, encourages me to request a few moments' audience, on another subject no less important to the two countries.—

The Packet Boat, now lying at New York, will be dispatched in a few days to England; and the King's Ministers will naturally look forward with a degree of interest and expectation to the first advices, which they shall receive after your accession to the Chief Magistracy of the Union, relative to the points in discussion between Great Britain and America.—I allude particularly to the stipulations of the Sixth Article of the Treaty of 1794, the complete execution of which has been hitherto delayed by the suspension of the Board, appointed to carry them into effect.

I hope, Sir, you will forgive the liberty I take on this occasion, in consideration of the earnest solicitude I feel to become in any manner the humble instrument of preserving and consolidating the friendship which happily subsists between the two countries;—and I beg you to accept the assurances of the profound respect, with which I have the honour to be,

Sir, Your most obedient humble servant,   EDWD THORNTON.

RC (DNA: RG 59, NL); at foot of first page: "The President of the United States"; endorsed by TJ as received 5 Mch. and so recorded in SJL.

Edward Thornton (1766-1852) first came to the United States in 1791 as secretary to British minister George Hammond. He became the British vice consul in Maryland in 1793, then was made secretary to the British legation in 1796. Since November 1800 he had been the acting British chargé d'affaires following the departure of minister Robert Liston and he continued to act in this capacity until the arrival of British minister Anthony Merry in November 1803. Thornton went on to a distinguished diplomatic career, which culminated in his appointment as ambassador to Portugal in 1819 (DNB; Charles Lanman, *Biographical Annals of the Civil Government of the United States, During Its First Century* [Washington, 1876], 616; Vol. 26:398).

The SIXTH ARTICLE of the Jay Treaty involved the settlement of claims by British merchants against American debtors. After months of acrimonious negotiations, the bilateral BOARD established to arbitrate these claims dissolved in July 1799 (Vol. 30:624-5n).

From Joseph Anderson

SIR,   George Town 6th March 1801
    Having been inform'd that Allen McLane Collector of the Port of
Wilmington, in the State of Delaware intends resigning his office—
I have been requested to mention Major Peter Jaquet of the County
of New Castle—as a Candidate for that appointment—he Served as
an Officer in the Delaware Regiment, through the whole Revolutionary War—Supported a fair Character, and has never appostatized
from his *former* principles—Other recommendations will no doubt be
offer'd to the President in favour of Mr. Jaquet. I am with Sentiments
of very great Respect your mo obt Servt   JOS: ANDERSON

RC (DLC); endorsed by TJ as received 7 Mch. and so recorded in SJL.

George Washington nominated ALLEN MCLANE as collector for the port of Wilmington in 1797. McLane did not resign the post. Peter Jaquett served in the DELAWARE REGIMENT from 1776 to 1781, retiring at the rank of major by brevet (Washington, *Papers, Pres. Ser.*, 2:69; J. Thomas Scharf, *History of Delaware. 1609-1888*, 2 vols. [Philadelphia, 1888], 1:208, 2:842, 845; JEP, 1:228; Vol. 19:403).

From Abraham Baldwin

SIR   Washington March 6th. 1801
    Since our conversation on the administration of the department of
the Postmaster General, I have made it my business to trace to their
causes, as far as was in my power, the complaints which, I find, are so
industriously circulated against that officer.
1. I have no doubt there is an intrinsic difficulty in the discharge of
the duties of that department, so as to give any good degree of satisfaction. A few years ago there were but 60 or 70 post offices in the
U.S. They are now not less than a thousand offices: the contracts and
correspondence necessary to keep such a vast circulation clear, is
become extremely laborious. Every session there is added from three
to five thousand miles of new post road, and waggon-loads of news
papers besides very bulky mails of dispatches from the general stamp
office and the other public offices are required to be carried through
roads scarcely passable, and in many parts of the country where there
are neither ferries, bridges nor causeways. These causes have already
rendered very difficult, and seem likely soon to render impracticable
a speedy conveyance of letters and public dispatches through the
principal places of business in the United States. The complaint
and ill affection which is always consequent on any want of perfect

punctuality in the conveyance of the mails, and the accumulation of these for so many years, must render the situation of the most faithful and laborious officer very disagreeable, if he fails in meeting the approbation of those who are best able to know his merits it must be very discouraging. Though the consequences fall on the officer, yet the remedy is only in the legislature.

2. Many persons are trying to injure him from personal disgust. For several years I have known unceasing efforts used by individuals to prevail on him to dismiss Mr Patton of Philadelphia, the postmaster at Newport, at Albany and in several of the eastern towns, on account of their political principles: they were so necessary to his department, that he could not dispense with their services or supply their places: several members, whom I could name if it were necessary, have persecuted him ever since, both in public and in private, with the most unrelenting bitterness.

He has been obliged to interpose, on several occasions, to prevent the abuse of the power of franking, which has proved a most pernicious evil in other countries, and to check it here was made his indispensible duty: there are some singular facts under this head, which if it were necessary I would state, and which would explain some of the present appearances.

3. This office is a very good item in the distribution which so many, at present, are engaged in planning. If they will allow me too to put in a word on the occasion, this will probably be the only word I shall wish to put in. If I do not deceive myself, personal considerations have not much share in it; you must have observed, for several years, there has been no remarkable intimacy between us. Were I now to feel myself at entire liberty to search for a man, in our two southern states, to fill that office, I think there is no one, whom it would be my duty to name sooner than him. Other names have lately been mentioned, I know them well, and believe that, on trial, they will not be found to be more laborious, more faithful, or more upright and disinterested. These are the principal qualities to be regarded, for the duties of the office do not require distinguishing genius or talents. I have known few men in my life, in whose character I found more perfect security against any dishonorable or dishonest action.

At a very early period in his life it was his good fortune to find a road opened which placed him on very high ground, in relation to our Union and Independence. He is one of three sons of the President of the King's council in Georgia, who were born in Savannah. After a direction seemed to have been given to the public sentiment there not to join with the other states at the commencement of our revolution, he and a company of volunteers which he commanded, by their energy and zeal were principally instrumental in bringing that state to take a part in the revolution, and send members to congress. If I mistake not he commanded the first regiment raised in that state for the continental service: from that time till now, his character, in the first stations in our councils and in the field, has, with respect to the principles of our revolution, been without a blemish. These things are generally known in both those states, his connexions in both are among the most respectable. I believe there is no man who would be more likely to be acceptable to them in that office, or in whose disgrace they would feel a more lively sentiment.

I have also found that a suggestion is circulated, that he is possessed of a constitutional obstinacy of character which will render it difficult to reconcile the administration of the duties of that department to such general systems as may be thought necessary. I have made it my business to enquire into this, and find the causes from which it has originated: Attempts have been made to treat that department as if it was a mere subordinate branch of the treasury department, which he has uniformly resisted, on the ground that collection of revenue is not the leading trait in the character of his department, and that the expressions of the law constituting the Post office department do not favour such an opinion. Whenever the President of the United States thinks proper to visit and inspect the manner in which his office is conducted, and gives him any verbal direction, or sends him any notice of his will in writing, it is invariably a law to him. I do not hesitate to pledge myself and him to you on that head that you could not wish a more ready compliance than you will always find.

As I am under the necessity of being on my return home immediately after the adjournment of the Senate, I have thus loosely sketched these remarks, which were more particularly stated in our conversation, from an apprehension that they might otherwise have been overlooked, in the multiplicity of more important concerns now pressing for your attention.

If however it should be thought best that some other person should hold that office, I hope it will not be found inconvenient to delay the measure till towards autumn, that it may not be too intimately associated with the change of the Administration, so as to unite with other causes to lay a foundation which may fix a party in that state, and that the manner of the transition may, as far as possible, be rendered easy to his feelings.

I am very respectfully Sir, your obt Servt   ABR BALDWIN

RC (DNA: RG 59, LAR); at foot of text: "Thomas Jefferson President of the United States"; endorsed by TJ as received 7 Mch. and so recorded in SJL; also endorsed by TJ: "Habersham."

A statute of April 1800 had created a GENERAL STAMP OFFICE to distribute stamps to revenue officers for the collection of duties under the 1797 Stamp Act. Congress abolished the stamp tax and the office in April 1802 (U.S. Statutes at Large, 2:40-2, 148-50; see also John Garland Jefferson to TJ, 17 Jan. 1801).

Robert PATTON had been postmaster at Philadelphia since 1789, Jacob Richardson at NEWPORT since 1784, and George Mancius at ALBANY since 1792. Republicans accused them of intercepting or interfering with the mail for political motives (Stets, *Postmasters* 173, 224, 229; Prince, *Federalists*, 190-1; Syrett, *Hamilton*, 20:115-16, 149).

From Columbia, South Carolina, Citizens

SIR   Columbia South Carolina 6th. March 1801

We rejoice in common, with the rest of our republican fellow Citizens, that the Clouds which lately overshadowed our Country, are happily dispelled, and our political horison again exhibits a serene aspect, in consequence of your accession to the Presidential Chair— It is with difficulty that we can refrain from expressing our indignation, at the nefarious efforts, which have been made, to defeat your election, and destroy the ardent hopes of a free and enlightned People.

Never was there a more alarming and dangrous combination concerted to subvert a Constitution dictated by the Wisdom and resting on the will of the people, and to involve a beloved Country in all the horrors of civil discord;—but thanks to the Almighty disposer of events, the Scene is changed, and our Prospects are brightned

Relying Sir, on the wisdom, virtue and disinterestedness, which have invariably characterized your public conduct, we now look forward, with the pleasing expectation that the national Constitution, the boast of our Country, will be preserved inviolate—that the malignant spirit of faction, which has long convulsed the United States, will be completely extinguished and that peace safety and concord, will revisit our native Land, and be long enjoyed by a people zealously engaged, in the Pursuit of blessings so essential to the happiness of mankind—

That the Supreme Ruler of the Universe may long preserve you as a blessing to our Country, and direct you in the discharge of the momentous duties of your office, is Sir, our unfeigned and unanimous wish—

Signed by Order of the Meeting   BN: WARING Chairman
                                         C. CLARKE
                                         Secretary to the Meeting

RC (DLC); in an unidentified hand, signed by Waring and Clarke; at foot of text: "To Thomas Jefferson President of the United States"; endorsed by TJ as a letter from Waring received 20 Mch. so recorded in SJL with notation "for a no. of cit. of Columbia & it's vicinity S.C." Enclosure: Minutes of a 4 Mch. meeting of citizens of Columbia and its vicinity, which chose committees to prepare congratulatory addresses to TJ and Aaron Burr and reconvened the following day at the State House to report and direct Waring as chairman to sign and forward the addresses on behalf of the meeting (MS in same; in Clarke's hand, signed by Waring and Clarke; endorsed by TJ).

Benjamin Waring (1741-1811), a leading citizen of Columbia, was a planter who also operated a cottonseed oil mill, tanyard, and paper mill. During the Revolutionary War he served as a captain in Francis Marion's brigade. He also sat in the state senate from 1787 to 1788 (*S.C. Biographical Directory, Senate*, 3:1677-8; John Hammond Moore, *Columbia and Richland County: A South Carolina Community, 1740-1990* [Columbia, 1993], 72). Caleb Clarke (1777-1849) was a native of Maryland who came to South Carolina around 1800. He studied law in Charleston and Columbia, was admitted to the bar in 1805, and then practiced law in the town of Winnsboro and Lancaster and Chester districts. He represented Fairfield District in the General Assembly from 1810 to 1813 and served as a solicitor of the Court of General Sessions and Common Pleas from 1815 to 1824 (*S.C. Biographical Directory, House of Representatives*, 4:116-17).

From Thomas T. Davis

Dʀ Sɪʀ,   Washington March 6th 1801

Permit me to assure you, that my not paying you a visit before I left this place, did not proceed from a want of due respect to you, or to the high office you fill.—taking upon yourself a trust of great weight—rendered more difficult by conflicting political opinions; I concluded your mind must be engaged on subjects highly interresting; from which it would be, wrong in any friend, to toll it by a visit of cerimony—accept this as a manifestation, of the esteem and confidence of your obt. Sert.   Tʜᴏ. T. Davis

RC (DLC); endorsed by TJ as received 7 Mch. and so recorded in SJL.

From Jonathan Dayton
and Aaron Ogden

Sɪʀ,   Washington March 6th. 1801

The Judges of the Supreme Court of the State of New Jersey, informed of Mr. Stockton's resignation of the office of the U. States Attorney for that district, have drawn up & unanimously signed the enclosed certificate in favor of Isaac H. Williamson Esq. with the hope that it might promote his nomination to fill the vacancy. Prior to it's rect. the late President had nominated Mr. Frelinghuysen, who has since been approved by the Senate. As however it is not probable that this gentleman will accept, & as it has been expected & requested that we should address to the Chief Magistrate, this certificate in behalf of Mr. Williamson, we now take the liberty of doing it, & at the same time sir, of assuring you, that we join most fully in the recommendation of the Honorable bench of Justices, & shall feel very much gratified if it should prove successful.

FC (MiU-C: Jonathan Dayton Papers); in Dayton's hand; endorsed by Dayton: "From Jona: Dayton & Aaron Ogden to President Jefferson in favor of Isaac Williamson for District Atty." Recorded in SJL as received 7 Mch. from "Dayton & Ogden." Enclosure: Certificate from James Kinsey, Isaac Smith, Andrew Kirkpatrick, and Elisha Boudinot, justices of the New Jersey supreme court, at Trenton, dated 25 Feb. 1801, recommending Isaac H. Williamson, a New Jersey attorney, as "a young gentleman one of the first in reputation & standing at the bar, and of irreproachable private character" (FC in same; in Dayton's hand).

Both Federalists from New Jersey, Jonathan Dayton served in the Senate from 4 Mch. 1799 to 3 Mch. 1805 and Aaron Ogden from 28 Feb. 1801 to 3 Mch. 1803 (*Biog. Dir. Cong.*). For the appointment of George Maxwell as U.S. ATTORNEY for the New Jersey district, see Notes on New Jersey Patronage, printed at 5 Mch.

To John Dickinson

Dear Sir   Washington Mar. 6. 1801.

No pleasure can exceed that which I recieved from reading your letter of the 21st. ult. it was like the joy we expect in the mansions of the blessed, when recieved within the embraces of our fathers, we shall be welcomed with their blessing as having done our part not unworthily of them. the storm through which we have passed has been tremendous indeed. the tough sides of our Argosie have been thoroughly tried. her strength has stood the waves into which she was steered with a view to sink her. we shall put her on her republican tack, & she will now[1] shew by the beauty of her motion the skill of her builders. figure apart, our fellow citizens have been led hoodwinked from their principles by a most extraordinary combination of circumstances. but the band is removed, and they now see for themselves. I hope to see shortly a perfect consolidation, to effect which nothing shall be spared on my part, short of the abandonment of the principles of our revolution. a just & solid republican government maintained here, will be a standing monument & example for the aim & imitation of the people of other countries; and I join with you in the hope and belief that they will see from our example that a free government is of all others the most energetic, that the enquiry which has been excited among the mass of mankind by our revolution & it's consequences will ameliorate the condition of man over a great portion of the globe. what a satisfaction have we in the contemplation of the benevolent effects of our efforts, compared with those of the leaders on the other side, who have discountenanced all advances in science as dangerous innovations, have endeavored to render philosophy & republicanism terms of reproach, to persuade us that man cannot be governed but by the rod &c. I shall have the happiness of living & dying in the contrary hope. accept assurances of my constant & sincere respect & attachment, and my affectionate salutations.   TH: JEFFERSON

RC (PHi); signature torn away, but supplied from PrC; addressed: "John Dickinson Wilmington"; franked and postmarked. PrC (DLC).

¹ Word interlined.

From Albert Gallatin

SIR   Washington 6th March 1801

By an act intituled "An Act to amend the act intituled "An act providing for the sale of the lands of the United States, in the territory north west of the Ohio, and above the mouth of Kentucky river," passed 10th May 1800, it is provided, that the purchase money shall be paid in four equal payments, the first payable within 40 days & the three last within two, three & four years respectively after the day of sale; that interest at the rate of six per cent a year from the day of sale shall be charged upon each of the three last payments, payable as they respectively become due; and that "a discount at the rate of eight per cent a year, shall be allowed on any of the three last payments, which shall be paid before the same shall become due, *reckoning* this discount always upon the sum, which would have been demandable by the United States, on *the day* appointed for such payment" See Sect. 5 —

It is agreed that the sum demandable by the United States consists of the principal & interest to *that day*, & that the discount or deduction, in case of prompt payment, must be calculated on that aggregate sum; but it is understood that, by instructions of the Treasury department to the Receivers of public monies, these are directed, in order to ascertain the sum payable, in that case by the purchaser, to deduct the sum thus ascertained to be the discount, not from the sum demandable by the United States on the day appointed for payment, but from the principal sum alone.

As the clause of the law, in the shape in which it now stands, resulted from a Comee. of conference, of which I was a member, I am enabled to say that the intention of the Legislature was that the discount should be deducted from the sum demandable by the United States including principal & interest; and it appears to me to be the strict & litteral construction of the law.

According to this last principle the difference between the purchaser who makes prompt payment & the purchaser who pays only on the day appointed for payment is precisely at the rate of eight per cent a year: according to the principle said to have been assumed by the Treasury Departt., that difference appears to be at the rate of about $14\frac{1}{2}$ per cent a year.

A bill intended to have removed any existing doubts on that subject passed the House of Representatives during the last session, but being objected to by the Senate, & there not being time for a conference, was postponed on the 3d of March late in the night & eventually lost.

The discretionary powers vested by that law in the Treasury department, being limited, (Sect. 11) to the prescribing such further regulations, in the manner of *keeping* books & accounts by the several officers as may appear necessary; it may be doubtful whether the several receivers shall think themselves bound by instructions which regulate the mode of *settling* the accounts of purchasers. And, as the difference to the United States may, in the course of the present year, exceed 50,000 dollars, I have taken the liberty of stating those facts to you. It seems important that the true legal construction of the clause should be ascertained & known to the receivers as early as possible. The land offices at Steubenville & Marietta have been opened since July & the public sales at Cincinnati shall begin on the first Monday in April next. Those at Chilicothe which are the most important will commence on the first Monday in May next.

I have the honor to be with great respect Sir Your most obt. & he. Servt.   ALBERT GALLATIN

RC (DLC); addressed: "The President of the United States"; endorsed by TJ as received 6 Mch. from "Departmt of Treasury."

On 26 Sep. 1800 Oliver Wolcott, Jr., sent INSTRUCTIONS and forms to the land office RECEIVERS for implementation of the Land Act of 1800. The House passed a bill designed to remove ANY EXISTING DOUBTS about "the mode of calculating discounts in case of prompt payment" on 28 Feb. 1801 and sent it to the Senate (JHR, 3:833, 837; Terr. Papers, 3:111-13; Malcolm J. Rohrbough, The Land Office Business: The Settlement and Administration of American Public Lands, 1789-1837 [New York, 1968], 23).

From Robert R. Livingston

DEAR SIR   Albany 6th. March 1801.

I recd your favor of the 16th. ult. just as I was leaving New York
for this place which has delayed till now my acknowledging the distinguished attention you have shewn me in procuring for me the
honor of a place among the American philosophers. The moment you
chose for doing has not a little encreased the obligation, since it
was one in which the whole American world (except the man who
employed their thoughts) were absorbed in reflection upon the great
event which they considered as of the last importance to their political welfare. permit me to offer you my sincerest congratulation upon
its issue, & my hope that it may be as productive of happiness to you,
by extending the sphere of your utility, as I am persuaded that it will
be to the community that have reposed their confidence in you. I beg
leave thro' you to return my thanks to the philosophical society for
the honor they have done me, & to assure them that I shall endeavour
as opportunity may offer, to contribute my mite to the promotion of
the objects of their very useful institution.

This subject naturally leads to one, in which, I fear you have before
this charged me with negligence, I mean the answer to your inquiries
relative to the bones of the Mammouth; for such I believe them to be.

The fact is that I wrote long since to an intelligent friend at Shaw-
ongunk to know how far it might be practicable to procure them;
his answer was as I had expected. "That the owner did not chuse to
part with them untill he shd have made another effort to procure the
remainder, after which I should have the refusal." This will probably
be effected in the course of the next summer. in the mean time I have
procured from Judge Graham an intelligent medical Gent who resides in that neighbourhood a full account of what bones have been
found, a copy of which I do myself the honor to enclose. There is
every reason to believe that the whole skeleton will be obtained so as
to clear up all doubts as to the distinction between this animal &
the elephant, which notwithstanding the ingenious reasoning of
Daubenton I concieve to be materialy different. The shape of the foot,
the articulation of the shoulder & the lateral junctions of the radius &
ulna (to say nothing of the teeth) appear to present specific differences, & such as can not be accounted for by sex or age. If, as I think
they will, the teeth should appear to differ from those of the Elephant, the usual answer that they may be assigned to the Hipotamus
will not be admitted here, because they are found connected with the
tusks & so much of the head as to prove that they belonged to a tusk

bearing animal none of which of any great size are known to exist except the Elephant & the Walrus.

While I am upon this subject I avail myself of the opportunity to inform you that I have just received information from our western country of the discovery of the bones of a non descript animal, unless it should turn out to be the magolanux. The incisors are described to me to be bent, & to shut upon each other in the same manner that the fingers of both hands would do if the nails were brought into contact, & to be much about that size, the teeth of the upper & lower jaws taken together exhibiting about five inches of ivory, above the parts that might have been covered by the gums. Those of the lion are in no sort to be compared with this. If this animal is extinct, it must have been very recently so, since not only the teeth but many of the bones were found above ground. I think it confirms your conjecture of the existance of the lion, or rather, of some animal of much superior size & strength, in the interior parts of this continent. I have taken such measures for collecting the bones as I hope will prove succesful. the Gent. who has the teeth has promised to send them to me. Should they appear to differ from those you have discovered I shall send them to the philosophical society. If they should be the same, the discovery may be rendered more useful by sending them to Sir Joseph Banks.

The Vortex of law, Legislation, & politics, in which I am engaged here prevents my considering with the attention it merits your proposition relative to the agricultural society. The subject is very important, & the advantages that would result from one such as ought not to be overlooked. I am perfectly of your sentiment relative to the power of Congress to endow or encorporate one, yet I fear that nothing can be effectualy done without some public aid. Might they not bring the states to make provission for such an object by recommending it to their attention, & calling, upon them to organize a society in each state; vested with power to form a general congress by members elected out of their body who should meet at the seat of goverment during the session of Congress?

My ideas on this subject are not however sufficiently digestd to commit to paper, & your time too precious to be farther encroached upon. I have the honor to be, Dr Sir, with the highest respect & esteem Your Most Obt hum: Servt   ROBT R LIVINGSTON

RC (DLC); endorsed by TJ as received 18 Mch. and so recorded in SJL. Enclosure: probably the "Further Account of the Fossil Bones in Orange and Ulster Counties: In a Letter from Dr. James G. Graham, one of the Senators of the Middle District, to Dr. Mitchill; dated Shawangunk, September 10, 1800" (DLC: TJ Papers, 107:18374-5; clipped from an unidentified publication that reprinted Graham's account from the *Medical Repository*, 4 [1801], 213-14).

To Robert Morris

DEAR SIR   Washington Mar. 6. 1801.

I am much obliged by the kind & prompt attention you have been so good as to pay to my letter of the 26th. your testimony and mrs Morris's in favor of mr Tate would have been decisive with me, but in the interval between that date and my receipt of your answer a proposition came to me of a very capital Maitre d'Hotel, whose character was so well vouched that I thought it imprudent to let it escape & engaged him. the rather as mr Gouverneur Morris's knowing nothing of any such person as Tate induced me to apprehend I had been misinformed on that subject. I am glad on his account that he holds a comfortable place.

I have ever been satisfied that you thought too justly to suffer your opinions of men, founded on your own knolege of them, to be changed by the discoloured representations of party spirit. I have changed no principle of politics or morality. the people were by art & industry, by alarm & resentment, wrought into a phrenzy, & led towards what they little imagined. they never meant to throw off the principles of 1776. they again recognise those who have never changed them; and I hope to see them again consolidated into a homogeneous mass, and the very name of party obliterated from among us. I will do any thing to obtain it short of abandoning the principles of the revolution. I rejoice at your expectation of [recovering] from your difficulties, and of seeing [us in] this quarter. no person [would] be more happy at recieving you here; as I have never ceased to entertain a just esteem for mrs Morris & yourself. be so good as to present her the homage of my respect & to accept yourself assurances of the constant esteem & regard of Dear Sir

Your most obedt. servt   TH: JEFFERSON

PrC (ViW); blurred and torn; at foot of text: "Robert Morris esq."; endorsed by TJ in ink on verso.

YOUR TESTIMONY: Morris to TJ, 2 Mch.

To Charles Pinckney

DEAR SIR   Washington Mar. 6. 1801.

Your favor of yesterday is just now put into my hands. it is so far from being improper to recieve the communications you had in contemplation as to arrangements in your state, that I have been in the constant expectation you would find time to do me the favor of calling & making them, when we could in conversation explain them better than by writing, and I should with frankness & thankfulness enter into the explanations. the most valuable source of information we have is that of the members of the legislature, & it is one to which I have resorted & shall resort with great freedom. I expect mr Madison daily, and shall with pleasure join in conferences with yourself & him. but this ought not to prevent previous conversations between us. if you can be contented with a bad tavern dinner, I should be happy if you would come and dine with our mess tomorrow, if convenient to you, or the next day, and if you could come a half an hour before dinner, I would be alone that we might have some conversation; say at half after two. or if this should not suit you any other time would be acceptable to me, but that I might be absent or engaged. accept assurances of sincere esteem & respect from Dear Sir

Your friend & servt   Th: Jefferson

PrC (DLC); at foot of text: "The honble Charles Pinckney."

From John W. Pratt

Sir   City of Washington March 6th. 1801

Should the office of Marshall for the District of Columbia become Vacant I beg leave to tender to you my services and to Solicit from you the appointment. Unknown to You my Self I have Sought for the Recommendation of those Whose Characters have been Respected. I have the Honour to inclose you letters from Mr. Duvall one of our Supreme Judges Mr. Duckett one of the Judges of our County Court Mr. Sprigg & Mr. Bowie two Gentlemen of Respectability and Mr. Mason & Mr. Sprigg two Lawyers of emenance at our Bar. Should I be deemed worthy of the appointment no exertions on my part Shall be wanting to discharge the duties of the Office with integrity and fidelity.—

I have the Honour to be Sir With Respect Your Obet. Servt.

John W Pratt

RC (DNA: RG 59, LAR); addressed: "Thomas Jefferson Esquire President of the United States"; endorsed by TJ as received 6 Mch. and so recorded in SJL; also endorsed by TJ: "to be Marshal of Columbia." Enclosures: (1) Gabriel Duvall to TJ, Annapolis, 2 Mch. 1801, recommending Pratt, with whom he has had a long acquaintance, noting that "he is a gentleman of good character, of industry and assiduity in any business which he undertakes" and that he has had experience with the office of sheriff, presently carrying out those duties in Prince George's County. (2) Thomas Duckett to TJ, Prince George's County, 3 Mch. 1801, stating that although unacquainted with TJ, he wishes to inform him that he has known Pratt all his life and has always considered him as a "Gentleman of character, industry, and assiduity in the departments in which he has been engaged"; he has no doubt Pratt would be "a faithfull good officer." (3) Osborn Sprigg to TJ, Prince George's County, 5 Mch. 1801, stating that Pratt was the most qualified person in the District of Columbia to discharge the duties of marshal, that he could testify to his integrity, having lived all his life as his neighbor until Pratt moved to Washington during the last year, and that "we never had the Sheriffs business so well done" as when he was the deputy sheriff. (4) Walter Bowie to TJ, Prince George's County, 2 Mch. 1801, stating that although unacquainted with TJ, he presumes that "information correctly Obtained" will be useful, and after a long acquaintance with the applicant, he can say that Pratt is a "man of fair Character industry & great attention to Business," who would be able to execute the duties of a marshal "with credit to himself and advantage to the Publick." (5) John T. Mason to TJ, Montgomery Court House, 5 Mch. 1801, introducing Pratt as "active diligent and attentive to business," with a reputation for integrity and as one who understands the routine business of a sheriff or marshal, having "discharged the duties of his office well" as a deputy sheriff. (6) Richard Sprigg, Jr., to TJ, Upper Marlboro, 2 Mch. 1801, stating that he has had a long acquaintance with Pratt, who, as acting deputy sheriff, executed his duties "with Credit to himself & advantage to the Community" (RCs all in DNA: RG 59, LAR).

In spite of the recommendations for Pratt, TJ appointed Daniel Carroll Brent to replace James M. Lingan as U.S. marshal for the District of Columbia (see TJ to Brent, 18 Mch. 1801).

In 1801 Thomas DUCKETT was serving as an associate justice of the First District Court in Prince George's County. GENTLEMEN OF RESPECTABILITY: as planters in Prince George's County, Osborn Sprigg resided at Northampton and Walter Bowie at Locust Grove. Bowie also owned the mercantile firm, Walter Bowie and Company of Bladensburg, Maryland, and served in each house of the state legislature. TWO LAWYERS: John T. Mason and Richard Sprigg, Jr. TJ nominated Mason to serve as the U.S. attorney for the District of Columbia in place of Thomas Swan, Adams's nominee for the office. After a hard-fought campaign, Mason had lost his bid for a seat in the Maryland House of Delegates in October 1800. Sprigg, a Republican congressman from Maryland in 1801, was appointed associate justice of the Maryland Court of Appeals in 1806 (JEP, 1:387, 402, 426; *Biog. Dir. Cong.*; Dauer, *Adams Federalists*, 312; Papenfuse, *Maryland Legislature*, 1:152-3, 283-4, 290-1; 2:764-5; Stevens Thomson Mason to TJ, 11 July and 17 Oct. 1800).

To Thomas Mann Randolph

TH:J. TO TMR.   Washington Mar. 6. 1801.

Harrassed with interruptions & worn down with fatigue; I take up my pen at midnight to scribble you a line. Mr. Nicholas who sets out by day light promises to call and give you the particulars of this place, & I will inclose a paper just recieved giving the details of an armistice between France & Austria, a second great victory, and the commencement of hostilities by England against Russia, Prussia, Sweden & Denmark.   your clover seed has been forwarded to Richmond some time ago, with directions to mr Jefferson to apply for it to Picket & Pollard & forward it to you. I still hope to get away in a fortnight or thereabouts. by the next post I shall probably desire that Davy Bowles may be got to bring my chair & two horses as far as Herring's a quarter of a mile this side of Strode's & there wait for me. I shall go on horseback that far. the notice for his departure will probably be very short.   my tenderest love to my dearest Martha & the little ones. and sincere & affectionate salutations to yourself.

RC (DLC); endorsed by Randolph. Enclosure not found.

The PAPER TJ enclosed has not been found, but on 2 Mch. the New York *Commercial Advertiser* printed the text of the convention detailing the armistice between Austria and France, news of victories of the French armies, and the British order in council of 14 Jan. that called for the embargo of Russian, Danish, and Swedish ports and vessels.

For DIRECTIONS on forwarding the clover seed, see TJ to George Jefferson, 4 Mch.

Beginning in 1800, TJ had employed DAVY BOWLES of Milton to convey his horses partway along the route between Monticello and the capital. HERRING'S: Herin's tavern in Culpeper County (MB, 2:1020, 1036; Vol. 31:360, 363, 474, 483).

From James Reed Dermott

SIR:—   City of Washington, March 7, 1801.

The knowledge which I have acquired by experience in the location, rise and progress of this city, from the year 1792, in the most difficult and trying times of the laying off of the same, and in which many deviations were made from the original design, all of which I opposed except those for the publick good, and the causes of which are known to very few others except myself, emboldens me, at this early period of your administration, to offer my services in any appointment, in *that* or any *other*, which may be conducive to restore harmony between the publick, and those purchasing under them, and the original proprietors; and also to reconcile seeming differences which now appear upon the carpet, between a plan made by me and signed by the late President, and one printed in 1792, before a general survey of the city had taken place. I acted as surveyor in the Commissioner's office, examined all the returns of squares made, made divisions between the original proprietors and the public, and, in short, had all the business in that respect nearly settled, when *principle* and *private* animosity took place, and caused me to quit my station in January, 1795.[1] I could not then, nor will I ever sacrifice justice to the caprice or speculative views of individuals, when these things are opposite to the just principles whereon I ought to act. Instead of resentment to the late Commissioners (who may extricate themselves as well as they can) I always afterwards gave them information to assist in doing them and the publick justice—and many things yet within my knowledge not communicated which may be conducive to peace and harmony, which I wish to communicate should I have a proper opportunity of so doing. Thomas Johnson, David Stewart, former Commissioners with whom I acted, will give an account of my integrity and abilities. Notley Young, Dan'l Carroll, Wm. Prout and James Barry, and *even* the *proprietors* in *Georgetown*, will own my abilities in the execution of the trust confided to me. Should you think me worthy of an appointment, a letter left at the post office will meet me, or a message directed to Mr. James Barry, or to myself at the Eastern Branch lower ferry, where I am laying off some ground for Mr. Barry, will be particularly attended to. This is but a preface to what I wish to say if entitled to confidence.

I have, sir, the honor to be Your sincere friend,

(Signed) JAMES O'DERMOTT

Tr (DLC); typescript; at head of text: "To Thomas Jefferson, Esq., President of the United States"; also at head of text: "(Copy)"; with note in ink by the collector William K. Bixby, 12 Apr. 1915. Tr (same); typescript, a different impression from the foregoing; identified by a note in an unidentified hand as a carbon copy presented to DLC by Cass Gilbert, April 1915. There are at least three other typescript (or carbon) copies of this letter bearing Bixby's notation, "Copy of original in my possession." Entered in SJL as a letter from James "Odermot" dated 4 Mch. and received on 8 Mch.

James Reed Dermott (ca. 1756-1803), a native of Ireland who did some teaching at academies in northern Virginia, produced a map of Alexandria by 1791. Employed from March 1792 in the surveying and platting of the Federal District, he prepared a comprehensive "Appropriation Map" that showed the city's lots and documented the form that L'Enfant's design was taking on the ground. His criticism of Andrew Ellicott, who was carrying out the field surveys, contributed to the dismissal of Ellicott and his assistants. They and others decried Dermott in turn as a troublesome, ill-tempered sot, and in January 1798 he too was discharged. The letter above is the only correspondence between Dermott and TJ recorded in SJL (Ralph E. Ehrenberg, "Mapping the Nation's Capital: The Surveyor's Office, 1791-1818," *Quarterly Journal of the Library of Congress*, 36 [1979], 284, 288-9, 291, 294-7, 304; Bryan, *National Capital*, 1:210-11, 300n; C. M. Harris, ed., *Papers of William Thornton: Volume One, 1781-1802* [Charlottesville, 1995], 296-7; *National Intelligencer*, 14 Sep. 1803).

[1] Thus in Tr and other known typescripts, but Dermott left the position in January 1798 (see above).

From John Hall

SIR   Philadelphia March 7. 1801.

From your Character for integrity which I have been taught to respect ever since I entered the Army of the United States in our revolutionary war in the year 1777, and from the excellent sentiments contained in your inaugural Speech, (every one of which is congenial to my heart) I have been led to believe no subordinate Officer of the General

Government who has not been defficient in duty, will be dismissed from his Office; But having heard that attempts are now making to exite in you an unjust opinion of my Official conduct, I have taken the liberty to enclose several Certificates from Gentlemen who have been witnesses, the nearest and best witnesses of my Conduct.

To those Certificates I submit the issue of a request to be continued in my present Office. Should further evidence be necessary of my impartiality in the selection of Juries, or should proofs be required of my early and uniform Attachment to the Cause of my Country, and to the genuine principles of true Republicanism as declared in your Speech, they shall be procured from Gentlemen of the most respectable characters in Pennsylvania, and transmitted to you by the earliest opportunity.

With sincere wishes that your administration may be conducted and end, with the auspicious circumstances of peace and Union to the Citizens of the United States with which it commenced on the memorable 4th. of March 1801.

I have the honor to be Most respectfully Your Excellencys Mot. Obt. Sevt   JNO HALL

Marshal of the US
for the District of Penna.

RC (DNA: RG 59, LAR); addressed: "The President of the United States"; endorsed by TJ as received 11 Mch. and so recorded in SJL. Enclosures: (1) Certificate of Richard Peters, 7 Mch. 1801, describing Hall as "diligent & punctual" and conducting himself with "Impartiality, in all Things," with no complaints of "Failure in his Duty, or of any improper Conduct" coming to his attention (MS in same; in Peters's hand and signed by him; endorsed by Hall: "Certificate of Richard Peters Judge of the District"). (2) Certificate of William Rawle, Philadelphia, 7 Mch. 1801, stating that Hall executed his duties as marshal with "integrity, diligence, perspecuity, promptitude and firmness" and that few would be found better qualified than he to hold the office (MS in same; in Rawle's hand and signed by him).

John Hall (1760-1826) of Harford County, Maryland, was the second son of Elihu Hall, a well-established landholder, and the son-in-law of John Ewing, pastor of the First Presbyterian Church at Philadelphia and provost of the University of Pennsylvania. In 1782 Hall married Sarah Ewing, a popular essayist who wrote for Joseph Dennie's *Port Folio*. Hall was secretary of the Pennsylvania land office from 1796 until 1799, when John Adams nominated him to replace William Nicholls as marshal of the district of Pennsylvania. Hall unsuccessfully petitioned Congress on 4 Feb. 1801 for relief of a settlement of his accounts with Treasury officers. TJ included him on a 28 Mch. list of removals for misconduct and delinquency, namely for packing juries (Sarah Hall, *Selections from the Writings of Mrs. Sarah Hall, Author of Conversations on the Bible, with a Memoir of Her Life* [Philadelphia, 1833], ix, xiii, xiv, xv, xxx, xxxi; JEP, 1:325, 403; JHR, 3:784-5, 841; PMHB, 84 [1960], 474n; *Maryland Genealogies*, 2 vols. [Baltimore, 1980], 2:34; Papenfuse, *Maryland Legislature*, 1:383; Appendix I, Lists 2, 3, and 4).

Hall's WITNESSES both received appointments during Washington's administration.

William Rawle, a prominent Federalist, served as U.S. district attorney from 1791 until 1800. Richard Peters served as a Pennsylvania district court judge from 1792 until his death in 1828 (Washington, *Papers, Pres. Ser.*, 7:250-1, 9:426; JEP, 1:86, 351).

In his letter to TJ on 8 Apr., Pierce Butler claimed that TJ had been "misinformed respecting the Marshal of Pennsylvania District. He is a Man of mild manners; and well qualified for the Office. I believe he has never been indellicate. I understand that the Family he Maried into indulge a latitude of unjustifiable expression; but I am persuaded that he disapproves of it. If I know You, it is not Your intention to remove good and qualified Men, if they even shoud not think exactly with Yourself on Publick good" (RC in DLC; endorsed by TJ as received 29 Apr. and so recorded in SJL).

From James Madison

DEAR SIR   March 7. 1801

Since my last which went by the mail in course, the papers of my deceased father have been opened. His will was made thirteen years ago, since which two of my brothers have died, one of them leaving a large number of children mostly minors, and both of them intestate. The will itself, besides the lapsed legacies, does not cover all the property held at the time; & valuable parcels of property were acquired subsequent to the will. The will is also ambiguous in some important points, and will raise a variety of questions for legal opinions if not controversies. Another circumstance in the case is that some memorandums preparatory to considerable alterations in the will were left in his hand writing; to which is to be added verbal intimations in his last moments of others wished by him. As the event took place also prior to the 1st. of March, an immediate division may be required if the parties interested so chuse. From this explanation you will judge of the task devolved on me as Extr, and in the other relations in which I stand; especially as much must necessarily be done by amicable negociations concessions & adjustments; and will be indulgent enough to combine it with the political lien to which I have subjected myself. I wait with anxiety for your answer to my last which I expect by the mail of wednesday next. I have nothing to add to that, but a repetition of the assurances with which I am most respectfully & affectionately

your friend & servt   Js. MADISON

RC (DLC: Madison Papers); endorsed by TJ as received 12 Mch. and so recorded in SJL.

MY LAST: Madison to TJ, 28 Feb. 1801. TWO OF MY BROTHERS: Ambrose and Francis Madison (Brant, *Madison*, 4:38). Madison was serving as executor of his father's will.

To James Monroe

Dear Sir Washington March[1] 7. 1801.

I had written the inclosed letter to mrs Trist, and was just proceeding to begin one to you, when your favor of the 6th. was put into my hand. I thank you sincerely for it, and consider the views of it so sound, that I have communicated it to my coadjutors as one of our important evidences of the public sentiment, according to which we must shape our course. I suspect, partly from this, but more from a letter of J. Taylor's which has been put into my hands, that an incorrect idea of my views has got abroad. I am in hopes my inaugural address will in some measure set this to rights, as it will present the[2] leading objects to be conciliation, and adherence to sound principle. this I know is impracticable with the leaders of the late faction, whom I abandon as incurables, & will never turn an inch out of my way to reconcile them. but with the main body of the Federalists, I believe it very practicable. you know that the maneuvres of the year XYZ. carried over from us a great body of the people real republicans, & honest men under virtuous motives. the delusion lasted awhile. at length the poor arts of tub-plots &c were repeated till the designs of the party became suspected. from that moment those who had left us, began to come back. it was by their return to us that we gained the victory in Nov. 1800. which we should not have gained in Nov. 1799. but during the suspension of the public mind from the 11th. to the 17th. of Feb. and the anxiety & alarm lest there should be no election & anarchy ensue, a wonderful effect was produced on the mass of Federalists who had not before come over. those who had before become sensible of their error in the former change, & only wanted a decent excuse for coming back, seised that occasion for doing so. another body, & a large one it is, who from timidity of constitution had gone with those who wished for a strong executive, were induced by the same timidity to come over to us rather than risk anarchy. so that according to the evidence we recieve from every direction, we may say that the whole of that portion of the people which was called federalist, was made to desire anxiously the very event they had just before opposed with all their energies, and to recieve the election, which was made, as an object of their earnest wishes, a child of their own. these people (I always include their leaders) are now aggregated with us, they look with a certain degree of affection & confidence to the administration, ready to become attached to it if it avoids, in the outset, acts which might revolt & throw them off. to give time for a perfect consolidation seems prudent. I have firmly refused to follow the counsels of those who have advised the giving offices to some of their leaders, in order to reconcile. I have given & will give only to republicans, under existing circumstances. but I believe with others that deprivations of office, if made on the ground of political principle alone, would revolt our new converts, & give a body to leaders who now stand alone. some I know must be made. they must be as few as possible, done gradually, & bottomed on some malversation or inherent disqualification. where we shall draw the line between retaining all, & none, is not yet settled, and will not be till we get our administration together: and perhaps even then we shall proceed *à tatons*, balancing our measures according to the impression we percieve them to make.—this may give you a general view of our plan. should you be in Albemarle the first week in April, I shall have the pleasure of seeing you there, and of developing things more particularly, and of profiting by an intercommunication of views.—Dawson sails for France about the 15th. as the *bearer* only of the treaty to Elsworth & Murray. he has probably asked your commands and your introductory letters. present my respects to mrs Monroe & accept assurances of my high & affectionate consideration & attachment.   TH: JEFFERSON

RC (NN); dated 7 Feb. (see note 1 below), but recorded in SJL under 7 Mch.; addressed: "Governor Monroe Richmond"; franked; endorsed by Monroe. PrC (DLC). Enclosure: TJ to Elizabeth House Trist, 7 Mch. 1801, which is recorded in SJL but has not been found.

Monroe's FAVOR OF THE 6TH was actually the letter of 3 Mch., which TJ received on the 7th.

TUB-PLOTS &C: in England in 1679 authorities identified as a concoction of forged evidence a supposed conspiracy to block any succession to the throne by James, the Duke of York. The spurious intrigue may have been an attempt by royalist Catholics to taint Protestant Whigs with sedition, a Whig ploy to give Catholics

the blame for the fabrication, or a bungled scheme by its perpetrators to win favor with influential patrons. The discovery of some of the forged papers in a tub of meal gave the affair its nickname, the "Meal Tub Plot" (Ronald H. Fritze, William B. Robison, and Walter Sutton, eds., *Historical Dictionary of Stuart England, 1603-1689* [Westport, Conn., 1996], 326-8; J. R. Jones, *The First Whigs: The Politics of the Exclusion Crisis, 1678-1683* [London, 1961], 109-13).

À TATONS: gropingly.

For the expected journey of John DAWSON to France, see TJ to Dawson, 12 Mch.

[1] Word interlined by Monroe in place of TJ's "Feb."

[2] Word interlined in place of "two."

From Wilson Cary Nicholas

DEAR SIR   March 7th. 1801

I have had a conversation with Genl. Sumpter in Genl. terms about his country man P—y. Sumpter says his standing in S.C. with our friends is not good, that he is not respected either as a public or a private man, that he has been made use of by the republicans, and that he has made use of them because they were convenient to each other—the opinion of one man cannot be conclusive, you will know how to appreciate it, and will I am sure pardon the liberty I have taken

with every sentiment of respect I am your hum. Serv.

W. C. NICHOLAS

RC (DLC); endorsed by TJ as received 7 Mch. and so recorded in SJL with notation "Geo. T."

P—Y: probably Charles Pinckney.

From Jonathan Williams

SIR   Mount Pleasant near Philadelphia March 7, 1801:

Wishing to submit my slender Performances to the candid Examination of those of my Philosophical Associates whose talents and acquirements inspire me with the utmost deference, and whose approbation is the first object of my Ambition, I took the liberty of sending you, among others, a Copy of my thermometrical improvements in Navigation.

Permit me now to ask a place in your private Library, for the inclosed translations of a System of Artillery and Fortification, which I believe to be the most approved, in a Country where these branches of the Art military are in the highest perfection.

You will give me credit, sir, for great Labour, & (I hope) for tolerable accuracy; but the technical nature of the works forbids any claims to literary honour. If they should tend to establish uniformity among the Artists of our Country, they will combine efficacy with Oeconomy, and eventually render us in this respect independent of foreign aid.

These Translations were gratuitously made at the request of the late Administration, but I have added to the latter one, an appendix of my own, with a model in Wood which I wish to deposit where it can best answer its object. It is, I presume, in compliment for these Services that the late President of the United States has honoured me with a Commission as Major in the Corps of Artillerists and Engineers, for I never made any personal Application of the kind. I have however accepted it with gratitude, and as long as I may be continued in Service, it shall be my pride, as it will be my duty, to contribute all in my Power to the perfection of that sort of national Defence, which, being in its nature permanent and not suddenly attainable, becomes important even in peace, being a preparative, which, if it should not avert, will at least render foreign attacks less formidable.

With the greatest Deference & Respect I have the honour to be Sir Your faithfull Associate & Servant   JONA WILLIAMS

RC (DLC); at foot of text: "The President of the American Philosophical Society"; endorsed by TJ as received 12 Mch. and so recorded in SJL. PrC (PPRF: Rush-Williams-Biddle Papers); closing and signature cut out. Enclosures: see below.

THERMOMETRICAL IMPROVEMENTS IN NAVIGATION: in January 1800 Williams sent TJ a copy of *Thermometrical Navigation*, his book on measuring water temperature to aid ocean navigation (Vol. 31:308).

Williams had made TRANSLATIONS for the War Department of two works previously published in French: *A Treatise of Artillery* by Heinrich Otto von Scheel and *The Elements of Fortification* by Guillaume Le Blond. Apparently both translations were printed in Philadelphia in 1800. Following the loss of most or all copies of *The Elements of Fortification* in the War Department fire in November 1800, that work was reissued in 1801. Williams added an APPENDIX to it as a brief practical explication, for an American audience, of some elements of Le Blond's theoretical discussion. Williams had made a MODEL IN WOOD of part of a

fortification to illustrate "at one view the exemplification of all the maxims and principles contained in this treatise" (*The Elements of Fortification: Translated from the French*, 2d ed. [Washington, 1801], 44-5; Theodore J. Crackel, *Mr. Jefferson's Army: Political and Social Reform of the Military Establishment, 1801-1809* [New York, 1987], 56-7, 198n; see Sowerby, No. 1161; Shaw-Shoemaker, No. 440).

On 16 Feb. the Senate had approved John Adams's nomination of Williams as a MAJOR in the Second Regiment of Artillerists and Engineers (JEP, 1:378, 380).

TJ replied to Williams on 14 Mch.: "Th: Jefferson returns his thanks to Major Williams for the books he has been so kind as to send him. he will be very happy to see the corps of which he is a member profit by his example and pursue the line of information he has so well pointed out. he prays him to accept assurances of his high consideration & respect" (RC owned by Gordon A. Block, Jr., Philadelphia, 1947, addressed: "Majr. Jonathan Williams Mount pleasant near Philadelphia," franked and postmarked; PrC in DLC).

From the Borough of Wilmington

SIR,   Wilmington Delaware March 7th. 1801

The corporation of the Borough of Wilmington beg leave to congratulate you, on your elevation to the first magistracy of the United States. The painful suspence previously suffered, serves but to enhance the triumph of sentiments in the final prevalence of the voice of the people, fairly and decidedly expressed. So far as acknowledged talents, examplary morals and disinterested patriotism can inspire hope, we have reason to expect from you, a wise, just and prosperous administration. And we pray that your political career may terminate in honorable fame, as well as public happiness.

In and on behalf of the corporation   NEHEMIAH TILTON
                                             JAS. BROBSON
                                             Burgesses

RC (DLC); in unknown hand, signed by Tilton and Brobson; endorsed by TJ as received 12 Mch. and so recorded in SJL.

From John Woodward

SIR,   Washington 7 March 1801

Permit me to state to Your Excellency that being desirous to obtain an employment under the Federal Government, I have thought the present a favorable and a pleasing opportunity to make application.

The Vice President, Sir, and the Honorable A. Galatin are acquainted with my Character. And the open testimonial addressed to General Muhlenberg I beg leave, as that Gentleman is absent from this place, to present for Your Excellency's perusal.

Should I be judged competent, Sir, and not altogether unworthy of an office in the Customs or Revenue at New York, Philadelphia or Washington, it would make me very happy. But any other designation of public appointment, which the President of the United States should direct, in any part of the Union, would be thankfully accepted.

I have the Honor to be with all Respect, Your Excellency's Most Obedient Servant,
                                             JOHN WOODWARD

RC (DNA: RG 59, LAR); at foot of text: "His Excellency Thomas Jefferson"; endorsed by TJ as received 7 Mch. and so recorded in SJL, where with a brace TJ connected this letter with one of 27 Feb. from William Barton at Lancaster (not found), probably carried to Washington by Woodward. Enclosure not found.

John Woodward (ca. 1742-1822), a New York merchant before the American Revolution, early joined the Whig cause serving as one of the first members of the New York City Committee of Correspondence. He fought during the Revolutionary War and served as an aide to Governor George Clinton. He lost most of his property during the Revolution. Woodward worked in Philadelphia as a Treasury Department clerk in 1792, but was forced to leave the next year after publishing a newspaper article in favor of the French Revolution. He later became a clerk in the

Pennsylvania comptroller-general's office at Lancaster, a position he held in 1803. Writing from Lancaster, James Trimble described Woodward as a "Gentleman of some talents, a good Democratic Republican, and an honest Man." Woodward married Ann Silvester. By 1801 their son, Augustus Brevoort Woodward, was a prominent attorney in the District of Columbia and an acquaintance of TJ (ANB, 23:821-3; Frank B. Woodford, *Mr. Jefferson's Disciple: A Life of Justice Woodward* [East Lansing, Mich., 1953], 98; Syrett, *Hamilton*, 11:392; 13:466; *Public Papers of George Clinton: First Governor of New York*, 10 vols. [New York, 1899-1914], 8:295; Gallatin, *Papers*, 4:656, 668-9; 8:672; Bryan to TJ, 26 Feb. 1801).

ACQUAINTED WITH MY CHARACTER: on 9 Mch., the day before he returned to Lancaster, where he was probably already employed as a clerk in the state government,

Woodward wrote Albert Gallatin a letter in which he outlined his career (Woodward to Gallatin, 9 Mch. 1801, in Gallatin, *Papers*, 4:668-9). On his trip to Washington he brought Gallatin a letter of introduction from Samuel Bryan. He also delivered documents from Bryan to the president (same, 4:653, 701-2).

To John Adams

Washington Mar. 8. 1801.

Th: Jefferson presents his respects to mr Adams and incloses him a letter which came to his hands last night; on reading what is written within the cover, he concluded it to be a private letter, and without opening a single paper within it he folded it up & now has the honor to inclose it to mr Adams, with the homage of his high consideration & respect.

RC (MHi: Adams Papers); addressed: "John Adams esquire Braintree"; franked; postmarked 9 Mch.; endorsed by Adams. Not recorded in SJL. Enclosure not identified, but see Adams's reply of 24 Mch.

To James Bowdoin

SIR   Washington Mar. 8. 1801.

I recollect with great satisfaction the acquaintance I had the honour of having with your most respectable father, and have seen with great pleasure the line of conduct you have yourself pursued, so worthy of him. the wonderful combinations of events, with the uses made of them, has been such as might lead even the best men from the true principles of free government. that you have not yielded to the delusion is as honorable to you as it will be for ever consolatory.

I thank you for your congratulations on the event of the late election. though it was a contest of principle merely, in the zealous friends of good government, yet as a name was necessarily to be connected with the contest I viewed with due respect & consolation my name selected for that purpose, and myself considered as the safe depository of the principle for which we were contending. but I see also with pain that more will be expected than my limited faculties can accomplish. I will do whatever they are equal to, & rely on that indulgence for all beyond, which I shall have occasion for.

In addressing a person whom I presume to be in habits of sociability with my venerable and ever esteemed friend Samuel Adams, I cannot refrain from asking leave to place here the tribute of my constant respect & affection for him, & that you will be so good as to be the channel of communicating it: and I pray you to accept yourself assurances of my high consideration & esteem.   TH: JEFFERSON

RC (MHi: Bowdoin and Temple Papers); addressed: "James Bowdoin esq. Boston"; franked and postmarked; endorsed by Bowdoin. PrC (DLC).

YOUR CONGRATULATIONS: Bowdoin to TJ, 24 Feb. 1801.

From Jeremiah Brown

DEAR SIR,   Providence March 8th. 1801

Inclosed you have Information of the most Important Discovery for Culture, Should immediate attention be paid it will increase the crop this year Sufficient to Feed $2\frac{1}{2}$ Millions of People, and by next year may be increas'd to 10 millions, which would be a great relief to the nations in Europe now in war, and add greatly to Harmonising this two much divided Country. I request you to see my Patent right secured at the patent Office agreeable to my Letter to president Adams the 9th. of 2nd. month. I request you to immediately acknowledge the Recept. of this Letter, Private reports represent your circumstance and Mr. Burrs to be embarrassed. Should that be the case I can with great ease and the utmost pleasure accommodate you with each an advance[1] of fifty or one Hundred Thousand Dollars, as may be to you most agreeable. A short description[2] of your Lands and whether Improved by slaves or free People will enable me to make such arrangement in Macheenary as will affectually water your Soil the principal Material to Effect which will be plank of different thicknesses and Logs suitably bored to form Tubes to throw the water any height Which the situation may require.—
I shall immediately answer yours and give you information how soon I can be at the seat of Government.

I am Dear sir your most affectionabley   JEREM BROWN

RC (DLC); endorsed by TJ as received 18 Mch. and so recorded in SJL. Enclosure not found.

Brown received a PATENT on 14 May 1800 for "Improvements in the construction of ships and vessels" (*List of Patents*, 22). In a 4 Feb. 1801 LETTER TO PRESIDENT ADAMS, Brown included a list of his inventions he wished to patent, including a device for "raising water for watering soil &c." as well as improved plows, cooking utensils, a fireplace, rudders, a churn, a bowsprit, and a grinding mill (MHi: Adams Family Papers).

[1] MS: "advace."
[2] MS: "desciption."

To Horatio Gates

DEAR GENERAL   Washington Mar. 8. 1801.

I have to acknolege your friendly letter of Feb. 9. as well as a former one. before that came to hand an arrangement had been settled; and in our country you know, talents alone are not to be the determining circumstance, but a geographical equilibrium is to a certain degree expected. the different parts in the union expect to share the public appointments. the character you pointed out was known to me & valued of old.—On the whole I hope we shall make up an administration which will unite a great mass of confidence, and bid defiance to the plans of opposition meditated by leaders,[1] who are now almost destitute of followers. if we can hit on the true line of conduct which may conciliate the honest part of those who were called federalists, & yet do justice to those who have so long been excluded from it, I should hope to be able to obliterate, or rather to unite the names of federalist & republican. the way to effect it is to preserve principle, but to treat tenderly those who have been estranged from us, & dispose their minds to view our proceedings with candour. this will end in approbation. I pray you to accept assurances of the high consideration & respect & the constant affection of Dr. Sir

Your most obedt. & most humble servt   TH: JEFFERSON

RC (NN); addressed: "Maj. General Gates New York"; franked and postmarked. PrC (DLC).

FORMER ONE: Gates's letter to TJ of 17 Dec. 1800 was carried to Washington by John Armstrong, who took his place as senator of New York on 8 Jan. 1801 (JS, 3:115). Armstrong was the CHARACTER Gates recommended as a worthy candidate for secretary of war in his letter of 9 Feb.

[1] TJ here canceled "whose conduct balanced."

From Thomas Leiper

DEAR SIR   Philada. March 8th. 1801

I ought to have attended to yours of the 23th. Ult: sooner but the 4th of March came in the way and to be plain with you it was impossible to think of any thing else till that business was finished—
Since I wrote you last I have often seen Jackson and Wharton and have again and again offered them for the whole of your Crop of Tobacco Seven Dollars pr Ct. and they have rejected the offer—This price is the extreme of the Market and I am offered by Messrs. Higbee & Milnor Two Invoice consisting of Twenty Five and Thirty Five Hhds of Richmond and Manchester inspection for seven Dollars

pr Ct. at 60 & 90 days credit with the liberty of rejecting it if I do not like it on reinspecting from this circumstance I imagine the Tobacco is very good for they know of their personal knowledge I am not easey pleased in that Article—

From what I have heard and seen respecting your tobacco in the hands of Jackson & Wharton you in conscience ought to make no discount on it and I believe they think so also for they inform me they have ordered their Agent to pay the money—

The joy feel't and expressed on the 4th of March exceed'd any thing I ever saw and your adress to your friends and fellow citizens has given a wonderfull cast in your favour with your Political enemies if they can be believed but for my part I doubt them still—The Body of the People of this country are sound but I believe at the same time we have citizens as perfectly Rotten as any on the face of the earth but I hope for the sake of human nature when they are compaired with the Mass they are few and I hope will daily grow less—A few nights ago at a meetting of the officers of the Militia Legion I signed a recommendation to you in favour of Lieutenant John Smith—Mr. Smith was certainly very active in forming the Militia Legion which had its use in the general scale and his father was and is still as good a Whig as any in Pennsylvania according to the powers he possesses—Mr. Smith has been a merchant and has been unfortunate an appointment to him in every sense of the word would be very convenient—some thing in the Pounds & pence line would be best formed to his abilities—

I am informed a number of our members in the Legislature mean to recommend Mr. Smith to you and as Dr. Logan will be one of the number I have no doubt but he will write you on the subject—

James Thomson Callender is casting a wishfull eye towards the Postmasters office at Richmond but he does not know how to go about it—he desires me to get the Governor and Major Butler to write you in his favor—He says the man who holds the office is a good man but prints a great deal of trash against you how he can reconcil the first and the last of this sentence I know not—Callender has three fine Boys which he is not able to provid for—I have been very Plain with him to forward me a certificate from his present Landlord who must have seen him late & early for nine months and if it was favorable I had no doubt but you would do some thing for him—I now beg for myself your personal friendship and your Crop of Tobacco at the market price for I think it is good as any I ever manufactured and if I have wrote any thing amiss I hope you will forgive it I am with the utmost esteem

Dear Sir Your most Obedient Sert   THOMAS LEIPER

RC (DLC); endorsed by TJ as received 11 Mch. and so recorded in SJL.

HIGBEE & MILNOR were located at Morris's wharf as were Jackson & Wharton (Stafford, *Philadelphia Directory, for 1801*, 200).

For the RECOMMENDATION of JOHN SMITH signed by Leiper, see Enclosure

No. 1 noted at Smith to TJ, 11 Mch. Leiper also wrote Albert Gallatin in Smith's behalf (Gallatin, *Papers*, 4:694-5).

POSTMASTERS OFFICE AT RICHMOND: occupied by Federalist Augustine Davis (Vol. 31:180-1n, 202n; Vol. 32:254).

From John F. Mercer

DEAR SIR   West River Mar. 8th. 1801.—

Amidst the Congratulations of an Extensive Continent, I persuade myself that those of an old friend will not be unacceptable & that you will believe tht. altho' others may have been earlier, none have been more sincere than those I now offer you—the final event of the late election has been highly gratifying to my personal feelings & by no Man in the United States will a political change be more sensibly felt than by myself—for altho' with great caution I escapd *prosecution*, yet on few has the discountenance (I may say) the malevolence of Administration bore more heavily than on myself—for twelve years, it has pursued me from the public Councils to the most sequesterd paths of private life & added gloom to obscurity.—

The earnest solicitations of Colo. John Gassaway of Annapolis, to be introducd to your notice, have induced me to add to what I know to be one of the most fruitful sources of perplexity that flow from the highest station.—And I have only done so from the hope that if the United States shoud want an Officer whose firmness & devotion may be entirely relied on, I may render service by mentioning the Gentleman to you—He distinguishd himself during our revolutionary war by prudence & intrepidity & for 14 years, from my personal knowledge has been unchangeably attach'd to Republican principles & measures—a character not very common here—As a military man I coud recommend him as one that will be found (altho' perhaps rusty now) equal to all Roster & Parade Duties— & beyond these Military education, never extended with us, at least to my knowledge.—

Having mentiond military Affairs, will you permit me to hazard a few remarks, to which I attach some importance? It is a fact that the higher Branches of the military Sciences (of which Engineering forms the basis,) the principles of Positions, Encampments, Posts, Attack, defence supply & what constitutes all the Duties of the Etat

Majeur, never became an object of Study with us—I have attributed this in a great measure to our habits of pursuing English examples— they have not an original work in their language on these subjects, unless a late one by Genl. Lloyd, who liv'd & died in foreign service, & lent a few translations of the meanest of the foreign Authors, that I ever coud find.—they have neglected & of course despis'd this & consequently they are the most contemptible Land Troops in Europe, the Spaniard & Portugais excepted—Improving on their model, I fear you will not be able to command the services of a native American who can construct a Redoubt on principle—to depend on Foreigners for what must command the fate of the nation, presents serious considerations; exclusive of their principles & attachments, Unless we have better luck than formerly, We shall get only the refuse of the rabble that follow the Armies of Europe.— I shoud hope to see this remedied either by a military School here upon moderate principles, or else by a Corps of Cadets, educated abroad.—

You will excuse this discussion to one who surely travells beyond his last, & permit me to hope that when public duties require a relaxation in Country scenes, I may sometimes see you at my humble Mansion,—its tenants will be renderd happy by the visit & the pleasure will be sensibly encreasd if you join Mr. Madison to your party, who public fame says is once more about to give those talents & acquirements to his Country which were never intended for a Negro-Driver in Orange County.—

With sentiments of sincerest friendship & respect I am y. Ob Hb Sv.

JOHN F MERCER

RC (DNA: RG 59, LAR); endorsed by TJ as received 30 Mch. and so recorded in SJL with notation "Gassaway."

Colonel JOHN GASSAWAY also received a recommendation from Gabriel Duvall. On 12 Mch. Duvall wrote TJ from Annapolis that as an officer Gassaway had served "with reputation" throughout the American Revolution and at the close held a commission as "Captain in the Maryland line." After the war he commanded a militia regiment, served for some time under collector Otho H. Williams in the customs house at Baltimore, and for the last 13 years as register of wills for Anne Arundel County. Having discharged these duties "with fidelity & integrity," Gassaway sought a position that would provide better support for his family. Duvall endorsed Gassaway as a "meritorious citizen," noting

"his private character is unexceptionable, & he is industrious & attentive to business" (RC in DNA: RG 59, LAR, at foot of text: "Thomas Jefferson, Esquire President of the United States," endorsed by TJ as received 30 Mch. and so recorded in SJL, also endorsed by TJ: "Gassaway"; JEP, 1:14; Papenfuse, *Maryland Legislature*, 1:290-1).

Welshman Henry LLOYD served with the French, German, Austrian, and Russian armies during a military career that spanned four decades. An accomplished writer on military theory and practice, he was best known for his two volume history of the Seven Years War and for *A Rhapsody on the Present System of French Politics*, first published in 1779, which analyzed the home defense of Britain against a hypothetical French invasion. Six posthumous editions appeared between 1790 and 1803 under the title *A Political and Military Rhapsody, on the Invasion and Defence of Great Britain and Ireland* (DNB; Patrick J. Speelman, *Henry Lloyd and the Military* *Enlightenment of Eighteenth-Century Europe* [Westport, Conn., 2002], 1-2, 89-92, 129-31).

Notes on a Cabinet Meeting

Mar. 8. 1801.

N.H.   restore Whipple & Gardner, Collector, & Commr. of loans. change no other except the recent
Livermore, Naval officer, to be removd. by & by, & George Wentworth to be put in his place.[1]

Mass.   change only the new District atty viz George Blake[2] for Otis

Maine.   Parker marshall, to be removed by & by, a very violent & influential & industrious fed. put in not very fairly.
Davis the Atty is expected to resign, & Silas Lee must be put in his place.
John Lee, Collector of Penobscot, bror of Silas, a refugee, a royalist, & very violent. to be removed when we appoint his brother Atty.

Conn.   mr Lincoln to consult Edwards &c as to removing Goodrich.

√Vermont.   marshall & Atty to be removd immedly. John Willard of Addison county to be marshal. examine hereafter Lyon's recomndn.[3] Fay rather approved for Atty.

New York.   postponed.

Jersey.   propose to Linn to accept Atty's place vice Frelinghuysen. mr Gallatin will write Oliver Barnet to be marshall when Lowry resigns.
turn out the tory Collector an atrocious appointment.[4]

Pensva   √Hall to be removd. Shee to be appointed.
George Reinhart to be keeper of public stores vice Harris.[5]
√Genl.William Irvine to be Superintendt. Military stores vice Hodgson.
Peter Muhlenbg supervisor vice Genl. Henry Miller. but not till after May.
√Dallas Atty of E. distr.
        Hamilton do. of W. distr.
√Presley Carr Lane marsh. W. district vice Barclay new appt.

Delaware.   the Collector Mc.lane to be retained.
enquire as to Marshal & collector.

Maryland.   Hopkins Marshall to be removd. & Reuben Etting to be appd.
also Zeb. Hollingsworth, & John Scott to be appd.

√Virginia.   D. Randolph to be removd. Scott to be appd.

S. C.   adopt C. Pinckney's nominations, but take time till after sessio
               Congress 1801-2.
Georgia.   only the collector to be questd. supposed a delinquent. Richar
               Wyley to be in his place.
               he is now loan officer.
Kentucky.   Colo. Joseph Crocket vice Mc.Dowell as marshal. but wait proof
               of extortion

----

general rule. remove no Collectors till called on for accts. that as many may b
               removed as defaulters as are such

----

               present Gallatin, Dearborn, Lincoln.
Mar. 8.   on application from an old Col. Wofford presented by mr Baldwin. h
               was settled near the Cherokee line, but supposed on our side. on run
               ning it however he was left on their side. some other families in th
               same situation. approved of Genl. Dearborn's writing to Hawkins t
               negociate for their quiet, and that we will within 2. or 3. months tak
               up the subject & give him final instrns.

MS (DLC: TJ Papers, 110:18892);
entirely in TJ's hand; with check marks
at those receiving appointment between
5 and 24 Mch. (see Appendix I, List 4)
and emendations added over several
weeks as additional information became
available (see notes below); on same
sheet as Notes on a Cabinet Meeting,
9 Mch.

In March 1802, TJ nominated
Nathaniel Folsome to replace Edward St.
Loe LIVERMORE as the NAVAL OFFICER
at Portsmouth, New Hampshire (JEP,
1:409). JERSEY: for the New Jersey
appointments, see Notes on New Jersey
Patronage, [ca. 5 Mch.-before June
1801]. James Powell of Savannah,
GEORGIA, was removed as collector

for delinquency in accounts, and in
September 1801 Thomas de Mattos
Johnson was appointed as his replacement (JEP, 1:341; Appendix I, Lists 3
and 4).

[1] Entry beginning with "Livermore"
interlined.

[2] Name interlined in place of "Sullivan," probably after TJ received Levi
Lincoln's letter of 16 Apr. 1801.

[3] Preceding sentence canceled by TJ,
probably after examining Matthew
Lyon's letter of 3 Mch. 1801. TJ then inserted the sentence on "Fay."

[4] Sentence interlined.

[5] TJ later added in the left margin "no.
see Beckley." See John Beckley to TJ, 18
Mch. 1801.

From Charles Willson Peale

DEAR SIR   Museum March 8th. 1801.

The terms of approbation with which you mention my Lecture and Museum, afford me much gratification; since I have scarcely a thought not devoted to the perfection of my scheme.

From my knowledge of the Interest which you have always felt in whatever concerned the comfort of Man or the Benefits of Society, I am induced to think that even in the important Station to which our Nation has called you; (upon which be pleased to receive my sincere Congratulations;) you may still find leisure to devote some attention to the Minutiae of public good, in objects which promise the economy, convenience, and comforts of Life. I therefore take the liberty to address you on Kitchen fire-places, a subject which has occupied all the leisure time this winter that could be spared from my Lectures.

To prepare our food for giving the most nourishment; to construct the cooking Utensils with such forms as will lessen labour, ward off danger, ensure cleanlyness, command the power of fire, and economise fuel; are certainly objects of no little consequence to the Citizens of America.

I have therefore neither spared labour nor expence to obtain these objects in my Kitchen, and have done something more than is realy necessary, in order to shew what conveniences may be obtained; and still am progressing with my experiment. I have embraced Count Rumfords Idea's, and combined them with other engenious inventions. Some parts I have constructed in the most simple modes, with a view of inducing others to follow my example, thereby to lessen the consumption of fuel which must daily become more scarce near large Cities. I have invited many Gentlemen and Ladies to see my Kitchen, who have admired the ease and economy of our cooking; —some few have determined to put the mode into execution.

But how extremly difficult is it to turn people generally from their old customs! there is a laziness in our natures, not easily overcome, and nothing but the example of many, can produce a reform, even when it meets their full approbation. In the article of fuel, independent of the many other advantages, there may be made a saving of one half the expence.

My Pots are all set in brick-work, with flues embracing them, the fire placed on a grate; the air admited from below, with a door to lessen the quantity, or wholy stop the draught; and a damper to retain the heat.

The Pots have all close covers, made double, with the space between, filled with charcoal-dust, in order to retain the heat.

Round one pot I have made a gutter, to hold water, with a lip to the cover falling into the gutter, whence it is perfectly air and steam tight. but, through all the covers is a tube to carry off the steam, which is connected with ease to another tube, communicating with the common flue of the chimney, by which the Kitchen is kept free of vapour. I have also Papins digesting Pots, fitted to rings in brick work, in form of a furnace—and although in a country of such plenty as we enjoy, we have no need to digest bones, yet such Pots are certainly much the best for all culinary purposes, and although they cost more at first, yet by their retention of heat, they soon repay the extra expence. *Homony* is a valuable food, but in the present mode of pre-pairing it, too expensive—If a large digesting pot were made use off, the expence of cooking would be lessened full two thirds, even in the common fire-place, as less fire will keep them boiling, and the corn made as soft in 6 hours as in 12 in the present mode practiced in Maryland & Virginia.

The practice of cooking with steam has many advantages over that of boiling flesh, Fishes, and vegetables generally. The juces are retained in fishes, flesh, and the sweetness in many vegetables. And most of my Pots have the covers so constructed as to receive different sized Steam kettles, and to use a number at the same time, if wanted. Thus a considerable part of our food is better cooked with heat which is wholly lost by former methods—and yet a surpluss even in this mode may be spared and conveyed by tubes to another apartment for warmth.

In the combination of all these advantages for the several kinds of cookery I have studied the placing the flues in such manner as to render it easey to clean them when necessary—and the steam pipes and covers have handles of wood to prevent them from burning the hands.—In short the Cook need have no fateague, nor a red face in cooking provi-sions for a large company, and the only trouble of the Kitchen falls on the scullion.

one very important consideration is, that, a Kitchen constructed in this manner is rendered warm in Winter, and very cool in Summer, this may appear an enigma, unless it is known that it is not the quan-tity of heat, but properly retaining it, that constitutes the difference between warm and cold rooms.

If these improvements were generally brought into use, the Mistress of a family and her daughters would rather find amusement than trou-ble or torments in conducting the affairs of their Kitchens.

Although stews are preferable to roasting, yet the latter mode perhaps must not be given up—yet the fire-place for that purpose need not be more than one third the size used, even in the latest built Houses.—They certainly ought not to be any wider than is necessary to admit the quantity of meats desired to be roasted, as the smaller, the less liable to smoke, and, if properly constructed, according to the plan of my Patent right, more heat may be thrown out than in any other mode.

I have three ovens—that imbraced in my Patent, has an opening in the crown with a sliding cover, to let the smoke pass, when it is necessary to make fire in the oven, and a small door in the larger door for supplying air. Another oven which is made of sheet Iron, the heat to pass round it, and a damper to check the draught. but that which forms the fire place under my soop-pot, is not the least useful, though small, as it is ready for baking every day after noon, it will hold two large loafs of bread, and it retains the heat so well as to admit twice baeking of Pies without additional heat.

Many persons who visited my Kitchen have supposed as I have a patent right for sundry improvements on fire-places, that I also had an Interest in the additions I have lately made, hence I have found it necessary to declare my motive for shewing it was only to induce others to follow my example and construct such, without my aid, with a view to the saving of fuel and its becoming a public benefit.

How, speedily, to introduce into common use these improvements is a matter of some difficulty. If I had more leisure I might give descriptions, drawings and Models with such directions as workmen would readily comprehend, and know how to execute them on different scales, according to the demand of families of different circumstances.

Under a beleif that you accord with me in opinion that this is an object of importance, I have been thus lenthy, and yet the whole I have written, is only an outline, which your immagination will readily fill up.

While engaged in making a Pacquet to you, I cannot refrain sending for the Amusement of Miss Jefferson, a piece of Music composed by Mr. Hawkins, the person whose patent Piano, she is in possession of; its effect may perhaps be improved from associating the two circumstances.—The words were written by my son Rembrandt, by request from the Committee of Arrangements; the reason for a fathers approbation of them, will be readily acknowledged.

I am with the highest respect, Dear Sir, your obliged friend and Humble Servant.   C W PEALE

RC (DLC); at foot of text: "His Excellency Thos Jefferson Esqr."; endorsed by TJ as received 11 Mch. and so recorded in SJL. Dft (Lb in PPAmP: Peale-Sellers Papers); dated 7 Mch.

YOU MENTION MY LECTURE AND MUSEUM: TJ to Peale, 21 Feb. 1801. Peale and his son Raphaelle designed fireplaces and stoves to reduce the loss of heat through the chimney, and they won a $60 premium from the American Philosophical Society for a design of a fireplace. Peale's system for a KITCHEN, similar to Count Rumford's plan, incorporated multiple fireplaces in a brick wall. Each unit was sized to match its purpose, and their flues all connected to a common chimney. Many of the Peales' innovations drew on methods already employed in Europe (Peale, *Papers*, v. 2, pt. 1:139-41, 192-7, 212, 215n, 252, 303-4n).

The DIGESTING POTS designed by Denis Papin in the 17th century were a form of pressure cooker (same, 303n; Vol. 8:574).

In November 1797 Peale received a PATENT for the design that won the prize from the APS. He recommended placing an OVEN in the kitchen wall to draw heat from the junction of a fireplace flue with the main chimney. A description that he published in the Philadelphia *Weekly Magazine* in 1798 gave some construction information for WORKMEN, noting also that permission to build fireplaces under his patent was available for a fee (*List of Patents*, 15; Peale, *Papers*, v. 2, pt. 1:209-15).

PACQUET: TJ received from Peale a printed handbill with lyrics of four "Pieces To be sung at the German Reformed Church, on Wednesday, the 4th of March, 1801." Peale made notations on the handbill giving Peter S. Du Ponceau credit for the first piece, a "Solemn Invocation," and identifying Peale's son Rembrandt as the writer of the lyrics of "The People's Friend," a song in praise of Jefferson's election. Peale did not name the writer of the third item on the handbill, titled "Chorus." He attributed the last song on the handbill to Georg Friedrich Händel (DLC: TJ Papers, 110:18848; see illustration). The music for "The People's Friend" was by John Isaac HAWKINS. He and Rembrandt Peale collaborated on at least three other songs, "The Beauties of Creation," "Dirge," and "Ode on the Death of Titian Peale." Charles Willson Peale incorporated those pieces into a public lecture on natural history that he gave at the University of Pennsylvania in November 1800 (Richard J. Wolfe, *Secular Music in America, 1801-1825*, 3 vols. [New York, 1964], 3:1008-9; Charles Willson Peale, *Discourse Introductory to a Course of Lectures on the Science of Nature; with Original Music, Composed For, and Sung On, the Occasion* [Philadelphia, 1800], 6-7, 19, 46-7, and appended musical scores; Charles Coleman Sellers, *Charles Willson Peale*, 2 vols. [Philadelphia, 1947], 2:115).

For TJ's purchase of a Hawkins PIANO for his younger daughter, see Vol. 31:365-6; Vol. 32:39, 538.

From Benjamin Ring

State of Penilvania Dalewer County
Birmingham township Near Chads ford on Brandewine
hed quarters the March the 8d *1801*

Most Noble Jefferson at the heering of thy Being Appoynted President was Caus of greate goy to Mee wich I inwardly felt I Love a tru & faithfull American who is tru to his Cuntry. Not Valuing his privite intrust Eaquel to that of his Cuntrys prosperytyes & groeath I thought it Must be Caus of greate Cunfort & greate goy to Say I hath bee faithfull & Just in that trust Reposed in Mee at the Close

I May inform thee at thy being Appoynted President is Caus of greate goy in oure part of the Cuntry for their is greate Confidence Reposed in thee wich I hath No Doubt will be Answarred According to Exspektatishon From thy Assured Friend Unknown but yet Real
BENJAM: RING

NB I Wish to be Remembrred to our tru Freind Curnell Bur A tru Ameraken in whome their is No gile From—   B: R

I wish to be Excused for my freedom.

RC (DLC); at foot of text: "For Thomas Jefferson President"; endorsed by TJ as received 13 Mch. and so recorded in SJL.

From William Lee

Boston [before 9] March 1801—

Encouraged by a most respectable circle of friends I am induced to address the President of the United States on a subject highly interesting to myself and family.—But even with the flattering support which, I have the honor to enclose, I cannot hazard my present application to the supreme magistrate of the american people, without refering him to other partial testimonies in my favor, which, I presume may be found on the files of the Secretary of State. Having been a resident in France for several years, and bred to mercantile pursuits, I have been persuaded to suppose myself qualified to discharge the Office of Consul, in some one of the principal seaports, of that Republic, particularly at Bordeaux where, I have resided at different periods.—Should I meet the approbation of the President of the United States, in such an appointment, I can only promise, that no Exertions, or diligence, shall be wanting to promote the true interests of my country, which, would then be rendered doubly dear, to me, in the obtainment of his confidence.—

With the highest Veneration I have the honor to be the Presidents faithful servant—   WILLIAM LEE

RC (DNA: RG 59, LAR); dated "March 1801"; at foot of text: "Thomas Jefferson President of the United States"; endorsed by TJ as received 9 Mch. and so recorded in SJL. Enclosures: (1) Lee to John Marshall, 14 Nov. 1800, with Lee's subjoined list of letters already in the secretary of state's office to support his quest for a consulship, including a letter by envoys Elbridge Gerry, Marshall, and Charles Cotesworth Pinckney, another from Gerry, two from Benjamin Lincoln, two from William Tudor, one from John Coffin Jones, and one "signed by most of the merchants of Boston." (2) Lincoln to John Adams, 16 Dec. 1800. (3) Tudor to

[Adams], 16 Dec. 1800 (all Trs in same, in Lee's hand).

William Lee (1772-1840) began his career as a commission merchant in Boston. In 1794 he married Susan Palfrey. Her father, William Palfrey, a Boston merchant who served as paymaster general during the War for Independence, had been made U.S. consul general to France but died in 1780 on his way to take up the post. In 1796 Lee journeyed to Bordeaux on business, traveling also in Britain and Holland and returning to the United States in 1798. Among the people he saw in Europe were Joel Barlow, Elbridge Gerry, and James Monroe. John Marshall, in Paris as a U.S. envoy, called Lee "a gentleman of good connections & good character." On his return voyage Lee carried letters from various sources directed to recipients in America. After Lee arrived in the United States Oliver Wolcott took possession of a portion of that correspondence, including at least one letter addressed to TJ. Lee hoped for a consular appointment even at that time, and on 3 June 1801 TJ made him commercial agent at Bordeaux. John Adams had named Isaac Cox Barnet to that post, but Barnet was one of the February 1801 nominees who never received letters of appointment after TJ took office. In January 1802 the Senate approved TJ's appointment of Lee. In 1811, while still holding the Bordeaux consulship, Lee acted as secretary of legation for Barlow, who had been appointed U.S. minister to France. Four years later, Lee schemed with others in an unsuccessful plan to evacuate the defeated Napoleon Bonaparte to America. Resigning his position at Bordeaux in 1816 and returning to the United States, Lee accepted an accounting position in the War Department and within a few months became second auditor of the Treasury. He lost that position in 1829 and spent the remainder of his life in Boston (Mary Lee Mann, ed., *A Yankee Jeffersonian: Selections from the Diary and Letters of William Lee of Massachusetts, Written from 1796 to 1840* [Cambridge, Mass., 1958], 2, 52-3, 117, 158-9, 186, 211-12, 233-4, 299-300; Marshall, *Papers*, 3:397; JEP, 1:402; Paul H. Smith and others, eds., *Letters of Delegates to Congress, 1774-1789*, 26 vols. [Washington, D.C., 1976-2000], 1:684; Smith, *Freedom's Fetters*, 194-6, 198; Ammon, *Monroe*, 351; Vol. 30:175, 183-7, 436, 499; Elbridge Gerry to TJ, 24 Feb., above).

From David Austin

RESPECTED SIR—   Philadelphia March 9th. 1801—

Though a stranger to your person, I doubt not but as a Gentleman of science, of benevolence & of regard to the pacification of the present jarring interests of the World, you will indulge me with a moment's attention on a very interesting theme.

The Nations need to be pacified. From what quarter shall the Olive Branch be seen to come!—For this the Nations are looking, & the pious are longing.—

To you, Sir, appertains, under God, the introduction of this exploit. From this nation went forth the arrows of war, & from us must go the healing leaf.—

The forwarding of the ratification of the late Convention to France, presents an avenue through which this design may be floated.—The impediments, hitherto, found to lie in the way of this Commission teach that there is something, yet in the wheel of providence to be presented.

A new Œra, under your administration, at the commencment of this New period of time, is about to discover the opening design.—The prophets of the last section of the Gospel Œconomy have expected that to them would appertain the overturning of the papal power, & the introduction of the pacification which was to follow. Providence hath disappointed their expectation. The deed hath been performed by National means.—By *National means*, the pacific Empire, to follow, is to be introduced. In your hand, it now lies to commission the man capable, under God, not only to consolidate the Union between the two Republicks, in question, but to suggest, not to say introduce that system of National fraternity, which *all wish to see displayed.*

The design gets its birth in this Country; but is to unfold its beauties & energies, on the European Theatre.

If Mr. Livingston excuses himself from the task, which all suppose he will do;—then, think of the pointings of providence; of the agonies of the World, of our Nation's glory, & of your own honor. It is in the hand that moves this pen to introduce, & to perform, thro' the instrumentality of yr. Commission, this exploit. I am at command.—

Excuse the liberty I take in forwarding a paper, struck this day, introductory to the object contemplated; even, though intellectual & moral influence, only, should be applied. I find a high interest in this City; & much mental preparation for the happy event.—

Your inaugurating speech has mightily calmed political tumult at home; it only remains that you perfect the begun enterprize by extending the Olive leaf to contending Nations.

National & diplomatic operations are much more pointed & operative than those that are merely suasive. If you let off the arrow, you will stand as a "Mighty Hunter before the Lord"—

Though I am to remove to the Union Hotel, Market street, in a few days, my address will remain at "the George Tavern."

with all due esteem.   DAVID AUSTIN

RC (DNA: RG 59, LAR); at head of text: "Th. Jefferson"; endorsed by TJ as received 13 Mch. and so recorded in SJL.

David Austin (1759-1831) was one of the most popular millennial preachers of his day. A native of New Haven, Connecticut, he graduated from Yale in 1779 and was ordained by the Presbytery of New York to a pastorate at Elizabethtown, New Jersey, in 1788. He published a number of tracts

and predicted that the second coming would take place on the fourth Sunday of May 1796. The failure of this prophecy and his increasingly erratic behavior led his congregation to request his dismissal. Austin resigned the following May and spent the next several years indulging his millennial enthusiasms through itinerant preaching and published writings. His millennialism was marked by his belief that the creation of the American republic was a precursor to the second coming and that the New Jersusalem would be erected on a "Washingtonian" base. During the first year of TJ's presidency, Austin wrote the president frequently to offer his views on national and international affairs and to solicit public office. After TJ's failure to reply did not dissuade the minister from continuing his one-sided correspondence, TJ wrote Austin on 21 Jan. 1802 and curtly requested that he cease writing. Austin wrote only a handful of letters to TJ after that. Austin's fanaticism waned by the 1810s. He became pastor of a Congregational church in Bozrah, Connecticut, in 1815, where he served until his death (ANB; Sprague, *American Pulpit*, 2:195-206; Ernest Lee Tuveson, *Redeemer Nation: The Idea of America's Millennial Role* [Chicago, 1968], 116-19; Cunningham, *Jeffersonian Republicans in Power*, 31-2).

FORWARDING A PAPER, STRUCK THIS DAY: the 9 Mch. edition of the Philadelphia *Aurora* included an appeal by Austin entitled "National Placitude" that called on Christians of all denominations to gather in Philadelphia for a series of 25 lectures by Austin, which would lay the "foundation" of an "intellectual and Moral" empire and reveal the "original plan of the Supreme Architect, in the total œconomy of his natural and moral administration."

Austin provided TJ with additional information on his plan for world pacification in an 11 Mch. letter, assuring TJ that although "the matter may appear mysterious," there existed "a river ... which bears on its surface 'the leaves of the tree of life wh. are for the healing of the Nations'—This stream must find entrance into the mechanism of the National Circles in order to convey its benign influence through its agitated parts" (RC in DNA: RG 59, LAR; addressed: "Thomas Jefferson Esqr. Pres: U: States Federal City"; franked and postmarked; endorsed by TJ as received 16 Mch. and so recorded in SJL).

To John Hargrove

SIR   Washington Mar. 9. 1801.

I beg leave to return you my thanks, & through you to the acting committee of the New Jerusalem church in the city of Baltimore, for your friendly congratulations. I deplore, with you, the present sanguinary & turbulent state of things in the Eastern world, & look forward to the restoration of peace & progress of information for the promotion of genuine charity, liberality and brotherly kindness towards those who differ from us in opinion. the philanthropy which breathes through the several expressions of your letter are a pledge that you will endeavor to diffuse the sentiments of benevolence among our fellow men, & to inculcate the important truth that they promote their own happiness by nourishing kind & friendly dispositions towards others.   Commending your endeavors to the Being in whose hand we are, I beg you to accept assurances of my perfect consideration & respect.   TH: JEFFERSON

PrC (DLC); at foot of text: "The revd. John Hargrove Minister of the New-Jerusalem church. Baltimore."

FRIENDLY CONGRATULATIONS: see the New Jerusalem Church of Baltimore to TJ, 4 Mch. 1801.

From Tobias Lear

SIR,   Washington, March 9th: 1801—

Permit me to offer you my services in the Naval Department.—It would be presumption in me to say that I am fully qualified to conduct the business of this Department; but, having passed a few years, on my first entrance into life, in maratime affairs, which included the building and fitting out Vessels, and having been latterly engaged, for some years, in commerce, I cannot say that I am wholly inexperienced in Naval Affairs: and with the aid of the judgment of others in the great arrangements, joined to an indefatigable industry, I should hope to discharge the duties with Credit.—Whether this should be a permanent or temporary appointment I would submit to your determination.—In either event; or in the event of this application being altogether rejected, you may depend, Sir, upon my full support of your Administration, so far as my abilities will permit, beleiving as I do, that it will be conducted with purity, and upon the genuine principles of Republicanism.—

With the highest respect & Sincere regard, I have the honor to be Sir, Your most Obedient Servant   TOBIAS LEAR—

RC (DNA: RG 59, LAR); at foot of text: "The President of the United States"; endorsed by TJ as received 9 Mch. and so recorded in SJL.

Lear probably sought an appointment because of the financial troubles he was facing as a result of the collapse of T. Lear & Co. in 1798. As private secretary to George Washington he was the caretaker of the former president's papers in the 1790s and the months immediately following Washington's death. Rumors circulated that in exchange for political preferments Lear turned over to TJ sections of Washington's diary and correspondence relating to TJ's controversial letter to Philip Mazzei (ANB; Ray Brighton, *The Checkered Career of Tobias Lear* [Portsmouth, N.H., 1985], 147-59, 169-81; Marshall, *Papers*, 6:34-40, 192-4; Lear to TJ, 26 Mch.; Vol. 29:80n).

To Thomas McKean

DEAR SIR   Washington Mar. 9. 1801.

I have to acknolege the reciept of your favor of Feb. 20. and to thank you for your congratulations on the event of the election. had it terminated in the elevation of mr Burr, every republican would I am sure have acquiesced in a moment; because, however it might have been variant from the intentions of the voters, yet it would have been agreeable to the constitution. no man would more chearfully have submitted than myself, because I am sure the administration would have been republican, and the chair of the Senate permitting me to be at home 8. months in the year, would on that account have been much more consonant to my real satisfaction. but in the event of an usurpation I was decidedly with those who were determined not to permit it. because that precedent once set, would be artificially reproduced, & end soon in a dictator. Virginia was bristling up as I believe. I shall know the particulars from Govr. Monroe whom I expect to meet in a short visit I must make home, to select some papers books &c necessary here, and make other domestic arrangements. I am sorry you committed to the flames the communication of details you mention to have been preparing for me. they would have been highly acceptable, and would now be very encouraging, as shouldered on two such massive columns as Pensva & Virga, nothing could be feared. if it were not too troublesome I would still sollicit the communication at some leisure moment. I am sorry to see the germ of division which shewed itself in the contest[1] on your late Senatorial election. having put down all things under our feet, & so reduced our enemy that he has hardly force to hoop us together, we have now to fear division among ourselves, and that the common enemy will, by throwing itself into either scale, recover their ascendancy by our aid.—I am sorry the Chevalr. d'Yrujo is destined to leave us. I would not stand in the way of his wishes or promotion, but shall thro' our minister at Madrid take care to let it be understood how agreeable to us would be the continuance of his residence here. perhaps it may be too late to have any effect.—I am anxious by availing the US. in some way of the honest worth of Genl. Muhlenburg to remove the danger of past or future divisions among you.—we propose to supercede Kittera by mr Dallas, the superiority of whose character will suppress all clamour. yet I am afraid we shall thereby deprive you of an able assistant. it is said however that the removal to Lancaster is inconsistent with his other business, & therefore that he meditates a resignation of his present office. you once told me you would take care of mr Cooper. it would be extremely gratifying to me; as I consider him on a line with the first men in America in talents, virtue, & republicanism. the power which controuls my nominations entertains[2] insurmountable prejudices against him. nothing will be spared on my part to harmonize our system, and to render the republican basis so solid as to defy the machinations of terrorism, illuminatism &c. accept assurances of my highest consideration & respect.

Th: Jefferson

RC (PHi); addressed "Governor Mc.kean Lancaster"; endorsed. PrC (DLC); first page only.

TO SUPERCEDE KITTERA BY MR DALLAS: TJ appointed Alexander J. Dallas to serve as the U.S. attorney for the eastern district of Pennsylvania in place of John W. Kittera, one of Adams's late-term appointments (JEP, 1:381, 383, 402).

[1] TJ here canceled "between."
[2] Interlined in place of "[bears?]."

From John Mitchell

SIRE Geo. Town 9th March 1801

I find the late President has not appointed a Collector to the Port of Geo. Town, I Respectfully Solicite that office; in this Extraordinary applacation I am unfortunatly Situated, in not having the Honour of the least Personal Acquantance with you, And Mr Mason being absent, who I am confident, would Render me every assistance in his power Consistent with a man of Honour, to get the Appointment

Permit a Compatriot who Served our Common country from the very begining to the End of the Revulution, A Captain in the Navy, to Request the favour of you not to fill the Appointment, Untill he has time to apply, to Some of those who laboured in the great and good Cause with him, for Recommendations, viz Genr. Smith, Colo. Stone, Colo. Forrest, Colo. Howard, and the merchants of this place, with Reall Respect

I am Sire Your Humble Servt. JOHN MITCHELL

RC (DNA: RG 59, LAR); endorsed by TJ as received 10 Mch. and so recorded in SJL.

John Mitchell served as an inspector in the collector's office at Georgetown. Fearful of a yellow fever outbreak in 1800, Georgetown officials appointed Mitchell and two others "to diligently attend the wharves and landing places of the town and to visit all vessels which may come into the river, and if infected persons are found to prevent them from landing" (RCHS, 11 [1908], 209-10; Mitchell to TJ, 19 Sep. 1801).

LATE PRESIDENT HAS NOT APPOINTED A COLLECTOR: Mitchell believed there was a vacancy at the collector's office in Georgetown because, on 28 Feb., Adams had nominated James M. Lingan, collector of the port since 1789, to be marshal of the District of Columbia (Washington, *Papers, Pres. Ser.*, 2:294-5; note to List of John Adams's Appointments, printed at 23 Feb. 1801). Lingan, however, did not resign his position to become marshal. Mitchell wrote Gallatin in September 1801 that he thought that "Mr. Adam's tho in the last Agonizing Gasp of his Political Death, had been Cautious Enough to Clothe" Lingan "with the Necessary formality of a Commission." That evidently was not the case. But the collector's office did become vacant in September when Lingan resigned. Mitchell informed Gallatin that along with other

"impertinant" comments, Lingan proclaimed "that he would descend to Act, no longer Under the Present Administration." Mitchell requested that the vacancy not be filled until he could renew his application and obtain recommendations from the Masons, Samuel Smith, and Samuel Hanson (Mitchell to Gallatin, 15 Sep. 1801, in DNA: RG 59, LAR, endorsed by TJ: "Mitchell John. to mr Gallatin to be made Collector of Geo. T."). On 19 Sep., Mitchell wrote the president explaining the circumstances at Georgetown and renewing his application for the collectorship, giving John Thomson Mason as a reference (RC in same; endorsed by TJ as received 20 Oct. and so recorded in SJL; also endorsed by TJ: "to be Collector vice Lingan"). Mitchell reiterated his desire for the collectorship in a letter to TJ dated 8 Oct. 1801. He encouraged the president to obtain references from John T. Mason, the only person "perfectly Acquainted with my Political Sentements," Samuel Hanson, and the "other Mr. Mason," probably Stevens Thomson Mason (RC in same; endorsed by TJ as a letter of 8 Oct. but received on the 7th).

TJ probably learned of Lingan's resignation on 17 Sep. when he received a letter from the collector dated 11 Sep. (recorded in SJL but not found). In early October, TJ appointed John Oakley to the Georgetown collectorship (Appendix I, Lists 3 and 4).

To Jonathan H. Nichols

SIR   Washington Mar. 9. 1801.

The proposition you are pleased to make of dedicating to me your Dictionary of elegant essays cannot but be grateful to me as it is an additional testimony of the esteem of my fellow citizens, and of one in particular, who without a personal knowlege, has been able to raise his mind above the ocean of calumny under which it has been thought expedient to endeavor to overwhelm my name. I am far from admitting that it can contribute to the recommendation of your book, the object & design of which is above such feeble aids. but you are perfectly right in believing me a sincere friend of science & of it's propagation and advancement. I consider these as the surest means of gratifying our fellow citizens to controul understandingly the proneness of their servants to pervert to their own advantage the trusts confided to them for the advantage of others.

So much public as well as personal mischief has ensued from the publication of letters either written or pretended to have been written by me, that I am obliged to accompany them with an express request that they may be guarded against that.

Accept my good wishes & salutations   TH: JEFFERSON

PrC (DLC); at foot of text: "John H. Nichols. Boston."

PROPOSITION: see Nichols to TJ, 24 Feb. 1801. Despite TJ's EXPRESS REQUEST that this letter be kept out of the press, an extract consisting of the first two sentences appeared in the *Washington Federalist* on 22 July 1801. William Rind had apparently found the extract along with a prospectus for the publication of Nichols's dictionary of essays in a Massachusetts newspaper. The editor ridiculed the author's prose and included a paragraph from the prospectus to give the reader "an idea of the taste, sense & judgment of the compiler." He included the closing to the prospectus: "Examined, and Dedicated by permission, to his Excellency Thomas Jefferson, Esquire, The President of United America; His Country's boast, the Friend of Science, and the advocate of Man." There is no indication that Nichols's work was published.

Notes on a Cabinet Meeting

9. prosecutions under Sedition law. remit the fines & enter Nolle prosequi in the prosecutns depending under that law. towit Callendar & Brown are in exn. Duane &   under prosecn. present as before.

mr Lincoln to consult Edwds. Granger Kirby Wolcot as to Goodrich's commn

Dawson to have 6. Dol. a day.

2 frigates to cruise in W. Indies, 2 in Mediterrann. 2 at Isle of Bourbon.

sign the decln proposd by Commrs. of Washn. continuing permission to build houses in certain forms.

MS (DLC: TJ Papers, 110:18892); entirely in TJ's hand; on same sheet as Notes on a Cabinet Meeting, 8 Mch.

PRESENT AS BEFORE: see Notes on a Cabinet Meeting at 8 Mch.

SIGN THE DECLN: see Commissioners of the District of Columbia to TJ at 4 Mch. and enclosure.

From Henry Roosen

March: the 9: 1801.

DEAR PRESIDENT!   Montgomery County. State of Pennsylvania

I wich your Ecellency may long live, in good heald allways surroundet with good Friends and no Fatterers. Some Time ago my Neighbour Benjamin Rittenhouse Esquire in formed me that he wass in tendet to write to your Eccellency I begged the Favor of him to write in my behalf lyke wyse, beggen the Precident to bestow on me a little Offices, Eqr. Rittenhouse atvised me to do it my selves, that your Ecellence wass a Gentllemen and Plain words would have moor efect by your Ecellence then hey Browing words, on this insurens I make bold to address your Ecellence beggen Humbly to bestow a little Office on me, and such a one that I can stay at home, by so doing you will faver a honest man advanset in Years, and blissing will attend your Ecellence, sertenly Sr it must appear Strange to you to be asket a Favor of a Mann you never heard his Name, but Joseph Nourse Esqr. in your City knows me, and by him your Eccellency may be in formed of my Caracter.

I have the Honour to call my self your Eccelency most Obidient Humble Servan   HENRY ROOSEN

RC (DNA: RG 59, LAR); addressed: "His Excellency Thomas Jefferson President of U States Washington"; endorsed by TJ as received 30 Mch. and so recorded in SJL.

Henry Roosen (1739-1803), a Mennonite, immigrated to Philadelphia from London sometime before 1765. A confectioner by trade, he had a shop on Chestnut Street before moving to Worcester Township after the Revolutionary War (*Bulletin of the Historical Society of Montgomery County Pennsylvania*, 11 [1959], 310; *Pennsylvania Gazette*, 13 June 1765).

To Samuel Smith

DEAR SIR   Washington Mar. 9. 1801.

By the time you recieve this, you will have been at home long enough I hope to take a view of the possibilities, & of the arrangements, which may enable you so to dispose of your private affairs, as to take a share in those of the public, & give us your aid as Secretary of the navy. if you can be added to the administration I am forming, it will constitute a mass so entirely possessed of the public confidence, that I shall fear nothing. there is nothing to which a nation is not equal where it pours all it's energies & zeal into the hands of those to whom they confide the direction of their force.[1] you will bring us the benefit of adding in a considerable degree the acquiescence at least of the leaders who have hitherto opposed us. your geographical situation too is peculiarly advantageous, as it will favor the policy of drawing our naval resources towards the center from which their benefits & protection may be extended equally to all the parts. but what renders it a matter not only of desire to us, but, permit me to say, of moral duty in you, is that if you refuse, where are we to find a substitute? you know that the knowlege of naval matters in this country is confined entirely to persons who are under other absolutely disqualifying circumstances. let me then, my dear Sir, intreat you to join in conducting the affairs of our country, and to prove by consequences that the views they entertained in the change of their servants are not to be without effect. in short, if you refuse, I must abandon from necessity, what I have been so falsely charged of doing from choice, the expectation of procuring to our country such benefits as may compensate the expences of their navy. I hope therefore you will accede to the proposition. every thing shall be yielded which may accomodate it to your affairs. let me hear from you favorably & soon. Accept assurances of my high & friendly consideration & esteem.   TH: JEFFERSON

RC (Mrs. Leonard A. Hewett, Louisville, Kentucky, 1944); addressed: "Genl. Samuel Smith Baltimore"; franked and postmarked. PrC (DLC). Not recorded in SJL.

[1] Word interlined in place of "efforts."

From John Stuart

SIR   Greenbrier March 9th. 1801

I was Honored with yours of the 14th. ulto. and the Diploma enclosed, and have to regret the want of qualifications that should entitle me to such a respectable mark of your favor.

I beg leave to Congratulate you on the late appointment to your High office, and am happy to inform you that in the small Circle of my acquaintance the final decision of Congress for President give universal satisfaction. Tho the People here are not yet such thorough Republicans as to loose all respect for the ruleing powers, or view opposition without horible dred of Anarchy, Principals which incline them to make reasonable allowance for the errors of Human nature in an Administration the uncurrupted choice of the People. The change however has a most auspicious prospect in reconciling the growing animosity of Zealous oppositions, the common misfortune of Republican forms of Government.

That it may terminate with the Highest satisfaction to yourself and the most sanguien hopes of the People is the sincere wish of one who has the Honor to be with profound respect your most obd. Humbl. Servt.   JOHN STUART

RC (DLC); endorsed by TJ as received 9 Apr. and so recorded in SJL.

From George Taylor

SIR   Alexandria March 9th 1801

The Citizens of Alexandria anxious for an opportunity of testifying *collectively* their high respect, for the chief Magistrate of the United States, have with an unanimous *voice* at a late meeting held for the purpose; expressed their desire that you will partake of a public Dinner, at as early a day as will be most convenient to yourself;—Less favoured than their brethren of the Eastern side of the District, as being more remote from the seat of Government, they Persuade themselves you will not suffer any unimportant considerations to oppose this real expression of the general sentiment

It is Sir with peculiar satisfaction and a perfect acquiscence on the wish of my fellow Citizens that I have the honour to make you this communication;—and I beg you to be assured of the confidence and regard with

Which I am Sir Your Most Obt. Hul. Svt.

GEORGE TAYLOR Mayor

RC (MoSHi: Jefferson Papers); at head of text: "Thomas Jefferson Esqr. President of the US"; endorsed by TJ as received 11 Mch. and so recorded in SJL.

George Taylor (ca. 1758-1851) was an active member of the Alexandria mercantile community, supporting a 1792 effort to establish a bank in the town and serving as a director of the Marine Insurance Company of Alexandria. He was appointed a justice of the peace for Alexandria County by John Adams on 2 Mch. 1801. Despite Taylor's "midnight appointment," TJ retained him in the post (*Alexandria Gazette*, 27 June 1851;

WMQ, 2d ser., 3 [1923], 206-8; *Federal Gazette & Baltimore Daily Advertiser*, 27 Jan. 1801; JEP, 1:388, 404; Appendix I, List 4).

The PUBLIC DINNER for TJ in Alexandria was held on 14 Mch. at Gadsby's Hotel. The event, which the Alexandria *Times* proclaimed to be the largest ever given in the city, was attended by TJ, the vice president, Secretary of War Henry Dearborn, Attorney General Levi Lincoln, and General James Wilkinson. TJ and his suite, escorted by two troops of cavalry, arrived around 2:00, then held a "numerous levee" before dining. When toasts were made, TJ offered "Prosperity to the town of Alexandria" (Alexandria *Times*, 16 Mch. 1801; *Alexandria Advertiser and Commercial Intelligencer*, 16 Mch. 1801).

From Benjamin Smith Barton

SIR,   Philadelphia, March 10th, 1801.

I take the liberty of introducing to your knowledge the bearer of this, Mr. Benjamin Rittenhouse. Mr. Rittenhouse is the brother of our late illustrious astronomer. He is a man of the most amiable character, and of pure, unsoiled republican principles.

Permit me, Sir, to congratulate your country upon the great event which has just taken place. To you, I am persuaded, the event is of much less importance than to the United-States, and to the world, at large. *Novus jam nascitur ordo.* May it be an order, a dispensation calculated to increase your happiness, as, I sincerely believe, it will increase the happiness of the union.

I acknowledge, with many thanks, the receipt of your letter of the 14th of February, and subscribe myself, with the greatest respect, Sir,

Your most obedient and most humble servant, and friend,

BENJAMIN SMITH BARTON

RC (DLC); endorsed by TJ as received 19 Mch. and so recorded in SJL.

NOVUS JAM NASCITUR ORDO: "a new order is now born."

From George Caines

SIR   New York 10th March 1801

I have to solicit permission to dedicate to You, the work, the proposals for which I take the liberty to transmit. It is intended to be of general utility to the people over whom You preside, & I know not, Sir, to what patronage it can be so properly directed, as to that of the Man who has so long, and so truly had at heart the interests of his Country. Suffer me then, Sir, to ask for the Lex Mercatoria Americana, that protection, which at Your hands America herself looks up to receive.

With unfeigned sentiments of real respect, impressed on my mind years before I had the Honor of being made known to You, I beg leave to subscribe myself,

Sir, Your most devoted and very Humble Servant

GEO. CAINES

RC (DLC); at foot of text: "The President of the United States"; endorsed by TJ as received 16 Mch. and so recorded in SJL. Enclosure: Prospectus for publishing *Lex Mercatoria Americana, or The American Merchants' Law* at eight dollars to subscribers with a request of a one dollar advance deposit (broadside in same).

George Caines (1771-1825), a legal scholar, author, and first official court reporter for the Supreme Court of New York, was practicing law in New York when the first volume of his *Lex Mercatoria Americana* was published anonymously in 1802. He intended to publish other volumes, but delays in printing and an indifferent reception to the work forced him to abandon the project (DAB).

From Tench Coxe

SIR   Philada. March 10th. 1801.

When I had the honor to write you upon the subject of an appointment, I did it with great reluctance from the numerous suggestions of names & applications that must necessarily embarrass and distress you. I will not suppress the expression of a consciousness, that I have undergone the most injurious and severe trials in the public service as a citizen lately, and before as an officer. My seniority in the treasury, had I not been removed would have given Me there, high claims. My habits in naval matters, and my too great attention to our public affairs might have justified my submitting myself to your consideration in that department, but it is my wish to receive such consideration as may be convenient. Should it happen that no object has been destined for me, I would wish it understood that some of the appointments in Pennsa. that may be soon vacant would be acceptable. Public Opinion has gone forth, that General Henry Miller will not continue in the office of "*Supervisor of the revenue*" in this State. The office is one of the sixteen, which as Commr. of the Revenue I superintended—besides the charge of the establishments for the safety & direction of shipping. Should it be placed in my hands, I trust there could be no doubt, that it would receive a correct administration. I will not consume your occupied time by saying more, nor have I chosen to assail you with indirect applications. My friend Mr. Dawson is the only man on earth to whom I have ever said a syllable to induce to a mention of my name—I do assure you,

Sir, I would not thus trouble you—I would wait the course of things—or decline public employment, but the inroads of our political enemies upon my property, late profession, and chances of [busin]ess, and the duties I owe [to] a very numerous family compel me to pay this attention to what I have little attended to——the emoluments of office—

I have the honor to be sir yr. most respectf. Servt

TENCH COXE

RC (DNA: RG 59, LAR); torn at seal; addressed: "The President of the U.S.";
endorsed by TJ as received 13 Mch. and so recorded in SJL.

From Samuel Hanson

SIR,   George-Town, March 10th; 1801

Knowing that my Friend, John T. Mason, would be out of Town all this week, I repaired to him immediately, for the purpose of communicating your commands on the Subject mentioned to me a few days ago. His Kinsman had set out for Philadelphia that morning. The result of our conference shall be laid before you at any moment that you shall appoint for me to wait on you—except the Hours between 10 and 3 O'Clock, when my official Duties require my presence here.

With due sensibility for the honour of being associated, in your consideration, with two such Men, I remain,

with perfect respect, Sir Your most obedt

S. HANSON of Saml

RC (DLC); endorsed by TJ as received 10 Mch. and so recorded in SJL.

On 5 Mch. TJ nominated JOHN T. MASON to serve as the U.S. attorney for the District of Columbia in place of Thomas Swan (Appendix I, List 3).

From Meriwether Lewis

DEAR SIR,   Pittsburgh, March 10th. 1801.

Not untill two late on friday last to answer by that days mail, did I receive your much esteemed favour of the 23rd. Ult, in it you have thought proper so far to honour me with your confidence, as to express a wish that I should accept the place of your private Secretary; I most cordially acquiesce, and with pleasure accept the office, nor were further motives necessary to induce my complyance, than that you Sir should conceive that in the discharge of the duties of that office, I could be servicable to my country, or ucefull to youreself: permit me here Sir to do further justice to my feelings, by expressing the lively sensibility with which I received this mark of your confidence and esteem.

I did not reach this place on my return from D,Etroit, untill late on the night of the 5th. inst., five days after the departure of Genl. Wilkinson, my report therefore on the subject of your letter was immediately made to Colo Hamtramck, the commanding Officer at this place; since which, not a moment has been lost in making the necessary arrangments in order to get forward to the City of Washington with all possible despatch: rest assured I shall not relax in my exertions.

Receive I pray you Sir, the most undesembled assureances of the attatchment and friendship of

Your most obedient, & Very Humble Servt,

MERIWETHER LEWIS.

RC (DLC); at foot of text: "Thomas Jefferson. President of the U. States"; endorsed by TJ as received 20 Mch. and so recorded in SJL.

From Henry Whetcroft

SIR   Washington 10th. March 1801

I beg permission respectfully to represent, that I have for some time past acted in the capacities of Justice of the Peace, and Notary Public of this City, under appointments by the Executive of Maryland, but discontinued in both those capacities by the late President, in his appointments under the late Acts of Congress, respecting the Jurisdiction of the District of Columbia.

In respect to the appointment of Justice of the peace, I am informed by a Gentleman of great respectability, who was present when the Nominations were made, that it was intended to continue all the old Justices, and that my name being accidentally omitted, in a list which was made out for the late President at his request, was the sole cause of my not being commissioned by him, as were all the other persons (one excepted) who were in Commission with me by the State.—Under those Circumstances, and lest the Omission above mentioned may operate to my disadvantage with those who might suppose it was designed, I respectfully solicit you Sir, to be pleased to continue me in Commission, which I flatter myself will be quite agreeable to my Fellow Citizens of this County.—

As to the appointment of Notary Public, the late President has commissioned one person only for this County, but I am informed the

Commission will be of no Effect, the power of appointing being vested in the Circuit Court of the Territory; altho' the Gentleman commissioned by the late President has for some time past been in commission for George Town, by the same Authority by which I was commissioned for Washington, yet I trust that if there be nothing incompatible with the Law, or objectionable to my Character or Conduct the President or the Court, as the law may provide, will at least deem it just and proper to grant me a Commission to act as heretofore within the City of Washington, or that part of Washington County containing the City.

I am not unmindful Sir, of the multiplicity of important Business which at this time necessarily occupies your Attention, and therefore do not presume to expect, or desire it to be turned to this trivial communication, 'till you are at leisure

I have the honor to be with Sentiments of perfect respect Sir Your mo. obdt. hu. Servt.   HENRY WHETCROFT

RC (DNA: RG 59, LAR); addressed: "The President of the United States"; endorsed by TJ as received 11 Mch. and so recorded in SJL.

On 2 Mch. 1801, John Adams made 23 nominations for the office of JUSTICE OF THE PEACE in Washington and 19 for Alexandria. For NOTARY PUBLIC he nominated Samuel Hanson for Washington and Henry Moore for Alexandria. In January 1802, TJ determined the nominations for justice of the peace too numerous and reduced the number of commissions to 15 each for Washington and Alexandria (JEP, 1:388, 404).

From William Bache

DEAR SIR.   Franklin March 11th. 1801.

I thank you much for yours of the 12th. Feby. and the inclosed pamphlet. No one can doubt the justice of a general maritime law, calculated to support neutral trade; but has not the author of common sense been rather fanciful in his detail. In the proposition of a law, which must necessarily be forced down the throat of the greatest maritime power extant, might not trivial aberrations from principle be over looked, to further its acceptance by the major part of commercial nations; does not the author, when he considers the neutral flag, as equal protection with neutral convoy, risk the opposition of the petty despots of the sea, who are never willing to give up the shadow of a power for the substance of a good. If however this right of visitation is admitted will not every objection be done away. It would be too large a stride towards truth to interdict naval armaments altogether, or the practice of medling with the floating property of friend or foe should be irrevocably condemned—

It is well that the American Conclave, not followg the favourite precedents of that of the Hats, have finally bethought themselves of the will of the people. But some comfort may still accrue to the sticklers for precedency, as it has not altogether been waved for the Cardinals once made choice of a Ganganelli. The People rejoice in the instalment of theirs; how far he should be joyful the cares of the first week will have already told him.—

If the fame of our new born has not yet reached your ears I now announce the birth of the young Benjamin Franklin Bache. May his name remind him of the patriotism of his predecessors, & may that remembrance stimulate him to an imitation of their virtues. For him and his sister I must endeavour to open better prospects. To you I refer. If there is any thing in your disposal, worthy my acceptance, and in which I can do justice by acquitting myself towards the people, I will thank you for it. If not you will still possess the affectionate regards of your sincere friend   WILLIAM BACHE

RC (DNA: RG 59, LAR); addressed: "Thomas Jefferson President of the U.S.A. Washington"; franked; endorsed by TJ as received 19 Mch. and so recorded in SJL.

Bache had named his Albemarle County property FRANKLIN in honor of his grandfather (Jane Flaherty Wells, "Thomas Jefferson's Neighbors: Hore Browse Trist of 'Birdwood' and Dr. William Bache of 'Franklin,'" *Magazine of Albemarle County History*, 47 [1989], 4). YOURS OF THE 12TH FEBY.: TJ's letter to Bache of 12 Feb. 1801 is recorded in SJL but has not been found; see, printed under that date, the similar letters in which TJ reported on the balloting by the House of Representatives and distributed copies of Thomas Paine's *Compact Maritime*.

In 1769 the conclave of Roman Catholic CARDINALS, divided over the Bourbon monarchies' opposition to the Jesuits, finally selected as the new pontiff Giovanni Vincenzo Antonio GANGANELLI. He had a record of close relations with Jesuits but seemed responsive to the Bourbon courts. As Pope Clement XIV he ordered the suppression of the Society of Jesus (*New Catholic Encyclopedia*, 2d ed., 15 vols. [New York, 2003], 3:793-7).

Bache's wife, Catharine Wistar Bache, had gone to Monticello for the birth of their son BENJAMIN FRANKLIN BACHE in February. The baby's older SISTER was named Sarah like her grandmother, Sarah Franklin Bache (Wells, "Jefferson's Neighbors," 7; *New England Historical and Genealogical Register*, 8 [1854], 374).

From William Brent

Commissioners Office, Washington

SIR   11th March 1801.

My friend and Relation, Mr. Richard Brent informed me some time ago, that he had signified my wish to you of becoming your private Secretary; and I make no doubt that his partiality for me induced him to give the highest colouring to my Pretensions to that

Office.   My Object in troubling you now, is respectfully to renew this Subject, though I do it with the utmost diffidence, and under the fear that I perhaps unnecessarily trespass upon your Time, in the liberty I take: But not having understood that any person was Yet appointed by you to the Office in question, and as I have very much at heart the success of this application in my behalf, I cannot but hope for your Indulgence, while I presume thus di[rec]tly to bring myself again under your notice, to solicit myself, an honor at your hands, which the friendship of another has been already exerted to procure for me. With sentiments of profound respect

    I am, Sir, yr. very Obt Servt   WM BRENT

RC (DNA: RG 59, LAR); damaged; at foot of text: "President of the United-States"; endorsed by TJ as received 12 Mch. and so recorded in SJL.

William Brent (1775-1848), a native of Stafford County, Virginia, was employed in Washington by the board of commissioners until May 1801. He was one of three commissioners designated to receive subscriptions for the Columbia Manufacturing Company in Washington. A member of the municipal council and a colonel of the militia, Brent declined an offer extended by Meriwether Lewis in 1803 to become TJ's private secretary, citing his intent to become established in a mercantile line instead. He agreed to render temporary service as needed to the president. Upon the death of Uriah

Forrest in 1805, he succeeded as clerk of the circuit court for the District of Columbia, an office he held for 38 years (Bryan, *National Capital*, 1:85, 411, 455, 555; Chester Horton Brent, *The Descendants of Collo Giles Brent Capt George Brent and Robert Brent, Gent Immigrants to Maryland and Virginia* [Rutland, Vt., 1946], 137-8; Brent to Meriwether Lewis, 25 Feb. 1803 [RC in DLC, endorsed by TJ]).

SOME TIME AGO: see Richard Brent to TJ, 14 Jan.

TJ's reply to William Brent of 13 Mch., recorded in SJL, has not been found. Brent also offered himself as a candidate for marshal of the District of Columbia in a letter to TJ of 17 Mch. (RC in DNA: RG 59, LAR; endorsed by TJ as received 17 Mch. and so recorded in SJL).

From Mary Glenholmes

Winchester March 11th 1801[1]

Great Monark—please to pardon my Boldness in troubling your Honour with those lines. I single Surcomstance hapened with in the Surcomferance of my acquaintance which I think worthy of notice— But Shold your wisdom—and prudiance think it not worthey of the Slightest Glance—I humbley submit to your Superior judgement in this Case—Being moved By this Surcomstance in pity to this famely about whom I am a going to mention—tho pity is all the tribute I Can pay to a man who processes intergity so wonderful as to hesitate no longer we will at once come to the point in hand—there is a Sertain man ho Resides in winchester—he desended from a good famely—tho a declining one as to this worlds goods—he is a Elder in the Methodist Republican Church one of Mr. C Relys Society—he Is now Employed in the buisiness of Scool keeping—he was always using his influence—and considering all things it was very powerfull—for he taught and all his Society Drank in to the same spirit many aristocrats under took to talk to him conserning it and he told them Rember the widows mite in days of Old was Excepted and tho his was But a mite comparitively Speaking—But he Bold it was a thousand times as much he Being a man of a tolarable degree of knolidg & generaly gave good Reasons why it Shold Be contended for—at length his landlord Being an Arest sent him word to desist for he was doing a vast of harm to the Cause, here we will pass over many things and not trouble you with such trifles—But he hel on—at lenth came the night of the Rejoyceing—an as I am told he alumanated sixty lites of glass—his lanlord Sent Strict word if the house was not darkned in a moment & he wold make use of all the Sevearity that in his power lay—and leave him not a Bed to lay his Sides upon for he was Behind hand in the Rent. But he Regardless of that Continued the lite—his wife Burst in tears and intreated him to darken the house—and urged the day was gained—and that wold neither ad nor Diminish—his Reply to her my Child you talk like one of the foolish woman—in days past to jobe—I will not Sacrifice my just principles to the ambition of mortal men—for as jobe said Nothing I Brought nor nothing I can take away for two hundred Dollers wold pay all my Debts and place me as well as I am now and I am willing to Suffer—if he will not in dulge me— I know I shall never want a friend—so Bid his wife to Be of good comfort the lord will provide—yes aded a chidd of three years old I will go and tell Mr jeferson on him an he will gave us a fine hous—for all the mother wass in tears She Smiled to hear the Child—But o my Babe aded she the presedent will Set in throned in this worlds grandure— and on the fifteenth of apriel these walls will Be Striped of all thay contain—and you and I must suffer for your fathers doings in this Case—as I live allmost joining houses with this family—they want nothing But outward acomplishments to Recommend them all most in any Company or any Business. my heart melted with in me and my Bowels yerned to wards them—But I am But a widow myself and am not in a capacity to administer to ther necessity—my persesions is small—one house and lot and 2 small children to Raise and I a lone or if it was with me as in times past I wold asist them against the fiftenth of apriel and Rescue them out of the mouth of the lion—I humbley Beg your pardon for troubleing your Exelency with those lines But my mind was so opresed in day by troughts and By Dreams at night hearing the complaints of that poor woman—now I shall be eased of a Burden that night I heard it pass I was Determed to Rite But then my intentions languished—and it was like the tide had its comings and goings—his name is John Bond flushed with the eidees of your Benevelence I submit to your Exelency   MARY GLENHOLMES.

RC (MHi); endorsed by TJ as received 23 Mch. and so recorded in SJL.   [1] MS: "8001."

From Samuel Hanson

SIR,   George-Town, March 11th., 1801
I have just conversed with a Gentleman well acquainted with Mr. Duvall's situation in Annapolis. He says that Mr. D. has little or no property in that place to attach him to it, on that account—that his present Salary, as a Judge,[1] is no more than $1600—and that he has no doubt that Mr. D. would accept the office of chief Justice of this District.

I take the liberty of communicating this information to you, with the hope of it's seconding the good intentions, expressed [to] you this morning, in favour of that honest [m]an and distinguished Republican. In [th]is freedom I am encouraged by the per[m]ission you had the goodness to grant me [i]n similar cases.

with the utmost respect I am Sir Your most obedt

S HANSON of Saml

RC (DLC); torn; endorsed by TJ as received 12 Mch. and so recorded in SJL.   [1] MS: "Jude."

From Samuel Kennedy

HONORABLE SIR   [11 Mch. 1801]
The artist & subscriber presumes to lay before you a Print to the Immortality of George Washington, for your Patronage; representing this Citizen ascending on light clouds from Mt. Vernon; on his Dexter hand are Portraits of the Heroes Warren, & Montgomery, taken from Trumbulls Paintings;—

In submitting this Print to your Protection, I must avail myself of this opportunity of wishing every Happiness to the worthy Chief Magistrate of America, & a series of good fortune to His Administration. I have the Honor to be Your Excellencies Ob Servt.

SAML. KENNEDY

RC (DLC); undated; at head of text: "To His Excellency Thomas Jefferson President of the United States"; endorsed by TJ as received 11 Mch. and so recorded in SJL.

In 1800, Samuel Kennedy of Philadelphia published a PRINT from a stipple engraving by David Edwin after Rembrandt Peale's *Apotheosis of Washington*. Advertised in the 20 Dec. 1800 issue of the *Temple of Reason*, the "elegant engraving" included a full-length portrait of Washington, "the Soldier, the Statesman, the Husband and the Friend." He was flanked on one side by "a figure of Cupid, suspended in the air, attentively admiring Washington" and on the other by the Revolutionary War heroes Joseph Warren and Richard Montgomery, taken from their portraits in PAINTINGS by John Trumbull, *The Death of General Warren at the Battle of Bunker's Hill* and *The Death of General Montgomery in the Attack on Quebec* (Harold Holzer, *Washington and Lincoln Portrayed: National Icons in Popular Prints* [Jefferson, N.C., 1993], 33, 35; ANB, s.v. "Trumbull").

From Samuel A. Otis

SIR   Washington. 11th March 1801

Agreably to your directions I send a copy of the record of the last session. The preceeding copy is in books deposited in the office of the late Secy to the President US or probably may be found in the office of the late Secretary for the department of State. I send you also a copy of everything printed during the Session as complete as is in my power. Should however any particular report be omitted be pleased to mention it and I will make a further effort.

Your goodness will excuse my taking this opportunity to mention my son Harrison G Otis Atty for the Massachusetts district; reinstated in the office by Mr Adams to which he was originally [app]ointed by Genl. Washington.

He resigned the office on being elected to Congress and sacrificed a business that at a moderate estimate would have yielded him 20,000 dollars. With a large and increasing family it became imprudent for him longer to continue in congress and peremptorily refused solicitation. On retiring Mr Adams reinstated him in his former office become vacant by Mr Davis's promotion; and in which should you be pleased to continue him, I am confident he will discharge the duties with honor & fidelity; and in doing which you will oblige an affectionate father &

Your most obedient humble Servt   SAM: A. OTIS

RC (DLC); torn; at foot of text: "The President of the United S[tates]"; endorsed by TJ as received 12 Mch. and so recorded in SJL.

REINSTATED IN THE OFFICE: Harrison Gray Otis was among those nominees submitted by President Adams on 18 Feb.; see List of John Adams's Judicial Appointments, printed at that date. On 3 Sep. 1789 Samuel A. Otis wrote George Washington a letter recommending his son for office, but the president did not make the appointment until 1796. Harrison Gray

Otis served as a Massachusetts congressman from 1797 to 1801 (*Biog. Dir. Cong.*; Washington, *Papers, Pres. Ser.*, 3:599). Considering Otis a midnight appointment, TJ appointed George Blake as U.S. attorney in his place (see Appendix 1, Lists 3 and 4, and Notes on a Cabinet Meeting, 8 Mch. 1801).

From John Smith

SIR,   Philadelphia March 11. 1801

So far as the enclosed Certificates may justify I presume to place myself before you as a Candidate for office, whenever it may be your pleasure, or occation may occur, to turn your attention to our state. In the Middle age of life, heretofore used to commercial pursuits, with a *wife* and family now distressed by the effect of political persecution, a Mind unambitious and Moderate Views, I should be thankful for Such employment in the service of the United States, as future Arrangements and your wisdom may direct—It might however be an injustice to myself, Sir, not to state that a Cruel report by some ill disposed person, that I have circulated a letter which proprosed to produce an opposition to Governor Mc:Kean and to favour the election of Genl. Muhlenberg, as Governor of this State, is totally destitute of truth.—

I have the honor to be with the highest respect your Obedient Servant

JNO SMITH

RC (DNA: RG 59, LAR); endorsed by TJ as received 16 Mch. and so recorded in SJL. Enclosures: (1) Commissioned officers of the Militia Legion of Philadelphia to TJ, 5 Mch. 1801, offering congratulations on the "revival of the republican conduct opinions and feelings which have procured to us the gratification and to our Country the benefit of your recent election" and recommending John Smith, a "uniform and active republican Character" who served "in advancing the cause of democracy" to the detriment of his business affairs, noting that it would therefore give "great Satisfaction if it should happen that Some appointment in the Service of his country were to be confided to him" (same; in Smith's hand, signed by Thomas Willis, William Duane, James McKean, John Shee, Thomas Leiper, James Stuart, William Jones, and 22 others, with signatures certified by Peter Christian, adjutant; at head of text: "To Thomas Jefferson President of the United States"; endorsed by TJ: "Pennsylva. Marshal"). (2) Members of the Philadelphia Committee of Arrangements and Correspondence to TJ, 5 Mch. 1801, offering congratulations and seeking an appointment for Smith with language almost identical to that of Enclosure No. 1 (same; in Smith's hand, signed by Hugh Ferguson, John Barker, William Rush, Frederick Wolbert, William Coats, James Kerr, and 12 others, with signatures certified by John Barker as chairman of the "General town Meeting"; at head of text: "To Thomas Jefferson President of the United States"; endorsed by TJ as received 18 Mch. and so recorded in SJL). (3) Certificate from John Beckley, 10 Mch. 1801, printed below.

John Smith, a Philadelphia merchant, served for many years in the militia and in June 1794 became a major in the Second Philadelphia Regiment led by Colonel John Barker. He resigned his commission a few months later in opposition to the excise law. In July 1798 he helped organize Philadelphia's Fourth Troop of Light Horse and was elected first lieutenant of the troop under Captain Thomas Leiper. Smith played a key role in getting out the vote for Republican electors in Pennsylvania in 1796. He strongly supported Thomas McKean in the 1799 gubernatorial campaign and was disappointed when he failed to receive an appointment in the new administration. Described as Tench Coxe's political lieutenant, Smith was again active in the Republican cause in 1800 and served as secretary of the committee of arrangements that planned the 4 Mch. inaugural celebration in Philadelphia. TJ offered Smith the position of marshal of the eastern district of Pennsylvania in late March after John Shee declined to serve (PMHB, 52 [1928], 378-9; Cooke, *Coxe*, 285, 346-7, 371n, Smith to Tench Coxe, 30 Oct. and 15 Dec. 1800, in PHi: Coxe Family Papers; Appendix I, List 4; Leiper to TJ, 8 Mch. 1801).

CRUEL REPORT BY SOME ILL DISPOSED PERSON: perhaps Israel Israel, the sheriff of Philadelphia, who Smith noted had become his "Enemy and the Enemy of many other Republicans." Israel boasted that he had kept Smith from obtaining a position under the McKean administration and that he also had "influence over Mr Jefferson," which he intended to use to prevent Smith's appointment "to any Office" (Smith to Coxe, 15 Dec. 1800, in PHi: Coxe Family Papers).

TJ received communications from two counties in Pennsylvania proposing Smith for an appointment. On 14 Mch. the citizens of Reading, in Berks County, sent congratulations, noting the election demonstrated the confidence the "warm Supporters of Democracy" had in TJ. They believed the newly elected president would advance the prosperity of the country through the encouragement of agriculture, commerce, and manufactures

and perpetuate "those Principles of Liberty upon which American Independance was founded." TJ could accomplish the goals if he carefully selected "suitable Characters to fill the Various departments of Public Office." With this in mind the signers wished to introduce Smith, a gentleman who "would fill any Appointment given him with Advantage to the Public and Credit to himself" (RC in DNA: RG 59, LAR; in unidentified hand, signed by Jacob Bright, Joseph Hiester, Jacob Schneider, and 12 others; at head of text: "To Thomas Jefferson President of the United States"; endorsed by TJ as received 21 Mch. and so recorded in SJL). In an undated letter, the citizens of Northumberland County, Pennsylvania, congratulated TJ and recommended Smith, introducing the same ideas in similar language as in the memorial from Berks County. The communication was signed by Daniel Montgomery and 14 others (same; at head of text: "To Thomas Jefferson, Esquire President of the United States").

In an undated note TJ wrote: "John Smith, Majr. of Phila. a 1st Lieut. in Leiper's corps of dragoons recommd by Dr. Leib as Marshall E. distr. Pensva" (MS in DNA: RG 59, LAR, 10:0408; entirely in TJ's hand).

Those supporting Smith did not specifically recommend him for the office of marshal. In fact, several who supported Smith recommended Andrew Geyer, Jr., of Philadelphia, as a candidate for the marshalship of the district. On 7 Mch., Philadelphians William Coats, Frederick Wolbert, Samuel Wetherill, and George A. Baker signed a recommendation for Geyer "as a Man of Good Character, a firm Republican" who was "well qualified" to fill the office (same; in unidentified hand; at head of text: "To Thomas Jefferson, Esquire, President of the United States"; endorsed by TJ as received 13 Mch. and so recorded in SJL; TJ later added "Geyer Andrew" to the endorsement and canceled "Coats & others").

Certificate from John Beckley

Philadelphia, 10th: March 1801.

Major, John Smith, of this City, and myself were in the Year 1796, Members of the General Committee of the State of pennsylvania appointed to promote the Election of Republican Electors for this State, of a president and Vice president of the United States. A special day of Election was appointed by law, of which, by the management of our political opponents, the people were kept in universal ignorance until a very late day, and, no state elections being called for, rendered the people still more listless and indifferent;—added to which, the law itself required a very short previous promulgation by Officers almost wholly fœderal, and it also demanded of every Voter a *written* ticket with the names of the 15 Electors. Under these discouragements the Committee commenced its operations.—they caused Copies of the law, Notices of the day and manner of Election, suitable addresses, circular letters and *50.000 written tickets*, to be prepared and distributed thro' every County of the State.—11 clerks were constantly employed—a Sub Committee of five of which the subscriber was one, was established with permanent sittings— Expresses were dispatched in every direction, and finally Major Smith, whose known influence and general knowledge of all the principal Republican Characters in the State, rendered his services extremely desirable, voluntarily offered his services to the Committee, to take a tour thro' all the principal Counties below the Allegheny Mountains, and personally animate the people to action—they were accepted, and Major Smith accordingly, at his own expense, employed 25 days immediately preceding the Election, and traversed the State in various directions, thro' a journey of 7 or 800 miles, with the loss of a very valuable horse killed by fatigue, and with a zeal activity, intelligence and exertion, seldom equalled, but never exceeded. To these exertions all of which were fully and intimately known to me, I have always believed and must ever believe, the success of that Election was principally, if not altogether produced.

Major Smiths uniform and active exertions since particularly in Governor Mc:Kean's & the late Election are also well known to me, and in justice to this highly meritorious & deserving Citizen, I with great pleasure render him this Certificate of my knowledge & testimonial of his conduct.

JOHN BECKLEY.

MS (DNA: RG 59, LAR); entirely in Beckley's hand.

From Benjamin Stoddert

[Navy Dept 11th. March 1801]

The Ship Ganges Captain Mullowny, of 24 Guns, sailed the 26th Jany. 1801 for Batavia, to cruise a few months in the Straits of Sunda for the protection of our East India trade the principal danger being from Privateers from the Isle of France, and to return with as many vessels under Convoy as could be collected. It was always intended to send after her, the Ship Connecticut, of the same size, now ready at New London—but she has not been ordered out, because it was thought that she should in the first instance wait for the fate of the Treaty. afterwards that she should carry out the ratification to the Isle of France; for the effect which might be produced by it on the Privateers of that place.—and latterly, because it was thought right, that she should wait for Instructions from the new Administration.

The Ganges, was ordered to treat in those distant seas, the armed Vessels of France, exactly as those Vessels treated the Vessels of the United States engaged in Commerce—

It seems proper, that the Connecticut should proceed as intended, or that her Men should be discharged. The effect which may be produced at the Isle of France by her carrying out the Treaty may be worth the expense of sending her. If no favourable effect should be produced, she would be of service in aiding the Ganges in the straits of Sunda.—and in Convoying back the American trade.

This is one of the things in the Navy Department which seems to require early attention. It is more than probable the French Government will have taken measures to restrain depredations on our Commerce from the Isle of France.—but it is uncertain whether their orders, if any have been given, may not have been intercepted, and it is also uncertain how far the orders from that Government will be regarded in the Isle of France, where the system has been to respect only those decrees of the French Nation, which promoted the Views of the ruling People of that Island. If the Connecticut goes on this Voyage, she will if depredations should have ceased on the part of Privateers from the Isle of France, return without delay. Should depredations continue, she will join the Ganges in the straits of Sunda, and after remaining there two or three months, return with the Ganges, and as many American Vessels under Convoy, as they may be able to collect.

[I have the honor to be with great respect, Sir, your most obt Servt.
(signed) BEN STODDERT]

RC (DLC: TJ Papers, 119:20547-8); undated, with date and closing in brackets supplied from FC; in unidentified hand; notation in Stoddert's hand "for the consideration of the President" briefly summarizing contents of the letter; recorded in SJL as received 12 Mch. FC (Lb in DNA: RG 45, LSP); at head of text: "To the President of the U, States."

French privateers from Île de France (Mauritius) had captured or attacked several American trading vessels in the STRAITS OF SUNDA between the Java Sea and Indian Ocean, near the primary Dutch trading post of BATAVIA (Djakarta) (Toussaint, *Mauritius*, 10-12).

The ship GANGES, Lieutenant John Mullowny, and the ship CONNECTICUT, Captain Richard Derby, both fell victim to the Peace Establishment Act before they could complete their East India mission. That law, approved on 3 Mch., ordered drastic reductions: except for 13 frigates, all vessels belonging to the navy were to be stripped of their guns and military stores and sold. Of the remaining frigates, 6 were to remain in active service and the others laid up in various ports. Only 9 captains, 36 lieutenants, and 150 midshipmen were to be retained, with those not on active duty receiving half pay. On 1 Apr. the *Connecticut* was ordered to New York, where its crew was transferred to the frigate *Essex* and the vessel sold. The *Ganges* was recalled and sold at Philadelphia. Derby resigned his commission on 8 May and Mullowny was discharged on 1 Oct. (NDQW, Dec. 1800-Dec. 1801, 134-5, 168, 203, 307, 325, 341; U.S. Statutes at Large, 2:110-11; Samuel Smith to TJ, 2 Apr. 1801).

From Samuel Smith

Sir/   [before 12 Mch. 1801]

Capt. William Buchanan has resided at the Isle of France for the last four or five years, [his] friends request me to solicit the Consulate of the Isles of France & Bourbon for him—An application for his appointment was presented by me lately to Mr. Marshall signed by the most [respec]table Merchants of both parties in this City—It was rejected because (as I understood) he was known to be my Cousin—& Mr. George Stacy was appointed—Mr. Stacy was a kind of Lawyer, serving the late Consul (Lewis) as his Chancellor—

Capt. Buchanan is a Man of liberal Education about 34 Years of Age & for whose good Conduct I will hold myself responsible—he has a fair Claim on his Country, having been shot thro: the Arm at St. Clairs defeat in a Charge on the Indians—at the Head of his Company—

From every information I Can have Mr. Stacy would do no honor to our Country—there is a ship bound from Philadelphia & will sail within a few Days for the Isle of France—If you think it proper to appoint Capt. Buchanan the Commission might go on immediately—

I will do myself the honor to write you fully on the subject of your Letter in a Week & am Sir/

your friend & Obedt. Servt   S. Smith

RC (DNA: RG 59, LAR); undated; frayed; endorsed by TJ as received [12] Mch. and so recorded in SJL; also endorsed by TJ: "Wm. Buchanan to be Consul at the I. of France."

ISLES OF FRANCE & BOURBON: when U.S. consul Jacob Lewis returned to the United States in 1799, George Stacey began serving as vice consul at the Île de France and subsequently submitted reports to Timothy Pickering, John Marshall, and James Madison. Although appointed commercial agent by Adams in February 1801, Stacey did not receive a commission and continued to sign his correspondence as vice consul. TJ issued a commission appointing William Buchanan commercial agent for the islands on 9 July 1801, but Buchanan did not learn of his appointment until January 1802. He enjoyed popularity in île de France and remained in office until 1816 (Toussaint, *Mauritius*, 10-13, 40-2, 62-4; Marshall, *Papers*, 4:240-1; Madison, *Papers, Sec. of State Ser.*, 2:104; TJ to Samuel Smith, 24 June and 9 July 1801).

To John James Barralet

SIR   Washington Mar. 12. 1801.

I recieved safely the portrait of mr Volney, which I find to be a perfect resemblance, & I pray you to accept my thanks for it. I am to ask the further favor of you to be so good as to take the trouble of calling on mr Richards, whose address will be noted below, and of recieving five guineas from him for the same. uninformed and unacquainted as I am of the proper compensation, if I make any blunder in that to your prejudice, I pray you to pardon and correct it, by better information. I pray you to accept my salutations & good wishes.

TH: JEFFERSON

PrC (DLC); at foot of text: "Mr. John Barralet engraver S. 2d. between Catherine & Queen streets"; endorsed by TJ in ink on verso.

For TJ's purchase of the drawing of VOLNEY by Barralet, see Barralet's letter of 31 Dec. 1800.

Pardon for David Brown

Thomas Jefferson, President of the United States of America,
To all who shall see these Presents, — Greeting:

Whereas David Brown, late of the District of Massachusetts, labourer, in the Circuit Court of the United States held at Boston for the said District on the first day of June in the year of our Lord one thousand seven hundred and ninety nine, was convicted of certain misdemeanors, in writing, uttering and publishing certain false, scandalous, malicious and seditious writings against the Government, Congress and President of the United States: and thereupon by the judgment of the same Court the said David Brown was adjudged to pay a fine of four hundred dollars to the Use of the United States, suffer eighteen months imprisonment and stand committed until the said judgment should be executed: And whereas the said David Brown hath suffered the said term of imprisonment, and it appears that from poverty he is unable to pay the said sum of four hundred Dollars or any part thereof. Now Therefore be it known, That I Thomas Jefferson, President of the United States of America, in consideration of the premises and of divers other good causes me thereunto moving, have pardoned and remitted and by these presents do pardon and remit to the said David Brown the misdemeanors aforesaid whereof he stood convicted and the judgment aforesaid of the said Circuit Court thereupon; and all pains and penalties incurred or to be incurred by reason thereof.

In Testimony whereof, I have caused the Seal of the United States to be hereunto affixed, and signed the same with my Hand.

Done at the City of Washington the Twelfth day of March, in the year of our Lord, one thousand Eight hundred and one; and of the Independence of the United States of America, the Twenty fifth.

TH: JEFFERSON
By the President
LEVI LINCOLN
Acting as Secretary of State

MS (Pierce W. Gaines, Fairfield, Connecticut, 1965); in clerk's hand, signed by TJ and Lincoln; with seal of the United States. FC (Lb in DNA: RG 59, GPR; in same clerk's hand).

David Brown, an itinerant Republican speaker and writer, was arrested in March 1799 under the Sedition Act for allegedly inciting the citizens of Dedham, Massachusetts, to erect a liberty pole that carried a sign declaring "No Stamp Act, No Sedition, No Alien Bills, No Land Tax; downfall to the Tyrants of America, peace and retirement to the President, Long Live the Vice-President and the Minority." Denounced by alarmed Federalists as a "wandering apostle of sedition," he was sentenced in June by Judge Samuel Chase to eighteen months in prison and fined $400 for "sowing sedition in the interior

country." Brown's sentence was the harshest imposed under the Sedition Act. Although he completed his prison term in December 1800, he remained in jail because he could not pay his fine. He sent petitions for pardon to John Adams in July 1800 and February 1801, but was unsuccessful on both occasions (Smith, *Freedom's Fetters*, 257-70). Apparently unaware of the above pardon, Brown petitioned TJ for his release on 23 Mch., pleading that two years' imprisonment was punishment enough for "an offence against a Law, which has now no existence, & which never perhaps had the decided approbation of the people over whom it was exercis'd" (MS in DNA: RG 59, GPR; in an unidentified hand, signed by Brown; certified by Oliver Hartshorn, underkeeper of the prison in Boston; enclosed in TJ to Levi Lincoln, 10 Apr. 1801).

To Stephen Burrowes

SIR   Washington Mar. 12. 1801.

I recieved in due time your favor of Mar. 2. and the saddle also is come safely to hand. I am well pleased with it, and take it willingly, but on the express condition that you permit me to pay for it. I have ever laid it down as an unalterable law to myself to accept of no present while I am in a public office. I assume that your own reflections on the tendency of the contrary practice will justify in your eye my adherence to this principle. I am sensible to your friendly intentions as if my situation had permitted me to accept of them, and I shall consider your conforming to this wish as an evidence the more of your favor to me. I take the liberty therefore of requesting you to call on mr Richards, whose address will be noted below, and who will pay you the price of the saddle. accept, I pray you, my salutations & friendly wishes. TH: JEFFERSON

PrC (DLC); at foot of text: "Mr. Stephen Burrowes 52 N. 2d. street"; endorsed by TJ in ink on verso.

To John Dawson

DEAR SIR   Washington Mar. 12. 1801.
We shall be ready for you by the time you can arrive here. I would therefore wish you to come on without delay. mr Madison will not be here for some time; so that we cannot wait for him. health & friendly salutations. TH: JEFFERSON

PrC (MHi); at foot of text: "John Dawson esq."; endorsed by TJ in ink on verso.

John Dawson (1762-1814), a Harvard-trained Virginia congressman and lawyer from Caroline County, served in the House of Delegates for Spotsylvania County from 1786 to 1789, was a delegate to the Continental Congress in 1788, and a member of the Virginia ratifying convention in 1788. He assumed James Madison's seat in the House of Representatives in May 1797 and served in the Fifth through Thirteenth Congresses until his death. His stepfather was also James Monroe's uncle and guardian, and Monroe and Dawson maintained a lifelong relationship as political colleagues.

Dawson had written to TJ on 7 Mch. 1801 requesting "the Secretary of state to drop me a line at Fredericksburg on his arrival at this place" (RC in MHi; endorsed by TJ as received 9 Mch. and so recorded in SJL). Madison did not meet with Dawson before the latter on 22 Mch. set sail for France with the amended convention for final ratification (ANB; *Biog. Dir. Cong.*; Leonard, *General Assembly*, 162, 166, 170, 174, 177; Madison, *Papers, Sec. of State Ser.*, 1:26, 33).

To Nicolas Gouin Dufief

SIR   Washington Mar. 12. 1801.
I recieved safely the books you were so kind as to forward me, and if you will have the goodness to call on mr Richards, whose address shall be stated below, he will pay you 5. D 80 c the amount of them. the one you propose being by it's bulk far beyond any time I can flatter myself with having to spare for looking into it, I must forbid myself the acquisition. accept my salutations & good wishes. TH: JEFFERSON

PrC (DLC); at foot of text: "M. N. Gouin Dufief. Philada 68. S. 4th. street"; endorsed by TJ in ink on verso.

ONE YOU PROPOSE: Grasset de Saint-Sauveur's *Encyclopédie des Voyages* (Dufief to TJ, 26 Feb.).

For the BOOKS that TJ had ordered, see his letter to Dufief, 9 Jan. 1801.

To Cyrus Griffin

DEAR SIR   Washington Mar. 12. 1801.

I return you my thanks for your friendly congratulations on my election to the chair of the Union. if it shall be in my power to effect a reconciliation of parties, I shall think I have not lived in vain. to effect this something must be yielded on both sides, and I hope there is a spirit of accomodation rising among us. I know the task is difficult, and cannot possibly be so executed as to give satisfaction to every one: but by suffering no passions of my own to intervene, I will give myself a right to the dispassionate judgment of others. I pray you to accept assurances of my high consideration & esteem.

TH: JEFFERSON

PrC (DLC); at foot of text: "The honble Cyrus Griffin"; endorsed by TJ in ink on verso.

YOUR FRIENDLY CONGRATULATIONS: Griffin to TJ, 4 Mch.

From Samuel Hanson

SIR,   George-Town, March 12th. 1801.

You were so obliging as to say that my Commission, as Notary-Publick of Washington County, should be made out. I beg leave to state that sundry instruments of writing have been put into my hands requiring Notareal Acts—and, among these, several promissory Notes for Protest. unfortunately for the present suspension of the Office, this last kind is supposed to admit of no delay, from an Opinion, generally prevalent, that a note must be protested in the last day of grace in order to bind the Endorser.

In this state of the business, you will, I trust, excuse the present intrusion upon your attention, occupied, as it is, by more important concerns.

with perfect respect, I am Sir, Your most obedt

S HANSON of Saml

RC (DLC); endorsed by TJ as received 12 Mch. and so recorded in SJL.

From Robert R. Livingston

DEAR SIR   Albany 12th. March 1801

I have this moment only received your favor the 24 Feby. It lay some days in the post Office at New York, from whence it was sent to Clermont & at last followed me to Albany. I hasten to express my gratitude for your frequent attentions to me. I had determined to take upon me no new Office, but to endeavour to promote your interest, which I believed to be intimatly connected with that of my country, in the Station I now hold. But flattered by your favourable opinions, & desirous of complying with your wishes, I will wh. pleasure undertake the mission you mention, provided I have at least two months notice before my departure to enable me to make such arrangments of my private affairs as so long an absence may render necessary. I write in haste least I should miss the post & am Dear Sir with sentiments of the highest essteem & respect

Your Most Ob hum: Servt   ROBT R LIVINGSTON

RC (DLC); endorsed by TJ as received 23 Mch. and so recorded in SJL.

To James Madison

DEAR SIR   Washington Mar. 12. 1801.

I offer you my sincere condolances on the melancholy loss which has detained you at home: and am entirely sensible of the necessities it will have imposed on you for further delay. mr Lincoln has undertaken the duties of your office per interim, and will continue till you can come. Genl. Dearborn is in the War department. mr Gallatin, though unappointed, has staid till now to give us the benefit of his counsel. he cannot enter into office till my return, & he leaves us tomorrow. in the mean time Dexter continues. Stoddart also accomodated me by staying till I could provide a successor. this I find next to impossible. R.R.L. first refused. then Genl. Smith refused. next Langdon. I am now returning on Genl. Smith, but with little confidence of success. if he will undertake 6. months or even 12. months hence, I will appoint Lear in the mean time. he promised, if Langdon would take it for 6. months, he would in that time so dispose of his business as to come in. this makes me hope he may now accept in that way. if he does not, there is no remedy but to appoint Lear permanently. he is equal to the office if he possessed equally the confidence of the public. what a misfortune to the public that R. Morris has fallen from his height of character. if he could get from confinement, & the public give him

[255]

confidence, he would be a most valuable officer in that station & in our council. but these are two impossibilities in the way.—I have ordered my chair & horses to meet me at Heron's on the 22d. inst. not that I count on being there punctually on that day, but as near it as I can. I shall be at home a fortnight. I hope you will find it convenient to come on when I do or very soon after. Dr. Thornton means to propose to rent his house to you. it will be some two or three hundred yards distant from your office, but also that much nearer towards the Capitol. we shall have an agreeable society here, and not too much of it. Present my esteem to mrs Madison and accept yourself assurances of my constant & sincere attachment.   TH: JEFFERSON

RC (DNCD); signature torn away, supplied from PrC; at foot of text: "Mr. Madison." PrC (DLC); endorsed by TJ in ink on verso.

R.R.L.: Robert R. Livingston. John LANGDON of New Hampshire had recently completed two terms in the United States Senate. He boarded at Conrad and McMunn's, and since no correspondence between him and TJ during February or March is recorded in SJL, it is likely that the two of them spoke rather than wrote to one another on the subject of the navy. During the Revolutionary War, Langdon had been on committees of the Continental Congress related to naval affairs and was a contractor for the construction of warships in Portsmouth. TJ wrote him on 23 May 1801 again to offer him the secretaryship of the navy (ANB; Lawrence Shaw Mayo, *John Langdon of New Hampshire* [Concord, N.H., 1937], 92-4, 99-100; Vol. 32:255, 392n).

From James Monroe

DEAR SIR   Richmond March 12. 1801.

I had yours of the 7th. by yesterday's mail. The danger of reaction is the evil to be fear'd from an energetic course, of disgusting and disuniting the republican party by an opposit one. These are the rocks, (to use a worn out metaphor) which you have to shun and which it is not easy to shun, but which may be done. On which side is the greater danger? In my judgement the latter. On which side if error is committed is it more pardonable, generous, and honorable? The latter. The royalist party has committed infinite crimes and enormities. The people have become sensible of this, comprizing all but the culprits and their more especially compromitted associates. It is scarcely possible that party shod. ever rise again, if the republican party is kept together. If it rises it will be by a union with the discontented members of the republican party, seeking a change in the admn. which can never take place, if the course of the admn. be in all respects sound at the present moment. The more complete the overthrow of the royalist party is I am persuaded the happier the effect will be; (by this I do not mean an unmanly pursuit of honest men in subaltern stations, who have differed with us in political sentiment as they had a right to do. I would oust all those who bore a part in the admn., or who held such a place in its councils, either at the seat of govt. or throughout the States as to form a kind of head or rallying point to the party or any portion of it). Whatever ground any of those men hold will be so much gained to the party, and will in like degree weaken the confidence of the republican party in yr. admn.[1] The more the turpitude of that party appears the less danger is to be apprehended from it. Under existing evidences it can scarcely ever raise its head. If other exists it ought to be shewn. It is known that the leaders only were guilty, not the mass of the people. Let the conviction be complete, and every honest man leaves them. To keep any person of note in power will not gratify those who have been deceived of their party, but embarrass them; since while such person is countenanc'd by the[2] admn. it checks the deluded federalist in coming over and acknowledging his errors. By such a course of conduct the royalist party must be overthrown. The republicans will be gratified since there will be no cause for well founded discontent. They will see it is a revolution of principle wh. is carried fully into effect: not a compromise of a few who[3] have come into office, stipulating with the enemy for personal tranquility, at the expense of principle, and of those who have labour'd in the common cause and contributed in their respective spheres their equal portion to bring abt. the late important change.

Removals from office is a different question. I am decidedly[4] of opinion, that where the officers have done their duty, a mere difference of political sentiment is not a justifiable motive. I do not think the republicans require it, nor wod. I do it, if they did: tho' I do not justify that partizanship wh. most in office have practic'd.

An energetic tone towards the leaders of the royalist party will keep the republicans & new converts together & gain strength daily to yr. admn. a different one will disunite them & put every thing afloat. Such a tone toward the leaders of that party will countenance the principles & opinion of misconduct wh. occasioned its overthrow.

It might be asked is it sufficient that the favor of the admn. shod. be with held only from the members of the latter and their most distinguished associates? Have they committed crimes or been calumniated by those who sought their offices? If the former is the case or presumeable ought such countenance to be shewn them as tended to stifle the publick resentment or check the freedom of enquiry, especially in the legislature? The deprivation from office is another question. There is a material difference between turning a man out of office, & giving him countenance. as there is between withholding countenance and persecuting him.

Much abuse is suspected to have been committed in every department, of the most gross and depraved kind; in the department, of State,

Be assured that every mild and benevolent sentiment wh. you express to or in favor of any of those people is treasured up & considered as a document in their favor, as a compact between you & them for ever; as a condition on wh. you accept the govt.

Dft (DLC: Monroe Papers); in Monroe's hand and endorsed by him: "Supposed to be a sketch of a letter sent or intended for Mr Jefferson—relating to parties." In SJL TJ recorded the receipt on 21 Mch. of a letter written by Monroe on the 12th.

[1] Monroe here canceled "I wod. never <put> leave a fort in the hands of the [army] taken in it to garrison it."

[2] Monroe here canceled "mass of the people."

[3] Preceding seven words interlined in place of "They will not be able to charge yr. admn."

[4] Preceding seven words interlined in place of "rest on a different ground. I do not think."

From Thomas Newton

DR SIR,   Norfolk March. 12. 1801—

I have just arived a consignment of old Madeira wines; Brasil Quality & London Particular, from a Portugeze house; who ships my wine for drinking. the Brasil kind is superior to any other sent here & such as is seldom imported; if you should want a supply, I will direct it to be saved for you by mr. Js Taylor Jr. to whom I have given up my business. be pleased to accept my best wishes for yr. health & happiness & I will with pleasure execute any commands you may have here, I am very respectfuly

Yr. Obt Servt.   THOS NEWTON

RC (DLC); endorsed by TJ as received 21 Mch. and so recorded in SJL.

Norfolk auctioneer James TAYLOR, Jr., was Newton's nephew (*Simmons's Norfolk Directory* [Norfolk, 1801], 31; Vol. 23:481).

From Charles Pinckney

DEAR SIR   Thursday Morning [12 Mch. 1801] Georgetown

On considering the offer You have been so good as to make me to go to the Court of Spain I have determined to accept it as I can at all times return whenever my friends in Carolina shall advise me that my presence may be useful or required there in support of the republican interest—

As it will be necessary for me to return to my family for a short time before I embark for Europe I will thank you to direct the Commission & instructions to be made out & to favour me with an introductory Letter or two to Paris as soon as they can conveniently be furnished, so as not to interfere with your other more important concerns & I will have the honour of calling on you on Sunday morning, if nothing should prevent—

With the greatest respect & regard I am dear Sir Yours truly

                                        CHARLES PINCKNEY

RC (DLC); partially dated; addressed: "To The President of the United States"; endorsed by TJ as received 13 Mch. and so recorded in SJL.

Pinckney's COMMISSION as minister plenipotentiary to Spain was dated 6 June. On that day also TJ and James Madison signed a letter of credence to the king of Spain informing him of Pinckney's appointment and of "our desire to cultivate the harmony and good correspondence, so happily subsisting" between the two countries (FCs in Lb in DNA: RG 59, Credences; in a clerk's hand). Madison sent those letters and Pinckney's INSTRUCTIONS to the new

minister on 9 June (Madison, Papers, Sec. of State Ser., 1:273-9; Pinckney to TJ, 8 July 1801).

About this time Pinckney prepared a brief, undated sketch of his public career perhaps to be used in consideration of his confirmation. In the final paragraph he observed, "I am now by the goodness of Providence & your friendship still further promoted," but, he concluded, "I should not I confess like to have my political ardour & pursuits damped by not being confirmed" (MS in DLC: TJ Papers, 119:20538; entirely in Pinckney's hand). The Senate confirmed the appointment of Pinckney on 26 Jan. 1802 (JEP, 1:404-5).

To Thomas Mann Randolph

DEAR SIR   Washington Mar. 12. 1801.

I mentioned to you in my letter by mr Nicholas that I should be able by this post to fix a day for the departure of Davy Bowles with my chair & horses, & that he should be in readiness. though it is impossible for me to say to a day when I can set out from hence, yet I expect it may be by the time you recieve this. I would therefore have him set off from Monticello on Saturday the 21st. inst. and come to mr Heron's in Culpeper, half a mile this side of mr Strode's, where he will arrive on Sunday the 22d. and will wait for me till I get there, which, if nothing unexpected occurs, will be on that or the next day. but circumstances might arise which might detain me longer, in which case he must wait there. it is probable mr Strode will press him much to go with his horses to his house, but he must be charged expressly to continue at Heron's which is a house of entertainment. my stay at home cannot exceed a fortnight, or a very few days over that. I am still at a great loss, mr Madison not having been able to come on as yet, mr Gallatin not agreeing to join us till my return, and not knowing as yet where to get a Secretary of the navy. Genl. Smith refused; so did mr Langdon. I am now pressing again on Genl. Smith, but with little hope of his acceding. in that case my distress will be very great. hitherto appearances of reunion are very flattering, in all the states South of New England. a few removals from office will be indispensable. they will be chiefly for real mal-conduct, & mostly in the offices connected with the administration of justice. I shall do as little in that way as possible. this may occasion some outcry; but it must be met. one removal will give me a great deal of pain, because it will pain you also. but it would be inexcusable in me to make that exception. the prostitution of justice by packing of juries cannot be passed over. embrace my dear Martha for me a thousand times, and kisses to the young ones. to yourself affectionate esteem & attachment. Th: Jefferson

RC (DLC); at foot of text: "T M Randolph"; endorsed by Randolph. PrC (MHi); endorsed by TJ in ink on verso.

LETTER BY MR NICHOLAS: TJ to Randolph, 6 Mch.

ONE REMOVAL WILL GIVE ME A GREAT DEAL OF PAIN: that of David Meade Randolph, U.S. marshal of the Virginia district, who was married to Thomas Mann Randolph's sister Mary (Daniels, *Randolphs of Virginia*, xvi, 130; Washington, *Papers, Pres. Ser.*, 3:104n).

From Benjamin Rush

Dear Sir,   Philadelphia March 12th: 1801

Your Character as a Philosopher & friend of mankind predominates so much more in my mind over that of your new station, that I cannot resist the habit of addressing you as I have done in my former letters. Your new official title has added nothing to my respect for your person. It could not add to my friendship for you.

You have opened a new Œra by your Speech on the 4th: of March in the history of the United States. Never have I seen the public mind more generally, or more agreeably affected by any publication.

Old friends who had been seperated by party names, and a *supposed* difference of *principle* in politicks for many years, shook hands with each Other, immediately After reading it, and discovered, for the first time, that they had differed in *Opinion* only, About the best means of promoting the interests of their common country. It would require a page to contain the names of all the citizens (formerly called federalists) who have spoken in the highest terms of your Speech. George Clymer (one of our colleagues in July 1776) and Judge Peters, have taken the lead in their encomiums upon it. A Mr: Joseph Wharton (an active, but republican federalist) has read it (he says) *seven* times, and with encreasing pleasure. I need hardly tell you how much every Sentiment, and even word in it, accord with my feelings, and principles. I consider it as a solemn & affecting address to your fellow citizens—to the nations of Europe, to all the inhabitants of the Globe, and to posterity to the latest generations, upon the great Subject of political Order and happiness. You have concentrated whole Chapters into a few aphorisms, into defence of the principles and *form* of our Government. It is owing to the long Sleep of such Sentiments in diplomatic performances, that the young men of our Country have been seduced from it, to admire, and prefer the British Constitution. It never occurred to them, 'till last week, that a Republic was a Government of *more* energy than a monarchy. It is equally true, though constantly denied by the monarchists of our Country, that national *stability* of opinion and conduct, with respect to public men, as well as national *integrity* & *humanity*, are more common Virtues in a Republic, than in Royal Governments. The *first* is proved by the Conduct of the Americans to their first Magistrates in all the States, not one of them having been dismissed by a general Suffrage from Office since the formation of our state governments in 1775. The *second* is proved by the general fidelity with which the duties upon imports are paid in every part of the Union. Mr Latimer assured me a few days ago, that in the course of three years, he had not detected a single American in an Attempt to elude the duty upon imported goods. The few Smuglers whom he had detected, & punished, were Europeans. In the United states every citizen feels the injury committed by public fraud, as done to *himself*. In a monarchy the mischief of fraud is said to extend only to the king, who by the common Sense of his Subjects is considered to possess millions of property not his own, & of course that it is not criminal to rob him. Both *national* humanity and integrity are proved by the manner in which the late election for the first magistrate of the United States was conducted by four millions of people. Not a dollar I beleive was expended in a bribe, nor was a black eye created by it in any part of the Union. Our newspapers like Chimnies, peaceably carried off the smoke of party rage[1] without doing any harm. This fact did not escape the Notice of the late British Minister Mr: Liston, and led him to remark in his farewell visit to my family, that it promised a continuance of our republican form of government "for many Ages to come."

In contemplating the change you have produced in the public mind, I have been carried back to an interesting conversation with you about two years ago in which you *predicted* it. I did not concur with you; for our country was then so much Under the influence of the *name* of — [2] the *plans* of — [3] and the *press* of Peter Porcupine that I despaired of a resuscitation of its republic Spirit. You said the death of two men (whom you named) would render your prediction *speedy*, as well as *certain*. They both died in 1799. In the third month of the year 1801 We have become "all Republicans—all federalists."

I fear I have trespassed upon time now more precious than ever by this long letter. I have only to add, that the pleasure created by your Speech has been encreased by your late appointments, and by your declaration to several of your friends that you did not intend to consider political Opinion or conduct as crimes in the present Officers of the Government.

Declining as I am in years, and languishing for retirement in Order more exclusively to pursue my medical researches, I can do nothing to render your administration easy, and[4] prosperous, but unite with thousands in imploring the direction and blessings of that Being upon it, to Whom you have publickly & solemnly committed the "destiny" of our nation.

From Dear Sir, with encreasing regard, your sincere, and faithful friend,

BENJN: RUSH

RC (DLC); endorsed by TJ as received 18 Mch. and so recorded in SJL.

PETER PORCUPINE: William Cobbett. BOTH DIED IN 1799: George Washington and Patrick Henry; for TJ's dissatisfaction with Henry in the period before the latter's death, see Lyman H. Butterfield, ed., *Letters of Benjamin Rush*, 2 vols. [Princeton, 1951], 2:833n, and Vol. 31:110, 114.

[1] Preceding two words interlined in place of "public resentment."
[2] Interlined by TJ above dash: "Washington."
[3] Interlined by TJ: "Hamilton."
[4] Rush here canceled "honourable."

From Benjamin Stoddert

SIR,   Navy Dep 12 March. 1801.

I fear you will think me too great an intruder on your attention—at a time too, when your mind must have full occupation.

In order to reduce the cost of the frames of ships, I introduced a method of getting the frames which had often been recommended, but never practised in England. There the method is to transport the logs to the ship yards, & at the ship yards to cut out of the logs, pieces for the different parts of the frame, of the size and shape required. By pursuing this practice, the live oaks of Georgia used in the three Frigates first built in this country, cost little less than four dollars per cubic foot. I thought the price of the live oak actually put into a ship, could be reduced to about a dollar & a half, by reducing in the woods, each piece of timber to the size & shape required to go into the ship, & by this means, avoiding the heavy expence of transporting first to landings in Georgia, & afterwards to ship yards great quantities of useless timber.

Thus impressed, I caused contracts to be made in Georgia for the frames of six 74 gun ships, reduced there to the moulds, & to be delivered at landings in Georgia, for three quarters of a dollar ℔ cubic foot—& in South Carolina, for two frames on the same terms. In South Carolina the contractor has procured about two thirds of one frame, & declares his utter inability to go further in the prosecution of the contract, from the difficulty of finding timber for the most difficult pieces which remain to be obtained; but still more, from the insufficiency of the price at which he had contracted. The contractor in Georgia has nearly completed his contract, & will complete it in the present spring—but he also has constantly contended that it will be attended with his ruin, if the government does not allow him more than his contract price, & that he proceeded in his contract, in full reliance on the justice of Government to make him a further allowance.

When these contracts were made, cutting timber to the moulds in the woods, was an untried experiment in this country. I limited the Agents to give no more than three quarters of a dollar. I sincerely beleive the contractors ought to be allowed, at least one dollar—perhaps one dollar & a quarter for the frames delivered at landings in Georgia—the whole expence of getting the frames from these landings to the different building yards from Norfolk to Portsmouth in New Hampshire, will be little less than $\frac{3}{4}$ of a dollar ℔ foot—altho freight alone will not exceed $\frac{1}{2}$ of a dollar—still the expense of frames by this new method, will not much exceed one half the expense of the old mode.

[263]

Mr Miller, the contractor in Georgia, has kept an account of his whole expences, to be laid before Government at the completion of his contract. Mr. Shrubeck the South Carolina contractor has already exhibited an account of his actual expenditures, exceeding considerably the sum he receives from Government without charging any thing for timber

I always intended, with the approbation of the President to do these people justice, & meant to make that account of real expences, which should appear to be most reasonable & most correct, the rule for settling with them both.

As I shall not be in office when these transactions shall be closed, I thought it incumbent on me, to make this representation to you, Sir, & to leave it on record in the books of this office.—I cannot doubt, that the rule I had contemplated, or some other equitable rule ought to be adopted, & therefore that it will be adopted in the settlement of them.

One thing more, & I have done. I am anxious before I quit office to send officially to Mr Marbury the Navy Agent here, the letter which I do myself the honor to enclose—the reasons I have endeavored in the letter itself fully to explain, that my successor in office may also know them. My first wish is, to act with propriety—my second, to appear so to act—and I cannot reconcile myself to the idea of being instrumental to the great injury, or ruin of any person. I do not expect nor desire that you Sir, who cannot be acquainted with this subject, should shield me from any of the responsibility attached to the step I propose to take with respect to the contracts at this place in 1799— it will be sufficient for me that you know it & do not forbid it—and the only evidence I require that you do not, will be a return of the letter to me.

For month's past applications have been made to me on the subject of these contracts. I supposed small losses only were to be sustained, & that these might arise from injudicious management on the part of the Contractors; but I have lately compared the list of prices furnished me at Philaa., with those actually given at Boston, & I find the latter for some principal pieces three times as high & in all instances greatly exceeding those of the former, & which governed the contracts here—From this & some other circumstances, I am led to suspect that the prices given me for those of Philaa, bore but little resemblance to the real truth—At all events, the contractors thought that they were getting the Philadelphia prices—they were so taught to think by the Agent, who also thought so—it is proposed that they shall receive those prices, and I beleive they could make good their claim, to those prices in a court of equity, but it is hard for an individual to contend against the public & the public ought to do strict justice, without compulsion.

I have the honor to be with great respect Sir Yr: most obed Svt.

BEN STODDERT

RC (DNA: RG 59, MLR); in clerk's hand, with closing and signature in Stoddert's hand; at foot of text in Stoddert's hand: "The President of the United States." FC (Lb in DNA: RG 45, LSP); in same clerk's hand. Recorded in SJL as received 12 Mch. Enclosure: Stoddert to

William Marbury, 12 Mch., authorizing and instructing Marbury to settle at Philadelphia prices with the gentlemen who contracted with the navy in 1799 to supply wood for a warship to be built in Washington (FC in same).

From Daniel Trump

DEAR SIR   Philadelphia March 12th 1801

I would have Answered your Letter Sooner but finding it Difficult to Procure a young man for you to Replace Mr Holms whose unfortunate Death I have Very much Regretted, but this Transitory Life is Very precarious and Death is the fate of Mortal man in Different forms I was almost Dispairing of getting one that would Answer you, but fortunately this Day I Received a Letter from Washington with an Application from a young man of the Name of James Oldham formerly of this City he Studied Architecture under Me and made Great Progress for the time he was with me, he mentions in his Letter of Applying to you Sir and the Answer you Gave him he is a Genteel well behaved young man and I have not a Doubt but he will answer you Very well. your Sashes are Making and we Shall Endeavour to Get them Done as Soon as Possible and Send them forward to Richmond Imediately we had to pay $\frac{30}{100}$ ℔ foot superficial measure for Mahogany you mentioned in your Letter of a friend of yours that wanted Sashes made like yours, if you'll Please Sir to forward the order they Shall be made for him if we Can Agree about the Price. I am Very Happy Sir in Congratulateing you to the Seat of the first Magestrate of the Union, we had a Grand Procession on the fourth of march and Celebrated the Day with Joy.

I Remain Sir yr Obt Hu Servt   DANIEL TRUMP

RC (MHi); endorsed by TJ as received 20 Mch. and so recorded in SJL.

ANSWERED YOUR LETTER: TJ to Trump, 21 Feb.

JAMES OLDHAM may have applied to TJ in person for a position at Monticello. The first correspondence between the two

men, recorded in SJL but not found, is dated 26 Dec. 1801. ANSWER YOU GAVE HIM: the president apparently requested recommendations. On 24 Mch. TJ agreed to employ Oldham as a house joiner at Monticello for $240 per year, plus expenses (MB, 2:1035).

To John Wright

SIR   Washington Mar. 12. 1801

I ought sooner to have acknowledged the receipt of your favr. of Feb. 20. which has been at hand a fortnight, but that the press of business in the intervening time has rendered it impracticable. I thank you for the offer of forwarding to me one of your cutting knives, as sincerely as if I were in a situation which would permit my acceptance of it. but I have laid it down as a rule to myself never to be departed from not to accept of presents while I am in any public office. you know the abuses to which the contrary practice leads in some countries, and [. . .] in all, and will therefore approve of the bar I oppose to them here. this takes nothing from the civility of your offer of which I am as sensible, & as thankful for it as I ought justly to be. accept, I pray you, my salutations & good wishes.

TH: JEFFERSON

PrC (MHi); blurred; at foot of text: "Mr. John Wright. 149. Market street"; endorsed by TJ in ink on verso.

From Nathaniel Anderson

DEAR SIR,   Richmond March 13th 1801.

I do most Sincerely Congratilate you on your Honorable Election to Preside over these United States, and it is with great pleasure I can inform you that your Conduct on the happy Occation, appears to give general satisfaction to all parties:—I beg leave to put you in mind of two young men, whose Interest I have a desire to promote, as I flatter myself, they are both Worthy: and are nearly Connected to me; The first is my son Overton Anderson who I expect is by this time in Liverpool, as he sailed from hence in a ship of his own the last of December; I have often heard him express a desire to settle in france as a Merchant, to which Business he has been regularly bred, his education has only been the English and french Languages. the latter he is thought to Understand pretty well, as he has done a great deal of Business in france, and been once to the Isle of france and Burboun, in the trading line, Connected with Mr. James Maury of Liverpool: If you should think him sufficiently qualifyed for a Consul and a Vacancy should take place for one in france, it strikes me that he would gladly Accept, as I suppose it would be a great Advantage to him in the trading line, of this you are the best Judge;—The second is my son-in-law Benjamin Rawlings, now living in Baltimore; regularly brought up to the same Business, he writes me that he should be glad to Accept any profitable business under Government. he has been to some of the Spanish Islands in the trading line, and is somewhat Acquainted with that Language. These two young men are steady; Attached firmly to their own Country and Government, and allways have been Attentive to Business perfectly Acquainted with Accompts, Should you find it entirely Convenient, and Consistent with your Judgment in every respect to prefer them, I should esteem it a favor. Otherwise I do not desire it: As I would by no means, have you to give them a preference, when others are to be had better Qualifyed—

I am Dear Sir with every sentiment of respect and Esteem Your Mo: Obdt. Servt.   NATHL. ANDERSON

RC (DNA: RG 59, LAR); at head of text: "Thomas Jefferson Esqr."; endorsed by TJ as received 18 Mch. and so recorded in SJL; also endorsed by TJ: "Overton Anderson for a Conslship in France Benjamin Rawlings. Spanish islds."

Neither OVERTON ANDERSON nor BENJAMIN RAWLINGS received appointments from TJ. A Richmond merchant in the Liverpool trade, Anderson died in Richmond on 19 Nov. 1809. Rawlings wrote TJ on 3 Apr. reiterating his interest in a consulship, specifically on the island of Guadeloupe (Fillmore Norfleet, Saint-Mémin in Virginia: Portraits and Biographies [Richmond, 1942], 138; Benjamin

Rawlings to TJ, 3 April 1801, RC in DNA: RG 59, LAR, endorsed by TJ as received 16 Apr. and so recorded in SJL with notation "Off.").

A native of Virginia and a childhood schoolmate of TJ, JAMES MAURY had been the U.S. consul in Liverpool since 1790. In 1801 he was a charter member and first president of the American Chamber of Commerce in Liverpool (Malone, Jefferson, 1:42; Gore's Liverpool Directory, 1800, p. 95; W. O. Henderson, "The American Chamber of Commerce for the Port of Liverpool, 1801-1908," Transactions of the Historic Society of Lancashire and Cheshire, 85 [1933], 2-3, 56; JEP, 1:48-9; Vol. 17:501-2n).

To Gabriel Duvall

DEAR SIR   Washington Mar. 13. 1801.

The office of Chief judge for the district of Columbia being become vacant by the resignation of mr Johnson, my desire to procure for offices of so much confidence, & permanence, persons whose talents & integrity may ensure to the public the honest benefits expected from them, and strengthen the mass of confidence which from the people at large [. . .] so necessary for their own service, has induced me to propose it for your acceptance. the office is during good behavior, & the salary 2300. Dollars a year. the first session for the county of Washington being fixed to the 4th. Monday (23d.) of this month, I will sollicit the favor of as early an answer as possible. accept assurances of my high consideration and respect.   TH: JEFFERSON

PrC (DLC); faint; at foot of text: "The honble Gabriel Duval." Not recorded in SJL.

Gabriel Duvall (1752-1844), a Revolutionary War veteran who was admitted to the Maryland bar in 1778, served as a Maryland congressman from November 1794 to March 1796, when he resigned to become chief justice of the General Court of Maryland. He promoted the Jeffersonian-Republican cause in Maryland, describing TJ as "the Friend of the People." As a presidential elector he cast his vote for TJ in 1796 and

1800. In 1802 TJ appointed Duvall the first comptroller of the U.S. Treasury, a position he held until 1811 when President Madison appointed him to the U.S. Supreme Court, where he served as an associate justice until 1835 (ANB; *Biog. Dir. Cong.*; Papenfuse, *Maryland Legislature*, 1:290-2).

The OFFICE OF CHIEF JUDGE FOR THE DISTRICT OF COLUMBIA was left unfilled when Thomas Johnson declined the appointment offered by Adams (Marshall, *Papers*, 6:90-1; JEP, 1:401; note to List of John Adams's Appointments, printed at 23 Feb. 1801).

To Andrew Ellicott

Mar. 13. 1801

Th: Jefferson having referred mr Ellicott's letter to the Secretary of the Treasury (mr Dexter) received from him the inclosed note. he leaves this place on the 21st. inst. to be absent one month, when mr Madison will also enter on his office. in the mean time mr Lincoln will have charge of the Secretary of state's office & will recieve any application from mr Ellicot, & do justice on it. he presents him his friendly salutations.

RC (DLC: Ellicott Papers); addressed: "Mr. Andrew Ellicot Philadelphia 16. N. 6th. str."; franked and postmarked. PrC (DLC). Enclosure not found.

Ellicott's LETTER has not been found but was probably one recorded in SJL as written on 5 Mch. from Philadelphia and received on the 7th.

From Carlos Martínez de Irujo

DEAR SIR   Philadelphia 13 March 1801

I arrived the day before yesterday to this City through muddy roads, & indiferent weather; but those litle inconveniences were smooth'd by the satisfaction of finding the smile of joi on every face, on account of your election—In my way I have convers'd with Tirians, & Troyans, high & low; & all to a man considers your exaltation as the triumph of merit & vertu; your Speech, which could not easely be heard in the room of the Senate, is making great noise & many conversions without doors; in fact you have had the fortunate talent of presenting truth on an irrisistible point of vue—

I wish you was equally succesful in the domestiquet concerns I was charg'd with—Since my arrival I have taken every step to procure you the excellent Cook living with Mr. Siemen, but, tho he has shewn great sensibility for the preference which was given to him, & he thought generous the offer made to him, he is obligd'd to decline it on account of his Wife being near laying in & his having already a numerous Family which he apprehends would not produce but trouble & inconvinience in your house—

Baffled on my expectations on this side, I directed my attention to Mr. Bingham's Cook, & the confidential person employ'd in the mission has just brought me the answer, that he would be very happy to have the honor to be in your Service, but Mr B. owes him about eight hundred Dollars, he cannot gett as yet from him; & he is afraid to loose every farthing if he was to leave him—It would appear as if the idea of the Family going to England was given up, no doubt on account of the storm which appears to be gathering over that devoted Island—

I have had the satisfaction to find my Family in perfect health & *all* overjoied with your succes—they *all* request me to present their compliments & respects to you—

To morrow I'll endeavour to find out my last Cook: he knows his profession very well, he is quite, sober & honest; but he is not so eminent as the one I had in view: in my opinion he could be got for 20 Dollars, & could be taken *en attendant* —

Accept, Sir, the sentiment of the most perfect consideration with which I have the honor to be Your mos obt. Servt.

LE CHEVALIER D'IRUJO

RC (CSmH); here and in other letters from Irujo, accents and other marks that he placed over some vowels have been omitted; addressed: "His Excellency Th. Jefferson President of the United States City of Washington"; franked; endorsed by TJ as received 18 Mch. and so recorded in SJL.

TO THIS CITY: the Spanish government, at the insistence of the Adams administration, had recalled Irujo from his position as minister plenipotentiary. He had not yet returned to Europe to take up his new diplomatic assignment. Irujo had ties to Philadelphia through his wife, the former Sally McKean (Vol. 30:194n; Joseph Yznardi, Sr., to TJ, 4 Jan. 1801; Thomas McKean to TJ, 21 Mch. 1801).

TIRIANS, & TROYANS: references to Tyrians and Trojans, here as an allusion for people of different origins and inter-ests, have their roots in Virgil's *Aeneid*. Irujo's spelling in English resembles the Spanish form of the expression, "tirios y troyanos." Cervantes, who had considerable interest in Virgil, used the phrase to open a chapter of *Don Quixote*, mirroring a line from a 16th-century Spanish translation of the *Aeneid* (Miguel de Cervantes Saavedra, *El Ingenioso Hidalgo Don Quijote de la Mancha*, ed. Vicente Gaos, 3 vols. [Madrid, 1987], 2:388; Michael D. McGaha, ed., *Cervantes and the Renaissance: Papers of the Pomona College Cervantes Symposium, November 16-18, 1978* [Easton, Pa., 1980], 34-6).

Étienne Lemaire, who later in the year succeeded Joseph Rapin as steward of the President's House, was a member of William BINGHAM's household staff (MB, 2:1053; Philippe de Létombe to TJ, 11 July, 1 Aug. 1801; TJ to Létombe, 29 July 1801).

EN ATTENDANT: in the meantime.

To Lafayette

MY DEAR FRIEND Washington Mar. 13. 1801.

I recieved a letter from you the last year, and it has been several since I wrote one to you. during the earlier part of the period it could never have got to your hands; & during the latter, such has been the state of politics on both sides of the water, that no communications were safe. nevertheless I have never ceased to nourish a sincere friendship for you, & to take a lively interest in your sufferings & losses. it would make me happy to learn that they are to have an end. we have passed through an awful scene in this country. the convulsions of Europe shook even us to our center. a few hardy spirits stood firm at their post, & the ship has weathered the storm. the details of this cannot be put on paper. for the astonishing particulars I refer you to the bearer of this, mr Dawson, my friend, fully possessed of every thing, as being a member of Congress & worthy of entire confidence. from him you must learn what America is now; or rather what it has been, for now I hope it is getting back to the state in which you knew it. I will only add that the storm we have passed through proves our vessel indestructible. I have heard with great concern of the decline of Me. de la Fayette's health; and wish anxiously to learn that it is getting better. having been at Monticello all the time your son was in America, I had not an opportunity of seeing him, & of proving my friendship to every one in whom I have an interest. present the homage of my respect & attachment to Me. de la Fayette, and accept yourself assurances of my constant and affectionate friendship.

TH: JEFFERSON

P.S. Mar. 18. this moment mr Pichon arrives & delivers me your letter of which he was the bearer.

RC (NIC: Fabius Collection); at foot of text: "M. de la Fayette." PrC (DLC).

A LETTER FROM YOU: the most recent one received by TJ was Lafayette's of 19 Apr. 1799, received in the closing days of that year. Lafayette's letter of 11 Nov. 1800 did not come to TJ's hand until July 1801. TJ had last written to Lafayette on 16 June 1792, when he envisioned his friend "at the head of a great army" on the verge of "exterminating the monster aristocracy, and pulling out the teeth and fangs of it's associate monarchy" (Vol. 24:85-6).

Lafayette's letter, carried by Louis André PICHON, was dated "20th Nivose," printed above in this series under 10 Jan. 1801.

From Francis Peyton

DEAR SIR,   Alexandria March 13th. 1801.

An invitation to Genl. Wilkinson was forwarded by express this morning, and I have this moment sent off a card for his aid Capt Huger,   I expect a delay of the dinner for even two or three days would be attended with serious inconveniences to Mr. Gadsby, I therefore hope if the day should be bad, it will comport with your convenience to come down in a carriage.

I find upon inquiry that Thomas Darne resides within the District of Columbia, and I am further confirmed in my opinion that he would be the most proper person to fill the office of magistrate in that part of the County, of Alexandria.

I am Sir with great respect Yr. Obt. Servt.   FRANCIS PEYTON

RC (DLC); endorsed by TJ as received 14 Mch. and so recorded in SJL.

Francis Peyton (ca. 1764-1836) was a prominent Alexandria merchant and a nephew of state senator Francis Peyton of Loudoun County, Virginia. On 2 Mch. 1801, in a "midnight appointment," John Adams nominated him a justice of the peace for Alexandria County in the District of Columbia. He was retained by TJ, however, who renominated him on 6 Jan. 1802. In that same year TJ also appointed Peyton a commissioner of bankruptcy for Alexandria County and a lieutenant colonel in the District of Columbia militia (CVSP, 8:345; JEP, 1:388, 404; RCHS, 5

[1902], 260, 279; 50 [1948-50], 388, 401; Horace Edwin Hayden, *Virginia Genealogies* [Washington, D.C., 1931], 500; Alexandria *Times*, 25 June, 9 July 1802; *National Intelligencer*, 31 Aug. 1836).

MR. GADSBY: John Gadsby, proprietor of Gadsby's Hotel in Alexandria.

On 6 Jan. 1802 TJ nominated THOMAS DARNE a justice of the peace for Alexandria County in the District of Columbia, but Darne declined qualifying for the office (JEP, 1:404, 417).

Peyton's letter is in response to one from TJ of 12 Mch. (PrC in ViW; blurred and faint, largely illegible; mistakenly endorsed by TJ in ink on verso as a letter of 12 May).

To Samuel Smith

DEAR SIR   Washington Mar. 13. 1801.

I recieved last night your favor on the subject of capt Wm. Buchanan. mr Madison not being to join us for some time & mr Gallatin gone, I have concluded only to dispatch such subjects as are of absolute necessity & to go home to make some necessary arrangements there preparatory to a final removal to this place. I count on leaving this on the 21st. and of our being all assembled here within 4. weeks from that time. for this reason we cannot take up the subject of Consuls till then; and in the particular case you mention there will then be a public occasion of conveying a letter to the isle of Bourbon if necessary. the circumstance of my intended departure induces me to press the promised answer to my last letter at the first possible moment, because whatever it be some important measures must be adopted relative to the navy before I can go away. in the wished for event of your acceptance, it would seem necessary you should be with us for 3. or 4. days to form those leading determinations which the laws & existing circumstances require respecting the navy. in hopes therefore of hearing from you soon as well as favorably I tender you assurances of my high & affectionate esteem.   TH: JEFFERSON

RC (ViU); addressed: "Genl. Samuel Smith Baltimore"; franked and postmarked. PrC (DLC).

MY LAST LETTER: TJ to Smith, 9 Mch.

To Benjamin Stoddert

SIR   Washington Mar. 13. 1801.

Your claims on my time need no apology certainly when the subject relates to the affairs of the government. to direct the conduct of these with the aid of the heads of departments constitutes the duties precisely for which I am placed here, & to which I cheerfully devote my whole time and faculties.

The subject of your letter received yesterday, respecting the contracts for ship timber would require a more minute information than I at present possess, or can acquire without more time & enquiry than present circumstances admit. your proposition to let the contract in South Carolina rest till a final settlement, only placing on the records of your office your opinion on the subject, is so perfectly just & proper that I am inclined to think it had better be done as to that with mr Marbury in this neighbourhood also. both appear to rest nearly on the same principles & to claim the same course of proceedure. the close of the contracts indeed seems the proper period for considering of indulgencies where terms are alledged to have been too hard. I think with you that on public, no more than on private contracts, we should never conduct ourselves with a rigour ruinous to individuals, nor make advantages from their undeserved ruin. it is also right that when the public or a private individual, wish, before they embark in an enterprize, to know the extent beyond which they are not to be carried, & therefore secure themselves by a contract, that this should be considered as something, and especially that we avoid establishing an expectation that it is a compact only in cases where we lose by it. the same degree of liberality should be practised for the public as would be done by a liberal & honorable man in his own case. as to this the justice of the administration, when the question shall necessarily come on, may be safely & properly trusted.

I will ask the favor of you to have me furnished with an authentic statement of the French prisoners in our possession, where they are, and in the custody of what officer, as something should be done without delay, as to their liberation & transportation.

Accept my respectful salutations.   TH: JEFFERSON

PrC (DLC); at foot of first page: "The Secretary of the Navy." FC (Lb in DNA: RG 45, LSP).

Late in 1800 the United States initiated the process of turning over to Philippe de

Létombe all captured French mariners held as PRISONERS in American ports (NDQW, Dec. 1800-Dec. 1801, 54, 103, 125, 131, 182).

From Elizabeth House Trist

DEAR SIR   Richmond 13th. March

Your favor received yesterday was quite Unexpected. It was not my intention by obtruding my admonitions upon you to draw you into a corrispondence, knowing how fully (particularly at this period) you must be occupied. altho to *you* business of every kind wou'd be as little irksome as to any one, yet every moment of leisure you shou'd embrace to promote your health and spirits—to hear that you enjoy'd both, wou'd be as grateful to my mind, as the proof you have given me of your attention and friendship

It is with delight I assure you that your speech is universally admired your opponants are relieved of a burthen by the concilitary sentiments it breathes and the republicans have not even complain'd of your philanthrophy on this occasion—all seem pleased and every testimony of has been exibited the country is capable of, the triumph of republickinism is celebrating in every part of this State. Albemarle has *shone*. its true for want of a feild peice they had to make a substitute not of a Jack Boot as *Trim* did but a peice of wrought Iron which they tied to one of the pillars of the Court House. it answered very well to anounce the glad tydings. I am obliged to relinquish the hope I had entertain'd of seeing you in Albemarle this spring if your visit is to be a short one, as it will not be in my power to leave this till the middle of next month, but I please my self with the hope the period will not be very distant when I shall have that pleasure

I am with every sentiment of Respect Your Sincere Friend

E. TRIST

[273]

RC (MHi); endorsed by TJ as received 18 Mch. and so recorded in SJL.

YOUR FAVOR: for TJ to Elizabeth Trist, 7 Mch., see TJ to Monroe, also of 7 Mch.

JACK BOOT: in chapter 20 of the third volume of Laurence Sterne's comic novel *The Life and Opinions of Tristram Shandy*, a character named Trim attempts to fashion siege mortars from a pair of military boots.

To Joel Barlow

DEAR SIR   Washington Mar. 14. 1801.

Not having my papers here, it is not in my power to acknolege the receipt of your letters by their dates, but I am pretty certain I have received two in the course of the last twelve months, one of them covering your excellent 2d. letter. nothing can be sounder than the principles it inculcates, and I am not without hopes they will make their way. you have understood that the revolutionary movements in Europe, had by industry & artifice, been wrought into objects of terror even to this country, and had really involved a great portion of our wellmeaning citizens in a panic which was perfectly unaccountable, and during the prevalence of which they were led to support measures the most insane. they are now pretty thoroughly recovered from it and sensible of the mischeif which was done, & preparing to be done had their minds continued a little longer under that derangement. the recovery bids fair to be complete, and to obliterate entirely the line of party division which had been so strongly drawn. not that their late leaders have come over, or ever can come over. but they stand at present almost without followers. the principal of them have retreated into the judiciary as a strong hold, the tenure of which renders it difficult to dislodge them. for all the particulars I must refer you to mr Dawson, a member of Congress, fully informed & worthy of entire confidence. give me leave to ask for him your attentions & civilities, and a *verbal* communication of such things on your side the water as you know I feel a great interest in, and as may not with safety be committed to paper. I am entirely unable to conjecture the issue of things with you. accept assurances of my constant esteem & high consideration.   TH: JEFFERSON

RC (NHi); addressed: "Joel Barlow esquire Paris by mr Dawson"; endorsed by Barlow. PrC (DLC).

The TWO most recent communications from Barlow were those of 15 Sep. and 3 Oct. 1800.

YOUR EXCELLENT 2D. LETTER: *Joel Barlow to his Fellow Citizens of the United States of America. Letter II* ; see Barlow to TJ, 3 Oct.; Sowerby, No. 3213.

From Albert Gallatin

SIR   Washington 14th March 1801

The weather having detained me here to day, I have employed it in making some rough sketches relative to our financial situation, which I have the honor to enclose.

Independent of the uncertainty arising from the fluctuation in the amount of duties on imports, which vary so much, as to have been two millions of dollars more in 1800 than the preceding year, I had neither time nor documents sufficient to give them even the degree of correctness of which estimates of that kind are susceptible.

No. 1 is an estimate of the probable receipts & expenditures for the year 1801, by which it would appear that we may have a surplus of above two millions of dollars applicable to the redemption of the debt. I am afraid that the revenue on imports is rated too high, although I have reduced it half a million less than last year, and it is not improbable that I may have supposed the savings for this year greater than will be found practicable. I find also a mistake of near 100,000 dollars in the marines; which arises from a part of the expense of that corps being blended with the general navy appropriation. But it is doubtful with me, whether you have not a power, in laying up the frigates; to discharge a number of those marines, grounded on the 2d. Sect. of the "Act for the establishing and organizing a marine corps" See 4th Vol. page 200, lines 3d & 4th. The simplest way of applying the surplus, whatever it may be, is, after making the necessary remittances to Holland for the purpose of discharging this & part of next year's instalments, to pay a part of the debt due to the Bank, which, by reducing the amount due to them, will enable them to assist us hereafter by temporary loans in equalizing the heavy instalments of the Dutch debt.

No. 2 is intended to show how far it will be necessary to reduce the naval & military establishments, in order to render a repeal of all the internal duties practicable, at the same time that we should apply one million yearly to the payment of the Dutch debt. That sum at least[1] is necessary in order to discharge the whole within the period for which it was originally borrowed. The payment of the British debts is perhaps the most untoward circumstance, as the result on that subject is not under our own controul. And if we shall be obliged actually to pay them, we must necessarily either redeem less debt or continue the internal duties. It is proposed in that sketch to continue those duties for the year 1802 because it seems necessary that Congress should have authorized a reduction of expense & that expense should have actually been diminished, before taxes can be lessened; and because the risk seems too great, to part altogether with that resource, before we have had the trial of another year.

No. 3 shows the present rate of expense for the army, and the intended plan of Mr Stoddard for the future expense of the navy. Although I have taken the liberty of suggesting in what manner the reduction might take place, it was merely in order to illustrate my meaning. The most eligible mode of making the reduction, and of applying & distributing amongst the several objects appertaining to those establishments the sums which shall ultimately be applicable to that purpose[2] must be the result of a strict investigation by the Gentlemen who understand the subject. All I wish to impress is the necess. of a great reduction there, if it be intended to repeal the internal duties. Savings in every department may be practicable, & must be attempted whenever practicable; but we can save but thousands in the other, & we may save hundreds of thousand in those two establishments. And that they are practicable to the extent proposed appears from this fact. In the year 1797 the military & indian departments including fortifications &c. cost only 1,062,000 dollars & the naval establishment 382,000—in all 1,444,000 dollars. The average of both for the years 1796 & 1797 was about one million and half. The lowest expence for the civil list, miscellaneous & contingent, foreign intercourse &c. was 1796 during which it amounted to 968,000 dollars. I have rated all those objects in No. 2 at only 900,000; which sum, unless the sessions of the Legislature shall be shorter, the judiciary Act repealed, & the diplomatic and Barbary expences curtailed, will not be sufficient.

I find that I have neglected another item of expense, vizt. the repayment of the 200,000 dollars loan guaranteed to Maryland for this city, & which will become due in four equal instalments, if I recollect right, within two years. And it is also to be feared that the city will draw from Congress additional sums.

Excuse, I pray, the very great hurry with which these observations have been written & believe me to be with great & sincere personal respect

Your most obt. & he. Servt.   ALBERT GALLATIN

The subject of the purchase of the navy yards seems to require attention. Is that at N. York completed? and if the appropriation does not cover the purchases, is there no remedy against the agents? The appropriation of 50,000 dollars for docks had not on the 30th Septer. last been touched & expired on the 31 Decer. The appropriation of 200,000 dollars was for timber, or lands on which timber was growing, & the President was, by the same law, authorized *to cause proper measures to be taken to have the same preserved.* But the appropriation extended to the purchase of timber & not to the expense attending those measures. Under colour of that appropriation, it appears that at least 186,800 dollars have been applied to navy yards & the balance to frames for two additional 74s. Mr. Stoddart in his report misquotes the word of the law & calls it an appropn. *for preparing proper places for securing the timber.* I enclose the report—

RC (DLC); addressed: "The President of the United States"; endorsed by TJ: "Finance." Enclosure: *Report of the Secretary of the Navy, Accompanying Sundry Documents Marked No. 1, to 5 inclusive, Relative to the Naval Establishment of the United States* [Washington, D.C., 1801]. Other enclosures printed below.

Gallatin based TJ's power to DIS-CHARGE A NUMBER OF THOSE MARINES on a sentence in Section 2 of the 1798 Marine Corps act which reads: "And the enlistments, which shall be made by virtue hereof, may be for the term of three years, subject to be discharged by the President of the United States, or by the ceasing or repeal of the laws providing for the naval armament" (U.S. Statutes at Large, 1:594-5).

PAYMENT OF THE BRITISH DEBTS: the commission established under Article 6 of the Jay Treaty to settle British prewar debt claims could not reach agreement and dissolved in 1799. In January 1802 a settlement was reached by which the U.S. agreed to pay £600,000 sterling, that is, $2,664,000, the sum to be paid in three annual installments (Madison, *Papers,*

Sec. of State Ser., 1:7-8; Miller, *Treaties*, 2:488-9; Perkins, *First Rapprochement*, 117-19, 140-1).

APPROPRIATION ... WAS FOR TIMBER: for the act "authorizing the purchase of Timber for naval purposes" passed by Congress on 25 Feb. 1799, see U.S. Statutes at Large, 1:622. In his report Stoddert noted that the appropriation for $200,000 had been expended on frames for two ships and "in preparing docks for receiving the timber, and wharves for building the ships." Stoddert explained that the Navy Department was in the practice of "drawing on one appropriation for all Navy purposes, until that appropriation is exhausted, leaving until the settlement of the agent's accounts, the charges against each appropriation for which the money has been expended" (*Report of the Secretary of the Navy*, 5, 6). Gallatin included the passage on the Navy Department's spending practices in his reference to pages in Stoddert's report in Enclosure No. 3.

[1] Preceding two words interlined.
[2] Preceding ten words interlined.

ENCLOSURES

I

Estimate of Receipts and Expenditures for 1801

Sketch &c.

Expenses & Receipts of 1801

. Interest & charges on public debt including repayt. on six p% & def. stock 5,325,000.
. Civil list, mint, military pensions, light houses, foreign intercourse, 900,000.
. Expenses attending land tax & census 100,000.

4. Extraordy. expenses attending for. intercouse vizt.

Protection of seamen	30,000	
Prize causes in England	64,000	
British Treaty	58,000	529,500 appropd.
Spanish do.	46,500	
Algiers & Barbary	256,000	
French prisoners	75,000	

But as all these items may, this year, be reduced, provided proper
& immediate attention is paid to them, they may be estimated at   400,000.

5. Army & Indian Departments   1,400,000

Fortifications	200,000	2,000,000 appd.
Cannon, arms, military stores	400,000	

     The same observation as in last item—may be estimated at   1,600,000.

6. Naval establisht. vizt.

2 large frigates & 4 smallest on war establisht. for 1 year   500,000

The whole estabt. exclusively of contingencies on shore,
marines, and building of ships, after deducting Insurgent
& Pickering supposed to be lost is   2,120,000.

                                    500,000

Deduct the six frigates retained   1620,000

       Remaining establisht.

By taking proper measures for promptly
recalling & disarming the ships not kept
in service, the expense for this year may

be estimated at $\frac{1}{3}$ of this whole or	540,000	
Expenses for laid up vessels say	36,000	
Contingencies on shore	37,000	
Marine corps	167,000	
Progressing with 74s—appd. 500,000, expend	300,000	

Purchase of navy yards, progressing with that at the
Eastern branch,— *no visible appropriation*
Purchases of timber—appropriation of 98 expired but
to pay contracts   say   50,000

                                         1,630,000

Total Expenses	9,955,000
7. Surplus applicable this year to paymt. of debt	2,400,000
	12,355,000

Receipts

Impost. for 1800 was	9,080,932.73—say for 1801	8,500,000
Internal	809,000.	800,000
Direct tax	734,000	1,000,000
Postage, dividends on bank stock, certs, fines &c.		200,000
Lands—very uncertain—say		300,000

Surplus in Treasury vizt
    Balance on 1st Jany. 1801 was   2,557,000   ⎫
Say that it is necessary to keep   ⎬ about 1,555,000
    always there about   1,000,000   ⎭

                                                      12,355,000

NB. The proceeds of the sales of vessels, about 300,000 dollars are not set down
    as part of the receipts, but allowed to cover contingencies, defalcations &
    mistakes—

        MS (DLC: TJ Papers, 110:18957); undated; entirely in Gallatin's hand; on verso
in Gallatin's hand: "No. 1."

II
Estimate of Receipts and Expenditures after 1801

Revenues exclusively of internal duties after 1801

Impost permanent may be estimated at	8,000,000
Postage, dividends &c	200,000
Sales of lands	300,000
	8,500,000

Expenses after 1801

1. Interest & charges on public debt will diminish about 40,000 dollars a year	about	5,200,000
2. Civil list &c. after probable reductions		800,000
3.⎫ 4.⎭ contingencies at home & abroad	say	100,000
7.[1] Payment (yearly) on foreign debt principal		1,000,000
5.⎫ 6.⎭ Balance applicable to army and navy		1,400,000
		8,500,000

Result

1. Internal taxes to be abolished after 1802
2. Public debt diminished in 4 years ending 31 Decer. 1804 about 10 or 11
million Ds.

1. surplus of 1801	2,400,000
2. internal duties of 1802	800,000

3. surplus of 1802-1803-1804 & interest	3,120,000
4. redemption of six p% & deferred stock pr. yearly paymt. of 2 p% on original stock	4,700,000
5. arrears of int. duties collected after 1802-Say	480,000
	11,500,000

The data on which that result rests are
1. That the impost shall not receive any considerable shock either from the want of a general peace or by our being involved in the war
2. That its gradual increase will cover any unforeseen contingencies other than that of an European war
3. That the strictest economy will be recommended by the Executive & adopted by Congress, and principally in the War & Navy establis ments, so far as to make reductions which will limit their expence to the 1,400,000 dollars
4. That the payment of British debts may be principally covered by our demands for spoliations since Jay's treaty

The only financial operation necessary is that of obtaining such temporary loans from the Bank, as may equalize the instalments of the Dutch debt.

MS (DLC: TJ Papers, 110:18958); undated; entirely in Gallatin's hand; on verso in Gallatin's hand: "No. 2."   [1] Number written over "5."

III
Estimate of Military Expenditures

Army
amounts now (exclusively of marines who are 1,100) to about 5400 men

The present expence is

1. Ordnance department including fabrication of muskets	100,000
2. Indian department & defensive protection of frontiers	100,000
3. Pay, subsistence, clothing &c. of army	1,000,000
4. Quarter master departt. & contingencies	200,000
	1,400,000

Congress had reduced the Army in 1797 to 3200 men
On the supposition of a similar reduction the expences may be

3. Pay, subsistence &c. $\frac{3}{5}$ of one million	600,000
4. Quart. master & contingencies $\frac{3}{5}$ of 200,000, but on account of abuses may be stated at one half	100,000
1. ⎫ Ordnance the same—indian & defens. protect. ⎬ say $\frac{4}{5}$ of prest. exp. or	180,000
2. ⎭	
	880,00●

Under the same head may be arranged
   1. Fortifications now 200,000 dollars—reduced $\frac{1}{2}$ 100,000
   2. Arms now 400,000—reduced to $\frac{1}{4}$ or 10,000 muskets a yr. 100,000   200,000

                            Proposed expense   1,080,000

Navy

The Secy. proposed a yearly expence of
   1. Six frigates in constant service, but on peace estabt.   387,257
      includ. the exp. of 7 laid up
   2. Marines on peace establishment   207,310
   3. For completing docks, building houses &c   400,000
      for finishing the six 74s   2,174,000
                                       2,574,000

          which he proposes completing in 4 years   643,500
   4. For yearly purchase of timber of one 74 & one 44   117,387
                                Total   1,355,454

Instead of which the sum allotted would allow only
   1. Two frigates in service, others laid up
      & pay of marines attached to the same   150,000
   2. Purchase of timber, finishing the dock here
      & perhaps one more   170,000   320,000
                                         1,400,000

This is grounded on a supposition that after this year Congress will not authorize the immediate finishing of the 74s. & that the other places purchased for navy yards, & the purchase of which was not authorized by law (a), will be sold
(a) See the law passed 25th Feby. 1799, authorizing the purchase of timber 4th Vol. page
267 & Stoddart's last report dated 12th Jany. 1801 page 5th from line 14th to line 32 &
page 6 from beginning to the words "been expended" at the end of 2d paragraph—

MS (DLC: TJ Papers, 110:18959); undated; entirely in Gallatin's hand; on verso in Gallatin's hand: "No. 3."

From Benjamin Galloway

Hagerstown, Washington County, Maryland, 14 Mch. 1801. He recommends Colonel Nathaniel Rochester, a 20-year resident of Hagerstown,
whose prudence, abilities, and public conduct "have secured to him, the good
Opinion, of all Descriptions, of his Fellow Citizens, within the Sphere of his
Movements." For "substantial Reasons" Rochester did not enter public life,
although he was encouraged to do so. At the last two congressional elections,
"when *Party Spirit* agitated the public Mind," he would have been elected
"*without Opposition*; both Parties having declared that if *he* would consent to

serve, they would unanimously support his Election." Rochester, who has a large young family and is advanced in age, visited "the Genesee" the previous summer and intends to move there. Galloway believes that Rochester would not move from Maryland if he received an appointment that would justify his staying. No person in the district "possesses the Confidence of all Descriptions of Persons, on so large a Scale, *as he does*." He exhibits unquestionable integrity "combined with great Industry, Suavity of Manners, and Fortitude of Mind." Rochester possesses the unrivaled confidence of his fellow Republican citizens "who have *paid you in Advance*." They would be pleased if he were nominated for a government office. Galloway reiterates that he is not related to Rochester "*by any Tie*, save only, *as a most worthy Man*, and a *good Republican*."

RC (DNA: RG 59, LAR); 3 p.; inadvertently endorsed by TJ as a letter of 21 Mch. received the same day, but recorded in SJL as a letter of 14 Mch. received the 21st. Enclosed in Galloway to James Madison, 14 Mch. 1801, with the request that it be delivered to "Mr. Jefferson" (RC in same).

Born in Virginia in 1752, Nathaniel Rochester grew up in North Carolina. About 1783, in conjunction with a business partner, he moved to Hagerstown, Maryland, rented a gristmill, and began the manufacture of nails and rope. According to his autobiography, Rochester served one term in the Maryland legislature but refused to serve again because he disliked "the intrigue and management among the members." In 1800 Rochester visited the Genesee country in western New York and purchased water-power sites near Dansville. He settled there in 1810 and established three mills and a wool-carding shop. In 1818 he moved to the Upper Falls of the Genesee River, where the city of Rochester developed (DAB; James Grant Wilson and John Fiske, eds., *Appletons' Cyclopaedia of American Biography*, 6 vols. [New York, 1887-89], 5:293-4).

From Abel Janney

SIR,   Alexandria March 14th. 1801.

Desirous to pay you every mark of respect due to the first Majestrate. of a happy free and Independant Nation, I have taken the liberty to march the Alexandria Rifle Company out to welcome you to Our Town, with a Sincere Satisfaction in the choice of our Fellow citizens. I thought it necessary to inform you of the reason of our not uniting With the Regiment on this Occasion, which will be under Arms for your Reception, it is in consequence of a Dispute of the right of Precedency which has arisen between the Compy I had the Honor to command, and on this particular Occasion take the Command of. (for the purpose above Recited) and the Light infantry. both attatched to the same Regt. I have From the little sirvice I had seen during the Revolutionary War, considered that Rifle Men were alway posted on the right And left of Regiments in Review. which post has been Denied me I have therefore considered it as an unprecedented Partiality in Our Colo. and cannot Consent To unite with the Regt., if Posted on the left. if I am under an Error of opinion of Military etiquaty You will pardon my error in Judgment and Accept These small marks of Respect we wish to make you A tender of

With due Respect I am Sir your Obedt. Hble. Sevt.

ABEL JANNEY

RC (DLC); at head of text: "Thomas Jefferson President of the United States"; endorsed by TJ as received 15 Mch. and so recorded in SJL.

Abel Janney (ca. 1755-1812) was an Alexandria merchant and member of the firm Janney & Paton, which went bankrupt in 1806. Janney was appointed tax collector by the Alexandria common council in 1808, a position he held until late 1811 when the corporation brought suit against him and his securities "for the balance due by his account" (Miller, *Alexandria Artisans*, 1:xxix, 234; *Alexandria Daily Gazette, Commercial & Political*, 28 July, 1 Aug. 1810, 1 Mch., 7 Nov. 1811, 14 Apr. 1812).

ALEXANDRIA RIFLE COMPANY: when TJ and his suite journeyed to the public dinner held in his honor in Alexandria on 14 Mch., Janney's company of riflemen met them at the northern boundary of the city. The remainder of the militia, commanded by Colonel George Deneale, and an artillery company were drawn up on King Street, where they honored the president with a 16-gun salute (Alexandria *Times*, 16 Mch. 1801; *Alexandria Advertiser and Commercial Intelligencer*, 16 Mch. 1801). Janney was dismissed from the 106th militia regiment in 1802 after a trial (Miller, *Alexandria Artisans*, 1:234).

From Walter Jones

DEAR SIR.   March 14th. 1801.

A variety of avocations have delayed for some, time, the Gratification of my desire, to Congratulate you on your final Election to the office of President.

It is with pleasure I am Conscious, that I can indulge my personal sentiments towards you, with perfect security to the Considerations I owe to the public welfare; as I am convinced that the Capacity, Experience & Principles of no Citizen in the U.S. gives him a more merited title, to the station you have attained.

For the remaining Part of this Letter, I must trust for an Excuse to its contents, as they relate both to motives & matter. it is true that the many admirable positions, for the conduct of Government, expressed in your inaugural speech, supersede the necessity of such an address, and forbid the hope that I can offer any thing useful to your view, which is not familiar: yet the Experience of Pleasure, from every effort to cast my mite into the common stock of social happiness, & my assurance that I could no where find for them, a more candid & indulgent depository, prompt me to proceed—permit me to add, that as a part of the primordial sovereignty of my Country, I feel, and incessantly cultivate the feeling, that it is my Right & my Duty to investigate, with decent freedom, any Topics connected with the common welfare—

The peculium indeed of power which belongs to each private Individual, is in quantity minute, & occasional only in Exertion. but for this very Cause it is, that each Individual should cherish and appreciate his peculiar Portion, with all its appendant Rights & Duties. for when the primary parts are vigorous, their collective force is irresistible, when they are sound, their collective agency is wise. when those parts are neglected or depraved, their collective force is impotent or mischeivous; their collective agency, partakes of the Impurity of the source. a *Nominal* sovereignty in the People, is borne down by the accumulated portions of power delegated to the few who rule; the Rulers soon disregard the popular origin & delegated nature of their Trust; and the Remembrance of them in the Community comes to be buried under every species of usurpation & oppression.—

That this dark Picture represents the general Condition of mankind as it has actually subsisted, is lamentably manifest from their History. how far may the fairer side of the Prospect be realised? how far may such Improvement in the intellectual & moral habits of a people become prevalent as to give them a wholesome reflective Sovereignty, and redeem them from their customary destinies, of being either the voluntary Dupes & victims of faithless representatives, or a Flock nurtured, driven, fleeced & slaughtered for the Behoof of royal Sheperds?—many very estimable men receive these questions, with much Doubt & dispondency, the most sanguine cannot but veiw them with qualified Hope—perhaps the Doubts of the first may be augmented, by the recent Experiment on these states.—

No people ever commenced their political Career, under Circumstances so favourable as ourselves: yet just as Power & Revenue have presented Temptations, men have been found so depraved, as to indulge a Lust of both, equal to the examples of any other Country, and so numerous, as to combine by system, into a faction, more dangerous to our freedom & happiness, than any other thing, by which I can concieve that we are menaced.—

But this difficulty, as it respects the Progress of Social Improvement, is more specious than solid. to the considerate & discerning, our boasted advantages will appear to have been of the negative kind.—we were exempt indeed from those great monopolies of wealth, Honours, privilege & Power, which in Europe, Ignorance had permitted to grow strong by time & usurpation. we had not Guidis & Montmorancis, Colignis & Rohans to split a nation into a few great sections, and to make each mass implicitly subservient to the Passions of its Leader; but we were replete with the Propensities that ingender the spirit of Oligarchy. we had caught from Europe her Cupidity of wealth & her Love of the Fashions, manners and distinctions it bestows. our spirit of Freedom, was rather a Passion producing a proud Impatience of Restraint, than a Principle founded in the understanding & moral habits, which can alone insure the durability & preserve, in purity, the nature of genuine Liberty.—

In your speech I was especially pleased, with your Comparative observations on religious & political Intolerance.—they are inestimable Truths, of which few men are aware & of which no man ought to be ignorant; they are congenial with the results of my best Judgment; they justify the view of your future administration, which I have always maintained, when I have heard the wild wishes & conjectures of some of the republican Party, conceived in all the fervor of vindictive Retaliation. In the objects which excite these systems of Intolerance, in the means they severally demand for their Execution, and in the Consequences that result from them, there is either a strong analogy or an exact similitude.—

in the Practice however, both of religious & political Forbearance, the Theory as in most other cases must be qualified in its extreme Latitude. when the People indeed, are called upon to elect, to a high & efficient office in Government, they are bound to investigate the opinions of the Candidates, with the most scrupulous attention, and universally to reject all those, whose Principles are equivocal, as they respect not only the spirit of the existing Constitution & Laws, but the progressive extension of individual Liberty, in proportion as the improved state of social morality will authorise a diminution of Taxation, Penalty & Coercion.—for example, a society of conscientious Baptists would act very absurdly in electing for their Pastor, a lutheran Priest, tho in other respects a pious & virtuous man. it would be no less absurd in a republican Society to place a man in a high & efficient office who professed opinions adverse to republican Principles & Institutions

Again, a President of the U.S. is compelled to act immediately with the higher departments of the Executive part of the Government; to them he must impart his Confidential counsels and Commit his official responsibility. it seems then to be the dictate of Common sense & self protection that no man, who has proclaimed his hostility to the Person & Principles of the chief Magistrate, ought ever to be appointed the head of those departments or be permitted to remain in them, even for a day

But in the lower & more remote offices of executive ministry, Talent, diligence & fidelity seem to bound the claims of the state, on the individual functionary—his private Judgment, should be left free of all control, except that of reason & conviction, and therefore to deprive a man of office, not for Incapacity or misconduct, but for his political opinions is to commit an act of Injustice against *him*, and to foster in *his Party* the implacable obstinacy of martyrdom, which grows out of Persecution.

Even in the original Promotion to office, political opinion seems to be an improper Test of exclusive Preference. considering the subject apart, it may be true, that one of two men, otherwise equal in their Pretensions may have a superior claim to Promotion, for the soundness of his political Principles: but upon a more liberal Calculation of moral Consequences, this ground of Preference ought occasionally to yield to considerations of greater moment. for while the avidity of wealth, and the vanity of Distinction are so prevalent, such an exclusive distribution of office, would be a grand Instrument of political Persecution—

Secondly. Free discussion, is the only possible medium thro which moral & political Truth can be developed & established.—the discussion of the *actual* Principles & Interests of men, in *opposite views*, excites the Passions & dissentions of Party.—it behoves the republican to allay & to bear these Evils as well as he can, but he is *bound*, at all hazards, to proceed in discussion & Inquiry.—on the troubled scene, thro which he must necessarily pursue his Course, it cannot but be wise, to exhibit occasional proofs, that he aims not at the Extermination but the Reformation of his adversaries, at a System of Comprehension not of exclusion, at the establishment of Truth on such Evidence, as must impress Conviction in every mind not eminently perverted, and gradually sink the spirit of Party, in a Common attachment to true Principles of Liberty & Right. The distinction & Emoluments of office, are so universally coveted, that a *judicious* distribution of them, among men of different Parties, would furnish a very useful Proof of the Conciliatory spirit of republicanism.

When we give the Reins to reflexion, on the diversity & complexity of the relations of associated man, of the ceaseless, rapid, & diversified action required of Government, the mind stands apalled at the difficulties of comprehending the first with clearness, and of transacting the latter with Precision.—among these difficulties, to me none appear to be of greater magnitude & importance, than those connected with our Commerce—

Various have been the means, in various ages, which accident or design have placed in the hands of the few, to depress the many—the spirit of Conquest & plunder, various forms of superstition, Rank, Titles, Privileges have all had their share; but they seem, at all times, to have been connected with & supported by the Cupidity of wealth.—in modern Times The Terrors of superstition have dwindled almost to ridicule; Conquest & Plunder have been limited, by changes in the art of war, and the Jealousy and frequency of national Intercourse; Rank Title & Privilege are daily offerings at the altar of reason & science—the Cupidity of wealth, supported by its associate Commerce, subsists in the utmost vigour and is the prominent, gigantic Fob of human happiness.—Improvements in navigation & ship-building, have given Commerce an extent, that brings it more & more into monopoly among bold adventurers and great Capitalists.—Monopoly makes them able, and the protection necessary for very distant & rapacious Trade, makes them willing to feed the Prodigality of Government—Government repays the obligation by enormous funds for their Loans, and by dispatching Navies to the remotest quarters of the Globe, either to acquire new fields of adventure for Commercial Monopolies, or to defend the oppressions inflicted on the old.—hence the tremendous Evils of Debts, Funds, and great Navies.—a Commerce so extended, calls for an immense supply of manufactures; and the demand, by very natural steps, tends to the monopoly of manufacturing Capital. accordingly in England, it is astonishing what numbers depend for employment on a few great manufacturing Capitalists—so that what with the Government, the landed aristocracy, the great commercial & manufacturing Capitalists, the people of England seem to have a greater variety of masters, than their progenitors found under the feudal system. and altho the latter might have had more direct & established power over the persons of their vassals, it is questionable, whether they posessed so many means of injuring the general Comforts & happiness of the peoples as the present Masters.—In that Country Commercial Cupidity has been ingrafted on military ferocity, and together they have generated a spirit more merciless & destructive, than any other, that ever afflicted mankind. If a very fair, &, of course, a very dreadful, detail of the sufferings inflicted on India & Peru could be exhibited to our review, I have no doubt, that a Considerable ballance of our detestation would be due to the former.—yet England is the Country which is held up to us as a model; whose Commercial spirit & naval Institutions we have been invited to imitate!

I am by no means a Competent judge, how far our Government may be able, to produce a pacific temper and habit of prudent adventure in the trading part of our Citizens; nor how far an extreme reduction or even abolition of our navy, may be expedient—I trust however that no subjects will Command, a more early or sedulous Consideration of the next Congress.—

I know to well the occupation & value of your time, as not to look even for an answer to this Letter, much less to make it the ground of a Correspondence.—I have much Interest in your personal happiness & the welfare of our Common Country—I could not suppress my desire of saying as much, & shall be happy if you accept this Letter as an Evidence of both—being with sentiments of very sincere & affectionate respect yours, dear Sir, WALT: JONES

RC (DLC); addressed: "The President of the U States"; endorsed by TJ as received 30 Mch. and so recorded in SJL.

Walter Jones (1745-1815) of Northumberland County, Virginia, was a college classmate of TJ's at William and Mary, departing in 1763 (a year after TJ). The two men also lodged together at the Philadelphia hotel of John Francis in 1797. An Edinburgh-trained physician,

Jones served in Congress from 1797 to 1799 and 1803 to 1811 as a Republican. In 1801 TJ appointed his son, Walter Jones, Jr., U.S. attorney for the district of Potomac (*List of Alumni*, 24; *Biog. Dir. Cong.*, 1282; DAB; Appendix I, Lists 3 and 4; JEP, 1:401; Vol. 1:12; Vol. 29: 469n). Jones's letter to TJ of 27 July 1799, recorded in SJL as received 30 Aug. of that year, has not been found.

To Tadeusz Kosciuszko

DEAR GENERAL   Washington Mar. 14. 1801.

I inclose you a letter from mr Barnes on the subject of your affairs here. a loan at an interest of 8. per cent having been proposed by our government, I thought it better to convert a part of your bank stock into that, which was done to advantage. all the details are in the hands of mr Barnes, who is worthy of all confidence.   This will be handed you by our friend mr Dawson. I can now hail you with confidence on the return of our fellow citizens to the principles of '76. and to their thorough understanding of the artifices which have been played off on them and under the operation of which they were while you were here. they are sensible of the dangers into which they were suffering themselves to be misled, and see the burthens of debt which they have imposed on them. the people have come over in a body to the republican side, & have left such of their leaders as were incurable to stand by themselves: so that there is every reason to hope that that line of party division which you saw drawn here, will be totally obliterated. it would give me infinite pleasure to have you here a witness to our recovery, & to recognise the people whom you knew during the war. for all particulars I refer you to mr Dawson, who, being an actor in the scene, can give you all the details. I have not been able to learn your exact situation since you were here. your letters are too barren of what I wish most to hear, I mean, of things relating to yourself. I am in constant expectation of recieving your commission to buy the hundred acres of land for you in my neighborhood. I am fixed here however for some time. continue to preserve my place in your esteem, and accept assurances of my constant and affectionate friendship.

Th: Jefferson

Mar. 18. This moment mr Pichon arrives & delivers me your letter of which he is the bearer.

RC (National Museum, Cracow, Poland); at foot of text: "Genl. Kosciuzko." PrC (DLC). Enclosure not found.

For the investment of some of Kosciuszko's assets in LOAN certificates offered by the U.S. government, see Vol. 31:587.

John Barnes having moved to Georgetown, TJ in February 1801 gave John Richards of Philadelphia substitute power of attorney to receive the dividends on Kosciuszko's STOCK in the Bank of Pennsylvania (PrC in MHi; entirely in TJ's hand and signed by him; blurred, day of month illegible; endorsed by TJ in ink on verso).

Pichon was the BEARER of Kosciuszko's letter of [10 Oct. 1800].

From Richard Parrott

Sir   Geo Town March 14. 1801

Presuming from the late appointment of the present Collector of the Port of George Town, that, that office will be vacated—I beg Permission to solicit the said office—and should it appear to you from any information recieved respecting me, that I am qualified therefor, I shall deem the appointment a very great obligation conferred on

Sir Yr: Mo: Ob: Servt.   Richard Parrott

RC (DNA: RG 59, LAR); at head of text: "Thomas Jefferson President U. States"; endorsed by TJ as received 18 Mch. and so recorded in SJL.

Richard Parrott (d. 1822), a prominent Georgetown manufacturer, later operated a ropewalk and spinning and carding mill in the city. TJ appointed him a justice of the peace for Washington County on 11 May 1805 (RCHS, 5 [1902], 279; 18 [1915], 89; 31-32 [1930], 98-9; Bryan, *National Capital*, 1:527).

THE PRESENT COLLECTOR OF THE PORT OF GEORGE TOWN: James M. Lingan.

Parrott's application was supported by a separate letter to TJ dated 14 Mch. and signed by 15 citizens of Georgetown, headed by Edward Gantt, which stated that Parrott's "industry, integrity, and knowledge of business, qualify him, to make a useful officer" (RC in DNA: RG 59, LAR; in Gantt's hand; addressed: "Thos. Jefferson Esquire. President of the U. States. Washington"; franked; postmarked 16 Mch.; endorsed by TJ as received 18 Mch.).

From Thomas Mann Randolph

Th:M.R. to Th:J.   March. 14. 1801.

We received yours by W.C.N. on the 11. inst: & feel for you most tenderly upon the necessity now of your sacrificing all private ease & comfort. We reflect however that it is according to Nature for the strongest to bear the Burthen; and we know well that your mind does from nature exult in grand scenes, in ample fields for exertion, in extraordinary toils, as much as the finest animal of the most exellent race of our noblest Quadrupedes must do in the length of the Course.

Martha & the children are well: *I* am now allways so: there has been no interruption of health among us indeed but her symptomatic complaints which are now very trifling & have all along been the slightest she ever knew.—Your Spanish Wine has turned up at last: 2 small casks of about 10 gallons each: we keep it in Milton for there is still a mystery about your Cellar: 80 gallons of Coles best Cider sunk, in 3 days exactly, under 2 locks & keys, without more than barely moistening the floor, to about 20: which is bottled for you.

with truest attachment   Th:M.R

RC (ViU: Coolidge Deposit); endorsed by TJ as received 19 Mch. and so recorded in SJL.

YOURS BY W.C.N.: TJ's letter of 6 Mch. delivered by Wilson Cary Nicholas.

From Benjamin Stoddert

SIR.   Navy Dept. 14th March 1801.

I have the honor to enclose an account of the French Prisoners in the United States, shewing where they are and in whose custody.

A Vessel has been provided at Newyork by Mr. Letombé, to carry away Prisoners. I know not how many the Vessel will carry.— Application has been made, to have those at Boston sent to Newyork to go in this Vessel, which I have directed to be done at the expense of the United States. It would seem by Mr. Letombés letters, that he was providing Vessels to take away the rest. He has been informed of the Numbers in our possession. I have written him, that they would be sent to any port or ports at the expense of the United States, where he might have Vessels to receive them.

I have the honor to be with great respect Sir yr most Obed Svt

BEN STODDERT

RC (DLC); in clerk's hand, with closing and signature in Stoddert's hand; endorsed by TJ as received 15 Mch. and so recorded in SJL.

ENCLOSURE

Account of French Prisoners

French Prisoners	
At Boston, under the care of S. Higginson & Co.	150
At New London, Norwick, Middletown & Hartford Connt. under the care of Philip B. Bradley Marshal.	100
At Providence (R I) under the care of Wm. Peck Marshal.	25
At Frederick Town (Maryland) under the care of Mountjoy Bayley	94
At Charleston. S.C. under the care of Wm. Crafts	8
At Newyork under the care of A. Giles Marshal.	8

MS (DLC: TJ Papers, 110:18943); undated; in clerk's hand.

From Benjamin Stoddert

SIR   Navy Depart. 14 March 1801.

I understand from the letter with which you honored me, of yesterdays date, that I am not to send the letter I proposed, to Mr Marbury—but that, as it makes a part of my representation to you, it may be recorded in the books of the office, which I will have done.

I confess it would have been more agreeable to me, to have sent the letter to Mr Marbury, because the contractors have been taught to expect that I would have the disputed point settled while I remained in office—not from an Idea that it would be the disposition of any person who might execute the duties of the Navy Department, under your administration, to deny them Justice—but from the apprehension that their claim to the Philadelphia prices, might not be so well understood as by the person under whose authority they made the contracts.

In the case of the Southern contracts, a positive rule could not well be applied at this time—& for any rule which mitigates the hardship of their case, they must be indebted to the Indulgence of Government—in the case of the contractors here, a rule could be applied, a rule too which the Contractors think and which I confess I also think, must in Justice govern in the settlement with them. I think it must govern, because both they & the Public agent who contracted with them, concur in agreeing that they were made to understand the prices agreed on, were the Phila. prices—even at these prices they will probably be loosers by their contracts.

I thought it due to the persons interested & to myself, to say this much in explanation—and have the honor to be, with

   great respect Sir yr. most obed. Serv   BEN. STODDERT

RC (DLC); endorsed by TJ as received 15 Mch. and so recorded in SJL. FC (Lb in DNA: RG 45, LSP).

Following the entries for Stoddert's correspondence with TJ of 12-14 Mch. recorded in the Navy Department letterbooks are entries for two documents regarding the disposition of the navy under the Peace Establishment Act. Neither document is addressed or signed, but they presumably record discussions between TJ and Stoddert, or perhaps other naval officials, on immediate steps to be taken to reduce the navy. The first document, which is undated, makes recommendations regarding the discharge and terms of enlistment of naval personnel, transporting a copy of the convention with France to the Île de France, and the recall of navy vessels still in the West Indies. The second document, dated 23 Mch. 1801, records that it is "Agreed with Mr. Stoddart" that the ship *Herald* shall be dispatched to recall vessels in the West Indies; that a copy of the convention be sent to the Île de France with Jacob Lewis, the former consul, who would travel in his own ship; and that the crews of the ship *Connecticut* and frigate *President* be discharged. The second document concludes with a list of the 13 frigates to be retained in service, with their current locations and dispositions, and a list of navy vessels in port and at sea to be sold (DNA: RG 45, LSP; NDQW, Dec. 1800-Dec. 1801, 145-6).

To the Borough of Wilmington

GENTLEMEN   Washington Mar. 14. 1801

I return you my thanks, & through you to the corporation of the borough of Wilmington, for your congratulations on my appointment to the first magistracy of the United States. as far as a disinterested and well intentioned conduct on my part may tend to produce a prosperous administration of our affairs, my fellow citizens may count on me with confidence. for all beyond this I shall have great need of their indulgence.

I pray you to accept yourselves and to tender on my behalf to the honourable corporation of which you are members, the assurances of my high consideration & respect.   TH: JEFFERSON

PrC (DLC); at foot of text: "Messrs. Tilton & Brobson."

YOUR CONGRATULATIONS: see Borough of Wilmington to TJ, 7 Mch.

From Joseph Yznardi, Sr.

EXELENTISIMO SEÑOR

Muy Señor mio, y de mi Respeto

Conforme á el permiso, de V.E le diriji mi Representasion Fechada en Philadelphia el 4 Corriente como parage de mi Residensia, despues de la qual por Motivos privados, y por venefisio de mi Salu me he retírado á este lugar esperando la llegada del Nuebo Secretario de Estado para qe segun VE tubo la vondad de ofreserme qe no existiendo Inpedimento legal qe lo estorvase, mi pretension Seria Atendido lo qe no dudo segun los documentos ya presentados, y por qe el Nombramiento de Mr. Preble, no hasido remitido, y asta el Aviso de V.E permaneseré en esta á quien suplico me diriga por escrito por Allarme algo endeble, y el tiempo es Crudo.

Aviendo Reflexado sobre la permanencia de Mr. Yrujo en esta Pais por Conoser Coviene para la Mejor Inteligensia de las dos Nasiones y Contemplar a V.E Instruido de Oficio de la Mutasion de Ministros en Madrid, y aver yo sido Comisionado por su Corte para Intermediar en la falta de Inteligensia, y demas Sircumstansias qe manifiestan, la Credensial entregada a V.E. en Copia

Aviendo diferidose la Contestasion por este Govierno, y no aver paresido el Nuebo Ministro de España, y qe desde mi llegada á este Pais en Cumplimiento, de mi encargo Informe á favor de Mr Yrujo en Honor de la verdad Conosiendo el poco fundamento, de las queras me allo en la presion de Suplicar á V.E qe tanto para provar el desempeño de la Mission a mi Cargo se dirijiese Solisitud por este Govierno por Escrit para el de España Reservada fundada en mi encargo, y por Supuesto resultaria la Satisfaccion de Mr Yrujo, y la Condesendencia de su permanencia

La Fragata que deve llevar el tratado para Fransia seria el Mejor conducto para dicha solisitud como para qe tragese la Respta con la demora de pocos, y por la qe con el permiso de V.E mandaré, yo mis despachos no dudando qe todo tendrá efeto á Cuyo Intento Escribo al Principe de la Paz, y no seria de estrañar segun mis representasiones, y el Inpreso de Mr Yrujo qe el Comercio, de la America Española se bolviese á Franquear durante la Guerra por beneficio de las dos Naciones Interes qe Sienpre he desseado

tengo el Honor de Repetir á VE mis Respectos George town 14 Marzo 801

Exmo. Señor BLM á V.E su mas Obedte. Servidor

JOSEF YZNARDY

MOST EXCELLENT SIR

My Dear Sir and with all due respect,

With Your Excellency's permission I addressed my petition to you dated the 4th of the present month in Philadelphia as the place of my residence, after which for personal reasons and for the benefit of my health I have withdrawn to this place awaiting the arrival of the new secretary of state; who according to Your Excellency had the kindness to offer, assuming that no legal impediment exists that might obstruct it, to attend to my request; which I do not doubt, according to the documents submitted already and because the appointment of Mr. Preble has not been remitted; and until notification by Your Excellency, I will stay here. I beg you to contact me in writing since I find myself somewhat weak and the weather is bitter.

Having reflected on the stay of Mr. Irujo in this country to familiarize himself with it, it is appropriate for the best intelligence of the two countries, and for Your Excellency's planning, to be officially informed of the change of ministers in Madrid; I being commissioned by the court to be an intermediary in the absence of a channel of information and from other circumstances—the credential having been submitted to Your Excellency in copy form.

The reply by this country being postponed and the new minister from Spain not having appeared, and in fulfillment of my responsibility in this country, I addressed the Spanish government in favor of Mr. Irujo. To tell the honest truth they know very little background about him, and about the complaints. I find myself under the pressure of imploring Your Excellency, as much to prove the work of the mission that I am responsible for, that a written petition might be addressed by this government to that of Spain—a reservation based on my charge that would, of course, result in Mr. Irujo's satisfaction and acquiescence in his remaining.

The frigate that should take the treaty to France would be the best conduit for that petition since it will bring the reply with little delay; and by this means, with Your Excellency's permission, I will send my dispatches, not doubting that all will be effective—for which purpose I am writing to the prince of the peace, and it would not be surprising if, as a result of my petitions and the effort of Mr. Irujo, the commerce of Spanish America should again open during the war for the benefit of the two nations' interests, as I have always desired.

I have the honor of repeating to Your Excellency my respects, at Georgetown 14 March 1801,

Most Excellent Sir, I kiss your Excellency's hands, your most Obedient Servant   JOSEF YZNARDY

RC (DLC); at foot of text: "Exmo. Sor. Dn. Thomas Jefferson"; endorsed by TJ as received 16 Mch. and so recorded in SJL.

MINISTROS EN MADRID: in December 1800 the Spanish government made Pedro Cevallos (or Ceballos) Guerra minister of state in place of Mariano Luis de Urquijo (Germán Bleiberg, ed., *Diccionario de Historia de España*, 2d ed.,

3 vols. [1968-69], 1:819; 3:851-2; Tulard, *Dictionnaire Napoléon*, 1694; David Humphreys to the secretary of state, 16 Dec. 1800, in DNA: RG 59, DD).

King Carlos IV had given his court favorite and chief adviser, Manuel Godoy, the title PRINCIPE DE LA PAZ (prince of the peace) for Godoy's role in arranging a treaty with France in 1795 (Bleiberg, *Diccionario*, 2:214-15).

From David Austin

RESPECTED SIR.   Philadelphia March 15th. 1801

Well knowing that the subject, on which my addresses are founded, is accompanied with difficulties, proportionate to its magnitude, I shall make no other apology for the continuation of the application.

I judge, that the bolt of foreign concerns is, by this time, shot into *another hand*. Suffer me to tell you, Sir!, that this bolt must be withdrawn, & committed to a legitimate hand. As the matter now stands a mistake is committed: foundation of confusion, in the order of providence, is laid; to be followed if persisted in[1] by the frowns of Heaven upon the concerned. Mr. Adams was visited by an application of this sort; & after long silence, through the obstacles in the way; & final resistance of the application; it pleased God to announce that he should *leave his chair*. This was signified to him before he left New England for the seat of government, the last time. The order of providence hath finished the prediction: and he is turned from his seat; not so much for inaccuracy of deportment in common things, as for having resisted the voice of God in respect to his designs of giving peace to the Earth.—

[295]

The dent, that hath been lately made in the top of the American Mount; is done, that the *waters of another flood* might be let in & *fresh trial* be made, in respect to the impression which a renewed application might make. Of consequence, you stand, in a state of trial before the God of all the Earth. At your door the power of the Prince of Peace now knocks: Its legitimate operation is found, only through the portals of the American Temple. The present is the moment, in which you are to finish your own honor, or to loose it, forever!—Already, hath it pleased God, that an exhibition of your tremulous situation should be given. Before the door of the visible administration of God, on Earth, you have been seen to pass. The form was that of "garments of the grave, & a removed Crown."—I, therefore, Sir, without the least hesitation state to you, in the name & by the authority of the Most High God, that you are a dead man, in case you refuse Obedience to the voice of Heaven.—And, that the utmost candor may be shown, on my part, I avow that the Commission, addressing you is that of the "Joshua" of the American Temple. In the overturning of the World, & in planting the standard of human relief, in which you have borne a part; it hath pleased God that the Œconomy of the Jewish redemption from the power of Babylon should have a more finished illustration in the redemption of these American tribes from the yoke of Great Britain. The Edifice built; in the Temple is found "the Olive Branch" in the hand of the "Joshua" of the Section.

In this Commission, & under the Authority of the God of our nation, & of all the earth, I again demand that you shut not the door of this American sanctuary against the legitimate knockings of the voice of the Almighty.

I demand a Commission to the Executive of France; & of Great Britain, that I may have legitimate authority to toutch those two Angles of the "political triangle" whose dimensions, no other man on the earth is capable to take; nor can any other make distribution of its parts. And this demand I make in the name & under the sanction above stated—   D. AUSTIN

P.S. That the Nation may judge between you & me, I shall give to this letter publicity.—

RC (DNA: RG 59, LAR); addressed: "Thomas Jefferson Esqr. Pres: U: States Fœderal City"; franked; endorsed by TJ as received 18 Mch. and so recorded in SJL.

Austin wrote TJ again the following day, this time implying that he could re-place Congressman John Dawson of Virginia in his commission to carry the ratified Convention of 1800 to France. "I submit the matter to the prudence of the Executive, & shall only add that the more extensive objects to which this application is directed, must be sufficient to outweigh any subordinate considerations, in the judgment of a mind, directed to the extensive objects of human felicity, such as yr Ex'ys communications appear to express" (RC in DNA: RG 59, LAR; at foot of text:

"Th: Jefferson"; endorsed by TJ as received 19 Mch. and so recorded in SJL).

[1] Preceding three words interlined.

From the Aliens of Beaver County, Pennsylvania

March 15th. 1801

The humble and most respectfull address of The Aliens of Beaver County and State of Pennsylvania

We although Considered as Strangers begs leave to express our Sincere joy And real pleasure which we enjoyed in common with our fellow Citizens on this occasion—And We Congratuate your Excellency and our Country on the happy Event of your Recent promotion, to that most Eminent Station which you so diservedly fill—And though our inslavers prevented us by their alien Bills from being instrumental to your advancement, Yet they Could not deprive us of enjoying a Secret happiness And partakeing of the general Joy, which prevailed (pretty generally.) among all real and true friends to this Country; and with the Lovers of freedom, We once more (to the mortification of some) Surrounded the Standard of liberty, and all as one United to Celebrate the gladsome day all rejoicing at the Sound And hopefull expectation of Freedom—the name of which is yet gratefull in our Ears, Why or for what cause are we deprived of the priviledges of freemen. We have not forfeited our rights thereto, by any act of ours. And what pretence or Right has any Nation under Heaven or any Goverment on Earth, to take away our liberties, are we not deprived of the Grand Charter of freedom and that which Constitutes a freeman Namely the rights of Suffrage, and what are we when deprived thereof but a kind of tollerated Slaves. Strange that the Boaster of liberty thus wishes to inslave others—The effects of these laws viz, the Alien and Sedition Bills, Laws never Sanctioned by the people at large, We say was the pernicious Consequence of them only confined to us as aliens We Would patiently submit to our burdens, But its to be more Regretted that not us alone, but all the union Severely feels the weight of them, A damage which we presume your Excellency well knows to be materially detrimental to these States that the Enemy (we mean the framers and Supporters of these very unpopular Laws) could not Countervail— We almost deem it needless to insinuate to your Excellency, how that

Slavery breaks the Spirit of Patriotism. Slaves will either become Seditious Rebels or vile Sycophants—besides innumerable other evils, Was it for this We left our native Lands and Braved the Boisterous ocean, Was it for this our Countrymen fought and bled, as we also Would have done, had we been here at that time, and must we now suffer for what was not in our own power to have done, We sought an Assylum on these happy shores from tyranny and oppression, but was disappointed. Where once every Stranger found protection safety and freedom Strange alterations now render our modern American Federal Despots—

But a Ray of hope appears another of Virginias Stars is now Risen whose gracious influence may yet preserve declining liberty, and disperse those political vapours from our horizon. Vapours which have too long prevented the growth of that Illustrious plant We Mean your Excellency promotion; And though aliens we look up to you as to our common Father for protection and redress, And that you would be instrumental in haveing the aforesaid hated Alien Law repealed or modified in such a manner as you in your Wisdom See meet. the promoters of Said Law we are persuaded meant the blow at the people, through us, and now have fixed and remains an eternal Stigma on themselves. We all look to thee not only as a Citizen of the Patriotic State of Virginia, but as a Citizen of the World, Whose Philanthropic Bosom generously Glows With ardent desire to promote the happiness of all Men, And We do with pleasure anticipate the happy moment when under your Excellencies Auspicious administration, We hope to See the fulfillment of our reasonable Wishes in the enjoyment of freedom, and abolition of Slavery, the Recovery of patriotism, and liberty: the downfall of delusion, fanatickism, Ambition, and falsehood; engines too long, too powerfully And too succesfully employed, in the Subjugation of Man; to Serve the purposes of a moment. These purposes have proved abortive, that moment is now fled, that Faction disappointed And through the gracious interposition of divine providence, in the instrumentability of the virtuous Majority, they are at last broke up, or we may Suppose very near it. the dark Vail of political Sophistry and deceit is rent and the Spell broke their imaginary airial Castles vanished. Truth and reason now assume their place and in spite of all opposition Liberty and true Republickanism universally triumphs, and like the palm Riseth and flourishes in spite of oppression—And it gives us the very sensible pleasure to hope that the time rapidly approaches, When peace and liberty shall universally prevail from East to West, from Pole to Pole, and your Excellency a happy instrument in the hand of divine

Providence, in the Completion thereof; and an end put to arbitrary despotism and Slavery for ever—And may your Excellency long enjoy peace health and happiness; With the Sincere love, and Esteem of your Country, the most Gratefull and affectionate Acknowledgment of us aliens, (though Strangers to your Excellency)—And When Called from this transitory Stage of action, May Almighty God of his infinite mercy Grant you the Crown of life prepared for the real and true Lovers of Virtue and liberty, And may you in the everlasting mansions above united With the Great, and good, of all Ages, enjoy Scenes of endless bliss—

Which is our most unfeigned desires and most earnest prayers And as in Duty, and Gratitude bound Shall and Will Ever be Signed by order of the meeting   HUGH WHITE, Chair
                                        WILLIAM BAKER, Sec.

RC (DLC); probably in White's hand, signed by White and Baker; at head of text: "To His Excellency Thomas Jefferson President of The United States"; endorsed by TJ as received 9 Apr. and so recorded in SJL.

From Charles Copland

SIR   Richmond 15 March 1801

Your favor of the 11th instant is recd, I can not better answer your letter, than by sending you a copy of my last letter to Mrs Randolph—at the time Mr Grymes confessed Judgt, the annuities of 150 pounds sterling were calculated up to the first day of January 1800—of course on the first day of January *last* 150 pounds was due for last years annuity, which I have not yet demanded of Mr Grymes not knowing whether I was to ask the whole or only half of that sum. of this you will be good enough to advise me—

I am Sir your obt Servt   CH S COPLAND

RC (MHi); addressed: "Thomas Jefferson Esqr City of Washington"; franked and postmarked; endorsed by TJ as received 20 Mch. and so recorded in SJL.

FAVOR OF THE 11TH: TJ to Copland, 11 Mch. 1801. TJ's letter indicated that Grymes had paid a sum and, before a release from judgment could be rendered, inquired whether the payment completed the moiety of the whole arrearages due to Ariana Randolph and how the amount was calculated (PrC in MHi; blurred; at foot of text: "Mr. Charles Copeland"; endorsed by TJ in ink on verso).

Charles Copland to Ariana Randolph

Madam   Richmond Virginia 31t Jany 1801

I wrote to you the 6th of October by the America, and sent (about a Month after that date) a duplicate by the Industry to that letter I refer you—Mr Philip L Grymes has this day paid to me a bill of exchange for four hundred and ninety pounds sterling, and nine shillings and a penny Currency as a further partial payment of the Judgment for your benefit rendered against him in the Federal Court in the name of the Jennings Executor—

The bill is drawn by Mr Grymes on Thomas Reeves of London at 60 days sight payable to Ralph Wormeley and by him endorsed to you—The first of the set I have this day sent to my friend George Weir of London, with directions to deliver it to you for an application, and for which you will sign a receipt—I have also instructed Mr Weir to pay you 6/10 sterling for the 9/1 Current money above mentioned—These payments now made by Mr Grymes, together with that stated in my letter of the 6th October is precisely one half of the Judgment aforesaid (acting exchange at $33\frac{1}{3}$) together with £6-5-6 Currency for Costs of the suit—and Mr Grymes now intends to get from Mr Jefferson a release from the other half of the amount of that Judgment agreeable to the power given by you to Mr Jefferson—I am in daily expectation of receiving a letter from you acknowledging the receipt of mine of the 6th October

I am &c   C Copland

Tr (MHi); in Copland's hand; at foot of text: "Mrs Ariana Randolph London."

From Tench Coxe

Sir   Philada. March 15. 1801.

Among the papers, which I possess in relation to the late transactions of the United states, there are several relative to the British treaty, which it may be useful to pass into your hands. The concessions, sacrifices, and losses of this country may become in some way topics either of argument or negociation, and the papers I refer to, may contribute to the defence of our conduct, or to the procurement of justice. In this view I will occassionally pass them, without trouble to yourself, into your hands. The present inclosure will contain the fullest discussion of the Negro question, which I have yet seen. The honor and interests of this country and particularly of the southern states did not appear to be untouched by the ground which Great Britain & her zealous friends took upon that point—

With perfect respect, I have the honor to be, sir, yr. mo. obt. & hum. Sert.   Tench Coxe

I beg leave to address this note to you merely in your private Character—

RC (DNA: RG 59, LAR); addressed: "Mr. Jefferson"; endorsed by TJ as received 18 Mch. and so recorded in SJL. Enclosure not found, but see below.

Coxe may have enclosed his own letters published in 1795 under the pseudonym "Juricola," three of which concerned the QUESTION of slaves lost to the British during the Revolution and the fact that the Jay Treaty did not address compensation for them. Coxe had previously sent the pieces to TJ in 1795 (Vol. 28:516-17). In October 1801, he enclosed them to Madison (Madison, *Papers, Sec. of State Ser.*, 2:180-1).

From Edmund Custis

RESPECTED SIR/   Baltimore 15 March 1801—

When I had the honor of waiting on you with a letter from my Frd. Colo. Cabell, I had intended myself the pleasure of calling on you again, but unavoidably left the City, earlier than was intended—Permit me, Sir to take the liberty of repeating that I have been among the Number of the Unfortunate & being Verging to the Stage of Old Age & of course less able to encounter the Toiles of life than Usual, Solicit a place within your Memory & at some convt. time a hope of experiencing your friendly patronage in favouring me with some employmt. that may enable me to support a family that has been accustom'd to better fate, & this I wou'd not presume to expect, were I not found as competent to the task as many who have had a preference.—I have the pleasing satisfaction of being well known by Gentn. of first respectability, Many of whom are now Members of Congress from Virginia, & with whom have long Serv'd in a legislative capacity,—I wou'd not presume to be pointed, but being now a Citizen of Baltimore,—Employmt. thereabt. wou'd be most desirable—I am with every Sentiment

of Respect, Your Mo. Obt. Servt—   EDMD. CUSTIS

RC (DNA: RG 59, LAR); endorsed by TJ as received 16 Mch. and so recorded in SJL.

Edmund Custis, serving as a delegate from Accomack County at the Virginia Convention of 1788, voted against ratification of the Constitution, as did Samuel J. Cabell, a delegate from Amherst County. They represented their respective counties in the Virginia House of Delegates from 1787 to 1789 (DHRC, 9:564, 907; Leonard, *General Assembly*, 164, 168, 172, 175).

LETTER FROM MY FRD. COLO. CABELL: in a partially dated letter, Samuel J. Cabell recommended Edmund Custis to TJ and noted that they had served together in the Virginia Assembly and the Virginia Convention of 1788. Cabell recalled that "no man exceeded" Custis "in firmness and Zeal in the cause of Republicanism" and he observed that few men ever manifested a higher regard for TJ's character (RC in DNA: RG 59, LAR; addressed: "Thomas Jefferson Esqr. President of the U States"; endorsed by TJ: "Custis Capt. of Baltimore Colo. Cabell's lre").

From Philippe de Létombe

Monsieur le Président,   Philadelphie, 15 mars 1801 (V. St.)

Aussitot après avoir reçu la lettre dont Vous avez bien voulu m'honorer, le 5 du courant, je me suis empressé de remplir votre Commission. Le porteur de la présente a eu malheureusement quelques affaires qui l'ont retenu ici plus longtems que je le voulois et dont il m'a témoigné ses regrets. Je compte toujours que Vous serez parfaitement satisfait de la fidélité et des services de votre Maître d'hotel, Joseph Rapin.

J'ai deux habiles cuisiniers à faire choix. Je Vous enverrai le plus habile: car l'on m'assure qu'ils sont tous deux très honnêtes gens. Mais Je desirerois que Vous vouliez bien m'informer quels gages Vous voulez lui donner; je ferois après ce que possible pour le meilleur marché. Je traite vos Interêts que Vous avez la bonté de me confier, comme les miens propres.

Je viens, Monsieur, le Président, de traduire votre Discours. J'en suis encore tout ému. J'oserai Vous dire que l'Antiquité n'offre rien d'aussi sage sur la Liberté et d'une Eloquence aussi sublime et aussi persuasive. La Postérité Vous en bénira. Vous êtes digne d'Elle. Vous vivrez éternellement dans la mémoire des hommes libres.

Daignez agréér, Monsieur le Président, mon profond Respect et permettez moi de partager la Gratitude que Vous doivent les bons citoyens de tous les Paÿs.   Létombe

---

EDITORS' TRANSLATION

Mister President,   Philadelphia, 15 March 1801 (Old Style)

As soon as I received the letter with which you kindly honored me on the fifth of this month, I hastened to fulfill your commission. The bearer of this letter unfortunately had some business that retained him here longer than I wished and for which he expressed to me his regrets. I am still presuming that you are completely satisfied with the faithfulness and the services of your steward, Joseph Rapin.

I have two skilled cooks to choose from. I will send you the more skilled, for I have been assured that they are both very honest people. But I should wish that you would be willing to advise me what wages you wish to give him; after that I will do my best for the best bargain. I treat your interests, which you kindly entrust to me, as if they were my own.

Mister President, I have just translated your speech. I am still very moved by it. I dare to say to you that antiquity presents nothing as wise on Liberty and with an eloquence so sublime and so persuasive. Posterity will bless you for it. You are worthy of it. You will live eternally in the memory of free men.

Kindly accept, Mister President, my deep respect, and permit me to share with the good citizens of all countries the gratitude owing to you.

LÉTOMBE

RC (DLC); at foot of first page: "Thomas Jefferson, President des Etatsunis d'Amérique"; endorsed by TJ as received 18 Mch. and so recorded in SJL.

LE PLUS HABILE: Honoré Julien, the cook recommended by Létombe, became chef at the President's House for a salary of $25 per month and remained through TJ's two terms in office (MB, 2:1035, 1040).

From Andrew Shepherd

SIR   Orange Ct H Virginia 15th March 1801

In consequence of my Absence last Post, the Mail was opened by a person not altogether as well acquainted with the business, who informed me a mistake was committed in dating a letter on the back addressed to the Presidant—in stead of dating it the 8th March it was dated the 8th Feby which might impress the Post Master at the Fedl. City with a belief that it was intended for Mr. Adams instead of yourself—I hope the Error will be attended with no unpleasant consequence

I am Respectfully Sir Y Obt Svt.   ANDW SHEPHERD JUNR
                                          Post Master O Ct H Va

RC (DLC); addressed: "The Presidant of the United States"; endorsed by TJ as received 19 Mch. and so recorded in SJL.

Andrew Shepherd, a storekeeper at Orange Court House, had served as postmaster since 1795 (Stets, *Postmasters*, 267; Madison, *Papers*, 16:123).

POST MASTER AT THE FEDL. CITY: Thomas Munroe (Stets, *Postmasters*, 107; Bryan, *National Capital*, 1:345-6).

A letter from TJ to Shepherd of 19 Jan. 1794 and one from Shepherd to TJ of 20 Jan., recorded in SJL as received from Orange Court House on 23 Jan. 1794, have not been found.

From Benjamin Vaughan

DEAR SIR,   Hallowell, March 15, 1801.

You will have received a sufficiency of personal congratulations to yourself & felicitations on the part of your country, for your election to the honorable post you now fill, to make every thing from me on that head superfluous. I know that your mind is of a nature to give the true interpretation to my feelings; every thing beyond which might occasion you the needless trouble of a reply, when your moments are too precious to be lost.

I proceed therefore to the only point which can be essential, if even that should be thought so, namely to tender to you my affectionate & unbought services. I live in a sequestered, but important part of the Union; & independent of any speculative opinions, may occasionally be able to report to you facts. Should the offer prove acceptable, the only return which I shall ask is, that my correspondence may rest unknown to *all* but yourself & me, & my brother John, who will be the easy channel through whom it may be conducted. If your letters pass to him under blank[1] covers, he will forward them to me, without trouble. Even though yours should be without direction to me, he will know what to do with them.

I trust that your administration will have few difficulties in these parts, provided it steers clear of religion. You are too wise & just to think of any official attacks upon religion, & too sincere to make any affected overtures in favor of it. You know where you are *thought to be* in this respect; & there it may be wise to stand.—If a ruler however at times acts with a view to accommodate himself to the feelings, in which many of the citizens for whom he takes thought, participate; this can neither be considered as a violation of truth or of dignity; and is not likely to prove unacceptable, if done avowedly with this view.—For example, it is not *in*, & is perhaps *without* the constitution, to recommend fasts & thanksgivings from the federal chair, at the seasons respectively when the New Englanders look for those things; & therefore you will not think it perhaps needful for you to meddle with such matters. But, if you did, this example will serve my purpose. You may then I presume safely & acceptably interfere with a view to name a time, when a large proportion of your constituents may be enabled to do the thing in question consentingly & cotemporarily. You certainly may make yourself in this an organ of the general convenience, without departing from any of your own principles; especially as you will take due care to use decorous language, should the occasion be used. I do not however see any necessity for a* federal fast or federal thanksgiving, when these things are open, to the states approving them, to order for themselves.—I treat the case therefore merely for illustration.—The religion of the New-Englanders will require to be touched with tenderness. Your opinions are known, & in defiance of those opinions you have your office: consequently you m[. . .] continue to hold them, as a privileged person. But it will be wise, as to these parts of

Note *I think it may be said of a fast, that it is "a Solemnity which of all others, least impairs our charity, our fortunes, & our understandings." Anonym.

the Union, to keep these opinions in the only situation in which they have hitherto been seen; a private one; & for the regulation of your private conduct.

I may venture to state one thing more, without entering into any general field, (for which I am not yet provided with the favor of your consent); namely, that in your public discourses, you should not be too diffident in your expressions of yourself. Christian humility may be becoming; but French humility, or the humility of phrases, may be spared you. Your choice, & your submission to that choice, as made by your constituents, have rendered superfluous any reference to such species of feelings. The public conceives too highly of your merits; to accede to your renunciation of them.[2] You are in a situation to *oblige* the public; & you are I hope well qualified with means & abilities for the purpose; although the absence of confidence may be wise in itself & satisfactory to the observer, yet a very little more than this will suffice. You are not in danger, in your proclamations, of writing "My people" & "My subjects" in large letters, as a certain king does beyond the Atlantic; and for the rest, nothing, or at least little more, is necessary, than a warm affection for the happiness & a firm attention to the rights of the Nation over which you preside.

I shall keep no copies of my letters, & it will be lost time to both of us to write them over again on account of corrections. I am dear Sir, with high esteem & respect, Yours affectionately.

RC (DLC); torn at seal; at head of text: "(Private.)," which Vaughan wrote again next to the seal after closing the letter; author's note written in top margin of page to which it refers; addressed: "Thomas Jefferson President of the United States, Washington," Vaughan having first written and partially blotted "Philadelphia"; endorsed by TJ as received 30 Mch. and so recorded in SJL. Enclosed in John Vaughan to TJ, 28 Mch. 1801.

SEQUESTERED, BUT IMPORTANT PART OF THE UNION: Vaughan lived in Maine after leaving Europe in 1797. CORRESPONDENCE MAY REST UNKNOWN TO ALL: the object of official scrutiny both in Britain (for his allegedly seditious activity) and in France (for his connections to Britain), Vaughan had for several years used false names and avoided calling attention to himself (ANB; Vol. 29:521n).

[1] Word interlined.
[2] Sentence interlined.

From Joseph B. Barry

Philada. March 16th. 1801

Sir, having had the honour of being employ'd by you while in Philadelphia, but fearing through the great press of business attendant on your Station; and the many applications likely to be made by people in my line, an obscure individual like me, might be pass'd by unnoticed. I am in hopes you will not think me impertinent for taking this method of reminding and solisiting a small part of your business; either in the cabinet or upholstery line: which if you will please to grant me, I will do my endeavour to give you Satisfaction, by paying the strictest attention to your orders—

I am with due respect Sir your humble servant

JOS. B. BARRY

RC (MHi); at foot of text: "To his Exellency, Th: Jefferson. President of the United States"; endorsed by TJ as received 20 Mch. and so recorded in SJL.

Joseph B. Barry (1757-1838), a cabinetmaker and upholsterer in Philadelphia, had a shop at 148 South Third Street in 1801. Born in Ireland, Barry advertised his training in London and his use of "the newest London and French patterns." Around 1810, Barry began to incorporate Egyptian and Gothic styles into his furniture (Stafford, *Philadelphia Directory, for 1801*, 60; Robert T. Trump, "Joseph B. Barry, Philadelphia Cabinetmaker," *Antiques*, 107 [1975], 159-63).

Between 1797 and 1800 TJ paid a total of $299.25 for furniture by Barry. One payment specified "for mahogany work" (MB, 2:964, 979, 986, 999, 1019).

A letter from Barry to TJ of 16 Sep. 1800, recorded in SJL as received on 2 Oct. 1800, has not been found.

From Carlo Bellini

ECCELLENZA   Williamsburge. 16. Marzo 1801.

Non v'è chi piu desideri il Bene di questi Popoli Americani, e le vostre Felicità: e s'io non fossi stato, a ciò fare, incoraggito o piuttosto stimolato, non averei ardito di tormentarvi; uno de' primi relativamente alla vostra esaltazione, e alla determinazione del Popolo a voler esser felice. Possa Egli persistere, giacché e' se n'è alla fine procurati i mezzi più efficaci, ed a eletto un Uomo che, oltre l'Abilità e la volontà, ne possede anco tutta la necessaria autorità.

Dopo che L'inclusa a fatto un viaggio considerabile in America, per pervenire al suo interessantissmo. destino, gli resta solo la vostra interposizione, posentissma. e si raccomanda a voi come Protettore de' bisognosi e come Tale, vi supplico, scongiuro e prego, adesso piu particolarmente, che io mi trovo oppresso dalla piu terribile persecuzione senza conoscere il Mio, o miei Persecutori. Non mi vergogno di domandare ad Uno che sa che *Nichil Difficile Potenti et Volenti*, e che sà che al buon' Intenditor poche parole, mal' concepite e peggio scritte sì, ma non men sincere, e cordiali. Se L'inclusa arriva a salvamento, com'io spero, mediante la Vostra protezione, non mi scorderò di quel favorimento, che io non mi vergogno di domandarvi, é che io ho molta, moltissima nécèsità di domandare a Voi ad esclusione d'ogne altro, e le ragioni son'ovvie.

Io sono, e sarò, come io fui, sempre, Ammirator sincero delle Vostre virtù   CARLO BELLINI

E D I T O R S'   T R A N S L A T I O N

YOUR EXCELLENCY,   Williamsburg, 16 Mch. 1801.
There is no one who more desires the well-being of these American people and your own happiness: had I not been encouraged, or better yet goaded, to do so, I would have never dared to bother you; one of the first, insofar as your exaltation and the resolution of the people to be willing to be happy. May the people persist, since they have finally availed themselves of the most efficacious means to that end by electing a man who, in addition to the capacity and the will, also possesses the necessary authority to achieve that goal.

After the enclosed has traveled a considerable distance in America in order to reach its most interesting destiny, it lacks only your most powerful intervention. It recommends itself to you as the protector of the needy, and as such, I beseech, implore and beg you, now more particularly since I find myself crushed by the most terrible persecution, without knowing my persecutor, or persecutors. I am not ashamed to ask someone who knows that *nothing is difficult to the person who is able and willing*, and who knows that "few words to a wise suffice," words which might be poorly conceived and worse written, and yet are no less sincere and from the heart. If the enclosed reaches safety, as I hope, through your protection, I will not forget the favor that I am not ashamed in asking and that I have a great, actually the greatest need to ask you, to the exclusion of any other persons, for reasons that are obvious.

I am, and will be, as I have always been, the sincere admirer of your virtues
                                                            CARLO BELLINI

RC (DLC); at foot of first page: "Sige. Tommaso Jefferson Washngn. City"; endorsed by TJ as received 21 Mch. and so recorded in SJL. Enclosure not found.

According to SJL, the letter above is the last correspondence between TJ and Bellini, who died in Williamsburg in June 1804 (WMQ, 2d ser., 5 [1925], 14).

A letter from TJ to Bellini of 11 May 1800 and one from Bellini to TJ of 19 May 1800, received from Williamsburg on 6 June of that year, are recorded in SJL but have not been found.

From Benjeman Bryen

                              Washington March the 16th 1801
Sir Understanding there is a Barracks to be built for the Marine Corps of the United States I take the liberty of addressing your

Excellency Hoping you will be so kind as too Write a few lines to the gentlemen Who is nomenated to let the above Work by So doing it Will Be a Means of my Getting in the above business Which At present I stand in much need off Owing to Sundry losses And Disappointments Which of late, I have Experenced.

Thomas law Esqr, By Whom I am known these five or Six years Back Will I hope give me a Charecter Which Will meet Your approbation.

Sir I hope you will not think it presumtious of me Who to You is an utter Stranger though I had the pleasure of knowing You When Governor of Virginia Which State has given me birth If I Should be so happy as to derive any advantage By your Kindness to me it shall be Ever gratefully rememberd. by Your Very humble and Obedient Servant.

BENJEMAN BRYEN

RC (DLC); at foot of text: "New Jersy Avenue—Washn'ton"; endorsed by TJ as received 16 Mch. and so recorded in SJL.

On 3 Mch. Congress appropriated $20,000 for the erection of a marine BARRACKS in Washington. Benjamin Stoddert left the choice of its location to the commandant of the Marine Corps, Lieutenant Colonel William Burrows. TJ accompanied Burrows on an inspection of potential building sites on 31 Mch. The location selected was a block near the Navy Yard bordered by Eighth and Ninth Streets and G and I Streets, S.E. An advertisement in the *National Intelligencer* of 3 Apr. offered a premium of $100 for the best plan of a barracks for 500 men and their officers, as well as a house for the commandant. On 8 May, the chief clerk of the Navy Department, Abishai Thomas, forwarded to TJ on behalf of Henry Dearborn, the acting secretary of the navy, "a plan of Marine Barracks." This had been submitted by Lieutenant Colonel Louis de Tousard, a French-trained military engineer and commander of the Second Regiment of Artillerists and Engineers (FC in Lb in DNA: RG 45, LSP). Tousard's plan was not chosen, however, and the commission instead went to George Hadfield, Maria Cosway's brother and earlier the superintendent of the U.S. Capitol. Calls for proposals for construction contracts appeared in the *National Intelligencer* on 13 May (U.S. Statutes at Large, 2:122-3; Karl Schuon, *Home of the Commandants* [Washington, D.C., 1966], 54-6, 61-4; Vol. 29:310n; Vol. 30:507-9).

From Aaron Burr

DEAR SIR   16 March 1801

From many hundreds of applications I have selected, as most worthy of your attention, those Contained in the enclosed sheet.

As there is in fact No Minister of the Navy, I take the Liberty to suggest through you to the gentleman who may fill that office, that all of those who have obtained Wealth and influence by Means of public appointment, James Watson, now Naval Agent at Nyork, is, to our Citizens, the Most obnoxious. Daniel Ludlow now Prest. of the Manhattan Co. would discharge the duties of that office with Economy, punctuality & discernment—to the satisfaction of Government & to that of Reasonable Men of all parties—He has a perfect knowledge of every thing Relating to the equipment of Vessels having fitted out more than any Man in our City—a Correct indefatiguable Man of business & of Mild amiable temper—

William Temple Broome is about 28 yrs of age—bred to the law— He is a Young Man of the Most classical acquirements and taste of any that know in our state & will probably be eminent as a literary Man—Son of our Republican John Broome who was long president of our Chamber of Commerce, but finally turned out by tory influence. Wm. T. B— would be useful & ornamental as Sec. to any foreign Minister & might thus become eminently qualified for promotion in that line—but his temper & Manners are not calculated to advance him in the popular line.

My brother in Law Joseph Browne is known to every Republican in NYork and my Stepson John B. Prevost, very particularly to Mr Monroe having been his Secy.—The fortifications detain me till tomorrow—

Respectfully & Affecy Yrs   A; BURR

RC (DNA: RG 59, LAR); torn; at foot of text: "[Th.] Jefferson [. . .] &c &c [&c]"; endorsed by TJ and recorded in SJL as received 16 Mch. Enclosure not identified; Kline, *Burr*, 1:531n.

Daniel Ludlow was appointed U.S. navy agent at New York in place of Ebenezer and James WATSON on 1 Apr. James Watson ran as the Federalist candidate for lieutenant governor in 1801

(Kline, *Burr*, 1:522-3n, 553n; NDQW, Dec. 1800-Dec. 1801, 172, 374).

FORTIFICATIONS: statutes passed from 1797 to 1799 allowed a state to undertake the fortification of its harbors in exchange for credit against the state's debt to the U.S. On 16 Mch. Burr agreed to review plans under way by New York State to augment the defenses of New York harbor (Kline, *Burr*, 1:527-8).

Pardon for James Thomson Callender

Thomas Jefferson, President of the United States of America,
To all to whom these presents shall come, Greeting:

Whereas James Thomson *Callender*, late of the District of Virginia, was lately convicted in the Circuit Court of the United States for the same District, of a misdemeanor or misdemeanors in making uttering and publishing certain false, scandalous and *malicious writings*; and thereupon the said James Thomson Callender was adjudged by the same Court, among other things, to be imprisoned for the space of eight months and to pay to the use of the United States a fine of two hundred Dollars as by the record thereof remaining in the same Court will more fully appear: Wherefore I Thomas Jefferson President of the United States of America, for divers good causes and considerations me thereunto moving, have granted, and by these presents do grant, unto the said James Thomson Callender, a full, free and entire pardon of the misdemeanor or misdemeanors aforesaid, and of the conviction and Judgment of the said Court thereupon: hereby remitting and releasing all pains and penalties incurred or to be incurred by him the said James Thomson Callender by reason thereof.

In Testimony whereof, I have caused these Letters to be made Patent, and the Seal of the United States to be hereunto affixed. Given under my Hand at the City of Washington the Sixteenth day of March, in the year of our Lord one Thousand Eight hundred and one; and of the Independence of the United States of America the twenty fifth   Th: Jefferson
By the President,
Levi Lincoln
Acting as Secretary of State

FC (Lb in DNA: RG 59, GPR).

From William Branch Giles

Sir   Amelia, Virginia March 16th. 1801

I sincerely congratulate you on your late election to the Presidential Chair; not because personal aggrandisement was ever your object, or is desirable in itself; But because in the most critical period, you have been solemnly called upon by the suffrages of your fellow-citizens, to reestablish American principles, to correct the manifold deviations of your predicessors, and to administer the government according to the original intent and meaning of the constitution; you have thus become the principal depository of the dearest rights of your fellow-citizens and to be instrumental in their preservation & security, must afford the highest of all gratifications; my congratulations therefore result from a sense of the important services, which you can, and which I have no doubt you will render to the Public, and the happiness, which you will necessarily derive from that circumstance.—

I have seen your Inauguration speech, and am highly gratifyed with its contents—I think the principles proposed for the administration, correct in themselves, happily enforsed, and peculiarly adapted to the present state of public opinion.—In fact it contains the only American

language, I ever heard from the Presidential chair—This I believe to
be a very general opinion; But I am still of opinion, that the success of
the administration, will depend very much upon the manner, in which
those principles are carried into effect.—

Many of your best and firmest friends already suggest apprehensions,
that the principle of moderation adopted by the administration, although
correct in itself, may by too much indulgence, degenerate into feebleness
and inefficiency.—This in my judgement would be the most unfortunate
circumstance, which could be attached to the administration, and ought
to be more guarded against, than any other.—It would produce general
and lasting disgusts in its best friends, and revive the hopes and enter-
prises of its enemies, for they are not dead.—They only sleep.—A pretty
general purgation of office has been one of the benefits expected by the
friends of the new order of things—and although an indiscriminate pri-
vation of office, merely from a difference in political sentiment, might not
be expected; yet it is expected, and confidently expected, that obnoxious
men will be ousted.—It can never be unpopular, to turn out a vicious
man & put a virtuous one in his room; and I am persuaded from the
prevalence of the vicious principles of the late administration, and the
universal loyalty of its adherants in office, it would be hardly possible to
err in exclusions; at the same time I highly approve of that part of your
speech which recognises justice, as the right of the minority as well as
the majority.—But I believe that justice would be the most formidable of
all terrors, to the discription of persons to whom I allude.—

It appears to me, that the only check upon the Judiciary system as it
is now organized and filled, is the removal of all its executive officers
indiscriminately—The judges have been the most unblushing viola-
tors of constitutional restrictions, and their officers have been the
humble echoes of all their vicious schemes, to retain them in office
would be to sanction the pollution of the very fountain of justice, taking it for granted therefore, that this salutary check will be applyed,
and particularly in this state where there has been as gross a violation
of the most sacred principle in the administration as can possibly
occur, I take the liberty of mentioning to you a Neighbour of mine, as
properly qualifyed to fill the office of Marshall for this district of
Virginia, when the same shall be vacated.—

The Gentleman to whom I allude is Mr. David Meade—a Gentleman
who has been firm and uniform in his principles in the worst of times,
of amiable and delicate mind & manners, and who is universally
respected by his acquaintances. He is connected to the sister of the
present Marshall, a lady extremely amiable and universally respected,
and permit me to urge the recommendation by one more observation;

that the emoluments of the office would be a material aid to Mr. Meade's pecuniary situation.—

I have taken the liberty, when suddenly called on by Mr. Meade, to make this frank communication to you, in the confidence that it will be well received, and duly appreciated—my sole view has been to give some intimations with candor, which I thought it material for you to receive, and I rely with perfect confidence that your desicions respecting them will be correct.—

Be pleased to accept my most ardent wishes for the success of your administration, and assurances of my most affectionate regards for your person.—   WM. B. GILES

RC (DCL); at head of text: "The President of the United States"; endorsed by TJ as received 21 Mch. and so recorded in SJL.

DAVID MEADE married his cousin Elizabeth Randolph, sister of David Meade Randolph (Daniels, *Randolphs of Virginia*, xvi-xvii).

From Samuel Hanson

SIR,   George-Town March 16th. 1801

I was with J. T. Mason last night. He says that Whetcraft, the late Magistrate in the City, is *not* a Republican.

I mentioned your wish that he Should accept the office of District-Attorney. He told me that he had no other objection than the following viz: It having been asserted, during his attempt to be elected to the Assembly, professedly with the view of opposing the legislative appointment of Electors of President, that his Zeal was occasioned by a desire to obtain some lucrative office, he was induced to deny it, and to declare that "he would not accept of any office, if offered to him." How far he is bound by a declaration, certainly not due to the adverse party, you will judge. That it did not procure his Election, is certain.

I find him perfectly agreed with me respecting Mr. William Kelty, the Gentleman whom I ventured to recommend as Chief-Judge of the District, in case Mr. Duvall should decline it. He is confident of his legal fitness for the office, as well as of his other merits. To these it may be added that Mr. Kelty is a man of small property, and therefore would thankfully accept the appointment.

Hoping that I do not, by the freedom of these remarks, abuse the privilege with which you have honoured me, I remain, with the utmost respect,

Sir your most obedt.   S HANSON of Saml

RC (DNA: RG 59, LAR); endorsed by TJ as received 16 Mch. and so recorded in SJL.

From Henry Knox

My dear sir   Boston 16 March 1801.

Even if the sincerity and cordiality which dictate this note should fail of giving it any value in your estimation, yet the consciousness of having performed an impulse of duty will afford me some gratification.

I cannot refrain from expressing to you, the heart felt satisfaction I have experienced in perusing your address of the 4th of the present month. The just manner in which you appreciate the motives of the two parties, which have divided the opinions, and which sometimes have seemed to threaten to divide the territory and government of the Country; and the strong incitements you display for cementing more closely our union, the esssential principle of our prosperity, evince conspicuously, at one view, your intelligence patriotism and magnanimity.

I rejoice at the early occasion you have taken to give publicity to your sentiments which in their operation, cannot but produce the just support of all true Americans.

Although my local situation has prevented any activity in the late contest for the election of a President, yet I was in favor of the continuance of Mr Adams, having always possessed an high opinion of his integrity, learning, and love of Country.

I mention this circumstance with freedom, in order to guard against the possibility of an idea arising in your mind, that this letter is dictated by motives of duplicity, which my soul abhors. The respect and attachment however, that I have ever entertained for you, enhanced by your acquaintance and confidence, have never been in the least impaired.

The great extent of our Country, & the different manners of the respective parts, claim forcibly, the superintendence, and direction of an enlarged mind, to consolidate their interests and affections. And if you should happily effect, this much to be desired object, an imperishable fame will be attached to your character.

I hope sincerely that you may experience more satisfaction, and less perplexity, in the exercise of the high duties committed to you, than you appear to anticipate; and that when you chuse to retire, you may receive a richly merited reward, similar to that bestowed by a grateful people on the much loved Washington.

I am my dear Sir, with respectful attachment Your Obedient Servant   H Knox

RC (DLC); at foot of text: "The President of the United States"; endorsed by TJ as received 25 Mch. and so recorded in SJL. Dft (MHi: Knox Papers).

From Robert R. Livingston

Dear Sir   ClerMont 16th. March 1801.

The delay that your favor of the 24th feby had met with induced me to write an hasty answer on the 12th. instant (the moment it came to hand) as the post was then going out. It appearing by the way bill that some free letters directed to Clermont had miscarried in their passage from New York least mine to you should have met the same fate I think it proper to repeat my grateful acknowledgments for this fresh mark of your attention & to assure you that tho I felt no solicitude about any appointment, yet, that there is none that it will give me more pleasure to discharge than the one you have so obligingly marked out for me. A conviction that no republicans reputation would be safe with the then administration alone induced me to decline the reiterated request of president Washington to accept a similar mission, I am now confirmed in my resolution to enter upon it, by as firm a persuasion, that in your friendship, & Mr. Madisons, I shall receive every indulgence for the deficiencies that may be found in my talents (none will be found in my endeavours) & every aid in fulfilling those duties it exacts, which your enlightened instructions can afford.

The time of my departure will be so far material, as I carry my whole family with me, & I could wish them to make their first voyage upon a summer sea, & as I must previous to it break up a family of near forty domisticks. It will be proper also to resign my state office so long before my departure as to enable me to go on to Washington that I may have the honor to receive your commands in person, & make myself acquainted with so much of the precedent negotiations with France as may serve to guide my future conduct. For these reasons if the public interest would not be prejudiced thereby I should prefer entering upon the duties of my mission so early as to sail in the months of june or July.

I have the honor to be Dr Sir with the greatest respect & essteem Your Most Obt hum: Servt   Robt R Livingston

RC (DLC); at foot of text: "Thomas Jefferson Esq president of the United States"; endorsed by TJ as received 25 Mch. and so recorded in SJL. Dft (NHi: Robert R. Livingston Papers).

Although Livingston resigned as chancellor, the New York state office that he had held since 1777, he would continue to be known by that title (anb).

From John Strode

WORTHY SIR   Culpeper 16 March 1801

Mr. Voss has just informd me that Your Horses & Carriage is in about Ten days to meet You at my Neighbour Herins; for Heavens sake, dont give this little Family the indiscribeable pain which we must Suffer on such an Occasion; make, for once more, I humbly beseech You Sir, this poor House Your Lodging for a night at least. I believe indeed it wd. afford You some degree of pleasure to know how happy such an honor wd make each individual of us—With all possible regard, and the most profound respect

I am most Worthy Sir Yr. very hble Servt.   JOHN STRODE

RC (MHi); addressed: "Thomas Jefferson Esquire President of the United States, Washington"; franked; postmarked at Fredericksburg, 21 Mch.; endorsed by TJ as received 24 Mch. and so recorded in SJL.

From Leonard Vandegrift, Sr.

SIR,   March 16th. 1801

Being one of those Citizens whose Politicks has ever been congenial with your own, and having long been a faithfull labourer in the Vineyard of Republicanism; beg leave on the Authority of the enclosed recomendatory Vouchers, to offer my Self as an Applicant for the Collectorship of the District of Deleware if not already C[overe]d.

I am Sir, with the highest consideration of regard for your Personal and Political welfare yours

LEONARD VANDEGRIFT SENR.

RC (DLC); torn; above date: "St. Georges Hundred New Castle County S. of Delaware"; at foot of text: "Thomas Jefferson President of the United States"; endorsed by TJ as received 20 Mch. and so recorded in SJL. Enclosure: probably an undated recommendation signed by Thomas FitzGerald and ten others proposing Vandegrift "as a suitable person for the office of Collector of the Port of Wilmington in Delaware" and noting that he had "a Large and promissing family of children" and had been a "uniform and active Republican" (MS in DLC: TJ Papers, 119:20529; in unidentified hand, with FitzGerald and four of the other signers identified as "Member's of the Legislature for the County of New Castle").

In a letter of 12 Mch. from Thomas FitzGerald to Israel Israel, Vandegrift was recommended "as a Gentleman Possessed of Genuine Political and Moraal principles, and Who Means to solicite for the office of Colector in this State Believing my worthy friend to have Considerable Influence with our Present worthy President." Israel appended a personal note to the letter and forwarded it to TJ: "I concider it improper to Recommend anyone that Resides in another State or I wold Oblige my freind" (RC in DLC; with note by Israel subjoined at foot of text).

From John James Barralet

SIR   Philadelphia March 17—1801.

I was honoured with your favour of the 12 Instant. I am happy that the portrait of Mr Volney drawn in Indian ink and black Chalk, meets with your Approbation. I return you many thanks for your kindness in sending to me a draught of five Guineas, which is double the value of the performance—Your kind acceptance would have been a Sufficient recompence, never thought of selling his likeness in the original Sheet—

I humbly request your leave to Insert your Name at the head of the Subscription list for the Apotheosis of General Washington, that Stands at present without a Patron. your acquiescence will be of the utmost Service there is an Overplus of monies, more than adequate for your Subscription. with Gratitude I remain

Sir/ Your most humble & Obedient Servt

JOHN JAMES BARRALET

Mr Chaudron has bought the Half of the plate Apotheosis at nine hundred and fith'ty Dollars. the size of the Engraving 24 inches by nineteen, the price to Subscriber's Seven dollars, to Non-Subscriber's[1] 9 Dollar's. I have been working these fourteen month's with the greatest attention. Shall not compleat it till the latter end of May next

RC (DLC); below date: "at the corner of Eleventh and Philbert Strs. next Market Strt."; endorsed by TJ as received 26 Mch. and so recorded in SJL.

For Barralet's engraving of the APOTHEOSIS of George Washington, see Simon Chaudron to TJ, 10 Jan. 1801.

[1] MS: "non Non-Subscriber's."

From Mathew Carey

SIR,   Philada. March 17, 1801.

With my most Sincere Congratulations on the train of recent & gratifying events, I request the acceptance of the enclosed, from him who is with due respect & esteem, your obt. hble. Servt

MATHEW CAREY

P.S. A few unimportant errors escaped in the former Editions.

RC (MHi); at foot of text: "Thomas Jefferson, president of the United States"; endorsed by TJ as received 19 Mch. and so recorded in SJL. Enclosure: probably Carey's third edition of the broadside of TJ's Inaugural Address (see Carey to TJ, 31 Mch.).

From Thomas Cooper

Sir   Philadelphia March 17th 1801

Calling to day at Governor McKean's, he was so good as to shew me part of letter from you respecting myself, couched in terms of higher approbation than I conceive myself to deserve: but praise from you will incite me to deserve it. Laudari à tam laudato viro, is too gratifying not to excite the wish for its continuance.

The Governor told me that knowing my desire of remaining at Northumberland, he meant to nominate me as a President Judge of that County under a new judiciary System which the republicans expect to carry in the next Session of our State legislature. This will be sufficient for me: so far as I am concerned I want nothing more. But I cannot help feeling much for the defalcation of income to the amount of about 300 Dollars a Year which a kind and honest man who has a family of 5 Children dependant upon him, has suffered from his uniform attachment to me. Genl. H. Millar, turned him out to make way for the man who was the Government-evidence against me on my trial, & whose Services on that occasion were not to be forgotten. I most sincerely hope, and earnestly request, that Mr. T. Hamilton of Northumberland (the person I allude to) may be reinstated in the humble post of Collector of the excise, which his attachment to me tho' a federalist has deprived him of. The loss of a trifling income to a man in his circumstances is a serious misfortune, nor, could any post you could give me, oblige me more than by his reinstatement.

Dr. Priestley who has been long ill and most dangerously ill, of a violently inflammatory fever, is now upon the recovery; but we dare not indulge him yet even with very weak chicken broth. You have not a more sincere and affectionate friend and admirer than he is. I am with sincere respect Sir

Your obedient Servant   Thomas Cooper

Should you happen to have time to write a line or two to Dr. Priestley, it will reach him at No 33 Spruce Street Philada. If he shd. be convalescent at the time, I really think it would have a good effect on his health.

RC (DLC); addressed: "Thomas Jefferson President of the United States at Washington"; franked and postmarked; endorsed by TJ as received 20 Mch. and so recorded in SJL.

LAUDARI À TAM LAUDATO VIRO: roughly translated as "to be praised so by a man who has himself been praised"; Cicero, *Epistulae Ad Familiares*, book v, no. xii.

Cooper referred to the LETTER that TJ wrote to Governor Thomas McKean on 9 Mch.

From Samuel Dexter

SIR,   Treasury Department March 17th. 1801

The case of Mr. Comte is not new to me—Heretofore an application was made to my Predecessor, in his behalf, for a remission of the forfeiture & penalties incurred; he determined not to remit. Since I came into the Treasury Department, a petition from Mr. Comte for a pardon passed thro' my hands to the late President, who it is presumed omitted to act on it from the press of business at the close of the last Session of the Legislature.   Possibly however it may appear at the Office of State that Mr. Comte was pardoned.   My own opinion was favourable to the Petitioner. I have the honor to enclose the petition & papers accompanying it, also the proceedings formerly had on the application for remission of the forfeiture & penalties, as from the particular Statement of the facts therein, the President will have the whole case before him & be enabled to determine on the propriety of granting or refusing pardon to Mr. Comte;—As there was pretty clearly an intent to defraud the Revenue, I presume he can hardly be thought to be entitled to a restitution of the property forfeited; but the loss of this added to his past imprisonment is perhaps a punishment adequate to his Offence.

I have the honour to be with very great respect Your obedient Servant

SAML. DEXTER

RC (DLC); in a clerk's hand, signed by Dexter; at foot of text: "The President of the United States"; endorsed by TJ as received 17 Mch. and so recorded in SJL. Enclosures not found.

In August 1800 Benjamin COMTE, a Swiss citizen, was imprisoned in New Castle, Delaware, for failing to pay the duty on imported watches, which he removed from a vessel. On 23 Mch. TJ signed an executive pardon for Comte with the provision that it should not be "construed as a remission of the forfeiture of the Watches" (FC in Lb in DNA: RG 59, GPR).

To Fayetteville Republican Citizens

GENTLEMEN   Washington Mar. 17. 1801.

Your felicitations on the issue of the late election are highly gratifying to me. I never doubted that the diversity of opinion, which for some time prevailed among us, proceeded from an honest diversity of view; while the good of our country was the common object of all. th[o'] I shall sincerely endeavor to merit the confidence which my fellow citizens have been pleased to repose in me, yet I shall deem it an injurious effect of that conduct were it to lull to rest that salutary jealousy and vigilance so effectual towards preserving integrity and attention in the public functionaries. however error or passions may at times [lead] us astray, I trust that the principles of '76. will forever form a point of union round which we shall learn to rally & to recognise one another encircling them with a mass of strength which the world cannot shake.

Accept for yourselves, & the republican citizens of the town [and] vicinity of Fayetteville, the tender of my high consideration & res[pect.]   TH: JEFFERSON

PrC (DLC); faint, with text in brackets supplied from New London *Bee*, 29 Apr. 1801; at foot of text: "Robert Cochran & Michael Molton esquires Fayetteville."

To Samuel Hanson

DEAR SIR   Washington Mar. 17. 1801.

I have by some accident mislaid the papers recommending mr Moore to be justice of the peace, & therefore cannot get at his Christian name. can you furnish it to me? in the mean time a person of the name of Amariah Frost has been recommended by many. as the vacant place is that of a republican member, is he of that [description]? & is he as good a man as mr Moore? if he be equal in other respects, his having been a justice heretofore ought to give him a preference. I am sorry to trouble you so often: but till I have been here long enough to see with my own eyes, I must avail myself of those of my friends who will advise me conscientiously. accept assurances of my respect & esteem.   TH: JEFFERSON

PrC (DLC); blurred; at foot of text: "Samuel Hanson esq."; endorsed by TJ in ink on verso.

MR MOORE: Benjamin More.

In a very brief letter to TJ on 16 Mch., AMARIAH FROST enclosed a subscription on his behalf (RC in DNA: RG 59, LAR; at foot of text: "Thos. Gefferson Esqr."; endorsed by TJ as received 16 Mch. and so recorded in SJL). The 27 subscribers recommending Frost noted that he had "been for some Time a Justice of the Peace in the City of Washington" and to the best of their knowledge had "discharged the Duties of that Office to the general Satisfaction of the Citizens." They urged his reappointment (MS in same; in unidentified hand, signed by William Rhodes, John Cunningham, William Tunnicliff, Thomas Webb, William Prout, and 22 others; at foot of text: "His Excellency—Thos Jefferson Esqr. President of the United States"). In a postscript the writer noted that a similar recommendation had been signed by Thomas Law and others and presented to the president "by Genl. Farnum." He undoubtedly referred to Joseph B. Varnum, the Republican congressman from Massachusetts. That recommendation, dated Washington, 3 Mch., and signed by Law, Richard Forrest, and Federalist congressmen John Reed, William Shepard, George Thatcher, Ebenezer Mat-

toon, and Nathan Read, acknowledged Frost's service as a justice of the peace in Massachusetts and Washington (same, in unidentified hand, endorsed by TJ: "Frost Amariah"; *Biog. Dir. Cong.*; Dauer, *Adams Federalists*, 323).

On 29 July TJ again received an application from Frost at Washington. Frost sought an appointment, citing his years as justice of the peace in Massachusetts and his commission in Maryland. He stated that he had "not received any Appointment in this City, since the 4th. March last" and wished "to be continued in the same Office, in which he hath acted so long, as he hath fixed his Residence in the City" (RC in DNA: RG 59, LAR; unsigned; in unidentified hand; at foot of text: "Thomas Jefferson Esqr."; endorsed by TJ: "Frost Amariah to be justice of the peace").

From Samuel Hanson

SIR,   George-Town March 16th [i.e. 17] 1801

I am told that Frost is a notorious Federalist, in the worst sense of that much-perverted term. Moore is a good man, a sensible man, a staunch Republican. He is also an unfortunate man—He made two attempts to establish a news-Paper in the City. The undertaking was premature on acct. of the then population of the place—but, I suspect, more so from the Complexion of his Paper.

I feel myself highly honoured by the confidence reposed in me— and that, if I may be permitted to say so, from considerations unconnected with the high Station in which you are placed.

Have the goodness to Excuse this Scrawl, which the fear of detaining your servant obliges me to send off in a hurry.

with perfect respect I am Sir Your much-obliged & obedt

S HANSON of Saml

RC (DNA: RG 59, LAR); endorsed by TJ as a letter of "Mch. 16 for 17. 1801. recd Mar. 17" but recorded in SJL as a letter of the 16th received the 17th.

From William Hardy

SIR   New York March 17th. 1801.

An old man who has faithfully Served the Republic during the revolution, who Suffered Severely for his attachment to it, in the distruction of his property by the British, and by an overweening confidence in Continental paper, begs leave to address himself to You, and to appeal to your kindness at this period, when the fond hope hope of his heart has been realised in Your elevation to the first Station in the Commonwealth.

To the Vice President he is well known, as well as to the most respectable Republicans in the Union, already has he written to Col. Burr; Genl. Armstrong &c intreating their friendship on the occasion, and intimating what his friends had Suggested would be Suitable for him

The office of Marshal for this District, Should it be vacant, would be most Eligible

he feels it an awkard task to Speak of himself, but the Same undeviating line of conduct which he and his Son while in office pursued will never be departed from, by him, Should he be So fortunate, as to receive the appointment, he will endeavour by a faithful discharge of its duties, to evince his gratitude who is with due defference, and high esteem, Sir, Your Most humble & Obt. Servant

WM HARDY

RC (DNA: RG 59, LAR); endorsed by TJ as received 21 Mch. and so recorded in SJL.

To David Humphreys, with Levi Lincoln

Department of State

SIR,   Washington [17] March 1801

Mr. Madison the Secretary of State being not yet arrived at this place, and a favorable apportunity of addressing you, offering itself by a government vessel going to France with our late convention with that country, I avail myself of it being authorized by the President of the United States to perform the duties of this department per interim. The Country in which you reside having as well in itself, as in its foreign possessions many interesting relations with ours, its government will naturally be anxious, on the late entire change of administration, to learn something of its dispositions towards that government. I therefore embrace this early occasion of authorising you to assure them on the part of the President that he considers the relations of friendship and commerce subsisting between the two nations as among the first in importance to the interests and prosperity of those over whom he presides, that he will cause to be observed with fidelity all the offices of good neighborhood towards the adjoining possessions of Spain, and particularly encourage the

Indians, neighbor to both countries, in the preservation of peace and friendship with its subjects, firmly persuaded, from the long established character of the Spanish government for rectitude and good faith, that it will reciprocate towards us dispositions which may so much contribute to mutual interest and prosperity.

The President learns with regret on his coming to the helm of government that the two countries will no longer be benefited by the intermediation of the Chevalier de Yrujo the present envoy of Spain residing here: the good sense, honor and friendly dispositions of that gentleman could not fail to render him an useful organ of communication between the two countries, and he will carry with him our best wishes for his personal welfare, this testimony in his favor is but an act of justice to him, and is rendered as such with sincerity and satisfaction. Be pleased to communicate it to his government. I am desired by the President to recall to your recollection that previous to your departure from New York on your appointment to the court of Lisbon, he informed you of a rule of practice which he had recommended to General Washington and which was approved by him, as one to which we would conform generally, that no person should remain in foreign mission beyond the term of six or seven years. In a country changing so rapidly as this does, one who has been absent that term knows little more of it than an entire stranger, you were probably sensible of this during the first, tho' a short term of your absence in Europe; You have now been absent nearly eleven years, the change has never been greater than within that period, of this you will be more sensible on your return than those who have remained here. The President on this consideration solely, proposes shortly to name a successor to you, of which this intimation is given at present that you may have the more time for those preparatory arrangements which such a circumstance may require, not doubting that yourself will be sensible of the expediency of observing a condition deemed useful for the public, and notified at the time of your appointment, the President wishes to consider this return as consistent with your own desires, and to make the nomination on that ground, this will take place at an early period, but the precise time of departure of your successor cannot now be ascertained, so however as to secure you time for a passage before the winter sets in.

I have the honor to be &c. LEVI LINCOLN

FC (Lb in DNA: RG 59, DCI); in a clerk's hand; at head of text: "David Humphreys Esqr."; day of month left blank in dateline, but Humphreys acknowledged this as a letter of 17 Mch. (Madison, *Papers, Sec. of State Ser.*, 1:361); in margin: "This letter should have been Recorded among the March letters." Not recorded in SJL.

For TJ's composition of this letter, see TJ to Thomas McKean, 26 Mch.

COUNTRY IN WHICH YOU RESIDE: Humphreys had been minister plenipotentiary to Spain since 1796. He was named minister to the Portuguese court at LISBON in 1791. He was already in Europe at that time. TJ may have told him about the RULE OF PRACTICE governing the tenure of diplomatic appointments in August 1790, when Humphreys, who had been George Washington's secretary, prepared to leave the United States on a secret diplomatic mission (ANB; Vol. 17:125-6; Vol. 19:294, 572-4).

On 6 June 1801 TJ addressed a letter to King Carlos stating that he had granted Humphreys permission to return to the United States and had directed the departing minister "to assure you of our friendship and sincere desire to preserve and strengthen the harmony and confidence, which so happily subsist between the two nations. We are persuaded, that he will do this in the manner most expressive of these sentiments and of the respect with which they are offered. We pray God to keep your Majesty under his holy protection" (FC in Lb in DNA: RG 59, Credences; in a clerk's hand, including TJ's signature and Madison's countersignature; at foot of text in Jacob Wagner's hand: "To our Great and Good Friend His Catholic Majesty").

From Robert R. Livingston

DEAR SIR   ClerMont 17th. March 1801

I not long since did myself the honor to inform you of the discovery of some bones near the surface of the earth in the Western parts of this State. of these I have as yet been able to obtain no description. by the polite attention however of Judge Williamson I have in my possession three very remarkable teeth which are evidently the dentis incisores of some enormous carnivourous animal. two of them from their shape & exact similarity to each other I believe to be the Lower front teeth. I am induced to think from the extream inequality of their surfaces that they belonged to the Mammoth in which particular they greatly resemble those grinders that have hither to been attributed to that animal—If so they conclusively esstablish your opinion and docr. Hunters—& prove beyond contradiction that he was carnivourous—Not having a safe conveyance at present I only send you a drawing of them & will retain the originals till I can transmit them to you & thro' you to the philosophical society to whom also the drawings may be of use if they should wish to have them engraved—

These teeth were in part[1] covered with a crust of calcarious earth which had nearly acquired the hardness of limestone & to this we may in some sort attribute their preservation—They have the following remarkable peculiarities—

1st. Their Size—2d the smallness of the root—3d. their structure which I shall notice—The drawing will show the two first & the extream inequality of their upper surface better than words. as well as that of the two sides—but it can not so well deliniate other circumstances in their formation in which they differ from those of any known animal—The outward & inner coat is composed of very strong bone which in its appearance exactly resembles unglazed China the polish (if it ever had any) may have been destroyed by the calcarious coating—each of these is somewhat more than $\frac{1}{13}$. of an inch in thickness the inner being somewhat thicker than[2] the outward coat. these are seperated by two other lamina of the same nature & thickness between each of which & between them & the two external coats there has originally been a space either entirely empty or filled with some soft substance which time has destroyed, the intervals being now filled by the same calcarious earth which adheres to the outside—These intervals are irregular owing to the shape of the ivory. Their dimensions & form will be assertained from the drawings which are exactly of the size of the originals—The Surface of the teeth differ then from those of all other animals in not being covered with enamel if this space was not filled then the teeth must have had the effect of four rows of cuting teeth & the wounds they gave have been the most dreadful in nature—But as it is evident, from the compartive smallness of the root (see the drawing) which is perfectly preserved & in no part rotted off that these teeth were the first & designed to be shed I am inclined to believe that their surface was covered with flesh the vessels for the maintenance of which passed thro' their intervals—This was absolutely necessary to preserve the mother from the otherwise too sharpe teeth of[3] her gigantic ofspring—This Idea is also confirmed by the extream sharpness of the teeth even now they not carrying with them the smallest mark of their having ever been used. indeed without a firmer support in the jaw than they appear to have had it must have been impossible to have used them either in browsing or holding their prey. so that I believe that they were only designed to close & form the mouth till they were replaced by stronger teeth when we consider the prodigous size of this mouth something of this kind will be found absolutely necessary if the lips in any sort resembled those of other carnivourous animals which in them are generally thin & movable— you will also observe Sir that the inner surface is much shorter than the outward one so that if the upper teeth had the same form they must have projected considerably, from a perpendicular—Viewing them then as the first teeth what must have been the size of the Animal to which they belonged when he had arrived at Maturity? taking into accont only their superficial measure above the gums (even of these infant teeth) they are more than thirty times the size of a lions of full age—they are twenty times larger than those of a horse in his prime if no attention is paid to the roots of the teeth in either animal, or to the superior thickness of these—Calculations upon these data would almost lead us to credit the tales of Stalembergh relative to the Russian Mammoth

These teeth however if they belonged to the Mammoth prove not only that he was carnivourous but that he had no trunk & of course if his imense volume is taken into consideration that he must have had some substitute for it—This could only be found in his claws or forefeet—which appear from the bones lately dug up in this state to have been formed like that of the racoon[4] Docr Graham whose accurate discount, made at my request, & which I have done myself the honor to send you informs us that the metatarsal bones are six or seven inches long which with the length of the phalanges[5] of which several are found evince this fact—Add to this that the radius & ulna are articulated laterally as in man & those animals whose arm has a considerable rototary motion which motion is also to be inferred from the Articulation of the shoulder bones of the same skeleton. Nothing conclusive as to the number of claws have yet been determined.[6] After these discoveries I think it can hardly be doubted that a carnivorous animal who was larger than the Elephant once subsisted in America & probably in the northern parts of the old world. That he had tusks but no hornes that his forefeet were so formed as to be a substitute for hands or a trunk.—

A vivid imagination may conclude from these discoveries that the animal was either shaped like a Baboon[7] or a bear. perhaps however it would be wisest to restrain its fervor, till the researches now on foot, & which we have reason to conclude will be crowned with success, shall give us more decided data to go upon.

That this Animal is extinct we have reason to belive & certainly to wish—The whole of our Country being continualy traversed by tribes[8] of hunters, & the greater part of it being uncovered by wood, an animal of such enormous bulk, & who would have too much confidence in his own strength, to fly at the approach of man, could hardly during the course of time in which we have had an intercourse wh. the aboriginal natives have concealed himself from their view, or our information. We should I think have had at least some more perfect traditions of him, or some such circumstances relative to him as those you have collected & which so strongly tend to establish[9] the present existance of the Megalonyx—An animal which appears at no time to have been so numerous as the Mammoth—the bones of but one of these having been yet discovered, while the traces of the Mammoth are innumerable—

Why Sir since the earth itself is undergoing perpetual changes should we find a difficulty in believing that Nature may form animals fitted for the different situations in which they are placed by those changes or without going quite so far why may we not admit the extinction of one animal to be necessary to the increase of another better adapted to the present circumstances of the earth—Many animals if not extinct have been so altered by the labour of man that the original stock can not now be traced by the most industrious naturalist—Where for instance is the dunhill fowl to be found except amidst the habitations of men—And it requires some ingenuity to trace many of kinds of domestic pegions[10] from any Stock now roving in our woods—There was a period when the existance of a very powerful carnivourous animal was necessary in America—The Moos the Bison & the Elk greatly over matched the wolf, or even the Jaguar of this country. A young Bison at New York was bated by 12 stout Bull dogs whom he beat off & destroyed with his hornes & his heels with the utmost facility not one of them having been able to fasten upon him—

In all parts of the globe providence has provided some means to prevent the degeneracy & perhaps the destruction of gramivorous animals that would be consequent on their multiplication beyond their regular means of subsistance. This useful purpose was probably effected in America by the Mammoth & the Megalonix whose strength was adapted to their prey while perhaps their mutual rivalry prevented the too great increase of either. When a race of Savage men were transplanted into our forests they were no longer necessary, on the contrary they were calculated to check the increase of a more noble animal—And we learn from you that the Indians[11] assign as a reason for the destruction of the Mammoth the havoc that he made among the Bison & the deer that the great man above designed for the support of his red Children. And do we not Sir see in the gradual but certain anihilation of those very red Children something like a similar dispensation of providence. No attempts to cultivate or soften their manners have succeeded—No arts can assimilate them to civilized man formed to wander in the forest they die at the approach of that new race that were created to cultivate the earth—And in less than 1000 years the existance of an Aboriginal American will not be less problematical than that of the Mammoth

I am Dr Sir with the sincerest Attachment & most perfect respect & essteem &c
                                                                    RRL

Dft (NHi: Robert R. Livingston Papers); at foot of text: "To Thomas Jefferson Esq pres: US: & pres: Ph: Socy. N.A."; endorsed by Livingston. Recorded in SJL as received 30 Mch. 1801. Enclosures not found. Enclosed in TJ to Caspar Wistar, 31 Mch. 1801.

HONOR TO INFORM YOU: Livingston to TJ, 6 Mch. 1801.

The prominent land promoter Charles WILLIAMSON was traveling between Bath and Geneva, New York, in July 1800 when he learned of the discovery of "some large teeth" near Flint Creek. The person who made the find brought Williamson three of the teeth. A "monstrous large horn"—probably a tusk— had also been found in the vicinity. Williamson, among other offices and activities, was a county court judge (John Maude, *Visit to the Falls of Niagara in 1800* [London, 1826], 74-6; L. B. Proctor, *The Bench and Bar of New-York* [New York, 1870], 178; DAB; Vol. 27:448n).

YOUR OPINION AND DOCR. HUNTERS: in 1768, after examining the teeth of the American "mammoth" or *incognitum*, the British physician William Hunter, prompted by his brother John, who was also an anatomist, opined that the animal ate flesh. For that and other reasons Hunter disputed assertions by Buffon and Daubenton that the animal was the same species as the modern elephant. In *Notes on the State of Virginia* TJ alluded to Hunter's views and also reported a tradition of the Delaware Indians that the mammoth or "big buffalo" was carnivorous (Paul Semonin, *American Monster: How the Nation's First Prehistoric Creature Became a Symbol of National Identity* [New York, 2000], 145-54; William Hunter, "Observations on the Bones, commonly supposed to be Elephants Bones, which have been found near the River Ohio in America," Royal Society of London, *Philosophical Transactions*, 58 [1768], 34-45; *Notes*, ed. Peden, 43-7, 54, 269).

TJ received the teeth early in May (see Livingston to TJ, 29 Mch., and Peter

Delabigarre to TJ, 18 Apr.). The American PHILOSOPHICAL SOCIETY accepted the specimens, and evidently the RC of the letter printed above, at a meeting in Philadelphia on 19 June 1801. The minutes of the meeting, which TJ did not attend, identified the specimens only as teeth of an extinct animal from New York State. The APS did not publish the drawings or Livingston's description. In 1849 the society transferred its collection of mammal fossils to the Academy of Natural Sciences of Philadelphia (APS, *Proceedings*, 22, pt. 3 [1884], 312; W. S. W. Ruschenberger, *A Notice of the Origin, Progress, and Present Condition of the Academy of Natural Sciences of Philadelphia* [Philadelphia, 1860], 56).

Philipp Johann Tabbert von Strahlenberg, a Swede who was in Siberia in the 1720s, had collected information and folk traditions about RUSSIAN mammoths (Semonin, *American Monster*, 73-4, 307-8).

BONES LATELY DUG UP IN THIS STATE: the mastodon remains found not far from Newburgh. For the account by James G. GRAHAM, see Livingston's letter of 6 Mch.

To support the notion that the MEGALONYX was not extinct, TJ cited woodsmen's anecdotes and apparent references by Native Americans to lions (Vol. 29:294-7, 415, 510).

WE LEARN FROM YOU: for TJ's recounting of the Delawares' story of the DESTRUCTION OF THE MAMMOTH, see *Notes*, ed. Peden, 43.

[1] Word interlined in place of "a great measure."
[2] MS: "that."
[3] Preceding seven words interlined in place of "while she nourished."
[4] Livingston here canceled "or bear."
[5] Livingston here canceled "of the toes."
[6] Sentence interlined in place of "This motion wd have been unnecessary."
[7] Preceding two words interlined in place of "an Ape."
[8] Word interlined in place of "nations."

To Philip Mazzei

MY DEAR SIR   Washington Mar. 17. 1801.

Your letter of Dec. 6. is just recieved, and a person leaving this place tomorrow morning for Paris, gives me a safe conveyance for this letter to that place. I shall depend on mr Short's finding a conveyance from thence. yet as I know not what that conveyance may be, I shall hazard nothing but small & familiar matters. my health, which wore a very threatening aspect at the date of the letter alluded to in your's, became soon reestablished, and has been very perfect ever since. my only fear now is that I may live too long. this would be a subject of dread to me.[1] it is customary here to 'wish joy' to a new-married couple, & this is generally done by those present in the moment after the ceremony a friend of mine however always delayed the wish of joy till one year after the ceremony, because he observed they had *by that time need of it.* I am entitled fully then to express the wish to you as you must now have been married at least three years. I have no doubt however that you have found real joy in the posses-sion of a good wife, and the endearments of a child. the vetches you were so good as to send by Baltimore came safely to hand; & being by that time withdrawn from my farm into public life again, I con-signed them to a friend.[2] the seeds which I sent you were of the Cym-ling (cucurbita vernucosa) & Squash (cucurbita melo-pepo) the latter grows with erect stems; the former trails on the ground altogether. the Squash is the best tasted. but if you will plant the cymling & pump-kin near together, you will produce the perfect equivalent of the Squash, & I am persuaded the Squash was originally so produced & that it is a Hybridal plant. I perceive by these enquiries in your letter as well as by your express mention, that my latter letters have not reached you. I have regularly written to you once a year, and in one of these I answered these same enquiries fully. should you be able to send me any plants of good fruit, & especially of peaches & *eating grapes*, they will be thankfully recieved, & will be forwarded to me from any custom house of the United states. they should leave your continent as early in autumn as they can be taken up. you mention that E. Randolph expected to recover from Alexander the value

[328]

of certificates left in the hands of Webb. Webb, Alexander and E.R. are all bankrupt, the first dead. that is desperate therefore; nor do I know of any thing unsettled of your's in this country, from which any thing is to be expected but the price of Colle, & Anderson's bill. I think I shall be able finally to settle the affair of Colle' on my return home, & to remit the amount of both to our friends V. Staphorsts. I meant to have sollicited this amount for Derieux & his wife, who are reduced to the most abject poverty. they have 8. or 10. children, who often need the first necessaries of life. he is living on a small farm in one of the Western counties, which some of us joined in buying a lease of for 20. years, & a horse &c to stock it. he had before exhausted us in the article of contributions; so that this was the last he could expect. how far the change in your own situation renders this aid reasonably to be expected, is now questionable. you will have time to say yourself—both the James Madisons, to wit, of Williamsburg & Orange are living & well. the latter is now Secretary of state, but not yet come on. his father of the same name being lately dead. he with Gallatin as Secretary of the treasury, Genl. Dearborn Secy. at war and mr Lincoln Attorney Genl. compose the new administration of the US. the person proposed as Secretary of the Navy has not yet accepted. I add no signature because of the perils by land & sea to which this may be exposed. But you can be at no loss from whom it comes. I shall be happy to hear from you often. accept assurances of my constant and affectionate friendship. Adieu.

RC (ViU); addressed: "Philip Mazzei at Pisa Italy"; endorsed by Mazzei as received 1 Apr. 1802; with added notation by Mazzei (see note 1 below). PrC (DLC). Enclosed in TJ to William Short, 17 Mch. 1801.

[1] Here in RC Mazzei made an asterisk keyed to a notation he wrote in the margin: "Precedentemente a queste 2 lettere l'ultima pervenutami era del 24 Aprile 1796, e in quella si espresse come segue: 'My health has suddenly broke down, with symptoms which give me to believe I shall not have much to encounter of *the tedium vitæ*'?" (translation: "before these two letters the last one that reached me was dated 24 Apr. 1796, and in that one he expressed himself as follows").

[2] TJ interlined the preceding two words in place of "mr T. Randolph my son in law."

Memorandum from Aaron Burr

[ca. 17 Mch. 1801]

New York

David Gelston, Collector, vice	Sands	⎫
John[1] Swartwout, Marshall, vice	Giles	
Theodr. Bailey,[2] Supervr.		
& Inspecr vice	Fish	
Matthew[3] L. Davis,		
Naval officer Vice	Rogers	
Edw. Livingston,		
dist. atty. Vice	Harison	

The Republicans of the NY. delegation in Senate & H. of R. are unanimously of opinion that these changes shouldbe made—they unite also in the arrangement here proposed, except that one Gentleman would prefer that Bailey and Davis should change places—Willett and Browne are also candidates for the Marshalls place and are both well qualified—all are personally known to a. Gallatin

Post Mr. at Esopus vice   Elmendorf ⎫ These are the suggestion
Gilbert Livingston Post Mr. at Poughkeepsie vice Powers[4] ⎬ of A.B. from personal
       ⎭ knowledge.

Connecticut

Gideon Granger, dist atty.	vice Edwards
Epraim Kirby—Marshall	vice Bradley
Munson Collectr. at N. Haven	vice Goodrich
John Rutherford Throop	
Surveyr. at Do.	vice Munson
Abm.[6] Bishop Post Mr at Do	Vice

This arrangement will be highly acceptable to our friends in Connecticut—all with whom I have had any Communication concur[5] heartily, and deem the three last to be immediately Necessary. Edwards and Bradley will resign.

If the office of P.M. Genl. should become Vacant and Hampton should decline, Kirby would fill it very ably and would be willing to accept—He consents to take the office of Marshall from public Motives only, the emoluments being in that State very inconsiderable—

Judge Bull of Hartford is recommended for Loan officer, in Case of Vacancy—[7]

S. Carolina

Danl. Doyley now treasurer of that State—

Collector, vice Simmons ⎫ Suggested by Pinckney and Alston
Col. Edw.Darrell   Supervisor vice Stephens ⎪ and *said* to have the Concurrence of
Dominick A. Hall ⎬ Hampton—The two former thought
Marshall Vice Wm. B. Cochran [8] ⎪ to be immedia[tely] and indispensbly
⎪ Necessary to our Interests
⎭ in S.C.

John J. Murray, formerly of Georgetown S.C. and a Member of the legislature of that State, has lately Married the only daughter of a very Wealthy Citizen of the State of NY. and has settled near his father in Law—Educated a Merchant and said to be of Respectable family and Connections—

—He wishes to be consul to Glascow or to some principal port in France—

—recommended by C. Pinckney & by Dr. Blythe one of the S.C. Electors,[9] A.B. concurs in this recommendation—

Jas. Glover Chenango County now a member of the Legislature of N. York—an active, intelligent, discreet man & decided republican—proposes to remove into the Mississippi Territory & wishes to have an Agency in the sale of Lands of the U.S. He is eminently qualified for any such employment and must, wherever he may reside, become a man of considerable influence—He is about 32 yrs. of age

MS (DNA: RG 59, LAR, 1:1339-40); undated; in Burr's hand, except for concluding lines from Tr in Gallatin's hand (see note 9) and check marks and notations in TJ's hand as noted below; frayed at edges; endorsed by TJ: "Colo Burr's last memm"; with notation by TJ in pencil on verso: "Chancellr. Livingston is against removing Rogers." Tr (same, 1:1336-8); undated; in Gallatin's hand; lacks TJ's notations; endorsed by TJ: "Colo. Burr's Memm. 1st. see 2d." and "from Colo Burr."

Burr probably gave this memorandum to TJ about 17 Mch., prior to his departure from Washington. As indicated in the notes below, TJ made notations on the document to reflect the status of the recommendations. He kept track of the pertinent appointments until the end of June. On 27 June, TJ appointed Samuel Osgood, who was allied with the Clintonians, instead of Theodorus BAILEY to serve as supervisor of the revenue. TJ noted this on the memorandum (see note 2 below). TJ did not, however, place a check mark at Gelston, who received his appointment on 9 July, as he did at John Swartwout and Edward Livingston (see note 1), who received their appointments on 28 Mch. The appointment of Samuel Bishop as collector at New Haven took place in May 1801 (ANB, 16:801; Kline, *Burr*, 1:535; Appendix I, Lists 3 and 4).

BAILEY AND DAVIS SHOULD CHANGE PLACES: TJ received an earlier list of New York candidates written in an unknown hand on the verso of an address leaf directed to "The Honorable Edward Livingston City of Washington," which was franked and postmarked 16 Feb. 1801. The candidates Swartwout, Matthew L. Davis, Gelston, and Bailey can be found on the list associated with the same positions as are indicated in Burr's memorandum above. Separated by a rule, the names appear again but with Bailey as naval officer and Davis as supervisor. Gelston's name, perhaps in TJ's hand, was added in front of the position of collector, which was originally blank, with "for consideration" in parentheses. At some point, "Davis, Supervisor" was canceled. "John Woodworth of Troy Atty. Gen." and "Solomon Southwick Albany Marshal," the last two entries on the document, are connected by a brace labeled "Albany District" (MS in DNA: RG 59, LAR, 1:1333; undated; endorsed by TJ: "New York. Officers"; see Kline, *Burr*, 1:534-5). Bailey, who had served as congressman from Dutchess County from 1793 to 1797 and during the Sixth Congress, returned to the House of Representatives in December 1801 after Thomas Tillotson resigned (*Biog. Dir. Cong.*).

Jacobus C. ELMENDORF served as postmaster at Esopus and Kingston from June 1796 until early 1803, when he was reportedly dismissed for being a "Federal Republican." Conrad I. Elmendorf then assumed the position. Levi McKeen, who was recommended by Gilbert LIVINGSTON, became postmaster at Poughkeepsie in January 1802 in place of Nicholas Power, editor of the *Poughkeepsie Journal*. This followed the administration's policy of prohibiting newspaper publishers from serving as postmasters (Stets, *Postmasters*, 181, 186; Kline, *Burr*, 1:543; Brigham, *American Newspapers*, 1:723).

For TJ's decision to appoint Samuel BISHOP collector at New Haven, see his notes of a Cabinet meeting of 17 May. See also note 6, below.

OFFICE OF P.M. GENL.: on 30 May TJ wrote South Carolina planter Wade Hampton to inquire whether he would accept the office of postmaster general. He declined (Wade Hampton to TJ, 26 June 1801).

S. CAROLINA: in September 1801 Burr recalled that Charles Pinckney had conversed with him on several occasions about changes to be made in the state. Burr noted: "I made a minute agreeably to his information, and having consulted

with one or two others, by whom it was approved, I handed it to the President, noting precisely the authority from which it came." Unable to locate a copy of the document, Burr only remembered that the collector, supervisor, and marshal were to be removed and that Daniel D'Oyley was one of those recommended (Kline, *Burr*, 2:623-4). For previous notes by TJ on D'Oyley, see Notes on Candidates for Public Office printed at 23 Dec. 1800.

In July 1801, at the urging of Governor John Drayton, young Charleston attorney Edward DARRELL agreed to serve as commissioner of the first division in South Carolina to provide for the valuation of land and houses and the enumeration of slaves under the Direct Tax. He received his commission but died before his appointment could be brought before the Senate (Charleston *City-Gazette and Daily Advertiser*, 13 Nov. 1801; Appendix I, List 4; John Drayton to TJ, 29 July 1801).

TJ appointed Charleston attorney DOMINICK A. HALL chief judge of the Fifth U.S. Circuit Court on 1 July. WM. B. COCHRAN: that is, Charles Burnham Cochran. When Cochran resigned his commission in October 1802 to look after "agricultural concerns," his brother Robert E. Cochran was appointed in his place (Madison, *Papers, Sec. of State Ser.*, 3:609; 4:31; Appendix I, List 4).

For Pinckney's part in the recommendation of JOHN J. MURRAY, see Kline, *Burr*, 1:520-1. Murray married Margaret Ryers DeHart, the ONLY DAUGHTER of Gosen Ryers from Richmond County, New York, and the widow of Stephen DeHart (Kline, *Burr*, 1:542, 545n). For Murray's appointment as consul at Glasgow, see Appendix I, Lists 1 and 4.

[1] TJ placed a check mark in front of this entry and the entry for "Edw. Livingston, dist. atty."

[2] TJ here interlined "Osgood" in place of "Theodr. Bailey."

[3] "Matthew" canceled with "X."

[4] Name lacking in Tr.

[5] Tr lacks remainder of this and next sentence.

⁶ TJ here interlined "Samuel" in place of "Abm." and added "rather collector vice Munson vice Goodrich."

⁷ Tr lacks preceding sentences, from the short horizontal rule to this point.

⁸ In Tr Gallatin added: "The district atty. is represented to be a discreet honest man."

⁹ MS ends at this point; remainder from Tr in Gallatin's hand.

Memorandum from Charles Pinckney

[ca. 17 March 1801]

Memorandum For South Carolina
Daniel Doyley to be Collector of Charleston in the room or place of James Simons

Edward Darrell to be Supervisor in the room of Daniel Stevens

Thomas Lehré to be offered the Marshals Place in the room of Charles B. Cochran—& if he does not accept Dominic A Hall to be appointed Marshal

John Splatt Cripps to be Navy agent in the room of *William Crafts*—indispensable[1]

MS (DNA: RG 59, LAR, 3:0377); undated; in Pinckney's hand, except as noted below; endorsed by TJ: "S. Carolina. Mr. Pinckney's 2d. memm."

Some of Pinckney's recommendations on South Carolina appointments were incorporated into Burr's memorandum of this date printed above. Pinckney probably left this memorandum with the president before he left for Charleston.

In letters to Madison and TJ on 26 May, Pinckney reiterated his recommendation that Daniel D'Oyley replace James Simons as COLLECTOR at Charleston. D'Oyley was Pinckney's cousin (Madison, *Papers, Sec. of State Ser.*, 1:230; Pinckney to TJ, 26 May).

A leading Jeffersonian in South Carolina, THOMAS LEHRÉ served in the state assembly

until elected sheriff for Charleston District in 1798, a position he held through 1803. He then returned to the general assembly (*S.C. Biographical Directory, House of Representatives*, 4:348-9).

In 1798 Charleston merchant JOHN SPLATT CRIPPS was appointed commissary general of purchases for the South Carolina militia. He also served as a director of the Bank of South Carolina. On 24 Sep. 1801 William Smith and Company received appointment as navy agent at Charleston in the place of WILLIAM CRAFTS, who resigned (*S.C. Biographical Directory, House of Representatives*, 3:268; Charleston *City-Gazette and Daily Advertiser*, 14 Feb., 4 Aug. 1798; NDQW, Dec. 1800-Dec. 1801, 374-5).

[1] Word in TJ's hand.

From James Monroe

DEAR SIR   Richmond 17. March 1801

Mr. Fenwick has requested me to state to you what I know of his conduct while acting under my ministry with the French republick. Altho' it wod. be more agreeable that no appeal shod. be made to me on subjects of the kind yet it is impossible to withhold my evidence where it is called for by the party interested, especially under circumstances like the present.

When I went to France Mr. Fenwick had more weight with the French govt. than any other American there. He was believed to be attached to the interest of his country & had weight in its concerns. His service in the case of the Bordeaux embargo is will known in both countries. Indeed his attendance at Paris, and attention to that object was generally spoken of abt. that time as forming a kind of epoch in our political history there.

He was afterwards denounc'd to our govt. for protecting in some form a shipment of money to this country the property of France, and I was empowered to enquire into the charge & suspend him if I thought fit. He made his explanation to me which I transmitted to the Executive for its decision, continuing him in office, unless the contrary shod. be directed. I never heard from the admn. afterwards on the subject, in consequence whereof he remained in office when I left France.

I heard disrespectful things said of Mr. Fenwick such as that he was engaged in privateering. But no denunciation was ever made agnst him to that effect to me or I shod. have communicated it to our govt. Nor was it ever said on such authority as to justify any attention or credit being paid to it by me.

On my own part I add with pleasure that I always found him, an active, able, and faithful publick officer. with great respect & esteem I am

yr. most obt. servant   JAS. MONROE

RC (MHi); endorsed by TJ. Recorded in SJL as received 23 Mch. Enclosed in Joseph Fenwick to TJ, 22 Mch. 1801.

In 1795 Joseph FENWICK, who was then the U.S. consul at Bordeaux, was accused of having improperly used his seal on a shipment to the United States.

Fenwick defended himself in a letter to Monroe on 28 Oct. 1795, which Monroe forwarded to Timothy Pickering, the acting secretary of state, on 6 Dec. of that year. Calling Fenwick a "valuable" officer and saying that "the error imputed to him might be the effect of judgment only," Monroe stated his readiness to support

Fenwick's removal if necessary but referred the question back to the administration. Monroe later consulted TJ about whether to include some of the correspondence on the subject in his *View of the Conduct of the Executive*. TJ—who from 1790 to 1795 had used Fenwick as his source for Bordeaux wine—replied that the charges of misconduct reflected "malversation in Fenwick if true." Fenwick was dismissed from his position as consul, the Senate approving his replacement in December 1797 (ASP, *Foreign Relations*, 1:727-8; JEP, 1:253; Preston, *Catalogue*, 1:52; MB, 2:831, 907; Vol. 17:493-4; Vol. 28:448-9; Vol. 29:563, 565).

BORDEAUX EMBARGO: the French detained more than 100 American merchant ships at Bordeaux from August 1793 to March 1794 (ASP, *Foreign Relations*, 1:748, 757-8; Syrett, *Hamilton*, 16:55n; Ulane Bonnel, *La France, les États-Unis, et la Guerre de Course* [Paris, 1961], 39-40; Vol. 27:192).

To Charles Pinckney

DEAR SIR   Washington Mar. 17. 1801.

I have duly received your favour agreeing to accept an appointment as Minister plenipotentiary to the court of Spain, and wishing to know when it would be expected you should take your departure. the convenience of Colo. Humphreys, the present minister there is the circumstance which must chiefly influence that question. you should be there as early in autumn as may admit his return to this country before the winter [sets] in. I presume therefore you ought to be there by the last of September and to give you time enough for this, I will see that your commission & letter of credence are forwarded to you in Charleston in the month of June. notice will also be given to mr John Graham, who is to be Secretary of the legation to you, to take his measures for meeting you at Madrid by the last of September.   Accept assurances of my high consideration & [respect].

TH: JEFFERSON

PrC (DLC); faint; at foot of text: "Charles Pinckney esq."

YOUR FAVOUR: Pinckney to TJ, 12 Mch. 1801.

From Benjamin Rittenhouse

SIR George Town March 17th 1801.

Permit a Brother of David Rittenhouse an Individual Citizen of the Immence Terretory over which you are now call'd by the Voice of your Country to Preside To Congratulate you on the Auspicious event

None but an enlarg'd Philosophick mind, such as you possess, can divest itself of those narrow Religious, and Political, prejudices so frequently to found with the best of men in common Life, and which so often Tend to disturb the peace and happiness of the World. From your Administration Sir the Genuine Republicans of the United States may presage the happiest consequences to our Common Country. Ambitious and desighning men have Oppos'd your Advancment to your present Station to the last, with unremited Zeal Fearing that your Stern Patriotism and Republican Virtue wou'd be a bar to those Views and measures, by which they Contemplated the promotion of thier own Agrandisment and prostration of the Liberties of their Country.

Thanks to the Great disposer of events their Indeavours have yet prov'd abortive and the Sun of freedom will once more rise in [splen]dor on this happy Land Pardon the Effusions of a heart yet Glowing with the feelings and Sentements of Seventy-Six never to be eradicated but by its dissolution. Altho I can Sollemly declare the little weight I had in the great polit
tical ballance to your advancment has been us'd without a Single Idea of personal Interest, but only for what I conciev'd the good and well being of the great family of mankind and from which I claim no Merit as deserving your particular attention and favor. Yet urg'd by some of my friends in the City of Philadelphia knowing the friendship you have expres'd for my Brother when living, and polite Attention to his family since his Death, And also knowing that I was a sufferer in the Revolutionary war, for which I never Ask'd or receiv'd any Compensation nor ever requested any Appointment to Office under Government. Thus impell'd by my friends I have been Induc'd to Solicit the Appointment to an Office To which you may concieve my Abilities may be adequate and such Appointment If a vacancy were wou'd be most agreable in my Native State. Shou'd You be induc'd from any Information Obtain'd of my Character to favor my present Application It will be remembered [with] gratitude by Sir

Your Most Obedient Humble Servant

BENJN RITTENHOUSE

RC (DNA: RG 59, LAR); torn at seal; at foot of text: "His Excellency Thomas Jefferson"; endorsed by TJ as received 19 Mch. and so recorded in SJL.

A younger brother of David Rittenhouse, Benjamin Rittenhouse (1740-1825) served as a captain in the Pennsylvania militia during the Revolutionary War from 1775 to 1777 and was wounded at the Battle of Brandywine. He superintended the state-operated gunlock factory in Philadelphia from 1776 to 1778, represented Montgomery County in the Pennsylvania Assembly from 1784 to 1788, and was appointed associate judge of the Montgomery County Court of Common Pleas in 1792. Like his late elder brother, Rittenhouse was also one of the nation's leading manufacturers of clocks and precision instruments. He was elected a member of the American Philosophical Society in 1789. He did not receive an appointment from TJ (Heitman, *Register*, 468; PMHB, 51 [1927], 298-9; Charles E. Smart, *The Makers of Surveying Instruments in America Since 1700* [Troy, 1962], 136-7, 142-3; *Pennsylvania Gazette*, 4 Feb. 1789).

To William Short

DEAR SIR   Washington Mar. 17. 1801.

This letter will be handed you by mr Dawson, an antient acquaintance & fellow collegian of yours, who goes as the bearer of the ratification of our late convention with France. this ratification being on conditions which will occasion some of the ground of the preceding negociations to be recurred to & trodden over again, messrs. Elsworth & Murray will be called to Paris again for that purpose.

You had been previously apprised that the proceedings of France with respect to this country had produced a sensible alienation from them in the people of this country. that these proceedings were artfully & industriously laid hold of here & played off in a thousand forms & with multiplied exaggerations to induce the people to consent to a war with France, & consequently then an alliance with England, and a disposition to approach ours more nearly to the forms of that government. the XYZ. mission wrought us up to a perfect frenzy. every principle of civil caution was lost sight of, and the Charlatans drove headlong as madness & wickedness prompted. but they were not able to keep up the bubble. some states had remained firm in their senses, and some portions of every state. the paroxysm with those who had gone into the delusion began to subside. in this state were things at the date of my last letter, wherein I stated to you the change which was working. it has kept pace fully with the expectations therein hinted. we have with us at this time a great majority, & the residue rallying so fast to their old principles that we have reason to believe all traces of the late party divisions will be obliterated; except that the leaders of the war party had committed themselves too far to change. but they will be without followers & therefore may be neglected. in this transition the New England states are slowest because under the dominion of their priests who had begun to hope they could toll us on to an established church to be in union with the state. even there however they are getting to rights and the probable election of Gerry by the republican interest will be the signal of it's ascendancy in Massachusets. these are the outlines only. I refer you to mr Dawson for the particulars, he being fully possessed of them. they will be well worth your minute enquiry, as they will give you some idea of our present character & pursuits, which are so different from what they were when you left this country, that no two nations are more unlike. he can particularly give you the true state of the late election which cannot be at all understood abroad. no endeavors will be spared on my part to reunite the nation in harmony and in interest.

Your letters of Aug. 6: & Sep. 18. has[1] been duly recieved: as were also the volumes of the Connoissance des tems for 1800. 1. 2. 3. except the additional part of 1800. which you expressed a hope of obtaining, and will be acceptable, as will the continuation of the work as fast as it appears. I am now here for a few days only, to set in motion some pressing measures which would not admit delay. I shall then go home for 3. or 4. weeks to make some arrangements there, necessary on my removal, and then become fixed here. as soon after my return as the first press of business will permit, I will resume the subject of your affairs here, and give you a statement in continuation of my last. in the mean time mr Barnes will have given you detached views from time to time. I now inclose a letter from him. Brown has paid up, & mr Jefferson of Richmond is in hopes shortly to get Moseby's money. Barnes is worthy of your entire confidence for his uprightness and his caution & safety. you had better join him in a regular power of attorney with me, for fear of my death.—I shall this summer send through you to mr Pougens a commission for some books, placing previously funds in Amsterdam to draw on, & I shall probably trouble yourself with some commissions. present me respectfully to our common friend, & accept yourself assurances of my constant & sincere affection.   TH: JEFFERSON

P.S. Just as I was about to seal my letter, mr Pichon arrives and puts into my hand yours of Dec. 9.—I must ask the favor of you to find a safe conveyance for the inclosed letter.

RC (ViW); addressed: "William Short esquire"; endorsed by Short as received 19 May. Enclosures: (1) John Barnes to Short, 12 Mch. 1801, stating that he must await information from Philadelphia before investing more of Short's capital in United States funds and noting that he has received no acknowledgment from Peyton Short of the letter that Barnes forwarded to him (RC in DLC: Short Papers, endorsed by Short as received 19 May; see Short to TJ, 6 Aug. 1800). (2) TJ to Philip Mazzei, 17 Mch. 1801.

MY LAST LETTER: TJ to Short, 13 Apr. 1800, particularly the addendum of 9 May containing an assessment of Republican prospects (Vol. 31:509, 512).

In 1801 Elbridge GERRY stood for election as governor of Massachusetts, as he had the previous year (George Athan Billias, *Elbridge Gerry: Founding Father and Republican Statesman* [New York, 1976], 301-4).

For Short's recommendation of bookseller Charles POUGENS of Paris and TJ's interest in the prospect, see Vol. 29:333, 464; Vol. 30:319, 481; Short to TJ, 18 Sep. 1800. OUR COMMON FRIEND: the Duchesse de La Rochefoucauld.

YOURS OF DEC. 9: Short's letter of 9 Dec. 1800, received by TJ on 18 Mch. 1801, enclosed one of 10 Dec. from Short to his brother Peyton. TJ forwarded that letter to Peyton Short on 18 Mch. with the following note: "The seal of the external letter having been exactly over the seal of this, they had melted together so that in disengaging the outer it brought off the inner seal. mr Short will do me the justice to be assured it was resealed without being opened" (RC in KyLo, addressed by TJ in a disguised hand: "Peyton Short Esqr. near Lexington in the State of Kentuckey," stamped, endorsed by Peyton Short; Peyton Short to TJ, 1 Aug. 1801).

[1] TJ first wrote "letter of Sep. 18. has" before altering the passage to read as above.

From Samuel Smith

SIR/   Baltimore 17th: March 1801

I am afraid I have Acted improperly by delaying to answer your letter so long.—I hope however It will be attributed to the real Cause,—to my anxiety & desire (if possible) to Comply with your wishes by accepting a Post that would have been at all times highly honorable, but during your Administration would have been *to me* particularly pleasing & gratifying—The Conflict with myself has been very great & I confess It is even now afflicting that my private affairs are Such, as to preclude the possibility of doing Justice to the Office. My Constituents also have expressed in Strong terms their disapprobation of my leaving them. under those Circumstances I am under the necessity of declining the Acceptance of the Department you have done me the honor to offer—Permit me to say, that I shall ever Consider myself under real obligations for the honor you have intended me,—

Mr. John Mason of George Town is a Man of good Understanding, bred a Merchant, is esteemed a Man of Integrity & honesty. I know nothing of his Abilities—perhaps on inquiry he may be found adequate to the duties of the Navy—

Should you not find a Mercantile Man to serve your purposes—&
are Compell'd to take a Gentleman from other Professions, I would
wish to recommend a Gentleman who perhaps with the Advice &
assistance of the three supernumerary Captains retained in service
by the late Law, might conduct the future Navy & would be of
great service as Council. I am sir with sentiments of high Regard &
Esteem

your friend & servt   S. SMITH

RC (DLC); endorsed by TJ as received
18 Mch. and so recorded in SJL.

THREE SUPERNUMERARY CAPTAINS: in
the act passed 3 Mch. providing for the
naval establishment during peacetime,

nine captains were to be retained in service, only six of whom would be needed to
command the six frigates to be "kept in
constant service" (U.S. Statutes at Large,
2:110-11).

To Benjamin Stoddert

SIR   Washington Mar. 17. 1801.

Mr Dawson a member of the late Congress is appointed to be the
bearer of the Convention with France, and will be ready to leave this
place, within two days, for Baltimore & thence to proceed immediately for Havre, which I think the most eligible port for him to land at.
I have therefore to ask the favor of you to give the necessary orders &
instructions to the Commander of the Maryland to recieve him. as
it is desireable that she should be back as soon as possible, that she
may be sold. mr Dawson will be instructed, immediately on his
arrival at Paris to prepare his first communications for us as quickly
as possible, on the receipt of which the vessel is to return immediately
to whatever port you shall direct. he is of course to have good accom-
odations in the vessel & a participation of such fare as is provided for
the officers themselves, his character being merely that of a confidential bearer of the Convention. accept assurances of my consideration
& respect.   TH: JEFFERSON

PrC (DLC); at foot of text: "The Secretary of the Navy."

COMMANDER OF THE MARYLAND:
Captain John Rodgers had commanded
the sloop *Maryland* since June 1799.
Writing to Rodgers on 18 Mch., Stoddert
instructed the captain to prepare his vessel for Dawson's imminent arrival and
departure for France. The *Maryland*
sailed from Baltimore on 22 Mch. and

arrived at Le Havre in early May. Returning to Baltimore in late August, the vessel
was sold in October and Rodgers was
discharged as part of the naval reduction
set forth in the Peace Establishment
Act (NDQW, Dec. 1800-Dec. 1801, 148,
292, 368; Charles Oscar Paullin, *Commodore John Rodgers: Captain, Commodore, and Senior Officer of the American
Navy, 1773-1838* [Cleveland, 1910],
68-70).

To Volney

DEAR SIR   Washington Mar. 17. 1801.

You left this country in a state of high delirium. the paroxysm was very [tense?], but has been shorter than I expected. it is now compleatly recovered. this has been effected by the better [. . .] conduct of your nation in a considerable degree, and by a development of the artifices & the objects of those who fomented the quarrel between us. our citizens are now generally returned to their antient principles, & there is the best prospect of an entire obliteration of that party spirit of which you were a victim when here. one of the first effects of this restoration of harmony which I hope for is the hearing from you, as nothing now forbids a communication between us. mr Dawson, the [bearer of] this, is I believe, known to you, as having been a member of Congress wh[ile] you were here. he is the near relation of Governor Monroe; and being intimately possessed of every thing relative to the affairs of this cou[ntry] will give you all the details you can desire. they will astonish you. he is a person of entire confidence, and I shall hope to recieve by him [a let]ter from you, informing me of whatever relates to yourself, as being [. . .] interesting to me, & such other matters as you may chuse to communicate. did you ever recieve the residue of the translation to the end of the [20th] chapter inclusive? it was sent through mr Mc.lure. literary news will be now & at all times acceptable. we have nothing to communicate hence [of] that kind. consequently my letters can only convey to you the expressions of my constant esteem & attachment. accept them [&] all the warmth [&] sincerity of my heart.   TH: JEFFERSON

PrC (DLC); faint; at foot of text: "M. Volney."

TRANSLATION: TJ translated into English the opening "Invocation" and at least the first 19 chapters of Volney's *Les Ruines, ou, Méditation sur les Révolutions des Empires*, which contained 24 chapters and had first been published in Paris in 1792. The "residue" mentioned by TJ above may have been chapters 13-19, since in his papers his retained copy of those chapters became separated from the earlier portions of the translation (PrC in MHi, 2 p. in TJ's hand with two emendations, consisting of the "Invocation," untitled, beginning "Hail solitary ruins"; PrC in same, 31 p. in TJ's hand with some emendations, consisting of chapters 1-12;

Dft in same, 23 p. in TJ's hand with extensive emendations, consisting of chapters 1-12; MS in DLC, TJ Papers, 234:41854-62, 18 p. in TJ's hand with some emendations, consisting of chapters 13-19). William Maclure was acquainted with both Volney and TJ by March 1798, when Maclure entertained the two of them, along with Julian Niemcewicz and Giambattista Scandella, at dinner in Philadelphia a few months before Volney returned to France. Maclure, who had retired from commerce to devote himself to science, left the United States in late summer or autumn 1799 to study the geology of Europe. He was in Paris in the spring of 1801, his travels having taken him first to Scandinavia and Prussia. Maclure and TJ did not correspond prior to July 1801, so it seems likely that TJ completed the "residue" of the translation before Maclure's departure in 1799 and that the traveler had the manuscript in his keeping until he met with Volney in Paris (Niemcewicz, *Under Their Vine*, 46-7; John S. Doskey, ed., *The European Journals of William Maclure* [Philadelphia, 1988], xxi; ANB; Vol. 30:396; Maclure to TJ, 3 July 1801).

Volney asked Joel Barlow to finish the translation of the *Ruines*. In the fall of 1802 the entire work appeared in two volumes titled *A New Translation of Volney's Ruins*. That version, leaving TJ's portion of the translation largely intact, alters some wording of his retained manuscripts. An unsigned "Preface of the Translator," no doubt written by Barlow, used the plural form "we" rather than "I," but the 1802 publication names neither of the translators. When Volney sent the translated "Invocation" to the United States in 1801 to excite interest in the forthcoming volumes, he kept the source of the translation secret. Asking TJ what to do with the manuscript translation following the publication of the book,

Volney received the reply: "it is desired that it may be burnt." Volney complied. The *Ruines* had already been translated into English once, in a 1792 London edition that had been reprinted several times. Barlow's preface to the *New Translation* asserted that the earlier effort had fallen well short of doing justice to the original. Volney's *Ruines* has been described as partly "un poème en prose," and in the preface Barlow said that the intent of the *New Translation* was "that as much of the spirit of the original be transfused and preserved as is consistent with the nature of translation" (*A New Translation of Volney's Ruins; or Meditations on the Revolution of Empires. Made under the Inspection of the Author* [Paris, 1802], v-viii; Gilbert Chinard, *Volney et l'Amérique d'après des Documents Inédits et sa Correspondance avec Jefferson*, The Johns Hopkins Studies in Romance Literatures and Languages, 1 [Baltimore, 1923], 110-13; Jean Gaulmier, *L'Idéologue Volney, 1757-1820: Contribution à l'Histoire de l'Orientalisme en France* [Geneva, 1980], 207; Sowerby, No. 1278; Volney to TJ, 24 June 1801, 21 Mch. 1803; TJ to Volney, 20 Apr. 1802).

From Thomas Waterman

SIR,   City of Washington, March 17th: 1801.

In the present crises of Affairs, should a vacancy occur, in the office of Commissioner of the revenue, or Accountant to the Navy department, I beg leave to solicit your confidence, in the appointment to either; possessed of a competent knowledge of business, I pledge myself to a just & faithful discharge, of those duties, you may please to entrust me with.—

Permit me Sir, shall you deem it worthy your attention, to refer you to John & Jno: T. Mason of Georgetown, Messrs: Anderson, Cocke & Mason of the Senate, & the republican members of the house of representatives from Pennsylvania.

It may not be amiss to observe to you that from a strict adherence, to certain principles imbibed at an early period of my life, I have been obliged to be contented, with a subordinate situation during the last administration, having at the same time an increasing family to support.—

I have the honor to be, Sir, with the highest respect & esteem, your obedt. hum. Servt: TH: WATERMAN

RC (DNA: RG 59, LAR); at foot of text: "Thomas Jefferson Esqre"; endorsed by TJ as received 18 Mch. and so recorded in SJL.

Thomas Waterman had moved with the federal government from Philadelphia to Washington, D.C., and in 1801 continued to be employed as a clerk in the Register's Office at the Treasury Department. He believed his salary had remained low under the Federalists because he possessed "certain political principles," and William Duane identified him as a Republican on a list of government clerks. In 1801 and again in 1802 he unsuccessfully applied for positions in the Treasury secretary's office. In 1803 Waterman wrote from Philadelphia, where he was employed as an accountant, seeking appointment as a bankruptcy commissioner for Pennsylvania. In 1808 he was selected to serve as a customs inspector at the port (Gallatin, *Papers*, 5:25; 6:355, 937; 7:649; 17:61, 104, 259; James Robinson, *The Philadelphia Directory for 1805* [Philadelphia, 1805], lxxii; same, *The Philadelphia Directory for 1809* [Philadelphia, 1809], liv; Waterman to TJ, 19 July 1803).

From John Beckley

DEAR SIR,   Philadelphia, 18th. March 1801.

I equally fear to be guilty of intrusion or importunity, well aware of the multiplied & incessant applications with which you are beseiged; but, the strong claim of friendship, has superseded my disinclination to forward you the enclosed, confiding, that there is nothing improper, in submitting the views of my friend, by this indirect mode, in his own language; at the same time that I presume to add, my knowledge of the fact, that he was the favored nephew, and confidential friend, of his Uncle Rittenhouse, who usually advised with and consulted him, in the first organization of the Mint establishment, as well as, on many other occasions, of Scientific and philosophical research; besides which, it cannot be questioned that a more exemplary private character than Mr: Bartons, is not to be found.

But in the instance that follows, I will make no apology, conscious that it is the first duty of a friend to guard you, against those surprises, to which you are liable.—Application, special or general, has been or will be made to you for appointment, by a certain Major Rhinehart of this City, under strong recommendations of most respectable characters, given, I presume, in perfect ignorance of his private and Moral Character, which you may be perfectly assured is this; that he is subsisted by a wife, from whom he had been five Years estranged, who keeps a house of illfame, and who, with him, has no other visible[1] means of support. I was inadvertently led to recommend this man as a decided republican character, to the notice of Colo. Burr, before I knew these particulars of his private life and character. It will be sufficient now to notice them, *only* for your own observation.

If on any other or future occasion, I shall discover similar attempts to deceive you, I will not hesitate, without other motive for so doing, to repeat the freedom now taken; being, with the most sincere regard and attachment, dear Sir,

Your friend and obedient Servant JOHN BECKLEY.

RC (DNA: RG 59, LAR); endorsed by TJ as received 20 Mch. and so recorded in SJL. Enclosure: William Barton to Beckley, 2 Mch. 1801, from Lancaster, noting his support for the Republican cause, mentioning his hope to obtain some "Office of a *secondary* class," preferably in Pennsylvania, to give him greater income for the support of his large family, and believing himself entitled to say "without any imputation of vanity" that he considers himself qualified to serve as supervisor of the revenue for Pennsylvania, should Henry Miller cease to occupy that post (RC in same); Barton was prothonotary of Lancaster County (Rowe, *McKean*, 344).

[1] Word interlined.

To Napoleon Bonaparte

CITIZEN FIRST CONSUL,

To testify to you the sincerity of the Government of the United States in its negotiations, I have transmitted to Oliver Ellsworth and William Vans Murray, two of the late Envoys Extraordinary and Ministers Plenipotentiary of the United States to the French Republic, the ratification of the Convention between the said States and the French Republic, signed at Paris on the 30th day of September last past, by your Plenipotentiaries and those of the said States: and the said Oliver Ellsworth and William Vans Murray or either of them are instructed to take the necessary measures for the exchange of the ratifications in convenient time, and to take upon themselves the execution of this business; in which case I beseech you, Citizen First Consul, to give full credence to whatever the said Oliver Ellsworth and William Vans Murray or either of them shall say to you on the part of the United States, concerning the same, and to receive the said ratification in the name of, and on the part of the United States of America, when it shall be tendered by them or either of them. I pray God to have you Citizen First Consul in his Holy keeping.

Written at the City of Washington this Eighteenth day of March, in the year of our Lord, one thousand Eight hundred and one.

TH: JEFFERSON

By the President
Levi Lincoln
Acting as Secretary of State.

FC (Lb in DNA: RG 59, Credences); in a clerk's hand; at head of text: "Thomas Jefferson, President of the United States of America, To the First Consul of the French Republic." Tr (NNPM: William Vans Murray Letterbooks); in Murray's hand; contains a blank in place of Lincoln's name (see John Dawson to TJ, 31 Mch.). Not recorded in SJL.

Napoleon Bonaparte (1769-1821) was first consul of France, the most powerful position under the constitution promulgated at his direction after the 18 Brumaire coup of November 1799. A professional army officer, he had previously gained notice for his role in dispersing the insurrection of 13 Vendémiaire in 1795, for his planning and command of the campaigns in Italy in 1796-7, and for leading the occupation of Egypt. He was proclaimed consul for life in 1802 and emperor in May 1804 (Tulard, *Dictionnaire Napoléon*, 1226-9; Stewart, *French Revolution*, 767-8, 773).

To Daniel Carroll Brent

SIR   Mar. 18. 1801.

Being to appoint a Marshall for the district of Columbia it has been intimated to me by a mutual friend that you might perhaps be willing to accept of that office. on this suggestion I take the liberty of proposing it to you. as a court is to be held here on Monday next, it becomes necessary for me to ask the favor of an answer by the bearer, mr M[ason]'s servant who goes expected for this purpose, because should you decline it, I shall still have to make an appointment before Monday. my anxiety to place in the offices men who will give weight to them & command the public confidence inspires an earnest desire that this may be acceptable to you. I am Sir

Your most obedt. sevt   TH: JEFFERSON

PrC (DLC); faint and blurred; at foot of text: "Daniel Carrol Brent esq."; endorsed by TJ in ink on verso.

Daniel Carroll Brent (1759-1814) was the son of Eleanor Carroll and William Brent of Richland, a plantation on the Potomac River, at Aquia Creek, in Stafford County, Virginia, and brother of Congressman Richard Brent. In 1782, Brent married Anne Fenton, daughter of Thomas Ludwell Lee. He served in the Virginia House of Delegates from 1785 to 1787, 1799 to 1801, and 1812 to 1813. Winning a hard-fought campaign to serve as elector in 1796, Brent cast his vote for TJ. As a nephew of Daniel Carroll, one of three commissioners appointed to superintend the construction of the new Federal City in 1791, Brent had a long-term interest in the development of Washington. He served as U.S. marshal for the District of Columbia for almost seven years, submitting his resignation in Nov. 1807. When the militia for the District of Columbia was organized in 1802, TJ commissioned him as a lieutenant colonel, commandant of the first legion, including militia companies north of the Potomac (Leonard, *General Assembly*, 157, 162, 217, 221, 271; Robert A. Rutland, ed., *The Papers of George Mason 1725-1792*, 3 vols. [Chapel Hill, 1970], 1:xxviii, xxxvi; Washington, *Papers, Pres. Ser.*, 2:354; VMHB, 17 [1909], 194-5; RCHS, 50 [1948-50], 387-8; Brent to James Madison, 4 Nov. 1807, in DNA: RG 59, RD; Vol. 29:193-5, 197n).

From Gabriel Duvall

Dear Sir,   Annapolis, 18 Mar. 1801.

Your letter of the 13th instant did not reach me until between 10 & 11 O'Clock at night on the 16th. & I was then twenty miles from this place. I embrace the earliest opportunity to express the high sense entertained, of the honour done me in offering me the office of Chief Judge of the district of Columbia;—for which, accept my thanks.

Many considerations lead me to accept the appointment, but as prudence forbids the making so great a sacrifice as must necessarily attend an acceptance, I am compeled, reluctantly, to decline it.—   Believe me to be with the highest sentiments of respect & esteem, your obedt. Sevt.   G. Duvall

RC (DLC); at foot of text: "The President of the United States"; endorsed by TJ as received 19 Mch. and so recorded in SJL.

To Oliver Ellsworth and William Vans Murray, with Levi Lincoln

                                                    Department of State
Gentlemen,   Washington [18] March 1801

Mr. Madison the Secretary of State being not yet arrived at the seat of Government I have been authorized by the President to discharge the duties of that office per interim; and among the objects which have claimed the earliest attention is the Convention signed by yourselves and General Davie with the government of France. This instrument was laid before the Senate on the 16th. of December and having met with considerable difficulties there, was under discussion till their final vote on the 3d of February, by which they advised and consented to the ratification of it with the suppression of the 2d article, and the addition of an Article limiting its duration. The term of change in the Administration being then approaching, this matter has rested to the present moment. Tho' the day agreed on for the exchange of ratifications will from these unavoidable causes have passed over, yet we apprehend that that exchange, being only a matter of form, will suffer no difficulty, and then it will take place on your receipt of this as a matter of course, if the modifications of the Senate meet with no objection as we hope they will not. It appeared from the documents you transmitted that the 2d article was chiefly of your own solliciting, and that its omission is not likely to be disagreeable to France. There was in the Senate a considerable diversity of sentiment on it, and as by our Consititution, one third of that body can negative a treaty or any particular article of it, there was found to be a sufficient number against this article to effect its negative. With respect to the additional article, limiting the duration, you will recollect there was an express instruction to that effect among those given to you. It is perhaps unwise policy in any nation to bind itself perpetually by an act which requires the consent of another nation to annul. It is most unwise in us, of all nations because the circumstances of our existence, and of our relations with others change so rapidly. What is now advantageous, may soon become otherwise: and our increasing strength is daily facilitating the command of just dispositions on the part of others. It has[1] therefore been the invariable policy of this country since the date of its earliest treaties to enter into none which shall not be limited to short terms, and now look forward with desire to the moment when we shall be free from compact with every nation, and have a right to govern ourselves with every one according to the principles of justice, and of a friendship proportioned to what we experience from them. We hope and trust these modifications by the Senate will meet with no difficulty, and you are accordingly desired to use your best endeavours to obtain an acquiescence in them on a final ratification in that form, nevertheless should the suppression of the 2d. article meet with obstacles on their part which we do not expect, rather than keep things between the two Countries in their present unsettled state, you might accept a ratification re-establishing the 2d. article only reserving to the Senate their consititutional right to advise or refuse a ratification in that form. But as to the additional article limiting the duration, it is a sine qua non from which we cannot depart. In every event we are carrying the convention into execution in all its parts. All hostilities on the sea have been forbidden, our vessels are returning into port, the prisoners in our possession are in a course of delivery to M. Letombe former Consul of France, he is notified that all those officers may resume their functions, commercial intercourse is restored, a number of our vessels actually cleared out and departed for France, and orders given for the restitution of vessels under the 3d. article of the convention, but I am sorry to say there is great reason to apprehend the Insurgente is lost together with a vessel of ours called the Pickering and all their crews. They were on a cruise together in the West Indies in the month of August last, since which neither have ever been heard of, should they return (which however we do not expect) the Insurgente shall be immediately restored according to the convention.

It is possible that these modifications of the Convention may give rise to new discussions between yourselves and those whom the government of France may authorize on[2] their part, and, as we observe that an armed coalition in vindication of neutral rights is formed, or forming in Europe, it is also possible that government may indulge a wish that we should take a part in it, and may make it an ingredient in the new discussions. In that case you are to set your faces against it at once, and to declare it a subject on which you have not a word to say, nor will say a word. In truth we are determined to take no part in European quarrels. we will endeavour by a rigorous observance of justice towards all nations to preserve peace and commerce with all; and we will not suffer our peace to be committed but by our own actions, or those of others immediately respecting ourselves. We shall endeavor to lead nations by their interest to observe all the terms of good correspondence and neighborhood with us, and if they fail in these to make it still their interest to return to them. To connect ourselves with the complicated combinations of the interests of Europe, would be to relinquish the most precious gift of nature, insulation from the power and politics of that continent.

As this matter will of course bring you into conference with the Minister of foreign affairs for that government, you are desired to avail yourself of that opportunity of conveying to the government assurances of the friendship of this Country to that, that the President will omit no occasion of proving to them his dispositions and wishes to cultivate harmony and good correspondence, by an observance of all those attentions and procedures which are found in respect, in justice and in usage between nation and nation, by a rigorous regard to justice in whatsoever may arise between us, and by every proof of friendship and favor which may be consistent with the justice due to others. he sincerely prays and hopes that the war in which that country is now engaged may be speedily terminated, and pledges himself during its continuance to observe a faithful and conscientious neutrality towards all the belligerent powers.

The honorable Mr. Dawson member of the late Congress from the state of Virginia will deliver you this with the treaty which is committed to his care. he will direct the vessel which carries him to return without delay; and awaiting the ratification on the part of France, he will receive it from you and take his passage back in some other vessel. You are desired to press for this ratification with as little delay as possible, and being obtained and delivered to Mr. Dawson you will consider it as closing your proceedings & powers: so soon as it is received here, a Minister Plenipotentiary will be sent on our part to reside with that nation.

I am Gentlemen &c. &c.   LEVI LINCOLN

FC (Lb in DNA: RG 59, DCI); in a clerk's hand; closing parenthesis supplied; at head of text: "Messrs. Ellsworth & Murray"; day of month left blank in dateline, but Murray acknowledged this as a letter of 18 Mch. (Madison, *Papers, Sec. of State Ser.*, 1:205); in margin: "This Letter should have been Recorded among the March letters." Not recorded in SJL.

TJ's authorship of this letter is suggested by its subject matter, the phrasing, and TJ's acknowledgment that he wrote to David Humphreys over Lincoln's signature on 17 Mch. That letter and this one are adjacent in the letterbook in DNA: RG 59, DCI, and out of sequence from the rest of March 1801.

EXPRESS INSTRUCTION: the instructions that John Adams and Timothy Pickering gave to Ellsworth, Murray, and William R. Davie in October 1799 called for a limit of no more than twelve years on most provisions of any treaty the envoys might conclude with the French (ASP, *Foreign Relations*, 2:306).

The French warship INSURGENTE had been taken by the *Constellation* in February 1799, then condemned by the federal district court at Richmond and put to use as a U.S. frigate. Dispatched on a long cruise to the West Indies in July 1800, the vessel never returned and was thought to have gone down in a gale in September of that year. The PICKERING, a U.S. revenue cutter, probably met the same fate. In a letter to the secretary of state on 19 Mch. 1801, Louis André Pichon suggested that the United States replace the *Insurgente* or pay compensation for it under the "spirit" of the Convention of 1800, the third article of which said that "public ships which have been taken on one part and the other, or which may be taken before the exchange of ratifications, shall be restored." TJ and Madison held to the view that the *Insurgente* had ceased to exist before the convention was signed and could not be included in the provision for the return of captured public vessels (NDQW, Dec. 1800-Dec. 1801, 54, 174, 311, 368-9; NDQW, June 1800-Nov. 1800, 149; ASP, *Foreign Relations*, 2:296, 431; Madison, *Papers, Sec. of State Ser.*, 1:399, 400n, 422).

MINISTER OF FOREIGN AFFAIRS: Talleyrand.

[1] MS: "is."
[2] MS: "or."

From John Wayles Eppes

DEAR SIR,   Bermuda-Hundred March 18th. 1801.

I have postponed writing until I could give you some information as to the horses—I have engaged Doctr. Walkers horse certainly—Mr. Bell has undertaken to send for the match & if I like him I shall have him also—So that you may count certainly on Bells horse and most probably a complete match—I examined Doctr. Shores pair also and drove them some miles. They are fine blood bays upwards of 16. hands high well made spirited & active. They match exactly in colour strength and spirit are gentle and steady—They are considered by many as equal to the famous pair bought by Colo. Hampton from Willis—Their price however is far beyond any thing I have ever heard of—800 dollars have been refused for them by Doctr. Shore and he holds them at 1000 dollars—Haxhall continues to keep his horse—I have employed others to sound him as to price and find that nothing less than 500 dollars would induce him to part with him—I think there are no other horses in this part of the state except Hax-halls & Shores whose figure & size would please you—Haxhalls as a parade horse from his gentleness and beauty would be equal to any that could be purchased & Shores pair are considered as the finest in the state—

I am sorry it will not be in our power to accept of the offer you are kind enough to make—So long a stay at Monticello would subject us to sepe-rations which we wish to avoid and your absence from it lessens much the desire we might otherwise feel to quit a spot on which we are at pres-ent fixed merely by motives of convenience.

The universal satisfaction with which your speech and the first acts of your administration have been received fill my heart with joy— Among all descriptions of persons it is admired extolled and quoted. The appointment of Dawson seems not to meet with such general approbation—The Feds who are just learning oeconomy object to it on that score & maintain that Mr. Livingston might carry the convention and save the expence—

Maria joins with me in the best wishes of affection. adieu yours

J: W: EPPES

RC (MHi); endorsed by TJ as received 26 Mch. and so recorded in SJL.

From Carlos Martínez de Irujo

DEAR SIR   Philadelphia 18 of March 1801

I have delay'd some few days writing to you a second letter on the *important* buiseness, trusted by you to my care, flattering myself to give you more satisfactory news than those imparted by my first, but I am sorry to tell you that no succes has crown'd as yet my endeavours—The Cook I had last, & of whom I spoke in my preced-ing letter, is gone to the Havana, & another who was recommended to me, tho a man of abilities, posses not other qualifications equally material—I am sorry then to tell you that Philadelphia does not offer the chance of a good Cook; perhaps by writing to New York you will be more fortunate—

You have heard officially perhaps of the late change which has taken place in the Spanish Cabinet—I am sorry my good Friend d'Urquijo is out, as he was a man of talent & vertu, & as this circumstance will probably banish my former *golden*, but *grounded* expectations. At all events the intended step on your part, tho probably too late, may be always of use, & of course I'll expect it with gratitude—

Poor Dr. Priestly has been & continues yet very sick: we apprehended three days ago for his life; but tho very ill yet, he appears to be on the recovery—

The Governor & all the Family joins me, in my best wishes for your good health & happiness for the sake of humanity & your friends, in whose number I'll take the liberty to include

your most obt. & he. Servt.   LE CHEVALIER D'IRUJO

RC (MoSHi: Jefferson Papers); at foot of text: "His Excellency Th. Jefferson"; endorsed by TJ as received 21 Mch. and so recorded in SJL.

INTENDED STEP ON YOUR PART: see TJ to Thomas McKean, 9 Mch.

GOVERNOR: McKean, Irujo's father-in-law.

To William Jones

SIR   Washington Mar. 18. 1801.

In providing an administration for our government I was led by every just consideration to wish that General Smith of Baltimore should undertake the Secretaryship of the navy, and accordingly proposed it to him. after taking time to consider of it, I have this morning recieved a letter from him informing me it is not in his power. in this case I have no hesitation in making the proposition to you, and of expressing my anxious wish that you would aid us with your skill and talents in this department. it is not for me to [offer?] considerations which I have no doubt will occur & influence your mind on this occasion with every possible disposition, & the most anxious desires, to provide a skilled & honest administration of public affairs for our fellow citizens, it will be impossible unless we can prevail on gentlemen duly qualified to avail this country of their talents. while I press your acceptance of this charge, I am forced at the same time to sollicit as little delay as possible in obtaining your answer. we had arranged the most pressing business in the other departments so as to permit us to go to our homes about the 22d. instant, in order to take measures necessary in our domestic affairs to enable us to return & fix here finally about the 18th. or 20th. of April. the delay of General Smith's answer has rendered it impossible for me now to go so soon, as there are some measures which must be set in motion in the naval department immediately, & consequently render it necessary not only that the department should be filled but that I wait to see & confer with the person before I can go away. consequently it is to me personally very interesting not only to obtain your acceptance, but an instantaneous visit if possible to this place, for two or three days, during which a view could be presented to you of what is pressing, which probably you could direct from your own dwelling, should your convenience call for your immediate return to it. between this & the 20th. or 21st. of April you might possibly find it practicable to remove here finally as we shall do. I shall be extremely anxious not only for an affirmative answer but to recieve it, or to see your self as soon as possible. I pray you to accept assurances of my high consideration & respect.

TH: JEFFERSON

PrC (DLC); blurred; at foot of first page: "William Jones esq."

William Jones (ca. 1760-1831) was a prominent Philadelphia merchant and an active participant in Republican politics. He served a single term in Congress (1801-3), during which time he twice declined offers from TJ to serve as secretary of the navy. Jones accepted the post under the Madison administration, serving with distinction from 1812 to 1814. He had a far less distinguished tenure as president of the second Bank of the U.S., serving from 1816 until his removal in 1819. He was collector for the port of Philadelphia from 1827 to 1829 and died in Bethlehem, Pennsylvania, in 1831 (ANB; Jones to TJ, 23 Mch., 20 May 1801).

From Ephraim Kirby

SIR   Litchfield Cont March 18th. 1801

I take the liberty to convey to you the enclosed Pamphlet.—It contains sentiments which I believe will meet your approbation. The author lives in my vicinity, and is an exception from the general character of the Connecticut Clergy.—In the great conflict of political opinion, he has suffered much for righteousness sake.

Permit me Sir, to mention, that if either the office of Post Master General, or Supervisor of the Revenue in Connecticut, should become vacant, I shall be willing to be considered a candidate for one or the other of them—If you know enough of my character, to confer upon me either of those offices, I shall endeavour to prove that your confidence is not misplaced.

I am most respectfully Your Obedt. Servt   EPHRAIM KIRBY

RC (DNA: RG 59, LAR); at foot of text: "The President of the U. States"; endorsed by TJ as received 9 Apr. and so recorded in SJL with notation "Off." Enclosure not found, but see below.

A Litchfield County native and Revolutionary War veteran, Ephraim Kirby (1757-1804) practiced law and compiled *Reports of Cases Adjudged in the Superior Court of the State of Connecticut from the Year 1785 to May 1788 with Some Determinations in the Supreme Court of Errors* (Litchfield, 1789; see Evans, No. 21914), noted as the first volume of state law reports to be published in the United States. Kirby speculated in land and helped organize the Connecticut Land Company. In 1791 he began serving in the state legislature. An outspoken critic of Federalist policies, he was prominent in the organization of the Republican opposition and stood as their candidate for governor in 1801 and the two following years. In July 1801, TJ appointed Kirby supervisor of internal revenue for Connecticut, a position he held until September 1802. In 1803 he was one of three commissioners appointed by the president to settle disputed land claims in Mississippi Territory. The commissioners met at Fort Stoddert. Before TJ heard of Kirby's untimely death from yellow fever, he wrote and offered him the governorship of Mississippi Territory (ANB; TJ to Kirby, 1 Dec. 1804).

The ENCLOSED PAMPHLET may have been Stanley Griswold's *Overcoming Evil With Good. A Sermon, Delivered at Wallingford, Connecticut, March 11, 1801; Before a Numerous Collection of the Friends of the Constitution, of Thomas Jefferson, President, and of Aaron Burr, Vice-President of the United States*, published in Hartford, Connecticut, in 1801. Griswold, a Congregational minister at New Milford, in Litchfield County, and a Republican, delivered the sermon as part of a celebration in honor of TJ's election (see Sowerby, Nos. 1664, 3263). For another pamphlet by Griswold, see Elijah Boardman to TJ, 1 Mch. 1801.

From James Monroe

DEAR SIR   Richmond 18. March 1801.

I acknowledged yours of the 7th. by Mr. Camp who went on some days since. I shod. have answered it more fully before this had I not been prevented by indisposition from wh. I am nearly recovered. Your address has been approved by every description of persons here. It is sound and strong in principle, and grateful to the opposit party. With your judgment views and principles it is hardly possible you shod. go wrong. Indeed I count on the good effects of yr. admn., being felt in favor of republican govt. abroad as well as at home. Still there are dangers in yr. way which it is necessary to shun. These are seen by you and therefore it may be useless for me to notice them. There have been two parties in this country, one whose views are honest, benevolent, republican; the other with views unfriendly to the rights of the people. The latter has enjoyed the govt. for 12. years past and greatly abused the trust. It was under a firm conviction of the misconduct and improper views of that party, that the people gradually withdrew their confidence from it, till at length they drove it from the government altogether. It was on this principle that the late change in the admn. was made, not by accomodation on the part of the republicans, who sought nothing unreasonable & therefore yeilded nothing, but by the honest part of the federalists abandoning their leaders when they saw their confidence was misplacd & uniting their force to that of the republican party. It was also on this principle that you came into the admn., one whose past conduct entitled him to the confidence of the republicans, and secured him the unrelenting hatred & persecution of their opponents. The object now is to restore the govt. to its principles, amend its defects, reform abuses and introduce order and œconomy in the admn. The republicans will of course unite in support of such a system, as I presume all those who lately came over likewise will. These *two* descriptions of persons may be considered as *one* in principle, I mean the bulk of them. Their seperation was momentary, may be trac'd to causes which no longer exist; their present union is therefore natural. If they are kept together, which will be easily done, the overthrow of the opposit party is as final as it is complete, since if they had sufficient strength to eject that party from the govt., when supported by the govt., now that they are in power they have little to fear from their adversaries, who are without power and without character. But new converts may shift again & go over to their former leaders. Some attention is due to them to prevent such a step on their part. I do not think there is much danger of such an event, or that the apprehention of it shod. produce much effect on the measures of yr. admn. What brot. them over lately to the republican side? A conviction of the misconduct of those leaders and the danger of the crisis to wh. they were brought, together with the firmness of the republicans. So strong was that sentiment that it broke the tie of former conviction, prevailed over former compromitment and enabled them to abandon old friends and unite with old political enemies. An union broken under such circumstances, with so much violence, is not easily repaired. It usually leaves a coolness, often a hatred between the parties. This is probably the case in the present instance. be it however as it may it is not to be presumed that these men will go back under your admn., wh. secures their persons and property, & cherishes their principles, which were lately jeopardized, to join those leaders who had brought them to the brink of ruin, and who on that acct. they abandoned. I admit however these new converts shod. be cherished, but it shod. be done with care so as not to wound the feelings of those who have deserv'd better of their country & of mankind. I am persuaded that any marked attention from you as yet, by which I mean advancement to office of any of those persons would be impolitick as it might lessen the confidence of the republicans in yr. admn. I am satisfied such a step in favor of a distinguished character on that side, wod. produce the worst possible effect, not with the uniform republicans only, but with those who have lately come over. The former wod. feel and express their disappointment; the latter wod. be confounded and begin to suspect they had abandoned their late leaders, if not without sufficient cause in point of principle, yet on an over estimate of the danger which impelled them to it. An attention of the kind referred to, to a distinguished character on that side, especially at the present time, wod. erect the standard of the party in yr. own admn., under yr. own auspices, with an invitation to its scattered members to rally round it.

But is it sufficient that the favor of the present admn. shod. be withheld from the members of the former one and its most distinguished associates? Have they committed crimes or been calumniated by their enemies? If the former is the case or even presumeable, ought such countenance to be shewn them, as tended to stifle the publick resentment, or check the freedom of enquiry especially in the legislature which has yet to pass on them? Much abuse is suspected to have been committed in every department of the most vulgar, gross, & corrupt kind. Ought not this to be probed into, and wod. not an impartial enquiry into it, contribute much to aid the republican cause & seperate for ever these new converts from their antient leaders. If the latter are really guilty, and it be proved, there is no danger to be apprehended from them afterwards. None who have already parted from, will ever rejoin them. And that they have been sufficiently guilty of one act or other of a reprehensible, if not criminal nature, to dishonor them for ever I have no doubt. The command of the political fortunes and treasury of America, by such subaltern low minded men was a trust, of wh. they were quite unworthy. We have much cause to believe they were not able to withstand the temptation. The evidence of their guilt it is supposed exists in each department, if not destroyd, & if destroyed that ought to be known. I do not urge the propriety of yr. taking a part in such concerns otherwise than by avoiding compromitment, leaving the door open to free investigation, and seperating the commenc'ment of yr. admn. by a distinct view in every departmt. of the actual state of things from that wh. preceded. Necker rendered an acct. when he left office. Ought not an acct. to be taken, considering what is passed, & rendered by the heads of departments to shew in what condition you found our affrs. when you came into office? Is it otherwise possible to do justice to yrself or those who preceded you?

Deprivation from office in subaltern grades is a different thing. The principle is sound that no man ought to be turnd out for mere difference of political sentiment, since that is a right in wh. he ought to be protected. Whether this shod. be construed, so as to cover and protect all those who gained their appointments by violence, at the expense of those who lost them on acct. of their inflexible virtue, or whether violence and partizanship alone when carried to great excess ought not to be made examples of are interesting points wh. merit great attention. I am persuaded that much of the unhappiness and misery to wh. our society has been subject, is owing to such conduct in the federal officers in every state. It is to be feared too, such men will never contribute much to the restoration of that harmony, in whose destruction, they had so distinguished an agency. By retaining them in office you will give a proof of tolerance, moderation, & forbearance, which must command the respect of the benevolent. Your situation is new and has its difficulties which I doubt not all parties will consider & make allowance for. I have trifled longer on this subject than I intended. I have done so from the interest I take in yr. own as well as the publick welfare, being sincerely your friend & servant

JAS. MONROE

It will give me pleasure to meet you in Albemarle if in my power, the first week in April, as I hope it will be.

RC (DLC); endorsed by TJ as received 23 Mch. and so recorded in SJL. Dft (DLC: Monroe Papers); dated 15 Mch.

Robert CAMP of Culpeper County, Virginia, who apparently carried Monroe's letter of 12 Mch. to TJ, had worked under John Beckley in the past and hoped to obtain a clerkship or other position in the federal government (Madison, *Papers, Sec. of State Ser.*, 1:13-14).

Jacques NECKER, shortly before resigning as the chief financial officer of the French government in 1781, issued a statement of the national finances (Stewart, *French Revolution*, 16-17; Vol. 6:191).

From Benjamin Nones

SIR   Philadelphia 18 March 1801.

When I contemplate the excellency of your Character, I feel satisfied that you will permit an old Soldier, and a republican Citizen of the United States, to approach you, with all the respect which your distinguished Virtues merit; and, if apology be deemed requisite to justify the present address, I flatter myself your Excellency will find an adequate one in what I shall have the honor to state to you.—

When the hostile armies of Great Britain invaded the United States to lay waste the fair rights of Freemen, I abandoned the place of my Nativity (Bordeaux in France) and arrived in Charleston South Carolina in the Year 1776 and in the presence of the Legislature of that State took the Oath of Allegiance to that State and to the United States. I immediately thereupon flew to the Standard of Liberty, and, under her banners, joined the valiant Sons of America in the defence of Freedom's Cause against her invading Foes. I was a Volunteer in the Militia of South Carolina under the Orders of General Lincoln, in which I served until the arrival of General Palaski when I became a Volunteer in the Corps under his command. From that time until the Surrender of Charleston to the British, I assisted to fight the battles of America, and deemed myself happy, at every hazard, in asserting, with my Sword, her Freedom and Independence. At the fall of Charleston I became a prisoner of war and continued so till the surrender of Lord Cornwallis when I was exchanged. The War being over which gave to America her Freedom and Independence; I felt the Country as near to me as if I had been born on her Soil, and possessed of the rights of a Citizen, I married in Philadelphia which became my home and where I have ever since resided. I have been blessed with thirteen Children of which nine are still living.—

Allow me, Sir, to say that, amidst all the revolutions of Opinion, my political principles remained pure and unchanged. I was always a republican and as a Freeman I glory in being a republican.—

But permit me to add that the few last years that are just gone have witnessed Events which justify the Conclusion that had I not been an inflexible republican my usual prosperity and Affluence would still have attended me and a large and young family.—

My Zeal & attachment to the republican Cause have been in some degree rewarded by a Major's Commission in the 25th Regiment of Militia of this City and County; but as a post of honor only it can add nothing to the means of enabling me to support a rising family.—

I hope, Sir, you will permit me to think that my Abilities may be useful to my Country, and, feeling as I do a sufficient degree of patriotism to lead me to Acts of disinterested honorableness, were the means in my power as they formerly were, it is due to Candor to state, that, under my present Circumstances, brought about chiefly by the tyranny of opinion, my present application to you for an Office is prompted by the united Wish to be useful to myself and the public.—

I therefore respectfully request your Excellency to honor me with such an Appointment as you in your Wisdom may think proper

I take the liberty to refer your Excellency to the inclosed Certifications of a few of my republican fellow Citizens, and have the honor to remain

Your Excellency's most obedient Servant   BENJ NONES

RC (DNA: RG 59, LAR); with sub-joined recommendation for Nones "as an honest man, and a Citizen of respectable Character, and qualified to fulfill the duties" of an appointment, in Nones's hand, dated 18 Mch., and signed by Israel Israel, William Duane, Samuel Wetherill, Samuel Wetherill, Jr., Mahlon Dickerson, Michael Leib, John Shee, and Joseph Clay; addressed: "The President of the United States Washington"; franked; postmarked 24 Mch.; endorsed by TJ as received 26 Mch. and so recorded in SJL.

Benjamin Nones (1757-1826), a Sephardic Jew, was a respected, if not prosperous, Philadelphia merchant and an influential member of the city's small Jewish community. He was also an active Jeffersonian and member of the Democratic Society and the Tammany Society. During the summer of 1800 he was the target of an anti-Semitic attack by the *Gazette of the United States*, to which

William Duane permitted him to reply in the *Aurora*. The statement by Nones declared, "I am a Jew, and if for no other reason, for that reason I am a republican." He went on to add, "In republics we have *rights*, in monarchies we live but to experience *wrongs*." Although he repeated his patronage request in an 11 Nov. letter, Nones did not receive an appointment during TJ's administration. He was, however, named a notary public and authorized interpreter by the governor of Pennsylvania in 1803 (Bennett Muraskin, "Benjamin Nones: Profile of a Jewish Jeffersonian," *American Jewish History*, 83 [1995], 381-5; William Pencak, "Jews and Anti-Semitism in Early Pennsylvania," PMHB, 126 [2002], 405-7; Edwin Wolf 2d and Maxwell Whiteman, *The History of the Jews of Philadelphia from Colonial Times to the Age of Jackson* [Philadelphia, 1957], 209-14, 216, 443, 444; *Aurora*, 13 Aug. 1800).

To Thomas Paine

DEAR SIR   Washington Mar. 18. 1801.

Your letters of Oct. 1. 4. 6. 16. came duly to hand, and the papers which they covered were, according to your permission, published in the newspapers & in a pamphlet, & under your own name. these papers contain precisely our principles, & I hope they will be generally recognized here. determined as we are to avoid, if possible, wasting the energies of our people in war & destruction, we shall avoid implicating ourselves with the powers of Europe, even in support of principles which we mean to pursue. they have so many other interests different from ours, that we must avoid being entangled in them. we believe we can enforce those principles as to ourselves[1] by peaceable means, now that we are likely to have our public councils detached from foreign views. the return of our citizens from the frenzy into which they had been wrought partly by ill-conduct in France, partly by artifices practiced on them, is [almost] entire, & will I believe become quite so. but these details, too [minute &] long for a letter, will be better developed by mr Dawson the bearer [of] this, a member of the late Congress, to whom I refer you for them. [he] goes in the Maryland[2] a sloop of war, which will wait a few days at Havre to recieve his letters to be written on his arrival at Paris. you expressed a wish to get a passage to this country in a public vessel. mr Dawson is charged with orders to the capt. of the Maryland to recieve and accomodate you with a passage back, if you can be ready to depart at such short warning. Rob. R. Livingston is appointed Min. Plen. [to] the republic of France, but will not leave this till we recieve the ratification of the Convention[3] by mr Dawson. I am in hopes you will find us returned generally to sentiments worthy of former times. in these it will be your [glory] to have steadily laboured & with as much effect as any man living. that you may long live to continue your useful labours & to [reap the] rewards in the thankfulness of nations is my sincere prayer. accept assurances of my high esteem & affectionate attachment.   TH: JEFFERSON

PrC (DLC); faint and blurred, with text in brackets supplied from *National Intelligencer*, 27 Apr. 1803; at foot of text: "Thomas Paine."

[1] Preceding three words interlined.
[2] Preceding two words interlined.
[3] Remainder of sentence interlined.

PAMPHLET: *Compact Maritime*.

From Henry Sheaff

HONOR'D SIR   Philada. 18 March 1801

I one of your fellow Citizens Rejoice; your being placed as Chief Magistrate at the Head of a free and enlighten Nation All Europe; must applaud, the Choice of the American people—that in successive Collectd Characters—who in the Feild and Counsel, Carried them threw a perilous struggle for there Liberties, against a powerfull, and ambitious nation—The Names of Washington Adams and Jefferson are known and Respected over all Europe—to you we look up to as a Father, and a Conciliator, to a people in the path of Ruin—My Confidence is placed in you as a Savior, that you will bring the ship to a Safe Mooring, to the Satisfaction of those concerned, and Establish that Harmony which ought to Exist in a powerfull Nation—

As Mr Dawson will soon sail for France, I make no doubt your order will accompany him, for your wines as I know your Taste and Judgement permit me to suggest to you, the Sparling Champn. should be Shipp'd in the month of october or November so as to be Landed here some time in January or February—Immediately plac'd on its arrival in your Cellar, Repacket and pack'd in sand on its Side—altho the still Champang is perferr'd in France the sparling in Amarica—this I experience in the Coarse of my Business—

Your opinion Respecting Burgundy as a Delicate wine will not stand the Sea. Will you order some for Trial Shipp'd at the same time say Cold season—If possible to have it packd in Saw Tust in the place of straw—I have seen some stand the Sea: was allow'd by Conniseurs to be equal with any they drank in France—Should it not prove to your Satisfaction; I shall take It at first Cost—

I should be happy to Receive your Commands: for any Kind of Wines or any other articles for your House Hold—untill your Stock arrives your orders shall be punctually compled with, Should the articcles not meet your Expectation they shall lay at my Risk—I have on hand the first quality of Made., Sherry, and the dry Lisbon, wine.

I was told by some Gentleman you wanted a Steward accustom'd to the French Cookery. I will mention to you Mr. Richardet and his wife. Many years lived with Mr Cazeno whose stile I make not doubt, you are acquant'd. for some time he kept the Coffe House in this City—

permit me to mention to your Excy. Genl. Thomas Proctor who has been a faithfull Revolutionary artillery officer, who in great measure has been neglected by your predecessors, whether from Political principal or Modesty [I can]not say. wishing you a Continuation of Good Health; with the greatest Respect I am

Your Excellencys most obedient Humble Servt.

Henry Sheaff

RC (MHi); addressed: "His Excy Thomas Jefferson Esqr President, U. States Washington"; franked; postmarked 23 Mch.; endorsed by TJ as received 26 Mch. and so recorded in SJL.

Henry Sheaff was a Philadelphia wine merchant at 180 Market Street (Stafford, *Philadelphia Directory, for 1801*, 15; MB, 2:809; Vol. 32:171, 406n).

From James D. Westcott

Sir,   Alexandria March 18th. 1801.—

Not claiming the pleasure of your personal acquaintance, it is with diffidence I presume to intrude upon your notice a subject of little importance. Occupied, as your attention must be, with the momentous affairs of the government an apology is necessary (and for that apology to your candor I cheerfully submit) for troubling you with the perusal of a statement in which no public question is involved, and in which individual feelings and interests are alone concerned.

Upwards of four years since, I commenced the publication of a Daily newspaper in the District of Columbia. 'Till within a few months past it has been the only diurnal print between Baltimore in Maryland and Charleston in South-Carolina. Nothing could have justified the embarking in an undertaking of so extensive and hazardous a nature, but a sanguine anticipation of the rapid increase of the wealth, population, and commerce of the town of Alexandria, and of the rising importance of the metropolis of the union:—Nothing could have induced a continuance, to the evident sacrafice of the interests of my family, after a prospect of a realization of my expectations had disappeared, but a conviction of duty to persevere in defence of those principles to which my paper had been devoted, in opposition to artfully-excited popular clamour. The eventual triumph of those principles for which my father, who is now connected with me in business, shared in the perils and the honors of the revolutionary war, and for which I have uniformly and unremittingly contended, affords a gratification of feeling amply sufficient to compensate for the difficulties I have been impelled to encounter while standing, *alone* of my profession in the District as the victim of political intolerance.

Apprized, however, of the intention of most of the printers within the territory of applying for the public work, I feel little hesitation in expressing a wish to participate in the public favors. Should I be so fortunate as to obtain a sufficient portion of your confidence as to warrant you in making "The Times, and District of Columbia Daily Advertizer," an organ of your official communications, or employing me to execute such a proportion of the public printing as it may be in my power to perform, no exertions shall be spared to merit every favour which may be assigned to me or every trust with which I may be honored. Should you conceive some other printer better entitled to the business I shall most cheerfully acquiesce in the decision of your Superior judgment, lamenting that my duty and my pecuniary interest continue to be unconnected, and that while a regard to my own conscience, impels me to discharge the one I am under the necessity of sacraficing the other.

I am with the greatest Respect Yours &c

JAMES D. WESTCOTT

RC (DNA: RG 59, LAR); at foot of text: "Thos. Jefferson Esqr. President of the United States"; endorsed by TJ as received 21 Mch. and so recorded in SJL; with notation by TJ: "to be handed for information to the heads of departments. Th: J. Mar. 22. 1801."

James D. Westcott and John V. Thomas established the Alexandria, Virginia, newspaper they called *The Times and Alexandria Advertiser* in 1797. Two years later the name became *The Times and District of Columbia Daily Advertiser*, and after Thomas's retirement Westcott continued in partnership with John Westcott until the partnership dissolved on 3 May 1802. Westcott discontinued the *Times* on 31 July 1802, when he began publishing a triweekly, but short-lived, paper, the *Columbian Advertiser; and Commercial, Mechanic, and Agricultural Gazette* (Brigham, *American Newspapers*, 1:492; 2:1107, 1110-11).

From Joseph Yznardi, Sr.

Exmo. Señor
Muy Señor mio, y de todo mi Respecto
En consequencia de la Orden de V.E me he presentado á el Secretario de Estado el qe me ha dicho no puede aser Nada hasta despachar la Fragata, y le Suplico tenga la vondad de prevenirle no me Olvide pues deseo retirarme á Philadelphia para despachar á mi Hijo á Concluir sus negocios en la Havana para regresarar á Cadiz á Continuar su Consulado
tengo encargadas oy Mismo tres medias Botas de Vino dos de Xerez una de Color, y otra Blanco, y la otra de Malaga especiales de Calidad, y propias para el gasto de su Mesa qe espero seran remitidas en primera Ocasion, y si V.E nessesita de otros Vinos de Europa tendra la bondad de prevenirmelo como quales quiera otra Cosa qe Nessesite
Mras tengo el Honor de Repetir á V.E mi Oba en George town 18 de Mazo de 1801
Exmo. Señor BLM de V.E. su mas Obte Serv

JOSEF YZNARDY

EDITORS' TRANSLATION

Most Excellent Sir
My most illustrious sir, and with all my respect
As a follow-up to Your Excellency's order I have presented myself to the secretary of state who has told me that he cannot do anything until the dispatch of the frigate, and I beg you to be so kind as not to let him forget me as I wish to go away to Philadelphia to send off my son to finish his business in Havana in order to return to Cadiz to continue his consulate.
Today I have ordered three half casks of wine, two from Jerez, one red, and another white, and the other from Malaga, distinctive for their quality, and worthy for consumption at your table, that I hope will be sent on first

occasion, and if Your Excellency needs other wines from Europe be so good as to notify me as you would with anything else you may need.

Meanwhile I have the honor of reiterating to Your Excellency my service in Georgetown 18 March 1801

Most excellent sir your most obedient servant kisses the hand of Your Excellency   JOSEF YZNARDY

RC (DLC); at foot of text: "Exmo. Sr.   LA FRAGATA: the *Maryland.*
Dn Thomas Jefferson"; endorsed by TJ
as received on the same day as written and
so recorded in SJL.

From Joseph Barnes

Messina March 19th. 1801 Sicily

In the postcript of my Last Feb. 22nd. I inform'd you, my best friend Mr Jefferson, that all the English Vessels at Naples had, from the order of the English Consul, withdrawn out into the Road—& most of the English were Shiping their property, which, tho' not then known here, was in consequence of the advancing of the French, who, having been met by commissioners from his Silician Majesty were Stop'd at the Limits of the Neapolitan States, and an armstice entred into; by *Virtue* of which all the English Vessels were Soon after order'd away from Naples—And, on the 2nd Instant all the English Vessels were order'd out of this Port in 24 hours!! pursuant to which, they have all Left this & every Port of Sicily—and a general prohibition of all provisions from being Ship'd by or for the English, Especially to Malta! Of consequence, circumstanc'd as the King of Naples is, he will be compell'd to continue the Ports of the two Sicilies Shut against the English 'till a general Peace; Should they not enter pr force, which is probable.—

Tis Said that a Treaty has Since been conclud'd between the King of Naples & the French, & is now before the King for his approof at Palermo—the purport of which however is not yet known—

Having now a Treaty with France, & being at Amity with the King of the two Sicilies, & the Princes of the Italian States; and having from the rights of Neutrality & Laws of Nations, full right, Should the English presume to prohibit our having free commerce into the Ports of France, Italy & Sicily, (except those Actually in a State of Siege,) hope the President of the Unit'd States will immediately Send a commissioner with full powers & Specific directions to remonstrate against demand & obtain free permission to entre all the Ports in question, not actually in a State of Siege, or the Ports of the Unit'd States Should be Shut against them—which at this moment would be ruin to England.—

Notice has been given here from the consul at Naples, that Should the Bay of Tripoli not receive Satisfactory answers to certain demands made by him of the Unit'd States before the 20th April ensuing, he will declare war against us—which hope may be Avoid'd by prompt proceedings of the U.S. in Sending Several Frigates & a commissioner to induce him immediately to pacific measures—To Pay well, will ever be found a Less evil than war with these Barbarians—or the consequences may be extremely Serious to our countrymen—for, not Long Since there were at once in this Port eight American Vessels! of course there must be many more in the Mediteranian—

With constant Solicitude for your health & happiness & preferment to the Presidency of the U.S I remain yours most respectfully

JOS: BARNES

P.S. Some doubts being entertain'd that Pennsylvan. will be depriv'd of Voting 'tis fear'd Mr Jefferson will Lose the Election—but, [Heavens forbid]—

RC (DNA: RG 59, LAR); endorsed by TJ as received 24 June and so recorded in SJL.

Barnes's LAST letter, dated 14 Feb. 1801, included the postscript of 22 Feb. and discussed the situation at NAPLES. Ferdinand, the king of Naples, was also monarch of the TWO SICILIES. Among other provisions, the treaty that he acceded to with France, signed at Florence on 29 Mch., closed the ports of his kingdoms to the British and called for garrisons of French troops in some ports (Tulard, *Dictionnaire Napoléon*, 729-30, 1225).

TRIPOLI and the United States signed a treaty in 1796 that the Senate ratified in June of the following year. Recognizing certain payments and gifts to Tripoli, the accord specified that the United States would not pay any ongoing annuity. On the arrival of James Leander Cathcart as the first American consul in 1799, however, the Tripolitans made additional demands, and by the spring of the following year Yusuf Qaramanli (Karamanli), who ruled as pasha and also commanded the country's military forces as bey, began to press for a new arrangement

with the United States. Yusuf had seized power in Tripoli not long before the negotiation of the treaty, following prolonged intrigue and warfare against his brothers, his father, and a rival from outside the country. As pasha he set out to enlarge Tripoli's power and demonstrate its autonomy, forcing several European nations to negotiate new tribute payments to protect their commerce from his fleet. He told Cathcart that he had agreed to unfavorable terms with the United States because of the influence of Ali Hassan, the dey of Algiers, to whom Yusuf had felt some obligation but who had died in 1798. Displeased by what he perceived as greater favor shown to Algiers and Tunis, Yusuf insisted that he get something "more substantial than compliments," as Cathcart expressed it, to prove the good will of the United States. In May 1800 the pasha sent John Adams an obliquely worded letter, making no outright demand for money but insisting that his country be treated as the equal of the other Barbary states. Showing a readiness to send corsairs against American shipping, Yusuf announced in October 1800 that if he did not have a response from the U.S. in six months he would declare war. Cathcart proclaimed Tripoli to be in violation of the treaty and requested the intervention of Mustafa, Ali Hassan's successor, since the treaty designated the dey of Algiers as the arbitrator of any dispute over the terms. Yusuf, hinting that he might lessen his demands if Algiers stayed out of the negotiation, stated that the price of a new treaty would be $225,000 plus continuing annual payments of $20,000. In January and February 1801, Cathcart notified other U.S. consuls that war appeared imminent and that the Tripolitans would likely begin seizing American ships before the announced April deadline. Noting that Tripoli had used captured ships and crews to exact high ransom and annuity payments from Sweden, Cathcart urged his fellow consuls to keep American merchant vessels out of the Mediterranean. John S. M. Matthieu was the U.S. consul at Naples (Miller, *Treaties*, 2:xx-xxii, 349-85; ASP, *Foreign Relations*, 2:347-57; Cathcart to Yusuf, 19 Feb. 1801, in DNA: RG 59, CD; NDBW, 1:314, 322-4, 330-2, 421-2; Madison, *Papers, Sec. of State Ser.*, 1:4-5; Kola Folayan, *Tripoli During the Reign of Yusuf Pasha Qaramanli* [Ile-Ife, Nigeria, 1979], 7-21, 25-35, 58; Robert J. Allison, *The Crescent Obscured: The United States and the Muslim World, 1776-1815* [Chicago, 1995], 56, 168-9; JEP, 1:209).

From Thomas Cogswell

State of Newhampshire
SIR   Gilmanton March 19th 1801

Permit me Sir altho a Stranger and at a remote corner of the United States to be among the Number of your Numerous Friends to congratulate you on your appointment to the first office in the United States—and while I admire the Tallents of a Washington—and the Abilities of an Addams—I am no less pleased with your Appointment to the Presidental chair of the United States of America, Especially at a time when Republicism to appearances was trembling to the very centre From this Expression permit me to observe that I marched at the head of a Body of Volunteers for Lexington Battle in 1775—that I shared in the fatigues of the Army at Bunkers hill—at New york and white plains was at the Surrender of Burgoin—was with Sullivan on the Island of Rhode Island was at the Battle of Monmouth and the Winter following took the charge of one of Principle Departments of the Quartermaster Under Mr Pickering and was at the Surrender of Cornwallis and closed my services on the 15 of January 1784 almost nine years. Dureing that Period I sowed the seeds of Republicinism so affectually as Never to be Eradicated and haveing a share in the Executive part of the army I was fully convinced that a Republican Goverment—*so pleasing in Theory*—might be fully put in practice in any Country provided those who were appointed to the Executive part of the Goverment Did not conclude that the Goverment Originated soley for there use to Agrandise themselves and

[365]

Families—Impressed with these Ideas—I retired to this place to enjoy that peace in Family Retirement so Agreable to most People after many years of fatigue and troble—I am no Candidate for any office Neither do I wish any Removed unless it is for Malepractice in office missconduct in life or against the States and United States Goverment—

And may your Administration be as Agreable to the United States as your appointment is Pleasing to your Numerous Friends is the wish and prayer of your Friend

and Most Obedient Humble Servant   THOMAS COGSWELL

RC (DLC); at foot of text: "Thomas Jefferson Esqr President of the United States of America"; endorsed by TJ as received 16 Apr. and so recorded in SJL.

During the Revolutionary War, Thomas Cogswell (1746-1810) attained the rank of lieutenant colonel of the 15th Massachusetts Regiment by 1779 and then served as wagonmaster general in the Quartermaster Department. A prominent Antifederalist, then a Republican, in New Hampshire he served as a judge on the court of common pleas from 1784 until his death (*Appleton's Cyclopedia of American Biography,* 11 vols. [New York, 1887-1928], 1:680; Lynn Warren Turner, *The Ninth State: New Hampshire's Formative Years* [Chapel Hill, 1983], 134, 142, 150).

To Philippe de Létombe

DEAR SIR   Washington Mar. 19. 1801.

I was honored last night with your favor of the 15th. by mr Rapin, and owe you a thousand acknolegements for the trouble you are so good as to take, & still to offer with respect to the procuring a cook. I mentioned to Rapin that you had your choice of two. he said he did not know who they were, but he imagined one was of the name of Julien, as he was known to M. Flamand, and he should prefer him to any one that he thought was to be procured in Philadelphia. I only mention this as his opinion, to which you will give as much attention only as your better judgment shall deem proper. I have understood that 20. Dollars a month is what is given for the best French cook: however the Chevalr. d'Yrujo having been so kind as to undertake to get the one which he deemed the best in Philadelphia, I authorised him to go [as] far as 25. Dols. the man was satisfied with the wages as liberal, but his engagements retained him. I should therefore think any one you would approve cheap enough at 20. Dollars, but would go as far as 25. rather than fail. Julien has a wife; but whether she can do any thing in the house Rapin does not know. if she can, I should be willing to make any addition for her services you should deem reasonable. you see, my dear Sir, what confidence I have in your goodness & friendship when I propose to employ them on such trifles. but we are such helpless creatures that if we did not aid one another, we should be in a dreary situation.—the cook may come at any time he pleases between this & the 15th. of April, only letting me know that I may depend on him. I leave this about the 29th. instant to be absent three weeks. I am sensible of your goodness in the civil things you say of my address. my object is to re-harmonize my countrymen, without abandoning republican principles.—accept assurances of my high consideration and affectionate attachment.

TH: JEFFERSON

PrC (MHi); torn; at foot of text: "M. Letombe"; endorsed by TJ in ink on verso.

From George Meade

MY DEAR SIR   Philada. March 19th. 1801—

After telling you, as Mr Jefferson, (not as President of the United States) that I am hurt that my letter of 17th Ulto has been Passed over in Silence,—Permit me to call Your Immediate & Pointed attention to the office of John Hall Esqr our Marshall. Common Fame says you are about Removing him. I hope as is often the Case, Common fame, will prove untrue. be it as it may, I request & intreat you Sir, not to Remove him. I ask this with as much earnestness, as if I was applying for the office for myself, he is a good officer, & an upright honest man, has a large family say 8 or 9 Children with a most Amiable Wife. Your Continuing him in office, without you can & will give him a letter, I shall esteem & deem a favor Conferrd on me—do let me without delay, have Your Answer on this business—

It was my full Intention to have Paid you my Personal Respects early next week. I am just told I should miss you, as you would be gone home— Mr Thornton, gave me this Information. Mr Tracey (who I never before exchanged one word with) was with Mr Thornton at the time. I freely told him, I reprobated the Conduct of the New England States, by not giving you one & all their Votes & their Country man, Mr Adams for making appointments, a few days indeed a Few hours before he went out of office (& as the Present Company was always exceptd) the Senate for Confirming them. Mr Thornton heard the whole Conversation & I added it was a Pity Mr. Adams had not learnt by his Travels abroad some little manners—as we were here told he left the Capital at 4 in the Morning. when You were to be Proclaimed President at 12—

I am Sorry You have Removed Mr Kittera. I have not much acquaintance, only a [Short] one, but I know he has always been friendly to our Government & if he had attended to his Law Practice he would have amply provided for his large family, say 6. or 7 Children & an Amiable Wife, if he had not unfortunately for them, gone into Congress.—do when you have an oppy., give him an Appointment equal at least to what you *have deprived him of.*

While your honor is in a giving humour any good office of 2, 3 or more Thousand Pounds a year during good behaviour, I would not Refuse myself. be believe me always My dear Sir

Your affn friend, obliged, devoted, & most Obedt. hble Servt.

GEO— MEADE

RC (DLC); at foot of text: "President of the United States"; endorsed by TJ as received 23 Mch. and so recorded in SJL.

TRACEY: Uriah Tracy, U.S. senator from Connecticut.

From Francis Peyton

DEAR SIR,   Alexandria 19th. March 1801.

When last at Alexandria you were pleased to express a wish that I would point out to you a character who in my opinion would be best calculated to fill the office of judge of the Orphans court, After reflecting on the subject I am induced to believe Colo. George Gilpin would be equal to the duties of that office, and would generally unite the confidence of the County. He is considered as possessing tolerable good abilities and great integrity, has resided in this place thirty years, upwards of twenty of which he has served in the commission of the Peace.

I would observe however that as this Office is not known under the laws of our state, but was created by the adoption of a law of Maryland I feel myself at a loss with respect to the qualifications requisite in a judge, and in my Selection of Colo. Gilpin have been influenced by an opinion that a legal education is not indispense necessary,

I am with great respect Yr. Obt. Servt.   FRANCIS PEYTON

RC (DNA: RG 59, LAR); endorsed by TJ as received 20 Mch. and so recorded in SJL.

TJ appointed Alexandria merchant and justice of the peace GEORGE GILPIN a

judge of the Orphan's Court of Alexandria County on 14 May in place of John Herbert, a "midnight appointment" of John Adams (Washington, *Diaries*, 4:141n; Appendix I, List 4; JEP, 1:388, 402, 404).

To Thomas Mann Randolph

TH:J. to TMR.   Washington Mar. 19. 1801.

I snatch half a moment to inform you that a circumstance has occurred which will inevitably keep me a week longer or thereabouts. in the mean time my horses will wait I presume at Heron's. my tender love to my dear Martha, & the little ones. Affectionate attachment to yourself.

P.S. I do not know if there is any merit in the music inclosed. It has been sent to me.

RC (DLC); endorsed by Randolph. PrC (MHi); lacks postscript; endorsed by TJ in ink on verso. Enclosure: "The People's Friend," music by John Isaac Hawkins (see Charles Willson Peale to TJ, 8 Mch. 1801).

From Hugh Rose

DEAR SIR   Winchester Virga. March 19. 1801

I flatter myself that your personal acquaintance with my Father and Family will be a sufficient apology for writing to you on the present occasition—At different times I have been in the army three years & Still continue to like a military life, though I confess my low situation is a mortification I am an orderly Serjeant doing the duty of An Officer without the pay—I have written to all my democrat friends to represent my situation to you & to beseech a Commission I coud get letters of recommendation from all the Officers who have Commanded, but think it needless as they are Adamites.

I am D Sir with regard & Esteem your Fre & Humble Servant

HUGH ROSE, son
of H Rose of Amhers deceased

RC (DNA: RG 59, LAR); endorsed by TJ as received 23 Mch. and so recorded in SJL.

Hugh Rose was the son of Hugh Rose of Amherst County, Virginia. TJ and his family stayed with the elder Rose after their flight from Monticello in 1781. Hugh Rose the younger did not receive a commission during TJ's administration and later moved to Augusta, Georgia (W. G. Stanard, *A Chart of the Ancestors and Descendants of Rev. Robert Rose* [Richmond, 1895]; Vol. 4:261; Vol. 23:503).

To Madame de Tessé

DEAR MADAM   Washington Mar. 19. 1801.

After so long a time & such various events, I take the liberty of recalling myself to your recollection. a letter I recieved yesterday from the Marquis de la Fayette informed me you were living in Paris. this is the only certain information I have recieved of the place where you were, except once by mr Gautier to whom I immediately addressed a letter for you, which I hope you recieved. I congratulate you sincerely on your return to your own country. from my knowledge of your physical & moral constitution I am sure you cannot be as happy in any other. from the same circumstances I have been satisfied your sufferings must have been great during your absence. I assure you with truth, Madam, that I have felt much for you, and partaken sincerely of the afflictions you must have felt. the convulsions of Europe have agitated even this country, & though in a small degree comparatively, yet more than I had imagined possible. we are now removed from them, & I hope from the public papers your country is also in a great degree. since my return, I have not been permitted to enjoy much those fine poplars of which you used to speak with such rapture. it would have been a great consolation to me on your account could I have known that your charming gardens at Chaville had been preserved to you unhurt. they have been the subject of my frequent enquiries, but without recieving information. I presume however they have suffered in the general run. perhaps you will now prefer adopting flowers, instead of trees, as promising earlier enjoiment. the very great civilities & even proofs of friendship by which you distinguished me in Paris, have made an indelible impression on my mind, and I shall for ever take an anxious concern in your happiness. it would give me great pleasure to learn that you are restored to the comforts of your former situation: that you enjoy good health, that M. de Tessé is also in health, and that you are both happy in the midst of your friends. accept I pray you the assurances of my constant and sincere affection, and the homage of my high consideration & respect.   TH: JEFFERSON

PrC (DLC); at foot of text: "Made. de Tessé."

LETTER I RECEIVED YESTERDAY: the letter from Lafayette printed at 10 Jan. 1801 (Vol. 32:427-32).

TJ had last written Madame de Tessé on 6 Sep. 1795, soon after learning from the banker Jean Antoine GAUTIER, who had written on 24 Mch. of that year, that the comtesse was still in Switzerland. TJ sent that letter to Madame de Tessé and one to Gautier of 7 Sep. in a communication to James Monroe, who was then in France; see Vol. 28:448, 451-4.

During TJ's residence in France and after his return to the United States he endeavored to obtain plants and seeds from Virginia, South Carolina, and elsewhere for the comtesse's formal garden at CHAVILLE, between Paris and Versailles. Before the French Revolution she had employed a British gardener and attempted to cultivate a variety of American plants and trees. In a letter to Lafayette on 16 June 1792, TJ wondered if Madame de Tessé might have preferred residing "under the Poplars of Virginia" to living in Switzerland (Vol. 9:228-30, 238, 253-5, 505-6; Vol. 10:xxvii, 178 [illus.], 514n; Vol. 11:121-2, 187, 233, 253; Vol. 13:xxx, 110, 137-8, 187, 476-7, 480 [illus.], 483-5; Vol. 16:223n, 226-8).

To Pierre Samuel Du Pont
de Nemours

Washington Mar. 20. 1801.

How many hard struggles, my dear friend, would it save me, had I really parted with my last vice on the 3d. of March. I thought you had known me better: but as you do not, I must endeavor to conceal, if I cannot eradicate, what remains amiss.

I recommended to the Secretary at war your proposition on the subject of clothing. he wishes to avail himself of it and has instructed the proper agent to apply to you on the subject. my respects & good wishes attend Made. Dupont and your other precious relations. their personal merit gives them a double right to my esteem. to yourself health, happiness & my sincere affections.   TH: JEFFERSON

RC (DeGH); addressed: "M. Dupont de Nemours New York"; franked; postmarked 21 Mch.

LAST VICE: see Du Pont de Nemours to TJ, 20 Feb. 1801.

Du Pont's PROPOSITION was an offer to purchase military clothing that might be "on hand in the public stores & not immediately wanted by the United States." He made the proposal in a letter of 1 Mch. received by TJ on the 6th. That letter has not been found, but is recorded in SJL and in the War Department's correspondence registers (DNA: RG 107, RLRMS).

From Andrew Ellicott

DEAR SIR   Philadelphia March 20th. 1801

I have enclosed the first 12 pages of my astronomical observations:—you will perceive they are intended as an appendix to another work, and which I fear, I shall not be able to put to the press in less than six, or seven months.—I began with the observations at this time, to make the trouble as little as possible, both to the printer, who is now at work upon the fifth volume of our transactions (in which they will appear) and to myself.—You will find the observations much more numerous than you expect;—the printer informs me that they will not occupy less than 150 or 160 pages.— there are certainly four, or five times as many, as were ever made by an individual in the same time, situated as I was.—The calculations were a work of great labour, and in which I had no assistance, and could derive none from any of the party except Mr. Dunbar, who was with us but a short time, and to whose uncommon talents I have endeavoured to do justice.—If you have no objection, I will forward the subsequent sheets as they are worked off, and if you should find any amusement in looking over them, I shall esteem it a singular favour if you would point out any material errors, that they may be corrected in the last sheet.

I have received your note of the 13th., and return you my most cordial thanks for the interest you have taken in my business, and as soon as the printer gets thro' with the observations, I shall repair to the City of Washington.—

I am sir with sincere esteem and regard your friend & Hl. Servt

ANDW. ELLICOTT

RC (DLC); at foot of text: "President of the U.S. and of the A.P.S."; endorsed by TJ as received 23 Mch. and so recorded in SJL. Enclosure: see below.

Ellicott's detailed record of astronomical and meteorological OBSERVATIONS

from the survey of the boundary between the United States and the Spanish territory of the East and West Floridas appeared in APS, *Transactions*, 5 (1802), 203-311; see also Ellicott to TJ, 28 May, 17 Oct., 21 Dec. 1800, 18 Jan. 1801.

To Albert Gallatin

Mar. 20. 1801.

The inclosed, tho' false and frivolous, yet requires to be answered with care. the other side of the medal requires to be shewn. we may safely admit there are talents of a certain kind on the other side; because all the talents which were venal have been bought up by the administration. Smith has refused. an offer is made to Jones. Duval has also refused & an offer is made to Kelty. health, respect & sincere attachment. I add no signature because unnecessary.

RC (NHi: Gallatin Papers); addressed: "Albert Gallatin esquire New Geneva"; franked; postmarked 21 Mch. Not recorded in SJL. Enclosure: Robert G. Harper to Constituents, 5 Mch. 1801 (printed on four folio pages in same; at foot of text in Harper's hand: "NB. I have omitted to mention that the federalists begat all the Children!").

REQUIRES TO BE ANSWERED: the circular by Robert G. Harper was a farewell address to his constituents. It was widely reprinted in pamphlet form (see *A Letter from Robert Goodloe Harper, of South Carolina, to His Constituents* [Providence, 1801]; Shaw-Shoemaker, No. 614). Harper reviewed the accomplishments of the Federalists in foreign and domestic policy from the establishment of the federal government in 1789 to the transfer of power in 1801, at which time the Republicans inherited "peace abroad; order and a well established government at home; a national character exalted; public credit firmly established; a respectable and increasing navy; a decreasing debt; a prosperous agriculture; a flourishing commerce; an augmenting revenue not felt by the people; and a balance in the treasury to the amount of two millions and a half of dollars." All the Republicans had to do was "preserve things in their present state" (Noble E. Cunningham, Jr., ed., *Circular Letters of Congressmen to Their Constituents, 1789-1829*, 3 vols. [Chapel Hill, 1978], 1:247-65).

To Joseph Mathias Gérard
de Rayneval

DEAR SIR   Washington Mar. 20. 1801

Mr. Pichon, who arrived two days ago, delivered me your favor of Jan. 1. and I had before recieved one by mr Dupont dated Aug. 24. 99. both on the subject of lands claimed on the behalf of your brother mr Gèrard, and that of Aug. 24. containing a statement of the case. I had verbally explained to mr Dupont at the time, what I presumed to have been the case, which must I believe be very much mistaken in the statement sent with that letter, and I[1] expected he had communicated it to you.

During the regal government two companies called the Loyal, and the Ohio companies had obtained grants from the crown for 800,000, or 1,000,000 of acres of land each, on the Ohio, on condition of settling them in a given number of years. they surveyed some & settled them; but the war of 1755. came on & broke up the settlements. after it was over they petitioned for a renewal. four other large companies then formed themselves called the Missisipi, the Ilinois, the Wabash & the Indiana companies, each praying for immense quantities of land, some [amounting] to 200 miles square, so that they proposed to cover[2] the whole country North between the Ohio & Missisipi, & a great portion of what is South. all these petitions were depending, without any answer whatever from the crown when the revolution war broke out. the petitioners had associated to themselves some of the [nobility] of England, & most of the characters in America of great influence. when Congress assumed the government, they took some of their body in as partners, to obtain their influence, and I remember to have heard at the time that one of them took mr Gèrard as a partner, expecting by that to obtain the influence of the French court, to obtain grants of those lands which they had not been able to obtain from the British government. all these lands were within the limits of Virginia, and that state determined peremptorily that they never should be granted to large companies, but left open equally to all: and when they passed their land law (which I think was in 1778.) they confirmed only so much of the lands of the Loyal company as they had actually surveyed, which was a very small proportion, and annulled every other pretension and when that state conveyed the lands to Congress (which was not till 178[4].) so determined were they to prevent their being granted to these or any other large companies, that they made it an express condition of the cession that they should be applied first towards the souldiers' bounties and the residue³ sold for the paiment of the national debt, and for no other purpose. this disposition has been accordingly rigorously made, and is still going on, and Congress considers itself as having no authority to dispose of them otherwise.

I will particularly note the errors in the statement of Aug. 99.[—]it says the Congress granted to the Wabash company the lands on that river dividing them into 82. lots—Congress never meddled with them (much less granted them) till after the cession of Virginia. the Company consisted perhaps of [82.] persons, & of course the lands, if they had been obtained, would have been divided into so many lots.—it says Congress made this grant to mr Gèrard as a proof of their esteem &c. Mr. Gèrard left this country in 1779. the cession of lands by Virginia to Congress was not till 1780.—it says that this intention of Congress was submitted to Louis [XVI.] who [au]thorised his minister to accept it. I believe the fact was that when the Wabash company proposed to associate mr Gèrard as a partner, he thought it necessary first to ask leave from his sovereign, who gave his consent. but in all this transaction Congress had nothing to do & meddled not.

I sincerely wish Sir, it had been in my power to have given you a more agreeable account of this claim. but as the case actually is, the most substantial service is to state it exactly, and not to foster false expectations. I remember with great sensibility all the attentions you were so good as to render me while I resided in Paris, and shall be made happy by every occasion which can be given me of acknowleging them, and the expressions of your friendly recollection are particularly soothing to me. accept I pray you the assurances of my high consideration & constant esteem   Th: Jefferson

PrC (DLC); faint and blurred; at foot of first page: "M. de Rayneval."

For a description of the STATEMENT that accompanied Gérard de Rayneval's letter of 24 Aug. 1799, see Vol. 31:175-6n. For TJ's involvement in the creation of the Virginia LAND LAW of 1778, see Vol. 2:133-67.

¹ TJ here canceled "presumed."
² TJ first wrote "they covered" before altering the clause to read as above.
³ Preceding nine words interlined.

From Christian G. Hahn

Boston, 20 Mch. 1801. He asks TJ's pardon for approaching him with a request. Two years ago he arrived in the U.S. and then had the misfortune of falling ill for 18 months, which depleted his little savings. He learned his trade from his father, the famous mechanic Pastor Hahn of Württemberg. After the death of his father, he went to Berlin and worked as a watch and clockmaker under a concession from King Frederick William II. Following the king's death, he went to America and desires nothing now except to reenter his trade. Lacking friends to help him obtain the 200 taler necessary to purchase tools, he asks if TJ would help him to make his living in this country, promising TJ his first sample of a mechanical watch. He also makes watches for ladies and a variety of other time pieces. A prompt reply and a patent are requested.

RC (DLC); 2 p.; in German; endorsed by TJ as received "about" 25 Mch.

Christian Gottfried Hahn (b. 1769) was the son of Philipp Matthäus Hahn, a minister, inventor, and maker of precision mechanical instruments, including clocks and one of the first mechanical calculating machines (Hans R. Jenemann, "Der Mechanicker-Pfarrer Philipp Matthäus Hahn und die Ausbreitung der Feinmechanik in Südwestdeutschland," *Zeitschrift für Württembergische Landesgeschichte*, 46 [1987], 117-61).

Hahn wrote TJ another letter from Boston on 4 May, which was translated from German by Jacob Wagner, a clerk in the State Department. Repeating his request for employment, Hahn wrote, "I am more than 31 years old and my character will not admit of my begging for money." He beseeched TJ "not to overlook my request, as I have neither friends nor relations and therefore I have sought a friend" (Tr in DLC, translation in Wagner's hand; RC in same, in German, endorsed by TJ as received 16 May and so recorded in SJL).

From John Hobby

Portland District of

MAY IT PLEASE YOUR EXCELLENCY.   Maine March 20th 1801.

Altho to you Sir I am personally unknown, I am induc'd from a consciencious belief that I have deserved a better fate to state to you my past services, & my present distressed seituation, flattering myself that if it is in your power it will afford you pleasure to relieve the distresses of an inocent family reduced to necessity & want, and if it is not, that you will not be offended with the following lines—Seven years of the best of my life was devoted to the service of my country during the Revolutionary War with the British Nation, received as a compensation fifty Cents on the pound being compell'd to dispose of my certificates to give support to an Aged Mother, after whose Death I sat down in this place in the mercantile line, as soon as the Genl. Government was established, & District Courts form'd, I received from Genl. Dearborn an appointment of Deputy Marshal after his appointment to Congress I received from President Washington a Commission as Marshal of the district of

Maine, in which office I remain'd nearly eight years, for several years the office but poorly supported my Horse expences, while other Marshals in large Capitols & Cyties were accumilating estates subjected to very little labor or fatigue. Experiencing that my public business frequently interfered with that of my private concerns, and the latter with the former, I perceived it necessary either to dismiss my private business or give up that of the public, but with a little ambition to soar above the commonnallity together with repeated assurances throug the medium of Mr. Adams's family that my name was first on the list for a more lucretive appointment induced me to prefer that of the public, while feeding myself with pleasing expectations, some intriguing incendiary and suppos'd low Character, prevailed on a Barber, & shoemaker, who owned part of a Vessell which I was obliged to take from them to secure a public demand to prefer without my knowlege in a most secret way, a complaint against me to President adams, who threw it into the hands of the then Secretary of the Treasury, & altho the complaint was founded on suspicion only, I was without warning—without time to adjust my accounts, without liberty of stating a syllable by way of defence, as it were with the stroke of a pen dashed out of office deprived of all means of support, & in this helpless seituation I have remain'd more than two years, during which I have had the painfull experience of long expensive sickness & repeated Deaths in my family. Expensive prosesses of a public as well as local nature is the natural result of misfortune, untill I am now reduced from a small but in[. . .] patrimony which was attched to my Wife not only to indijent circumstances, but almost to a Morsel of Bread, and am still by a C[. . .] [. . .]eferres brot in Debt to the goverment, a sum I never can discharge but by the De[t] of nature, unless I can be discharged from my present state of painfull suspence and enter into some business that may ena[ble m]e to do it some few years hence.—From a consideration of a life having been almost intirely devoted to public service with little or no compensation I have been induced to have recource to your Excellecy's clemency praying if it is not inconsistant with the duties of the important office you sustain, that my mind & the wants of a tender family dear to me, who naturally look to a Parent for support, and who had once a right to believe themselves born to a better fate may be restor'd to quietude & peace by either a limited or entire discharge of the public demand on me that I may be an enabled to embrace the first offers of any kind of decent business. Genl. Dearborn to whom I have been long personnally known & to whom I have related some particulars of the treatment I have received & the consequent misfortunes which followed will I believe substantiate this statement so far as he has been acquainted or inform'd.—

I am Sir with great respect & Esteem for your Excellencys name & Character your most obedt. Hble Sert   JOHN HOBBY

RC (DNA: RG 59, LAR); torn; at foot of text: "President Jefferson"; endorsed by TJ as received 30 Apr. and so recorded in SJL.

John Hobby (ca. 1750-1802) was an officer in the Continental Army from 1777 to 1784, holding the rank of captain in the 16th Massachusetts Regiment at the end of his service. He succeeded Henry Dearborn as federal marshal for the district of Maine in April 1793 and was reappointed to the same post in January 1798. He was replaced by Isaac Parker in March 1799. In 1801 the U.S. government obtained a judgment against Hobby to recover monies he received while marshal for use of the federal government amounting to $5,834.67. Imprisoned, he unsuccessfully petitioned Congress in December 1801 for his release, citing his past service, advanced age, and declining health. He was deceased by the following May (Heitman, *Register*, 40, 61, 293; *Letter from the Secretary of the Treasury, Accompanying His Report on the Petition of John Hobby, Late Marshal of the District of Maine* [Washington, 1802], 5-7; Shaw-Shoemaker, No. 3321; JEP, 1:142, 144, 258, 325, 327; JHR, 4:16, 49, 73; *Jenks' Portland Gazette*, 4 Jan., 10 May 1802; Vol. 25:316-17).

From Henry Ingle

SIR/   Fryday March 20th 1801

The bearer hereof is a young man who has a mind to enter into your employ at Monticello, he came well recommended to me, and I am rather inclined to think that he is a good workman,   his step father is a very ingenious and good workman he did the work of those large houses belonging to Mr Miradith at the corner of ninth and markett street in Phila. and likewise of those which were built by Mr Cook at the corner of third and markett street, from the fathers abilities—and the son's learning with the father, and from his being employed to do the stare case in the presidents house I make no doubt but what he will sute you, his father by the approbation of Mr Trump has recommended him to me requesting I would endeavour to get him employ—

If you should have occasion of a carpenter to attend your house here and are not already suted, I beg leave to recommend Mr James Grimes, he is at present at work for me and I believe he will give you satisfaction both in attention and execution.

I am Sir Your Obdt Servt   HENRY INGLE

RC (MHi); at foot of text: "Mr Jefferson"; endorsed by TJ as received 20 Mch. and so recorded in SJL.

Henry Ingle (1764-1822), a Philadelphia cabinetmaker who did work for TJ during the 1790s, moved to Washington, D.C., in 1800. He established a hardware store on New Jersey Avenue near the Capitol where TJ purchased tools and ironmongery (*National Intelligencer*, 8 Dec. 1800; *Daily National Intelligencer*, 3 Oct. 1822; RCHS, 33-4 [1932], 210-11; MB, 2:810, 1132).

BEARER HEREOF: James Oldham (Daniel Trump to TJ, 12 Mch. 1801; MB, 2:1035).

A letter from Ingle to TJ of 21 Jan. 1800, recorded in SJL as received the same day, and TJ's response of 28 Jan. have not been found.

From Jacob Lewis

Washington, 20 Mch. 1801. A sense of duty prompts him to present this memorial. He was appointed consul to the Île de France and Bourbon Island a few months before communication was interrupted between the United States and France. He departed with his family planning to make his permanent residence there; after a six-month passage he arrived and immediately purchased and furnished a house. Expenditures for the move amounted to at least $15,000, which he hoped to recover through mercantile transactions. Shortly after he settled there the passage of the nonintercourse act cut off the means he "had Calculated on, for a Subsistence." He received no news from the U.S. government. He became "obnoxious" to the French colonial government and was left with the "ungracious Task of remonstrating, Claiming, petitioning, & defending, property belonging to american Subjects arrested in that Quarter of the Globe, but all to little effect." Finding he could neither render his countrymen satisfaction nor his country service, he resolved to return to the United States. He borrowed money, purchased a vessel, and received permission from the governor-general to depart. When he arrived in Boston, his native city, the president requested that he return to the French islands on a special mission, a request he declined for health reasons. He was then asked to suggest to Secretary of State Pickering measures "to prevent the Isle of france from depredating on our Commerce." When he arrived in Philadelphia, Lewis found that the secretary of state had already appointed "a person, recommended by Willings & Francis the British Agents for their West India Colonies" and fixed the principles for the negotiations. Lewis predicted that the mission would not succeed and "lost the good graces" of the secretary of state. He soon learned from friends that efforts were being made to replace him because of his political opinions although when asked about the appointment, Adams assured Lewis that his commission was permanent. When Lewis learned that the French islands were ready to negotiate with the U.S. government, he tried to return but could find no "flag of Truce, with french passengers" and he abandoned the project. In the meantime the U.S. commissioners arrived from France and Lewis prepared to return to his consular position as soon as the convention with France was ratified. On his way to receive instructions from the state department, he learned from a newspaper that George Stacey, who was serving as his agent, had been named to replace him. He inquired of the acting secretary of state "whether the appointment was peremtory, or whether Intended to fill the Vacancy in the Consulate, during my Absence." With the consular commission in his pocket and the "positive assurance" given by President Adams, he had already sent instructions to the Île de France to prepare for his arrival. He suggests four reasons for the former president's actions: 1. "Incompetency." 2. In the presence of Adams's friends, he had declared "that there lives In America, a greater man than himself." 3. In the congressional election in Massachusetts he supported men not of Adams's choice. 4. Because he is a "Federal Republican" and dares think for himself. He has sacrificed half his fortune while in the service of his country and now is "threatned by a Cruel unprecedented Act of revenge by the Ex President, *at the last moment of his expiring power.*" He pleads with TJ to find some way to relieve his situation, noting "you will Render an Infinite servise *to one who ever has, & ever will, support you.*" If necessary he will obtain letters of recommendation from a number of TJ's friends, including John Mason, the bank president, James Martin, "*whose Tallents and pen, has long been devoted to you,*" and Elbridge Gerry.

RC (DNA: RG 59, LAR); 4 p.; at head of text: "Thomas Jefferson President of the United States"; at foot of text: "at John Mason Esqre"; endorsed by TJ as received 20 Mch. and so recorded in SJL.

On 31 May 1797, John Adams nominated Jacob Lewis, a Boston merchant, as consul for the Île de France. The next day Lewis's commission was issued, which he registered with the authorities of the Île de France and Bourbon Island on 21 Feb. 1798. About six months later, he protested against excessive duties imposed on American ships by the colonial government. The interruption of U.S. commerce with the French colonies led Lewis to seek permission from Governor Malartic to return with his family to Boston, where he arrived by June 1799. In August,

Secretary of State Pickering sent Samuel S. Cooper on a special mission to the Île de France to restore commerce. Cooper returned in early 1800, before receiving a reply to his proposal. The Senate's qualified approval of the Convention of 1800 in February 1801 brought the resumption of trade with the French islands, but Lewis learned that he had been replaced. In July 1801 TJ appointed him consul to Calcutta, but Lewis learned in London in March 1802 that the British government had refused to issue him an exequatur and he returned to the United States (Toussaint, *Mauritius*, 10-12, 18-19, 36-48, 56-60; JEP, 1:242; Madison, *Papers, Sec. of State Ser.*, 2:40, 3:96; Appendix I, List 4; Samuel Smith to TJ, [before 12 Mch. 1801]).

From John Thomson Mason

DEAR SIR George Town 20th March 1801.

Mr William Kelty is a man of learning, of sound knowledge in the law, of exemplary life, unexceptionable character, and much respected in the State of Maryland. Altho' a man of real worth, he does not possess that address and readiness of expression or action, which compel all who see him to acknowledge his merit, those who know him well value him highly. I know no man in this State or in the neighbourhood of this place, in the other State, that would accept the appointment, so well calculated to fill it. In Virginia you are much better acquainted with the characters of professional men than I am. I do not think Mr Kelty upon a level in point of talents, with such men as Messrs George Hay, John Wickham, and some others I could mention, at the bar of your State Courts. I have no hesitation however to say that he is superior to what Mr T. Johnson now is, or to either of those named for his associates.

No letter addressed to Mr Kelty by post can reach him in time to have his attendance here on Monday. The direct post to Annapolis left this yesterday, and goes but once a week. From Baltimore to Annapolis the Mail goes twice a week, on Mondays, and on Saturdays, so that no letter by that rout can reach him until Monday night.

Accept the best wishes of one who is with real respect & esteem Your Obedt Servt JOHN T. MASON

RC (DNA: RG 59, LAR); endorsed by TJ as received 20 Mch. and so recorded in SJL; TJ later canceled "Mason John T." and added "Kilty" to his endorsement.

John Thomson Mason (1765-1824), younger brother of Virginia Senator Stevens Thomson Mason, was a Georgetown attorney who actively campaigned for TJ in the elections of 1796 and 1800. He was defeated for a seat in the Maryland House of Delegates in 1800. Shortly after TJ took office, he appointed him U.S. attorney for the District of Columbia (Bryan, *National Capital*, 1:411-12, 414;

Madison, *Papers, Sec. of State Ser.*, 1:66; Vol. 29:197n; Vol. 30:13n; Stevens Thomson Mason to TJ, 5 Sep. and 17 Oct. 1800).

For the appointment of Thomas JOHNSON as chief judge for the District of Columbia and James Marshall and William Cranch as HIS ASSOCIATES, see List of John Adams's Appointments, 23 Feb. 1801, and JEP, 1:386-7.

On this date TJ sent a LETTER by express to William Kilty offering him the office of chief judge of the Circuit Court of the District of Columbia. Kilty accepted the position (see William Kilty to TJ, 23 Mch. 1801).

From Sarah Mease

SIR. Philadelphia March the 20th 1801.

I feel that an apology is necessary for my intruding one moment on your time, and it is not without extreme reluctance and much hesitation that I have been induced to do so. But the motive is strong; and the obligation we are all under to promote the good of others as much as, even within the smallest sphere, we can, has prevailed over other considerations.

An opinion is generally entertained here that Mr Hall, the Marshall, will be dismissed from his office. He is under that apprehension himself, and is made, I have been told, very unhappy by it. I have little knowledge of Mr Hall, nor have I enquired what was his conduct under the late Administration. Of this, I doubt not, you are well informed, and must be the best judge; but I have learnt that he has a very large family, eight children, who depend entirely upon his salary for support; and, should that cease, he has no other probable means of skreening them from distress. Several gentlemen were requested to communicate to you the circumstance: they declined interfering. I can not view it in that light; but only as stating a fact, probably unknown to you, which may, perhaps, outweigh circumstances that would otherwise have determined you.

Mr. Hall, I have understood, is not personally violent; on the contrary, a man of mild manners, and private worth. The unfortunate state of dependance on an illiberal and intollerant party, which left not its agents always at liberty to act with moderation, or according to their own inclination may palliate his official conduct, if as represented to you, it was improper. And I have no doubt of his subscribing to, and acting in conformity with the more just and equitable principles which now predominate.

I can not on the present occasion refrain from expressing the pleasure I feel at the ascendency of principles, which I have ever warmly admired since the moment that political subjects, or human happiness began to interest me; and at the first fair experiment of a good government; every peoples best care, and which ages have taught us, "is necessary to close the circle of their felicities"

I pray you, Sir, to accept of my best wishes and highest respect.

SARAH MEASE

RC (DLC); endorsed by TJ as received 23 Mch. 1801 and so recorded in SJL.

Sarah Butler Mease (1772?-1831) was the eldest child of Mary Middleton Butler and Pierce Butler, a wealthy planter and a U.S. senator from South Carolina. Sarah ("Sally") was an avid reader, except of the Bible, and was the favorite of her father, who in 1784 took her to London to receive a classical education. He commented that

although her "manners and disposition are perfectly feminine, Her mind is Masculine." With her July 1800 marriage to James Mease, a prominent Philadelphia physician mentored by Benjamin Rush, and the son of a tax collector held in low regard, Sarah fell out of favor with her father and family. She forbade her children to read the Bible although she allowed her family to attend the Unitarian Church. Of her six children, two sons later changed their surnames to

Butler in order to ensure the inheritances from their maternal grandfather. Upon her estranged father's death in 1822, Sarah received a bequest in trust which was to be "free from the control and interference of her husband." At the time of her own death in 1831 she was alienated from her brother and sisters (Malcolm Bell, Jr., *Major Butler's Legacy: Five Generations of a Slaveholding Family* [Athens, Ga., 1987], xvi, 44-5, 203-6, 209, 229, 484-5; ANB; DAB).

From Samuel Smith

SIR/   Baltimore 20th. March 1801

I do myself the honor to transmit to you an Address from the Republican Citizens of Alleghany County (Maryland), which they have thought proper to request me to present—Should you return an answer, they request It may be done thro: me & that the Address & Answer may be published in one of our Papers—

Mr. Dawson will sail on sunday the ship being perfectly ready—. He mentions that I am wanted at Washington—if so—pray Command me. I will wait on you at any time—Nay I would (if consistent with the Law) do the Duties of the Department (but without salary) for one, two or three Months, or even untill the Meeting of Congress, if better Cannot be done—

I understand from Mr. D that Mr. Duval declines the offer of Chief Justice of the Territory of Columbia—if so—pray would not the office suit Mr. John Nicholas—No Man deserves better—

I sincerely wish you Could Concieve it proper to give Genl. Wilkinson the Government of the Natchez because I Concieve him to be precisely the kind of Character adapted to a People who have been so long under a spanish Government—and exactly the Character to keep the spanish Conduct Correct towards our Government— I am sir.

With the highest Respect your friend & servt   S. SMITH

RC (DLC); endorsed by TJ as received 21 Mch. and so recorded in SJL.

ENCLOSURE

From Allegany County Republican Citizens

SIR,   Cumberland March. 4th 1801

Truly sensible of the importance of the late Political Contest; and Actuated by the most pure and unalterable Zeal for the Wellfare of Our Country; We the republican Citizens of Allegany County in the State of Maryland, beg leave, to offer you our most Cordial Congratulations on your election to the office of President of the united States: And bid you a sencere and unfeigned welcome to the Chair as our Chief Magistrate. We freely Committ Sir, to your management and direction the helm of our political affairs, under the most firm and perfect reliance that that Spirit, which dictated the declaration of our independance; and that those sentiments which have so eminently distinguished you amongst the Number of American Patriots; Cannot fail to produce an Adminstration, founded on the basis of the genuine principles of the federal Constitution, and Consonant with the true interests of America.

We rejoice, that notwithstanding the deep laid schemes of the enemies to our freedom to disunite us, there is a display of virtuous Courage, and a Manifestation of Zeal for the support of our Country's Independance, dignity and Honour which evidently pervades the united States, and fully proves that the Citizens of America, so far from being dismay'd by any efforts or Threats hostile to thier liberty, are animated to a degree that arouses thier Contempt as Citizens, and thier spirit as Soldiers. With unspeakable pleasure we anticipate the enjoyment of those blessings which necessarily result from the due Adminstration of wise and wholesome laws, such as are warranted by the letter and spirit of our inestimable Constitution, and Calculated to give peace and unanimity to our Citizens at home, and respectibility to our nation Abroad.

We draw Sir, the happiest presages in favour of your Adminstration, fondly hoping that no imperious threat from Abroad will draw your attention from wise and necessary domestic regulations; And firmly believe that nothing will be wanting on your part to promote and increase the liberty, prosperity and true happiness of the united States.

With Sencere wishes for your good health and[1] happiness, We, on the part of, and by order of the republicans of Allegany County beg leave to Subscribe ourselves—with the utmost respect Your Most Obt. Servants

HANSON BRISCOE Chairman
ROB SINCLAIR—Secy.

RC (DLC); in unidentified hand, signed by Briscoe and Sinclair; at head of text: "To Thomas Jefferson, President of the United States of America."

[1] MS: "and and."

To Warren County Inhabitants

SIR   Washington Mar. 20. 1801

I tender my thankful acknolegements to the inhabitants of Warren county for their congratulations on my election to the chief magistracy of our country. I am duly sensible of the obligations imposed on me by the public will, as well as by the election made by the House of Representatives in the manner pointed out by our constitution, and no [endeavors] of mine shall be wanting to fulfil them.

Nothing is more important to the interests of this country than the absolute exclusion of every degree of foreign influence; and nothing more essential to it's happiness & permanence than to [disarm] all tendencies to [faction] by justice & firmness.

To your kind applications on my behalf to the almighty ruler of worlds, permit me to add mine for your future welfare, & for the future and prosperity of our country to the latest ages. Accept for yourself & the inhabitants of Warren county the assurances of my high consideration & respect.   Th: Jefferson

PrC (DLC); at foot of text: "W. A. K. Falkner"; blurred, with words in brackets supplied from New London *Bee*, 29 Apr. 1801.

From Joseph Yznardi, Sr.

George town
Exmo. Sor. Dn. T. Jefferson   20. de Marzo de 1801.

V.E. tiene pruevas infinitas desde el principio de mi conocimiento, de mi lealtad y cordial afecto de amistad.

Desde Philadelphia dirigi a V.E. copia de mi credencial traducida y al propio tiempo manifestandole pruevas de mi addiccion á su partido, visto que la eleccion recaeria ciertante en persona tan digna como lo deseava, considerando que el Govierno que cesava no era el mas favorable á los intereses comunes de mi Soverano, y que a mi llegada á Esta repeti verbalmente á V.E. como mis deberes, representando lo util que seria Separar los casos de perjuicios Causados durante la Guerra por Corsarios Franceses, que llevaron las presas á Puertos Españoles, cuya defensa hice como Consul en los Puertos Principales de España, con el justo fin que los Dueños fuesen á reclamarlos de la Republica, por quanto S.M.C. habia puesto de su parte todos los medios para evitarlos; sobre cuio punto como en el contenido de mi encargo, no dudava de la rectitud y buen deceo de amistad de V.E. merecer una respuesta conque manifestar (sin faltar á la confianza que merezco á este pais, y Su Govierno) el desempeño de la mision que se me ha confiado—   Josef Yznardy.

E D I T O R S '   T R A N S L A T I O N

Georgetown
Most Excellent Señor Don T. Jefferson   20th of March 1801

Your Excellency has infinite evidence of my loyalty and my cordial profession of friendship since our first meeting.

From Philadelphia I dispatched to Your Excellency a copy of my translated credentials, and at the same time revealing to you evidence of my devotion to your party, seeing that the election would certainly go to such a dignified person as I hoped, considering that the government that just ended was not the most favorable to the common interests of my sovereign, and whose opinion I verbally reiterated to Your Excellency upon my arrival here as my duties require, keeping in mind how useful it would be to separate cases of damages caused during the war by French privateers who took prizes to Spanish ports, the defense of which I was in charge of as a consul in the major ports of Spain, with the just purpose that the owners reclaimed them from the French Republic, as His Catholic Majesty had used all possible means in order to prevent the cases; an issue about which, as in the mandates of my assignment, I had no doubt to deserve a response on account of the rectitude and the good wishes of the friendship of Your Excellency (without betraying the confidence that I owe to this country, and your government) to demonstrate the completion of the mission that has been entrusted to me.　　　　　　　　　　JOSEF YZNARDY

Tr (Lb in AHN: Papeles de Estado, legajo 3891 bis, expediente 1, no. 109); in a clerk's hand.

From Joseph Yznardi, Sr.

EXELENTISIMO SEÑOR

Muy Señor mio, y de mi Respecto

He acudido dos Veses personalmente á el Secretario Interino, y una por escrito, y Siempre le encuentro Ocupado en Asuntos mas Inportantes, y por Miedo de la ausiencia de V.E antes de mi despacho, me estimulo a repetir mi Suplica

la presente Cubre el Asunto de presas en Cadiz, y contuinuasion de la Correspondencía del Viceconsul hasta 8 de Dicienbre qe dirijo á V.E por si Conviniese Adelantar Algo con la llegada del Ministro de la Republica á esta Capital, y el qe prevenga, yo Instruiciones a el dicho Vice Consul consequente á lo qe V.E me Ordene para evitar Confusiones en pretenciones tan Claras y Justas pues la Causas pendian sin dession de tribunal, y reclamadas á mi Instancia por el Govierno Español

tengo el Honor de Repetir á V.E mi Respecto en George town 20 De Marzo de 801 Exmo. Señor BLM de V.E su Obediente Ser[vidor]　　　　　　　　　　JOSEF YZNARDY

EDITORS' TRANSLATION

MOST EXCELLENT SIR

My most illustrious sir, and with all my respect

I have tried to contact the acting secretary twice in person, and once in writing, and I always find him busy in matters more important, and for fear of

Your Excellency's absence before my departure, I am compelled to repeat my request.

This letter deals with the issue of prizes in Cadiz, and follows up on the correspondence of the vice consul until the 8th of December, which I forward to Your Excellency in case it would be convenient to put forth something before the arrival of the minister of the French Republic at this capital, and in order that I give instructions to the aforementioned vice consul in accordance to what Your Excellency mandates to avoid confusion in such clear and just claims given that the trials were pending without a decision from the court, and appealed at my instance by the Spanish government.

I have the honor to reiterate to your excellency my respect in Georgetown 20 March 1801 most excellent sir your obedient servant kisses the hand of Your Excellency JOSEF YZNARDY

RC (DNA: RG 59, CD); at foot of text: "Exmo. Señor Dn Thomas Jefferson Precidente de los EU de Ame."; translation in Jacob Wagner's hand in margin; endorsed by Wagner; endorsed by TJ as received 21 Mch. and so recorded in SJL; also endorsed by TJ as referred to the secretary of state on 22 Mch. Enclosure: Anthony Terry to J. B. Millet, 8 Dec. 1800, Terry as United States vice consul in Cadiz responding to a letter from Millet, the French chargé d'affaires for commerical relations for that region of Spain, concerning four American ships seized as prizes and their status under the articles of the Convention of 1800 (Tr in same; in Terry's hand, in Spanish; with Tr of Millet's letter of 14 Frimaire Year 9 [5 Dec. 1800], in French, subjoined).

EL SECRETARIO INTERINO: Levi Lincoln, as acting secretary of state. In a letter to Madison written at Philadelphia on 21 May, Yznardi again took up the issue of American ships held as prizes at Cadiz (Madison, *Papers, Sec. of State Ser.*, 1:220).

MINISTRO DE LA REPUBLICA: Louis André Pichon.

From David Austin

SIR   Philadelphia March 21st: 1801—

Casting my eye upon a News paper of this morning, I observed the following remark: "We understand that the announcing of Mr. Wagner's appointment, as private Secretary to the President is premature."

The remark suggested an idea, that if the President contemplated such an appointment, it would, if obtained, afford an happy opportunity for a more explicit and convincing exposition of the subject of former communications.

I submit the matter to the consideration of the President; & as it is probable little may be known of the abilities of the applicant for the discharge of the duties of this office; he may be pardoned for suggesting that so far as a Liberal education; a tour through several parts of Europe, a general acquaintance with men & things, & a close attention to the affairs of our revolution may be plead as qualifications, so far, the President might rely on the accuracy of the appointment should it be thought necessary or proper.

If the President should judge that the services of such an one would at all aid to lighten the burthen, or at all to accommodate the duties of his high Commission; it is sufficient, that notwithstanding subordinate & increasing engagements in this City, it be said, that those services are at the President's command.

Should this place be filled, & there be found other vacancy near yr. Excellency, the Objects of this address might be equally well answered.—

After the communications on the subject of foreign affairs, your Excellency will have the goodness to excuse the seeming vanity of the expression; that the superintendancy of either of the departments is not deemed beyond the reach of my abilities; at the same time, it is of little moment what the appointment may be, so be, it brings me, in honor, into the Councils of yr. Excell'y—

There is a most interesting game soon to be played amongst the Nations; & I miss my guess; if all the wisdom than can be collected will not be needful to preserve our own barque in safety during the tremulous scene.

With sentiments of high esteem   DAVID AUSTIN
"Geo: Tavern."

RC (DNA: RG 59, LAR); at head of text: "Th: Jefferson, P. U. States:"; endorsed by TJ as received 25 Mch. and so recorded in SJL.

A NEWS PAPER OF THIS MORNING: *Poulson's American Daily Advertiser*, 21 Mch. 1801.

From Samuel Bryan

SIR,   Lancaster 21st. of March 1801

I had the honor of writing to you some weeks ago on the subject of an appointment, and transmitting sundry documents to sustain my pretensions to your notice—Mr. William Findley one of our most distinguished characters wrote a letter to your Excellency in which he gave a detailed statement of my conduct in the Office I have held for six years past that of Register General of the State, an office in which all accounts are settled, and the Finances of the State yearly arranged & reported to the Legislature; this letter he sent under cover to Mr. Gregg with a request to deliver it in person—

This day I wrote to Mr. Gallatin on the same subject, but after my Letter was put in the Post-Office I heard that he had left Washington for some weeks, which determined me to take it out and enclose it to your Excellency to hand to Mr. Gallatin when he returns & for the purpose of your looking over it.

I have the honor to be, With high esteem and regard, Your humble. Servt. SAML. BRYAN

RC (DNA: RG 59, LAR); at foot of text: "His Excellency Thomas Jefferson, President"; endorsed by TJ as received 2 May and so recorded in SJL with notation "Off." Enclosure: Bryan to Albert Gallatin, 21 Mch. 1801; seeking appointment as supervisor of the revenue for Pennsylvania, he reiterates the contribution he made to the success of the Republican ticket in 1800 with his "Sketch of an Address," as testified to by Solomon Myers and William Reed; to support his expertise in financial affairs he notes that as register general of Pennsylvania he made many enemies by his "persevering resolution against a host of delinquents," and that when he took office almost one thousand accounts were open, but only six of any importance remained in arrears, because he "introduced a habit of punctuality in the rendering of the current revenue accounts and in the payment of the monies received into the State Treasury" (RC in NHi: Gallatin Papers).

Bryan's letter to TJ requesting an APPOINTMENT is printed at 26 Feb. On the same date WILLIAM FINDLEY wrote TJ recommending Bryan.

From Stephen Burrowes

SIR Philadelphia March 21 1801

I received your highly esteemed favor of the 12 Inst which demands my greateful acknowledgments. It is impossible not to admit the propriety of your reasons for not accepting the Saddle as a present Thay did not however occur to me in time or I Should not given you the trouble of Stating them I have thearefore made out the bill at thirty five Dollars & presented it to Mr Richards who immediately paid the money

Premet me now Sir to congratulate you on filling the first office in the world which affords a great deal of happiness to those who have long been anxious and Struggling for the event

That the supreme Being may long preserve you life and health as a blessing to our highly favored Country is the Sencere wish of Sir your very Humble Servant STEPHEN BURROWES

RC (DLC); at foot of text: "Thomas Jefferson President US"; endorsed by TJ as received 25 Mch. and so recorded in SJL.

To George Caines

SIR   Washington Mar. 21. 1801.

The desire you express to prefix my name to the work you are about to publish is gratifying to me as an additional testimonial of that approbation of my fellow citizens which is so consoling to me. the matter of your work possesses too much self importance to need any adventitious aid from external circumstances. it cannot fail to recommend itself to a very general attention. I ask the favor of you to consider me as one of the subscribers to it, & to accept my friendly & respectful salutations.   TH: JEFFERSON

PrC (DLC); at foot of text: "George Caines esq. N. York."

DESIRE YOU EXPRESS: see Caines to TJ, 10 Mch.

Caines proceeded to dedicate his work on commercial law to TJ and included a letter to the president in the front matter of his initial volume: "As that which might be of some utility to these States, whose welfare I know you have so truly at heart, I begged leave to dedicate to you the following sheets. For the obliging manner in which the permission was accorded, you have long had my private, and I am happy now to offer my public acknowledgments. In affixing your name to this publication, it is very possible, Sir, I may preserve the title-page long after the work itself is forgotten" (*An Enquiry into the Law Merchant of the United States; or, Lex Mercatoria Americana, on Several Heads of Commercial Importance* [New York, 1802]; Shaw-Shoemaker, No. 1978).

From Levi Lincoln

                                              Department of State
SIR   Washington March 21. 1801

I have thought it my duty to submit to your consideration two letters, addressed to the Secretary, containing the application of Major Thomas A Dyson, for the office of marshal of this District of Columbia, as also Stephen Moylan's letter of congratulation. Mr Gelsten's[1] having in view similar objects, is also submitted. The office, is informed by a letter from Mr Sitgreaves,[2] that he declines accepting of the office of judge of the circuit court of the 5th. circuit of the U.S.—I am sorry to add, by a Letter from Philadelphia addressed to Genl. Wilkinson, stating conversation with Mr Jones, on the supposition of his being appointed Secretary of the navy, then there is too much reason to beleive he will not accept. The note addressed to Mr Lincoln by Mr Stoddert was handed him, last evening, he regrets adding to the weight of business with which you are constantly pressed by this difficult matter. I have further to state that there were two Alexanders, the father & the son, for whom Mr Adams made a commission of the Peace. It still remains to distinguish between the two —

with the most perfect respect Sir I have the honor to by your most obt. Humble Sert.   LEVI LINCOLN

RC (DLC); at head of text: "The President of the United States"; endorsed by TJ as received 21 Mch. and so recorded in SJL. Enclosures: (1) Michael J. Stone to [secretary of state], 19 Mch. 1801, recommending Major Thomas A. Dyson, and noting that as a lawyer and judge he could evaluate Dyson, who had served for six years as sheriff of Charles County, Maryland, as "a Man of Firmness, Honour and Integrity" and as "active and Deligent" (RC in DNA: RG 59, LAR). (2) George Dent to James Madison, 20 Mch. 1801, recommending Dyson as well qualified for the office of marshal of the District of Columbia, having observed him as an army officer during the Revolutionary War and as sheriff of Charles County (same; endorsed by TJ: "G. Dent (for Dyson) to Jas. Madison"; TJ later canceled "G. Dent"). (3) David Gelston to same, 13 Mch. 1801 (same; see Notes on New York Patronage, printed after 17 Feb. 1801). (4) Memorandum from Benjamin Stoddert to Lincoln, [21 Mch.

1801], reporting on the substance of an earlier conversation in which Stoddert observed that his continuance in office was disadvantageous to the public and that until a new secretary of the navy could be named, it would be better for Lincoln or Dearborn to be charged with the duties of the office, although Stoddert would be ready to provide any information in his power to the acting secretary (MS in DLC; undated; in Stoddert's hand; endorsed by TJ: "Stoddert Benj. to L. Lincoln. Mar. 21. 1801"). Other enclosures not found.

TWO ALEXANDERS: Adams nominated Charles Alexander and Charles Alexander, Jr., as justices of the peace for the County of Alexandria on 2 Mch. (JEP, 1:388).

[1] TJ wrote "Gelston" in the left margin adjacent to this line of text.
[2] TJ wrote "Sitgreaves" in the left margin adjacent to this line of text.

To George Logan

DR SIR   Washington Mar. 21. 1801.

An immense press of business has prevented my sooner acknowleging your favors of Feb. 20. & 27. I join you in congratulations on the return of republican ascendency: and also in a sense of the necessity of restoring freedom to the ocean. but I doubt, with you, whether the US. ought to join in an armed confederacy for that purpose; or rather I am satisfied they ought not. it ought to be the very first object of our pursuits to have nothing to do with the European interests & politics. let them be free or slaves at will, navigators or agricultural, swallowed into one government or divided into a thousand. we have nothing to fear from them in any form, and therefore to take a part in their conflicts would be to divert our energies from creation to destruction. our commerce is so valuable to them that they will be glad to purchase it when the only price we ask is to do us justice. I believe we have in our own hands the means of peaceable coercion; & that the moment they see our government so united as that [we] can make use of it, they will for their own interest be disposed to do us justice. in this way we shall not be obliged by any treaty of confederation to go to war for injuries done to others.

I will pray you to make my affectionate respects acceptable to mrs Logan, & to recieve yourself assurances of my constant esteem & attachment. TH: JEFFERSON

PrC (DLC); faint; in ink at foot of text: "Logan Dr."

From Thomas McKean

DEAR SIR, Philadelphia March 21st. 1801.

Had Mr; Burr been elected President by the Representatives of a majority of the States, the Republicans of Pennsylvania would certainly have acquiesced, as you mention in your favor of the 9th. instant, but they would not have submitted to an appointment, of any other person than one of the two elected by the Electors, either by the Senate or an Act of the Congress: Fearing the latter would be attempted, a proclamation was framed by myself, enjoining obedience on all officers civil & military and the citizens of this State to you as President and Mr; Burr as Vice-President, in case you should so agree the matter between yourselves (as expected); a resolution was also prepared for our House of Representatives to adopt, approving the proclamation and pledging themselves to support it, and an instruement to be signed by the eleven Senators, in case we could not prevail with one of the party in opposition, which would have made a majority in the Senate, as a Mr; Potts belonging to them had left the House thro' indisposition; he is lately dead. The Militia would have been warned to be ready, arms for upwards of twenty thousand were secured, brass field-pieces &c. &c. and an order would have issued for the arresting & bringing to justice every member of Congress, or other person found in Pennsylvania, who should have been concerned in the treason; and I am perswaded a verdict would have been given against them, even if the jury had been returned by a Marshall. These are the outlines of what I alluded to as committed to the flames, on my receiving the pleasing intelligence of the Election. I thank God for the event, for otherwise the consequences might have been deplorable indeed.

The changes you have made in officers in this State are highly approved here, not only by the Republicans but others. If General Muhlenberg should be put in the place of Henry Miller, supervisor of the Excise &c. it would fully gratify him, and, I firmly believe, a more popular removal and appointment could not be made. I take the liberty of suggesting this, from the favorable expressions you have been pleased to use—respecting him: this would effectually settle all the divisions occasioned by his late election to the Senate. The conduct of the supervisor has been as hostile and provoking as that of the Commissary of military stores.

It is with reluctance, I confess, that I part with Mr; Dallas, more[1] on account of his talents than his fidelity; however, as the office you have given him is more convenient for him, tho' not so profitable as that of Secretary, I submit, for I wish his happiness; he desires, that I would make his grateful acknowledgments on the occasion. Messrs. Coxe and Beckley seem to me to hope you will hold them in remembrance, as at present they have but a bare subsistance, and I can hardly better their condition. I offered Mr; Cooper the offices of Prothonotary, Register of Wills & all the Clerkships in the new county of Centre, the day after he was liberated from durance vile, but he declined them on account of his attachment to the society of Doctor Priestly, from whom he would have been removed near eighty miles, and because the tenure was during the pleasure of the Governor for the time being: next winter I expect to have it in my power to make him Presiding Judge of a District, the salary D 1600 a year, payable quarter yearly, with the prospect of which he is quite satisfied, as the tenure is during good behavior; in this way I shall imitate my friend, late President Adams, in *securing* my friends offices, from which they cannot readily be removed, however unworthy, only my intentions favor an amiable & learned man: until this period arrives I shall make other provision for him.

I sincerely thank you for your polite & friendly conduct towards the Chevalier de Yrujo; nothing would be more agreeable to me than his remaining in this country, for I love him as a child and never expect to see my daughter after their departure for Europe. Happy should I be if your kind interference should arrive in time at Madrid to prevent his removal. He has expressed a wish that he might have a passage for himself & family in the Frigate that will convey Chancellor Livingston to France; he means to pay the Captn. the same as if in a private vessel, and I have reason to believe it would be very agreeable to both Ministers.

Accept, dear Sir, my best wishes for your health, honor & happiness, and if I can contribute to them, or render you any other service, I beg you will freely impose your commands.

I am, dear Sir, Your friend & most obedient

THOS M:KEAN

RC (DLC); at foot of text: "His Excellency Thomas Jefferson Esquire, President of the U.S."; endorsed by TJ as received 25 Mch. and so recorded in SJL. FC (PHi); dated 19 Mch.; in clerk's hand.

COMMITTED TO THE FLAMES: see McKean to TJ, 20 Feb.

TJ discussed some of the CHANGES he was making IN OFFICERS in Pennsylvania in his letter to McKean of 9 Mch. TJ appointed William Irvine to replace Samuel Hodgdon, COMMISSARY OF MILITARY STORES (see note to McKean to TJ, 10 Jan. 1801).

[1] FC: "not more."

To Joseph Priestley

DEAR SIR   Washington Mar. 21. 1801.

I learnt some time ago that you were in Philadelphia, but that it was only for a fortnight, & supposed you were gone. it was not till yesterday I recieved information that you were still there, had been very ill but were on the recovery. I sincerely rejoice that you are so. yours is one of the few lives precious to mankind, & for the continuance of which every thinking man is solicitous. bigots may be an exception. what an effort, my dear Sir, of bigotry in Politics & Religion have we gone through. the barbarians really flattered themselves they should even be able to bring back the times of Vandalism, when ignorance put every thing into the hands of power & priestcraft. all advances in science were proscribed as innovations. they pretended to praise & encourage education, but it was to be vain the education of our ancestors. we were to look backwards not forwards for improvement, the President himself declaring in one of his answers to addresses that we were never to expect to go beyond them in real science. this was the real ground of all the attacks on you: those who live by mystery & charlatanerie, fearing you would render them useless by simplifying the Christian philosophy, the most sublime & benevolent, but most perverted system that ever shone on man, endeavored to crush your well earnt, & well deserved fame. but it was the Lilliputians upon Gulliver. our countrymen have recovered from the alarm into which art & industry had thrown them, science & honesty are replaced on their high ground, and you, my dear Sir, as their great apostle, are on it's pinnacle.[1] it is with heartfelt satisfaction that, in the first moment of my public action, I can hail you with welcome to our land, tender to

[393]

you the homage of it's respect & esteem, cover you under the protection of those laws which were made for the wise & the good like you, and disclaim the legitimacy of that libel on legislation which under the form of a law was for sometime placed among them.[2] as the storm is now subsiding & the horison becoming serene, it is pleasant to consider the phaenomenon with attention. we can no longer say there is nothing new under the sun. for this whole chapter in the history of man is new. the great extent of our republic is new. it's sparse habitation is new. the mighty wave of public opinion which has rolled over it is new. but the most pleasing novelty is it's so quickly subsiding, over such an extent of surface, to it's true level again. the order & good sense displayed in this recovery from delusion, and in the momentous crisis which lately arose, really bespeak a strength of character in our nation which augurs well for the duration of our republic, & I am much better satisfied now of it's stability, than I was before it was tried. I have been above all things solaced by the prospect which opened on us in the event of a non election of a president; in which case the federal government would have been in the situation of a clock or watch run down. there was no idea of force, nor of any occasion for it. a Convention, invited by the republican members of Congress with the virtual President & Vice President, would have been on the ground in 8. weeks, would have repaired the constitution where it was defective & wound it up again. this peaceable & legitimate resource, to which we are in the habit of implicit obedience, superseding all appeal to force, and being always within our reach, shews a precious principle of self-preservation in our composition, till a change of circumstances shall take place, which is not within prospect at any definite period.—but I have got into a long disquisition on politics when I only meant to express my sympathy in the state of your health, and to tender you all the affections of public & private hospitality. I should be very happy indeed to see you here. I leave this about the 30th. inst. to return about the 25th. of April. if you do not leave Philadelphia before that, a little excursion hither would help your health. I should be much gratified with the possession of a guest I so much esteem, and should claim a right to lodge you should you make such an excursion. accept the homage of my high consideration & respect, & assurances of affectionate attachment.   TH: JEFFERSON

PrC (DLC); faint; at foot of first page in ink: "Priestley Dr. Joseph."

HAD BEEN VERY ILL: while visiting Philadelphia to settle his affairs and to attend a meeting of the American Philosophical Society, Priestley became seriously ill with "a bilious fever with pleurisy" and was treated by Benjamin Rush. Although he returned to Northumberland, Priestley never fully recovered his health and spent his last years completing and publishing religious pamphlets and other works (F. W. Gibbs, *Joseph Priestley: Adventurer in Science and Champion of Truth* [London, 1965], 242, 246-7; Edgar F. Smith, *Priestley in America 1749-1804* [Philadelphia, 1920], 144-5).

ONE OF John Adams's ANSWERS TO ADDRESSES refers to his reply to "the Young Men of the City of Philadelphia" of 7 May 1798 (see Vol. 30:341-2; Vol. 31:129).

Priestley made a copy of this letter and enclosed it in one to John Wilkinson, his brother-in-law in England, on 30 Apr. 1801 (RC and enclosure in Municipal Library, Warrington, England; with photostats of both in DLC). Priestley's transcript was later published in London in 1812 in the appendix of Thomas Belsham's edition of the *Memoirs of the Late Reverend Theophilus Lindsey* and became a source of embarrassment for TJ in his renewed friendship with John Adams (Lester J. Cappon, ed., *The Adams-Jefferson Letters: The Complete Correspondence Between Thomas Jefferson and Abigail and John Adams*, 2 vols. [Chapel Hill, 1959], 2:288-9, 325-6; see also Sowerby, No. 1661).

[1] Preceding two words interlined in place of "[the top of the] pyramid."

[2] TJ wrote "[Alien law]" in the margin alongside this passage.

From Henry Rose

DEAR SIR   Fairfax 21st March 1801

Having understood that Coll: C Simms of Alexandria has sent in his Commission as Collector of the revenue for that Port—I take the liberty of presenting myself to your Excellency as a candidate for that Office.

If I have waved what may be the usage on occasions of this Kind, that of being represnted by some distinguished pesonage, it has arisen from an impression that you were sufficiently acquainted with my charecter, to place the asked confidence, independant of collateral interference— —

Should my information have been incorrect or the ground I have taken in introducing *myself* to your notice be indecorous, I shall rest assured of your indugence and am with every assurance of the highest respect and esteem

Your most obedient and very humble Servant   HENRY ROSE

RC (DNA: RG 59, LAR); endorsed by TJ as received 24 Mch. and so recorded in SJL; also endorsed by TJ: "to be Collector Alexa."

Henry Rose (d. 1810), a 1794 graduate in medicine at the University of Pennsylvania, practiced his profession in Alexandria. He owned an estate in Fairfax County and valuable lands along the Little River Turnpike Road, as well as shares in the turnpike company. In 1801 he sold land near Alexandria and 1,000 acres in Amherst County. In that year he won election to the Virginia House of Delegates, representing Fairfax County for one term (Miller, *Alexandria Artisans*, 2:87-8; Wyndham B. Blanton, *Medicine in Virginia in the Eighteenth Century* [Richmond, 1931], 82; Alexandria *Times*, 8 Apr. 1801; Leonard, *General Assembly*, 223, 859).

From Stephen Sayre

SIR   Philaa 21 Mar: 1801—

I have been lately in New York, & think it my duty to inform you—
that there has been a purchase of 10 acres of land, on Long Island,
made by the agent, acting for the navy, at the enormous price of
40000. dollars. This agreement was the subject of conversation, &
astonishment, in all companies, & of all parties—universally declaring, that, any private person might have bought it, for one fourth of
the amount. If not too late, you will, of course not only investigate,
but set aside this shameful transaction.

I can have no interest, either to reform, or inform—nor should I have
deem'd it my particular duty, to point out abuses in this, or any other
department of our general government had they not been, long since,
too evident, to my own eyes, & too flagrant to be tolerated.

Mr. Stoddert, in augt. 1799. employd me to designate a proper
place for dry docks, the most eligible for building ships, & to report
a true state of facts as to, depth of water tides, rocks, shoals &c &c. to
the eastward.—this I undertook, & reported, faithfully—he express'd
full satisfaction.

I know it was his opinion, at the time, not to trust any part of our
navy, or means to create it, on any part of Long Island—I made him
fully sensible, that an enemy could instantly destroy, such establishment—
having numberless places in the continent, equally convenient—he
therefore did not instruct me to examine the Island—but tho he may
have changed his opinion, must he employ an agent so ignorant as not
to know, that any proprietor of land could afford to give away a part, to
inhance the value of the rest, twenty fold—I told Mr S. this Watson
was as ignorant, as to any thing respecting ships, as a common nigro—
but, he might have known how to buy land—I also told him, how I saw
the nation plunder'd by his other agents—I presume he was offended—
for he has not changed them, tho he confess'd the fact.

I must, do Mr Gibbs of R.I. the justice to say—he is intelligent, &
honest. Those in Boston & Portsmouth, were Tories, in our revolution—
they would have deem'd it meritorious to have ruin'd us there—can
they now be supposed to tout our government? better than their own
interest? were there no intelligent men to be found who had served
their country?—

I had no opportunity to know the merits of Mr Hubbert & Mr
Howland, agents in Connecticut. The Ship Connecticut, built by
contract, is an abortion—she has neither room to fight her guns,
accommodation for her officers, or the properties, necessary for

a Merchant—she lay at New London—I examined her accurately—&
I ought to know every quality of a good ship—having built two, in
1780. in St Petersburg of 1200 Tons each, acknowledged to have
been equal, to any on the ocean, in all points, & superior in sailing to
any Merchantmen, tho' under less masts & sparrs—I have also had
opportunity of making my remarks on the finest ships in Plimouth,
being there 10 days—I was three weeks at Brest—have seen the
docks, & arsenals of Toulon, Cronstadt, & all the inferior ones, of the
rest of Europe—what I now say therefore, respecting the Connecticut, I know to be true—when the United States was going out, I predicted, that she must carry away her Bowsprit—she did so—has lost
a second—and may lose two more.

I have always had my doubts whether a navy could, under any circumstances, be profitable—I know that in bad hands it is dangerous—
under wicked men destructive—I am confident you will, if continued,
make the best use of *it*—but to do this, you must order your secretary to
adopt another mode, & employ other men—otherwise the nation will
curse your navy, & your own reputation will not escape censure—
Dont imagine I wish to be employ'd under this department—I have
seen too much—where ignorance, & roguery are united an honest
man finds no peaceable abode—If you were to offer me the most
profitable agency in the navy I would not accept it—the system is
wrong—it gives security & patronage to baseness, peculation, &
fraud. and I am sorry to say, that we have no grounds to reproach the
most venal nation in Europe with want of virtue.
It was my intention, when I began this letter, meerly to give you *that*
information, which my opportunies have given me, respecting some
public abuses, that knowing them, you may apply a remedy; but I
will now trouble you with a few words on another subject.
You have named Chancellor Livingston to France—he is every way
worthy. Let me ask whether you cannot, make me still useful there. If
I was sure of your future patronage, I should accept of a secondary
employment. Can the commercial agency be united with secretary
of legation? can a salary be annex'd to such appointment, worth my
acceptance? could I expect to become his successor, should Mr L.
return—which I presume he will wish to do, after our most important concerns, are settled?
I am so far fixd in opinion, that, a great measure may be brought into
operation, such as I hinted in my former letter, that, I should prefer the
opportunity of promoting it, to any thing which could be offer'd. I am
as obstinate in the belief, as Columbus was in his, of an undiscover'd
continent. Let me request you not to decide against it, untill you have

the canvass fill'd up, with all its features—a Skeleton, promises neither, beauty, or perfection.

Should it never be adopted you will lose no reputation—but if accomplish'd, you will gain much—

If the powers of Europe do not percieve, the lasting, & extensive benefits of this proposition, they may be instructed, & prevaild upon to do it. you must know, having resided so long among public functionaries, how few there are, who, conceive, or contemplate a great & solid system. Kings are ignorant—their Representatives, are like themselves. I lived among them, from 1777. to 1782, & never found above two men of superior talents. You do not know the influence, of your own name, & character in Europe, if you suppose yourself unable to bring this subject under universal, & serious consideration. under the sanction of your name, & supported by your instructions, *I, even I*, could settle the affairs of a trouble'd world; perhaps forever

I wish you had named Mr Livingston for St James's—*Kings* cannot be expected to serve republicans with fervor, or sincerity—

I am most respectfully   STEPHEN SAYRE

RC (DNA: RG 59, LAR); at foot of text: "Thomas Jefferson Esqr President of the United States"; endorsed by TJ as a letter of 27 Mch. received 16 Apr. and so recorded in SJL.

Sayre, employed by Benjamin STODDERT in 1799 as inspector to examine shipyard transactions, denounced agents in Boston and Portsmouth as grafters and was himself removed from his post by Stoddert. TJ eventually ordered a dockyard investigation, however, responding in large part to Sayre's advice (John R. Alden, *Stephen Sayre, American Revolutionary Adventurer* [Baton Rouge, 1983], 187-9).

The SHIP CONNECTICUT, built under contract at Middletown, Connecticut, was launched on 6 June 1799 (NDQW, Dec. 1800-Dec. 1801, 365).

To James Warren

SIR   Washington Mar. 21. 1801.

I am much gratified by the reciept of your favor of the 4th inst. and by the expressions of friendly sentiment it contains. it is pleasant for those who have just escaped threatened shipwreck, to hail one another when landed in unexpected safety. the resistance which our republic has opposed to a course of operation for which it was not destined, shews a strength of body which affords the most flattering presages of duration. I hope we shall now be permitted to steer her in her natural course, and to shew by the smoothness of her motion the skill with which she has been formed for it. I have seen with great grief yourself and so many other venerable patriots, retired & weeping in silence over the rapid subversion of those principles for the attainment of which you had sacrificed the ease & comforts of life. but I rejoice that you have lived to see us revindicate our rights, & regain manfully the ground from which fraud, not force, had for a moment driven us. the character which our fellow citizens have displayed on this occasion gives us every thing to hope for the permanence of our government. it's extent has saved us. while some parts were labouring under the paroxysm of delusion, others retained their senses,[1] and time was thus given to the affected parts to recover their health. your portion of the union is longest recovering, because the decievers there wear a more imposing form: but a little more time, and they too will recover. I pray you to present the homage of my great respect to mrs Warren. I have long possessed evidences of her high station in the ranks of genius: and have considered her silence as a proof that she did not go with the current.

accept yourself assurances of my high consideration & respect.

Th: Jefferson

PrC (DLC); in ink at foot of text: "General Warren. Plymouth."   [1] TJ here canceled "and the country."

From Washington, D.C., Inhabitants

Sir—   [ca. 21 Mch. 1801]

We the inhabitants of the City of Washington having experienced great inconvenience last Year in hauling Wood Coal &ca. from the nearest landing place on the Eastern Branch in consequence of the steep ascent near the Capitol & having also perceived that some Members of Congress resided[1] three miles off although there were empty houses about half a mile below the Hill on New Jersey Avenue because that Avenue in its present impaired and rugged Condition rendered it inconvenient, respectfully request that some portion of the 10,000 Dollars expressly appropriated to the accomodation of Congress may be applied to levelling & paving to facilitate a communication with the Eastern Branch—and should there not remain assets from that fund we request that the Commissioners of the City of Washington may be instructed to aid this part of the City as they have aided other quarters—

Strongly impressed by a conviction of the Necessity of making the situation of the Members of Congress more comfortable next Session we rely upon your fostering attention & encouragement & as the Sum required will not be large, we trust that such an appropriation will be granted as it will be attended with the most beneficial effects.

THOMAS LAW

RC (DLC: TJ Papers, 111:19117-18); undated; in unidentified hand, signed by Thomas Law, Henry Ingle, Thomas Herty, John Minchin, Samuel H. Smith, and 40 others; at head of text: "To His Excellency Thomas Jefferson President of the United States of America"; endorsed by TJ as received 21 Mch. and so recorded in SJL with notation "Law, Thos. & others—petn."

For work completed on NEW JERSEY AVENUE, "including a good Road up the Hill," see District of Columbia Commissioners to TJ, 24 Aug. 1801.

[1] Canceled: "in George town."

To Isaac Weaver, Jr.

SIR   Washington Mar. 21 1801.

I was duly honoured with your favor of Feb. 25. and am [from] duty bound to return my thanks for the expressions it contains of confidence and respect to myself. I perfectly agree with you that while it is necessary to clothe public magistrates with powers sufficiently nervous for order & defence that every surrender of power beyond that is improper. I believe too that a great deal more than usually is, might be left to private morality in the regulation of our[1] own nature without mischief, and that the public opinion would step in, in those cases, as a supplement to the laws, more effectual than laws themselves. we see this take place as to the duties of gratitude, of parental & filial duties, of respect, of decency &c and it is a general truth that legislatures are too fond of interposing their power & of governing too much. the right of election by the people shews itself daily more and more valuable. it is a peaceable means of producing reformation, which if we suffer to be withdrawn or evaded, they will have no resource but in the sword. how long [have] we seen them remaining quiet under violations of their constitution, [looking] forward to the moment when they could rectify things by their votes, when nothing could have preserved peace, had that expectation been cut off. I wish them more frequent than they are, especially in some of the public functionaries. I pray you to accept assurances of my high consideration & respect.

TH: JEFFERSON

PrC (DLC); faint; at foot of text: "Isaac Weaver esq. Speaker of the H. [R.] of Penna."

[1] Word interlined in place of "[their]."

From John Dawson

DEAR SIR,   Baltimore March 22d 1801.

I recievd your letter and the enclosures on friday night, but not any by the last evenings mail.

All things are ready, and we expect to sail at Eleven—it is probable we shall be delayd on Hampton road, as I learn from the Capt. that some of his offices are at Norfolk—

I deem it my duty to forward to you Colo: Barbours letter, recievd at this place.

With much Esteem Your real friend,   J DAWSON

RC (DLC); endorsed by TJ as received 23 Mch. and so recorded in SJL. Enclosure not found.

YOUR LETTER: no letter from TJ to Dawson is recorded in SJL between 12 and 22 Mch.

THE CAPT.: John Rodgers.

To Joseph Fay

DEAR SIR   Washington Mar. 22. 1801.

Your favor of Feb. 21. has been too long unacknoleged. the press of business on a first entrance into office must apologize for me. it contains much to thank you for. while the esteem of my friends is dear to my heart, I see that their expectations are painfully too high; and especially in a scene of such vast extent, where we must of necessity depend on information not inspection. the symptoms of a coalition of parties give me infinite pleasure. setting aside a few only, I have been ever persuaded that the great bulk of both parties had the same principles fundamentally, and that it was only as to our foreign relations there was any division. these I hope can be so managed as to cease to be a subject of division for us. nothing shall be spared on my part to obliterate the traces of party & consolidate the nation, if it can be done without abandonment of principle; which I believe the more as I think we agree in principle. the late crisis, so alarming generally, presented comfort to me as it opened to our view a peaceable resource, which will ever be in our power, and controul & supercede all appeals to force. had no president been chosen, we should have considered the general government as a clock run down; the sincerely well disposed to it would have invited a convention, which could have been on the spot in 8. weeks, and wound up the machine again. to this I have no doubt there would have been universal obedience; and that we may consider this as a resource which can never fail us under any political derangement, until our habits are changed more than can happen in any definite period. Mr. Madison will not be here till late next month, till which time I shall shortly be absent myself, to make some domestic arrangements preparatory to my final settlement here. I will be the bearer of your respects to him. accept assurances of my high consideration & esteem.   Th: Jefferson

PrC (DLC); at foot of text: "Joseph Fay esq. N. York."

From Joseph Fenwick

Sir   George Town 22 March 1801.

Having communicated to Mr. Monroe my application to be continued in the Consulate at Bordeaux, and asked his testimony on the manner I had filled that office during his residence in France—he has been pleased to forward the inclosed letter for you, which I have the honor to transmit.

As my intention is to avoid importunity, I shall add nothing to what I have already said on this business—relying, that as soon as the public service permits you to make an election, you will cause the same to be communicated to me thro' my friend Mr. John Mason, shou'd the liquidation of my concerns require my absence from this place.

With the greatest respect I have the honour to be Sir your most obedient Servant   Joseph Fenwick

RC (DLC); at foot of text: "Thomas Jefferson Esquire President of the U.S."; endorsed by TJ as received 23 Mch. and so recorded in SJL. Enclosure: Monroe to TJ, 17 Mch. 1801.

liquidation: Fenwick and John Mason were dissolving their Georgetown mercantile partnership (MB, 2:831n).

To Elijah Griffiths

Dear Sir   Washington Mar. 22. 1801

Your letter of July last was delivered to me at Monticello, from which place I had nothing new, or worthy the subject of an answer. that of Feb. 22. is now to be acknoleged. I have considerable hopes that our government will go on with less opposition than preceding occasions have called for. I rather expect that several circumstances latterly have brought over & consolidated with us a large body of the people who had left us on the XYZ fable, but [. . .] beginning to be sensible they had got with leaders whose views were different from theirs. we [see] strong symptoms of this return in almost every quarter. we have to apprehend most trouble from the English. however their present situation must render peace with us very desireable, & if we meet them with frank & sincere demonstrations of friendship, it is not within the ordinary principles of human calculation that they should reject them. it is true we have [. . .] points to settle with them, which nothing but a disposition to do what is just on both sides can facilitate. the disposition shall not be witheld on our part.

I am sorry to hear of your long continued indisposition. the approaching season may perhaps relieve you. accept my sincere wishes for it, with my friendly salutations. TH: JEFFERSON

PrC (DLC); faint; at foot of text: "Mr. Elijah Griffiths." Recorded in SJL under 21 Mch.

To Nathaniel Niles

DEAR SIR   Washington Mar. 22. 1801.

Your favor of Feb. 12. which did not get to my hands till Mar. 2. is entitled to my acknolegements. it was the more agreeable as it proved that the esteem I had entertained for you while we were acting together on the public stage, had not been without reciprocated affect. what wonderful scenes have passed since that time! the late chapter of our history furnishes a lesson to man perfectly new. the times have been awful, but they have proved an useful truth that the good citizen must never despair of the commonwealth. how many good men abandoned the deck, & gave up the vessel as lost. it furnishes a new proof of the falsehood of Montesquieu's doctrine that a republic can be preserved only in a small territory. the reverse is the truth. had our territory been even a third only of what it is, we were gone. but while frenzy & delusion, like an epidemic gained certain parts, the residue remained sound & untouched, and held on till their brethren could recover from the temporary delirium. another circumstance has given me great comfort. there was general alarm during the pendency of the election in Congress, lest no President should be chosen, the government be dissolved, & anarchy ensue. but the cool determination of the really patriotic to call a convention in that case, which might be on the ground in 8. weeks, and wind up the machine again which had only run down, pointed out to my

mind a perpetual & peaceable resource against force in whatever ex-
tremity might befal us: & I am certain a convention would have commanded immediate & universal obedience. how happy that our army
had been disbanded! what might have happened otherwise [is
more] a subject of reflection than explanation.—you have seen your
recommendation of mr Willard duly respected. as to yourself I hope
we shall see you again in Congress. Accept assurances of my high respect and attachment.

PrC (DLC); faint; at foot of text: "Nathanial Niles esq."

TOGETHER ON THE PUBLIC STAGE: Niles served in Congress during TJ's last years as secretary of state (*Biog. Dir. Cong.*).

From Joseph Allen Smith

SIR,   Paris March 22d. 1801.

I do not hesitate to trouble you with a letter on a Subject, which
I think of importance to the tranquillity & happiness of our Country.

Spain has ceeded Louisiana to France, & an expedition is preparing
to take possession of New Orleans, & to plant a Colony in that country. Genl. Collaud, who is to command it, sails in a few days for
Philadelphia, & will proceed by land to the Missisippi—The force destined for the execution of this project, consisting, I believe, of three or
four frigates, will follow as soon as possible—The intention, *at present*,
is to keep the whole a Secret from the government of the United
States.

I have done every thing, which attachment to his Country could
suggest to a private individual, to suspend the execution of this
enterprise; & have been seconded by General Lafayette, & by
Mr. Victor Dupont. The enclosed are copies of a memorial & a note,
which I addressed to Joseph Bonaparte—they were received by him
this morning. I had been told that he would receive me with pleasure
today, but finding, probably, that the execution of the project was
resolved upon, he has by a second note, deferred our Interview until
his return from the Country. I have since heard, indirectly, in answer
to the memorial which I presented, "that it would produce no change
in the determination of the government."

I had, in the mean time, requested of Genl. Lafayette to speak to Citizen Talleyrand on the Subject. The Minister began by observing, that
the fears of Americans as to the results of such an expedition, were ill

founded, but finding that these Assurances were unsatisfactory, he desired him to declare on *his Authority*, that the government had no thoughts of carrying it, into execution & this, at the Very moment that I had the most positive information to the Contrary.

I have not only written, but have sent off a Confidential person to apprise Mr King.

The Execution of this project cannot fail to produce consequences extremely disagreeable to those who are desirous that perfect harmony should exist between France & the United States; but there is this Consolation, that we have every reason to expect from the government of our Country that Energy, Patriotism, & Consistency, which insure Security at Home, & establish national character abroad—

Permit me, Sir, to offer you my Sincere Congratulations on your Election, & to assure you of the perfect respect with which I have the Honor to be

Yr Most Obt Hmbe. St:

JOSEPH ALLEN SMITH of So. Carol.

RC (DLC); endorsed by TJ as received 27 Aug. and so recorded in SJL. Enclosures: (1) Memorial, dated Paris, 30 Ventose Year 9 [21 Mch. 1801], stating that an expedition to take possession of Louisiana will bring conflict with the United States, fostering insubordination in the western United States and raising the prospect of a slave revolt in the southern states; Spain's administration of Louisiana has lessened the Americans' apprehension, but if threatened by civil war and a situation similar to that of Saint-Domingue they will engage in a prolonged war to assure their independence, even against the country that helped them to gain it; Great Britain will exploit the opportunity to make common cause with the Americans, suppress the armed neutrality and control all seaborne commerce, and mount an expedition to capture New Orleans that Spanish colonists, fearful of losing their slave property, will support; yet it suits the genius and peaceful nature of Napoleon Bonaparte to avert these evils by letting the Americans determine the fate of Louisiana, keeping the province available to France as a source of wood for shipbuilding, provisions for the West Indies, and land for settlement; Smith urging the prudence of suspending plans for an expedition during this time when ratification of the convention between France and the United States is pending and the United States is without a resident minister in France (MS in same; in French, in Smith's hand, with no signature or addressee; at head of text: "Copy"). (2) Smith to Joseph Bonaparte, 1 Germinal Year 9 [22 Mch. 1801], Hotel d'Orsay, Rue de Varennes, asking him to excuse the liberty that Smith takes seeking an interview, but Smith is certain that Joseph Bonaparte will want to preserve the harmony that he has done so much to restore between France and the United States; Smith, knowing for some days now that Spain has ceded Louisiana to France, understands that the government plans an expedition to take possession and establish a colony; Smith's disposition usually keeps him apart from political matters, but he hopes to prevent the alienation of the Americans from France; he asks that Joseph Bonaparte read his memorial and, if the request is not too indiscreet, to communicate his views to the first consul; Smith asks only that the project be suspended until the matter can be discussed with people who have knowledge of the situation in America, including Rufus King, William Vans Murray, Lafayette, and Victor du Pont (MS in same; in French, in Smith's hand

and signed by him; at head of text: "Copy"). Enclosed in James C. Mountflorence to TJ, 26 Mch. 1801, from Quay Malaquais No. 1, Paris, the body of which reads in its entirety: "The Packet herewith was particularly recommended to me by Mr. Smith, with a Request that I would beg Mr. Olsen to deliver it personally" (RC in DLC; at foot of text: "His Excellency The President of the United States of America—Washington"; endorsed by TJ as received 27 Aug. and so recorded in SJL); according to SJL this letter was the last correspondence between TJ and Mountflorence; Peder Blicher Olsen was on his way to the United States to serve as resident minister and consul general of Denmark (Emil Marquard, *Danske Gesandter og Gesandtskabspersonale indtil 1914* [Copenhagen, 1952], 459; Madison, *Papers, Sec. of State Ser.*, 1:452, 489; 2:206n).

Joseph Allen Smith (1769-1828), a halfbrother of William Loughton Smith, traveled in Europe from 1793 to 1807, collecting prints, paintings, and casts of gems, medals, and statuary. After his return to the United States he lived in Philadelphia, where items from his collection became part of the early holdings of the Pennsylvania Academy of Fine Arts. The letter above is the only correspondence to or from Smith that TJ recorded in SJL (E. P. Richardson, "Allen Smith, Collector and Benefactor," *American Art Journal*, 1, no. 2 [1969], 5-19; George C. Rogers, Jr., *Evolution of a Federalist: William Loughton Smith of Charleston (1758-1812)* [Columbia, S.C., 1962], 338-40).

By a secret preliminary treaty signed at San Ildefonso on 1 Oct. 1800 the Spanish crown agreed to cede the vast province of LOUISIANA back to France. Spain was also to provide the French with six 74-gun warships. In return for these concessions France agreed to create a kingdom of 1,200,000 subjects in northern Italy for King Carlos's son-in-law, Louis of Parma. The new kingdom of Tuscany—subsequently called Etruria—was recognized by a confirming treaty signed at Aranjuez on 21 Mch. 1801. That treaty contained formal acknowledgment of the cession of Louisiana to

France (Parry, *Consolidated Treaty Series*, 55:375-8; 56:45-9; Tulard, *Dictionnaire Napoléon*, 944).

GENL. COLLAUD: like Smith, William Constable, a New York merchant and land speculator who wrote to Alexander Hamilton from Paris on 23 Mch., spelled the general's name "Collaud." Although there was a French general named Colaud, Smith and Constable evidently meant Victor Collot, who was the person named by Rufus King in London and by Robert R. Livingston when he corresponded with King from Paris in December 1801. A few years previously Collot had gathered military intelligence and topographical information in the Mississippi Valley, apparently in anticipation of a return of Louisiana to French control and the potential joining of the western United States to that province. Whether Collot, on the basis of that experience, was a candidate for command of an expedition to take possession of Louisiana is uncertain. Constable thought that Collot, a former governor of the island of Guadeloupe, was to be the governor of Louisiana, which Livingston also understood to have been the original intention. But King heard only that Collot might lead "a considerable number of disaffected and exiled Englishmen, Scotchmen and Irishmen" to the United States. King thought that any link between that rumor and the retrocession of Louisiana to France was "mere conjecture." Collot had been away from France from 1792 to 1800, and according to Livingston he was "out of favor" in Paris by late 1801. When France did assemble an expedition during 1802, Collot was not named as the *capitaine général* of Louisiana to lead it (Syrett, *Hamilton*, 25:372-3; Madison, *Papers, Sec. of State Ser.*, 1:55-6, 228-9; Michaël Garnier, *Bonaparte et la Louisiane* [Paris, 1992], 48; Tulard, *Dictionnaire Napoléon*, 200-1, 435-6, 1092, 1717; Vol. 30:300, 361-2n; Vol. 31:467-9).

TO APPRISE MR KING: on 29 Mch. King wrote to the secretary of state to confirm "the rumours of the day" about the Louisiana cession. Without naming his source, King also reported the rumor about Collot (Madison, *Papers, Sec. of State Ser.*, 1:55-6).

By Express from the City of Washington ! !

To the EDITORS of the TIMES.

THIS moment the election is decided. Morris, from Vermont, absented himself, so that Vermont was for Jefferson. The four members from Maryland, who had voted for Burr, put in blank tickets. The result was then ten for Jefferson.

I hope you will have the cannon out to announce the news.

Yours,

N. B. This was the second ballot to-day. Bayard is appointed ambassador to France.

Tuesday, two o'clock.

Broadside

Friends & fellow citizens

Called upon to undertake the duties of the first Executive office of our country, I avail myself of the presence of that portion of my fellow citizens which is here assembled, to express my grateful thanks for the favor with which they have been pleased to look towards me, to declare a sincere consciousness that the task is above my talents, & that I approach it with those anxious & awful presentiments which the greatness of the charge & the weakness of my powers so justly inspire. a rising nation, spread over a wide & fruitful land, traversing all the seas with the rich productions of their industry, ... in commerce with nations .... advancing rapidly to destinies beyond the reach of mortal eye; when I contemplate these transcendent objects & see the honour, the happiness, & the hopes of this beloved country, ... to the issue & the auspices of this day, I shrink from the contemplation, ... before the magnitude of the undertaking. utterly indeed should I despair, did not the presence of many, whom I here see, remind me, that in the other high authorities provided by our constitution, I shall find resources of wisdom, of virtue, & of zeal on which to rely under all difficulties. to you then, gentlemen, who are charged with the sovereign functions of legislation, & to those associated with you, I look with encouragement for that guidance & support which may enable us to steer with safety the vessel in which we are all embarked, amidst the conflicting elements of a troubled world.

During the contest of opinion — .... through which we have past, the animation of discussions & of exertions has sometimes worn an aspect which might impose on strangers unused to think freely, & to speak & to write what they think. but this being now decided by the voice of the nation, enounced according to .... the rules of the constitution, all will of course arrange themselves under the will of the law & unite in common efforts for the common good. .... that will to be rightful must be reasonable; that the minority possess their equal rights, which equal laws must protect, & to violate would be .... let us then, fellow citizens, unite with one heart & one mind, let us restore to social intercourse that harmony & affection without which liberty & even life itself are but dreary things. and let us reflect that having banished from our land that religious intolerance under which mankind so long bled & suffered, we have yet gained little if we countenance a political intolerance, as despotic, as wicked & capable of

Revised Draft of Jefferson's First Inaugural Address

Creamware Pitcher

View of the Capitol

Jefferson Banner

PIECES

To be sung at the German Reformed Church,

On *WEDNESDAY, the 4th of MARCH,* 1801.

by Mr
DuPonceau

SOLEMN INVOCATION.

LET our songs ascend to thee,
God of life and LIBERTY :
For grateful songs our tongues employ,
The transports of a Nation's joy.

THE PEOPLE'S FRIEND.

Rembrandt
Peale

NO more to subtle arts a prey,
Which, fearful of the eye of day,
A Nation's ruin plann'd :
Now entering on th' auspicious morn,
In which a people's hopes are born,
What joy o'erspreads the land !

While past events portended harm,
And rais'd the spirit of alarm,
Uncertain of the end :
Ere all was lost, the prospect clear'd,
And a bright star of hope appear'd,
The People's chosen Friend.

Devoted to his country's cause,
The Rights of Men and equal Laws,
His hallow'd pen was given :
And now those Rights and Laws to save,
From sinking to an early grave,
He comes, employ'd by Heaven.

What joyful prospects rise before !
Peace, Arts and Science hail our shore,
And thro' the country spread :
Long may these blessings be preserv'd,
And by a virtuous land deserv'd,
With JEFFERSON our head.

CHORUS.

REJOICE, ye States, rejoice,
And spread the patriot flame ;
Call'd by a Nation's voice,
To save his country's fame,
And dissipate increasing fears,
Our favourite JEFFERSON appears.

Let every heart unite,
Th' eventful day to hail ;
When from the Freemen's Right,
The People's hopes prevail ;—
That hence may horrid faction cease,
And honour be maintain'd with PEACE.

AFTER THE ORATION.

Handel

'TIS LIBERTY, dear LIBERTY alone,
Which gives fresh beauty to the sun ;
That bids all nature look more gay,
And lovely life with pleasures steal away.

18848

"Pieces To be sung at the German Reformed Church"

"The People's Friend"

Candidate	Residence	by Office recommended?	by whom recommend	Date.
Munson William.	New Haven.		Pierp[.] Edwards	1800. Dec. 16.
Meade Everard				
Cranch Wm. nephew Mrs. A.	Washington	Commr. vice Scott.	William Thornton	Dec. 31.
Barnes Joseph.	Hamburg	Consul Genl. of 2 Sicilies.		
Paine Thomas.	Paris	Commr. of indemnities		Oct. 4
Thomas Cooper	161. Chestnut Street. or Northumbd	Supervisor of Distr. of Pensva. less Genl. miller		
Hamilton	Northumbd. Penova	Collector of Excise. less Prieurs who was put less Hamilton unjustly	Thomas Cooper.	
Dist[.] Tho[s]. J. Vandyke		Superintend[.] of Chactaw nation	David Campbell	Dec. 28.
William Brent	Addl. to Commr. of Washington	less maj. Tho. Lewis my private Secretary	Richd. Brent	
Stephen Sayre	Philada.	Commr. in the negociation	himself & Govr. McKean	1801. Jan. 16.
Genl. Wm. Irvine	Carlisle	Supervisor of the excise	Gov[r]. McKean	Jan. 10. 12. &c. Feb. 5.
Robert McKean	Philada.	in the customs	Gov[r]. McKean	Jan. 10.
Zantzinger Paul.	Lancaster	in the revenue &c.	Barr. S. Barton.	Jan. 10.
Sullivan.	Boston	district judge	I. Langdon.	Feb.
Genl. Muhlenberg		Supervisor of revenue	delegates of Pensva.	Feb. 20
Genl. Irvine			Mr. Brown.	
I. Beckley		Comptroller vice Steele	do.	
Claiborne		Gov[r]. Missi. territory	Gregg Davis	
Charles Wilkins	Kentucky	marshal vice McDowell	Innes. Short. S.Brown. I. Brown	Feb. 23.
John Jouett	do.	do.	Innes. Todd. Breckenr. Hopkins	
Muhlenburg F. A.	Phila.	Collector Phila. vice Latimer	himself.	Feb. 11
Adam & Rhoades	Boston	Printing	Genl. Varnum.	Jan. 20.
Dr. John Villard				
Genl. Isaac Clarke	Vermont	Marshal Vermont & Fitch	M. Lyon	Mar. 1.
Dr. James M'Neill				
Lane. George.	Dumfries.	Marshal of Columbia.	Richd. Brent -	Feb. 22.
I. John Page	Rosewell	Director of Mint		
Tho'. Tudor Tucker	S. Caro[l].	Treas[r]. of mint	I. John Page	Feb.
John Caldwell. Shr.	N. Jersey	Consul in St. D[?]	Boudinot. Rush.	21.
Joseph Fenwick	English. S.C.	Consul Algiers	Piere Butler	
Lewis S. Pintard.				
Edw. Livingston		Consul Wadeira.	I. M. Pintard. Burr	
Mr. James	Madeira.	do.	Burr	
Barnet	Bordeaux	do.	Fitzsimmons. Stoddart.	
Dorr Mr. Grayson. Shrpt	Washington	Consul at Bordeaux.	mr. A.	
Lee Wm.	Boston	do.	Wall. Jones	
Wm. Forbes.	R. I.	or Havre	mr. A. Monroe. Genl. Lincoln Fendn. I.C. Jones Russell. Dexter. Mint	
Peter D. Abel	Phila.	do.	Perry. marshal Lynhburg. I. Foster. Monroe? Dexter.	
Theodore Peters.	Bordeaux.	do.	Dr. Vidar.	
Thorn Stephen.		do.		
La Motte.	Havre.	Consul at Havre.		
John Mitchell.		do.		
Skipwith	Paris.	do.		
Mountflorence	do.	Consul Genl. France.		
Jas. Swan. Shrpt.	do.	do.		
Nathan?		Consul in France	Ja. Monroe.	
Wm. E. Halings.	N. Orleans.	Consul at N. Orleans.	Wm. Jones Phila.	
Lewis Dab.		do. Isle of France		
Stacy George		do.		
Wm. Buchanan.	Baltimore	do.	app[.] by mr. A. recent.	
Henry Preble.	Boston	do. Cadiz	Genl. Smith.	
Blake James.	Phila.	do.	nam[d]. by mr. A.	
Prevost	N.J.	do.	Dr. Stevens.	
John Caldwell Shrpt	N.J.	do.	Boudin[ot]. Rush. I. R. Smith	
Jacob Mayer	Penova.	St. Domingo	McKean. W.Barton. Duane.	
Henry L. Rutledge		Span. colo[nies]		
Edw[r]. Jones.	Geo. ?	Guadaloupe	the Mason. Stoddart.	
Anthony Van Mannevelt	Phila.	Antwerp.	Baron de Beelen Bartholf. Wm. Innes &c	
John I. Murray.	N.Y.	Glasgow	Burr. C. Pinckney.	
Thomas Aborne	Dunwich	Cayenne	Theodore Foster.	18557

List of Candidates

Memorial from Eliakim Littell and Squier Littell

[before 23 Mch. 1801]

His Excelency Thomas Jefferson Esqr. Presedent of the United States Of America:

The Memorial of Eliakim Littell:

Humbly Sheweth that as earley as the Year 1776 your Memorilist took an active part against the Common Enemy of the United States of America, By Entering on Board the Schooner General Putnam as Master after Returning from Said Vessel, He then Raise'd a Company of Rangers at his Own Expence which Prove'd of Service In Defence of his Contry, He then Engaged in the year 1777, as first Lieut. In the first New Jersey Regiment Commaned By Coln. Matthias Ogden, And Inlisted Fifty Six men during the war for Said Regimen and Paid Each Soldier his Bounty at his Own Risque, and Continued with the Army until July 1778 at which time He Sustaind Great fatigue and Losses and Resigne'd my Commision my health then being much impared, after a Short tim Recoverd his Health again and then took the Command of a Company of Militia Artilery in the year 1780 in June at the Battle of Springfield your Memorist Receivd the approbation of Genl. Washington together with Genl. Dayton and many other Field Officers, After this nothing Material Until April, 1791. Then Receivd a Lieuts. Commission Under Capt. Philne in Levies Raised in New Jersey to Join Genl. St. Clair, on the Western Expedition against the Hostile Indians. In which Battle himself and son Suffered Great danger and hardships being Numbered among the dead. But now your Petitioners having Recoved his heath wishes if it be agreeable with Your Excelenceys Approbation to Join the Western Army in what Station your Honour would think most Proper your Petitioner having had three Lieuts. Commissions and two Captains, In the Last Revolution War, and has Fought in Five General Engagements and Fourteen Scurmages Both by Land & Sea In Defence of American Rights Said Petitioner has a Son which was Bred to Practice of Phisic and Surgery which would wish a Birth in Some Regiment as he Bears a Reputable Character as any young man in the State of New Jersey, Your Compliance with the above Requests will much Oblidge your humble Petitioner—your Excellency & Country Ever to serve—

ELIAKIM LITTELL
&. SQUIER LITTELL Surgn.

State. of New Jersey County of
County of Essex. Township of Springfield.

RC (DNA: RG 59, LAR, 7:0283-4); undated; probably in Eliakim Littell's hand; addressed: "A. Petition To the President of the United States"; endorsed by TJ as received 23 Mch. and so recorded in SJL.

Eliakim Littell (d. ca. 1805) resided at Hobart's Hill between Chatham and Springfield, New Jersey. His sixth and youngest child, Squier (1776-1849), moved to Butler County, Ohio, around 1800, where he became a successful physician and served as a justice of the peace and judge. Neither received a commission or appointment during TJ's administration (John Littell, *Family Records: or Genealogies of the First Settlers of Passaic Valley, [and Vicinity,] Above Chatham* [Feltville, N.J., 1852], 218).

From Joseph Louis d'Anterroches

Elizabethtown, New Jersey, 23 Mch. 1801. His recollection of the kindness shown by TJ as minister plenipotentiary to France encourages him to write. Born into a noble French family in 1753, D'Anterroches was at the age of eight placed under the supervision of his uncle, a bishop, to be educated for a life in the church. At 15 he hoped to begin a career in the army but was sent to the University of Paris, where he became acquainted with Talleyrand in the seminary of St. Sulpice. At the age of 20, still wanting to pursue a military career but finding his family, with the exception of his mother, firmly opposed to the idea, he made his way to England, where he obtained a commission in the army. Sent to Quebec with his regiment during the American Revolution, he was taken prisoner with Burgoyne's army, then married a woman from the vicinity of Elizabeth and at his earliest opportunity gave up his British commission to settle in the United States. He and his wife had nine children but he has been cut off from all support from France. He asks for a government job, noting that he was meant to have a consulship "previous to the change of government" and had the support of La Luzerne, France's former ambassador to the U.S., and of both Lafayette and George Washington. General Lee can attest to his service as an adjutant general with the expedition to western Pennsylvania in 1794. D'Anterroches also commanded his town's volunteer company as part of the provisional army, a responsibility that he would have avoided had he realized how expensive it would be, and he encloses a letter relating to that service. His simple "political Creed" is adherence to the Constitution, which he will gladly defend even against insurrection or invasion. His friend Lafayette, whom he expects soon in the United States as minister of France, can verify the facts of his early life, and if desired D'Anterroches can provide testimonials of his conduct during his residence in America.

RC (DNA: RG 59, LAR); 4 p.; at foot of text: "His Excellency Thomas Jefferson Esqr. President of the United States"; endorsed by TJ as received 28 Mch. and so recorded in SJL. Enclosure: probably Harry W. Ogden and Thomas Loval to D'Anterroches, 28 Jan. 1799, regarding his command of the Elizabethtown company of volunteers (Tr in same; in D'Anterroches's hand).

As minister to France, TJ helped D'Anterroches's mother contact her son (Vol. 9:289, 311-12, 323-5; Vol. 10:188;

Vol. 14:588, 684-6; Vol. 15:51, 86). For D'Anterroches's career, see Emeline G. Pierson, "Some Records of the French in Elizabethtown," *Proceedings of the New Jersey Historical Society*, 2d ser., 13 (1895), 165-70.

To Columbia, South Carolina, Citizens

GENTLEMEN   Washington Mar. 23. 1801.

The reliance is most flattering to me [whic]h you are pleased to express in the character of my public conduct; as is the expectation with which you look forward to the inviolable preservation of our national constitution, deservedly the boast of our country. that peace, safety, & concord may be the portion of our native land, & be long enjoyed by our fellow citizens, is the most ardent wish of my heart; & if I can be instrumental in procuring or preserving them, I shall think I have not lived in vain. in every country where man is free to think & to speak, differences of opinion will arise from difference of perception, & the imperfection of reason. but these differences, when permitted, as in this happy country, to purify themselves by free discussion, are but as passing clouds overshadowing our land transiently, & leaving our horizon more bright & serene. that love of order & obedience to the laws, which so considerably characterizes the citizens of the United States, are sure pledges of internal tranquility, and the elective franchise, if guarded as the ark of our safety, will peaceably dissipate all combinations to subvert[1] a constitution dictated by the wisdom, & resting on the will of the people. that will is the only legitimate foundation of any government, and to protect it's free expression should be our first object. I offer my sincere prayers to the supreme ruler of the universe, that he may long preserve our country in freedom & prosperity, and to yourselves, gentlemen, & the citizens of Columbia & it's vicinity the assurances of my profound consideration & respect.

TH: JEFFERSON

PrC (DLC); blurred; at foot of text: "Benjamin Waring esq. Columbia. S.C."

YOU ARE PLEASED TO EXPRESS: see Columbia, South Carolina, Citizens to TJ, 6 Mch.

[1] TJ here canceled "our."

From Tench Coxe

Philadelphia Mar. 23. 1801

A gentleman of this place called upon me to day and stated to me the receipt of a letter by him evidencing some kind intentions towards me. There appears to be a necessity of making some remarks and explanations, which I hope will be excused.

The reason of mentioning the object in a letter (covered to the Secy of State) from this place, was the certainty represented to me of a vacancy—the appearances of good reasons—and the inexecution of the various, numerous and extended duties of the office. It is certain that it has never been well executed in the district in question—nor in more than one third of the districts throughout the US., nor will the person in question, and now employed ever accomplish them. He is far from being enough of an office man. A review of his management from the beginning will prove this, and an inspection in the proper department by the head of it will establish these Suggestions. This case, I mention it with deference, appears to call for early attention, that the proper Conduct by Decr. may at once ameliorate the affairs of the Office, & conciliate the government, in certain parts, to the new appointment. As the principal difficulty in settling the proposed appointment of the head of that Department at Washington merits particular attention, the change in the district would be best made before the first of May. The Gentleman now charged with it is fixed, & it seems generally expedient that all the changes throughout that department & the districts in connexion with it, should be made in the temporary service of the present incumbent. This Idea, it is conceived, merits particular attention. The disorderly state of the district, in that line, requires great and early exertions.

If the three offices in the other line were vacant, it is conceived that the second would be more agreeable to the person than the first of them, because it has less pecuniary responsibility, and indeed none. The first is however the most valuable & would be generally the most desired, but in this case less so than the second. The third does not appear eligible to the person—

The most eligible is that mentioned in the former letter of about the 10th. instant. It will be ever found the most difficult *district* office to fill well—This may be relied on, as well from experience as from the nature of the office.

Another point has been mentioned—an abolition of a class of internal revenue officers. The Inspectors of Surveys can be better spared, than the Supervisors. The present System is—Collectors for

Counties connected in the number of 5, 7 or 9 under an inspector of a Survey, of which there are four in Pennsa. for example. These Inspectors are covered under the Supervisor of the Revenue for the district, and the Supervisors under the Commr. of the Revenue.

It is certain that an able and active supervisor would at one time have done better without Inspectors than with them. How it would be now I forbear to say. If either class should be abolished it should be (as is conceived) the Inspectors of Surveys. The action of a proper Supervisor on the Collectors would be greater than that of most of the Inspectors. The person favored by the Kindness mentioned would prefer a residence in his state in either of the two or even of the three, to more power, rank, & emolument at Washington. But if neither of them prove disposable, he would *reluctantly* move—but it would be reluctantly.

This much is said, Sir, because it seems to be desired that the person should explain.

RC (DNA: RG 59, LAR); in Coxe's hand; endorsed by TJ as received from Coxe 26 Mch. and so recorded in SJL.

PERSON IN QUESTION: Henry Miller occupied the office of supervisor of the revenue for the district of Pennsylvania, the position described by Coxe (JEP, 1:164-5). HEAD OF THAT DEPARTMENT AT WASHINGTON: Commissioner of the Revenue William Miller, who had been appointed to the office after Coxe's dismissal (JEP, 1:259-60; Washington, *Papers, Pres. Ser.*, 10:367; Coxe to TJ, 10 Mch. 1801). By the THREE OFFICES IN THE OTHER LINE Coxe probably meant the positions of collector, naval officer, and surveyor, those responsible for the collection of external revenues. For the compensation connected with those offices in Philadelphia in 1800, see ASP, *Miscellaneous*, 1:271.

From Theodore Foster

DEAR SIR,   New York March 23d. 1801—

When I last had the Honor to be in Company with you, I took the Liberty to mention that I was *personally* acquainted with *John M: Forbes Esqr.* of this City, who was lately nominated, by President Adams, and with the Concurrence of the Senate was appointed *Commercial Agent, for the United States at Havre, in France*. I then proposed to write to your Excellency, on his case, upon my Arrival, in this City, where his Brother and Partner in Trade Mr. R. B. Forbes resides, to which you was pleased to consent.—

John M. Forbes Esq before named was born at Boston, in Massachusetts, and had a liberal Education at Harvard College at Cambridge in that State.—He graduated there about the Year 1787, after which he pursued the Study of the Law—was regularly admitted to the Bar, and was sometime in Practice in New England.—But his Brother of this City, being largely concerned in Commerce, particularly with France, and wanting a Partner to assist him in Business, they formed a Commercial Connexion, under the Form of *John & Bennet Forbes* when the former went to reside in France to transact the Concerns of the Company there.—He was there when the Controversy commenced between that Country and the United States, and was one of the Committee of the Citizens of the United States then in France, who presented an Address to Mr. Munroe Decr. 6th: 1796 published by him, near the Close of the Volume, respecting his Embassy to France. In Consequence of the Troubles between the Two Nations Mr. Forbes returnd to this, his Native Country.—But as Commercial Intercourse is again opened he proposes to return to France, and it will very acceptable to him to be continued, in his before mentioned Appointment.—

I have Reason to think that Mr. Forbes is much esteemed in France:—and that he possesses genuine, republican Principles, in Politicks.—And as he speaks the French Language,—Sustains an excellent Character,—possesses a well informed, comprehensive Understanding, with an engaging Deportment, and agreeable Manners, at a Period of Life, when his Judgment, ripened by Experience, will not be likely to be led astray, I am induced to beleive that Mr. Forbes's Appointment, as Commercial Agent will give Satisfaction to all who know him, and that but few native Americans can be found to go to reside, in France, more capable, or more disposed honorably to discharge the Duties attachd to the Office.—

Mr. Forbes would prefer an Appointment to reside at Bourdeaux where he is well acquainted, to one at Havre.—But will be obliged by one to either Place, and in either will be disposed to render the American Government all the Services in his Power.—

I have the Honor to be, with great Esteem and Respect, your Excellencys most Obedient Servant   THEODORE FOSTER

RC (DNA: RG 59, LAR); at head of text: "To the President of the United States"; endorsed by TJ as received 30 Mch. and so recorded in SJL.

Theodore Foster (1752-1828), an attorney, judge, and antiquarian, was a U.S. Senator from Rhode Island from 1790 until March 1803. He was the brother of Dwight Foster and the son-in-law of Arthur Fenner (DAB). For earlier correspondence from

Foster to TJ that has not been found, see Vol. 25:415n.

On a slip of paper filed with Foster's letter TJ wrote:

"Forbes. see Monroe's lre Mar. 23. 1801.
a federalist
well enough.
named by mr A."

On 18 Feb., John Adams had named John Murray FORBES to be commercial agent at Le Havre, France. The Senate confirmed the nomination on 24 Feb., but Forbes was one of the late-term appointees who did not receive a commission. TJ named another person to the post at Le Havre but appointed Forbes in February 1802 to succeed Joseph Pitcairn as U.S. consul at Hamburg (JEP, 1:381, 385, 402, 406-7).

Forbes's BROTHER, Ralph Bennet Forbes, wrote to TJ from New York on 20 Mch. 1801 to enclose a letter from Monroe in support of John Murray Forbes and to assert that his brother was, contrary to "gross misrepresentation," a native of the United States, their family having lived in Boston and its vicinity "since the begining of the last Century." On the subject of political alignments R. B. Forbes could say only that his brother was "no partizan and that his *Americanism* will bear the most rigid Scrutiny" (DNA: RG 59, LAR, at foot of text: "The President of the United States," endorsed by TJ as

received 25 Mch. and so recorded in SJL; enclosure: Monroe to TJ, 22 Feb. 1801, regarding which see Monroe's letter of 23 Mch.). The brothers' father, a Church of England clergyman born in Scotland, was for many years a resident and government official of British East Florida, but his wife was from Massachusetts, where they married (DAB, 6:505-6). The letter of 20 Mch. is the only correspondence to or from R. B. Forbes recorded in SJL.

The ADDRESS by U.S. citizens in Paris praised Monroe and expressed regret at his recall from the position of minister to France. John Murray Forbes and R. Bennet Forbes were among the 70 people who subscribed their names to the memorial (James Monroe, *A View of the Conduct of the Executive, in the Foreign Affairs of the United States, Connected with the Mission to the French Republic, During the Years 1794, 5, & 6* [Philadelphia, 1797], 401-2).

To William Branch Giles

DEAR SIR   Washington Mar. 23. 1801.

I recieved two days ago your favor of the 16th. and thank you for your kind felicitations on my election; but whether it will be a subject of felicitation permanently will be for chapters of future history to say. the important subjects of the government I meet with some degree of courage & confidence, because I do believe the talents to be associated with me. the [honest] line of conduct we will religiously pursue at home & abroad, and the confidence of my fellow citizens [drawing on us], will be equal to these objects. but there is another branch of duty, which I must meet with courage too, tho' I cannot without pain; that is the appointments & disappointments as to office. Madison & Gallatin being still absent, we have not yet decided on our rule of conduct as to these. that some ought to be removed from office, & that all ought not, all mankind will agree. but where to draw the line perhaps no two will agree. consequently nothing like a general[1] approbation on this subject can be looked for. some principles have been the subject of conversation but not of determination e.g. 1. all appointments to civil offices during pleasure, made after the event of the election was certainly known to mr A. are considered as nullities. I do not view the persons appointed as even candidates for the office, but make others without noticing or notifying them. mr A's best friends have agreed this is right. 2. officers who have been guilty of official mal-conduct are proper subjects of removal. 3. good men, to whom there is no objection but a difference of political principle, practised only as far as the right of a private citizen will justify, are not proper subjects of removal, except in the case of Attornies & Marshals. the courts being so decidedly federal, & irremovable, it is believed that republican Attornies & Marshals, being the doors of entrance into the courts, are indispensably necessary as a shield to the republican part of our fellow citizens, which I believe is the main body of the people. these principles are yet to be considered of, and I sketch them to you in confidence. not that there is objection to your [mooting?] them as subjects of conversation & as proceeding from yourself, but not as matters of executive determination. nay further I will thank you for your own sentiments & those of others on them. if recieved before the 2[0]th. of April, they will be in time for our deliberation on the subject.—you know that it was in the year XYZ. that so great a transition from our to the other side took place, & with as real[2] republicans as we were ourselves. that these, after getting over that delusion have been returning to us, and that it is to that return we [owe] a triumph in 1800. which in 1799. would have been the other way. the week's suspense of the election before Congress, seems almost to have compleated that business, and to have brought over nearly the whole remaining mass. they now find themselves with us, & separated from their quondam leaders. if we can but avoid shocking their feelings by unnecessary acts of severity against their late friends, they will in a little time cement & form one mass with us, & by these means harmony & union be restored to our country, which would be the greatest good we could affect. it was a conviction that these people did not differ from us in principle, which induced me to define the principles which I deemed orthodox, & to urge a reunion on those principles; and I am induced to hope it has conciliated many. I do not speak of the desperados of the quondam faction, in & out of Congress. these I consider as incurables, on whom all attentions would be lost, & therefore will not be wasted. but my wish is to keep their flock from returning to them.—on the subject of the Marshal of Virginia, I refer you confidentially to Majr. Egglestone for information. I leave this about this day sennight to make some arrangements at home preparatory to my final removal to this place from which I shall be absent about three weeks. accept assurances of my constant esteem, & high consideration & respect.   Th: Jefferson

PrC (DLC); faint; at foot of first page: "W. B. Giles esq."

[1] Written over "federal."
[2] Word interlined in place of "[firm?]."

MARSHAL OF VIRGINIA: see Joseph Eggleston to TJ, 2 Mch. 1801.

From Joseph Habersham

SIR,   March 23 1801

Mr John H Barney in a letter to the Comptroller of the Treasury states that he intends to prefer a complaint against the Postmaster General for rejecting his proposals for carrying sundry mails during the last summer. As I was necessarily absent at that time & that business was done by the Assistant Postmaster General he has thought it necessary to state his reasons for rejecting those proposals & has requested me to submit them to your consideration which I have now the honor to do As his letter goes fully into the subject it is only necessary for me to add that on my return I examined the business alluded to, & was fully convinced that it was properly conducted. Should any other charges have been prefered by Mr Barney I have to request the favor of being furnished with a copy that I may have an opportunity of replying to them. I am

J. H.

FC (Lb in DNA: RG 28, LPG); in clerk's hand; at head of text: "Thomas Jefferson Esqr. President of the United States." Recorded in SJL as received 23 Mch. Enclosure not found.

In 1800 JOHN H. BARNEY moved from Havre de Grace, where he had served as postmaster from 1789 to 1795 and had invested in a stage line from Baltimore to Philadelphia, to the Columbian Inn in Georgetown. He continued his investment in a stage line between Philadelphia and Alexandria with James Bryden of Baltimore. In 1800, Barney submitted a bid to carry the mail between Baltimore and Washington for $200. The contract instead went to William Evans and his partner, who bid $1,400 for the route. In submitting the bids to John Steele,

comptroller of the Treasury, the postmaster general noted that Barney had "deceived the public in a former contract & by neglecting his duty was the occasion of much complaint, inconvenience, and disappointment" (RCHS, 50 [1952], 15, 19-23, 39n; Stets, *Postmasters*, 138; DAB, 17:557). Upon learning that Habersham was to resign, Barney wrote TJ a short letter from Georgetown on 1 Oct. 1801, in which he noted that if "you think me Compitent and deserving, I shall be Happy in the Appointment" (RC in DNA: RG 59, LAR; addressed: "The President of U,S,"; endorsed by TJ as received 1 Oct. and "to be postmaster Genl." and so recorded in SJL).

ASSISTANT POSTMASTER GENERAL: Abraham Bradley, Jr. (ASP, *Finance*, 1:813).

From William Jones

SIR   Philadelphia 23d March 1801

Deeply penetrated with the confidence you are pleased to evince in proposing to me the Secretaryship of the Navy, I entreat you to believe that I have weighed with mature deliberation all the considerations which ought to influence my decision in a case so important to the public interest and the honor of the administration

To be associated with private worth and exalted talents such as compose your administration, would be no less grateful to my feelings than honora[ble] to myself, and tho my skill and talents in that department have been much too highly estima[ted] I would with pleasure have contributed my humble efforts to promote the great end you have in view but for obstacles of a private nature which I find irresistible.   I am fully sensible of the duty we owe our country and the administration of our choice [and would] [. . .]ly forego private consider[ations to] any reasonable extent.   I regret the necessity that impels me to decline the proffered honor, and trust my motives will be so appreciated as to preserve for me the favorable sentiments you are pleased to express.   With earnest wishes for the prosperity of your administration and your personal happiness

I am very respectfully and faithfully Yours   WM JONES

RC (DLC); frayed at margins; at foot of text: "Thomas Jefferson Esqr. President of the United States"; endorsed by TJ as received 26 Mch. and so recorded in SJL.

From William Kilty

                    Washington Rhodes's Hotel

SIR   March 23d. 1801

I had the Honour of receiving your letter of the 20th. proposing to me the office of Chief Judge of the Circuit Court of the district of Washington; but it did not reach me till yesterday at one oclock, being forwarded by express from Annapolis to Charles County where I was attending Court.

I avail myself of the earliest occasion to make you my respectful acknowledgement for the offer of the appointment and to Signify my Willingness to accept it

At the same time I must express my diffidence in entering on an office the duties of which appear to be of an arduous, and I may say, of a Novel Nature; and I can only pledge my endeavours for the performance of them

My Business at the Court in Charles County was not entirely finished, but as it appeared essential that I should attend here to day I Set out immediately on the arrival of the express

I shall wait your further Commands at this place, and shall pay my respects to you in Person before I leave the City

I have written this letter in some haste as the Court is to Sit so soon, and I have addressed it to you directly, instead of Sending it thro the Medium of the Secretary of State in pursuance of the Manner in which the notification was addressed to me

I am Sir with Great Consideration and respect Your obedient Servant

WILLIAM KILTY

RC (CSmH); at foot of text: "Thomas Jefferson Esqr"; endorsed by TJ as received 23 Mch. and so recorded in SJL.

Born in London, William Kilty (1757-1821) came to Maryland with his family shortly before the American Revolution. He served as an army surgeon during the war and was one of the founders of the Society of the Cincinnati. He studied law and entered the Maryland bar. In Annapolis in 1799 he began publication of his multivolume *The Laws of Maryland* (see Sowerby, No. 2171). In 1801 the two-volume edition of the Maryland laws was advertised as having "been prepared with great labour, and distinguished accuracy and ability." Kilty served as chief judge of the Washington circuit court until 1806 when he resigned to become chancellor of Maryland, the position he held until his death (Papenfuse, *Maryland Legislature,* 2:510; *Maryland Gazette,* 23 Apr. 1801;

Kilty to [James Madison], 27 Jan. 1806, in DNA: RG 59, RD).

On Friday, 20 Mch. 1801, TJ wrote William Kilty offering him the OFFICE OF CHIEF JUDGE OF THE CIRCUIT COURT at Washington, a position left unfilled when Thomas Johnson declined it. TJ noted that Kilty already knew the "emoluments" of the office as provided by law and hoped that he could be induced "to accept the appointment." Observing that the first court was "to be held here on Monday next," TJ requested that if Kilty agreed to serve he should arrive in Washington on the 22d for preparation of his commission (PrC in DLC; faint and blurred; at foot of text: "William Kelty esquire").

COURT IS TO SIT SO SOON: on Monday, 23 Mch., the *National Intelligencer* reported that the newly organized district court had met that day with Kilty presiding as chief judge.

From James Magoffin

HONOURED SIR,   Philada. March 23d: 1801—

Having once had the pleasure (in company with Mr. Fleming) of hearing you speak favourably of Chipmans Principles of Goverment—and at the same time signify your desire to be in possession of it—I beg Sir you'll accept of the inclosed Copy being one of six presented me by a friend in Boston—From your remarks on the work

I felt a more than common desire to give it an attentive perusal and must confess I became involuntarily struck with a peculiar boldness of Investigation—an ardent attempt to examine first principles with Candour & Impartiality which accompany and I think is inseperable from true Genius—and which undoubtedly does honor to the Writer—For but a small knowledge of the progress of Science will serve to convince a candid mind—that nothing tends more to retard the progress of Truth than that disposition so prevalent in the mass of Mankind to receive principles at second hand—especially if sanction'd by a name possessing Celebrity or glossed over with a more than common degree of plausability—The most absurd prejudices increase and become venerable by age—Antiquity seems as it were to consecrate Error—and men choose rather to follow the beaten paths that reason & Humanity on a deliberate examination would explode than wade through a deliberate research or what some has called the drudgery of Investigation—For my pa[rt] Sir I cannot help feeling a degree of esteem for a man who even dares at attempting to shake popular opinions—Should this small Treatise have the effect of tempting men to think more for themselves it would be desirable— For Truth only demands a candid search & seldom fails to reward our labours—

Those with a variety of other reasons have induced a few of us to get the work reprinted and give it Circulation through this State—as it appears unknown—Whatever may in the least tend to disseminate the remaining films of prejudice & Error—give energy to and accelerate the reign of those Sentiments & principles which have for their Basis, Justice, Humanity, & universal Benovelence, with a true knowledge of the most Sacred *rights of Men*—whatever may have the happy, the desirable tendency of spreading and causing those Sentiments to become as universal as the Scale of Human Beings must inevitably draw forth the energy and exertion of every Virtuous mind—Excuse Sir the liberty of those few thoughts, probably straind by the premature effusions of inexperienced youth———It no doubt will be agreable to hear that the prosperity of this City appears to revive—I just mention the Circumstance of every Shipyard in this City being engaged for one or two Ships this approaching Spring— which principally takes its rise from the prevailing hopes of a Speedy & permanent understanding being establish'd between this Country & France—Permit me Sir to add mine to the ardent wishes of your Country for your personal Health & Happiness & beleive me to be with every Sentiment of Esteem

Your mo: obedt. Servt.   JAMES MAGOFFIN

RC (ViW); frayed at edges; endorsed by TJ as received 31 Mch. and so recorded in SJL; used as blotting paper by TJ.

Magoffin was most likely of Magoffin & Son, merchants, on 12 South Front Street in Philadelphia (Stafford, *Philadelphia Directory, for 1801*, 50).

CHIPMANS PRINCIPLES OF GOVERNMENT: Magoffin enclosed a copy of Nathaniel Chipman's *Sketches of the Principles of Government*, a title which TJ often included on his lists of recommended reading (Sowerby, No. 2361; Vol. 31:68).

From James Monroe

DEAR SIR   Richmond 23. March 1801.

My present and past employments have made me acquainted with many deserving men whose demands I cannot resist to make themselves & their views known to you. I must mention several at present with whom I stand in that predicamt. lest by withholding their pretentions longer, a reliance on me for that service might possibly expose them to injury.   David Gelston of New Yk. wod. be happy to accept the collectorship of that city shod. it become vacant. He was a firm patriot in our revolution. I knew him in 1784. when he was a Senator of that State, which office he has generally held since, as I believe he did for several years before. He was always a republican and a bold supporter of the cause when it was most dangerous to support it. He is a merchant who trades within his capital, of respectable abilities and unimpeachable integrity. I became acquainted with him the year you went to France in a trip to fort Stanwix with Govr. Clinton himself & others. Govr. Clinton and I presume many others will write in his favor if necessary.   William Lee of Boston lately nominated by Mr. Adams consul to Marseilles. He is a sensible deserving man, sound in his principles and amiable in his manners. He was nominated reluctantly by Mr. Adams at the instance of Mr. Gerry, who put him at a post where he cod. do nothing. He wishes to be brot. more into the busy world, as he has a family dependant on his industry & success. He is the person who brought Pichons pamphlets wh. gave occasion for so much noise & scandal at the time. That transaction has been explained much to his honor, and his conduct since has justified the good opinion I formed of him in Paris.

Mr. Forbes of New Yk. formerly Mass: had a letter from me to you. He likewise was nominated by Mr. Adams to some port in France. I think him an honest man, of good understanding, and worthy attention. Tho' friendly to Mr. Adams's admn. yet he was disliked by him & those under him for his liberality.   I enclosed to Mr. Madison Mr Skipwiths letter to me mentioning his & the wish of Joel Barlow for

employment. They are both known to you.   I hinted to you I was persuaded Mr. Ervine wod. be gratified with some employment abroad wh. wod. enable him to advance his own fame in support of yr. admn. I have the highest opinion of his honor, his principles, & merit. His pretentions are moderate, and altho he wod. like some diplomatic agency, such as chargé des affrs. or even secry.ship at London or Paris, yet he wod. act as consul genl. to London. His delicacy wod. not permit me to penetrate so far into this as, was necessary to explain correctly his views. You are doubtless informd of his standing at Boston, and what his pretentions growing out of it are. I think I mentioned Mr. Prevost, Mr. Beckly & some characters in this State in a former letter.
      sincerely I am dear Sir yr. friend & servt   JAS. MONROE

RC (DLC); endorsed by TJ as received 27 Mch. and so recorded in SJL. Dft (DLC: Monroe Papers); first paragraph only, with revisions.

TRIP TO FORT STANWIX: in 1784 Monroe, a member of Congress, observed conferences between Indian tribes and New York State commissioners before continuing his travels into Canada (Ammon, *Monroe*, 45-7).

PICHONS PAMPHLETS: the papers that William Lee handed to Oliver Wolcott in June 1798 included a packet addressed to Benjamin Franklin Bache. Wolcott's interception of the packet, which bore the seal of the French ministry of foreign affairs, prompted speculation that it contained subversive correspondence. After some delay, when Bache finally received the unopened packet it was found to hold only two anonymous pamphlets relating to Great Britain and France, *Lettre d'un Français á M. Pitt, ou, Examen du Systême Suivi par le Gouvernement Britanique Envers la France* (1797) and *Seconde Lettre d'un Français á M. Pitt* (1798). Authorship of the works has been attributed to Louis André Pichon, who was an acquaintance of Bache and sent the pamphlets to him. The pamphlets were published by the print shop that Dupont de Nemours had in Paris during that period (James Tagg, *Benjamin Franklin Bache and the Philadelphia Aurora* [Philadelphia, 1991], 382-5; *Catalogue Général des Livres Imprimés de la Bibliothèque Nationale. Auteurs*, 231 vols. [Paris, 1897-1981], 136:646; Saricks, *Du Pont*, 242, 278).

LETTER FROM ME TO YOU: a letter that Monroe wrote on 22 Feb. 1801, received on 25 Mch. and recorded in SJL with TJ's notation that it pertained to "Forbes," has not been found. That communication was an enclosure to one from Ralph Bennet Forbes to TJ of 20 Mch.; see note to Theodore Foster to TJ, 23 Mch. 1801.

Monroe had forwarded to James MADISON Fulwar Skipwith's letter requesting employment for Skipwith and Joel Barlow. In June TJ named Skipwith the U.S. commercial agent at Paris in place of James C. Mountflorence, whom John Adams had nominated for the post (Madison, *Papers, Sec. of State Ser.*, 1:11-12; JEP, 1:384, 403; Appendix I, Lists 3 and 4).

To Thomas Newton

DEAR SIR   Washington Mar. 23. 1801.
      I duly recieved your favor of the 12th. inst. and thank you for the information respecting the receipt of a consignment of old Madeira

wines. I will gladly take a pipe of the Brazil quality which you mention to be the best: and should hope a means of conveying it hither would occur. the price I presume I shall be able to remit by a bill on the Collector of your port.

We [hear] nothing very late from Europe. I believe it to be certain that the emperor has ordered the signature of a treaty with France, but [we do] not yet know of it's actual signature. it is also said that England is making overtures for treating separately. the danger of famine will no doubt increase her desire for peace.

I am sensible of your goodness in offering to attend to my little [wants] in your place, should I have any. I have too long experienced it, not to avail myself of it should there be occasion. I pray you accept assurances of my constant esteem & high consideration and respect.

Th: Jefferson

PrC (DLC); faint and blurred; at foot of text: "Colo. Thomas Newton"; endorsed by TJ in ink on verso.

From Jonathan H. Nichols

Sir,   Boston, March 23, 1801.

I had the honor of receiving yours of the 9th inst. for the obliging terms of which, be pleased to accept my sincerest thanks:—Permit me, sir, to congratulate my country & yourself, upon your election to a trying and great office; may that Being who has raised you to preside over the affairs of a free & great nation, continue you long in that eminent usefulness, which has ever commanded the gratitude, affection and confidence of the republican Citizens of America. Pardon me if I join the plaudits of all who have any ideas of Literary elegance, of Sentimental excellence, and exalted moderation, in saying, that your late Speech is one of the most happy speciments of that nobility of mind, and superiority of talent, which the envious & unjust have endeavor'd to envelope in the dull mists of neglected merit;—But the pinions of slander are clipt, and malicious calumnies hover over the abys of disgrace.

I lament that I have neither the honor nor happiness of being personally acquainted with you, Sir, yet I am happy in recollecting the Name of one, whom fame Justly pronounces the friend of human Nature.

Want of property seems to have doom'd me to perpetual obscurity, but the happiest moment of my life would be that which offered an opportunity of evincing my attachment to the President, by active service. I fear you will suspect me to be a servile, courting, flatterer, never contented with undeserved favors. when you see me come forward with a second request, presuming too far upon your kindness.

Should I be so fortunate as to obtain your consideration, I have the vanity to hope, that I may one day inherit a Share of your esteem. I am young—possess a Small portion of literary knowledge, *I have political sentiments*—some little *Nautical experience*—and ambition, which is the parent of human action, has so strong dominion in my mind, that I almost forget what I do, when I continue to trouble you with solicitations—forgive me Sir, but if you recollect any *trifling office* or employment which would enable me more conveniently to procure subsistence, and at times, recreations in the pursuits of Study—your remembrance will be another addition to those kindnesses which you delight to bestow on your fellow citizens—for an answer to this I can hardly ask,

Mean while I remain, with grateful esteem, your obedt & hmbl. Servt. JONA H NICHOLS

RC (DNA: RG 59, LAR); addressed: "Th: Jefferson, Esq. President of the U.S. City—Washington"; franked; postmarked 26 Mch.; endorsed by TJ as received 16 Apr. and so recorded in SJL with notation "Off."; also endorsed by TJ: "some small office."

To John Page

MY DEAR FRIEND   Washington Mar. 23. 1801.

Your's of Feb. 1 did not reach me until Feb. 28. and a press of business has retarded my acknoleging it. I sincerely thank you for your congratulations on my election, but this is only the first verse of the chapter. what the last may be nobody can tell. a consciousness that I feel no wish but to do what is best, without passion or predilection, encourages me to hope for an indulgent construction of what I do. I had in General Washington's time proposed you as Director of the Mint, and therefore should the more readily have turned to you had a vacancy now happened. but that institution continuing at Philada, because the legislature have not taken up the subject in time to decide on it, it will of course remain full till this time twelvemonth. should it then be removed, the present director would probably, & the Treasurer certainly resign. it would give me great pleasure to employ the talents & integrity of Dr. Tucker in the latter office.

I am very much in hopes we shall be able to restore union & harmony to our country. not indeed that the desperado leaders can be brought over. they are incurables. but I really hope their followers may. the belief that these last were real republicans, carried over from us by French excesses, induced me to offer a political creed, & to invite to conciliation on that plan. and I am pleased to hear, that these principles are recognised by them, and considered as no bar of separation. a moderate conduct therefore, which may not revolt our new friends, which may give them time to cement with us, must be observed. some removals must take place; but on such principles as will not shock them.

Present my respects to mrs Page, and accept assurances of my constant and affectionate esteem.   TH: JEFFERSON

RC (Charles E. Kern II, South Merritt Island, Cocoa, Florida, 1956); addressed: "John Page esquire Rosewell near Gloucester. Virginia"; franked and postmarked; endorsed by Page as received 29 Mch. PrC (DLC).

As a congressman in 1792 Page had been active in the debates over the creation of the MINT and successfully argued that an image of Liberty, rather than a portrait of the president of the United States, should appear on U.S. coins. Early in 1793 TJ sent Page a copy of David Rittenhouse's report on assays of foreign coins. TJ probably suggested Page as director of the Mint in 1795 when Rittenhouse resigned and his successor, Henry William DeSaussure, left the post after four months. Elias Boudinot received the appointment. Benjamin Rush, who had declined to succeed Rittenhouse as director, became TREASURER of the Mint in 1797 on Boudinot's recommendation. In the autumn of 1801 TJ offered Thomas Tudor TUCKER, who had served in Congress with Page, the position of treasurer of the United States (George Adams Boyd, *Elias Boudinot: Patriot and Statesman, 1740-1821* [Princeton, 1952], 170, 198, 224-5, 232-3; *Biog. Dir. Cong.*; Vol. 25:33n; TJ to Tucker, 31 Oct. 1801).

To Moses Robinson

DEAR SIR   Washington Mar. 23. 1801.

I have to acknolege the reciept of your favor of the 3d. inst. and to thank you for the friendly expressions it contains. I entertain real hope that the whole body of our fellow citizens (many of whom had been carried away by the XYZ. business) will shortly be consolidated in the same sentiments. when they examine the real principles of both parties I think they will find little to differ about. I know indeed that there are some of their leaders who have so committed themselves that pride, if no other passion, will prevent their coalescing. we must be easy with them. the eastern states will be the last to come over, on account of the dominion of the clergy, who had got a smell of union between church & state, and began to indulge reveries which can never be realized in the present state of science. if indeed they could have prevailed on us to view all advances in science as dangerous innovations and to look back to the opinions & practices of our forefathers, instead of looking forward, for improvement, a promising ground work would have been laid. but I am in hopes their good sense will dictate to them that since the mountain will not come to them, they had better go to the mountain: that they will find their interest in acquiescing in the liberty & science of their country, and that the Christian religion when divested of the rags in which they have inveloped it, and brought to the original purity & simplicity of it's benevolent institutor, is a religion of all others most friendly to liberty, science, & the freest expansions of the human mind.

I sincerely wish with you we could see our government so secured as to depend less on the character of the person in whose hands it is trusted. bad men will sometimes get in, & with such an immense patronage, may make great progress in corrupting the public mind & principles. this is a subject with which wisdom & patriotism should be occupied. I pray you to accept assurances of my high respect & esteem.　　　　　　　　　　　　　　　　　　　TH: JEFFERSON

PrC (DLC); at foot of text: "Moses Robinson esq."

From Andrew Rounsavell

Fairfax County March 23d 1801

Sir haveing Spent considerable time in Study uppon a plan for riseing the water above its leavel So as to give the water to the inhabetance of a town, without labour: also to put it in the power of the Farmer to water his meadow ground in much larger quantity, by the hight he gains by the Rise of the water, and after a number of conjectors of a Simmelar nature am of opinnion the thing is plactable But Never the less have Some doubts wich ocation me to call on your honner to know your oppinion of the matter and if you think the thing practabel After Seeing my plan—your assistance in putting it in to execution—as my circomstance will not Admit my trying the experiment: wich will not in my opinion cost much to try the experiment uppon a Small Scale: my want of experience will I trust apologise for the want of formallety of my letter: that the Grate an first Cause may grant you health: and peace plenty & unity with the people you preside over is the prayrs of your petitioner

ANDREW ROUNSAVELL

PS Sir if the absurdety of the thing Should ocation your honor to think it not worth your notice: I wish you to think over the following philosophisical Ideas: first that the would is a Sphere Second that it turns round once in twenty four hours
3d that no one part can be said to be uppermost

4th that the water apears to have life wich it perservs by runing: when If confin'd Standing becomes Stagnate:

5th that we See the water come out of the top an exceding high mountain in large quantity and must have Some cause

6th that we See the power of Suction by the clouds drawing the water out of the Rivers in large quantity

---

Sir after you have read the above I trust you will heare my Reasons & look at my plan as I have Shewn my plan to Severl people wich might take advantage of it by making applycation or experiment before me: I therefore Send this Sooner to you then I intend: wishing to make you my deposit as I under Stand you are presedent of the philosophical Society:[1] thereby to Secure any advantages may be Receivd. by it

I at first thought to Send my letter but am at preasant at your Door myself. A ROUNSAVELL

RC (ViW); addressed: "To Thomas Jefferson Esq President of the United States"; endorsed by TJ as received on the same day as written, and so recorded in SJL.

Andrew Rounsavell (d. 1826) resided in Alexandria, at least in the latter part of his life, and on various occasions in his later years he served as a jailer there. Before the creation of the District of Columbia, Alexandria was part of Fairfax County, and the separation had only been formalized by a statute of 27 Feb. 1801 (Patrick G.

Wardell, *Alexandria City and County, Virginia, Wills, Administrations, and Guardian Bonds, 1800-1870* [Bowie, Md., 1986], 104; T. Michael Miller, *Portrait of a Town: Alexandria, District of Columbia, Virginia, 1820-1830* [Bowie, Md., 1995], 12, 119, 139, 205, 270, 354, 375, 385, 488; Emily J. Salmon, ed., *A Hornbook of Virginia History*, 3d ed. [Richmond, 1983], 104; U.S. Statutes at Large, 2:105).

[1] Rounsavell here canceled "that is in case you Should not fraternise in the [. . .] tor of a citizen."

To Andrew Rounsavell

SIR   Washington Mar. 23. 1801.

I am sincerely sorry it is not in my power to attend to the explanation of your invention for raising water. but my duties to the public now require that I deny myself every gratification of that kind, however fond of it from inclination. objects of a very different nature require the whole of my time & attention, & the whole is not sufficient. I hope you will be so good as to accept of this apology with the candor with which it is made. I am Sir

your most obedt. servt   TH: JEFFERSON

PrC (DLC); at foot of text: "Mr. Andrew Rounsavell."

From John Adams

Sir   Stony Field, Quincy March 24, 1801

I have recd your favour of March 8 with the Letter inclosed, for which I thank you. Inclosed is a Letter to one of your Domesticks Joseph Dougherty,[1]

Had you read the Papers inclosed they might have given you a moment of Melancholly or at least of Sympathy with a mourning Father. They relate wholly to the Funeral of a Son who was once the delight of my Eyes and a darling of my heart, cutt off in the flower of his days, amidst very flattering Prospects by causes which have been the greatest Grief of my heart and the deepest affliction of my Life. It is not possible that any thing of the kind should hapen to you, and I sincerely wish you may never experience any thing in any degree resembling it.

This part of the Union is in a State of perfect Tranquility and I See nothing to obscure your prospect of a quiet and prosperous Administration, which I heartily wish you.

With great Respect I have the honor to be Sir your most obedient and very humble Servant   John Adams

RC (DLC); at foot of text: "President Jefferson"; endorsed by TJ as received 9 Apr. and so recorded in SJL. FC (Lb in MHi: Adams Papers). Enclosure not found.

According to TJ's financial memoranda he first gave wages to Joseph Dougherty on 31 Mch. 1801, paying him $14. Dougherty oversaw the stable and performed other tasks at the President's House (MB, 2:1036, 1118).

Funeral of a son: Charles Adams (b. 1770) had died in New York late in the autumn of 1800 from causes related to alcoholism. His father had had no direct contact with him in the year preceding his death (John Ferling, *John Adams: A Life* [Knoxville, Tenn., 1992], 322-3, 386-8, 402, 405-6; Edith B. Gelles, "'Splendid Misery': Abigail Adams as First Lady," in Richard Alan Ryerson, ed., *John Adams and the Founding of the Republic* [Boston, 2001], 221-2).

[1] Sentence interlined.

From Charles Burrall

Sir,   Baltimore March 24. 1801

I have the honor to inform you that Mr. Dawson sailed from this port on Sunday about 2 OClock PM, and yesterday I received a letter in the mail from Washington City addressed to him in your hand writing. Previous to his sailing he requested me to forward all letters that might arrive at my office for him to Hampton in Virginia—I have therefore returned your letter in the mail of this day addressed to him at that place. Supposing it may be of importance, and considering it doubtful whether he will receive it, I have thought proper to advise you of this circumstance. I do not close a mail for the southward on Mondays which will account for my not returning your letter yesterday.—

I am Sir, with great respect, your obedient servant

CHAS: BURRALL

RC (MHi); at foot of text: "The President of the United States"; endorsed by TJ as received 25 Mch. and so recorded in SJL.

In 1791 Charles Burrall served as the clerk in the general post office in Philadelphia alongside his brother Jonathan Burrall, who was the assistant postmaster general. Not long after his brother took the position as cashier of the New York branch of the Bank of the United States in 1792, Charles Burrall became the assistant postmaster general. In 1798, Burrall submitted a report to Congress that was published in Philadelphia as *A Letter from the Assistant Post Master-General* (see Evans, No. 34903). It was his re-

sponse to a House committee inquiry calling for recommendations for changes to the law establishing the post office. In early 1800, Burrall became the postmaster at Baltimore, a position he held throughout TJ's presidency (Joseph Habersham to Charles Burrall, 4 Feb. 1800, in DNA: RG 28, LPG; Syrett, *Hamilton*, 12:79; 14:546-7; Leonard D. White, *The Federalists: A Study in Administrative History* [New York, 1959], 180; Stets, *Postmasters*, 135; ASP, *Miscellaneous*, 1:289; ASP, *Finance*, 1:813; Clement Biddle, *The Philadelphia Directory* [Philadelphia, 1791], 158).

TJ's LETTER IN THE MAIL addressed to Dawson is not recorded in SJL.

To William Findley

DEAR SIR   Washington Mar. 24. 1801.

I have to acknolege the receipt of your favors of Feb. 28. and Mar. 5. I thank you for the information they contain, and will always be thankful to you for information in the same line. it will always be interesting to me to know the impression made by any particular thing on the public mind. my idea is that where two measures are equally right, it is a duty to the people to adopt that one which is most agreeable to them; & where a measure not agreeable to them has been adopted, it is desireable to know it, because it is an admonition to a review of that measure to see if it has been really right, & to correct it if mistaken. it is rare that the public sentiment decides immorally or unwisely, and the individual who differs from it ought to distrust & examine well his own opinion. as to the character of the appointments which have been & will be made, I have less fear as to the satisfaction they will give, provided the real appointments only be attended to, and not the lying ones of which the papers are daily full. the paper which probably will be correct in that article will be

Smith's, who is at hand to get his information from the offices. but as to removals from office, great differences of opinion exist. that some ought to be removed, all will agree. that all should, nobody will say: and no two will probably draw the same line between these two extremes; consequently nothing like general approbation can be expected. mal-conduct is a just ground of removal: mere difference of political principle is not. the temper of some states requires a stronger proceedure, that of others would be more alienated even by a milder course. taking into consideration all circumstances we can only do in every case what to us seems best, & trust to the indulgence of our fellow citizens who may see the same matter in a different point of view. the nominations crouded in by mr Adams after he knew he was not appointing for himself, I treat as mere nullities. his best friends do not disapprove of this. time, prudence & patience will perhaps get us over this whole difficulty. accept assurances of my high esteem & best wishes; and let me hear from you frequently,[1] tho' it will be impossible for me to reciprocate frequently.   TH: JEFFERSON

PrC (DLC); at foot of text: "William Findley esq."

LYING ONES: on 25 Mch. the *National Intelligencer* printed corrections to some of the "erroneous" statements on appointments published in Baltimore, Philadelphia, and New York, including rumors that John Dawson was appointed minister to Portugal in place of William Loughton Smith and that "Mr." Muhlenberg—perhaps Frederick, who had applied for the position in February—had replaced George Latimer as collector at Philadelphia (see Appendix I, List 1).

[1] Word interlined.

To Philip Ludwell Grymes

DEAR SIR   Washington Mar. 24. 1800. [i.e. 1801]

Before I could answer your letter of Feb. 9. I had to write to mr Copeland & await an answer from him. this has been recieved some days, and I hereby, by virtue of the power of attorney from mrs Ariana Randolph to mr Boardley & myself jointly & severally, do release to you the one moiety of the judgment you conferred to Jenning's executors on her behalf, satisfactory evidence being produced to me of your having actually paid the other moiety. this judgment I understand settled the annuity to the end of the year 1799. though mrs Randolph readily came into my proposition, made on the ground of justice, of releasing you from one half the judgment, yet I am not certain whether different views of the subject presented her from another quarter, may have left her as well contented at this time. with respect therefore to the annuity incurred and incurring, for the year 1800. & subsequent, I can do nothing, till I know from mrs Randolph whether she continues to view the subject in the same light. my agency having been yielded on a sense of moral duty to a family with which I had formerly been in habits of great intimacy, will of course cease whenever the measures to be pursued do not accord with my ideas of justice. in that case the applications to you will be from some other quarter. in the mean time I would recommend to you to write to mrs Randolph yourself on the subject. probably if you will regularly remit to her annually the moiety of the annuity, you may obtain a quietus against the other moiety. the duties in which I am now engaged will render it impossible for me to multiply letters. accept assurances of my esteem & high respect. TH: JEFFERSON

RC (U.S. District Court for the Eastern District of Virginia, Richmond); addressed: "Philip L. Grymes esq. at Brandon near Urbanna"; franked and postmarked; added in unidentified hand: "24 March 1800 Thomas Jefferson—Washington—Release to me of one Moiety of a Judgment Confess'd to Jennings Executors on behalf of Mrs Ariana Randolph—by virtue of a Power of Attorney from her to Mr Jefferson." PrC (DLC). Recorded in SJL at 24 Mch. 1801.

TJ wrote to Copland on 11 Mch. and received his ANSWER of the 15th on 20 Mch.

To Joseph Habersham

SIR   Washington Mar. 24. 1801.

I duly recieved your favor of yesterday. mr Barney's memorial had before been delivered in. you may rest assured that no suspicions or distrust of the offices will be hastily admitted. I propose to consider the Post office as within the department of state, to which I have ever been of opinion it more properly belongs than to the treasury. the laws certainly do not contemplate it as a subject of revenue. when mr Madison arrives therefore I will propose to him to examine and satisfy himself as to the general arrangements, which I have no doubt he will find quite satisfactory. particular complaints may be a subject of conversation & enquiry from time to time. complaints are very numerous. many I have no doubt are groundless. some I presume are founded. whenever these are discovered, removals will of course be expected. Accept assurances of my high respect & esteem. TH: JEFFERSON

PrC (DLC); at foot of text: "Colo. Habersham. Post Master Genl."

For TJ's OPINION that the post office should be under the jurisdiction of the State Department, not the Treasury, see Vol. 23:184, 187n.

To Carlos Martínez de Irujo

DEAR SIR   Washington Mar. 24. 1801.

Your favor of the 18th. is recieved. in the meantime you will have recieved one of the 19th. from me. I have inserted in a letter to Colo. Humphreys what might be said with effect on the subject mentioned in your letter. if in time, I hope it will weigh. if not, when you take leave, you will of course recieve a letter, the tenor of which shall do you the justice due to you. I am in hopes however the occasion of that letter may be long delayed. Made. d'Yrujo will have time to meet mrs Madison here about the latter end of April. present her the homage of my respects, and accept yourself my best wishes & high consideration.

TH: JEFFERSON

PrC (DLC); at foot of text: "The Chevalr. d'Yrujo"; endorsed by TJ in ink on verso.

ONE OF THE 19TH. FROM ME: writing from Washington on 19 Mch. TJ acknowledged Irujo's letter of the 13th and thanked him for his efforts to assist TJ in finding a cook—"a [Minister] of the kitchen." Reporting the prospect of employing Honoré Julien for that position on the suggestion of Philippe de Létombe, TJ noted that he might have to ask for Irujo's "immediate interference" to persuade Julien to accept: "you see how much I count on your friendship."

TJ also responded to Irujo's comments about the "coalescing" effects of his inaugural address. If TJ could help achieve "harmony" in the nation without compromising "our republican priniciples," then "I have not lived in vain." Acknowledging that some of his allies as well as some opponents might find fault with his policy toward removal or retention of officers, he wrote that "in time I hope both parties will judge with less passion" (PrC in MoSHi: Jefferson Papers; badly blurred; at foot of text: "The Chevalier d'Yrujo"; endorsed by TJ in ink on verso).

See TJ's letter to David HUMPHREYS, over Levi Lincoln's signature, at 17 Mch.

To Peter Legaux

SIR   Washington Mar. 24. 1801.

This is the first moment, since the reciept of your favor of the 4th. inst. that it has been in my power to acknowlege it, and to thank you for the kind offer of a number of vines. by this time I presume the season is too far advanced for their removal, & consequently that I must decline till another year availing myself of your liberality. and even then I would confine it to a few only, & of the eating kind preferably, my absence from home and other circumstances excluding me from the possibility of becoming a winemaker.   I am not able to say why Govr. Monroe has failed to answer your letter. it is probable he found himself unable to say any thing effectual, & in that case men who recieve more letters than they can answer, select of preference those which can be answered with effect.

The Botanico-meteorological observations shall be forwarded to the American Philosophical society. Accept assurances of my respect and high consideration.   Th: Jefferson

RC (Facsimile in Harmers of New York Catalogue, sale 2858, 12 June 1990); at foot of text: "M. Legaux." PrC (DLC); endorsed by TJ in ink on verso.

BOTANICO-METEOROLOGICAL OBSERVATIONS: one of the tables that Legaux sent on 4 Mch. had this title. In it, for the growing seasons of 1787 through 1800 Legaux recorded information about temperatures, the dates on which grapes in his vineyard reached certain stages of maturation, and the dates on which other crops reached full development.

Writing to TJ in French from Philadelphia on 25 Mch., Legaux indicated that he needed to promote enrollment in the subscription that had opened in 1794 under the authority of the Pennsylvania General Assembly to form a company for the development of his vineyard. He hoped that TJ would join the subscription and act as the project's sponsor—its "protecteur spécial"—so that viticulture and the production of wine, brandy, ether, and tartar could be among the benefits to America from TJ's presidency (RC in DLC; at foot of first page: "Monsieur Le Président des Etats unis de Lamérique"; endorsed by TJ as received 28 Mch. and so recorded in SJL). Legaux enclosed a copy from the company's subscription book of an authorization made on 16 Mch. 1801 by the state's commissioners for the subscription. The authorization empowered Legaux to accept subscriptions at a minimum payment of $1 per share, with the remainder of the $20 price of each share to be paid when requested by the company's managers following its incorporation. John Vaughan, Benjamin Smith Barton, Benjamin Henry Latrobe, Caspar Wistar, Simon Chaudron, and Stephen Girard were among the 12 commissioners making that authorization. Legaux also enclosed extracts from the subscription book listing the names of subscribers since 1794, yielding a total of 210 shares and payments of $1,745 to date. Legaux observed that his venture was opposed by wine merchants and by others, including Pennsylvania Chief Justice Edward Shippen, Judge Richard Peters, and William Bingham: "the Medium Classe of the people appear more please of this improuvement than the richer." In a final note Legaux stated that although several people who subscribed in 1794 had died or left the country, a moiety of their subscriptions had been paid, yet Bingham, who had put in for 5 shares, refused to make any payment, forcing Legaux to seek redress through the commissioners (MS in same; dated 25 Mch. 1801; in English, final note in French; in Legaux's hand, signed by initials; at foot of first page: "Copie pour Monsieur Jéfferson President des Etats unis de L'Amerique"). On 12 Apr. Legaux wrote a brief letter in French from Philadelphia, covering a prospectus of the subscription plan for his vineyard and stating that it would be his great pleasure to fulfill the request made by TJ in the letter printed above (RC in same; at foot of text: "Monsieur Le Président des Etats unis de L'Amerique"; endorsed by TJ as received 24 Apr. 1801 and so recorded in SJL). For Legaux's efforts to gain support for his vineyard, see also Vol. 30:41-2.

From James Linn

SIR   Trenton 24th March 1801

I have been informed that Mr. Kitchel and Mr. Condit of New Jerey have stated to the President the necessity of displacing the Supervisor of that state, and I have reason to believe that friendship has induced them to recommend me for that appointment—

I have also understood that the partiality of some gentlemen hath led them to mention my name for the office of postmaster general— In either case I shall consider myself honored by the attention of government. But if I may be permitted to express a wish on the occasion—A residence at the seat of government would be most agreeable to me—But as private interest ought ever to give way to public good—I am disposed to sacrifice all personal considerations to those of a more general nature—

I am your most Humble Servt.   JAMES LINN

RC (DNA: RG 59, LAR); at foot of text: "President of the United States"; endorsed by TJ as received 28 Mch. and so recorded in SJL.

James Linn (1750-1821) was born in New Jersey, the son of Alexander Linn, an Irish immigrant who became a prominent judge in Somerset County. A Princeton graduate, Linn studied law and in 1771 married Mary Livingston, daughter of New Jersey Governor William Livingston. Linn served as a major in the militia during the Revolutionary War, practiced law, and was active in state politics. In 1790 he was elected to the state legislature and in 1793 became a leader of the Republican movement in New Jersey. In 1798 he won election to Congress as a Republican from a Federalist district. Viewed as the swing vote in the five-member New Jersey delegation during the vote for president in the House of Representatives, Linn declared his support for TJ. In June 1801, TJ appointed him supervisor of the revenue for the New Jersey district. As a prominent political organizer in the state, Linn published weekly essays for the Republican cause. His election as secretary of New Jersey in 1805, a position he held until 1820, strengthened his control of the party in the state (*Biog. Dir. Cong.*; Harrison, *Princetonians, 1769-1775*, 28-31).

Aaron Kitchell and John CONDIT, Republican congressmen from New Jersey, served with Linn in the state legislature in 1793 and were part of the early opposition to the Federalists in the state (*Biog. Dir. Cong.*; Walter R. Fee, *The Transition from Aristocracy to Democracy in New Jersey, 1789-1829* [Somerville, N.J., 1933], 71). On 28 Feb. they wrote TJ noting that complaints against Aaron Dunham, supervisor of the revenue, were circulating in the state. They recommended Linn as a "Suitable person" to fill the office if a change was "thought Expedient" (RC in DNA: RG 59, LAR; in Kitchell's hand, signed by Kitchell and Condit; at foot of text: "Honle Thomas Jefferson"; endorsed by TJ as a letter from John Condit, received 3 Mch., and so recorded in SJL; TJ later added: "Linn Jas." to the endorsement and canceled Condit's name).

To Robert R. Livingston

DEAR SIR   Washington Mar. 24. 1801.

Your favor of the 12th. is just now at hand. with respect to the time of your departure it will depend on the return of mr Dawson with the ratification of the Convention. we may expect this in 4. months: so that you may have time enough to prepare for your departure soon after his arrival. we shall join with you a Secretary of legation, to guard against any accident happening to yourself: and as we consider it advantageous to the public to make these apprenticeships prepare subjects for principal duties hereafter, such a character has been sought out as will form a proper subject of future expectation. the elder son of Genl. Sumpter from his rank in life & fortune, from an extraordinary degree of sound understanding & discretion, and the amability of his temper & gentlemanly manners, has attracted our attention; it is proposed therefore to give him a commission of Secretary of legation to accompany you. but it is not known that he will accept. if he does, he will probably meet you there, or more likely precede you.

Accept assurances of my constant esteem, & high consideration & respect.   TH: JEFFERSON

RC (NNMus); addressed: "Robert R. Livingston Clermont New York"; franked; postmarked 25 Mch.; endorsed by Livingston. PrC (DLC).

From Rembrandt Peale

SIR   [Philadelphia, 24 Mch. 1801]

I take the earliest opportunity of informing you that the Copy is now finished & shall be disposed of according to any Orders you may send. In order to have furnished you with an accurate likeness, as well as to be myself possessed of one more to my Satisfaction, I could have wished for an opportunity, without imposing too disagreable a task, to have made some improvement in both with an hour or two of your leisure. The Room in which I painted last Winter was the worst calculated for the purpose; it would have added infinitely to my Satisfaction and Success to have done it in a high light & large room: This I dispair of getting without building; which would require quite a different order of things from those which now prevail. Possess'd therefore as I am with the Desire to be eminent if at all engaged in Painting, I must either persevere in hope & wait a favorable concurrence of Circumstances; or by some bold & successful attempt, distinguish & force myself into Notice—The first is discouraging in the extreme, and Confines the whole of my hopes to the latter which must be accomplished either by a Visit to the Riches of Europe—or the consequence of some other employment at home, which, in relieving me from the Necessity of Painting the most disagreable Subjects, may enable me to devote an occasional hour to the powerful Instructions of more pleasing Nature.

I hesitated before I could address you this letter, from the apprehension it might appear impertinent after what I had already said when I address'd a few lines to the late President; but I had not then fully expressed my desire, alluding only to the Intercourse with France. My desire then was & now is—either to Visit England, France or Italy; or, to make my Industry, Attention & perseverance beneficial at home, without encroaching on the Merit of others—or undertaking what my habits have rendered me improper for.

I should not have the Vanity thus to present myself, did I not know that all Appointments to Offices originate either from personal Acquaintance or private Recommendation—And from my Solitary & Domestic Mode of living, having few other than Social friends, I am tempted to speak in my own favor. I have sometimes thought of a Situation in one of our Banks, but this requires which I have not, Interest among the Merchants.

I know the delicacy of your Situation, the difficulty of Selection, and the importance of your Decisions, & shall therefore form no improper hope—at the same time that I beg of you to excuse the freedom which I have taken in troubling you so much with my own affairs.

RC (DNA: RG 59, LAR); closing and signature cut away, dateline supplied from postmark and endorsement; addressed: "His Excellency Thomas Jefferson Esquire Washington"; franked and postmarked; endorsed by TJ as a letter of 24 Mch. from Rembrandt Peale received on 27 Mch. and so recorded in SJL.

A FEW LINES TO THE LATE PRESIDENT: see Peale to TJ, 17 Dec. 1800, regarding the artist's letter of that date to John Adams.

To Thomas Perkins

SIR   Washington Mar. 24. 1801.

I recieved in due time your favor of Feb. 6. but never till now have had a moment's leisure to make you my acknolegements for the permission to use your invention. my nailers are employed in hammering nails, except one cutter for four pennies only, our neighborhood requiring no other cut nail. so that it is but a small business with me. still I like to see even small things done to the best advantage. I am not certain that I perfectly understand the manner of making the vice for holding and pushing up the hoop iron; tho I have some idea of it; and you do not mention whether you cut your hoop cold or warm. I cut it warm, in which case the frequent changes necessary would waste time. perhaps you can add to your former favor by taking time to drop me a line of information on this subject which will be thankfully recieved by Sir

Your humble servt   TH: JEFFERSON

RC (Thomas J. Perkins, Easton, Maryland, 1946); addressed: "Mr. Thomas Perkins Naaman's creek mills near Wilmington Delaware"; franked; postmarked 25 Mch.

Thomas Perkins received a patent for manufacturing nails in February 1794. He may have been the person of that name who was sheriff of New Castle County, Delaware, 1809-11, and who represented that county in the state assembly, 1803-5, and the state senate, 1807. Naaman's Creek, a tributary of the Delaware River near the Delaware-Pennsylvania boundary, had been the site of water-powered grain milling since the beginning of the eighteenth century. The Perkins family had been in the locale even longer (List of Patents, 8; Henry C. Conrad, History of the State of Delaware, 3 vols. [Wilmington, Del., 1908], 1:264, 272, 293; 2:451-2, 458).

FORMER FAVOR: a letter from Perkins to TJ, dated 6 Feb. 1801 and recorded in SJL as received from Naaman's Creek Mills on the 20th of that month, has not been found.

A LINE OF INFORMATION: Perkins wrote TJ from the mills on 8 May 1801; that letter, recorded in SJL as received on 16 May, has not been located. It was enclosed in a brief communication written by Benjamin Perkins to TJ, dated at Washington on 15 May: "The Letter Inclosed Came to me with a Request to furnish you with a Drawing of a Michene for Cutting Nails for which My Brother Obtained a Patent—the Drawing Shall be Handed to you & any Explanations Necesry given by wednesday Next—By your Obt Svt" (RC in MHi; at foot of text: "New York avenu near Mr Taloes Building"; addressed: "Thomas Jefferson President of the United States Washington City"; endorsed by TJ as received 16 May 1801 and so recorded in SJL).

From Andrew Rounsavell

washington march 24

Sir I Rec:d your note of the 23d and am Sincerely Sorry, and am Sencible of the improiety of trobeling you in the Station you are now in: with any thing that Requires So much Study

as I Said in my letter I had Some Doubts: I must now do my Self the justice to Say I have none: and am happy to State that I have fell uppon a Cheap plan: and an old aquaintance both able and willing to assist me in trying the experiment: and in Looking over the the city have found a Spring form:d by nature to try the experiment and if you give or procure me the promition to put my plan into Execution: I mean to make the experiment in the month of may when the watters are Reduc:d to their natulal Strength Should you not See me untill I leave this place wich I Shall do this Day a note Directed to me: and to the care of Robt young Eqr. in allexandria Can not fail being Rec:d by me

I mean a letter of permition wich if not got here I shall elswhere Seek

yours ANW: ROUNSAVELL

RC (DLC); addressed: "Mr Thos: Jefferson Esqr President of the United States"; endorsed by TJ as received 24 Mch. and so recorded in SJL.

To Benjamin Rush

DEAR SIR   Washington Mar. 24. 1801.

I have to acknolege the reciept of your friendly favor of the 12th and the pleasing sensations produced in my mind by it's affectionate contents. I am made very happy by learning that the sentiments expressed in my inaugural address give general satisfaction, and hold out a ground on which our fellow citizens can once more unite. I am the more pleased, because these sentiments have been long & radically mine, and therefore will be pursued honestly & conscientiously. I know there is an obstacle which very possibly may check the confidence which would otherwise have been more generally reposed in my observance of these principles. this obstacle does not arise from the measures to be pursued, as to which I am in no fear of giving satisfaction: but from appointments & disappointments as to office. with respect to appointments I have so much confidence in the justice and good sense of the federalists that I have no doubt they will concur in the fairness of the position, that after they have been in the exclusive possession of all offices from the very first origin of party among us to the 3d. of March at 9. aclock in the night, no republican ever admitted, & this doctrine openly avowed, it is now perfectly just that the republicans should come in for the vacancies which may fall in, until something like an equilibrium in office be restored; after which 'Tros, Tyriusque nullo discrimine habeatur.' but the great stumbling block will be removals, which tho' made on those just principles only on which my predecessor ought to have removed the same persons, will nevertheless be ascribed to removal on party principles. Imprimis I will expunge the effects of mr A's indecent conduct in crouding nominations after he knew they were not for himself, till 9. aclock of the night, at 12. aclock of which he was to go out of office; so far as they are during pleasure. I will not consider the persons named, even as candidates for the office, nor pay the respect of notifying them that I consider what was done as a nullity. 2. some removals must be made for misconduct. one of these is of the marshal in your city, who being an officer of justice, entrusted with the sacred function of chusing impartial judges for the trial of his fellow citizens placed at the awful tribunal of god & their country, selected judges who either avowed, or were known to him to be predetermined to condemn. and if the lives of the unfortunate persons were not cut short[1] by the sword of the law, it was not for want of his good will. in another state I have to perform the same act of justice on the dearest connection of my dearest friend, for similar conduct in cases[2] not capital. the same practice of packing juries & prosecuting their fellow citizens with the bitterness of party hatred, will probably involve several other marshals & attorneys. out of this line, I see but very few instances where past misconduct has been in such a degree as to call for notice. of the thousands of officers therefore in the US. a very few individuals only, probably not 20. will be removed; & these only for doing what they ought not to have done. 2. or 3. instances indeed where mr A. removed men because they would not sign addresses &c to him, will be rectified, & the persons restored. the whole world will say this is just. I know that in stopping thus short in the career of removal, I shall give great offence to many of my friends. that torrent has been pressing me heavily, & will require all my force to bear up against. but my maxim is 'fiat justitia, ruat coelum.' after the first unfavorable impressions of doing too much in the opinion of some, & too little in that of others, shall be got over, I should hope a steady line of conciliation very practicable, & that without yielding a single republican principle. a certainty that these principles prevailed in the breasts of the main body of federalists was my motive for stating them as the ground of reunion.—I have said thus much for your private satisfaction, to be used even in private conversation, as the presumptive principles on which we shall act, but not as proceeding from myself declaredly.—information lately recieved from France gives a high idea of the progress of science there. it seems to keep pace with their victories. I have just recieved for the A.P. society 2. volumes of Comparative Anatomy by Cuvier, probably the greatest work in that line that has ever appeared. his comparisons embrace every organ of the animal economy, and from Man, to the rotifer.

accept assurances of my sincere friendship & high consideration & respect.   TH: JEFFERSON

RC (Frederick M. Dearborn, New York, 1949); addressed: "Doctr. Benjamin Rush Philadelphia"; franked; postmarked 25 Mch. PrC (DLC).

TROS, TYRIUSQUE: in the *Aeneid*, 1:574, "Tros Tyruisque mihi nullo discrimine agetur," or "I shall allow no difference between the Trojan and Tyrian." John Hall was MARSHAL of the district of Pennsylvania (Hall to TJ, 7 Mch.). DEAREST CONNECTION OF MY DEAREST FRIEND: David Meade Randolph (TJ to Thomas Mann Randolph, 12 Mch.). FIAT JUSTITIA, RUAT COELUM: "let justice be done, though heaven should fall." Lord Mansfield, as chief justice of the Court of King's Bench, had invoked this expression in the noted *Somerset*

slave case in 1772. TJ, unhappy with many of Mansfield's legal decisions, noted the judge's "most seducing eloquence" (Paul Finkelman, ed., *The Law of Freedom and Bondage: A Casebook* [New York, 1986], 31-3; Vol. 9:71; Vol. 13:649).

The American chemist Thomas Peters Smith, who was in Europe, had sent the American Philosophical Society the *Leçons d'Anatomie Comparée* (Paris, 1800) of Georges CUVIER. TJ later obtained a copy for his own library (Sowerby, No. 999; APS, *Proceedings*, 22, pt. 3 [1884], 310; Vol. 31:291n).

[1] Preceding two words interlined in place of "taken."

[2] TJ first wrote "in a case."

To Samuel Smith

DEAR SIR   Washington Mar. 24. 1801.

I have to acknowlege the reciept of your favor of the 20th. the appointment of Secy. of the navy, was immediately on receipt of your letter declining it, proposed to mr Jones of Philadelphia. I cannot have an answer from him till the night of the 26th. but I have great reason to expect a negative. in that case I will gladly for the public accept your offer to undertake it for a time. besides that it will comprehend important operations to be immediately carried into effect, it will give us time to look out for a successor. I mention it now in hopes that in the moment you recieve notice from me of mr Jones's refusal, if it takes place, you may be so good as to be in readiness to come here for a few days. if I recieve Jones's refusal on Thursday night, you shall hear from me Friday night, & may be here I hope yourself on Saturday night. Sunday & Monday will probably suffice for the first decisions necessary, so that I may get away on Tuesday, which now becomes very urgent.

I inclose you the answer to the address you forwarded me. though these expressions of good will from my fellow citizens cannot but be grateful to me, yet I would rather relinquish the gratification, and see republican self respect prevail over movements of the heart too capable of misleading the person to whom they are addressed. however, their will, not mine, be done.

Mr. Kilty is appointed judge in the room of mr Duval. mr Nicholas's being a Virginian is a bar. it is essential that I be on my guard in appointing persons from that state.—I sincerely wish Genl. Wilkinson could be appointed as you propose. but besides the objection from principle that no military commander should be so placed as to have no civil superior, his residence at the Natchez is entirely inconsistent with his superintendance of the military posts. this would then devolve on Hamtramck, who is represented as unequal to it. we must help Wilkinson in some other way. be pleased to present my respects to mrs Smith, & to accept yourself assurances of my high consideration & esteem.   TH: JEFFERSON

RC (ViU); addressed: "Genl. Samuel Smith Baltimore"; franked and postmarked; endorsed. PrC (DLC).

ENCLOSURE

To Allegany County Republican Citizens

GENTLEMEN   Washington Mar. 23. 1801.
I am sensible of the kindness of the republican citizens of the county of Alleghany in Maryland, in their cordial congratulations on my election to the office of President of the United States, and I pray you to be the organ of my acknolegement to them. the confidence reposed in me on committing to my management the helm of our political affairs, shall not be abused; but, to the best of my skill & judgment, I will administer the government according to the genuine principles of our inestimable constitution, & the true interests of our country; sparing no effort which may procure us peace & unanimity at home, & respectability abroad.

I rejoice with them in the display of virtuous courage & zeal for the support of our independance, dignity & honor, which pervade the United States, & that our countrymen, undismayed by any efforts hostile to their liberty, will meet them with the animated courage of citizens & souldiers. the union of these characters is the true rock of our safety, and should be the pride of every man who is free, & means to remain so.

accept, I beseech you, for yourselves & the republican citizens of Alleghany the homage of my high consideration & respect.   TH: JEFFERSON

PrC (DLC); at foot of text: "Hanson Briscoe esq. Cumberland."

THEIR CORDIAL CONGRATULATIONS: see the address of 4 Mch. enclosed in Smith's letter to TJ of 20 Mch.

To Thomas Sumter

My Dear General   Washington Mar. 24. 1801.

Chancellor Livingston has accepted his mission to France, but will not proceed till mr Dawson returns with the ratification of the Convention. I have thought it useful to the public, instead of permitting ministers to take a private Secretary of their own choice,[1] to name a Secretary of legation, who will do the duties of the private Secretary, and on the same salary (of 1350. Dollars)[2] but on the death of his principal would become Chargé des affaires, with the salary of 4500. Dollars. the character of Secretary of legation gives an entrance into all diplomatic societies, which the private Secretary has not, and the public making the appointment, can thus fix their choice on persons who from their station & circumstances in life, their talents and good dispositions, will after these apprenticeships make good subjects for principal missions or other employments in future. in this view of the subject I have cast my eye on your son to be Secretary of legation to France, if the appointment shall be acceptable to him, as I hope it will. he will of course be one of mr Livingston's family, so that the salary, moderate as it may seem, will not be insufficient for his other expences. mr Short was 7. years with me on the *same salary* & found it sufficient. I must ask the favor of you to make the proposition to him, & if accepted, let me know it immediately, and the commission & every thing else necessary shall be forwarded to him without delay. tho' mr Livingston will not go in 4. or 5. months, I think it would be better your son should proceed immediately; because they have sent a Chargé here; because he will be recieved there in that quality, and act as principal till mr L. arrives, which will give him an advantageous standing, and because, [acquiring] previous acquaintance there, he may be prepared to make himself useful to mr Livingston on his arrival, and lay a foundation in his esteem, by friendly offices, which may be very favorable to their harmony and his situation. Accept assurances of my sincere affection, & high consideration & respect.   Th: Jefferson

P.S. from the time of departure till the arrival of mr L. in Paris, mr Sumpter's salary will be at the rate of 4500. Dollars a year, because his character during that period will be Chargé des affaires.[3]

RC (Jacques De La Ferrière, Paris, 1991); addressed: "General Sumpter S. Carolina," with "Statesburg" added in unidentified hand; franked; postmarked 25 Mch. PrC (DLC).

Thomas Sumter, Sr. (1734-1832), earned acclaim during the Revolutionary War as a militia general and partisan leader in the South Carolina backcountry. In March 1792, TJ suggested Sumter as commander of the army fighting Indians in the Northwest Territory, but the command went instead to Anthony Wayne. Elected to Congress from South Carolina in 1788, Sumter served from 1789 to 1793 as an Antifederalist and 1795 to 1801 as an ardent Republican. In December 1801 he was appointed to the U.S. Senate seat vacated by Charles Pinckney's appointment as minister to Spain. In the Senate, Sumter remained a loyal supporter of the

Jeffersonians until his retirement in 1810 (ANB; Vol. 23:242, 244).

YOUR SON TO BE SECRETARY OF LEGA-TION: see Thomas Sumter, Jr., to TJ, 20 Apr.

¹ TJ here canceled "to avail."
² Parenthetical phrase interlined.
³ Postscript written perpendicular to text in left margin.

To Joseph Yznardi, Sr.

DEAR SIR   Washington Mar. 24. 1801.

In your favor of the 18th. you mention having for disposal two casks of white & red Sherry, and one of Malaga. if the Sherry be dry, I will gladly take them, as also the Malaga. if you could order for me a pipe of dry Pacharetti, and one of dry Sherry of the first qualities, to be forwarded from Spain by the first safe occasion I should be obliged to you. I presume you have persons there on whom you can rely for the quality, tho' absent yourself. I wish the wines as old as could be got, so as to be ready for immediate use. accept assurances of my great esteem and respect.   TH: JEFFERSON

PrC (DLC); at foot of text: "Joseph Yznardy esq."; endorsed by TJ in ink on verso.

GLADLY TAKE THEM: in May, TJ recorded the receipt from Yznardi of a 126-gallon pipe of Pedro Ximenes "Mountain" sherry, 30 gallons of "Tent" (from "tinto" or "tintillo de Rota"), which was a dark red sherry, and a keg of sweet pajarete, a Malaga wine that TJ called PACHARETTI or pacaret. He later had 424

bottles drawn from the pipe of Pedro Ximenes wine and shipped them to Monticello. Yznardi ordered for TJ more sherry, a pipe of dry pajarete, and a 60-gallon tierce of lágrima, a dark, sweet wine from Malaga. The lágrima, which arrived at Baltimore late in 1801, was of 1755 vintage. TJ received the sherry and the pajarete in February 1802 (MB, 1:674n; 2:1037, 1060-1, 1064, 1115; Yznardi to TJ, 7 Apr., 17 July 1801, 15 Jan. 1802).

From Gideon Granger

SIR—   Suffield Mar: 25. 1801.

Inclosed I have both the Honor and Pleasure to transmit the Address of a Number of Gentlemen. It originated not merely from fashion, but from those high transports of Joy produced by the preservation of Our happy Constitution, the probable restoration of social harmony, and the guaranty of personal Liberty—   It speaks in plain language the just confidence and feelings of it's Authors—

It it with great Satisfaction that I embrace this opportunity to congratulate you, Sir, upon the great events we have lately witnessed. Events which must be peculiarly pleasing to you, not because the Station is elevated, for it is attended with great evils, high responsibility & much personal anxiety and solicitude; but because by nobly surmounting all it's difficulties, you will be enabled to place the Liberties of Our Citizens upon a durable foundation, and in a great degree, to calm the tempestuous passions of party. The anxiety of the People of this part of New England at the time of the Struggle in the House of Representatives was wholly inexpressible. The Yeomanry viewed with astonishment acts the utility and object of which, they could not in any degree comprehend—

The Countenances of the warm federalists were marked with great Solicitude; the same expression mingled with Indignation was exhibited by every Republican.

The inaugural Speech was read by the body of the people with delight & Satisfaction. The deceitfull appearance of a spirit of Accomodation is assurred—This will soon be cast off, if the temper of the people will allow of it. But in that the Monarchists will be disappointed. The same habits of submitting quietly to the Acts and Opinions of their Rulers which led the people to approve of a System dangerous to liberty & destructive to property, will surely lead them to approve of One founded upon the true principles of the Constitution, and protecting both their rights & property—yet from What I see and hear I am fully persuaded that in the Course of a few weeks the opposition will begin to show itself. I think they are forming a plan of Operation—In Connecticut we appear to be stationary. In Massachusetts the Republicans are gaining Strength greatly— Newhampre. is improving slowly & I calculate Rhode Island with Us. A great effort will be made to return Republican Senators for Vermt:—The election is very doubtfull, But I am inclined to think the Chances are in Our favor.

Give me leave to suggest that a Gentleman of this County a reputable Lawyer of fair Character, wishes to be considered a Candidate for a Seat on the bench in the N.W. or Mississippi Territory—The best part of his life is run & his Republican principles forbid his enjoying any of the honors or offices of his Native State. He may probably apply in person with further Recommendations. It is not for me to solicit in his favor—but at his desire I make this Communicatn. I avoid mentioning his Name, for fear this Letter (like many others) may Miscarry—I have never heard from my friend Erving but once, nor recd. any Letters from the Southward for Months—

With sincere Esteem & Respect   GIDN. GRANGER

RC (DLC); addressed: "Thomas Jefferson Esq President of the U States Washington"; endorsed by TJ as received 24 Apr. and so recorded in SJL.

From Suffield Citizens

SIR,   Suffield, State of Connecticut, March 16th. 1801

The People of the United States, assisted by the experience of past ages, have established a Constitution of Government, founded on the genuine principles of Republicanism, Wisdom and Virtue—

The important offices which you have sustained with dignity, and discharged with integrity under this Constitution, warrant us to believe, that you will employ Your talents and influence to preserve the same inviolate and uncorrupted.—We trust that your Prudence will harmonise the discordant opinions, which exist in some parts of the union; and that, by your wisdom, you will conciliate the affections of all the Citizens of these States.—Impressed with these sentiments, the Inhabitants of This and the neighboring Towns, here assembled, Congratulate You, Sir, on your Advancement to the first Office of Government in the United States.—

May You be happy in the general tranquillity of the Republic, & satisfied with the gratitude of the People, who have placed you in this exalted Station: May the blessings of the People over whom you preside, be the certain Pledge of a sure reward in Heaven, for the services you have rendered them here: And may the Supreme Being, whose Guardian eye has ever watched over this Land for good, still protect the United States.

By Order
ALEXR: KING CHAIRMAN.

RC (DLC); in unidentified hand, signed by King; at head of text: "The Citizens of This and the neighboring Towns, assembled in Celebration of the Election of a Republican President and Vice President of the United States, Alexander King Esqr. Chairman, unanimously adopted the following Address and requested that the same might be transmitted to the President" and "Thomas Jefferson, President of the United States"; on separate sheet, in Granger's hand: "If Mr. Jefferson should deem it proper to transmit an Answer to this address—he is requested to Send it—under Cover—addressed to his friend & humle. Servt. G Granger"; endorsed by TJ as received 24 Apr. and so recorded in SJL. FC and Dft (CtHi), lacking sentence at head of text.

From John Gregorie

Sir Embden 25 March 1801.

When application was made to you some Years ago in my favor at the time you were at the Head of the State Department, for a Consular Appointment (that had previously been dispos'd of) you had the goodness to say, that I should not be forgot at some future Period—

I now beg leave to Solicit a Commission of Consul General for the County of Embden & Ports of East Friesland:—This Sovereign State was under the protection of the Dutch Government 'till the Year 1744 when that right was purchased by the King of Prussia; but the Inhabitants still consider themselves Independent & are Governed by Laws enacted by their own Magistrates.—

At present I bear a Commission from Mr. Freidr. Wilh. Lutze Consul at Stettin, directed to his Prussian Majesties Governors, & Officers, Appointing me Consular Agent for this Port & all others of East Friesland.—

I am respectfully Sir Your most Obedient humble Servant

JOHN GREGORIE
of Petersburg Virginia

RC (DNA: RG 59, LAR); at foot of text: "His Excellency Thomas Jefferson President of the United States"; endorsed by TJ as received 13 Aug. and so recorded in SJL with notation "Off." Enclosed in David Meade Randolph to TJ, 8 Aug. 1801.

Gregorie unsuccessfully sought a CONSULAR APPOINTMENT to Dunkirk in 1793 (see Vol. 25:409-10; Vol. 27:9).

From Joseph Habersham

Joseph Habersham presents his compliments to Mr. Jefferson & has the pleasure to say that the letter inclosed to him yesterday was addressed to the proper office & will be duly forwarded.

The postmaster general several years since authorised the employment of Letter-Carriers (penny posts) in this city; and one was employed for some time: but the emoluments being found inadequate to the labour it was relinquished by the person employed and no other could be prevailed upon to undertake it. Two applications were made yesterday to the Postmaster who will be glad to appoint a proper person, both for his own convenience and the public.

Letter Carriers receive two cents, for each letter delivered, of the individual to whom it is addressed, no other allowance can be made him by the postmaster general but the postmaster might pay him something for assistance as a clerk in the office; this was suggested to him but he did not meet with a suitable person

March 25. 1801

Having received some hurt by a fall from his horse yesterday, J. Habersham begs to be excused for not calling personally to state the above:

RC (DLC); in Abraham Bradley's hand; dateline above postscript; endorsed by TJ as received 26 Mch. and so recorded in SJL.

The LETTER INCLOSED to Habersham on 24 Mch. has not been identified. SUGGESTED TO HIM: Thomas Munroe, the postmaster at Washington. See Andrew Shepherd to TJ, 15 Mch.

To John Strode

DEAR SIR   Washington Mar. 25. 1801

I recieved your kind favor of the 16th. yesterday only. I certainly always meant to claim the antient hospitality of you as I pass along. but when it became necessary to have horses & a servant posted on the road, where they might have to wait for me a week or weeks, my departure being so liable to be controuled by unexpected events, I could not possibly think of quartering them on you. for this reason they were ordered to mr Heron's, on board as it were, and my purpose was to go on myself to your house. indeed it is possible I may find it convenient to keep a pair of horses always thereabout to facilitate my occasional visits home, which in that way might perhaps be effected in two days.—I am in hopes of being with you on Monday, Tuesday or Wednesday, which will be as early as you get this letter; but I may be still detained by occurrences not yet foreseen. if my servant is waiting at Heron's, as I expect, I should be glad he should know this. accept assurances of my great esteem & best wishes.

TH: JEFFERSON

PrC (MHi); at foot of text: "Mr. Strode"; endorsed by TJ in ink on verso.

MY SERVANT IS WAITING AT HERON'S: on 2 Apr. TJ paid $15 for the board of Davy Bowles and two horses for 12 days at Herin's tavern. The daily rate was 50 cents per horse and 25 cents per servant (MB, 2:1036).

From John Sutton

Alexandria 25 of 3 mo 1801

not being in any business at present that will find me meat and cloathes, i write to thee with the view of recommending myself to thy notice for some employment to answer that purpose. i do not pretend to any superior republican patriotism or love for the country i am in which causes me to apply to thee—but some appointment would suit my present situation; and, if i could procure one i would indeavour to make such talents as i possess suit the appointment

i never saw thee, nor dost thou know me: some who call themselves thy friends, were they to speak of me would speak disrespectfully— thou knowest how much thomas jefferson hath been traduc'd and abus'd, because he had the misfortune to be rob'd, plunder'd, and oblig'd to pay debts three times over; therefor i need not expect less, who have been cheated of near ten times the sum for which thomas jefferson has sustained so much calumny—but, stevens thomson mason, and john thomson mason never having to my knowledge either cheated, or assisted in cheating me, they can have no motive to speak of me, other than truth—i cannot have much hope of attracting they friendly attention; but, if in the course of events thou do me a service i shall be oblig'd to thee—   JOHN SUTTON

RC (DNA: RG 59, LAR); at head of text: "Thomas jefferson president of the United States"; endorsed by TJ as received 9 Apr. and so recorded in SJL with notation "Off."; also endorsed by TJ: "for office."

In a letter to William C. C. Claiborne in August 1805, JOHN THOMSON MASON described Sutton as an "Old quaker" with whom he long had been friends and who, with his sons, had always "been steady uniform decided republicans" (Tr in same).

From Samuel Hanson

SIR,   George-Town March 26th 1801

In stead of apologizing for my frequent intrusions upon your time, every moment of which must, at this juncture, be peculiarly precious, may I be permitted to trespass, once more, on your indulgence in requesting an audience, at some hour of this day, the most convenient to yourself, after 3 O'Clock?

My Friends Genl. Mason, and Mr. Baldwin, having informed me that they had mentioned me to you as a Candidate for Office, it is proper to assure you that a solicitation on that head is not the object of the meditated Interview. On the contrary, I conceive that any attempt, directly or indirectly, to elicit from your breast any determination you may have formed upon that point, would be highly indecorous; and, of course, entirely incompatible with those Sentiments of perfect respect and Esteem with which I beg leave to subscribe myself

Sir Your much obliged and most obedt. Servt

SM HANSON of Saml

RC (DLC); endorsed by TJ as received 26 Mch. and so recorded in SJL.

To Tobias Lear

DEAR SIR   Washington Mar. 26. 1801.

I have to appoint a Consul to reside near Toussaint in St. Domingo, an office of great importance to us at present, and requiring great prudence. no salary is annexed to it: but it is understood to be in the power of the Consul, by means entirely honorable, to amass a profit in a very short time. Dr. Stevens is said to have done so, but perhaps [by] additional means not so justifiable. it would give me great satisfaction if you would accept of the appointment, as I should have entire confidence in the prudence with which you would conduct it, & which will be so necessary. a very early departure would be requisite, & if you accept it, it would be necessary I should see you within 2. or 3. days, being about making a short visit to Monticello, & having communications to make of which I have been the special deposit. accept assurances of my high esteem & best wishes

TH: JEFFERSON

PrC (DLC); at foot of text: "Tobias Lear. esq."; endorsed by TJ in ink on verso.

John Adams had named Edward STEVENS the U.S. consul general for the island of Santo Domingo in February 1799 (Vol. 31:45n).

From Tobias Lear

DEAR SIR,   Walnut Tree Farm, March 26th: 1801—

I have been this moment honored with your favor of the present date, and feel grateful for the attention you have been so good as to pay me, by an offer of the Consulship in St. Domingo; and am highly flattered by the confidence which you repose in my prudence and discretion.—But, how ever desireable such an office may be to me, either in a pecuniary point of view; or from a wish to serve my Country, I must, at present, decline it, as the situation of my own Affairs will not permit me to leave the United States immediately; for although an attention to them would not occupy my whole time; yet some part of them are so circumstanced as not to allow of my committing them, at this time, to the charge of another person.—

Although I have always avoided, as much as possible, giving recommendations for Office; yet I should do an injury to my own feelings, and perhaps injustice to my Country, not to call your attention, on this occasion, to Mr. Bartholomew Dandridge, who has lately been appointed Consul for some of the Southern Ports of St. Domingo, and in whose prudence and discretion I have as full a confidence as I have in my own.—This Gentleman, you will recollect, was in the Family of General Washington during his Presidency, and after I left him, acted as his private Secretary to the end of his Administration, when Mr. D. went to the Hague with Mr. Murry as his Secretary, and that Climate not agreeing with his health, he went to England, where he held the same place under Mr. King, 'till about 12 mos. ago, when he came to Alexandria and established himself in the mercantile line until his appointment.—He has not yet sail'd.—I recd. a letter from him dated the 15th inst. informing me that he should not sail till the middle of April.—

But I will not take up more of your time at present, as I intend being in the City on Saturday, when I will have the honor of paying my respects to you.—And, if it is not really necessary to make this appointment before that time, you will do me a favour by delaying it; for I confess if it should *be possible* for *me* to receive it I should most readily embrace it.—

Be assured, Dear Sir, of the Respect, Esteem & Attachment of Your Obliged Friend   Tobias Lear.

RC (DLC); at foot of text: "The President of the United States"; endorsed by TJ as received on the 26th and so recorded in SJL.

WALNUT TREE FARM, also called River Farm, was one of the plantations of Mount Vernon. George Washington's will gave Lear lifetime tenancy of the property (Ray Brighton, *The Checkered Career of Tobias Lear* [Portsmouth, N.H., 1985], 166, 168).

CONSULSHIP: on 31 Mch. TJ signed a commission for Lear as consul general for the island of Santo Domingo. According to a note on the State Department's copy of that commission, it was replaced by another certificate issued on 11 May. The second commission, following the nomenclature contained in the Convention of 1800, named Lear general commercial agent for the island (both commissions in Lb in DNA: RG 59, PTCC; in a clerk's hand, including note in margin of 31 Mch. commission: "The Commission of which this is a copy, was suppressed and the one on the opposite page substituted"; two copies in clerks' hands of the 11 May commission are in NHi: Robert R. Livingston Papers). In January 1802 the Senate approved Lear's appointment (JEP, 1:401, 405).

Bartholomew DANDRIDGE had received the appointment as consul for what was designated the southern district of Santo Domingo, including the ports of Cayes and Jérémie, in December 1800 (JEP, 1:357).

From Philippe de Létombe

Monsieur le Président,   Philadelphie, 26 mars 1801. (v. st.)

Je ne puis Vous être utile dans les grandes choses; mais pour les petites, je m'y prends de zèle, même d'enthousiasme, et j'aurai regret bientot de n'avoir plus d'occasions de Vous être de quelque utilité.

Julien est en effet celui que J'ai choisi. M. Flamend a fait séévérement son enquête de son côté; la mienne lui a été aussi favorable; et il en résulte que Vous aurez un habile Cuisinier Agé d'environ 42 ans, honnête homme. Il gagne, dans la Maison où il est aujourd'hui, 25. dollars par mois et il a les graisses pour profit. Il en vouloit 30; un dollard par jour lui parroissoit équitable. Mais M. Flamend ayant découvert qu'il n'en gagnoit que 25 chez le feu Général Washington oû il a servi pendant les quatre derniers mois de sa Présidence, Nous l'avons déterminé à accepter le même prix, avec la Condition que ses frais de route lui seront remboursés. Il ne pourra partir que dans dix ou douze jours pour se rendre chez Vous, parce qu'il lui faut ce tems pour que la Personne chez laquelle il travaille puisse le remplacer et J'ai applaudi à cette délicatesse de sa part.—Quant à sa femme, Elle pourra aller le joindre, lors que satisfait du mari Vous voudrez bien, Monsieur, ordonner à ce dernier de l'appeller auprès de lui pour remplir le genre de service auquel Elle sera destinée dans votre Maison. Enfin, J'ai lieu de croire, d'après les renseignemens que J'ai pris, que Vous serez satisfait de ces deux Serviteurs et, d'autant plus qu'ils veilleront à vos Intérets de concert avec Rapin dont ils sont connus.—Je Vous prie de m'honorer d'une réponse, le plûtot possible, pour que Je puisse le faire partir d'ici dans 10 ou 12 Jours. Si même il est libre plûtot, Je l'enverrai à Washington pour qu'il ne reste pas, ici, oisif et avec des motifs de demander une indemnité.

Pour difficile qu'il soit d'accorder les hommes, même sur leurs Intérets mutuels les plus palpables, Je ne doute pas que Vous n'y parveniez ici, même, en y fortifiant les principes republicains. Ce sera là votre Gloire. Vous les subjuguerez par vos vertus, par vos talens, par votre Grand art de Gouverner et Vous serez porté comme en triomphe dans les écrits de vos Contemporains. Déja je lis ce Couplet dans une Ode "sur les évenemens du nouveau Siècle":

> Ainsi le Siècle se prépare
> A consoler l'humanité
> Qu'une politique barbare
> Enchainoit à l'Adversité;
> En France, un héros magnanime
> A surpassé l'effort sublime

Des Caton, des Léonidas:
En Amérique, un nouveau Guide
Avec les vertus d'Aristide
Gouverne de nombreux Etats.—

Voilà mon suççesseur installé. Je suis aujourd'hui sans fonctions. Je retournerai dans ma Patrie par le premier parlementaire, vers le mois de Juin. Mais je serai pénétré toute ma vie des bontés dont Vous m'avez honoré pendant seize ans. Si J'étois moins vieux, Je pourrois me flatter encore de pouvoir venir Vous admirer. Privé de cet espoir, permettez moi de Vous être attaché Jusqu'au dernier moment de ma Vie.

Daignez, Monsieur le Président, agréér mon dévouement et mon profond Respect.

LÉTOMBE

EDITORS' TRANSLATION

MISTER PRESIDENT,   Philadelphia, 26 March 1801 (old style)

I cannot be useful to you in great things; but for the small ones, I go about them with zeal, even enthusiasm, and I shall soon regret no longer having occasions to be of some utility to you.

Julien is in fact the one I have chosen. Mr. Flamand made a stern investigation; mine was also favorable to him; the result is that you will have a skillful cook about 42 years old, an honest man. He earns in his present house 25 dollars per month, and he has the fat and grease for his perquisite. He wanted 30; a dollar a day seemed reasonable to him. But Mr. Flamand having discovered that Julien earned only 25 with the late General Washington, where he served for the four last months of his presidency, we convinced him to accept the same amount, with the proviso that his travel expenses will be reimbursed to him. He can leave only after 10 or 12 days to go to you, because he will need that time so the person in whose home he is working can replace him, and I applauded that scruple on his part.—As for his wife, she will be able to join him when you, being satisfied with the husband, are willing, Sir, to order him to call her to fulfill whatever service may be allotted to her in your residence. Finally, I have reason to believe, according to the information I have found, that you will be satisfied with these two servants, and all the more so that they will watch over your interests in harmony with Rapin to whom they are known.—I beg you to honor me with a reply as soon as possible so that I can send him on from here in 10 or 12 days. If he is free even sooner, I shall send him to Washington so that he does not remain here with nothing to do and with some cause to request an indemnity.

As difficult as it may be to make men agree, even on their most obvious mutual interests, I do not doubt that you will succeed here, even while fortifying republican principles. That will be your glory. You will subjugate them by your virtues, by your talents, by your great art in governing, and you will be borne as in triumph in the writings of your contemporaries. Already I read this stanza in an ode "on the events of the new century":

[450]

Thus the century prepares
To console the humankind
That barbarian politics
Chained to adversity;
In France a great-souled hero
Has surpassed the sublime efforts
Of Cato, of Leonidas:
In America, a new guide
With the virtues of Aristides
Governs many states.—

My successor is now installed. I am today without a function. I shall return to my homeland via the first diplomatic vessel, around the month of June. But I shall be imbued all my life by the kindnesses with which you have honored me during 16 years. If I were younger, I could imagine that I might still be able to come and admire you. Deprived of that hope, allow me to be devoted to you until the last moment of my life.

Be pleased, Mister President, to accept my devotion and my deep respect.

LÉTOMBE

RC (DLC); endorsed by TJ as received 30 Mch. and so recorded in SJL.

SA FEMME: Honoré Julien's wife worked in the President's House for at least three months in the summer and fall of 1801, earning $8 per month (MB, 2:1045, 1054, 1056).

Simon Chaudron penned the ODE in commemoration of the new century. The poem consisted of six stanzas, one of which Létombe transcribed in the letter above. Philadelphia printers Thomas and William Bradford published the work as a broadside dated 4 Mch. 1801. Chaudron probably composed the verses not long before that, since in them he mentioned the French victory at Hohenlinden. The poem extolled that battle and the movement toward armed neutrality in northern Europe as checks on the expansive power of a tyrannical and corrupt Great Britain. Without naming either leader, Chaudron's verses hailed Bonaparte as the hero of France and TJ as the new leader of America. TJ received a manuscript copy of the poem, either from Chaudron or by other means (MS in MHi, in French, apparently in Chaudron's hand, endorsed by TJ: "Chaudron M."; *Poésies Choisies de Jean-Simon Chaudron, suivies de l'Oraison Funèbre de Washington, par le Même Auteur* [Paris, 1841], 6-9; Moses Robinson to TJ, 3 Mch. 1801).

From Levi Lincoln

SIR   Washington March 26. 1801.

with the letter, and the associated papers from Mr Porter, and three from Gent. in Alexandria recommending Capt Moore as register of wills in that district, I take the liberty of submitting to your inspection a letter of a more private nature just recd. from Boston—By it, my friends, it is easy to be perceived, have agreed to confuse. Explanations, it is to be hoped will remove the impressions, which I was sure would be made. The effects of the public measures, and the elections of Bacon and Smith as stated towards the close of my friends letter, being interesting events, must apologize for the freedom taken in troubling you with a private correspondence.

with sentiments Sir of the highest respect I have the honor to be your most obt Hum Sevt   LEVI LINCOLN

RC (DLC); at head of text: "The President of the United States"; endorsed by TJ as received 26 Mch. and so recorded in SJL. Enclosures: (1) David Porter, Jr., to James Madison, Baltimore, 23 Mch. 1801, requesting appointment as an officer in the U.S. Navy (RC in DNA: RG 59, LAR; endorsed by TJ: "David Porter:—Navy departmt."; enclosures not found). (2) Elisha Dick to Levi Lincoln, Alexandria, 26 Mch., recommending Cleon Moore, a Revolutionary War veteran who claimed the confidence of the people of Alexandria as register of wills for the county. (3) George Gilpin to same, Alexandria, 26 Mch., noting that he has known Moore for 30 years and that the candidate, with experience as a notary public and a practicing lawyer, was "fit to fill the office" of register of wills. (4) George Taylor to same, Alexandria, 26 Mch., introducing Moore as "an old and respectable Citizen" of Alexandria

qualified for appointment (RCs in same). The "letter of a more private nature" has not been identified.

On 2 Mch. John Adams nominated Cleon MOORE as register of wills and justice of the peace for Alexandria County. Not having his commissions, Moore engaged the support of "Mr. Fitzhugh" (probably William), who had agreed that if he saw the president he would mention Moore's nomination. In a statement dated 25 Mch., Moore reviewed his Revolutionary War experience and his need for the "Small emoluments" from these offices to support his large family (MS in DNA: RG 59, LAR, in Moore's hand and signed by him, endorsed by TJ: "Cleon Moore, Register of wills"; JEP, 1:388). TJ signed a commission, dated 30 Mch. 1801, appointing Moore register of wills at Alexandria (Lb in DNA: RG 59, MPTPC; Appendix I, List 4).

To James Madison

TH:J. to J.M.   Washington Mar. 26. 1801.

I am still here. three refusals of the Naval Secretaryship have been recieved,[1] and I am afraid of recieving a 4th. this evening from mr Jones of Phila. in that case Genl. Smith has agreed to take it pro tempore, so as to give me time; and I hope the moment it is in either his or Jones's hands, to get away; but this may be yet three four or five days. Lincoln is doing the duties of your office. he & Dearborn will remain here. health, respect & affectionate attachment.

RC (DLC: Madison Papers, Rives Collection); at foot of text: "James Madison"; endorsed by Madison. PrC (DLC); endorsed by TJ in ink on verso.

[1] MS: "reieved."

To Thomas McKean

DEAR SIR   Washington Mar. 26. 1801.

I recieved last night your favor of the 21st. and thank you for the communication it contained. I value it as a historical fact, as well as a strong evidence of the obligations I am under for the partiality of my country men to me: but rejoice with you that the views of the constitution were otherwise fulfilled.   satisfied that the departure of the Chevr. d'Yrujo & his family must be a circumstance of the most tender sollicitude to you & them, it was among my earliest attentions to address a letter to our Minister at Madrid in which I stated the exchange meditated by that court, & the regret it would excite here. this letter was written by myself, tho' in the name of, & signed by the Secretary of state. this was sent by mr Dawson, who was to forward it as speedily as possible from Paris to Madrid. still this being an official letter, the terms of it were, as of usage, restrained within the limits of self-respect & public formality. I therefore availed myself of a conversation which had passed between mr Yznardi & myself, as giving an occasion to write him a letter. considering that conversation as confidential to myself on the part of his court, & a mark of friendship, I chose to take it out of the line of official correspondence, & to make it the subject of a private letter to him, to be used as a confidential answer from myself for the inspection of his court. in this way I was free to urge the retaining of the Chevalier much more freely & fully. In doing this I was the more gratified as it was in perfect unison with my public duty, being myself so well satisfied of the good faith & good sense of the Chevalr. that I would rather have to transact the interests of this country through him, than through any other person they could possibly send. I only fear these letters may be too late. — I have been anxiously attentive to the merits of mr Coxe & mr Beckley, and the more uneasy as there has been absolutely nothing which could be done for them as yet, nor any immediate prospect. I mentioned to you the important motives on which P. Muhlenberg must take the place of Miller. the principles of removal, are to be settled finally when our administration collects about the last of April. some, on unquestionable principles are made & making in the mean time. a few minutes conversation with those gentlemen would possess them fully of the state and prospect of things. but that is impossible, & the trusting such matter by letter equally so. since you have been so good as to mention them in your letter, will you add to it by communicating to them so much of this as respects them? Accept assurances of my high consideration & respect

TH: JEFFERSON

RC (PHi); addressed: "Governor Mc.Kean Philadelphia"; franked; postmarked 27 Mch.; readdressed at Philadelphia, in unknown hand: "His Excellency Thos. Mc.Kean Esq. Governor of Pennsylva. Lancaster"; postmarked 12 Apr.; endorsed in clerk's hand. PrC (DLC).

THIS LETTER WAS WRITTEN BY MYSELF: see Levi Lincoln to David Humphreys, 17 Mch. 1801. SUBJECT OF A PRIVATE LETTER: see TJ to Yznardi, 26 Mch.

To Sarah Mease

DEAR MADAM   Washington Mar. 26. 1801.

I am honoured with your favor of the 20th. inst. on the subject of mr Hall, and I readily ascribe honor to the motives from which it proceeds. the probable sufferings of a wife & numerous family are considerations which may lawfully weigh in the minds of the good, and ought to prevail when unopposed by others more weighty. it has not been the custom, nor would it be expedient for the executive to enter into details of justification for the rejection of candidates for offices or removal of those who possess them. your good sense will readily percieve to what such contests would lead. yet my respect for your understanding & the value I set on your esteem, induce me, for your own *private & personal* satisfaction *confidentially* to say that an officer who is entrusted by the law with the sacred duty of naming judges of life & death for his fellow citizens, and who selects them exclusively from among his political & party enemies, ought never to have in his power a second abuse of that tremendous magnitude. how many widows and orphans would have been this day weeping in the bitterness of their losses, had not a milder sense of duty in another stayed the hand of the executioner. I mean no reflection on the conduct of the jurors. they acted according to their conscientious principles. I only condemn an officer, important in the administration of justice, who selects judges[1] for principles which lead necessarily to condemnation. he might as well lead his culprits to the scaffold at once without the mockery of trial. the sword of the law should never fall but on those whose guilt is so apparent as to be pronounced by their friends as well as foes. pardon, my dear, Madam, these rigorous justifications of a duty which has been a painful one to me, and which has yet to be repeated in some cases of greater feeling. you will see in them proofs of my desire to preserve your esteem, and accept assurances of my highest consideration & respect.

TH: JEFFERSON

RC (PHi); at foot of text: "Mrs. Sarah Mease." PrC (DLC).

[1] Word interlined.

From John Miller

Sir/   Pendleton Court-House S.C. March 26, 1801.

The Man who in London between the Periods of 1770 and 1781, in his London Evening Post, for seven Years laboured *in decrying and exposing the Wickedness and Folly of the accursed American War*, (as he told Lord Mansfield when receiving Sentence) Now, from under the Mountains in South Carolina, has the heartfelt Satisfaction of offering his Congratulations to the President of the United States on his Call, by the glad Voice of his Country, to his present all-important and dignified Post. He adds his most fervent Wishes, which shall ever be accompanied by his Prayers, that a gracious Providence may continue to the President the Blessing of uninterrupted Health in the Discharge of his infinitely interesting Functions—and that, ever beloved, his Administration may be truly tranquil and singularly happy.   With sincerely affectionate Regard he will ever be the President's most humble servant.   J. Miller

☞   Mr. Miller's Imprisonment (which during fourteen years this last Time made the eighth) was terminated by the coming into the Ministry, of his Friend Mr. Fox.

RC (ViW); at foot of text: "His Excellency the President of the United States"; endorsed by TJ as received 5 May and so recorded in SJL.

Noted for his pro-American views, John Miller (ca. 1744-1807), printer of the *London Evening Post* and the *London Courant*, faced libel charges five times between 1770 and 1781 and was jailed on several occasions. He published a series of articles in the *London Courant* in October and November 1781 criticizing the treatment of Henry Laurens, who had been captured on his way to Europe in September 1780 and was held in the Tower of London under the charge of treason until 31 Dec. 1781. Arrested, tried, and jailed again in late 1781, Miller began making plans to leave England. Carrying a letter of recommendation from Laurens, he arrived in the United States in January 1783. Miller settled in Charleston, South Carolina, where he established the *South-Carolina Gazette and General Advertiser* and served as the official state printer. He sold the newspaper in 1785 and settled with his family in Pendleton District. In 1795 he became the corresponding secretary of the Franklin Society of Pendleton, a Democratic-Republican Society for which he wrote "stirring anti-Federalist resolutions" and voiced opposition to the Jay Treaty (*London Courant*, 23, 29 Nov. 1781; Philip M. Hamer and others, eds., *The Papers of Henry Laurens*, 16 vols. [Columbia, S.C., 1968-2003], 15:xvii, 380; 16:4; *S.C. Biographical Directory, House of Representatives*, 3:498-500; D. H. Gilpatrick, "The English Background of John Miller," *The Furman Bulletin*, 20 [1938], 14-20; Eugene P. Link, *Democratic-Republican Societies, 1790-1800* [New York, 1973], 58, 90-1, 132; Brigham, *American Newspapers*, 2:1039).

Miller delivered the statement on the accursed american war on 28 Nov. 1781, immediately after being sentenced to a year in prison for "copying a paragraph respecting the Russian Ambassador" from a morning newspaper into the *London Evening Post* (*London Courant*, 29 Nov. 1781).

Charles James fox, an outspoken opponent of the war with the American colonies, became foreign secretary in

[455]

March 1782, when Lord North resigned and the Rockingham administration came into power. Miller was released from prison in May 1782 (DNB; *The Furman Bulletin*, 20 [1938], 18-19).

To Thomas Mann Randolph

TH:J. to TMR.   Mar. 26. 1801. Washington

I am still here, & not yet absolutely certain of the moment I can get off. I fear I shall this evening recieve a 4th. refusal of the Secretary-ship of the Navy. should it take place, I have fixed on a temporary arrangement, & in any event expect to get away in the course of 3. or 4. days, so as to be with you by the time you recieve this or very soon after. it is the getting the Naval department under way which alone detains me. my tenderest affections to my ever dear Martha and to the little ones. friendly attachment to yourself.   TH: JEFFERSON

RC (DLC); endorsed by Randolph. PrC (MHi); endorsed by TJ in ink on verso.

To Samuel Smith

DEAR SIR   Washington Mar. 26. 1801.

According to what I had augured, I have this moment recieved mr Jones's refusal of the Secretaryship of the navy. in mine of two days ago, I mentioned to you this fear, & that in that event I must avail the public of your kind offer to accept the office for a while. I now take the liberty of repeating my request that you will be so good as to come on on Saturday, that we may have a consultation on the measures imme-diately to be taken. the urgency arises not only from the state of sufferance in which the department is, but from the necessity of my departure immediately, lest the assembling of our administration at the time agreed on should be delayed which would be very injurious to the public. accept assurances of my great respect & esteem.

TH: JEFFERSON

RC (ViU); addressed: "General S. Smith Baltimore"; franked. PrC (DLC); en-dorsed by TJ in ink on verso.

To Joseph Yznardi, Sr.

Dear Sir   Washington Mar. 26. 1801.

The Secretary of state is proceeding in the consideration of the several matters which have been proposed to us by you, & will prepare answers to them, and particularly as to our vessels taken by French cruisers & carried into the ports of Spain, contrary as we suppose to the tenor of the convention with France. tho' ordinary business will be regularly transacted with you by the Secretary of state, yet considering what you mentioned as to our Minister at Madrid to have been private & confidential, I take it out of the official course, & observe to you myself that under an intimate conviction of long standing in my mind, of the importance of an honest friendship with Spain, and one which shall identify her American interests with our own, I see in a strong point of view the necessity that the organ of communication which we establish near the king, should possess the favor & confidence of that government. I have therefore destined for that mission a person whose accomodating & reasonable conduct, which will be still more fortified by instructions, will render him agreeable there, & an useful channel of communication between us. I have no doubt the new appointment by that government to this, in the room of the Chevalr. d'Yrujo, has been made under the influence of the same motives. but still, the Chevalr. d'Yrujo being intimately known to us, the integrity, sincerity & reasonableness of his conduct having established in us a perfect confidence, in no wise diminished by the bickerings which took place between him & a former Secretary of state, whose irritable temper drew on more than one affair of the same kind, it will be a subject of regret if we lose him. however if the interests of Spain require that his services should be employed elsewhere, it is the duty of a friend to acquiesce; and we shall certainly recieve any successor the king may chuse to send, with every possible degree of favor & friendship. our administration will not be collected till the end of the ensuing month: and consequently, till then, no other of the mutual interests of the two nations will be under our view, except those general assurances of friendship which I have before given you verbally, & now repeat. accept I pray you assurances of my high consideration & respect.   Th: Jefferson

RC (AHN: Papeles de Estado, legajo 3891 bis, expediente 1, no. 126); at foot of text: "Don Joseph Yznardi." PrC (DLC).

A former secretary of state: Timothy Pickering; see Vol. 30:53-5.

From Alexander Boyd

SIR Philadelphia 27th March 1801

As it is Generally Expected that a Change of officers will take place in the Custom house of this port, a large Circile of my friends have encouraged me to apply to your Excellency for the place of naval officer now filled by Genl. William Mc.Pherson—I flatter myself that such Credentials & Recommendations Can be obtained in favour of my public Character & private Life as will Give General Satisfaction—I am a pensylvanian by Birth & I served my Countrys Cause during the whole Revolutionary war—In the year 1789 I was appointed inspector for this port and for Eight years in that office I faithfully Executed the trust Reposed in me—as Soon as party Spirit began to Run high my Known Republican principles Rendered me Odious to the Colletor and Surveyor of the port—and when I Dared to Exercise my Rights openly as a freeman on an important Election in this City I was abruptly Dismissed from office, with no other Reason assigned than that I had Voted for a man Esteemed an Enemy to the Administration—These Circumstances make me the more Bold To Come forward with my present application—

I hope I may be thought worthy of that or Some other office in the Custom house of this port—and that my application will meet with Every attention it deserves I Can Entertain no Doubt—

With the most profound Respect and Esteem I am your Excellencys Most Obt. and most Humbl. Servt. ALEXR. BOYD

RC (DNA: RG 59, LAR); at foot of text: "Thomas Jefferson, presedent o U States"; endorsed by TJ as received 16 Apr. and so recorded in SJL with notation "Off."

Alexander Boyd was a major in the Pennsylvania militia during the Revolutionary War. A Philadelphia innkeeper, Boyd made his boarding house an unofficial gathering place for Antifederalist members of the Pennsylvania legislature who opposed the calling of a state convention to consider the new federal Constitution (*Pennsylvania Gazette*, 27 Nov. 1782; John Bach McMaster and Frederick D. Stone, eds., *Pennsylvania and the Federal Constitution, 1787-1788* [Philadelphia, 1888], 3, 13, 204).

Ardent Federalists served as OFFICERS of the Philadelphia Custom House: Collector George Latimer, Naval Officer William McPherson, and Surveyor William Jackson. Boyd would not receive an appointment from TJ, but the president replaced Latimer with Peter Muhlenberg in 1802 and Jackson with William Bache in 1804. McPherson retained his position until his death in 1813 (Prince, *Federalists*, 85-94; JEP, 1:432, 471; PMHB, 5 [1881], 91-2).

To Catherine Church

Washington Mar. 27. 1801.

I owe you a letter, my dear young friend. it is a debt I pay with pleasure, & therefore should not have so long delayed but for the importunity of others more urging & less indulgent. I thank you for your kind congratulations on the proof of public esteem lately bestowed on me. that you write in these sentiments renders them more dear to me. the post is not enviable, as it affords little exercise for social affections. there is something within us which makes us wish to have things conducted in our own way, and which we generally fancy to be patriotism. this passion is gratified by such a position. but the heart would be happier enjoying the affections of a family fireside.—It is more than six weeks since I heard from Maria. this is a proof of her aversion to her pen, & must be her apology for not answering your letter, which she recieved in due time & resolved to answer every day for a month before I parted with her last. she continues to love you as much as ever, and would give you, as she does me, every proof of it, except writing letters. she is in a fair way to be again a mother. this will prevent her meeting me at home, in a short excursion I am about making thither. mrs Randolph always recollects you with her former affection. she is the mother of four children, and half of another. I shall endeavor to persuade them to come & see me here sometimes, & will not be without hopes it may tempt you to take a flying trip, which, in summer, is of three days only. present my friendly respects to mr and mrs Church, & accept yourself assurances of my constant and affectionate attachment.   TH: JEFFERSON

RC (ViU); address sheet torn; addressed: "Miss Catharine Ch[urch] New York"; franked; postmarked 29 Mch. PrC (MHi); endorsed by TJ in ink on verso.

YOUR KIND CONGRATULATIONS: Catherine Church to TJ, 23 Feb.

To John Wayles Eppes

DEAR SIR   Washington Mar. 27. 1801.

According to the plan I had proposed of each of us answering immediately on reciept of a letter from the other, by which means we should keep up a continued correspondence, & hear mutually about once a fortnight, I was waiting a letter from you, and began to be very uneasy, when yesterday yours of the 18th. came to hand. I set out the last day of this month for Monticello, where I shall remain three weeks only, and sincerely lament we cannot all be together there; and that I have no chance of seeing my dear Maria till August. the cause which prevents her now going to Monticello, will I suppose forbid me to expect what I much wished, a visit here. whether I could take a flying trip of one week to Monticello in June is doubtful.—as soon as I arrive there I will send to you for Dr. Walker's & Bell's pair of horses. draw your bills at 90. days, as I desired in my last, on Gibson & Jefferson, who are instructed to accept them. tho I am disposed to give 500. D. for Haxhall's as a riding horse, yet it is too much for carriage horses. I would give 800. for Dr. Shore's. if Haxall's can be bought for 500. D. about the 1st. of May at 90. day's, and Dr. Shore's pair on the same credit about the 1st. of June, it would bring the paiments within my accomplishment: tho' it would have been convenient to me to have recieved Haxall's with the two first, to save a second sending for him. but that would be to propose 120. days credit instead of 90. which he would not like. will Doctr. Shore's match in colour with Dr. Walker's?

I am happy to learn from all quarters that the ground proposed by me in my inaugural address is considered as a ground of union. the accession to us since the 11th. of February has been immense. I am in hopes our administration will give satisfaction. the[1] mission of Dawson is only disapproved because misrepresented. I had determined to send a Lieutt. or an ensign, merely as a messenger, & allowing him moderate expences in addition to his pay. the enquiry for a proper one, became known to Dawson, who offered to go on the same scale of allowance. he was preferred, because known, worthy of all confidence, honest & intelligent: and because his known character would answer the additional purpose of giving verbal assurances of our friendship to that government and useful statements of the state of things here. if absent 4. months, his allowance for expences will be 720. Dollars, whereas Livingston's, had he gone, would in the same time have have been 3000. D. besides the inadmissibility of sending a minister there before the ratification of the treaty. Livingston will not recieve his *commission* till Dawson returns. the lying appointments published in the newspapers are another source of discontent. I recommend to you to pay not the least credit to pretended appointments in any paper,[2] till you see it in Smith's. he is at hand to enquire at the offices, and is careful not to publish them on any other authority. but what there will be the most difference of opinion about will be removals. that all former officers should be removed, no man thinks; that some should, all agree. But no two draw the same line. mr Adams's last appointments, made just as he was going out of office, are treated by me as nullities (except the judges.) I appoint others instead of them generally. Marshals & attorneys who have packed juries or committed other legal oppression on our citizens are under a course of removal. officers in every line who have been guilty of misconduct & abuse of office, will be removed. but for mere difference of principle, I am not disposed to disturb any man. this is exactly what we have complained of in the former administration. some acts of injustice in that way by mr Adams, I shall redress. these removals, tho' unquestionably just, will be thought too much by some, too little by others. so that on that ground I can expect nothing like a general approbation. still I shall hope indulgence when it shall be seen that removals are on fixed rules, applied to every case without passion or partiality. the rule may be disapproved, but the application shall be beyond reproach.—my tenderest love to my dear & ever beloved Maria; and to yourself health happiness & affectionate esteem.   TH: JEFFERSON

P.S. Gibson & Jefferson will pay you £16-4-9 for your 902. ℔ tobo. whenever called for.

RC (ViU); addressed: "John W. Eppes. at Bermuda Hundred near City point"; franked and postmarked. PrC (Hamilton Cottier, Princeton, New Jersey, 1948); second page only.

IN MY LAST: TJ to Eppes, 22 Feb.

[1] TJ here canceled "appointment."
[2] TJ first wrote "the papers" before altering the words to read as above.

To Gibson & Jefferson

DEAR SIR   Washington Mar. 27. 1801.

In the last letter recieved from mr Lieper (Mar. 8.) are these words. 'from what I have heard & seen respecting your tobo. in the hands of Jackson & Wharton, you in conscience ought to make no discount on it, & I believe they think [so also for] they have refused 7. D. which I offered them, & inform me they have ordered their agent to pay the money.' and again 'I would now beg for myself your crop of tobacco (of 1800) at the market price, for I think your tobaccoes as good as any I ever manufactured.' what would be given in Richmond for the last year's crop? tobacco sells here at 6. D. I should suppose the best crops at Richmond would always be a third more than the market price here. I ask your information because perhaps the spring price, may by the opening of the French market, be as good as the price in autumn.—I set out for Monticello on the last day of this month, to stay there three weeks. while there I shall have occasion to draw on you perhaps beyond the funds which remain free of

Jackson & Wharton's paiments or rather M. & F.; and not being in my power to know till I get there what demands I shall have, I cannot now direct mr Barnes as to the remittance; but will endeavor to do it in time to meet my draughts. of the tobo sold to Mcmurdo & Fisher £16.4.9 (for 902. lb) belonged to J. W. Eppes, which now be pleased to pay him. my part is therefore £797-15 or 2659.17 of which I had engaged 1000. D. to Tazewell, 1000. D. to Lyle & 450. for T M Randolph. consequently there remain but 209.17 & I do not know how stands our balance on other accounts. but my orders on mr Barnes shall be sufficient, & I hope early enough for my draughts whatever they may be. mr Eppes will draw on you on my account for some such sum as 600. D. at 90 days, say payable the beginng. of July perhaps for [like sum], or less, or larger, for the beginng. of Aug. & Sep. these will be for horses, should he buy them for me. I pray you to accept the draughts, & to rely that they shall be covered with effects placed with you in due time to prevent advances. Accept assurances of my constant & affectionate esteem.

TH: JEFFERSON

P.S. If you can immediately send up 1. doz. bottles of Syrop of punch to Monticello, I will thank you.

PrC (MHi); blurred; at foot of text: "Mr. G. Jefferson"; endorsed by TJ in ink on verso as "Gibson & Jefferson" and so recorded in SJL.

From George Hadfield

SIR   Washington. March 27th. 1801.—
Be pleased to allow me to lay before you, the case of an artist who chearfully quitted his occupations and prospects in London, to accept through Colonel John Trumbull; the invitations of the Commissioners of Washington to visit this country, for the purpose of superintending the building of the Capitol.—

After having continued in that Office, for three years, and superintended the execution of the most difficult part of that building; I was abruptly dismissed to the great injury of my professional reputation.

Sensible, that such treatment could not fail to cause me to experience very serious consequences. if left unnoticed: I hastened to lay my situation before the late President of the United States, but after considerable delay and anxiety, I found that I had no hope of redress, in consequence of which I have had the painful mortification, not only of seeing my work remain for the praise and reputation of those, who have meditated and effected my ruin: but also, of having my productions for Public buildings surreptitiously taken from me and executed, without my receiving any compensation for them.

I hope that I shall not be thought too presumptuous if I am desirous to shew, that the great increase of expence in consequence of the unnecessary alterations made in the Capitol: after I had left it, as well as the present leakiness and other defects of that building: arise from an entire ignorance of the plans & mode intended by me, and of course lost in consequence of my dismission.

And I will further venture to say, that had I been permitted to superintend my work & designs in the building of the Executive Offices, that the late unfortunate fire in one of them, would not have happened from the causes, by many supposed & alledged; and it appears, that those buildings, from the manner of their execution, will always be subject to similar accidents, if suffered to remain in their present state.

I shall not, Sir, at present trouble you, with a tedious detail of particulars, but should you think my case worthy of your notice, I trust that I shall be able to substantiate my assertions, supported by some of the most respectable characters in this City

I shall only say for the present that I suffer considerably through the oppressive treatment which I have received from the Commissioners of the City: but encouraged as I am, by letters lately received from Colo. Trumbull in Europe, and by other friends here, and presuming that the advantages I have had during the pursuit of my studies might be of further utility in the present state of the City, I have taken the liberty thus to lay my case before you, with no other view, Sir, than to endeavour to make myself useful, and thereby obtain a subsistence in a country which I have chosen to spend the remainder of my life in.—

I have the honor to be with most profound respect, Sir, your very obedient humble servant—   GEORGE HADFIELD

RC (DLC); at foot of text: "The President of the United States"; endorsed by TJ as received 27 Mch. and so recorded in SJL.

The younger brother of TJ's friend Maria Cosway, George Hadfield (1763-1826) studied architecture at the Royal Academy in London before superintending work on the U.S. Capitol. He held the post from 1795 until his dismissal in 1798. The founder of both an architectural academy and manufacturing company and the designer of many public buildings in the District of Columbia, he became a naturalized U.S. citizen in 1802 (ANB; Harris, *Thornton*, 294, 327-38, 454; George S. Hunsberger, "The Architectural Career of George Hadfield," RCHS, 51-2 [1955], 46-65).

From William Hylton

DEAR SIR!   Morris-Ville Pensylva. 27th March 1801—

Having occasion to address you upon the subject of my intended departure for Europe—permit me to avail of it, to pay the Tribute of congratulation *due* to you, as a man, a patriot and a Statesman, from every friend of our common Country; whose voice has called you to the most exalted Station of it!

Although probably among the *latest*—I am not the *least* sincere in rejoicing at the Triumph, Reason and Right, have had over Prejudice and Faction!

The contemplation of the happy Results assured, by the mildness and wisdom of the administration, has strengthened my determination to release myself of foreign property; by the immediate disposal of my Jamaica Estate; which will afford me a moderate Independance; and the satisfaction of releiving my unfortunate Brother.

With these views I mean to depart for Europe, soon as I shall have procured such Letters to Hamburgh & London, as may give necessary responsibility to my negotiation.   At present one *is* onfoot, with Sir William Poultney & myself for productive property in Genessee.   whatever Letters of protection or recommendation, you will please to honor me with, *I* shall be grately thankful for!   If Sir I can be useful to you *individually*, as a friend—or to my Country as a Citizen—please to faver me with your Commands!

I lately saw the propriety of your *silence*, respecting my Son— while I felt the *inadvertence*, my sollicitude as a Father, *led* me into! I trust it will plead my apology!

my Son is now appointed a Soldier! His Conduct, I hope, will render him deserving of the attention his Country and friends may honor him with.

With sentiments of great Respect and much Consideration I have the honor to be Dear sir

Your very obliged friend & obedt. servt.   WM. HYLTON

I leave this for Baltimore

RC (DLC); at foot of text: "His excellency Thomas Jefferson Esqr"; endorsed by TJ as received 30 Mch. and so recorded in SJL. Dupl (same); in Hylton's hand; at head of text: "Copy"; lacks postscript.

MY UNFORTUNATE BROTHER: Daniel L. Hylton.

On 1 June Hylton wrote again to TJ requesting LETTERS of recommendation for England, Holland, and Hamburg, in advance of Hylton's proposed visit to Europe in anticipation of selling his Jamaican estate (RC in DLC; endorsed by TJ as received 5 June and so recorded in SJL).

For Hylton's SON John, see William Hylton to TJ, 20 Jan. 1801 (Vol. 32:495).

To George Jefferson

DEAR SIR   Washington Mar. 27. 1801.

I have to acknowlege the receipt of yours of Mar. 4. and to express to you the delight with which I found the just, disinterested & honorable point of view in which you saw the proposition it covered. the resolution you so properly approve had long been formed in my mind. the public will never be made to believe that an appointment of a relative is made on the ground of merit alone, uninfluenced by family views. nor can they [. . .] see with approbation offices, the disposal of which they entrust to their president for public purposes, divided out as family property. mr Adams degraded himself infinitely by his conduct on this subject, as Genl. Washington had done himself the greatest honor. with two such examples to proceed by, I should be doubly inexcusable to err. it is true that this places the relations of the President in a worse situation than if he were a stranger. but the public good which cannot be effected if it's confidence is lost, requires this sacrifice. perhaps too it is compensated by sharing in the public esteem. I could not be satisfied till I assured you of the increased esteem with which this transaction fills me for you. accept my affectionate assurances of it.   TH: JEFFERSON

PrC (DLC); faint; at foot of text: "Mr. George Jefferson."

To Henry Knox

DEAR SIR   Washington Mar. 27. 1801.

I recieved with great pleasure your favor of the 16. and it is with the greatest satisfaction I learn from all quarters that my inaugural Address is considered as holding out a ground for conciliation & union. I am the more pleased with this, because the opinion therein stated as to the real ground of difference among us (to wit, the measures rendered most expedient by French enormities) is that which I have long entertained. I was always satisfied that the great body of those called Federalists were real Republicans as well as federalists. I know indeed there are Monarchists among us. one character of these is in theory only, & perfectly acquiescent in our form of government as it is, & not entertaining a thought of disturbing it merely on their theoretic opinions. a second class, at the head of which is our quondam collegue, are ardent for the introduction of monarchy, eager for armies, making more noise for a great naval establishment than better patriots who wish it on a rational scale only, commensurate to our wants & our means. this last class ought to be tolerated but not trusted. believing that (excepting the ardent Monarchists) all our citizens agreed in antient whig principles, I thought it adviseable to define & declare them, & let them see the ground on which we could rally: and the fact proving to be so, that they agree on these principles, I shall pursue them with more encouragement. I am aware that the necessity of a few removals for legal, oppressions, delinquencies and other official malversations, may[1] be misconstrued as done for political opinions, & produce hesitation in the coalition so much to be desired; but the extent of these will be too limited to make permanent impressions. in the class of removals however I do not rank the new appointments which mr A. crouded in with whip & spur from the 12th. of Dec. when the event of the election was known, (and consequently that he was making appointments, not for himself, but his successor) until 9. aclock of the night, at 12. aclock of which he was to go out of office. this outrage on decency, shall not have it's affect, except in the life appointments which are irremoveable. but as to the others I consider the nominations as nullities & will not view the persons appointed as even candidates for their office, much less as possessing it by any title meriting respect. I mention these things that the grounds & extent of the removals may be understood, & may not disturb the tendency to union. indeed that union is already effected from N. York Southwardly almost completely. in the N. England states it will be slower than elsewhere from peculiar circumstances better known to yourself than me. but we will go on attending with the utmost sollicitude to their interests, & doing them impartial justice, & I have no doubt they will in time do justice to us. I have opened myself frankly because I wish to be understood by those who mean well, and are disposed to be just towards me, as you are; & because I know you will use it for good purposes only, & for none unfriendly to me.—I leave this place in a few days to make a short excursion home where some domestic arrangements are necessary previous to my final removal here, which will be about the latter end of April. be so good as to present my respects to mrs Knox, & accept yourself assurances of my high consideration & esteem. Th: Jefferson

PrC (DLC); at foot of first page: "General Knox."

¹ TJ here canceled "excite."

QUONDAM COLLEGUE: Alexander Hamilton.

From Ralph Mather

Calais, 27 Mch. 1801. While awaiting a passport for Paris, he wishes to congratulate TJ on his "late preference and appointment to the government of the U.S." He trusts that TJ recollects their introduction in 1792 by Mr. Muhlenberg at the instance of "the late Mr. Miller, my wife's father, the oldest settler or one of them in office in Philadelphia." He showed TJ some half-cent coins at the request of Matthew Boulton and then mentioned the desire of Lee & Son of Smyrna to offer their assistance in the matter of the Algerine corsairs. TJ was good enough to peruse a letter relating to it. Arriving from England as the representative of English commercial interests, Mather did well until "politics became unsettled, thereby trade convulsed." In 1797 he shipped a valuable cargo that was taken and condemned by the infamous Judge Cambould at the vice-admiralty court at Môle St. Nicolas. Despite the severe loss, he still maintains land in the Genesee Valley of New York that he purchased in 1794 from Sir William Pulteney. Coupled with new business connections near Leeds and at London and Staffordshire, he does not doubt his ability to recoup his losses. He is an agent for Baron Luigi La Greca of Naples and Messrs. Willinks of Amsterdam, and suggests that an appointment as acting consul at Le Havre "would help a *great sufferer*." He asks no compensation "but merely the influence to be derived" from the office. In a conversation with an English baronet he learned that Britain has no intention of negotiating a peace with France or a treaty with the Baltic nations. The baronet also blamed grain and flour shortages in England on bounties and government interference in trade. For a long time, Mather has known that better and cheaper modes of procuring cloth for the government could be employed and has stated that fact to Rufus King. He particularly recommends the textile firm of J. J. J. & William Taylor of Leeds as "*real* makers" who would "give goods on lower terms." Samples have been sent to Mr. Whelen, and Mather includes a price list for different types of cloth. He also recommends the work of hatmaker Joseph Tilstone at Newcastle, Staffordshire, whom he expects will write Mr. Whelen as well. Tilstone has a contract for 48,000 hats for a house in London, which will sell them abroad. Copper, iron bolts, and slops are best obtained in London, but better and cheaper shirts can be had at Lisle in Flanders, where he also

[467]

recommends purchasing linens and bleaching them to reduce the price. In France, flax is cheaper and best for the price, while Abbeville cloth of Spanish wool is not exceded by Britain. Sail cloth, once established in France, will soon be made better and at a lower price than in England. In this manner, savings can be as high as twenty percent and a greater number of soldiers clothed at the same expence. Such direct orders also ensure a better quality cloth than the defective goods and refuse generally sent to the American and West Indian markets. In conversation with Pulteney, Mather condemned the "violence and Spirit" made by British officials in the West Indies, he being among the sufferers, which has suspended insurance and been a great inconvenience to American trade. Pulteney asked for information on the most obnoxious offenders, which he promised to show to persons of influence. Pulteney added that it was difficult to find first-rate men willing to accept a post abroad. Mather responded that the United States had a stronger claim in the West Indies than before American independence and that British efforts to subjugate such foreign territories by force had not justified the cost and left the country in a weakened condition. Pulteney was impressed with Mather's arguments and proposed a meeting with members of the council. Mather relates these conversations to TJ to demonstrate how little British cabinet leaders know of the spoliations carried out in the West Indies. Mather also remarks "that a certain honorable judge in his treaty of 94" had been outwitted by Lord Grenville due to his lack of commercial knowledge, as proven by Article 12 of the treaty. Judges and lawyers should expound law, merchants discriminate in commercial arrangements, manufacturers set prices and select their materials, and agriculturists choose their seed and land adequate to each season and former produce. Pitt made himself a master of every argument by learning from persons in their several trades and professions. Answers to questions of trade should come from "*assured* quarters." In a postscript he states Pulteney has informed him that an order has been given to lay before Parliament every specific vessel taken by the British. An annexed list of prices for foodstuffs in England and France demonstrates their cheapness in the latter place.

RC (DNA: RG 59, LAR); addressed: "The honble. T. Jefferson Esqr. President of the *United States*"; also on address sheet in Mather's hand: "No. 1 via Hamburg: *Speed*" and "forwarded to & in the care of John de Cheauprouge Esqr. Hamburg by his Servant R: Mather late of Philadelphia"; franked; postmarked Philadelphia, 28 May; endorsed by TJ as received 30 May and so recorded in SJL with notation "Off."

Merchant and landholder Ralph Mather resided in Philadelphia between 1794 and 1797, occupying various addresses, the final one of 12 and 13 Quarry Street. Struggling financially in recent years, he advertised his Genesee land for sale in 1799 and had a house in Philadelphia auctioned off at a sheriff's sale in 1801. When TJ was secretary of state he and Mather discussed coinage (Edmund Hogan, *The Prospect of Philadelphia, and Check on the Next Directory* [Philadelphia, 1795], Evans, No. 28845, p. 72; *Gazette of the United States*, 27 Dec. 1794; *Columbian Centinel*, 8 Oct. 1796; *Pennsylvania Gazette*, 22 Mch. 1797; *Federal Gazette &*

Baltimore Daily Advertiser, 19 June 1799; *Poulson's American Daily Advertiser*, 4 Nov. 1800, 16 June 1801; Vol. 16:341-2).

Mather wrote TJ again from Calais on 7 Apr., repeating his recommendation of J. J. J. & W. Taylor as supplier of clothing for the army, adding that Rufus King would second their application to the government. Mather likewise reiterated his intention to settle in France and repeated his request for a consular post at either Le Havre or Antwerp, being "more inclined to fix" at the latter port. In summarizing his qualifications, Mather described himself as "a merchant of some experience," fluent in English, and an American citizen with considerable property in New York and connections with a merchant house in Norfolk. He described the French as "very partial" to the United States and felt confident that the conciliation of France and America "will produce very happy consequences."

America should nevertheless continue to assert its trading rights as a nation, wrote Mather, and keep "at an awfull distance from the cabals & intrigues of foreign emissaries." After requesting the favor of a reply from TJ to be sent to the post office at Paris, Mather added as a postscript an extract from a letter he received from Sir William Pulteney in London, dated 24 Mch. In it, Pulteney reported that the Privy Council had responded favorably to Mather's assertions regarding British spoliations in the West Indies (RC in DNA: RG 59, LAR; addressed: "The Honble. T. Jefferson Esqr. President of the United States"; also on address sheet: "⅌ Havre" and "Forwarded by Your very humble & respectfull Servant Philadelphia May 14th 1801. Petit de Villers"; franked; endorsed by TJ as received 16 July and "to be Consul at Havre or Antwerp," and so recorded in SJL).

From Joseph H. Nicholson

SIR   Centre-Ville (Md.) March 27. 1801

As no Secretary to the Navy has yet been appointed, and as I am entirely ignorant who will be at the Head of that Department, I beg you to excuse me for addressing myself personally to you, as the Subject of my Letter will, I trust, be considered a sufficient apology.

By an Act of Congress passed at the last Session, nine Captains only are to be retained in the naval Service, and from some Information received yesterday from the Seat of Government, I am induced to believe that an attempt will be made to impress you with the Propriety of including Captain Nicholson in the Number of those who are to be discharged. As he is an old and experienced Officer I should have been very much at a Loss for the Reason of his being pointed at, if I did not know that deep rooted and illiberal Prejudices exist against him in New England; from which quarter I have Reason to suppose the Attack will be made upon him.

The Object of the present Letter is two fold in its Nature. I wish to ask in the first Place that if Representations injurious to Captain Nicholson should be made to you, they may not be suffered to operate against him untill he has had an Opportunity of shewing them to be groundless—I am sensible that he has no *Right* to require this; yet in his peculiar Situation it is an Indulgence that may perhaps without

Impropriety be granted him. Although the Executive is authorized to dismiss at Pleasure, all the Officers of Government, Judges excepted, yet I believe this authority is seldom, perhaps never, exercised towards military or naval men of high Rank, unless previously sanctioned by the Sentence of a Court-martial, where the Party charged has it in his P[ower] to vindicate himself. It is true that some of the Officers of the Navy, very deserving men I have no Doubt, must now be dismissed without any Imputation of Misconduct, but this arises *et Necessitate Rei*, and will I presume generally apply to the youngest in Commission. I hope it may not be deemed improper in me to remark that it will at least wear the Appearance of Hardship, if a man originally commissioned to and yet holding the second Rank in the Ser[vice,] an old, intelligent and faithful Officer, who has acted with his Countrymen in every War in which they have been engaged since he was able to "pull a Rope," from that of 1756 to the present Period, should now be dismissed unless upon the most substantial Grounds and without knowing what part of his Conduct has been impeached.

I beg leave also to mention to you the only Charges which I have ever heard made against Captain Nicholson, (and I have taken some Pains to learn all that could be said against him) and to shew you that these Charges were acknowledged to be groundless by the late Administration, although they entertained strong Prejudices against him arising from other Causes.[1]

For the first charge I refer you to the Copy of a Letter from General Wilkinson to Captain Nicholson, herewith transmitted, marked A, in which he says that strong Prejudices exist against Captain Nicholson at the Seat of Government on Account of a Capture which he made and the Consequences that ensued. I enclose this Letter for the purpose of shewing that this Capture was used by *some one* in the administration to the Injury of Captain Nicholson, although Mr. Stoddert afterwards repeatedly in Conversation with me declared it was no Ground of Charge.—Capt. Nicholson captured an armed Ship of 20 Guns, called the *Niger*, which he carried into Norfolk, where she was not condemned on the Plea of her being British Property. I think his Justification will be very apparent if his Letters are referred to, now filed in the Navy Office, giving the Secretary an account of the suspicious Circumstances under which the Ship appeared when the Capture was made. These Circumstances were so strong that the Ship was lib[erated] *without Costs* or *Damages* in the District Court, although, upon Appeal the sentence was reversed by the Circuit Court as far as related to Cost[s and] Damages. From the Tenour of General Wilkinson's Letter I am persuaded that Mr. Stoddert mentioned this Capture to him as a ground of [charges] against Captain Nicholson, although he afterwards denied it to me saying he did not know from whom General Wilkinson could have his Information, and although I had seen a Letter (or rather the copy of a Letter) from Mr. Stoddert, where he says that "Capt. Nicholson was strictly within the Line of his Duty in bringing this Ship into Port."— [2] If [in] passing through Richmond you should have an Opportunity of conversing with Mr. Tazewell, of the House of Representatives, it may be in his Power to convince you that the true Grounds on which the Ship was liberated were not totally unlike those upon which Jonathan Robins was surrendered by Judge Bee.—If however the adm[inis]tration really believed Capt. Nicholson to be culpable, a Court martial ought to have been held upon him, and if guilty he ought to have been dismissed from the Service—If they really [thought] him chargeable with Misconduct, I do not see why it was denied to me, unless indeed the Reason may be discovered from *one* Expression in General Wilkinson Letter.

For another Charge I refer you to a Paper marked B w[hich] is the Copy of a Communication made by me to Captain Nicholson giving the Substance of a Conversation with Mr. Stoddert relative to him. In Relation to this Paper it is necessary to remark that in the Winter of '99, 1800 Captain Nicholson came to Philadelphia for the Purpose of demanding the Reasons of his being divested of his command; as he appeared very much irritated at the Conduct of the Administration towards him, I was apprehensive that he might use some Expressions which would furnish an Excuse for dismissing him altogether, and therefore prevailed on him to let me manage the Affair for him—This Charge you will see was mentioned by Mr. Stoddert himself, not as one made, or indeed entertained by the Government, and answered as fully by him at the same Time as it could be by Capt. Nicholson himself.[3] Permit me to add that the only Laxity of Discipline with which the Citizens of Boston could be acquainted must have been confined to the Port and visible there only; and if there was a Want of due Subordination on shore, I think I am justified in saying that this Imputation does not rest on Capt. Nicholson alone, for I believe there is scarcely a Port in the Union frequented by our Ships of War in which some of the inferior Officers have not committed the most shameful Outrages.—The Conversation above alluded to was reduced to writing on the Evening of the Day on which it was held, at the Request of Capt. Nicholson as he wished to relieve the anxieties of his Family and answer friends who thought his Prospects very unfavorable at that Period.[4]

The only other Charge which I have ever heard, was [mentioned] to me by my friend Captain Murray, and I thought it of too degrading a Nature to make it the Subject of a formal Vin[dica]tion, particularly as Capt. Murray told me he had entirely [remo]ved it—This was, that Captain Nicholson was in Habits of Intoxication; than which a more base and infamous Falsehood never was propagated against any man.

In a former part of my Letter I have observed that Prejudices of some kind or other against Capt. Nicholson had their Weight with the late administration—If I know myself I [hope] I should be one of the last Men in the World to make a Remark of this kind to you at the present Juncture, if I did not con[sider] it necessary to the complete Establishment of his Innocence—My own Feelings convince me that his Case will be decided as it ought to be, entirely upon its own Merits. But if it app[ear] that these Prejudices were entertained, that Mr. Stoddert's Professions of Friendship and Promises of Service, were mere Prof[essi]ons and Promises, that he treated Capt. Nicholson with neglect the most pointed, and omitted no opportunity of wou[nding] his Feelings; that he did not regard, in the slightest Manner his repeated Applications to be again called into active Service and that to all this, personal Insult was added by the late President, it clearly proves to my Mind that they entertained a strong Enmity towards him; and feeling this Enmity the fair Presumption is that they would have given it the fullest scope if any Charges of a serious Nature could have been brought to bear upon him.

In the Document marked B already referred to, it appears that Mr. Stoddert made repeated Professions of Friendship to Captain Nicholson, and spoke of Mr. Adams as feeling the same Disposition towards him; that he promised to give him with Captains Barry and Tingey some further Emoluments; that these were afterwards specified to me in the same conversation and a Promise made that they should be given if the thing was practicable. I thought it reasonable, as it would make no Difference to the United States and would be affording a Compensation for the Loss of all Chance of Prize money, arising from their not being in actual Service. The Paper marked [C.] is in Reference to this Head, and contains a Letter from me to Mr. Stoddert repeating the Request, and his Answer repeating the Promise, to which he adds "I will endeavour to make Captain Nicholson's Situation as good as I can"; a kind of Language seldom used in Relation to a Man whose Conduct we think merits our Disapprobation.—That this Promise has never been complied with to this Day, nor the slightest Notice taken of Captain

Nicholson's Letters reminding him of it, I consider as an Evidence of Mr. Stoddert's Duplicity and inimical Disposition towards him.

A Court martial has been *twice* held at or in the Neighbourhod of Boston (one on Board the *Constitution*), Officers sent from a Distance to compose it, and no Notice taken of Captain Nicholson, thereby wounding his Feelings in a Point of very great Delicacy with military men.—Mr. Stoddert likewise sent men from Philadelphia at a very great Expence to survey the Shore, sound the Bottom and give the Depth of Water of the very Spot before Captain Nicholson's Door,[5] leaving him entirely unnoticed, and evincing a Want of Confidence which has been used very much to his disadvantage—No Documents from me are necessary to support [these] Facts, as they are of Record, I presume.

In the Paper marked D it will be found that Capt. Nich[olson] made two Applications to the Secretary of the Navy to be again [called] into Service, which Applications have hither remained unanswered; and the Paper marked F shews the manner in which [the] late President treated the Application when personally made to him.

The Paper marked G I do not consider as very much connected with this Subject, but I transmit it because it contains some facts which ought to be enquired into by the next Secretary of the Navy— It is the Copy of a Memorandum from a Mr. Gibbs, the [Clerk] of the Navy Yard at Boston, delivered by Capt. Nicholson to the late President for the Purpose of shewing that the Agents Stephen Higgin[son & Co.] had defrauded the United States. He deemed a communication of this kind to be a part of his Duty, although I believe it has not been enquired into.

From all this I think it fair to infer that the late Administration were inimical to Capt. Nicholson, and inasmuch as he [has] never been charged before a Court Martial, nor dismissed from the Service, it may reasonably be concluded that he is really innocent. That Representations unfavorable to him may have been made [from] the Town of Boston, and injurious Reports circulated in other Por[ts of M]assachusetts, I can readily believe. He is a Man of nice feeling and high Sense of Honour, with a Haughtiness of Demeanour that has refused to bend with his declining Fortune—to this Circumstance together with that of his being a Southern Man I can readily ascribe the local Prejudices which may have been conceived against him; but I have no Hesitation in saying that I look to another Cause for those entertained by the late Executive. Although in common with many others both in the army and Navy, he felt [a strong] Disposition to accommodate himself to the Views of those under whom his "narrow

Fortune" obliged him to act, and therefore took very little Part in the political Differences of the Day, yet he was unfortunate in his connection with Men who never concealed thier unalterable attachment to the Principles of the Revolution: I mean Mr. Gallatin and Commodore Nicholson of New York; his other Freinds were too obscure to attract Notice.[6]

I have thus, Sir, laid before you as briefly as I could, the Case of a Man who appears to me to have some little Claim, if not upon the Bounty, at least upon the Justice of the Country, and who I am satisfied will not be discarded upon light and trivial Grounds. In May 1799 he was divested of his Command under the Pretence of favoring him; but the subsequent Conduct of the Executive has convinced me that they wished to get clear of him by compelling him to resign— His Necessities overcame his feelings and obliged him to continue in a Situation where every Day produced new Indignities. If he is now to be dismissed, his Case will be peculiarly hard—He [has] already passed his sixtieth year, and has spent his best Days in the Service of his Country—His Family is large, his Resources small, and he is now too far advanced in Life to engage in any other Business.—Under these Impressions permit me to express a Hope that he will not be thought unworthy future Confidence—

I have the Honor to be Sir with very high Respect—Yr. Ob. Servt.

JOSEPH H. NICHOLSON

It is not my Wish that you should consider this as a confidential communication, but that you will feel yourself at perfect liberty to shew the whole or a Part of it, to any Person who you think will be able to add to or diminish the Weight of the Observations I have made—

RC (DNA: RG 45, MLR); text obscured in margin supplied in brackets from Dft or by Editors; endorsed by TJ as received 16 Apr. and so recorded in SJL. Dft (DLC: Shippen Family Papers); lacks postscript; at foot of text: "The President of the United States." Enclosures: Memorandum from Caleb Gibbs to Samuel Nicholson, 9 July 1800, outlining the improprieties he observed as clerk of the navy yard at Boston, including the delivery of "Kent-ledge" or scrap iron for the *Massachusetts* to J. & T. H. Perkins; the delivery of 50-foot-long plank sawed for the Navy but used for masts of the *Globe*, a ship owned by Perkins; sale of the *Constitution's* launch for $150; the purchase of ballast for $110 per ton, being iron not fit for use for a ship of war; and pilfering of U.S. property by boatmen (Tr in DNA: RG 45, MLR, in Samuel Nicholson's hand, with notation by Nicholson that the memorandum was made "for the express purpose of informg. the prest. how his business was Carry'd on at Boston"; *The Boston Directory, Containing the Names of the Inhabitants, Their Occupations, Places of Business, and Dwelling-Houses* [Boston, 1798], 53, 90). Other enclosures not found.

INFORMATION RECEIVED YESTERDAY: on 27 May, Nicholson observed that he wrote the president immediately after he received a letter from Albert Gallatin warning that Captain Samuel Nicholson's situation was "extremely critical." Nicholson hoped that writing the president directly was "not contrary to *Court Etiquette*," declaring that he was "not quite so much of a Democrat as to wish to break through established Rules" (Gallatin, *Papers*, 5:46).

As a navy captain Samuel Nicholson watched over the construction of the U.S. frigate *Constitution* in Boston and commanded the ship's first two voyages in 1798 and 1799. In September 1798, NICHOLSON CAPTURED AN ARMED SHIP, the *Niger*. Finding the ship to be a British vessel, the courts ordered its release and the payment of an $11,000 indemnity to the ship's owners. Congress appropriated the money for the payment in April 1799. In that year Nicholson was relieved of command of the *Constitution* and appointed to oversee the construction of a 74-gun ship at Boston (ANB; Palmer, *Stoddert's War*, 44-9, 110-12). The decision was made to retain Nicholson as one of the nine captains. He became the first superintendent of the naval yard in Charlestown, Massachusetts (ANB; NDBW, 1:488).

UNFORTUNATE IN HIS CONNECTION: Samuel Nicholson was the uncle of Gallatin's wife, Hannah, whose father, Commodore James Nicholson, was a Republican party leader in New York City (Palmer, *Stoddert's War*, 111-12; ANB, 8:640).

[1] In Dft Nicholson here canceled: "I[n] May 1799 Capt. Nicholson was divested of his Command of the *Constitution* and ordered to remain on shore for the Purpose of superintending the building of a Seventy four at Boston—This was done under a Pretence of favoring him, and the Secretary of the Navy, Mr. Stoddert has always in Conversation with me declared that this was the Intention—I do not hesitate to say that I disbelieve it, although I once entertained different Impressions—."

[2] In Dft Nicholson wrote: "Perhaps indeed she might have been condemned, if Mr. Stoddert had not written 'that she must be liberated at all Events,' as Mr. Tazewell who was Capt. Nicholson's counsel on the occasion, informed me he certainly did." Dft lacks remainder of paragraph.

[3] In Dft, in place of the preceding sentence, Nicholson wrote: "in this Paper you will find that Mr. Stoddert declared that the Prejudices against him were confined *solely to Boston*, from which Place unfavorable Representations had been made, but he considered them in a great measure groundless."

[4] Dft lacks preceding sentence.

[5] In Dft Nicholson here added: "which has been since purchased for Navy and Dock Yards."

[6] In Dft Nicholson added: "although I cannot help feeling myself glanced at, possibly by Mr. Stodderts Request in an Expression in Genl. Wilkinson's Letter—It produced however no other Effect than that of exciting Disgust."

To Providence Citizens

GENTLEMEN   Washington Mar. 27. 1801.

I return my sincere thanks for your kind congratulations on my elevation to the first magistracy of the United States.   I see with pleasure every evidence of the attachment of my fellow citizens to elective government, calculated to promote their happiness, peculiarly adapted to their genius, habits & situation, and the best peaceable corrective of the errors or abuses of those entrusted with power.   The constitution, on which our Union rests, shall be administered by me according to the safe and honest meaning contemplated by the plain understanding of the people of the United states at the time of it's adoption: a meaning to be found in the explanations of those who advocated, not of those who opposed it, and who opposed it merely lest the constructions should be applied which they denounced as possible. these explanations are preserved in the publications of the time, and are too recent in the memories of most men to admit of question.   The energies of the nation so far as depends on me, shall be reserved for improvement of the condition of man, not wasted in his destruction. the lamentable resource of war is not authorised for evils of imagination, but for those actual injuries only, which would be more destructive of our wellbeing than war itself. peace, justice, & liberal intercourse with all the nations of the world, will, I hope, with all nations, characterize this commonwealth. Accept for yourselves, gentlemen, & the respectable citizens of the town of Providence, assurances of my high consideration & respect.

TH: JEFFERSON

RC (C. H. Merriman, Charlottesville, Virginia, 1965); at foot of text: "Messrs. Eddy, Russell, Thurber, Wheaton, & Smith, Providence." PrC (DLC). Enclosed in TJ to Samuel L. Mitchill, Washington, 27 Mch., stating that because Mitchill had transmitted the letter from the "several gentlemen of Providence," he wished to avail himself "of the same channel for returning the answer," and requesting that Mitchill provide the protection of his "cover and such an address as may carry it safely to it's destination" (RC in N, lacks inside address; PrC in DLC, at foot of text: "Doctr. Mitchell," endorsed by TJ in ink on verso).

KIND CONGRATULATIONS: see Providence Citizens to TJ, 5 Mch.

From Stephen Sayre

SIR   [Phila]a. 27th Mar: 1801

Mr D. informs [me], that you gave him reason to beleive, you were disposed to do [me] that justice, which my country has, so long deny'd me—I m[ea]n, so far as you have power to do it—at the same time, he advises me to inclose you, one of his papers, in which, my case is stated in part—but after you have done me the honor of reading it, with attention,—beleive me—*the half has not been told you.*

Yesterday, I had some conversation with Chavalier D.U—he has advised me to think of the Natches—says he will, in the course of some few weeks, speak to you on the subject—let his reasons for doing so be what they may—you will give them weight no farther, than you deem me capable of doing you honor, & service to the nation.

My long experience might, probably, be very useful in an infant government—I should exert all my faculties, to give it, the great principle of honor, & plant the seeds of virtue, in its virgin soil.

Much will depend on your governor—he may do injury, to our national character, or raise it into dignity, among our neibours, by giving a proper, or improper tone, to the manners of the people.

I am respectfully   STEPHEN SAYRE

RC (DNA: RG 59, LAR); torn at fold; at foot of text: "Thos. Jefferson Esqr. P. of U. Sta[tes]"; endorsed by TJ as received 16 Apr. and so recorded in SJL as "Mar. 27. & 27.," indicating that two letters of that date were received, with the notation "Off. N." Enclosure not found, but see below.

According to SJL and TJ's endorsements, on 16 Apr. the president received two letters from Sayre dated 27 Mch. Sayre, however, clearly dated the first letter that TJ received on 16 Apr. as one of 21 Mch. In neither letter did Sayre make reference to an enclosure from Anthony F. Taylor, a Jeffersonian from Bordentown, New Jersey. But TJ's endorsement on a letter from Taylor to Sayre of 26 Dec. 1800 indicates that it was

enclosed in Sayre's letter of 27 Mch. Taylor reported on election returns in the eastern part of New Jersey, concluding that "the Feds will be Jefferson'd & Burr'd." He had just received news that there would be a Republican majority in Monmouth County and observed in closing that "The Feds are Cursedly in the Dumps here" (RC in same; endorsed by TJ on verso of address sheet: "Sayre Stephen inclusa in his lre of Mar. 27. 1801"). In April 1801, Sayre wrote Gallatin recommending Taylor for an appointment in New Jersey (Gallatin, *Papers*, 4:762-3).

MR D.: probably William Duane (Vol. 32:457). CHAVALIER D.U: Sayre referred to the Chevalier de Irujo as "Chavalier de Urico" (Sayre to TJ, 5 Feb. 1801, noted at Vol. 32:457n).

From Joseph Yznardi, Sr.

EXMO. SEÑOR   George Town 27th. March 801

Muy Señor mio de todo mi Respecto

Por Respuesta a su Apreciable de 24 recivida en este Momento devo desir á V.E qe las tres Medias Botas de Vinos, ya pedidas deven ser de la Mas Celecta Calidad, y gusto de V.E pues las tengo encargadas a las Mejores Casas

en Philadelphia tengo el Paxarete y Vino tinto qe tanbien he pedido, y deseado Saver á qe nombre devo dirijirlas á esta pensava tener el gusto de Aver Visitado á V.E oy, no lo he virificado por averme Indispuesto, y confio aserlo en la Semana, y para darle la enhorabuena en la posesion de su Alogamiento Nuebo como pasage propio que Obstenta la Dignidad de su Condecorasion, y Mientras deseo verlo lleno de Satisfacciones

Ojalá pudiera tener el gusto de Visitar su quinta qe tanto por la Situacion Celebrada como por el Conosimiento qe VE adquiria en Italia deve Allarse en buen estado, y si para su Mayor Aumento gusta de Plantas Semillas u Arboles de Europa me encargaré con gusto de su Remesa, Mras tengo el Onor de repetirme a su Oba.

Exmo. Señor BLM de V.E su mas Obedte Servr.

                                   JOSEF YZNARDY

Si Mr. Yrujo no ha encontrado Cosinero para V.E yo puedo prestarle el Mio Mras allo uno á proposito, es un Frances, Honorado, sin Vicios y buen repostero qe con su aviso le Mandaré venir pues Nada hace en Philadelphia y ase 5 años qe lo tengo

E D I T O R S '   T R A N S L A T I O N

MOST EXCELLENT SIR   Georgetown 27 Mch. 1801
My most illustrious sir and with all my respect
As a response to your esteemed letter of the 24th just received, I ought to tell Your Excellency that the three half casks already requested should be of the most select quality, and to Your Excellency's liking, because I have ordered them from the best wineries.

In Philadelphia I have pajarete and red wine that I have also ordered, and wishing to know to whom I should address them in this city, I was thinking of having the pleasure of visiting Your Excellency today; I have not done it because I became indisposed, and I trust that I will visit you this week; also to congratulate you on the possession of your new dwelling as a proper outlet that deserves the merit of your decoration, and meanwhile I wish to see you full of satisfaction.

I hope that I can have the pleasure of visiting your estate as much for its celebrated location as for the good style that it must have on account of the knowledge about architecture that Your Excellency acquired in Italy, and if for its further enhancement you would like plants, seeds, or trees from Europe, I will with pleasure see to it that they be sent to you; in the meantime I have the honor of reiterating my services to you.

Most excellent sir your most obedient servant kisses the hand of Your Excellency   JOSEF YZNARDY

If Mr. Irujo has not found a cook for Your Excellency, I can lend you mine while I find one fit for the purpose. He is French, honorable, without vice, and a good pastry maker, for whom I will send on your behest, as he is doing nothing in Philadelphia and I have had him for five years.

RC (DLC); at foot of text: "Exmo. Señor Dn Thomas Jefferson Presidente de los EU de America"; endorsed by TJ as received 27 Mch. and so recorded in SJL.

From John Barnes

SIR   Geo Town 28th, March 1801.
The $1500 to Messrs G & J. shall be remitted to them on Monday—or Tuesday if US. Bank paper is to be Obtaind. from the B. of Columbia—Rapine & Co., Carpenter S H Smith & Stewarts—shall be Attend to on Monday—as well the Currt. Exps of Househd. I have sent, by Mr. Dougherty $70. in the smallest change Obtainable—my several a/c Copies are looking up—in Order to correct errors & Omissions—
I am sir mst Respectfully yr Obedt.   JOHN BARNES

RC (ViU); at foot of text: "Thomas Jefferson Esqr, President"; endorsed by TJ.

MESSRS G & J.: Gibson & Jefferson. For TJ's account with Thomas CARPENTER, see 31 Mch. below. STEWARTS: James Stuart was the stepfather of John Holmes, a carpenter who had died from a fall at Monticello in January 1801 (Vol. 32:482; TJ to Stuart, 12 May 1801).

EXPS OF HOUSEHD.: that is, expenses of household.

On 6 Mch. TJ wrote an order on Barnes to pay John H. Barney for portage of a box from Philadelphia (MS in CtY, written and signed by TJ, endorsed by Barnes showing payment of $1.50). On 11 Mch. Barnes, as TJ's agent, submitted a request to the Treasury for payment to TJ of $861.11 as his compensation from 1 Jan. to 3 Mch., prorated from the vice president's annual salary of $5,000 (MS in DNA: RG 217, MTA; in Barnes's hand, endorsed by Patrick Ferrall for the auditor's office).

From Thomas U. P. Charlton

SIR,   Savannah March 28th. 1801

Permit a man who has ever held in high veneration those principles which have uniformly characterised your official conduct, to express his congratulation on your appointment to the presidency of the Union:— and to indulge himself with an expectation, that the measures of your administration may ultimately prove as beneficent, as they are at present anticipated by a majority of your Countrymen—

It was time, Sir, that the rights of the freemen of America should be rescued from the grasp of domestic usurpation; and the idea is fondly cherished, that the influence of your experience,—your wisdom, combined with the energies of a regenerated Legislature, may, eer the fiat of nature snatches you from your post, bring back our institutions to their original purity—May Almighty God direct your decisions, and may you long continue to act in the Station to which the voice of your Country has elevated you, is,

Sir, the devout wish, of your fellow Citizen

THOS U P CHARLTON

RC (DLC); endorsed by TJ as received 24 Apr. and so recorded in SJL.

Thomas Usher Pulaski Charlton (1779-1835) of Savannah was an aide-de-camp and protégé of Governor James Jackson, the leading Republican in Georgia. Elected to the Georgia House of Representatives in October 1802, Charlton went on to enjoy a distinguished career as a politician, jurist, and writer. In 1804 Jackson wrote TJ an unsuccessful recommendation of Charlton for the post of U.S. district attorney at New Orleans,

describing him as "a determined Republican, & friend of the present administration." Charlton published a laudatory biography of Jackson in 1809, three years after his mentor's death (Kenneth Coleman and Charles Stephen Gurr, eds., *Dictionary of Georgia Biography*, 2 vols. [Athens, 1983], 1:184-5; George R. Lamplugh, *Politics on the Periphery: Factions and Parties in Georgia, 1783-1806* [Newark, Del., 1986], 150, 166, 176-8; *Georgia Gazette*, 7 Oct. 1802; Jackson to TJ, 26 Mch. 1804).

From the District of Columbia Commissioners

Sir   Commissioner's Office, 28th March 1801.

Deeply impressed with the necessity of bringing the Business of the Commission as near as possible to a close, previous to the meeting of the next Congress, and of promoting the Interest of the City in the mean Time, we have had under consideration the means of accomplishing those objects; but the Difficulties which occur are so great as to prevent an unanimous opinion of the Board with regard to the Measures to be pursued—We therefore find ourselves under the necessity of stating the Subject of disagreement to the President for his Direction.

We have already advertised for Sale on the 12th Day of May next all the Property purchased by Morris & Greenleaf which we consider as liable to be resold for non-payment of the purchase money, except such as has been already sold for the same cause; but there remains other Property liable to be resold, either purchased at private Sales, or at public Sales of Property resold for non-payment of the original purchase Money;—of the last Description the Sum of Dolls $33,802\frac{97}{100}$ exclusive of Interest is due on four[1] notes drawn by Uriah Forrest— one for $16,407$\frac{94}{100}$ endorsed by Benjamin Stoddert, one for $6,269$\frac{92}{100}$ endorsed by Gustavus Scott & two endorsed by John Templeman and Benja. Stoddert, one for \$6641 & the other for \$4,485, and the Sum of Dolls $1675\frac{68}{100}$ drawn by William Thornton and endorsed by Mr. Blodget—It is to be observed that the said Gustavus Scott, William Thornton and Uriah Forrest together with James M. Lingan, are sureties for the Sum of 50,000 Dollars United States six per cent Stock, borrowed of the State of Maryland, under the circumstances stated to the President in a Representation of the Commissioners dated 28th Janry last on the Affairs of the City of Washington, an Extract from which is enclosed (A)—and it is urged that they ought not to pay these Sums, until the Money becomes due to the State of Maryland, they paying into the Hands of the Commissioners a Sum equal to the Interest in the mean Time, which we admit they have exceeded, and have had Property equivalent conveyed to them, which consequently cannot be resold. It is admitted that a payment to the State of Maryland or an exoneration of the public for so much, would be considered a payment for the Property purchased, and in giving their notes, these Gentlemen reserved to themselves time to negotiate that Business with the Legislature of Maryland; but we do not find that it was accomplished.

The points on which we wish the decision of the President are, whether we shall immediately pursue the most efficacious Measures for the recovery of Debts generally? Whether there shall be an exception of those above mentioned, and if not, whether it will be most eligible to bring Suits on the Notes or to sell the Property, agreeably to the summary mode authorised by the Act of the Assembly of Maryland, and if the latter, whether the Sale shall be for ready money or on credit; and finally, whether it would be better to postpone the sale now advertised, and unite the whole Property in one advertisement; or to suffer the Sale to take place on the 12th of May on the Terms published, and to advertise a Sale for ready money of the remainder of the Property which is liable to be resold at as early a Day as circumstances will admit—and here we would observe, that we think that if payment of the Debts due from the Gentlemen who stand Sureties to the State of Maryland is enforced,[2] provision ought to be made for meeting the Demands of that State which may with more certainty be done by Sales on credit than for Cash. We are, with sentiments of the highest respect, Sir, yr. Mo: Obt Servts

WILLIAM THORNTON
ALEX WHITE
TRISTRAM DALTON

RC (DLC); in William Brent's hand, signed by Thornton, White, and Dalton; at foot of text: "The President." FC (DNA: RG 42, DCLB); at foot of text: "Since writing the above, General Forrest has written a Letter to the Board, a copy of which we think proper to transmit to the President for his consideration." Enclosure: Extract of District of Columbia Commissioners to John Adams, 28 Jan. 1801, not found, but for a printed copy of the letter, see ASP, *Miscellaneous*, 1:219-21.

Tristram Dalton was appointed to the Board of Commissioners by John Adams to fill a vacancy in Mch. 1801 (Bryan, *National Capital*, 1:415).

For the failures of real estate speculators Robert MORRIS, James GREENLEAF, and John Nicholson, see TJ to Alexander White, 10 Sep. 1797, and TJ to Van Staphorst & Hubbard, 30 Apr. 1798.

The Board of Commissioners of the District of Columbia was concerned about insolvency due to NON-PAYMENT for lots in the federal city, the declining value of unsold lots, and the commission's indebt-

edness to the state of Maryland. According to the commission's REPRESENTATION to the president of 28 Jan. 1801, the value of the 4,682 unsold city lots (out of the total 10,000) was approximately $850,000. The Maryland legislature approved several loans to the commission in U.S. stock with six percent interest for $200,000 in total between 1796 and 1797 and for $50,000 in 1799 (Bryan, *National Capital*, 1:271-2, 299, 329, 415-17).

In a letter to the commissioners of 28 Mch., Uriah FORREST proposed an arrangement for the sale of his lots and payment to the commissioners that he hoped would avoid "controversy with the Board." Forrest stated that at the next meeting of the Maryland legislature, he would "get the commissioners exonerated to the amount of what I may owe them." The commissioners transmitted a copy of the letter to TJ (Tr in DLC; at head of text: "(Copy)"; endorsed by TJ: "Commissioners of Washington"). For an account of Forrest's role in the 1799 loan from the state of Maryland, see John Thomson Mason to TJ, 31 Mch. 1801.

On 30 Mch., TJ replied to the commissioners: "Th: Jefferson will take the liberty of calling on the board of commissioners at their hour of meeting this morning, to confer on the subject of their paper lately sent him. as some questions of law are involved, he has asked the favor of the Attorney general to accompany him. he tenders to the board his high consideration & respect" (RC in DLC: District of Columbia Papers; addressed: "The Board of Commissioners"; endorsed by clerk as received the same day; not recorded in SJL).

[1] Word interlined in place of "three."
[2] Canceled: "we think."

To John Wayles Eppes

DEAR SIR   Washington Mar. 28. 1801.

I wrote to you the day before yesterday, since that I have taken a more correct view of my [probable] receipts & expenditures and find that I may venture to take Haxall's horse immediately at 500. doll. paiable at 90. days. it would be a great inconvenience to have to send from Washington for directions; & on the [other hand] a convenience to have [. . .] brought to Monticello by the messenger who will go for [Walker's] & Bell's. be so good as to engage him at once, if to be done on that [verdict], and have them ready for me. if you could write me a line to Monticello as soon as possible, to give [me] an idea of the time at which I may send for them, I will thank you. I still flatter myself with getting from here on the 31st. a thousand endearing assurances to my beloved Maria, to whom I [. . .] in a letter from Kitty Church to present her affectionately. [health,] happiness & sincere attachment to yourself.   TH: JEFFERSON

PrC (CSmH); faint and blurred; at foot of text: "Mr. Eppes"; endorsed by TJ in ink on verso.

I WROTE TO YOU: see TJ's letter to Eppes of 27 Mch. The letter from Catherine CHURCH is printed at 23 Feb.

From John Vaughan

DR SIR   Philada 28 Mar: 1801

The enclosed was just recieved by me under cover, should any reply be necessary & be forwarded under cover to me, it will be safely conveyed to its destination—

I have the pleasure of informing you that our much valued friend Dr Priestly is now on his recovery from a most dangerous Illness, & will I hope in two or three Weeks be able to resume his pen & his Labors—

The plates to the 4th Vol. of our Transactions are completed & the 5th Vol. in the press & I believe nearly printed—Dr Barton withdrew most of his pieces, saying he wished to render them more perfect, I am inclined to think he contemplates a separate Work, or Collection of Tracts—

The Society have sent a Set of its Transactions to Count Rumford for the Royal Institution—

I cannot but flatter myself that your Elevation will tend much to the encouragement of Science in this Country—Pecuniary rewards are not to be had in the present state of Society here—we therefore more Strongly require patronage & Countenance—It has hitherto been sparingly given if not witheld altogether

I remain with the highest respect Dr Sir Your obt Serv

JN VAUGHAN

RC (DLC); at foot of text: "His Exy. Thomas Jefferson President of the United States"; endorsed by TJ as received 30 Mch. and so recorded in SJL. Enclosure: Benjamin Vaughan to TJ, 15 Mch. 1801.

The fifth volume of TRANSACTIONS of the American Philosophical Society appeared in 1802. It contained one paper by Benjamin Smith BARTON, on poisonous honey (APS, *Transactions*, 5 [1802], 51-70).

From Joseph Yznardi, Sr.

EXELENTISIMO SEÑOR   George town 28 Marzo 801
Muy Señor mio, y de mi Respecto
con el qe devo me allo Obligado a Manifestar á V.E la Sensivilidad de mi gratitud por Repuesta a su apreciable de 26 del qe Acava disiendole qe desde los primeros Anuncios de su Eleccion di Noticias al Ministro de Estado de S.M.C en la Corte de Madrid, como de las favorables Circunstancias, pues que proporsionarian la Mejor Inteligencia á los dos Goviernos, qe he ratificado con Motibo de la Alterasion de Ministerio desde mi recidencia en este Pais, a el Exmo. Señor principe de la Paz como la persona mas Immediata á S.M, agregando aver tenido efecto tan dichosa Eleccion, y a el qe transferiré Copia de dicha su apreciable a la Verdad la mas propia para prueba de mis preedicciones, llenandome de gloria ser el Conducto de Sentimientos tan benevolentes adornados de Candor, y por aver sido el Organo por cuya Voses se espresaron los deseos de mi Soverano nada Menos Cordiales, y Sinceros en Conservar aquella reprosicidad qe merese la Fee de su Real Caracter siguiendo el encargo puesto á mi Cuidado por la Credensial qe me Autor[iza] Manifestada á V.E y dirigidole tradusida

El Cavallero Nuebo Ministro Cuyas circunstancias son Notorias espero Será de la Misma Opinion pues sean los qe fuesen enpleados en el Gavinete Español Sienpre se Conserbó en el Consequencia Constante de Rectitud Manteniendo la Ofertas con que Liga, y con Mayor motibo Mediando Interes locales Utiles a los dos paices que deven Conservarse en lo posible

por lo qe ase al Cavellero de Irujo tengo dicho á V.E aver cumplido con mi Honrades Asiendole la Justicia qe Merese

deseo á V.E larga Vida, y el Mejor asierto en su Administracion, para la perfecta organisasion de los Cuerpos que precide, pa Conservarlos con Felicidad Unidos, y Conformes, á los deseos de una Paz General permanénte, por el bien de la humanidad, y Mras tengo el Honor de ser

Exelentisimo Señor su mayor, y mas Obediente Servr

JOSEF YZNARDY

EDITORS' TRANSLATION

MOST EXCELLENT SIR   Georgetown 28 Mch. 1801
My most illustrious sir, and with my respect
With what I owe, I find myself obliged to manifest my feelings of gratitude in response to your esteemed letter of the 26th of this month by telling you that, since the first news about your election was announced, I notified the minister of state of His Catholic Majesty in the court at Madrid of it, as well as of the favorable circumstances of it, which provide the best understanding between the two governments. I have ratified this, on the occasion of the change of ministers since my residence in this country, to the most excellent prince of the peace as the person closest to his majesty, adding that such joyful election has been completed. And to him I will send a copy of the above mentioned esteemed letter of yours, truthfully the most appropriate as proof of my predictions, filling me with glory to be the conduit of your benevolent and candid feelings, and to have been the person through whose voice were expressed the wishes of my sovereign, no less cordial and sincere, to conserve that reciprocity that deserves the trust of his royal person, as I have followed the orders that were placed in my care by the credentials that give me authority, credentials that I showed to Your Excellency and sent to you translated.

I hope that the new gentleman minister, whose circumstances are well known, is of the same opinion. No matter who is appointed to the Spanish cabinet, he always behaved with rectitude maintaining that with which he was bound, and with more reason when dealing with local interests that are useful to both countries and that must be preserved as much as possible.

Concerning the Chevalier de Irujo, I have told Your Excellency that I have behaved honorably, rendering to him the justice that he deserves.

I wish Your Excellency long life and the best wisdom in your administration for the perfect organization of the bodies that you preside over, in order to keep them happily united and in agreement, in hope of a general and lasting peace, for the good of humanity; and in the meantime I have the honor to be

Most excellent sir your greatest, and most obedient servant

JOSEF YZNARDY

RC (DLC); at foot of text: "Exmo. Sor. Dn Thomas Jefferson Presidente de los E.U de Amea."; endorsed by TJ as received 30 Mch. and so recorded in SJL. Tr (AHN), in a clerk's hand.

From Joseph Yznardi, Sr.

George town 28. del Mzo. 1801.

Despues de mi ultima he recivido Carta de Madrid, del nuevo Minro de Estado, cuia copia incluyo, para que V.E. vea la buena disposicion del Rey mi Sor. para con este Govierno, y los efectos de mi mision; y no dudo que en vista de lo que escribo al Exmo. Sor. Principe de la Paz, ⅌ la Fragata, surtiran efectos favorables entre las dos Naciones que consoliden una amistad de mutua utilidad, y como tal permanente.

Haviendo reflexado sobre la permanencia que V.E. desea del Cavallero Yrujo en este pais, por creer convenir para la mexor inteligencia de las dos naciones, y que V.E. se halla instruido de la mutacion de Ministerio en Madrid, y como he sido comisionado para intermediar en la falta de inteligencia, y demas circumstancias que manifiesta mi credencial, participo á V.E. haver informado, desde los principios de mi llegada favorablemente á dho Cavallero, y si consequente á ello se dirigiese oficio por este Govierno para el de España, pidiendo su permanencia, es consequente esperar su permanencia.

La Fragata que debe salir para Francia sera el mexor conducto para dirigir dha solicitud, y la que podria esperar la respuesta de Madrid, que en breves dias la tendria; y no dude V.E. logrará sus deseos, pues al intento me veo en obligacion, si conocidamente es para el interes del Estado, de representarlo, como dho llebo, al Principe; incluiendole la Carta de V.E. en copia, si me lo permite, pues como hombre de bien por lo qe. Yo anhelo es el bien de las dos naciones, como siempre lo he manifestado, conociendo efectos favorables—

J. YZNARDY

EDITORS' TRANSLATION

Georgetown 28 Mch. 1801

After my last, I received a letter from Madrid, from the new minister of state, a copy of which I am enclosing in order that Your Excellency sees the goodwill of the king my lord towards this government, and the effects of my mission; and I do not doubt that in light of what I will write to the excellent gentleman, the prince of the peace, by the frigate, there will be favorable outcomes that will consolidate a friendship between the two nations that will be mutually beneficial, and therefore permanent.

Having reflected on Your Excellency's wishes that the Chevalier de Irujo remain in this country, believing it to be advantageous for the better understanding between the two nations, and that Your Excellency has been informed of the change of the ministry in Madrid, and as I have been commissioned to act as intermediary during the interruption in communication, and in other circumstances that are stated in my credentials, I inform Your Excellency that ever since my arrival I have favorably reported to the aforementioned gentleman, and if as a result an official note is sent by this government to that of Spain requesting his continued stay, it is logical to expect that he will remain.

The frigate that should be leaving for France will be the best conveyance by which to send the aforementioned request, and could wait for an answer from Madrid, which should arrive within a few days; and Your Excellency should have no doubt that your wishes will be fulfilled, because in that regard I feel the obligation, since it is in the interest of the state, to represent the matter, as I have said, before the prince; giving him a copy of your excellency's letter, if you would permit me, given that as a good citizen, what I hope for is the welfare of the two nations, something that I have always demonstrated and with favorable results.   J. YZNARDY

Tr (AHN); in a clerk's hand; at head of text: "Sor. Dn. Thomas Jefferson." Enclosure not found.

Pedro Cevallos had written to Yznardi from MADRID on 25 and 29 Jan. (Miguel

Gómez del Campillo, comp., *Relaciones Diplomáticas entre España y los Estados Unidos*, 2 vols. [Madrid, 1944-46], 2:499-500).

From Joseph Yznardi, Sr.

EXMO. SEÑOR   George town 28 Marzo 801

Muy Señor mio, y de mi Respecto

Suplico á V.E dispense la Livertad qe me tomo en dirigirle la Inclusa para el Cavallero Secretario de estado Interino para qe tenga la vondad de leerla, y Mandarsela, esperando qe sus Efectos favoreserán mi Justa Solisitud pues al Contrario se me Causarian Incomodidades paresiendo desairada la Confiansa qe de Nuebo pone á mi Cargo, y por la qe repito los Sentimientos de mi Mayor gratitud como provar la Ratificasion del desenpeño de mi dever en el Consulado restituido á mi Hijo

Esperaré oportunamente las disposiciones de dicho Secretario respecto a los Asuntos de presas como Regulaciones en el Manejo futuro del Oficio Consular segun V.E tubo la vondad de Ofreserme, y he pedido con frequencia a los Antsesores con el deseo de Condusirme con asierto, y con lo que Respondo a su apreciable de 26 del que acava, y tengo el Honor de Repetir a V.E mi obligasion en ser

Exmo. Señor Su mas atento y Obte. Servidor

JOSEF YZNARDY

EDITORS' TRANSLATION

MOST EXCELLENT SIR   Georgetown 28 Mch. 1801

My most illustrious sir, and with all my respect

I beg Your Excellency to forgive me for taking the liberty to forward to you the enclosed letter intended for the acting gentleman secretary of state so that you may be kind enough to read it, and send it to him, in hopes that its content will be favorable to my just request; since otherwise they will cause me inconvenience though it may seem disrespectful of the trust that you have once more placed in my care, and for which I reiterate the sentiments of my greatest gratitude as proof of your endorsement of my performance as consul in my son's place.

I will patiently wait for the decisions of the aforementioned secretary regarding the issue of the prizes, as well as the policies for the future management of the consular office as Your Excellency had the generosity of offering me, and that I have frequently requested from your predecessors with hopes that I carry it out properly; and with this I respond to your esteemed letter on the 26th of this month, and have the honor to repeat to Your Excellency my duty to be,

Most excellent sir your most attentive and obedient servant

JOSEF YZNARDY

RC (DLC); at foot of text: "Exmo. Sr. Dn. Thomas Jefferson Precidente de los E.U de Ama."; endorsed by TJ as received 30 Mch. and so recorded in SJL. Enclosure not found.

To Samuel Adams

Washington Mar. 29. 1801

I addressed a letter to you, my very dear & antient friend, on the 4th. of March: not indeed to you by name, but through the medium of some of my fellow citizens, whom occasion called on me to address. in meditating the matter of that address, I often asked myself, is this exactly in the spirit of the patriarch of liberty, Samuel Adams? is it as he would express it? will he approve of it? I have felt a great deal for our country in the times we have seen: but individually for no one so much as yourself. when I have been told that you were avoided, insulated, frowned on, I could but ejaculate 'Father, forgive them, for they know not what they do.' I confess I felt an indignation for you, which for myself I have been able under every trial to keep entirely passive. however, the storm is over, and we are in port. the ship was not rigged for the service she was put on. we will shew the smoothness of her motions on her republican tack. I hope we shall once more see harmony restored among our citizens, & an entire oblivion of past feuds. some of the leaders who have most committed themselves cannot come into this. but I hope the great body of our fellow citizens will do it. I will sacrifice every thing but principle to procure it. a few examples of justice on officers who have perverted their functions to the oppression of their fellow citizens, must, in justice to those citizens, be made. but opinion, & the just maintenance of it shall never be a crime in my view; nor bring injury on the individual. those whose misconduct in office ought to have produced their removal even by my predecessor, must not be protected by the delicacy due only to honest men.—how much I lament that time has[1] deprived us of your aid: it would have been a day of glory which should have called you to the first office of the administration. but give us your counsel my friend, and give us your blessing: and be assured that there exists not in the heart of man a more faithful esteem than mine to you, & that I shall ever bear you the most affectionate veneration & respect.   TH: JEFFERSON

RC (NN); at foot of text: "Samuel   [1] TJ here canceled "withdrawn."
Adams." PrC (DLC).

From Jabez Bingham

Washington County Pennsylvania
RESPECTED SIR   March 29—1801
    I am sensible of the amazing distance there is between the first Magistrate of a Great, free and Powerfull Nation, and a Citizen of the Lower Order, who is poor and always liv'd in Obscurity, and ondly known by a few of his Neighbours, this is my situation, for I never sought to be known by the Great, and have Ondly studied to be Usefull in my small Speir, A great veriety of Circomstances have combined to Imbolden me to Ask favour, and Imployment from the Father of my Country, I have no great and Powerfull Friends to Interceed or make Interest for me, or even to speek in my favour—I also know the difficulty of Obtaining Imployment under Government, that will be of any considerable advantage without such Aides and assistance—I am also sensible that there are a sufficient number always ready, that can be recommended to fill all posts of Honour and prophet—under all these discouraging circomstances, I have ventered to make my supplication, for some Imployment in the Republick. As this is the first time in my life that I ever made the least Overture, or request for any kind of Office what ever, I hope your Excellency will be kind enough to pardon my presumtions, and if you

[488]

have any Imployment in the Western Territories, or Amongst the Indians (with whoom I have some knowledge) or in any other quarter, though ever so Hazardous—I shall be happy to serve my Country with my best Abilities and will do all in my power not to dishonour your confidence in the Appointment—I was a Great sufferer in the time of the British war, and more latly have suffered much by Contracts made with the Contractors for the Western Army by the Immediate vice of provisions, in the time of the Western Insurrection—by those means, and some other losses I am brought low, which makes me seek for some prophetable Imployment from the United States—May I hope your Excellency will think of me in your devotions, and not forget me in your most Convivial Hours—Pleas to permit an honest man to congratulate you on your Advancment to the first Magistracy in the United States, we already begin to feel the good affects of Our Choice, by a reunion of the different parties—that over baring Sperit of opposition seems to subside, confidence, friendship, and Brotherly love seems to be gaining ground, all will soon be quiet—may God almighty grant you Health and a long and peaceble Administration which is the sincear wish of your

most obedient Humble Suppliant   JABEZ BINGHAM

RC (DNA: RG 59, LAR); at foot of text: "His Excellency Thomas Jefferson Esqr. President of the United States"; endorsed by TJ as received 6 May and so recorded in SJL with notation "Off."

To Pierpont Edwards

SIR   Washington Mar. 29. 1801.

You will doubtless have long ago learned that the office which was the subject of your two favors to me was filled by mr Adams some days before he went out of office. I have not considered as candid, or even decorous, the crouding of appointments by mr A. after he knew he was making them for his successor & not for himself, even to 9. aclock of the night, at twelve of which he was to go out of office. I do not think I ought to permit that conduct to have any effect as to the offices removeable in their nature. of course this would leave me free to fill mr Goodrich's place by any other person. this is a subject worthy of mature consideration, & therefore Judge Lincoln will ask of yourself, & some few of your fellow laborers, who best know all [the] circumstances which ought to weigh, to consult and advise us on this subject; taking a broad view of it, general as well as local. if it be thought that there may be a [character], which might prevail in a comparison with mr Goodrich's, and whose appointment would better further the progress of republican opinion, be so good as to favor us with your sentiments either addressed to myself directly, or to mr Lincoln. and in all cases I invite, and shall recieve with great thankfulness, your opinion & that of others on the course of things, and particularly in the suggestion of characters who may worthily be appointed to vacancies which happen within your knolege. your spontaneous[1] information too would be desireable, without waiting for the sollicitation of those who wish office. my other occupations may not permit me to return you my thanks on every special occasion of recieving your information, & therefore I much hope it on the score of public, not personal favor; & refer you for the acknolegment to the effect which you may be assured your opinions will have. Accept assurances of my high consideration & respect.

Th: Jefferson

PrC (DLC); blurred; at foot of text: "Pierpoint Edwards esquire."

recommending William Munson who sought the collectorship at New Haven.

your two favors to me: Edwards to TJ, 16 Dec. 1800 and 6 Feb. 1801, both

[1] TJ here canceled "opinion."

To Elbridge Gerry

My Dear Sir   Washington Mar. 29. 1801.

Your two letters of Jan. 15. and Feb. 24. came safely to hand and I thank you for the history of a transaction which will ever be interesting in our[1] affairs. it has been very precisely as I had imagined. I thought, on your return, that if you had come forward boldly and appealed to the public by a full statement, it would have had a great effect in your favor personally, & that of the republican cause then oppressed almost unto the death. but I judged from a tact of the Southern pulse. I suspect that of the North was different and decided your conduct: and perhaps it has been as well. if the revolution of sentiment has been later, it has perhaps been not less sure. at length it is arrived. what with the natural current of opinion which has been setting over to us for 18. months, and the immense impetus which was given it from the 11th. to the 17th. of Feb. we may now say that the U.S. from N.Y Southwardly are as unanimous in the principles of 76. as they were in 76. the only difference is that the leaders, who remain behind, are more numerous & bolder than the apostles of toryism in 76. the reason is that we are now justly more tolerant, than we could safely[2] have been then, circumstanced as we were. your part of the union, tho' as absolutely republican as ours, has drunk deeper of the delusion, & is therefore slower in recovering from it. the aegis of government & the temples of religion & of justice have all been prostituted there to toll us back to the times when we burnt witches. but your people will rise again, they will awake like Samson from his sleep & carry away the gates & the posts of the city. you, my friend are destined to rally them again under their former banners, and when called to the post, exercise it with firmness and with inflexible adherence to your own principles. the people will support you, notwithstanding the howlings of the ravenous crew from whose jaws they are escaping. it will be a great blessing to our country if we can once more restore harmony and social love among it's citizens. I confess, as to myself, it is almost the first object of my heart, & one to which I would sacrifice every thing but principle.[3] with the people I have hopes of effecting it. but their Coryphaei are incurables. I expect little from them. I was not deluded by the eulogisms of the public papers in the first moments of change. if they could have continued to get all the loaves & fishes, that is if I would have gone over to them, they would continue to eulogise. but I well knew that the moment that such removals should take place, as the justice of the preceding administration ought to have executed, their hue & cry would be set up & they would take their old stand. I shall disregard that also.—mr Adams's last appointments when he knew he was naming counsellors & aids for me & not for himself, I set aside as far as depends on me. officers who have been guilty of gross abuses of office, such as Marshals packing juries, &c I shall now remove as my predecessor ought in justice to have done. the instances will be few, and governed by strict rule, & not party passion. the right of opinion shall suffer no invasion from me. those who have acted well have nothing to fear, however they may have differed from me in opinion: those who have done ill, however, have nothing to hope; nor shall I fail to do justice, lest it should be ascribed to that difference of opinion. a coalition of sentiments is not for the interest of the printers. they, like the clergy, live by the zeal they can kindle, & the schisms they can create. it is contest of opinion in politics as well as religion which makes us take great interest in them, and bestow our money liberally on those who furnish aliment to our appetite. the mild and simple principles of the Christian philosophy, would produce too much calm, too much regularity of good, to extract from it's disciples a support for a numerous priesthood, were they not to sophisticate it, ramify it, split it into hairs, and twist it's texts till they cover the divine morality of it's author with mysteries, and require a priesthood to explain them. the Quakers seem to have discovered this. they have no priests, therefore no schisms. they judge of the text by the dictates of common sense & common morality. so the printers can never leave us to a state of perfect rest and union of opinion. they would be no longer useful, and would have to go to the plough. in the first moments of quietude which have succeeded the election, they seem to have arroused their lying faculties beyond their ordinary state, to reagitate the public mind. what appointments to office have they detailed which had never been thought of, merely to found a text for their calumniating commentaries. however the steady character of our countrymen is a rock to which we may safely moor: and notwithstanding the efforts of the papers to disseminate early discontent, I expect that a just, dispassionate, and steady conduct will at length rally to a proper system the great body of our country. unequivocal in principle, reasonable in manner, we shall be able I hope to do a great deal of good to the cause of freedom & harmony. I shall be happy to hear from you often, to know your own sentiments & those of others, on the course of things, and to concur with you in efforts for the common good. your letters through the post will now come safely. present my best respects to mrs Gerry, & accept yourself assurances of my constant esteem & high consideration.　　Th: Jefferson

RC (Mrs. L. Carstairs Pierce, Bryn Mawr, Pennsylvania, 1950); at foot of first page: "Mr. Gerry"; endorsed by Gerry. PrC (DLC).

Gerry's letter of 15 jan. and another one on the 20th of that month responded to TJ's of 26 Jan. 1799 and discussed Gerry's role in the XYZ affair.

[1] TJ here canceled "history."

[2] Preceding two words interlined in place of "ought justly to."

[3] TJ here canceled "but I know."

To Gideon Granger

Dear Sir　　　　　　　　　　　　　Washington Mar. 29. 1801

I have long been indebted to you a letter; but it has been because you desired me to write by mr Ervin the bearer of yours who is not yet gone back. but in the mean time I trust that the post is become a safe channel to and from [me]. I have heard indeed of some extraordinary licenses practised in the post offices of your state, & there is nothing I desire so much as information of facts on that subject, to rectify the office. if you can be the means of furnishing them to me they will be thankfully & usefully esteemed. nothing presents such difficulties of administration as offices. about appointments to them, the rule is simple enough. the federalists having been in exclusive possession of them from the first origin of party among us to the 3d. of Mar. 9. aclock P.M. of the evening, at twelve of which mr A. was to go out of office, their reason will acknolege the justice of giving vacancies as they happen to those who have been so long excluded, till the same general proportion prevails in office which exists out of it. but removals are more difficult. no one will say that all should be removed, or that none should. yet no two scarcely draw the same line. I consider as nullities all the appointments (of a removeable character) crouded in by mr Adams when he knew he was appointing counsellors and agents for his successor & not for himself. persons who have perverted their offices to the oppression of their fellow citizens, as Marshals packing juries, attornies grinding their legal victims, intolerants removing those under them for opinion sake, substitutes for honest men removed for their republican principles, will probably find few advocates even among their quondam party. but the freedom of opinion, & the reasonable maintenance of it, is not a crime, and ought not to occasion injury. these are as yet matters under consideration, our administration having never yet been assembled to decide finally on them. however some of them have in the mean time been acted on in cases which [pressed.] there is one in your state which calls for decision, and on which Judge Lincoln will ask yourself & some others to consult & advise us. it is the case of mr Goodrich, whose being a recent appointment, made a few days only before mr Adams went out of office, is liable to the general nullification I affix to them. yet there might be reasons for continuing him: or if that would do more harm than good, we should enquire who is the person in the state who, superseding mr Goodrich, would from his character & standing in society most effectually silence clamour, & justify the executive on a comparison of the two characters. for tho' I consider mr G's appointment as a nullity in effect, yet others may view it as a possession & removal, and ask if that removal has been made to put in a better man? I pray you to take a broad view of this subject, consider it in all it's bearings, local & general, & communicate to me your opinion. and on all subjects & at all times I shall highly prize your communications to me, & sollicit them earnestly. the immense pressure of my other duties will not allow me to write letter for letter; but you must excuse that, & consider it as a sacrifice you ought to make to the public service; especially assured, as you may be, that your letters, tho unacknoleged, will not be unattended to in their effect. I particularly ask your opinion of characters suitable for any office which becomes vacant within your knolege: and would rather recieve your voluntary & spontaneous information, than that which is extorted by sollicitation of parties interested. accept assurances of my perfect esteem & high consideration & respect.   TH: JEFFERSON

PrC (DLC); faint and blurred; at foot of first page: "Gideon Granger."

INDEBTED TO YOU: on 7 Nov. George W. Erving delivered Granger's letter to TJ of 18 Oct. 1800.

From John Garland Jefferson

DEAR SIR,   Amelia Mar. 29th. 1801.

I have before me a letter from my brother to you dated Mar. 4th. and I feel anxious to acquit myself of the imputations to which that letter subjects me. I might perhaps deem it necessary to apologyze to you for what may be called an intrusion but for an assurance you have often given that you shoud be pleased to hear from me at any time I might think proper to write. Under this privilege which has never been abused, I beg leave to make a few remarks to my brother's charge of a want of reflection and of delicacy on my part. I am glad that his confidence in my candor is such that he can undertake to thwart "my wishes" without fear of blame whenever they appear improper or censurable. He seems however, to have mistaken my anxiety to avoid all appearance of indelicacy for an extreme solicitude for office.

I had some doubt myself that my application might carry with it at first sight the appearance of impropriety which my brother so much condemns. But I was pressed by some of my friends who think differently on that subject, and who offered to write on my behalf. Mr. Giles who is your most zealous friend, and who is as averse to appointments originating in partiality, or family attachment as any man can be approved of my application. My brother's idea that a man who has made the law his profession is incompetent to the discharge of an executive office is of a nature most singular and novel. I will place his idea in a more striking point of view by changing the form only whilst the substance is retained. He seems to conceive that a man who has a knowledge of the law, is thereby rendered unfit to carry that very law into effect. I will forbear to comment on this idea. But he says that I ought to have concluded from what you have already done for me, that if there was any office in your gift to which I was competent, and there was no other objection, that you woud have recollected me. He woud have been correct in this if you had possest a spirit of divination, and coud have forseen that it was my wish to abandon the practice of the law, and to accept of an appointment under you, otherwise he appears to me to be incorrect. I foresaw the objections which my brother's overscrupulous attention to punctilios woud raise. I thought our relationship too remote to render you liable to censure, which seems to be admitted by him as far as relates to just censure; and to exclude a man from office because he had the misfortune to be called by a particular name, for in that case it might be considered by some as a misfortune, woud appear extremely hard to say no more. That there are but few of the name woud make rather in favor of the application than against it, because it renders it probable that if you were to make an appointment in this case, that it might be the only one you woud ever make to one of the same name. This however can be but of little weight. I knew that if your enemies were to attempt to injure you in consequence of the appointment, that the publick might easily be set right, and that there was no danger of incurring odium by false statements when the subject was left free to investigation.

You will not my dear Sir consider this as a repetition of my former application. I believe that I feel as little solicitude on that head as any one woud do in the same situation. When I wrote to you before, it was my wish rather to obtain your opinion on that subject, than to urge you to any particular act; and I declared my willing acquiessence in that opinion whatever it might be. I think it unnecessary to make any apology for the length of this. The subject of which it treats is before you, and you will be good enough to make the best of it. I am dear Sir with the most grateful esteem,

Your most obliged servant   JNO. G. JEFFERSON

RC (ViU: Carr-Cary Papers); addressed: "The Honourable Thomas Jefferson President of the United States"; endorsed by TJ as received 15 Apr. and so recorded in SJL with notation "Off."; also endorsed by TJ: "office."; with unrelated numerical calculations by TJ on address sheet.

MY APPLICATION: John Garland Jefferson to TJ, 1 Mch.

From Henry Knox

MY DEAR SIR   Boston March 29. 1801.

Among the most perplexing, and thankless acts of your high station will be that of appointments to offices. You will be assailed by all sorts of arguments by applicants to obtain their ends; and even with all possible caution and wisdom errors may be committed. I ask pardon for these observations which I am persuaded have already occurred in full force, and also for the trouble I am about giving you. Perhaps were a secretary of the navy appointed, I should not in this instance have intruded.

It has been suggested that it is probable that a new appointment of Naval Agent will be made for this department. I know not how true this may be, but on condition that it should be so, I beg leave to suggest the name of my particular friend General Henry Jackson as one highly worthy to fill the office. He possessed it before the person who now holds it, and was superseded by some management in the year 1798.[1]

Under the direction of General Jackson the Constitution was built, one of the finest frigates floating on the Ocean. Abundant and perfect evidence could be adduced of his zealous industry, oeconomy, and integrity in the performance of that business. Indeed his competence in all respects to execute the duties of the station cannot be questioned with propriety. I shall only add that if another appointment should be made, I shall gratefully acknowledge the favor, if it be given to General Jackson.

I am my dear Sir with great attachment and respect Your obedient humble Servant   H KNOX

RC (DNA: RG 59, LAR); at head of text: "private"; at foot of text: "The President of the United States"; endorsed by TJ as received 16 Apr. and so recorded in SJL; also endorsed by TJ: "Genl. Jackson to be Navy agt." Dft (MHi: Knox Papers).

Knox, as secretary of war, had been responsible for implementing the construction of the frigates authorized by Congress in 1794. Knox's good friend HENRY JACKSON received the appointment as navy agent for the building of the Constitution, although Stephen Higginson, Sr., became the agent for subsequent projects at Boston. Knox and Jackson had known one another for many years. Jackson supervised the construction of Knox's large residence in Maine and suffered considerable financial loss in 1798 when Knox, for whom Jackson had cosigned promissory notes, was unable to pay his creditors (NDBW, 1:76, 78; NDQW, Feb. 1797-Oct. 1798, 10, 166, 179; Palmer, Stoddert's War, 26-7; North Callahan, Henry Knox: General Washington's General [New York, 1958], 28, 304-5; Vol. 30:610, 612n, 614).

[1] Preceding six words written over an erasure. Dft: "by Mr Wolcott when secretary of the treasury."

To Thomas Leiper

DEAR SIR   Washington Mar. 29. 1801.

I propose in two or three days to make a short excursion home to make some arrangements previously neecessary to my final settlement here. I cannot go till I have thanked you for the trouble you took in the late case of my tobo. which as to the complaints I suppose had it's origin in feelings no way derived from the quality of the tobo. my crop of the last year, about [40,000] is lying at Richmond; but I have never heard from the [weigher?] as to it's quality; and when that is, from the season, rendered [secondary], I never think of offering it to you. indeed latterly the difference between the prices at Richmond and Philadelphia has hardly been equal to the expense, trouble, & risk of transportation. I have not heard the prices at Richmond lately, but they ought for the best crops to be considerably higher than here, where 6. D. are given. to correspond with this 7. or 8. should be given there.—the office for which you recommended Major Smith had been offered to Colo. Shee, who refusing it, it has been given to Major Smith. accept assurances of my high esteem & best wishes.

Th: Jefferson

PrC (MHi); faint and blurred; at foot of text: "Majr. Thomas Leiper"; endorsed by TJ in ink on verso.

From Robert R. Livingston

Dear Sir   Clermont 29th. March 1801

I avail myself of Mr. DeLaBegarre's going to Washington to send you the teeth found in the western part of this state, drawings of which, I had before done myself the honor to transmit to you. May they not have belonged to the hippopotamus? The front teeth of that animal in the lower jaw being described "as projecting, furrowed & pointed, & as formed rather to tear than cut." Fab: Columna. 32.—The Gent who will have the honor to deliver them is attatched to natural history, & havg. (in my name) taken a patent for making paper from the conferva, he is now endeavouring to repeat, & perfect my experiments on a larger scale, at the paper mills, & will shew you samples of the plant which may have escaped your observation.

At the request of Mr. Vander kemp, a Clergy man of much learning who resides in this state, I enclose an essay of his for your perusal without any observations thereon. The author is a man of much reading and enthusiasm. Hurried away by the Spirit of Liberty on the first attempt of his country, (the United Netherlands,) to free itself from the fetters of its old constitution He exchanged his gown for a uniform, & his pulpit for a troop of horse. exiled by the prusians, he has retired to the western part of this state with the wrecks of a large fortune, & devotes his winter to study, & the rest of the year to hard labor, for the support of a very numerous family.

I have the honor to be Dr. Sir with the greatest respect & the most perfect attachment Your Most Obt hum: Servt

ROBT R LIVINGSTON

RC (DLC); at foot of text: "Thomas Jefferson Esq President of the U:S:"; endorsed by TJ as received 1 May and so recorded in SJL. Enclosure: see below.

FAB: COLUMNA: Fabius Columna—that is, Fabio Colonna, a Neapolitan who from the 1590s through the early decades of the 17th century studied and wrote on various topics of natural science (Nicoletta Morello, "De glossopetris dissertatio: The Demonstration by Fabio Colonna of the True Nature of Fossils," Archives Internationales d'Histoire des Sciences, 31 [1981], 63-71). For Livingston's interest in making paper from CONFERVA, see Vol. 31:397. VANDER KEMP: in Paris in 1788, Baron van der Capellen van de Marsch sent Francis Adrian Van der Kemp, a Dutch Mennonite who was on his way to take up residence in the United States, to see TJ.

At Capellen's request, TJ wrote to Madison to introduce Van der Kemp. In March 1790 TJ, as secretary of state, responded to a letter from Van der Kemp to George Washington about means of reclaiming his property in the Netherlands. Van der Kemp and TJ exchanged a number of letters from 1812 until TJ's death (Washington, Papers, Pres. Ser., 1:18n; 5:243-5; Vol. 12:632-3, 655-6; Vol. 16:285).

If the ESSAY was a published work, it was perhaps the Speech of Fr. Adr. Van der Kemp, at a Meeting, the First of June, One Thousand, Seven Hundred and Ninety-Five, at Whitestown, for the Institution of a Society of Agriculture (Whitestown, N.Y., 1795) or Van der Kemp's eulogy of Washington, Lofrede op George Washington, te Oldenbarneveld, den 22sten van Sprokkelmaand 1800, in Oneida district, staat van New York (Amsterdam, 1800).

From David Austin

SIR/.   Philadelphia March 30th. 1801

In revising the order, & judging of the properiety of certain appointments, at the conclusion of the late administration, your indulgence will bear with a request, that the Commission of Collector of the Revenue, at New Haven, State of Connecticut may not be forgotten.

The duties of this Office had, from its commencement been discharged, with exactist fidelity by my Hond: father; & for a few years, during his last illness, through the aid of my brother, who, acted as Assistant Collector in the duties of the office, & who stood in the expectation of the Citizens, & of all acquainted with him, as the unrivalled expectant of the Office, at my fathers death. —

The expectations of my brother were blasted by the transfer of this Office into the hands of Elizur Goodrich:—No ground of complaint was ever heard, & no supplanting ever expected; unless it arose from an idea of a supplanting exertion on the part of the Goodriches. My brother is left to bemoan the loss of his father, & of his expectations, a family young & tender upon his hands, & no means of professional support. He commands an honorary independent Company of Artillery, composed of the young Gentlemen of the place; who feel not a little this loss of honor & of emolument, on the part of their Captain. Your Excellency can readily perceive the predicament into wh. my brother is cast by this unexpected event: To yr. Ex'y it still appertains to redress this grief—No objections to my Brother, on the score of political principle was ever made; & if any shadow of objection was ever found; it was *only* that some of the Most reputable members of the General Assembly of the State of Connecticut, of republican principles lodged at my Brother's, during the Octobr. session;—I shall only add, that there are reasons to believe, that my brother was supplanted on this account.—

If your Ex'y will be so good as to restore the Name of John P. Austin to its former lustre; & heal his wounded bosom from the wounds of unprovoked ambition & conspiracy, you may rest satisfied in having performed a worthy deed, & of being in full possession of the good wishes of all good men.—With all due esteem.

D: AUSTIN

RC (DNA: RG 59, LAR); at head of text: "Th: Jefferson Esqr:"; endorsed by TJ as received 9 Apr. and so recorded in SJL with notation "Off."

MY HOND: FATHER: David Austin (1732-1801) was a prominent merchant and banker of New Haven. He served as collector of customs for the port of New Haven from 1793 until his death on 5 Feb. 1801. JOHN P. AUSTIN was his youngest son. He did not receive an appointment during TJ's administration (Donald Lines Jacobus, comp., *Families of Ancient New Haven*, 3 vols. [Baltimore, 1981], 1:91-2; Rollin G. Osterweis, *Three Centuries of New Haven, 1638-1938* [New Haven, 1953], 166, 167, 171, 186, 259; Theodore S. Woolsey, "The Old New Haven Bank," *Papers of the New Haven Colony Historical Society* 8 [1914], 312-13).

From Samuel Dexter

SIR,   Washington 20th. [i.e. 30] March 1801

On the late change in the administration of the government of the United States I thought it would be improper in me instantly to resign the office of secretary of the treasury, as it would look like a refusal to submit to the public will, & might leave an important department destitute of necessary superintendence. I therefore took an early opportunity of submitting to your consideration the propriety of my retiring from office; &, if such was your desire, the time & manner of doing so. For the obliging terms in which you informed me of your wishes on this subject be pleased, Sir, to accept my thanks. In conformity thereto I have continued in office until, as I presume, you have made such an arrangement that my services will not be necessary after the 20th. day of April next; & in pursuance of the same principle I now request that my resignation of the office of secretary of the treasury of the United States may be accepted, to take effect from & after that day.— Give me leave, Sir, on this occasion to express my most cordial wishes that your administration of the government may greatly promote the true interests of our Country & your honor, & the very great respect with which I have the honor to be

Your ob. servt.   SAML. DEXTER

RC (DLC); at foot of first page: "The President of U. States"; endorsed by TJ as received 31 Mch. and so recorded in SJL.

YOU INFORMED ME: see TJ to Dexter, 20 Feb.

To Enoch Edwards

DEAR SIR   Washington Mar. 30. 1801.

I have a commission to be executed in Philadelphia which would be the better at least of being done with taste and convenience,[1] and to whom [. . .] I apply in a question of taste & convenience so justly as to yourself, who are full of taste, and aided by that of mrs Edwards? the only scruple is on what ground I can claim a right to lay your taste under [contribution?] for my benefit? to this I acknolege I have not one word to say. but I will put into your mouth the words of the benevolent man in Terence, 'Homo sum, humani nil a me alienum puto' and will suppose the scruple answered. I wish a handsome chariot to be made for me in Philadelphia, and give on the inclosed paper the only directions material, as to it's conveniences. the colour, form, and every thing about it which is taste I leave absolutely to yourself.   wishing always to have as many enjoiments for my money [as it will procure] [. . .] to have any just surplus to give to some greater object of charity than the workman generally is, I, of course, wish to get things as cheap as I can. therefore it may be proper not to say for whom the carriage or harness is, till prices are fixed. I should want this as soon after the 1st. of May as possible, because till then I shall be absent in Virginia. draughts for the price or any part of it to be made on John Barnes of Georgetown, payable in Philadelphia, at such periods of the work, after the 1st. of May, as you shall authorise. perhaps you may find a carriage ready made, or at least advanced, & to your mind. still it would not be wanting till the 1st. of May, nor would prompter paiments than the 1st. of May & June, in moieties, be convenient. I would not have trespassed on you with this commission, but that as the fine season is approaching, you will of course be sometimes going to Philadelphia, and certainly will not need to go once merely for this object. an eye on the work now & then, en passant, will be a sufficient security for it's faithful & tasty execution. I am not fond of splendid things; but of chaste neatness. this is as applicable to the harness as to the carriage.

I wish I could offer to reciprocate services here. but the state of the arts here is too far behind Philadelphia to afford anything of that kind; I must therefore let it rest on the mere ground of charity.

I trust we may now exchange congratulations on a continent at peace in Europe: and the change of the ministry in England is a strong proof to me that they also are for peace. the attitudes of the maritime powers furnishes a ground of hope that something favorable to neutral rights may be established. present my respects to mrs Edwards, and accept yourself assurances of my best wishes & great consideration. TH: JEFFERSON

PrC (DLC); faint and blurred; at foot of first page: "Doctr. Edwards"; with enclosure letterpressed perpendicularly below signature; endorsed by TJ in ink on verso.

Edwards and TJ first exchanged letters in 1793, shortly before Edwards and his wife, Frances Gordon Edwards, left the Philadelphia area to begin a three-year

tour of France and Britain (Vol. 25:671-2; Vol. 29:230).

HOMO SUM, HUMANI NIL A ME ALIENUM PUTO: "I am human, so nothing human is alien to me," from Terence's play, *The Self-Tormentor*, act 1, line 77.

[1] Preceding two words interlined.

ENCLOSURE

Instructions for a Carriage

A handsome chariot for both city & country use, consequently to be made very light, and to be hung absolutely low, without any regard at all to the modern fashion, as low as they came in former times, which the dangerous roads of the country absolutely require.
a very[1] large semicircular light behind.
quadrantal lights in each hind quarter.
Venetian blinds and glasses[2] to all the lights, & spring curtains
calico lining
plated beads & cypher.
qu? plated caps to the hubs of the wheels.
a driver's box to be taken off or on easily. by 4. screws.
a light boot to be off or on at pleasure. in this, have no regard to the ridiculous fashion of enormous boots.
no lantherns.
2 pr. plated harness, with both pads & postillion saddles, to be easily changed.

PrC (DLC); blurred; letterpressed to second page of enclosing letter.

¹ Word interlined.
² Preceding two words interlined.

To Benjamin Stoddert

SIR   Washington Mar. 30. 1801.

In your letter of Feb. 18. you were so kind as to tender your continuance in office till I could provide a successor, expressing a [wish at] the same time to be relieved as early in this month as should be p[ossible to do.] it has not been in my power to do this as early as you wished. Genl. Smith is now arrived to take charge of the department, at such particular moment as you may think proper to designate. I beg [leave] to repeat here my acknolegements for the time & leisure which [your ac]comodation has furnished me for [fill]ing a department of [. . .] difficulty & importance. Accept assurances of my high [consideration] & respect.   TH: JEFFERSON

PrC (DLC); faint and blurred; at foot of text: "Benjamin Stoddert esq"; endorsed by TJ in ink on verso.

From Mathew Carey

SIR,   Philada. March 31. 1801.

Agreeably to your directions, I enclose a copy of your speech on Satin—and am, Sir,

with due respect your obt. hble. servt.   MATHEW CAREY

RC (MHi); at foot of text: "Thomas Jefferson, President of the United States"; endorsed by TJ as received 9 Apr. and so recorded in SJL. Enclosure not found, but see below.

For TJ's SPEECH ON SATIN, see our editorial note on the First Inaugural Address, printed at 4 Mch.

Statement of Account with Thomas Carpenter

Thomas Jefferson Esq.

    1801   To Thomas Carpenter Dr.
January 1st.

        Repairing a Surtout Coat   Drs.0.25
        To Making a pr Breeches and materials, with pocketts   2.62

	$1\frac{7}{8}$ yds Superfine Black Cassimeer @ 22/6		5.62
	To Making a Coat, trimings, stays, pocketts &c		4.25
	Silk Sleeve Lynings and velvet Collar		3.25
	20 Steele Buttons		1.75
	$2\frac{1}{4}$ yds Superfine Blue Cloth @ 48/9		14.62
Febry. 14	Facing a Waistcoat and Silk		1.25
28.	Making a Coat & materials		4.25
	Silk Sleeve Lynings & velvet Collar		3.25
	Making a Waistcoat and materials		3.25
	$6\frac{1}{2}$ yds Superfine black Cassimeer @ 22/6		19.50
	Facing an under Waistcoat and Silk		1.25
	Repairing Breeches		25
March 30	Making a Coat and Materials		4.25
	Silk Sleeve Lynings Velvet Collar and Steele Buttons		5.—
	5 Yards Superfine blue Cassimeer @ 22/6		15.—
	Making a Great Coat and materials		4.25
	Silk Sleeve Lynings and Velvet Collar		3.25
	$3\frac{3}{4}$ yards Milled blue Cloth @ 45/		22.50
	Making the Servant's Coat and materials		4.—
	Making his Waistcoat and materials		2.50
	Making his Pantaloons and materials		2.25
	2 Yards blue Cloth @ 30/		8.—
	1 Doz Coat and 1 Doz small Gilt Buttons		90
	Scarlet Cloth for Collar and Cuffs		1.—
	A Corded Waistcoat Pattern		1.50
	3 yards Velvet for Pantaloons @ 11/3		4.50
		$	144.26

Mar. 31. 1801.   servants   *24.65*

Mr. Barnes will be pleased to pay this   *119.61*
Th: Jefferson

MS (ViU); in Carpenter's hand, words and figures in italics added by TJ, who also endorsed the statement on verso with Carpenter's name and addressed it "Mr. Barnes"; notation in a clerk's hand alongside Carpenter's total, "Exd. JB," refers to an examination of the account in John Barnes's office, and checkmarks next to all of Carpenter's figures, not shown here, were probably added during that review; at foot, Barnes wrote and Carpenter signed an acknowledgment of payment in full on 2 Apr. 1801; endorsed by Barnes and a clerk.

Thomas Carpenter, who had moved to the capital city from Philadelphia, was the proprietor of a Washington tailoring business that employed several workmen. In the early months of 1801 he was in partnership with Charles Varden. They had shops on Capitol Hill and Pennsylvania Avenue. Later in the year the two businesses separated, Varden opened a shop on New Jersey Avenue, and Carpenter's operation occupied the Capitol Hill and Pennsylvania Avenue locations (*National Intelligencer*, 26 Jan., 11 Mch., 20 July 1801, 4 Jan. 1802;

Washington Federalist, 11 Dec. 1801; MB, 2:1063n).

The final eight entries of Carpenter's statement, beginning with the cost of MAKING THE SERVANT'S COAT, comprised the total of $24.65 that TJ noted as charges for servants' clothing. In his financial memoranda for March, TJ noted that Edward Maher was to have two suits of clothes in addition to his monthly pay as porter. Some months later the expenses for the presidential household included clothing for seven servants, five of whom wore livery made in Carpenter's shop (MB, 2:1035, 1058, 1063; Josph Rapin to TJ, 3 Apr. 1801).

From John Dawson

DEAR SIR,   Henry and Charles. March 31. 1801.

A strong gale from the East detained us untill this moring at sunrise, [on?] Hampton roads we are now under sail with a wind N.W. we have every prospect of a quick and agreeable passage.

On looking into the papers delivered to me by the Secretary of State, I find that the one described to the first Consul is signd by yourself but not by Mr. Lincoln, altho the words "acting Secretary of State" are at the bottom—this I presume has been an omission, and you can well judge, on knowing the fact, how far it may have an Effect, & whether it will be necessary to take any step to remedy it.

With most respect and Esteem Your friend & sevt

J DAWSON

RC (DLC); at foot of text: "Mr. Jefferson"; endorsed by TJ as received 16 Apr. from "the Capes" and so recorded in SJL.

TO THE FIRST CONSUL: see TJ to Napoleon Bonaparte, 18 Mch.

To Henry Dearborn

SIR   Washington Mar. 31. 1801.

Mr. Stoddart, Secretary of the Navy having early in this month informed me by letter of his desire to resign that office, and having continued in it ever since, on my request only, I hereby authorize & appoint you to recieve the charge of the department from him, and to perform the duties of it until a Secretary of the Navy shall be formally appointed. Accept assurances of my high consideration and respect.

TH: JEFFERSON

RC (MH); at foot of text: "Genl. Henry Dearborn, Secretary at War." PrC (DLC).

To Samuel Dexter

Sir   Washington Mar. 31. 1801

I am this moment favored with yours of yesterday's date expressing your wish that your resignation might be accepted to take place on the 20th. of the ensuing month. after continuing so long as an accomodation to myself as well as the public, I can not urge your convenience further, tho' it would have been materially advantageous if you could have continued a fortnight longer than the time you mention, as I cannot have a successor in place earlier than that, and shall not myself be able to return hither till the last days of the month. leaving therefore to your own pleasure this extension of the term, your resignation shall operate from the 20th. or any later day to which circumstances will permit you to remain. with many thanks for [the] continuance of your services, and wishes for your health & happiness I pray you to accept assurances of my high consideration & respect

Th: Jefferson

PrC (DLC); faint; at foot of text: "Samuel Dexter esq. Secretary of the Treasury."

To William Evans

Dear Sir   Washington Mar. 31. 1801.

Being in the moment of departure for Monticello where it is necessary for me to be two or three weeks previous to my final settlement here, I cannot go without thanking you for the trouble you were so good as to take as to James & Francis. I supposed I saw in the difficulties raised by James an unwillingness to come here, arising wholly from some attachment he had formed at Baltimore; for I cannot suspect an indisposition towards me. I concluded at once therefore not to urge him against inclination, and wrote to Philadelphia, where I have been successful in getting a cook equal to my wishes. I am glad Francis remains there, as I cannot bear a servant who drinks, & on the whole am supplied to mind. I would wish James to understand that it was in acquiesance to what I supposed his own wish that I did not repeat my application, after having so long rested on the expectation of having him. Accept assurances of my best wishes & sincere esteem.   Th: Jefferson

PrC (MHi); at foot of text: "Mr. William Evans"; endorsed by TJ in ink on verso.

For TJ's hire of Honoré Julien as the cook, see Philippe de Létombe to TJ, 15 Mch.

To Walter Jones

DEAR SIR   Washington Mar. 31. 1801.

I was already almost in the act of mounting my horse for a short excursion home, when your favor of the 14th. was put into my hands. I stop barely to acknolege it, and to thank you for your kind congratulations, and still more for your interesting observations on the course of things. I am sensible how far I should fall short of effecting all the reformation which reason would suggest and experience approve, were I free to do whatever I thought best. but when we reflect how difficult it is to move or inflect the great machine of society, how impossible to advance the notions of a whole people suddenly to ideal right, we see the wisdom of Solen's remark that no more good must be attempted than the nation can bear, and that will be chiefly to reform the waste of public money, & thus drive away the vultures who prey on it, and improve some little on old routines. some new fences for securing constitutional rights may, with the aid of a good legislature, perhaps be attainable.   I am going home for 3. weeks to make some final arrangements there for my removal hither. mr Madison & mr Gallatin will be here by the last of the month. Dearborne & Lincoln remain here, & Genl. Smith entered yesterday on the Naval department, but only pro tempore & to give me time to look for what cannot be[1] obtained, a permanent officer, equal & willing to undertake the duties. accept assurances of my constant and affectionate respect   TH: JEFFERSON

RC (DLC); addressed: "Doctr. Walter Jones Kinsale Westmoreland Virginia"; franked; postmarked 6 Apr. PrC (DLC).

SOLEN'S REMARK: probably TJ's rendering of a statement related in *Plutarch's Lives*, when the Greek statesman and poet Solon was asked if he had enacted the best laws for the Athenians. He replied "the best they would receive" (*Plutarch's Lives*, trans. Bernadotte Perrin, 11 vols. [London, 1914-26], 1:443). See Sowerby, Nos. 68-9.

[1] TJ here canceled "found."

To Philippe de Létombe

DEAR SIR   Washington Mar. 31. 1801.

I recieve your favor of the 26th. just in the moment of my departure for Monticello, from which I shall not return till the last week of April. I have therefore but barely time to acknolege the receipt of your letter, to thank you for the trouble you have taken to aid me in my domestic administration, and to rejoice in the success which has attended your endeavors. it is a great matter to get small things put out of our way, that our efforts may uninterruptedly be applied to great.—Julien may come at any time before the 28th. of April, at his own pleasure. it places me at ease to know that I may depend on finding him here on my return. accept my sincere wishes for your health, happiness, and safe return to your native country & long days of life & enjoiment. be assured I shall preserve with constancy the memory of your merit and my sincere esteem for it, & accept my affectionate consideration & respect.   TH: JEFFERSON

PrC (MHi); at foot of text: "M. Le Tombe"; endorsed by TJ in ink on verso.

To Meriwether Lewis

DEAR SIR   Washington Mar. 31. 1801.

I have been in hopes you would arrive here in time, with me, to make a little excursion to Albemarle, where I supposed it would be as agreeable to you to see your friends, as necessary to me to make some arrangements for my final removal hither. I shall stay there till the 29th. & then return. the time of your arrival here therefore, & your own inclinations will decide whether you follow me thither, or await my return here. if the latter, you will take up your lodgings in the President's house, and the steward (mr Rapin) whom I leave in it, will provide for you. I write this by duplicates, one to remain here, & one to go to Fort Pitt. Accept assurances of my best wishes & friendly esteem.   TH: JEFFERSON

PrC (DLC); at foot of text: "Capt. Meriwether Lewis."

To Charles Little

SIR   Washington Mar. 31. 1801

Mr. White, one of the Commissioners of this city, informs me that he has heretofore had conversations with you on the subject of a road we have been wishing to get from this place to Slaterun church as direct as can be had tolerably level; for levelness is a still more important consideration than distance. it is become more interesting now to me to find such a course. as I am setting out tomorrow for my own house, and shall be on horseback, I propose to endeavor to find the best road. for this information I must ask leave to trouble you. I therefore send my servant as far as Colo. Wren's this evening, with orders to deliver you this letter in the course of the evening. I shall set out by sunrise in the morning, breakfast at Colo. Wren's, and ask the pleasure either of seeing you there, or[1] permission to call on you at your own house, to obtain from you, not only directions for my present course, but to consult on the best means which can be pursued to find out a good direction for a future road. accept assurances of my best wishes and respect.   TH: JEFFERSON

PrC (MoSHi: Jefferson Papers); at foot of text: "Colo. Little"; endorsed by TJ in ink on verso.

Charles Little (ca. 1744-1813), an immigrant from Scotland, settled in Virginia in 1768. He purchased Cleesh, an estate in Fairfax County, southwest of Alexandria, and served as a militia officer. In the 1790s he frequently visited at Mount Vernon and he served as one of Washington's pallbearers (Washington, *Papers, Pres. Ser.*, 9:411n; Washington, *Diaries*, 4:275n; 6:304-5n; Preston, *Catalogue*, 1:107; CVSP, 8:487).

SUBJECT OF A ROAD: see Alexander White to TJ, 5 Dec. 1800. James Wren, a prominent Fairfax County resident, kept a tavern near present-day Falls Church (MB, 2:975, 1036).

SEND MY SERVANT: probably John Freeman, to whom TJ gave $5 on 31 Mch. TJ hired Freeman, a slave about 20 years old, from William Baker, a Maryland physician, for $8 a month. He became a dining room servant at the President's House, and, in August 1801, began accompanying TJ on his journeys to Monticello. On this trip he probably traveled as far as Herin's tavern, where Davy Bowles was waiting for TJ. In 1804, TJ purchased Freeman from Baker for $400, with the stipulation that he would be freed in 1815. When Freeman did not want to leave Washington in 1809, TJ sold the remainder of his term to James Madison (MB, 2:1036, 1043, 1059; Stanton, *Free Some Day*, 80, 129, 185n; Lucia Stanton, "'A Well-Ordered Household': Domestic Servants in Jefferson's White House," *White House History*, 17 [2006], 8-9, 14, 19; RS, 1:156; TJ to John Strode, 25 Mch. 1801; John Freeman to TJ, 2 Mch. 1809).

[1] Canceled: "leave."

From John Thomson Mason

George Town 31st. March 1801

George Town and the City of Washington was the Stage upon which Morris & Nicholson acted the last scene of swindling and imposition. They contracted debts and issued notes to an immense amount here, and such was the folly of a numbers of our inhabitants that just before they sunk, they bought up their paper to a very great amount, which paper had been issued a considerable time before.

Morris & Nicholson apprized of these circumstances, and finding that they could no longer raise money in their ordinary modes of negotiation, proposed as they termed it, to fund their debts. That is they agreed & proposed, that if any holder of their paper would advance to them in cash one third of the amount of the paper so held, they would secure the whole sum by a Mortgage on their city property.

U. Forrest, Benjamin Stoddert, Gustavus Scott and Philip B Key formed a company, united the paper they held, made the advance demanded, and received the proposed Mortgage. The Mortgage which they thus received included a number of lots sold by the Commissioners to Morris Nicholson & Greenleaf, for which they had not made full payment. The Bal. due to the Comrs, for the purchase money of these lots, amounted, I am told, to $35,000; no doubt it amounted to a very large sum of money. By the terms of sale, made by the Commissioners to Morris Nicholson & Greenleaf, these lots were to be resold for any default in the payment of the purchase money. This default happened, the lots were resold, and Uriah Forrest purchased them for the benefit of the funded debt as above stated, that is for himself, Scott, (one of the City Commissioners) Stoddert, & Key,[1] upon a credit I believe of sixty days. After this purchase, and before the day of payment came round as I have always understood, and beleive, the Maryland Legislature met. Uriah Forrest a Senator proposed to the Legislature to make a loan of $50,000 to the Commissioners of the City, to enable them the better to provide for the reception of Congress, and thereby to secure the residence of that body upon the Potomac. His efforts were a long time unsuccessful, however just before the close of the session, when many of the Members had gone home, to the great astonishment of many, he succeeded, procured the loan, and also procured himself to be taken as one of the Securities to the State for the repayment of the money.

When he returned home, it was whispered and beleived, that he prevailed upon the Commissioners to consent, that the money which he owed them should not be drawn from his hands, except to pay the debt to the State of Maryland for which he stood bound as Security. This trick was supported upon the plausible pretext, that as Forrest was bound for them in a large Sum of Money, it was necessary to secure him for the risque he run, and that could not be better done than by letting him hold as an indemnity the money he owed them. Scott and Thornton it is said thought this reasonable, White it is said remonstrated. Two however made a majority, and the result was, that the Legislature of Maryland, to promote the progress of the City, and secure the residence of Congress, loaned to Uriah Forrest and others 35,000$ and to the Commissioners $15,000, and they became mutually bound for each other to repay the money.

That Scott should think this a proper arrangement, no person wondered, but Thorntons conduct excited great surprize, until it was understood, and I believe it is true, that Thornton too was a purchaser of lots upon credit, that finding indulgence necessary, he found no means of gaining it so easy and so certain as that of a mutual exchange of favours with his brother Commissioner Scott. It was also said that Thornton owed money in Bank, to continue his paper there he needed an indorser, he found it difficult to get one, and was upon the point of being denied further credit, and called upon for payment, when U Forrest very generously came forward and indorsed for him. This was a friendly act and merited some return

I this moment heard that you were at this time deliberating upon this very subject. I accidentally saw a note from Doctor Thornton to his friend, in which he mentions that U Forrest had written you a letter upon this business, and that he Thornton had made some statement upon the subject, which had been handed to you. I thought I saw a settled design to deceive you by false statements. An enemy to fraud I felt it my duty to represent to you the transactions as they have been represented among us, and as they are beleived in truth to be.

The time when Forrest purchased these lots, the terms of credit given to him, the time when the State loaned the money, and the amount of the Debt from Forrest to the Commissioners will certainly appear from their books. Whether Thornton is a purchaser upon credit and has remained undisturbed for the payment, tho' the time in which it ought to have been made has passed, may be also seen there. I will state it as a fact within my own knowledge that Scott was interested with Forrest in these purchases, if that fact does not appear from the Commissioners proceedings

I have the Honor to be with great respect and esteem Your Obedt. Servt   JOHN T. MASON

RC (DLC); endorsed by TJ as a letter of 31 Mch. received on [30] Mch. and so recorded in SJL.

On 12 Dec. 1799 the MARYLAND LEGISLATURE received a petition from the District of Columbia Commissioners requesting a loan of $70,000. Philip B. Key, a member of the House of Delegates from Annapolis who was appointed to the committee to consider the petition, reported a resolution six days later calling for a $50,000 loan to the commissioners in U.S. stock bearing 6 percent interest "upon the said commissioners giving such real and personal security as the governor and council shall approve" for payment of the principal by 1 Feb. 1803. On 21 Dec. the resolution failed in the house by a 33 to 35 vote. When it was considered again two days later, with the modification that the loan was to be paid by 1 Nov. 1802, the resolution passed, 34 to 30. It passed the state senate the same day. The legislature adjourned on 3 Jan. 1800 (*Votes and Proceedings of the House of Delegates of the State of Maryland. November Session, 1799* [Annapolis, 1800; Evans, No. 37895], 2, 56-7, 69, 71-2, 75-6; *Votes and Proceedings of the Senate of the State of Maryland. November Session, 1799* [Annapolis, 1800; Evans, No. 37896], 23, 45).

FORREST HAD WRITTEN YOU: according to SJL, TJ did not receive correspondence from Uriah Forrest during March 1801, but for Forrest's letter to the District of Columbia Commissioners of

28 Mch., which was sent to TJ, see note to District of Columbia Commissioners to TJ, of the same date.

[1] Phrase of six or seven words here heavily canceled and illegible.

To Benjamin Vaughan

DEAR SIR   Washington Mar. 31. 1801.

Your favor of the 15th. is put into my hand, just as I am mounting my horse for Monticello, where I shall be about three weeks making some domestic arrangements for my final settlement here. I stop to thank you for your kind congratulations & still more for your judicious observations on the circumstances of my position. one counsel will be very difficult, to draw the veil of confidence over a consciousness that it ought not to exist. your frequent letters will make me very happy, & lay me under the greater obligation as I foresee that private correspondence will be to me practicable in but a small degree. still it would be calamitous were that to deprive me of the[1] information & counsel of the wise & good. accept assurances of my sincere esteem, & high consideration & respect.

TH: JEFFERSON

RC (Mrs. Langdon Marvin, Hallowell, Maine, 1944); addressed in John Vaughan's hand: "Benjamin Vaughan Esqr Hallowell Maine Massachussets";

stamped; postmarked Philadelphia, 3 Apr. PrC (DLC).

[1] TJ here canceled "aid."

To Caspar Wistar

DEAR SIR   Washington Mar. 31. 1801.

By the preceding post you will have recieved some Observations transmitted [here] by Mr. Legaux, [& also] two precious volumes of Comparative anatomy presented to the Society by mr Cuvier, the author. I now inclose you a letter from Chancellor Livingston on the subject of the large [bones] lately found [in New York] with a drawing, & also a paper enclosed me in a former [private] letter, but referred to in this. Accept assurances of my high consideration & respect

TH: JEFFERSON

PrC (DLC); faint; at foot of text: "Doctr. Wistar"; endorsed by TJ in ink on verso. Enclosure: Robert R. Livingston to TJ, 17 Mch.

The American Philosophical Society received Peter Legaux's meteorological OBSERVATIONS and the work by CUVIER during a meeting in Philadelphia on 3 Apr. (APS, *Proceedings*, 22, pt. 3 [1884], 310). TJ apparently sent the items to Wistar without a cover letter.

PAPER: see the enclosure listed at Livingston to TJ, 6 Mch.

Jacob Wagner's Memorandum on State Department Clerks

[March 1801]

Mr. Kimball keeps the accounts of the Department; and, when not so engaged, does such other current business as is assigned to him.

Mr. Thom fills up patents for Virginia Military lands and for useful discoveries and inventions, and does such other copying and recording as is assigned to him.

Mr. Miller records the foreign and domestic letters written by the Secretary of State, and does such other copying and recording as is assigned to him.

Mr. Pleasonton fills up patents for U.S. military lands, and does such other copying and recording as is assigned to him.

Mr. Crawford is employed in copying, recording and assisting Mr. Brent in collating.

Mr. Brent for the present is engaged only in collating.

J. Wagner has been employed in filing away the papers, making copies of the most confidential of them, when necessary; receiving applications about the current business and having them executed; collating the laws and superintending their publication and distribution; the receipt and management of complaints for captures and impressments of American citizens, when they do not embrace such peculiar circumstances as render them worthy of the particular attention of the Secretary; drafting commissions, formal official papers and answers to such letters of inferior consequence, as the Secretary may charge him with, &c. &c. It is not easy to comprehend every particular of his duty in a concise sketch: but the above will serve to give a view of the general nature of his usual employment, the design of which is, by saving the attention of the Secretary, as much as possible, from matters of routine and small importance, to enable him to devote[1] his time to objects of greater magnitude

MS (DLC: TJ Papers, 235:42188); in Jacob Wagner's hand, except as noted below; endorsed by TJ: "State. department of. Clerks."

TJ probably requested this information regarding clerks in the State Department shortly after he took office, when Levi Lincoln was looking after the department, and before he left, on 1 Apr., for Monticello. Timothy Pickering appointed to the clerkship Jacob Wagner, an acknowledged Federalist, whose role as chief clerk under James Madison has been described "as something of an assistant secretary of state." Hazen KIMBALL resigned his post on 14 Nov. 1801. Noting their allegiance to Pickering, William Duane characterized Wagner, Kimball, and Christopher S. THOM as "Complete Picaroons." Duane described John C. MILLER as "Modest," Stephen PLEASONTON as a "Nothingarian," William CRAWFORD as a "Hamiltonian," and Daniel BRENT as a "Nincumpoop." In 1807 Wagner, Thom, Pleasonton, and Brent still held their clerkships. Wagner resigned that year and became the editor of a Federalist newspaper in Baltimore (Cunningham, *Process of Government*, 94-5, 178, 328; Madison, *Sec. of State Ser.*, 2:427n; Gallatin, *Papers*, 6:354).

[1] Remainder in TJ's hand, supplying Wagner's words cut off at bottom of page.

Notes on South Carolina Patronage

[March-November 1801]

S. Carolina

1. James Symonds. Collector. violent federalist. commands great interest.
2. Edwd Weyman. Surveyor[1] fed. nothing known amiss of him.
   [3. Daniel Stevens. Bostonian. fed. Supervisor. very active & commands great interest
4. Thomas Waring. Naval officer. good man. no more federalist than would keep his office. never meddles.
5. Wm. Crafts. Navy agent. a Bostonian. bitter fellow. very influential.
6.   Cockran. marshall.[2] Goodwin says 'Eastern man, dupe of Eastern politics, factious, wrong headed, youngster, partial selection of juries'; Ramsay says 'intolerant & indiscreet youth.' a very good man. federalist, but not medling. has no power in selecting even grand juries.
       Thos. Lehré recommended by C. Pinckney and   Goodwyn by P. Butler & by Ephraim Ramsay[3]
7.   Parker. fed. & able, but good & unmedling. Attorney of district.[4] brother in law of Drayton the Govr. who is a violent republican. therefore let him stand till further enquiry.

---

1. Daniel Doyley (now state treasurer) able & estimable man. vice Symonds
[3. Edwd. Darrell.[5] Supervisor v. Stevens. a lawyer & Notary public. has been persecuted as a lawyer by the merchts.

5. Thomas Lehré.[6] now Sheriff Charleston district. a steady republican.[7] may perhaps refuse
John Splatt Cripps by C. Pinckney
Ramsay & Darrell dead

MS (DNA: RG 59, LAR, file of James Symonds [i.e., Simons], 10:0777); undated; entirely in TJ's hand, written in several sittings, over several months, as indicated by interlineations and last entry; opening brackets perhaps added by TJ at the time of Darrell's appointment in July or at the receipt of Pierce Butler's letter of 3 Sep. 1801; closing quotation marks supplied by Editors; endorsed by TJ: "S. Carolina."

In early March 1801, TJ decided to postpone changes in federal offices in South Carolina until after the close of the upcoming session of the Seventh Congress, that is, the spring of 1802. As the months passed, pressure increased to appoint Republicans to offices in the state, but TJ wanted to wait at least until Congress met, when he would have the "broad counsel" of South Carolina's congressional delegation. These notes clearly indicate the president's efforts to sort out patronage questions in the state (Notes on a Cabinet Meeting, 8 Mch. 1801; TJ to Gallatin, 7 Aug. 1801).

Edward WEYMAN became surveyor and inspector of the port of Charleston in 1793 upon the death of his father, who had served as surveyor since 1789. TJ learned more about Weyman from a letter written by South Carolina judge and former congressman Aedanus Burke to Madison on 13 Sep. 1801. Burke noted that through "some mistake or other" Republicans in Charleston feared Weyman might be removed. Burke described the surveyor as a man of Republican principles who did not waiver during the XYZ affair. "During the reign of Terror in 1798. & 99.," Burke observed, "there were not ten men to whom I dare speak my mind; there were not, I declare before God, there were not half a dozen men, yet Weyman never quited the Ground; and I expected every week nothing less than, than his removal." TJ endorsed the letter "Weyman Edw. Surveyor Charleston"

and interlined "Surveyor" in place of Burke's description of Weyman as "inspector." Weyman remained surveyor until shortly before his death in 1813 (RC in DNA: RG 59, LAR; Washington, *Papers, Pres. Ser.*, 11:615-16; Madison, *Papers, Sec. of State Ser.*, 2:108-10; *Biog. Dir. Cong.*).

GOODWIN SAYS: see Charles Goodwin to TJ, 30 Apr. 1801. RAMSAY SAYS: see Ephraim Ramsay to TJ, 2 May 1801.

As secretary of state, TJ provided Thomas PARKER with his commission when Washington appointed him U.S. district attorney for South Carolina in October 1792. Parker continued in the office until his death in 1820 (Washington, *Papers, Pres. Ser.*, 11:264-5).

In August, TJ still described Daniel D'Oyley (DOYLEY), Charles Pinckney's candidate for collector at Charleston, as a "most respectable republican" and as "one of those destined for office." But when James Simons complied with Gallatin's directions in rendering accounts, the Treasury secretary observed that perhaps it would not be necessary to remove him. Simons retained his office until 1806, when Simeon Theus became collector (JEP, 2:16; Daniel D'Oyley to Gallatin, 29 July 1801, in DNA, RG 59: LAR; Memorandum from Charles Pinckney, 17 Mch.; TJ to Gallatin, 7, 21 Aug. 1801; Gallatin to TJ, 10 Aug. 1801).

RAMSAY & DARRELL DEAD: both young South Carolina Republicans died in November 1801. Ramsay was 35 and Darrell was 31 years old (*S.C. Biographical Directory, House of Representatives*, 4:465; Charleston *City-Gazette and Daily Advertiser*, 13 Nov. 1801).

[1] Word interlined.

[2] Interlined from here through "indiscreet youth."

[3] Entry beginning with "Thos. Lehré" to this point interlined.

[4] Remainder of entry added at later sitting.

⁵ TJ here interlined "dead" at a later sitting.

⁶ Interlined by TJ in place of "Leary" probably after he received Pinckney's memorandum printed at 17 Mch.

⁷ From here through "C. Pinckney" possibly added at a later sitting.

From Jean Chas

paris ce 11. germinal l'an 9. ou
Le 1er. avril l'an 1801.

MONSIEUR LE PRESIDENT

Daignés accepter un exemplaire de mon histoire politique, et philosophique de La revolution de L'amérique Septentrionale. cet ouvrage a eté presenté et dedié au premier consul de La republique francoise. J'ai obtenu Les Suffrages, et Les felicitations des savans et des philosophes. Mon ouvrage a eu Le plus grand succès. J'en suis seul L'auteur, quoiqu'il porte Le nom d'un Second cooperateur.

J'ai exposé a L'admiration publique L'histoire d'un peuple qui a donné a L'univers Le spectacle de L'heroisme, du courage et de toutes les vertus; et qui presente Le tableau consolant du bonheur et de La prosperité. Recevés ici, monsieur Le president, L'hommage de ma profonde veneration.

Vous vous rappellerés, monsieur Le president, que dans Le tems ou vous etiés ambassadeur des etats unis auprès de L'ancien gouvernement francois, j'eus L'honneur de vous voir plusieurs fois, que je vous remis mon manuscrit, et que vous me fites des observations dont j'ai su profiter. Des circonstances penibles ne m'ont point permis jusqu'ici de faire paroitre mon ouvrage; je l'ai publié, c'etoit un besoin pressant de mon coeur. Je voudrois bien pouvoir les visiter ces heureuses contrées que vous habités, et contempler un peuple si heureux, et puiser des connoissances qui me manquent encore. mais je ne vis que de mes travaux Litteraires, et La fortune s'oppose a un desir que je conserverai toujours. Pour remplir ce voeu de mon coeur, j'aurois besoin d'encouragements qui me manquent. Je conserve une quantité d'exemplaires de mon ouvrage que je destine pour L'amerique. J'attend de connoitre vos intentions pour remplir cet objet.

Votre nom, vos talens, vos vertus sont connus en europe, monsieur Le president. Vous jouissés d'une grande reputation en france; vous y etes honoré et estimé. on a appris avec plaisir votre nomination à La place eminente que vous occupés. vous remplirés avec fidelité les grands devoirs qui vous sont imposés, et vous donnerés L'exemple de ces vertus sublimes qui ont placé wasingthon au rang de ces hommes privilegiés que La nature destine a illustrer et a honorer leur Siecle par Leur genie et leurs vertus. Que Le ciel benisse vos travaux et conserve vos jours!

Je vis isolé Loin du tumulte, et des passions des hommes; je trouve dans la solitude et dans La meditation ce bonheur que je ne trouverai point dans le fracas d'une grande Societé. je suis pauvre, mais je suis Libre et independant; cependant je recevrai avec reconnoissance Les marques de votre bienveillance. Le titre d'un bienfaiteur tel que vous flatte, honore, console L'homme de Lettres.

Je vous prie, monsieur Le président, d'accepter un exemplaire des Synonymes de d'alembert, de diderot, et de jaucourt. dont je suis Lediteur, et de mon ouvrage sur bonaparte.

je suis avec un profond respect monsieur Le president, votre tres humble et très obeissant Serviteur   J CHAS

Mr. President

Paris, this 11th Germinal, Year 9. or 1st April of the year 1801.

Kindly accept a copy of my political and philosophical history of the American Revolution. This work has been presented and dedicated to the first consul of the French Republic. I have obtained the approval and the congratulations of scholars and philosophers. My work has had the greatest success. I am its sole author, even though it bears the name of a second coauthor.

I have exposed to public admiration the history of a people that has given to the universe the spectacle of heroism, courage, and all the virtues; and that presents the comforting picture of happiness and prosperity. Accept now, Mr. President, this tribute of my profound veneration.

You will recall, Mr. President, that at the time you were the United States' ambassador to the former French government, I had the honor of seeing you several times, that I handed over to you my manuscript, and that you made some observations from which I was able to draw advantage. Painful circumstances prevented me until now from bringing out my work; I published it because it was an urgent need of my heart. I wish I could visit those fortunate regions where you live and to look upon such a fortunate people and gain knowledge still lacking to me. But I live on my literary work alone, and fortune is opposed to a desire that I shall always have. To fulfill this heart's desire I should need encouragement lacking to me. I am reserving a number of copies of my work to send to America. I am waiting to know your intentions to accomplish this project.

Your name, your talents, and your virtues are known in Europe, Mr. President. You enjoy a great reputation in France, where you are honored and esteemed. We learned here with pleasure that you were chosen for the eminent position you occupy. You will faithfully fulfill the great duties imposed upon you, and you will give the example of those sublime virtues that placed Washington in the ranks of those privileged men whom nature designates to render illustrious and to honor their epoch through their genius and their virtues. May Heaven bless your work and preserve your days!

I live in isolation, far from the tumult and passions of men; I find in solitude and meditation that happiness that I should not find in the uproar of a great society. I am poor, but I am free and independent. Nevertheless, I should receive with gratitude the marks of your benevolence. The title of a benefactor such as you flatters, honors, and comforts the man of letters.

I beg you, Mr. President, to accept a copy of the Synonyms of D'Alembert, Diderot, and Jaucourt, of which I am the publisher, and of my work on Bonaparte.

I am with deep respect, Mr. President, your very humble and very obedient servant
J CHAS

RC (DLC); below signature: "rue du bout du monde n 184"; endorsed by TJ as a letter of 1 Mch. received on 6 Aug. 1801 and so recorded in SJL (11 Germinal Year 9 was 1 Apr. 1801).

MON HISTOIRE: *Histoire Politique et Philosophique de la Révolution de l'Amérique Septentrionale* (Paris, 1801); see Sowerby, No. 485, and Vol. 10:442-3, 571. The book identified Chas's collaborator only as "Citoyen" Lebrun. For TJ's limited OBSERVATIONS on the work in manuscript, see his letter to Chas of 7 Dec. 1786 (Vol. 10:580).

The work by Denis DIDEROT and his fellow encyclopedists Jean Le Rond d'Alembert and Chevalier Louis de Jaucourt was *Synonymes Français* (Paris, 1801); see Sowerby, No. 4833.

MON OUVRAGE SUR BONAPARTE: *Sur Bonaparte, Premier Consul de la République Française*, written by Chas and published in Paris in 1800.

From Auguste de Grasse

charleston Caroline du Sud
Ce 1er. d'avril 1801.

MONSIEUR LE PRÉSIDENT

J'Etais fort Jeune Lorsque Vous allates a Paris, mais je me Rapele parfaitement bien D'avoir Eu L'honneur de Vous y Voir plusieurs fois chez mon Pere.

Lorsque j'arrivai ici En 1793 fuyant avec ma famille les dangers qui nous menacaient à St. domingue, ou je m'Etois rendu avant la Revolution pour y prendre possession des biens qui m'y Etoient devolus par la mort de mon Pere, Je n'aurois Certainement pas manqué de Cultiver Votre Connoissance Si les Circonstances Eussent dirigées mes pas vers philadelphie. Votre accession a la chaire Présidentiel du Gouvernement des Etats-unis de L'amérique, m'offre l'occasion de me rappeler a Votre ressouvenir et de Vous feliciter d'avoir enfin réuni des Suffrages tant merités par le devouement que vous n'avés jamais Cessé de temoigner pour le bien de Votre pays.

En arrivant dans ce Continent, J'ai Eprouvé les bienfaits du Gouvernement Sous le titre de Sous-Ingenieur, mais je ne Scais par qu'elle fatalité ces Secours m'ont Etés Subitement retirés au moment ou je m'y attendois le moins, forcé D'attendre ici la paix Générale, Comme le Seul Evenement qui puisse nourir nos Esperences sur le Sort de St. domingue, mon desir Seroit, dans cet interval dont la durée Est incertaine, D'Etre Employé utilement pour les Etats-unis Et assés avantageusement pour L'Existance de ma famille. Le Colonel Sinf qui Vient de partir pour philadelphie, devoit se charger de Vous remettre Cette Lettre Et de Vous parler de moi, mais Son depart à Eté si précipité que je n'ai pû En profiter, permettés moi au nom de la mémoire de mon pere, que Vous honnoré de quelques Considerations, de reclamer Votre bienveillance Et votre appui Et Soyés convaincu Du Zêle avec le quel j'e m'Efforcerai de les meriter.

J'ai L'honneur D'Etre avec un profond Respect Monsieur Le président Votre trés humble Et trés Obeissent Serviteur

AUGUSTUS DE GRASSE

Charleston, South Carolina,
MR. PRESIDENT · this 1st of April 1801.

I was very young when you went to Paris, but I remember perfectly well having had the honor of seeing you several times at my father's house.

When I arrived here in 1793, fleeing with my family the dangers that threatened us in Saint-Domingue—whither I had gone before the Revolution to take possession of the estate that had come down to me through the death of my father—I should certainly not have failed to make your acquaintance if circumstances had directed my steps towards Philadelphia. Your accession to the post of president of the government of the United States of America offers me the chance to recall myself to your memory and to congratulate you for having finally gained the approval so well deserved by the devotion that you have never ceased to manifest for the good of your country.

Upon arriving on this continent, I experienced the beneficence of the government under the title of sub-engineer, but through I know not what fatality, this assistance was suddenly withdrawn from me at the moment when I least expected it. Forced to await here the general peace as the sole event that can nourish my hopes for the fate of Saint-Domingue, my desire would be, in this interval of unknown duration, to be employed usefully for the United States and advantageously enough for my family's existence. Colonel Senf, who has just left for Philadelphia, was to take charge of delivering this letter to you and to speak to you about me, but his departure was so precipitated that I could not take advantage of it. Permit me, in the name of my father's memory, whom you honored with certain marks of esteem, to lay claim to your kindness and support. And be assured of the zeal with which I shall exert myself to deserve them.

I have the honor to be with profound respect, Mr. President, your very humble and very obedient servant   AUGUSTUS DE GRASSE

RC (DLC); endorsed by TJ as received 24 Apr. and so recorded in SJL.

MON PERE: the writer of the letter above, Alexandre François Auguste de Grasse, was the son of Comte François Joseph Paul de Grasse, the French admiral who in 1781 prevented the British fleet from reaching Cornwallis's army at Yorktown. TJ and the younger De Grasse corresponded briefly in 1788, when the admiral died and his son succeeded him as comte. According to SJL, the letter above was the last correspondence between TJ and De Grasse, who returned to Saint-Domingue by sometime in 1802, served as an officer with a French expeditionary force in the West Indies, was a British prisoner of war, and returned to France in 1804 (*Dictionnaire*, 16:1059-60,

1063-5; Vol. 12:516, 519-20, 521-2). In 1795 Congress had given Auguste de Grasse's sisters $4,000 in recognition of their father's role in the American Revolutionary War. TJ considered that grant to be "unjustifiable largess." Congress added to it, however, agreeing in January 1798 to pay annuities of $400 a year for five years to each of the admiral's four daughters (U.S. Statutes at Large, 6:31; Vol. 28:498, 500n, 613; Vol. 29:7).

LE COLONEL SINF: John (Jean) Christian Senf, who had been the principal military engineer for the defense of Virginia against the British while TJ was governor, lived in South Carolina and was involved in the construction of canals (Washington, *Diaries*, 4:345-6n; Vol. 4:11n).

From Benjamin Hichborn

SIR   Boston 1 april 1801

It is with no Small degree of Reluctance that I consent to tax you with an additional Correspondence, when I know you must already have many more than can be profitable to you—but while I feel conscious of a friendship, as disinterested as any man's on Earth can be; (for it is coupled with no hope of personal benefit) & find myself in a Circle of as respectable Patriots as the Country can boast, all of whom are actuated by the same political Sentiments & feel the same zeal with myself to render your administration briliant & prosperous, I realize a species of duty mixt with the right, to make every Communication which may subserve those important objects—at present every thing wears the appearance of Complacency, & some of your worst Enemies, have pretended to be charmed with your public address on the 4 of March, but this cannot continue long.—I am however, pleased with the necessity they seem to be under of assuming this mask, as it has a strong tendency to confirm the public approbation, which wou'd have been irresistable without it—we have every reason to expect that Mr Gerrey will be Governor this year & that a correspondent Reform will take place in the two branches of the Legislature, indeed were the same Members to be returned, their Conduct woud be very different this Year, from what it was the last, in short we beg to flatter ourselves that the degraded Reputation of New England will begin to revive.—I shoud not have troubled you with this Letter to day, but for a peice of Information I received this Morning (in which I have the fullest relyance) that Mr Higginson is making the most expensive Contracts preparatory to the building of a Navy-yard at Charlestown in this Neighbourhood if these things are done with your Knowledge, this advice will be at least harmless— I shall never trouble you with Recommendations, (much less with Solicitations) for the appointment of any Persons to office any farther than I may feel it my duty to give you the best Information I can obtain, to enable you to form a just estimate of the Character who may offer himself as a Candidate for office. I beleive Mr Higginson himself does not expect long to hold his office as Navy agent in this Department, shoud he be removed, I understand that General Jackson (who held that office before him & was displaced without any motive being assigned) will offer his pretentions to be reappointed I have been long acquainted with the General & beleive him to be as honest a Man as lives, he is certainly very industrious & œconomical, & always attended personally to the minutest objects of his agency he has been uniformly republican, tho' not so ostensibly, as he wished to be, on account of his positions; he has no other pursuits; is not given to speculation & has no Stores of Merchandize to mix in, with public property, & I beleive is perfectly acquainted with the business of that Department—he has a handsom property which is at present locked up in the lands of General Knox, he has no embarrassment of his own, but I beleive is still jointly answerable with Genl: Knox for some of his Debts, how far this may be an objection to him I will not undertake to say, but I beleive Genl: Lincoln is on the same obligation, & I understand that some arrangement has been made with Knox's Creditors, in favor of these Gentleman, I conceive however that in no Case coud the public money be exposed, (shoud any be on hand) as the agents accounts are always kept seperately in the bank— I am requested by my Friend Mr Bowdoin (whose character I presume you are well acquainted with) to mention to you the wishes of Mr William Wetmore, to succeed Mr Davis in the office he held as

the United States attorney in the District of Maine, & which he
has or will give up to enable him to hold a new appointment, which
he prefers, under our State Government—Mr Wetmore is a cotem-
porary of mine & practised law with reputation while I was at the
bar—he has for many years been too much embarrassed with the purchase of Georgan lands & other speculations to aim at any political
Character, perhaps you may remember that Mr Adams nominated
him as one of the Judges of the District Court at the Natchez, but
I beleive he was rejected by the Senate on account of those Embarrassments, which I understand he is now adjusting under the
bankruptlaw—Mr Wetmore has an amiable family & respectable
Connections, but there is not one of them, who woud wish an impro-
proper thing in his favor; General Derbon I beleive is well acquainted
with all the law Characters in that District & can of Course give
the best Information—I hope we shall soon have it in our power to
send you the Compliments of the State—with much esteem & respect
I am yrs   B HICHBORN

RC (DNA: RG 59, LAR); at head of
text in Hichborn's hand: "Genl. Jackson";
endorsed by TJ as received 24 Apr. and
so recorded in SJL with notation "Off." ;
also endorsed by TJ: "Genl. Jackson to be
Navy agent."

For the nomination of WILLIAM
WETMORE as a judge of Mississippi

Territory and the subsequent withdrawal
of his name by President Adams, see Vol.
30:280-1. TJ had already decided to appoint Silas Lee in place of Daniel Davis as
the U.S. district attorney for Maine (JEP,
1:401; Notes on a Cabinet Meeting,
8 Mch. 1801).

From Robert Leslie

SIR   Philada April 1st 1801
   your favour of Feby 8th was duly recieved, I hoped before this
time, to have had the honour of thanking you in person, for you
attention to me.   as I intend visiting the City of Washington,
agreable to your recommendation, before I settle, but have been
detained here longer than I expected, in winding up the old consern,
and have not yet finished, but wish to do it, before I leave the place,
which I expect will be in a few days,
   I should not take the liberty of troubleing you with this, but in
consequence of a paragraph which appeard in the Aurora of yesterday, which I here inclose, in the postscript to my last, I mentioned
that I had made myself acquainted with the machanical operation of

the Mint, but declined entering into perticulars, least it should be considered as offering my service to fill an office, at that time, not vacant. but if it is as stated in the inclosed, and Mr Rittenhouse is not yet actuly appointed; nor promised the office, I hope you will not think me too forward in offering myself as a candidate for the office of director of the Mint, haveing no doubt but if the Abilities of Mr R and myself, are fairly investigated, I shall be found at least as well qualifyed to conduct the business as him, as I am in posession of the whole of Mr Boltons method of Coining, which he communicated to me at his mint, near Birmingham, whare I spent a few weeks not long before I left England. Mr. Bolton also engaged, that if I should be appointed to that office in this Country, and not be able to get the necesary machinery made here, he would send me the whole, or any part of it, that I should write for, at a very moderate price, Mr Boltons method of coining is now acknoledged to be superiour to any in the world, and if you think it would be worth while to adopt it in America, it is now at your service togeather with the best endevers of your very obliged, and Humble Servent

ROBERT LESLIE

RC (DNA: RG 59, LAR); endorsed by TJ as received 16 Apr. and so recorded in SJL with notation "Off." Enclosure not found, but see below.

YOUR FAVOUR OF FEBY 8TH: TJ's letter to Leslie of 8 Feb., recorded in SJL, has not been found. PARAGRAPH WHICH APPEARD IN THE AURORA OF YESTERDAY: "It is reported that *Benjamin Rittenhouse*, of Montgomery county, brother of the late celebrated David Rittenhouse, is to succeed to the direction of the Mint; Mr. Elias Boudinot being about to retire from that situation" (Philadelphia *Aurora*, 31 Mch.).

Matthew Boulton, a prominent manufacturer of Birmingham, set up steam COINING presses at Soho and in 1797 produced a new copper coinage for Great Britain (DNB; Clarence Blair Mitchell, *Mitchell-Boulton Correspondence 1787-1792 Relative to Coinages for South Carolina and the United States* [Princeton, 1931], 1-2).

From "A. B."

SIR   Philadelphia, April 2d. 1801.

A paragraph lately appeared in a Gazette of this City, relative to the resignation or removal of the Director of the Mint; should this be founded in truth, I will take the liberty to remind you of *one* among many deserving Candidates for Office, whose modest, unassuming merit, you will know how to appreciate—I mean Doctor Thomas Tudor Tucker, whose warm attachment to your Person & Politics he has uniformly expressed for many years: his circumstances, I am sorry to say, as well as his merit, claim your friendly patronage.— Should he be so fortunate as to meet your approbation, I have little doubt but your choice will secure you the applause of the virtuous of all parties, & I have still less that his talents, integrity and attention, will richly entitle him to all they can bestow upon him. I have mentioned the Doctor's name for this appointment, because I know it is one which would be particularly pleasing to him, & one which his turn of mind would be found admirably calculated to manage the concerns of to advantage:

I am an obscure person in a humble station, and unknown to you, for which reason I shall not add my real name.—I have been befriended in my humblest station by this good man & know no way of returning his kindness, better than by soliciting unknown to him, that favor which he deserves & which he liberally gave to me.

With sentiments of Esteem I am, [Dr.] Sir, Yr. obt Hble. Servt.

A. B.

RC (DNA: RG 59, LAR); torn; at head of text: "Thomas Jefferson, President of the United States"; endorsed by TJ as received from "Anonymous" on 16 Apr. and so recorded in SJL with notation "Off"; also endorsed by TJ: "Tucker T. T. to be."

From Thomas Cooper

SIR/   No 161 Chesnut Street Philadelphia April 2. 1801

Since my last I find that the office which was lately filled by Genl. Millar, is (if report be true) offered to Genl. Muhlenburgh. I hope that your numerous and important avocations have not driven entirely from your recollection the case of Mr Hamilton of Northumberland. But lest it should be so, I write to you again on the Subject, without making *to you* any apology for reiterating the claims of Justice and Humanity. I have nothing to ask for myself, and I am sure you will excuse those who trouble you on behalf of persons who have some right to attract your attention. nor will the comparative insignificancy of the request be a reason with you for not attending to it, when you are informed that it is very important to the Person who, applies for it, through me, his friend.

Mr Thos. Hamilton of Northumberland was collector of excise under the Inspector of the district. He had ever been attached to me, tho' what is usually called a federalist Genl. Millar deprived him of his paltry office of 300 Dollars a Year, expressly to give it to a rich man who had recommended himself by becoming the voluntary evidence against me. A fortnight before Mr Hamilton's deprivation, Genl. Millar had so far approved of his Conduct as to appoint him also Collector of the Assessed Taxes. Mr Hamilton has Six children. I request of you to write to Genl. Muhlenburgh to reinstate Mr Hamilton, who *I know* was removed from political motives only. Oblige me in this, and believe me with sincere respect

Yr. obedt. Servt   THOMAS COOPER

RC (DLC); addressed: "To the President of the United States at Washington"; franked and postmarked; endorsed by TJ as received 16 Apr. and so recorded in SJL.

MY LAST: Cooper to TJ, 17 Mch.

From Thomas Lomax

DEAR SIR   Port-Tobago Apl. 2. 1801.

This will be delivered to you by my second Son. You will be pleased to accept of my acknowledgment, and Thanks for your favour of the 25th. of Feby, 'tho it did not reach me till that Day four Weeks; happening probably from its direction near Urbanna, instead of Pt. Royal. I accord most heartly with you in indeavouring to harmonise and bring back the deluded part of our Citizens, to their only true Interest and happiness. I call it delusion; because I know many who seemed to have been correct in Principles; but were drawn from them by Artifices, too highly gilt to discover the Poison concealed within, and the highest Varnish was a *Name*. The Man is now dead, and I sincerely wish that Peace, and Quiet may mingle with his Ashes. His Virtues we will imitate, and his Errors, if not buried in the Grave with him, let them be Beacons to avoid the Shoals, and Quicksands on which they ran. There is but one consideration which can induce me chearfully to pay my contribution towards the erection of a Mausoleum, and that is, that it should be an everlasting Sepulchre, for all political Vices & Follies.

Those Men who have been drawn from us by our Enemies, we ought to pity; and avail ourselves of their first Wish to return to the Bosom of their true Parent. A deluded Sinner, I think should be met with a chearful Countenance, soothed, and comforted; for it is sufficient Satisfaction that he has discovered, and returned from his Delusions. But there are some amonst us, whom I must confess,

I beleive to be incorrigable; and therefore sincerely wish, the Eyes of our Eagle may be always sensibly awake, and every Citizen a watchful Centinel—A pure Representative Governmt. I have ever thought to be the most natural, rational, and best adapted to secure to Man his Rights, Liberties, and to make him feel his own Importance, and that he is not a Being barely removed from the Beasts of Burden. Ours I think approaches nearer to it than any other, yet in my Judgmt. the Constitution is in some Important Parts defective. If I stood in need of any Thing to strengthen my belief that the Govt. I have mentioned, was best to promote our happiness, I would look no farther than the Obsticles; which are always thrown in the way to prevent, the beneficial Operations of such a System, by Tyrants and their miscreant Hirelings. They know if it can ever take a proper effect, that it would be the certain Means of discovering to Mankind, how they have been cheated for Ages. There never was yet a Rogue or Theif, who would not do every Thing in his Power to prevent a discovery of his Artifices. Be pleased to excuse the crudeness of these Thoughts, and to accept of my sincere Wishes for your Health and happiness. I am with Real Esteem & Regard

Yor. Friend & Hmbe. Servt.   Tho. Lomax

P.S. The intended Bearer of this, has been prevented from going to Washington.   T. L.

RC (DLC); endorsed by TJ as received   a name: George Washington.
6 May and so recorded in SJL.

From Louis André Pichon

Washington City—12 Germinal an 9 (2 avril 1801)

Le Cit. Pichon prend la liberté de prier Monsieur le Président des Etats Unis de vouloir bien agréer l'expression du regret qu'il a eprouvé d'apprendre le depart de cette ville de Monsieur le Prèsident avant d'avoir pu lui présenter ses devoirs. Le Cit. Pichon, avait cru entendre de la bouche de Monsieur le Secre. d'Etat que Mr. jefferson devait rester jusqu'a vendredi prochain; L'equivoque dont l'expression est Susceptible a trompé le Cit. Pichon qui prie Mr. Le Prèsident des Etats Unis de vouloir bien accepter l'assurance de sa respectueuse consideration.

[525]

EDITORS' TRANSLATION

Washington City—12 Germinal Year 9 (2 April 1801)

Citizen Pichon takes the liberty of begging the president of the United States to be so kind as to accept the expression of regret that he felt on learning of the president's departure from this city before being able to present his respects. Citizen Pichon had thought he understood from what the secretary of state said that Mr. Jefferson was to remain until next Friday; the misunderstanding to which the expression is open deceived Citizen Pichon, who begs the president of the United States to accept the assurance of his respectful esteem.

RC (DLC); at foot of text: "à Monsieur le Prèsident des Etats Unis"; endorsed by TJ as received on 9 Apr. and so recorded in SJL.

Louis André Pichon (1771-1854) presented his credentials on 18 Mch., and the next day TJ signed an exequatur recognizing him as commissary general from France for commercial relations and extending all privileges "as are allowed within the United States to the Consuls of the most favoured nations." When Bonaparte appointed Pichon on 26 Oct. 1800 he also authorized him to act as chargé d'affaires until such time as France might send a minister plenipotentiary to the United States. Pichon was no stranger to America: beginning in 1791 he was a secretary in the French legation to the United States, where he served for five years under three ministers to the U.S., Ternant, Genet, and Fauchet. Returning to France in 1796, he recommended a policy of "clandestine" aggressiveness to force changes in U.S. policy without an open war. He became the assistant head of a division of the Ministry of Foreign Affairs. Sent to the French legation at The Hague, he conveyed to William Vans Murray, with whom he was acquainted, Talleyrand's message that France would welcome new American envoys in the aftermath of the XYZ debacle. In the ensuing negotiation, which resulted in the Convention of 1800, Pichon was the secretary of the French delegation and acted as an intermediary between the two sides. In 1804, Bonaparte abruptly recalled Pichon, who had failed to prevent the marriage of Bonaparte's brother Jerome to Elizabeth Patterson, from his posting in the United States. Jerome Bonaparte and, later, the restored kings of France appointed Pichon to various positions after his return to Europe, and the career diplomat and government official also wrote tracts on public affairs (FC in Lb, DNA: RG 59, Exequaturs, TJ "To all whom it may concern," 19 Mch. 1801, in a clerk's hand including signatures of TJ and Levi Lincoln; Tulard, *Dictionnaire Napoléon*, 1329; *National Intelligencer*, 23, 30 Mch. 1801; Jean B. Duvergier and others, eds., *Collection Complète des Lois, Décrets, Ordonnances, Réglemens, avis du Conseil-d'État*, 108 vols. [Paris, 1834-1908], 12:319; *Gazette Nationale ou le Moniteur Universel*, 7 Brumaire Year 9 [29 Oct. 1800]; Albert H. Bowman, "Pichon, the United States, and Louisiana," *Diplomatic History*, 1 [1977], 257-8; Michel Poniatowski, *Talleyrand et le Directoire, 1796-1800* [Paris, 1982], 19; Michel Poniatowski, *Talleyrand et le Consulat* [Paris, 1986], 27, 461-2, 480, 487-8; Vol. 31:44-50, 55).

From Samuel Smith

SIR/   Washington 2d. April 1801

A Report prevails & is believed that a fracas took place between the sailors of the French ship at Norfolk & the English & American sailors. I presume no Lives were lost, as I have no Account from Norfolk on the subject—

I progress with as much dispatch as possible in putting the Navy in the situation the Law has directed—

My son Louis. Buchanan. Smith will go to Europe in two Weeks. permit me to request that you will send me for him if not too Inconvenient such Letters of Introduction as might be of Utility to him while on his Travels—& believe me to be with the greatest respect—

your Obed Servt.   S. SMITH

RC (DLC); endorsed by TJ as received 9 Apr. and so recorded in SJL.

Norfolk newspapers apparently reported nothing about the 22 Mch. FRACAS between the crew of the French frigate *La Sémillante* and British sailors. Other newspapers printed widely varying accounts with exaggerated initial casualty figures (New York *Daily Advertiser*, 30 Mch.; *National Intelligencer*, 1 Apr.; *Aurora*, 11, 15 Apr.; New York *American Citizen*, 11 Apr. 1801).

THE SITUATION THE LAW HAS DI-RECTED: the reduction of the navy under the Peace Establishment Act.

From Enoch Edwards

DEAR SIR.   Frankford 3 April 1801—

I received your Favor of the 30 March, and am much gratified by the Confidence you have in my Judgment—It is with the greatest Pleasure I shall embrace the opportunity of excuting that Commission or any other for you, that may be in my power—in doing which Mrs. Edwards will chearfully join me. entertaining however as well as Myself an opinion that you overate our Taste—

I shall begin by observing your Caution. to say Nothing about who it is for, that will be necessary probably for some time after the contract. there are many Extra's, & frequently alterations of Orders. in a good Carriage which some Workmen will take Advantage of, if they know who it is for—this however can be left to my Judgment of the Prudence of the Man I employ—for if he is a clever Fellow to inform him a little while after he has engaged may possibly do good—

When I enter into Contract (or get the Terms of the Maker) which shall be done by describing on Paper minutely what I want. I will send it to You—I think I have taken exactly your Idea. It must be a good, a strong, a neat elegant Carriage—without any Finery about it—my utmost shall be done to have it so—& to relieve you from Apprehension of giving me Trouble, I now inform you that it will not put Me to the least possible Inconvenience—but more likely be of Service to Me as my health is the better for some Amusement—

One of the principle Difficulties in starting—will be for the Workman to satisfy Me by his drawings—as to the Proportions—Your Quarter-Light must not be over large, or the bottom part will be heavy in order to let the blinds go down. The Elegance of a Carriage depends much on the handsome Sweep below—too full & square is as bad as too light—there must be a Compromise here that will best please the Eye—I will attend to that—

The caps over the Hubs must be plated. they make them very neat—The drivers Box—as you say,—& the Fashion is to fix them lower than formerly— I should like to know your opinion about Collars, & breastplates. the former is rather more fashionable, the latter shews the horse to more Advantage, & is much cheaper—the best Leather that can possibly be found must be applied to that Use,—even at a price extraordinary—

The Wheels should I think be rather large & 'tho light the Hub ought not to be too small. for the outside half Inch gives more strength to it. than almost all the rest of it.—I should like to know whether you mean for the calicoe lining to be immediately over the Canvass, or over a cloth Cover—the other Trimmings, Color &c. shall be spoken of as the work is going on.—

I think you cannot calculate safely on having it sooner than in all June.—unless I find you a Body already done or nearly so. which I doubt of being able to do—

I will certainly attend & that frequently on the Thing en passant as you say, I know a great deal depends on that as to the Goodness of the Materials—I would not have a Carriage if I could help it, that I did not see before the Inside work was covered, or the Paint laid on,   excuse if you please the length of this Letter—it is done that you may have all my Ideas before you—to give or vary any Order at your Leisure—& thereby save you Trouble—

I heartily rejoice with you, for the Sake of Humanity—& our own Country in particular at appearances in Europe—& hope that the neutral Nations will finally establish what they have so laudably undertaken—and permit me to assure you I rejoice on your Account—as I hope Peace there will render your administration less painful & troblesome to you—and afford the time I well know you are anxious to bestow to heal the Wounds inflicted on the Country already so much indebted to you—with the highest & most perfect Respect I am your

obedt hmble Serv.   ENO. EDWARDS

RC (DLC); endorsed by TJ as received 16 Apr. and so recorded in SJL.

From George Helmbold

HONOURED SIR,   Philadelphia, April 3. 1801

I hope you will not deem me impertinent if I take the liberty of addressing you:—I am editor of a german gazette in this place, and have uniformly supported the republican cause, but have been rather unsuccessful in my undertaking, owing to the rapid innovation of the english upon the german language; which makes it indispensible to proffer an application to you for an appointment to an Office, not of great profit, for I do not soar so high, but one that will enable me to pursue my avocation with more alacrity—

Some few months ago I was in hopes of my not being necessiated to make any application for an Appointment, from the prospect of success I had in view from publishing a full length portrait of yourself; but those prospects have in a great degree be rendered a nullity or illusion from another person setting up one in opposition to me, so that I shall merely clear whatever I may have expended—

From circumstances so complicated and disagreeable I am compelled to make this first application for any reward (for I do not act from sordid motives) and that too without any recommendation; for if I should be unsuccessful I should not be able to combat the sneers of my enemies or neglect of my friends—If your excellency will please to take my case into consideration you will confer a lasting obligation on

Your humble Servant   GEORGE HELMBOLD

RC (DNA: RG 59, LAR); endorsed by TJ as received 16 Apr. and so recorded in SJL with notation "Off."

George Helmbold (d. 1821) was the son of a German immigrant papermaker and an active Republican. Since 1799 he had published the *Neue Philadelphische Correspondenz*, but would garner greater success as publisher from 1807 to 1812 of the comic newspaper *The Tickler*, for which TJ took out a year's subscription in November 1808 (Brigham, *American Newspapers*, 2:926-7, 954-5; *Aurora*, 28 Feb. 1801; David E. E. Sloane, "The Comic Writers of Philadelphia: George Helmbold's *The Tickler*, Joseph C. Neal's 'City Worthies,' and the Beginning of Modern Periodical Humor in America," *Victorian Periodicals Review*, 28 [1995], 186-98; MB, 2:1235).

In September 1800, Helmbold began advertising in the *Aurora* his proposal for a full-length portrait of TJ. The engraving was to measure 14 by 22 inches and cost $6.00. Delivery was expected to take place in five months. On 20 Feb. 1801, however, ANOTHER PERSON, framemaker Augustus Day, announced the publication of a full-length portrait of TJ by engraver Cornelius Tiebout. Also about this time, printer Mathew Carey began to sell a bust portrait of TJ. Helmbold did not publish his full-length portrait until July 1801 (*Aurora*, 8 Sep. 1800, 20, 28 Feb., 2 July 1801; PMHB, 63 [1939], 173-5).

Helmbold wrote TJ again on 7 Apr., requesting appointment to the office of purveyor of public supplies and offering to forward recommendations from Peter Muhlenberg, William Irvine, or others "of respectability" if TJ so desired (RC in DNA: RG 59, LAR, endorsed by TJ as received 16 Apr. and so recorded in SJL with notation "Off").

From Meriwether Lewis

SIR   City of Washington, April 3rd. 1801.

I arrived at this place on the 1st. inst., a few hours only after your departure, Mr. Rapin presented me your very friendly letter of the 31st. ult., and in complyance therewith I have taken up my lodgings in the President's house, where I feel myself much pleased, and extreamly gratifyed with the attention paid, as well by the Steward, as your other domesticks, to all matters which regard my comfort—I must think you extreemly fortunate in the selection you have made of a Steward. I should have reached this place two days earlyer, had not the lameness of my horse, added to the excessive bad state of the roads prevented me. I fear I shall be obliged to relinquish the eydea of visiting Albemarle, this event altogether depends on the return of Lieut. Pinckney from Baltimore, who has been appointed to succeed me as Pay Master to the 1st. Regt. of Infty, to him therefore I shall be obliged to transfer my official documents, before I can perfectly acquit myself of military concerns; his return is uncertain, and I am compelled to wait it. You will find enclosed a note from the Steward—

I am with much esteem Your most Obt. & very Humble Servt.

MERIWETHER LEWIS.

RC (DLC); at foot of text: "Thomas Jefferson. President of the U. States"; endorsed by TJ as a letter of 5 Apr. received on 9 Apr. and so recorded in SJL. Enclosure: the following document.

From Joseph Rapin

washinton Ce 3me avril a 4 heure après Midi

Depuis que votre Exelence est parti Eduard na parut a la Maison qu'une demi heure pour prandre Son diner C'etoit yer. M'onsieur McMan qui est venut voir la Maison Ma dit qu'il avoit veu a sa

Maison Se plaignant que vous aviez donnéz la prefference a un Naigre pluto qua lui pour vous Suivre. Je Lait entendu Moimême Mur-
murer disant qu'il ne porteroit pas un habillement Sanblable a Celui
qu'un Naigre porte en parlant de la Livrée. Le Capitaine Louis peut
me dire vos intention. a ce Sujet vous vous Souviendrez qu'il est très
Matinal et que votre Cabinet Ce trouve arrangé le Mattin a Six heure
Lorsque vous dessendez. Le Capitaine Louis a pour domestique un
jeune Soldat dont il en est tres Content il me Serat tres util pour
Laver les fenetres jai dessendu les Rideaux qui ont Besoint detre
Blanchi; Cinq appartement ont Besoint de Letre aussi Les platreurs
qui doivent aller travaillier a Monti Celo vont Les Blanchir a 5 do.
chaque chambre.

EDITORS' TRANSLATION

Washington this 3d of April at 4 in the afternoon
Since Your Excellency left, Edward has appeared at the house for only one
half hour to eat his dinner. That was yesterday. Mr. McMunn, who came to
see the house, told me that he had seen him at his house, complaining that
you had given the preference to a Negro rather than to him to accompany
you. I myself heard him murmuring that he would not wear similar clothing
to what a Negro wears, while speaking of the livery. Captain Lewis can tell
me your intention. On that subject you will remember that he is an early riser
and that your office is all in order at six o'clock when you come downstairs.
Captain Lewis has a young soldier for a servant, with whom he is very
pleased. He will be very useful to me for washing the windows. I took down
the curtains that need washing; five suites also need it. The plasterers who
are going to work at Monticello will whitewash them at 5 dollars for each
room.

RC (MHi); endorsed by TJ as a letter
from Rapin received 9 Apr. and so
recorded in SJL. Enclosed in Meriwether
Lewis to TJ, 3 Apr. 1801.

When Joseph Rapin and his wife began
working at the President's House on
18 Mch., TJ recorded the husband's function as "steward" and the wife's as "femme
de charge" (housekeeper). They agreed to
receive 100 guineas ($350, at the rate of 6
Virginia shillings per dollar) as annual
pay for the two of them together. By mid-
June, however, the couple decided to give
up their positions at the President's House

and return to Philadelphia. Rapin remained as steward until September when
his successor, Étienne Lemaire, could assume his responsibilities (MB, 2:1035,
1045-8, 1053-4; Stafford, *Philadelphia Directory, for 1800*, 68; Philippe de Létombe
to TJ, 16 June, 5 Aug. 1801; John Barnes
to TJ, 7 Sep. 1801).

EDUARD: Edward Maher, a member of
the domestic staff of the President's House
since 12 Mch. Lemaire later referred to
Maher's position as that of a porter (MB,
2:1035; Lemaire to TJ, 10 May 1802).

UN NAIGRE: John Freeman (see TJ to
Charles Little, 31 Mch.).

From "A Vermont Republican"

Sir,   April 3d. 1801.

A man, who inhaled with his first breath the genuine spirit of republicanism, and who never abandoned or dissembled his principles in the darkest period of the late administration, a man who has long been a most zealous admirer of the name and character of the illustrious citizen who penned the immortal declaration of his country's independence; whose predictions have been fulfilled, and whose most ardent wishes have been realised, in the election of the present President of the United States, solicits the privelege of addressing that illustrious magistrate. No personal considerations could have induced him to the measure; but it is consonant with the republican simplicity which all unprejudiced men attach to the character of Mr. Jefferson, to suppose that he will listen to decent representations, on subjects which involve the public concerns, even from obscure men, unconnected with the administration, and undignified by office. As the writer of this will ever conceal his name from the great man whom he addresses, he cannot accuse himself of a too great share of vanity, when he assures the President, that in knowledge of the political concerns of the State of Vermont, the state of the political opinions of her citizens, and the characters of all her most distinguished men, he yields to very few men in the State.

The day, Sir, on which your administration commenced, was anticipated, by the writer of this Letter, with a degree of pleasure which he never experienced, till the voice of the majority of your fellow citizens unequivocally designated you as "the safe depository of their rights." Regret would have mingled itself with the sublime satisfaction which he derived from an event so glorious for his country, if he could have been made to believe that Mr. Jefferson would suffer men to continue in office under him, or would appoint men to office, whose political sentiments are known to be hostile to the fundamental principles of our constitution, and who have laboured with infernal industry for years to poison the minds of the people, and convince them, that their best and greatest fellow citizen is an anarchist and an atheist. That such would be the result of your accession to the Presidency, he never believed. His predictions and wishes to the contrary were realised in the appointment of able and virtuous republicans to fill the highest vacant offices, on the fifth of March and in the subsequent removal from subordinate stations, of men who deserved any thing rather than the confidence of the present President. The appointments to fill the vacancies occasioned by those removals, in every State but Vermont, according to the writers best information, have been made with great judgment. But permit me, Sir, with the highest deference to observe, that the unequivocal and universal voice of all informed and unprejudiced men, of all parties, within this State, denies to Mr. Fay and Mr. Willard, the possession of those talents and that respectability of character, which ought to be attached to those offices in which they are destined to serve.

The people of Vermont, Sir, at least the majority of them, repose the highest confidence in your abilities and integrity; but in the instance to which I have presumed to invite your attention, they declare unanimously that you have been unfortunately influenced. The writer, Sir, is personally a friend to Mr. Fay, and while he esteems him as an amiable man, he is constrained to mingle his voice with that of all his fellow citizens, who declare that gentleman utterly incompetent to discharge the duties of his office with dignity, or even with decency. Possessing very little genius, and still less application to legal studies, he has frequently appeared ridiculous as a lawyer, even in the county court of Bennington. There exists, Sir, in Vermont, a very artful and powerful party who are devoted to aristocracy; and nothing could have been so inauspicious to the best of causes, nothing could have so much contributed to perpetuate the depression of the republican side in this quarter, as the appointments alluded to. They furnish a theme of satire and reproach against the President, which occasions his friends the keenest pain and regret.

He, Sir, who has now the honour to address you, is also a warm friend to Mr. Lyon, to whose influence many attribute those appointments. No man has been more indignant at the unjust and cruel treatment which that unwavering republican received from the late Attorney and Marshal. But, if it be true that Mr. Lyon has had influence with the present Administration, either directly or indirectly, it is equally true that he has, I would hope unintentionally, postponed the public good and the reputation of the administration, to his personal attachments.

Permit the writer of this address, Sir, to apologize for having arrested your attention for a moment. Nothing but a strong, an irresistible sense of duty; of duty to his country and her first magistrate, could have induced him to it. He has no views of a personal nature, for he never anticipated or solicited any personal advantages from the change of administration. "For his country he rejoices at the beams of peace," at the prospect of the extinguishment of the "divisions which have been artificially excited," and at the fresh lustre of the Sun of Liberty, emerging from the dark cloud by which its rays have been transiently obscured. Devoted, not less from disposition and habit, than by his humble fortune, to literary and professional pursuits, he finds consolations in the shade of retirement, which he is not anxious to exchange for public honours. As he has taken upon himself, however, a task which no one ought to assume, who does not possess some influence in society, he begs leave to observe that he has not been, at all times, unhonoured by the suffrages of a very large and respectable portion of his fellow citizens.

With the highest and most unqualified respect [for your] person and character, I have the honour to be, Sir, Your most obedient humble Servant   A VERMONT REPUBLICAN.

RC (DNA: RG 59, LAR); words in brackets obscured by seal; addressed: "Thomas Jefferson Esquire, President of the United States Washington"; franked; postmarked Washington, 12 Apr.; endorsed by TJ as received from "Anon." on 24 Apr. and so recorded in SJL; also endorsed by TJ: "Fay Willard."

The writer took the quotations on the SAFE DEPOSITORY of rights and "divisions which have been artificially excited," near the close of the letter, from TJ to John Vanmetre, 4 Sep. 1800, a letter published in Republican newspapers throughout the United States (see Vanmetre to TJ, 28 Feb. 1801).

LATE ATTORNEY AND MARSHAL: Amos Marsh and Jabez G. Fitch (JEP, 1:403).

From Matthew Lyon

SIR—   Washington April 4th. 1801

You'll doubtless be surprised to see a letter from me dated at this place and at this time. An unforeseen accidental bussness led me to Philadelphia and another peice of bussness brought me this far out of my road from there to N Geneva—

The purport of this is to request that Our Minister at the Court of London be directed to pay the necessary attention to the case of General Ira Allen and his claims for Justice there, his case is pending before the Lords of Appeal respecting some arms he had fairly purchased in France and was bringing to this Country but taken by a British man of War & without even a pretext condemned in the lower Court. Had Mr Adams & his Secretary done half they promised me in May 1797 I should have had no occasion to troubled you at this time, Mr Adams promised me that Mr Pickering should write & they both Assured me that he had writen in such a manner to Mr King that General Allens bussness should be made easy to him, it now appears from the copy of them instructions that they were dictated by the same submissive policy which in one respect guided the late Administration and that they were calculated to do more harm than good. The Aspect of Affairs now in Europe seams favorable to any reasonable demands made by this Country on Britain, which will be increased on their knowledge that the Affairs of this Country are in the hands of those who are by no means disposed to crouch to them, All this tends to cherish a hope that an application on the part of this Government in behalf of General Allen will be effecatious; and I trust that he will meet with that Countenance from the Goverment which an Important and Patriotic Citizen of this Country deserves

I have had the pleasure of seeing the smile of Approbation on every republican countenance I saw in Philadelphia, they are pleased much both with the moderation and decission of the new Administration, they Hope much also, the Custom house Officers are an Eye sore to them, it has been a great source of Corruption, it has been and still is a terror to the midling merchants who are in secret pleased with the change & wish to shew themselves when they dare; without a change in the Custom house the Republicans say they can not be sure of the Elections. The late appointment of Marshal has undoubtedly given them fresh Joy, the News had not arrived when I left there Major Smith however expected it, and the Republicans with whom I conversed hoped for it, & wished it most anxiously, he is really a Worthy Meritorious capable & respectable man—

The papers on both sides make more of the Opposition much more than the people do—I mixed more than ever with the Aristocrats they seem cool & conciliateing, I rode on Monday last to Lancaster in the Stage with Mr Yates chief Justice of Pensilvania he is strongly federal however he approved of all that had been done by the new Administration: speaking of Mr Galatin he said despised all that had been said in the papers against him; that he was so highly esteemed for his tallents that every honest man of either party, looked out on the change to see him at the head of the Treasury department,

Mr Tenche Coxe rode with us, I was happy to find him disposed to be patient in his present situation until things get in a more setled state, indeed I ventured to commend him for that patience and to concur with him in opinion that an immediate appointment given to him would be very unpopular

I have lately received a letter from Mr Southwick of Albany in which he expresses much gratitude for the favor intended him, with a hope that if he should obtain he shall be able to fulfill the duties with honour to himself and Justice to his Country, this is not an answer to the letter in which I informed him agreably to your permission that his appointment was agreed upon—

Within a few days I shall take another Start for the Western waters I expect to be detained a week or two at N Geneva & then proceed to Cumberland river, wherever I shall be it will always give me pleasure to hear of your welfare, and the popularity of your Administration will be a constant source of Satisfaction to your very hble Servt

M LYON

RC (DLC); at foot of text: "The President of the United States"; endorsed by TJ as received 16 Apr. and so recorded in SJL.

In 1796 IRA ALLEN, Vermont land speculator, entrepreneur, and youngest brother of Ethan Allen, purchased arms in France, ostensibly for the Vermont militia. On Allen's return voyage in the ship *Olive Branch*, the British captured the vessel and confiscated the arms. Allen sought the intervention of Rufus King, U.S. MINISTER AT THE COURT OF LONDON, in late 1796. King, however, informed Secretary of State Pickering that rumors indicated that the muskets and cannon carried by Allen were destined for a French project in Canada, not for the state militia. PICKERING SHOULD WRITE: in 1797 Congressman Lyon and the senators from Vermont visited the secretary of state and brought evidence favorable to Allen's claims. On 15 June, Pickering wrote King: "Upon the whole, it is the real wish of the Executive of the U. States that the arms and military stores in question may be restored to General Allen, to be brought to the U. States" (ANB, 1:330-1; King, *Life*, 2:123-4, 187-8; James B. Wilbur, *Ira Allen: Founder of Vermont, 1751-1814*, 2 vols. [Boston, 1928], 2:119-20). For an account of Allen's case, see J. Kevin Graffagnino, "'Twenty Thousand Muskets!!!': Ira Allen and the Olive Branch Affair, 1796-1800," WMQ, 3d ser., 48 (1991), 409-31.

In a short letter to TJ written from Washington on this date, Allen noted that he had twice applied to Levi Lincoln regarding his case. Lincoln replied that he needed instructions from the president before he could do anything. Arguing that his misfortunes in Europe were related to the "American War, and his continued attachment to the Liberties of the United States," Allen trusted that TJ would act in his favor and that "proper Instructions" would be immediately forwarded to King in London (Tr in VtBW; at foot of text: "The President of the United States"; recorded in SJL as received 24 Apr.). Allen, abroad since 1795, had arrived in Philadelphia on 2 Jan. 1801. Before 9 Mch. he called on TJ, who reportedly requested Allen's opinion on conditions in Europe. On 14 Apr., Allen wrote King and enclosed a letter written by Lincoln on his behalf dated 8 Apr. (John J. Duffy and others, eds., *Ethan Allen and His Kin: Correspondence, 1772-1819*, 2 vols. [Hanover, N.H., 1998], 2:695-6, 699; Wilbur, *Ira Allen*, 2:309, 313-14). For two of Allen's pamphlets in which he presented his case to the public, see Sowerby, Nos. 3306 and 3538. A previous letter from Allen to TJ of 4 Nov. 1797, recorded in SJL as received 21 Feb. 1798 from London, has not been found.

MR YATES CHIEF JUSTICE: Jasper Yeates was an associate justice of the Pennsylvania Supreme Court (*Martin's Bench and Bar*, 23).

From Oliver Pollock

Sir   Philada. 4th. April 1801.

however unwilling to add to the troubles you experience from numerous Applications to office, Yet compeled as I am by my present unfortunate situation I must throw my self upon your indulgence & Rely on the benevolence of your disposition, not only to excuse this intrusion but to listen favourably to my Request. I had some years since retired to a verrey fine estate in the country, there expecting to enjoy in ease & happiness the fruits of former industry— the duty which a parent owes to his offspring, brought me to this city, in Order to set off & promote the interest of my eldest son & in an evil hour, I was in this pursuit led into an intimacy with the late John Swanwick Esquire, who prevailed on me to join him in bonds to the custom House, for duties arrising to the Goverment upon importations, in which I had no concern or interest, I then had no doubt of his ability or inclination to discharge his bonds as they became due, and my only motive for joining him in them, was, to afford the facility he wanted & asked for. He died insolvent & my estate was Seized, Sold & sacrificed to pay a debt of his contracting to the U.S. My estate called Silver Springs in Cumberland County Pensya. was sold for $33,000—Respecting the seizure & sale of this estate I corresponded with the late Secrty. & present Comptroller of the Treasury, who thought themselves from Official considerations bound to pursue the measures of severity, 'tho I had reason to believe that Other motives than that of Official duty Opperated on the minds of those Gentlemen,—I was Opposed to them in politics, and had they submitted the Sale to my management it would have produced from 60 to $70,000—In like manner an estate of mine in this city was sold for $6,700 which under my own direction would have brought 9 to $10,000—I give this detail to shew the cause of my looking for Office at a time of life when I might have indulged in ease & independance, in consequence of former exertions; exertions which for a long time was intented to promote the interest of the U.S. & of suffering the loss of a large & valuable property to pay the Goverment, a debt due to it by an other person, I ground some degree of pretension to an employment that may give bread to a distressd family—some part of the circumstance above alluded to have fallen within your knowledge, and the experrience I had of your Official conduct in another station not only Attached me to your person & character but gives more vigour to my hopes than I should otherwise indulge. I am too far advanced in life to begin the world in a commercial line, especially without money & under circumstances of a ruined credit by Marshalls & sheriffs advertizements & sales; an Office is therefore become most desireable, what Office I cannot say but such as my ability is competent to execute, shall be attended to, to the honor interest & content of the Goverment, as my desire is by faithfull & honest services to earn the emolument—It would suit me best to be fixed in this City, but I am willing to serve in any seaport Town in the U.S., where my services can be most usefull & I beg you when a suitable vaccancy occurs to think of a friend that venerate your character & classes himself amongst your most ardent wellwishers.

Altho my fortunes are so greatly injured yet thank God there was under all the disadvantages of the sales sufficient to pay my debts, so that I shall be free from incumbrances and I have friends that will become security in case of an appointment to any Office in which security is required for faithfull performance.

Should you incline to favour my request and wish for further information on the subject, I beg leave to referr you to the Governor of this State, Genl. Wm. Irwin of Cumberland Pensya. & Genl. Wilkison who has been often at New Orleans where probably he may have heard of my exertions with that Goverment in favour of this country during the contest with Great Britain.

Pardon the length of this letter and permit me to profess the sincerity with which I have the honor to be Dear sir

Your Most faithfull & Obedient servant   OLR. POLLOCK

RC (DNA: RG 59, LAR); at foot of text: "Thomas Jefferson President of the United States"; endorsed by TJ as received 16 Apr. and so recorded in SJL with notation "Off."

One of Philadelphia's wealthiest merchants during the early 1790s, JOHN SWANWICK, an urban Republican, won election to Congress in 1794 and 1796. He died INSOLVENT on 31 July 1798, one of the earliest victims of the yellow fever outbreak in Philadelphia that year (ANB; Philadelphia *Aurora*, 2, 3 Aug. 1798).

FORMER EXERTIONS: Pollock had served as a commercial agent at New Orleans obtaining supplies for Virginia and the Continental Congress during the Revolution and in Cuba from 1783 to 1785. He still had outstanding claims against Virginia and the United States in 1801, which would not be settled until the next decade (ANB; Madison, *Papers, Sec. of State Ser.*, 2:192-3). Pollock last wrote TJ in 1792, seeking aid to recover debts owed him in Cuba (see Vol. 23:162-3).

From Tench Coxe

Sir   Lancaster Pa. April 5th. 1801

Public Business having called me to Philada. on the 10th. of March, I did not receive your favor of the 11th. Feby till the 31st. ultimo. The book accompanied it. It was my intention that the papers N. 1. to 8 should have remained in your library, as I have another copy of the Book, and the question of the commencement of violations of neutral trade is very important. The rise and progress of that business was a subject to which I had constantly attended; and I found the facts, when offered to men of opinions opposite to my own, often produced impression. I have therefore sent the Book to Mr. Madison and asked him to retain it. Every thing that will refresh his memory of events before his retirement, will be useful.

It is only in consequence of the request of the gentleman with whom I was bred to Business, that I take the liberty to mention his name and character, & his son in law to you. The former, Moore Furman Esquire, is a native & again a resident of New Jersey. He was many years a partner of my father in trade at Philada., but has since returned to Trenton. He is a man of Business, and excellent private Character, a good merchant in the foreign & domestic line, quick in correspondence and accounts, a sincere and steady whig & republican from 1775 to this hour. He was a quarter Master in Jersey under Genl. Greene, has been, many years since, Sherriff of Hunterdon and since the War, Mayor of Trenton.

His Son in Law Col. Peter Hunt is of the same principles and lives in the Lamberton part of Trenton. I believe the Jersey Legislature deprived them both of offices on that account.

I am very apprehensive from your last letter (of 26 Mar) to the Governor, that he has repeated his notice of me to you. I do assure, Sir, that it was without my request or knowledge, and much against my wishes. I have never taken a measure to procure an application to you, but in the case of Mr. Dawson. My views then were only to facilitate your communications thro a gentleman, that venerates you and regards me as a friend. I cannot expect to escape those violent jealousies, which energy and zeal excite among my own party; and which have shewn themselves in force, but in vain, in our state government. I thought it prudent therefore to provide an unexceptionable channel thro which I might be afforded an opportunity of explanation. The Governors distance from you rendered him unsuitable, otherwise I believe I should have found him a partial friend.

From his particular station, I thought it improper to trouble him.—
With perfect respect, I have the honor to be, Sir,

yr. mo. obdt & hble Servt TENCH COXE

RC (DNA: RG 59, LAR), at foot of text: "Mr. Jefferson"; endorsed by TJ as received 24 Apr. and so recorded in SJL with notation "Off."; also endorsed by TJ "Furman Moore" and "Hunt Peter."

BOOK: *The American Museum: or, Annual Register of Fugitive Pieces, Ancient and Modern. For the Year 1798*, published in Philadelphia in 1799 (see Sowerby, No. 4900).

PARTNER OF MY FATHER: in May 1776 Tench Coxe became an equal partner in the firm and it became Coxe, Furman, & Coxe. The partnership dissolved in 1780. PETER HUNT married Moore Furman's daughter Maria in 1798. In 1804 he was appointed adjutant general of New Jersey (*The Letters of Moore Furman Deputy Quarter-Master General of New Jersey in the Revolution* [New York, 1912], viii, 107; Cooke, *Coxe*, 18, 52).

From Samuel Hanson

SIR, George-Town, April 6th., 1801.

It would have been difficult, some weeks ago, to persuade myself that any motives, however imperious, could urge a modest Man—such as I feel myself to be—to tax your liberality in the manner that I have done. On sight of my signature, you will have reason to complain that a temporary retreat from the cares of Government has failed to shelter you from the persecution of my Addresses. The Apology that I am about to make for my new transgression is, perhaps, of all others, the worst that could be offered; namely, your uniform indulgence to me, and, particularly, your kindness at my last Interview. Considerations, such as these, should prompt me to consult your repose, rather than to disturb it. But, Sir, it is the fate of Generosity to encourage, instead of repressing, additional claims to favour.

Your voluntary introduction of the subject in which the colour of my temporal fate is involved, releases me from the silence which I had imposed upon myself. It is to cherish, and, at the same time, to justify your good intentions in my favour that I am tempted once more to intrude upon your privacy, in order to state that my Friend, J. T. Mason—who was never yet, *knowingly*, the friend of any dishonest Man—waited on you, the day before your departure, for the sole purpose of urging my Claims to your favour. In this he was prevented by the presence of others. It is to apprise you of this Circumstance, so reputable to me, that I have taken the liberty now to address you. My pretensions would be very defective indeed, were they to be unsupported by the advocation of that virtuous and enlightened Man.

I have already taken the liberty to state to you the irksomeness of my present employment; the uncertainty of the tenure by which it is held, and the Causes of that uncertainty: One of which is the Hostility of my Employers; the other, such as is not proper to be repeated on paper. Not to dwell on the confinement, little short of that of a Gaol, rigorously expected, if not exacted, from me, think of the state of a Man, addicted to Letters, doomed for life to the insipid occupation of writing his name, or of passing through his fingers Slips of Paper, uninteresting to every Human Being except the real Owner; Employments that neither require, nor permit, the Exercise of the mind! This, however, might be borne. But what shall I say of my Sufferings arising from another Source? Possessing, perhaps, too keen a sensibility, if possible, on that score, who can describe the situation of an honest man exposed, *ex officio*, to be a daily, yet involuntary, witness, of improprieties, of Knaveries, which [he must] neither censure nor reveal? "*A witness*", did I say? I am more. In these inequitous scenes I am compelled to be an Agent, if not an Accessary.

Good Sir, I have done. Excuse this, which Shall be my last offence. when I reflect on the date of the Acquaintance with which you have honoured me, I am struck with my temerity. I am impelled to it, contrary to the natural timidity of my temper, by a Species of despair; a despair produced by the helpless situation of a large family. This last plea for forgiveness will not, I trust, be urged in vain. Sir, you, too, are a *Father*!

With sentiments of perfect respect and Esteem, I remain Sir Your much-obliged Servt   S HANSON of Saml

P.S. Enclosed is a voucher for my integrity, the more weighty, as being, in a manner, obtained from my Enemies. These were all the Tories, both Foreign & Native, of that period; whom, by resisting certain usurpations, I had grievously offended. I have only to add that my invitation was declined—and *that* from tenderness to themselves, not to me.

RC (DNA: RG 59, LAR); damaged; addressed: "The President of The United States Monticello"; endorsed by TJ as received 17 Apr. and so recorded in SJL with notation "Off." Enclosure: see below.

Hanson ENCLOSED the printed text of a 6 Nov. 1793 letter he had placed in the classified section of an unidentified newspaper that year. In it he acknowledged the civility of seven-eighths of the inhabitants of Alexandria during his nine-year residence. In an effort to leave town with his reputation and good name intact, he asked forgiveness for having offended any inhabitants and extended an INVITATION to those with any charges against him to print them in the next issue of the newspaper and to present any outstanding claims against him by 14 Nov. 1793 (same).

From George Jefferson

Dear Sir   Richmond 6th April 1801

Your favor of the 27th. ultimo came duly to hand. The current Cash price of Tobacco is now from 35/. to 36/.— 42/. has however been given where it has been opened and approved of; which price I was to day offered for yours in that way—and suppose the person would give it on my receiving an answer from you. I do not think it probable though that you will approve of such a plan, as it operates very disadvantageously, where any is rejected—no person wishing to purchase under such circumstances, except at a very reduced price— and it may be observed too that it very frequently is refused, tho' of good quality, the purchaser wanting only a particular kind, as is the case in the present instance.   Excepting this, the best offer I have had is 7$: payable in 4 months, which I am of opinion it would be advisable to take; for as the European markets do not in my opinion justify such a price at present, I should certainly be for securing this price in preference to taking the chance of a rise; which nothing I think can occasion, except it is the planters holding up their crops— & to that I should not like to trust much longer.   I am surprised at the small difference there is just now between the price in George Town and in this place—I suppose however it may be accounted for in some degree by the purchasers in G:T. intending it for the French markets, where I have been informed the most inferior quality commands as good a price as the best James River.

Tobacco I understand is even dull in N. York at $6\frac{1}{2}$.$:—in Philadelphia it is 7 & $7\frac{1}{2}$.$:—but I am told that little, if any, is bought by the shippers—the manufacturers being the only purchasers.

Should you conclude to take the price now offered at 4 months you will be pleased to say so by return of the post, as the persons who make the offer bind themselves to take it if we can then decide.

I shall leave home in a day or two and be absent for some weeks, but this business, as well as Mr. Eppes's drafts will in the mean time be attended to.

The syrup of punch was forwarded some days ago by Hendersons boat.

I am Dear Sir Your Very humble servt.   Geo. Jefferson

RC (MHi); at foot of text: "Thos. Jefferson esqr."; endorsed by TJ as received 15 Apr. and so recorded in SJL.

From Michael Leib

Sir Philadelphia April 6th 1801

Presuming that the inspector of the Revenue for this district will be removed, permit me to express a wish, that the vacancy may be supplied by my brother John L. Leib

My friend General Muhlenberg has authorised me to say, that it would be highly gratifying to him, that my brother should be placed in this situation. The relation subsisting between the Supervisor & inspectors renders it desireable to him, that persons in whom he has confidence should fill the offices subordinate to the one which he is to occupy, & he has been kind enough to assure me, that he prefers my brother to any one who has been named for this district

It is with considerable reluctance, Sir, that I approach you in this way; but you will pardon me, when you consider, that I have presumed upon your indulgence at the instance of a brother, & one too who has suffered in his professional pursuits on account of his zeal for our cause—

With Sentiments of sincere respect I am, Sir, Your obedient Servant

M Leib

RC (DNA: RG 59, LAR); at foot of text: "Thomas Jefferson Esqr. President of the United States"; endorsed by TJ as received 16 Apr. and so recorded in SJL with notation "Off."

Michael Leib (1760-1822), son of a German immigrant, studied medicine with Benjamin Rush, received a commission as a surgeon in the Philadelphia militia in 1780, and after the Revolution became one of the leading physicians in the city. He began his transition to politics in 1793 as a founding member and secretary of the German Republican Society in Philadelphia and as an active member of the Democratic Society of Pennsylvania.

An early advocate of Jeffersonian principles, he served in Congress from 1799 to 1806 and in the Senate from 1809 to 1814. In the factionalism that emerged in Republican politics in Pennsylvania after the election of 1800, Leib joined with William Duane against Governor McKean and Tench Coxe. He later split with Gallatin and the Madison administration (*Biog. Dir. Cong.*; ANB).

JOHN L. LEIB was admitted to the Philadelphia bar in 1795 (*Martin's Bench and Bar*, 286). The four revenue inspectors in Pennsylvania were not removed in 1801 (JEP, 1:400-4; ASP, *Miscellaneous*, 1:282).

From James Monroe

Richmond April 6. 1801

Jas. Monroe is happy to inform Mr. Jefferson that Joseph Scott the person lately appointed Marshall for this district, is the brother of Genl. Scott of Kentuckey. He was an officer through the revolutionary war, dangerously wounded in one of its battles by which he lost the use of one of his arms, is respectable for his talents, of fair and upright character, and sound in his political principles. He is also indigent in his circumstances. It was perhaps impossible to find another man in the state who had so many and such high pretentions to the office, who had so few enemies among those who were opposed to him, and whose appointment wod. give such general satisfaction to the community at large.

RC (DLC); "April" in dateline interlined by Monroe in place of "March"; endorsed by TJ as received 15 Apr. and so recorded in SJL.

From John Page

My Dear Sir   Rosewell April the 6th. 1801

I have to acknowledge the Receipt of your highly flattering & friendly Letter, & to return as I do my best Thanks for it.

That you should have proposed to hold me up as worthy of being the Successor of Rittenhouse in the Office of Director of the Mint, is to my Feelings in my present Situation highly gratifying, & to be informed of this in the manner I was, has afforded me much Consolation. This Circumstance has in a great Measure removed those painful Sensations I was exposed to, whenever I reflected on the Application I made.

Without Flattery I can assure you that your Creed was viewed by all, both Whigs & Tories in these parts, as excellent, & satisfactory; & that I look upon your Address as an admirable Compendium of Republican Principles, & a striking Confutation of the Objections to free elective Governments: & that I view it as a well timed, delicate Advance towards a Conciliation of Parties, which must have a very happy Effect. The desperado leaders however can never be reconciled — they have so long & so grievously injured their opponents that they can never forgive them.   Your Ideas respecting Removal from Office are generous, consistent with the System you have resolved to pursue, & ought to go far in the benevolent & patriotic work of Conciliation. Heaven grant that it may!

Should you ever have leisure to favor me with another Letter, send it directed to me at York Town; or near York, & I shall receive it a week sooner than by a Mail to Gloucester Court House. That I may not intrude too much on your pretious Time, I will conclude, wishing you the Accomplishment of your Wishes, & the Enjoyment of every Blessing, & assuring you that I am sincerely yours

                                                                    John Page

RC (DLC); endorsed by TJ as received 24 Apr. and so recorded in SJL with notation "Off." YOUR HIGHLY FLATTERING & FRIENDLY LETTER: TJ to Page, 23 Mch.

From Samuel Smith

SIR/ Baltimore 6 April 1801

The Inclosed from Mr Dawson I have this Instant received—The fracas at Norfolk commenced with some English & French Sailors & terminated with some very severe broken heads but no lives lost—

Previous to my leaving this City (on Sunday) I had ordered all the ships (for sale) that were in Port to be Sold without delay—I directed two 44 gun ships one of 32 guns & a Schooner to be got ready for Sea & to rendezvous at Hampton Road on the 1: May—I fear [the] Philadelphia cannot be quite so soon prepared—[I] have dismissed a few of the Masters Commandant, that the Law does not Contemplate Retaining—

I have ordered the General Green from New Port to the Eastern Branch—I wish she may get [. . .] the Lieutenant, who had been ordered to fathom the Potomack, reports that at low Water there is 19 feet [at] Maryland Point—at Muttawiming but 18 feet & [. . .] the Drain or Channel at the Mouth of the E. Branch be only 18 feet at low tides $\frac{1}{2}$ of the Width of a large ship—Mr. Lear (who was present) said he had seen a ship aground Head & Stern & the Channel under her Center—I directed the Lieut. & Pilot to return & make an Accurate survey of the length of the Drain & its Breadth—If their Report should be true, It will operate against Compleating the Navy yard—indeed I fear that all operations relative to ships will progress slowly at Washington—

I returned here for a few days—but find it impossible for me to leave my own affairs before next Sunday—In this Manner I shall frequently be compelled to act or Injure my private affairs too much Such Inattention will not Comport with the Navy Department—I therefore again take leave to represent the necessity of fixing on some Character to fill the place—It never Can answer to Conduct it for longer than five or six weeks in this Manner—I am certain that a gentleman of Business would soon very soon make himself Competent[1]—

Against the 15 May all the ships for sale may be disposed of—the seven intended to be laid up may be placed in a state of security, and the Squadron under Truxtun nearly ready for sea—At which time I trust my services may be dispensed with

And am Sir with the greatest Respect your Obedt Servt.

S. SMITH

Mr. Dent has accepted.

RC (DLC); frayed at margin; addressed: "Thomas Jefferson Esqr. President of the United States Monticello"; franked; postmarked 7 Apr.; endorsed by TJ as received 16 Apr. and so recorded in SJL. Enclosure: possibly Dawson to TJ, 31 Mch.

On 1 Apr., acting under directions from the president, Smith began issuing orders to READY FOR SEA a naval squadron consisting of the frigates *President, Philadelphia,* and *Essex* and the schooner *Enterprize* for a 12-month cruise under the command of Thomas Truxtun. The vessels were to carry full complements of sailors and marines and rendezvous at Hampton Roads on 1 May, with the intention of sailing on 10 May (NDBW, 1:425-7; Abishai Thomas to William Burrows, 1 Apr. 1801, in DNA: RG 45, MLS).

THE LIEUTENANT: on 10 Mch. 1801 Benjamin Stoddert and Thomas Truxtun wrote Lieutenant Josias M. Speake, directing him to sound the channel of the Potomac River and ascertain its width and depth from the Eastern Branch (Anacostia River) to Maryland Point, then below until reaching a point where the depth of the remaining channel was known to be at least five fathoms at low water to the mouth of the river (FC in Lb in DNA: RG 45, LSO).

MUTTAWIMING: Mattawoman Creek.

MR. DENT: Maryland Congressman George Dent accepted the post of marshal for the district of Potomac, but soon after resigned the position (Levi Lincoln to TJ, 9 Apr.; TJ to Francis Peyton, 24 May).

[1] Smith here heavily canceled four lines of text.

From Alexander White

SIR,   Washington 6th April 1801.

Agreeably to a Resolution of the Board of Commissioners of the 30th. Ulto, I went to Annapolis on Thursday last. The Governor was in Virginia and not expected to return soon. Mr. Shoaff, one of the Council was likewise absent, but expected on friday Evening. I waited on the other Members of the Council, and procured a meeting on Saturday when all the Members in the City attended, but Mr. Shoaff had not arrived. I presented to them the Commissioners' letter (of which a Copy is enclosed) and conversed fully on the Subject of my Mission, in presence of the Agent and Auditor of the State, who had been notified to attend. It appeared that the State had found it necessary to borrow thirty thousand Dollars to answer the current expenses of the last Year, and that without the Interest of the Money lent to the City, their funds were inadequate to the Expenses of the present Year, even though they should not pay any part of the Money borrowed—Under these Circumstances the Council were against granting any Indulgence with respect to the payment of that Interest

I also presented a note (of which a Copy is enclosed). The Council wished not to act on the subject of that Note till Mr Shoaff should be present, as some legal Difficulties were suggested. I did not think it necessary to attend their Deliberations, having said all that appeared proper for me to say—the result I expect to receive by post tomorrow.

I am, with sentiments of the highest respect, Sir, Yr mo: Obt Servt.

ALEX WHITE

RC (DLC); in William Brent's hand, signed by White; addressed: "President of the United States"; endorsed by TJ as received 16 Apr. and so recorded in SJL. FC (DNA: RG 42, DCLB). Enclosures: (1) Tristram Dalton and William Thornton to Benjamin Ogle, 31 Mch. 1801, requesting "some indulgence" on the payment of loan interest due to the state of Maryland in 1801 (Tr in DLC). (2) Alexander White to the governor and council of the state of Maryland, 4 Apr. 1801, stating that the sureties to the state of Maryland for the 1799 loan of $50,000 proposed "an exoneration of the Commissioners in their individual and public capacities" from a large part of the debt (Tr in same).

On 30 Mch. the BOARD OF COMMISSIONERS resolved to apply to Governor Benjamin Ogle and the Council of Maryland for modification of debts owed to the state (DNA: RG 42, PC). For the names of the sureties for the 1799 loan, see District of Columbia Commissioners to TJ, 28 Mch. 1801.

From John Dickinson

MY DEAR FRIEND,   Wilmington the 7th of the 4th. Month 1801

Thy Letter of the 6th of last Month I received with all the pleasure that arises from every Testimony of Regard given by a person highly Esteemed on Considerations of private and public Import. My Mind is much at rest with what relates to my Country; tho I shall allways lament, that thy predecessors did not discover this all important Truth, that after France had declared herself a Republic, our Safety depended on her maintaining herself in that Character. Had that single position been taken by us, and our movements regulated by a Reference to it, the two Back doors of our Country might have been closed, through which now open, in Case of certain Changes, incalculable Evil may enter. The favorable moment was suffered to pass unimproved. If any policy can yet compensate for the neglect, look for it from the existing administration.

Now I am to address thee on a Subject, which I am compelled to mention by affections and Circumstances too powerful to be resisted.

I have known the Treasurer of the United States about forty Years, and he has allways been esteemed, very justly in my opinion, an honest worthy Man.   He is married to a first Cousin of mine, a truely excellent Woman, and has an amiable Family consisting of five Daughters and a Son.   One of the Daughters is married to John Read, Agent for Claims, a young Man exceedingly estimable, the Son of George Read, my intimate Friend from Youth to age, many Years a Member of Congress in the most distressing Times, and since Chief Justice of this State, and between whom and thyself, I believe, a pleasing acquaintance subsisted.

The two Gentlemen before mentioned, I beg Leave most earnestly to recommend to thy Notice; and judging of my Heart by what I feel on this occasion, I trust, that the Liberty now taken will be forgiven. With every respectful Recollection I am thy affectionate Friend,

JOHN DICKINSON

2d Dft (PHi); endorsed by Dickinson: "Letter to the President 7th of the 4th Month 1801." Dft (same); dated 7 Mch. 1801; unsigned; written on verso of unrelated address sheet; endorsed by Dickinson: "Copies of Letters to Jefferson and Madison and McKean 1801." Recorded in SJL as received 24 Apr. with notation "Off."

TREASURER OF THE UNITED STATES: Samuel Meredith, who was married to Dickinson's FIRST COUSIN, Margaret Cadwalader.

JOHN READ, U.S. agent to settle claims made under Article 6 of the Jay Treaty, was the husband of Martha Meredith (DAB; Vol. 30:428n).

From George Jefferson

DEAR SIR   Richmond 7th. April 1801

I am desired by Mr. Hanson to request that you will authorise some one to receive of him six bonds of yours which are discharged, as he intends in the course of next month to leave this Country for Europe. he says that he wrote to you upon this subject some time ago, and as he has not since heard from you, concludes his letter must have miscarried.

I am Dear Sir Your Very humble servt.

GEO. JEFFERSON

RC (MHi); at foot of text: "Thomas Jefferson esqr."; endorsed by TJ as received 17 Apr. and so recorded in SJL.

The last letter recorded in SJL from Richard HANSON was that of 23 Oct.

which TJ received 3 Nov. 1800, but it has not been found. For TJ's earlier arrangements to receive the discharged bonds from Hanson, see TJ to George Jefferson, 8 Nov. 1799 (second letter).

From "A Married Female"

SIR   philadelphia april 7

a firm confidence in your indulgence for my presumtion in addressing you, will I hope plead my excuse—I have for years wished for the houner of your acquaintence, the only houner I have been often heard to say (owing to my Independence of mind) I supose I could arrive at on this side the grave, as my veneration for your virtues are quite enthusiastick— I cannot read your address upon that great event which emancipated our country, without tears of admiration & joy, the long wished for blessing heaven has at last granted to my prayrs—in giveing us so great so good a father—I fear you will be percicuted for one office after another till quite wearied out, as your freinds have so many of them risked their lives & allmost ruined their fortunes in your behalf—which I hope will in your benevolent heart plead their excuse, I feel in a tender point this subject, yet mean not to urge in behalf of any one, yet I could expaceate, there was a person a relation of Mr S—the Mr S— who is Mr Gallitins freind, travelled night & day, spent many anxcious hours in the 1796 in your cause—but I will not dare not mention names—Indeed I would not let any one know I write to you for the world—I have been thinking If their was five dollors tax upon every thousand dollors received by people in office as a paticulor tax, It would be but little felt but be a great emolument to the States, a hint from a weak head will not allways be taken wrong by those of unerring judgment

 I subcribe my self your subject   A Married Female

RC (DNA: RG 59, LAR); addressed: "Thomas Jefferson president of the united States"; endorsed by TJ as received from "Anon." on 24 Apr. and so recorded in SJL.

From Joseph Yznardi, Sr.

Exelentisimo Señor   G. town 7th. April 801
Muy Señor mio, y de todo mi Respeto
A el dia Siguiente qe diriji á V.E mi Ultima pasé á darle gracias (por qe sin duda por su Orden Mr Lincoln aunque no, el todo, me proveyo con parte de mi Credito con lo qe me Conpondré asta la llegada de Documentos pedidos) quando supe en su Palacio le Avia dejado aquella mañana para essa encontrando, en el a su Nuebo Secretario Sugeto a mi ver de Apreciable Circumstancias.

 Mr. Barnes me ha Visto, y quedó entendido de todo, y si la Pipa de Vino Paxarete, y Barril de tintillo de Rota, qe deve venir de Philadelphia llegase á esta Antes de mi partida, yo Mismo Instruire a su Mayordomo, del Modo qe deve Manejar el Cuidado de Vinos, para qe sus Calidades se Mejoren

 Escrivi á Xeres por los qe de Nuebo V.E me encargó ádemas de los demas, ya pedidos por mi

 Mande Copia tradusida de su Estimada Carta de 26 del pasado (Mediante su permiso) á el princípe de la paz, con el Sincero deseo de qe el Rey Sepa la Generosidad de los de V.E, y Renovando el Asunto del Sr. de Yrujo &ca

 Infinitas Gracias por la Orden qe me Mando para el Retratato del qe haré el aprecio, qe Devo, y mientras le deseo Regreso Felis á esta

Capital en la qe no teniendo el Honor de verle, no dudo me Considerará aunque Ausente como su protegido

Como á tal recomiendo á V.E el Asunto qe esta Aconpaña como lo espero de su Vondad mientras tengo el Honor

Señor Exelentisimo de ser su mas Obediente Servidor

JOSEF YZNARDY

EDITORS' TRANSLATION

MOST EXCELLENT SIR   Georgetown 7 Apr. 1801

My most illustrious sir, and with all my respect,

The day after I sent Your Excellency my last letter, I passed by to thank you (because without question your orders to Mr. Lincoln, though not entirely, did provide me with part of the credit with which I will make do until the arrival of the requested documents). At your mansion I found that you had left that morning for your other residence, and I saw your new secretary, who is in my opinion worthy of esteem.

Mr. Barnes has seen me, and he has been informed about everything. If the cask of the pajarete wine and the barrel of tent from Rota that should come from Philadelphia arrive here before my departure, I will instruct your butler myself on how to care for the wines so that their quality improves.

I wrote to Jerez with regard to your recent request in addition to the ones that you previously desired from me.

I sent a translated copy of your esteemed letter of the 26th of last month (by your permission) to the prince of the peace with the sincere hope that the king would know about the generosity of your excellency's desires, and to renew the matter concerning Señor de Irujo, etc.

Many thanks for the order that you sent me concerning the retraction, which I will give the attention that I should; and meanwhile I wish you a happy return to this capital in which, should I not have the honor to see you, you will doubtless grant me your protection though you may be absent.

Counting on that, I refer to Your Excellency the matter that accompanies this letter in hope of your kind consideration; meanwhile I have the honor

Most excellent sir to be your most obedient servant

JOSEF YZNARDY

RC (DLC); at foot of text: "Exmo. Sor. Dn Thomas Jefferson"; endorsed by TJ as received 16 Apr. and so recorded in SJL.

VINO: under 8 Apr. in his financial memoranda TJ made a notation that "the wine from Yznardi is 34. bottles Pacharetti 55. do. Ruota Tenta" (MB, 2:1037).

From Stephen Cathalan, Jr.

SIR   Marseilles the 8th. april 1801

Permit me of embracing this opportunity of Forwarding dispatches from tripoly & Tunis, to the Secretary of State, to present you my best Respects and Sincere Congratulations, on your Election to the Presidency of the united states of america, assuring you, Sir, that my old Father, Mother and family as well as I, are much rejoiced Since we have heard that very Important and agreable event, tho' the official New has not yet Reached me.

I have the honour of asking you, as a Peculiar favour (and a Continuation of that Friendship you have honoured me[1] with, Since many years,) your kind Protection, towards me;—I will Study my Self to fulfill the Duties of my office, as long as my best Services will Continue to be agreable to you, as much as it may be in my Power, to deserve your approbation, & Satisfaction;

I have the honour to be with Great Respect Sir your most Obedient humble & Devoted Servant   STEPHEN CATHALAN JUNR.

RC (DLC); at foot of text: "The honourable President of the United States of America Thos. Jefferson Esqr. City of Washington"; endorsed by TJ as received 29 June and so recorded in SJL. Dupl (same); in Cathalan's hand, appended to his letter to TJ of 10 Apr. 1801. Enclosed in Cathalan to secretary of state, 8 Apr. (see below).

FORWARDING DISPATCHES: with a letter of this date to the secretary of state, Cathalan sent two packets of papers from the U.S. consul at Tunis, William Eaton, and acknowledged receipt of a circular from James Cathcart warning of the probable commencement of hostilities against the United States by Tripoli (RC in DNA: RG 59, CD; Madison, *Papers, Sec. of State Ser.*, 1:77; Joseph Barnes to TJ, 19 Mch.).

[1] Word lacking in MS, supplied from Dupl.

To John Wayles Eppes

DEAR SIR   Monticello Apr. 8. 1801.

I arrived here on the 4th. inst. and found the family at Edgehill all well. we are now all together at this place, and only want the addition of your's and my dear Maria's company to be entirely happy. I shall leave it pointedly on the 25th. if not some days before. mr Overton is married & settled adjoining us. Nancy Jefferson is said to be about marrying Charles Lewis. this is our only small news. I am not able to tell you any thing of your affairs, the 3 days of my stay here having been Sunday, Court-day, and a day of rain. but I presume all are well as I have heard nothing to the contrary.—I shall send off for the horses on Sunday the 12th. so the messenger will be with you on Monday or Tuesday. I wish you may have got the three. the two I count upon according to your & my last letters.—the public news you have in the papers: but there is one article not yet I believe published. the British government has promised us to suppress all their courts of admiralty in America; to establish two new ones in Jamaica & the Windward islands, to send out men of character as judges & give them independant salaries: and the orders were actually dispatched. this will relieve us from their spoliations to a certain degree. at any rate it shews a disposition to be friendly & just. my tenderest love to my dear Maria, in which her sister joins me. let us know when she expects to come up. accept yourself assurances of sincere & affectionate esteem.   TH: JEFFERSON

RC (MoSHi: Jefferson Papers); addressed: "John W. Eppes at Bermuda Hundred near City point"; franked; postmarked Charlottesville, 11 Apr. PrC (MHi); endorsed by TJ in ink on verso.

OVERTON IS MARRIED: probably Richard Overton, who married Sarah Johnson of Louisa County, Virginia (WMQ, 1st ser., 22 [1914], 278-9; VMHB, 26 [1918], 105). NANCY JEFFERSON: the proposed marriage of TJ's niece Anna Scott Jefferson to her first cousin Charles Lewis did not take place (Merrill, *Jefferson's Nephews*, 85, 388n). YOUR AND MY LAST LETTERS: see 18 and 28 Mch., respectively.

On 23 Jan., Rufus King wrote the secretary of state that after repeated notes and conferences the BRITISH GOVERNMENT had agreed to reform the admiralty courts in the West Indies. He then cited the measures described by TJ and noted that the ORDERS had been DISPATCHED the preceding day (Dupl. in DNA: RG 59, DD; in clerk's hand, signed by King; at head of text: "Duplicate"; endorsed as received 3 Apr. 1801). The newspapers began carrying reports on the judiciary reforms in the British West Indies in early May (*National Intelligencer*, 6 May; *Boston Gazette*, 11 May 1801).

From Peter Jaquett

Sir

Long Hook New Castle County State of Delaware April 8th. 1801.

Having served during the whole course of the late Revolutionary War [. . .] Regiment raised by [the] State of Delaware, I am encouraged by your known attachment to the principles of that Revolution and to those men who were the firm and active supporters of it, to offer myself to your Consideration as a candidate for any office under your administration that may become vacant, and for which I may be found qualified.

Not having the honor of a Personal acquaintance with your Excellency, I must beg leave to refer you for information on my Character should you think it necessary, to Joseph Anderson Esqr: member of the Senate for the State of Tenesee; who has had opportunities of knowing me in the respective Characters of Citizen and Soldier—

Doct[or] Ja[. . .] John Dickeson Esquire [. . .] from a long acquaintance with me are competent to form a just opinion of my Character; and my Capacity for office and I have no doubt will report favorably thereon! Should You incline to Honor me, or wish further evidences of my Zeal for the public Welfare—my confidence in your administration, and my capacity for discharging with care & fidelity such trust as you may be inclined to repose in me, your Commands addressed to me near the Borough of [Wilmington] Delaware, will be received & attended to with respect. I am Sir With high Esteem Your Obedt. Servt.

PETER JAQUETT

RC (DNA: RG 59, LAR); torn; endorsed by TJ as received 29 June and so recorded in SJL.

For Jaquett's claims to civil and military experience, his unsuccessful efforts to receive an appointment in George Washington's administration, and his previous connection with Joseph ANDERSON, who had written to TJ on his behalf on 6 Mch., see Vol. 19:387, 392-9.

From Levi Lincoln

SIR   Washington April 8th 1801

I omitted to mention that there was a mistake in making out the commission for Ray Greene of Providence. the design was, to appoint him to the office of a district Judge, the commission to him is, as judge of the circuit court—he has sent it back, & wishes to have it rectified. It is probable that Bourn was the judge of the district court. when the appointment was made—of course there was no vacancy—this letter of acceptance is dated the 23d of March—

I am Sir most respectfully yours.   LEVI LINCOLN

RC (DLC); at head of text: "The President of the United States"; endorsed by TJ as received 16 Apr. and so recorded in SJL.

RAY GREENE resigned his seat in the Senate on 5 Mch. on the presumption that he had received a commission from John Adams as district judge of Rhode Island.

Because of a technicality, he was not appointed and Christopher Ellery was elected to serve the remainder of his Senate term. Benjamin Bourne was appointed district and then circuit judge of the U.S. Court (*Biog. Dir. Cong.*; JEP, 1:395, 401; JS, 3:155; List of John Adams's Judicial Appointments, printed at 18 Feb.; Appendix I, List 4).

From Gouverneur Morris

DEAR SIR   Morrisania 8 April 1801

I never was so long in my Life going the same Distance as on my Return from the City to this Place nor were there ever much worse Roads. This will excuse me I hope for what might otherwise seem neglect—The Service of Plate which I mentioned to you weighed in Paris six hundred and twenty two Marks making about 408 Pounds Troy which at $1\frac{1}{3}$ per Oz or $16 per Pound will amount to $6528. There may perhaps have been packed up with it one or two Pieces that do not belong to it. if so we can easily arrange that afterwards. By the Time this Letter reaches your Hands you will I expect be established in your Palace accept thereon my Congratulations and the sincere wish that you may be happy in it—

I have the Honor to be with perfect Respect your obedient Servant

GOUV MORRIS

RC (DLC); at foot of text: "His Excellency Thomas Jefferson Esqr. Washington"; endorsed by TJ as received 24 Apr. and so recorded in SJL. FC (Lb in DLC: Gouverneur Morris Papers); in Morris's hand.

THIS WILL EXCUSE ME: according to the TJ Editorial Files, a letter from TJ to Gouverneur Morris, 21 Mch. 1801, was sold at auction in 1929, but the letter is not recorded in SJL and has not been found. Morris finally sold the SERVICE OF PLATE to Robert R. Livingston (Morris to TJ, 23 Oct. 1801).

From Thomas Newton

DEAR SIR   Norfolk April 8. 1801

Your esteemd favor I received of 23. Ulto. the wine shall be sent up by Capts. Willis or Moore who will be here in a few days; the Brasil wine is highly esteemd here, it is superior to the London particular, & shall send one of it. the latter is fine 3 years old & shiped (wracked off), by a Portugeze house in Madeira. you will find it clear, let the cask be ever so much shaked. we have very late arivals here from Europe, the news by them you will receive by the papers from this place & N York where some of the same fleet is arived. it will ever give me pleasure to be attentive to any commands you may have here, there are several packets from Alexandria & this place who ply every week, with good accommodations & reputable Capts. that any thing you may require from this can be sent by them—I beg you'l accept of my best wishes for your health & happiness & am respectfully

Yr Obt Servt   THOS NEWTON

RC (DLC); endorsed by TJ as received 3 May and so recorded in SJL.

On this day Newton also wrote two letters of introduction to TJ. One was for Dr. Lewis Hansford, "a worthy citizen of this place, who is desirous of seeing his own Country" (RC in same; endorsed by TJ as received 3 May and so recorded in SJL). The other letter was carried by Dr. Robert B. Starke, a citizen of Norfolk who served aboard the U.S. frigate *Chesapeake* and hoped to continue in that position. Newton recommended him "as a young gentleman high in reputation here, and one that I have no doubt will do honor to any appointment in the line of his profession" (RC in same; endorsed by TJ as received 3 May and so recorded in SJL). Starke had received an appointment as a surgeon's mate in the spring of 1800. He was retained in the navy under the Peace Establishment Act (JEP, 1:341-2; NDQW, Dec. 1800-Dec. 1801, 351).

To Archibald Stuart

DEAR SIR   Monticello Apr. 8. 1801.

I arrived here on the 4th. and expect to stay a fortnight in order to make some arrangements preparatory to my final removal to Washington.—you know that the last Congress established a Western judiciary district in Virginia, comprehending chiefly the Western counties. mr Adams, who continued filling all the offices till 9. aclock of the night, at 12. of which he was to go out of office himself, took care to appoint for this district also. the judge of course stands till the law shall be repealed, which we trust will be at the next Congress. but as to all others, I made it immediately known, that I should consider them as nullities, and appoint others: as I think I have a preferable right to name agents for my own administration, at least to the vacancies falling after it was known that mr Adams was not naming for himself. consequently we want an Attorney & Marshal for the Western district. I had thought of mr Coalter, but I am told he has a clerkship incompatible with it by our laws. I thought also of Hugh Holmes; but I fear he is so far off he would not attend the court, which is to be in Rockbridge, I believe. this is the extent of my personal knowledge. pray recommend one to me, as also a Marshal; and let them be the most respectable & unexceptionable possible; and especially let them be republican. the only shield for our Republican citizens against the federalism of the courts is to have the Attornies & Marshals republicans. there is nothing I am so anxious about as good nominations, conscious that the merit as well as reputation of an administration depends as much on that as on it's measures.

Accept assurances of my constant esteem & high consideration & respect.   TH: JEFFERSON

RC (ViHi); at foot of text: "A. Stuart esq." PrC (DLC).

For the nomination of Samuel Blackburn as district attorney and Robert Grattan as marshal of the newly formed WESTERN JUDICIARY DISTRICT IN VIRGINIA, see List of John Adams's Appointments, printed at 23 Feb. 1801. JUDGE OF COURSE STANDS: Charles Magill (JEP, 1:385-6).

HE HAS A CLERKSHIP: John Coalter began serving as clerk of the Virginia District Court in Staunton in 1793 (see Vol. 31:192n). HUGH HOLMES, of Frederick County, served in the Virginia Senate from 1795 to 1799 and in the House of Delegates from 1802 until the 1805-6 term, when he resigned to become a judge of the General Court. He was elected speaker of the House in 1803, 1804, and 1805 (Leonard, *General Assembly*, 202, 206, 210, 214, 227, 231, 235, 239, 240).

From Caspar Wistar

DEAR SIR, [before 9 Apr. 1801]

Permit me to offer you my most sincere & affectionate congratulations on the recent election, which I hope will contribute to your individual happiness as much as I am certain it will to the benefit of our beloved Country—Sensible of the laborious task which is now imposed upon you, it is with great reluctance that I intrude upon your valuable time, & beg from your good nature an indulgence which I am not entitled to in justice. Mr. Peter Dobel a respectable Young Gentleman of this City, after returning from a tedious detention in the Isle of France, (being captured on a voyage to India) resolved to settle at Bourdeaux, expecting to avail himself there of the knowledge of French Commerce which he had acquired during his residence in the aforesaid Colony; with this view he determined to solicit from the President the appointment of Consul at that Port, & to strengthen his application a recommendation of him was signed by a large number of very respectable Merchants of Philada. & ready to be presented, when an appointment was made by the late President—He is impressed with a belief that another Consul is to be appointed, & as in that case he would beg leave to prefer his request, & lay his recommendations before you, he has applied to me to procure him information whether a new appointment is about to be made—If you can favour me with one line on this subject it will greatly oblige me indeed—

I regret that it is not in my power to communicate to you any thing which is new & interesting, the last publication here was the Presidents Speech, which besides an immense multiplication in the News Papers, has undergone several Editions—

Private letters from England state their distresses more strongly than the public prints—they inform that many have certainly died with famine—

In my last I had the pleasure of inclosing the printed accounts of the great bones found in the State of New York, & specifying those parts which I thought would be most useful I hope we shall not lose our chance of them by the departure of Chancellor Livingston.

With[1] anxious hopes that you will excuse the liberty I have taken I beg leave to subscribe with sentiments of most respectful attachment Your obliged friend   C. WISTAR JUNR.

RC (DNA: RG 59, LAR); undated; at foot of text: "His Excellency T. Jefferson"; endorsed by TJ as received 9 Apr. and so recorded in SJL; also endorsed by TJ: "Dobel Peter."

In June, TJ named Peter Dobell (DOBEL) commercial agent at Le Havre, and the Senate approved the nomination in January 1802; see JEP, 1:402, 405, and Appendix I, Lists 1, 3, and 4.

THIS CITY: Philadelphia.
MY LAST: Wistar to TJ, 18 Feb.

[1] Before this word Wistar first wrote, then partially erased, "I again request."

From Levi Lincoln

SIR   Washington April 9th 1801

I have the honor to forward for your consideration several setts of papers on subjects to which the attention of government has been pressed by the applicants.

Priestman's case will appear fully from his papers. Judge Peters certificate on the back of a former petition prefer'd to the treasurys office, excludes the idea of intentional wrong, for which purpose I have procured, & forward it. It seems at the time, when the transaction took place, there was a doubt on the construction of the law, since which the necessity of a permit is argued. And even now I am informed by Mr Lyon the collector refuses permits, & that goods are transported as by Priestman, without permits— It appears Mr [. . .] refused releif, because there had been time for the law to be known— the difficulty was, it could not be understood—From a supposition that you would think proper to pardon, a blank, is forwarded for that purpose—I have written to the marshal to stay proceedings untill your pleasure would be known in the subject—

Mr Yznardi, is like the importunate widow his applications are incessant. I have consented, notwithstanding a deficiency of vouchers, to pay him the further sum of $2,000, on account. It appearing highly probable that that sum on a final settlement, will be found his due. From the statement of Mr Dallas of the two suits against

Mr Yznardi, I can contemplate no principles, upon which I think it would be right for the Executive to interfere in reference to the one in favor of Mr Israel. The cause of this action, is traced very remotely, & very incorrectly, to a regular exertion of consular authority. Mr Israel's letter contains some weighty, altho common reasons against an interference.

It may be reasonable that the defence of Pentards action should be at the public expence. Or that the defendant should ultimately be indemnified. His conduct which is the ground of this process, appears to have been proper & meritorious.

The letter of Govr. St. Clair and the therein inclosed papers state a most outrageous violation of the rights of society. As the subject is important, I thought it my duty to forward it—opportunities may present for inquiries—

The Spanish ministers communication refering to papers was unattended with any, he has been written to on the subject—

Dent has accepted of the office of Marshal for the district of Potomac— Jones has been written to, from not having recd an answer, it is probable he is from home—Judge Bee has declined accepting of the office of Cheif Judge of the fifth circuit court of the United States, assigning as a reason his inability to undergo the fatigue incident to that office—the late Governor Lee of Maryland declines accepting of his commission as a justice of the peace—

I take the liberty of enclosing the national Intelligencer, have deferd observations on the propriety and expediency, of withholding the commissions with a view of availing myself of the opportunity of considering remarks, which I expected would have been made, on the discussion of its legality. I however have not heard or seen a syllable on the subject—

My private letters from the State of Massachusetts state a general approbation of the measures of Govt. and a great prevalence of the principles of republicanism. They say Gerry will be Governor. I perceive republican candidates a pushed for the Senate—By the address of our Legislature to Mr Adams, it appears that a renovation is necessary—

Genl. Smith is elected by a very great majority It is said & generally credited, that a Mr Sprigg is elected in the room of C Thomas—great is the power of truth, it must prevail—

I have Sir the honor to be most respectfully your most obedient Hum Sert.   LEVI LINCOLN

RC (DLC); at head of text: "President of the United States"; endorsed by TJ as received 16 April and so recorded in SJL. Enclosures not found, but see below.

William PRIESTMAN'S CASE involved a merchant who imported to Baltimore watches valued at $3,385 and who, in 1797, moved his wares to Philadelphia in violation of section 19 of the February 1793 act regulating imports, specifically movement of goods from one port of entry to another. The watches were confiscated and U.S. attorney William Rawle prosecuted the case. TJ ultimately pardoned Priestman in June 1801 and ordered a return of the seized watches (DNA: RG 59, GPR; Madison, *Papers, Sec. of State Ser.*, 1:314).

The letter of Governor Arthur ST. CLAIR and the enclosed PAPERS have not been found, but St. Clair, writing to James Madison on 9 Mch., asserted that in December he had sent "information that a very violent violation of the Territory had been committed by the British near to Detroit, and a man carried away by force and murdered." A grand jury of the Northwest Territory indicted British Sergeant Levy P. Cole for the murder of suspected deserter Francis Poquette (William Henry Smith, ed., *The St. Clair Papers: The Life and Pub-*

lic Services of Arthur St. Clair, 2 vols., [Cincinnati, 1882], 2:532-3; Madison, *Papers, Sec. of State Ser.*, 1:9-10).

Thomas BEE returned his commission as chief judge for the Fifth Circuit Court, claiming fatigue of long journeys and a desire to continue to serve as district judge in South Carolina (Madison, *Papers, Sec. of State Ser.*, 1:28).

The 3 Apr. 1801 issue of the *National Intelligencer* contained a front-page critique of a letter published in the *Philadelphia Gazette* of 25 Mch., the writer of which claimed that TJ had been illegally WITHHOLDING THE COMMISSIONS of justices named by Adams.

Richard SPRIGG, Jr., was elected in place of Federalist Congressman John C. THOMAS to represent Maryland's second district in the Seventh Congress (*Biog. Dir. Cong.*; Dauer, *Adams Federalists*, 323, 328).

From Joseph Whipple

SIR   Portsmouth New Hampre. April 9th. 1801

Penetrated with the most lively sensations of gratitude to that Being who has preserved this country a second time from the fangs of tyranny by your elevation to the station of chief Magistrate—Permit me Sir to express my joy on the Occasion and to declare in the openness of an undissembling heart that no event of my countrys prosperity—not even the acknowledgment of its independancy has ever given me more sincere satisfaction—since it is a re-establishment of an independance which was tottering and a restoration of the public mind to the principles which produced our emancipation from the chains of Britain.—

The gradual introduction of aristocratical principles & the increasing power & elevation of the opposers of our independence and of republicanism had brought our country to the verge of ruin—the abuse of those who had uniformly supported the principles of our independance had become intollerable—& those abuses were extended even to that character who had penned the instrument of its declaration, on which account their malice had been exercised to a degree of unprecedented licentiousness—particularly in this State by disseminating false & scandalous reports by means of the gazettes exclusively in their power—This has been the course for the last four years—but the people are now happily emerging from the delusions obtruded upon them and their second independence will be more glorious than the former.—May you live Sir not only to see its full Accomplishment but to enjoy the view of its extensive blessings diffused through a gratefull country.—

Nor have I, Sir though acting in a subordinate sphere escaped the Malice of the enemies to the measures of 1776, but experienced in the late Administration through the influence of old Tories a dismissal from an office executed by me ten years without a charge of error thereby fixing on me a disgraceful stigma of demeret—of treachery or of infidility—and this office & several others particularly that of Commissioner of loans formerly held by Col. Gardner who was dismissed for possessing sentiments similar to mine are filled by persons who have been uniformly inimical to our government (except the 4 last years administration) & to republican principles & who were the most inviterate Tories in time of our Revolution—who have been constantly in the habit of exciting the contempt and indignation of the deluded multitude against the new President and vice President & those who have been named for the first offices of the State—these are the persons who hold in New Hampshire every Office under the United States and whose continuance would be greviously humiliating to every republican.—

Since I have been led to this point, I will take the liberty to add that—should it be your pleasure—I should esteem a reestablishment to the office which I held (that of Collector of the Customs for the Port of Portsmouth) as a healing specific to a wound maliciously inflicted through the influence of the enemies of our countrys peace & independence. I do not solicit this, Sir from pecuniary considerations—it proceeds from an earnest wish founded on political principles to participate in the execution of the government under your administration and the enjoyment of the felicity of a justifiable triumph over your enemies & the enemies of our country.— Nor would the reinstatement of Mr. Gardner in the particular Office which he held be less grateful to my feelings & to those of every republican who consider these dismissals as shafts levelled at the principle in the persons of those who possess them.—Mr. Langdon (late of the Senate) his knowledge both of Mr. Gardners character & mine & of the facts mentioned herein authorize a reference to him for their truth.—

Although I have not the happiness to be known to you Sir, yet your character has been long familiar to me, that of a public nature by the eminent services you have renderd your country—that of a more private—through a dear friend & brother many years since deceased who acted with you in the memorable era for July '76 & whose republican virtues congenial with yours I am happy in appretiating— These considerations I pray you will have the goodness to admit as an apology for my addressing a private letter to you.

I have the honor to be with the most profound respect Sir Your faithful & Obedt. humble Servant   JOSEPH WHIPPLE

RC (CSmH); at foot of text: "Thomas Jefferson, President of the United States"; endorsed by TJ as received 6 May and so recorded in SJL.

Joseph Whipple (1737-1816) was appointed the first federal collector of customs at Portsmouth in 1789. Initially a Federalist, by 1795 he had followed the lead of U.S. Senator John Langdon and defected to the Republican camp. New Hampshire Federalists, led by U.S. Attorney Jeremiah Smith and state Representative William Plumer, arranged for Whipple's removal in 1798, along with the removal of Commissioner of Loans William GARDNER, Naval Officer Eleazer Russell, and revenue cutter Captain Hopley Yeaton. Whipple's successor was Thomas Martin, the surveyor and inspector of customs and a loyal Federalist, who quickly replaced 20 of 23 customhouse subordinates. Shortly after his inauguration, TJ restored Whipple and Gardner to their former offices (Chester B. Jordan, "Sketch of Col. Joseph Whipple," *Proceedings of the New Hampshire Historical Society*, 2 [1888-95], 289-320; Prince, *Federalists*, 46-56; JEP, 1:9, 13, 103, 283, 403).

DEAR FRIEND & BROTHER: William Whipple, a member of the Continental Congress from 1776 to 1779 and a signer of the Declaration of Independence, was Joseph Whipple's elder brother and business partner. In 1784 he assisted TJ in his efforts to secure a moose skeleton. He died in 1785 (DAB; Vol. 7:22, 28-30, 318).

From Joseph Barnes

Messina Sicily April 10th. 1801

In my Letter dat'd Feb. 14th., to you my best friend Mr Jefferson, I Specified the circumstances in which I presumed the English expedition to Egypt would prove *Abortive*—which is the result—

In consequence of the great despot of the East having guarranteed the French in Egypt, &, of the powerful influence he had over the Ottoman Court, the Grand Siegnor has *refused* permission for the English to Land in Egypt!! Consequently, Should they not take possession of Some of the Islands, Candia, Cyprus or others, they must immediately return to Malta—

I also anticipat'd, in Said Letter, the views of the French relative to the Ottoman Empire—It appears they have Stipulat'd in their Treaty with the Emperor of Germany to march an Army of 60.000 men thro' his dominions in order to meet a much greater Army of Russions at Constantinople, no doubt with the view of *dissolving* the Ottoman Empire—

And, 'tis Suggest'd, with the further view of attacking the English possessions in the East—this however is to be prov'd—The convention of Neutrality of the Northern Powers has been formally ratified—in which I am happy to find, the contracting parties engage to enforce as far as may be in their power. the *Great principle of Neutral bottoms making Neutral property*—as Stipulat'd between the Unit'd States and France.—

To complete the Stroke against the British Commerce & Manufactures, the French have forced the Portugees into an Alliance with Spain and France, to the exclusion of the English—What will be the event is at present difficult to calculate—England cannot exist Long without vent for its manufactures, nor can its opponents, especially Portugal & Danemark Stand it Long without Commerce.—

As all these circumstances operate in favor, and render America Still more Essential, Should England, which no doubt it will being So prevalent at Sea, declare the ports of its enemies in a State of blockade, hope the Executive of the Unit'd States will embrace the Oppertunity, and by an *energetic* remonstrance thro' the means of a proper Envoy *obtain* permission to exercise the rights of Neutrality & Laws of Nations, by Navigating into *every* port of each Country not in an *Actual* State of Siege, or *Shut* the ports of the Unit'd States against & Let them take the consequences—I Should glory in Such an agency, to have it in my power to Speak the Language which the representative of a great Republic Aught to do, tho' not yet done, to a Nation So *imperious* as the English—having practical knowledge from four years residence in London.—

Having just read an English paper dated London Feb. 7th. containing a Paragraph purporting, that the Prosperity Arrived at Dublin in 29 days from Philada. had brot. the *confermation* of the *Election* of *Mr Jefferson* and Mr Burr, & the presumption being of course the first is President, I do exulting again most heartily Congratulate Mr Jefferson, & felicitate myself & fellow Citizens on the *happy event* & *flattering prospect* which expands before us; not doubting but all the objects Suggest'd in my former Letter will be effect'd, and whatever may tend to promote the *true* interest & happiness of Citizens of the Unit'd States, at Least attempt'd.

Enclos'd with this you have an Address, unsolicit'd, of Several Citizens of the Unit'd whose names are thereto Subscrib'd, Recommending me, from the circumstances therein Specified, to the approbation of the President of the Unit'd States to fill the office of Consul general or *Commercial Agent* of the Unit'd States to the two Sicilies—and, as Mr Jefferson is President, every attention due will follow of course

I Should however prefer the office of general Commercial Agent in France—or residence at Marseilles, or Bourdeaux in Some capacity— With constant Solicitude for your health & happiness, & Long continuence in the Presidency Mr Jefferson I remain yours most respectfully   Jos: Barnes
                                                                of Virginia

P.S. Any Agency or Services in my power to promote the interest &c of the People of the United States & of the Government may be command'd at all times either at home or abroad.— Director of the Mint or of the Public works in & for the Unit'd States would be a favorite object—

The Neopolitans disgust'd at the degrading treaty made with France desire the English—& as the French insist on Sending a garrison to Naples & this place—tis impossible to Say what will be the result—

RC (DNA: RG 59, LAR); addressed: "Thomas Jefferson Esqr. P. of the U.S Washington," with notation that the letter was to be carried by David Sawyer, commander of the snow *Fox* of Boston (who was a signatory of the enclosure); franked; postmarked at Boston, 23 June; endorsed by TJ as received 29 June and so recorded in SJL; also endorsed by TJ: "to be Consul of the two Sicilies." Enclosure: Memorial signed at Messina, 4 Mch. 1801, by Robert H. Rose of Pennsylvania and five American ship captains urging the appointment of Barnes as consul general for the Two Sicilies (MS in RG 59, LAR, addressed: "His Excellency The President of the United States," endorsed by TJ as received 29 June and so recorded in SJL; Dupl in same, in Barnes's hand including signatures, one of which is lacking, Barnes adding notations stating that he would send the original MS by post through England, endorsed by a clerk as "Recommendatory of Joseph Barnes").

Despite Barnes's expectations, the ENGLISH EXPEDITION TO EGYPT was successful. After landing at Aboukir Bay in March, the British forced the French garrisons at Cairo and Alexandria to surrender in June and early September, respectively (Piers Mackesy, *British Victory in Egypt, 1801: The End of Napoleon's Conquest* [London, 1995], 67-77, 196-7, 221-4). GREAT DESPOT OF THE EAST: Emperor Paul of Russia (Barnes to TJ, 14 Feb.

1801). Paul sought a formal compact with France, contemplated a partitioning of the Ottoman Empire, and dispatched a military column with the intention of attacking the British in India (Roderick E. McGrew, *Paul I of Russia, 1754-1801* [Oxford, 1992], 315-16; Ehrman, *Pitt*, 397-400).

CANDIA: Crete.

GRAND SIEGNOR: the Ottoman sultan, Selim III. The Turks negotiated with the British over the landing site in Egypt, but did not forbid the invasion and in fact sent an army to assist (Mackesy, *British Victory*, 21-6, 178-9; Tulard, *Dictionnaire Napoléon*, 1277).

Sweden, Denmark, and Prussia made conventions with Russia in December 1800 to form the league of armed NEUTRALITY. An article in each of those pacts guaranteed the free passage of ships and protected the cargoes of neutral vessels. Those provisions appeared also in a treaty between Russia and Sweden in March 1801. The convention between the United States and France included similar guarantees, Article 14 declaring "that free ships shall give a freedom to goods" (Parry, *Consolidated Treaty Series*, 55:354-6, 411-37; 56:1-23; Vol. 32:296-7).

Preliminary articles of alliance between SPAIN and France in January 1801 contained an ultimatum requiring Portugal to abandon its friendly relationship with Great Britain and yield other concessions or face an immediate invasion. Portugal failed to comply with the demands and Spain declared war in March, although it was some weeks more before Spanish troops, supported by French reinforcements, attacked (H. V. Livermore, *A History of Portugal* [Cambridge, 1947], 389-91; Parry, *Consolidated Treaty Series*, 55:467-73).

By a treaty concluded between France and the Two Sicilies late in March, the ports of NAPLES and Sicily remained closed to British ships. Secret articles of the pact allowed French troops access to the territory of Naples in transit to other locations (Parry, *Consolidated Treaty Series*, 56:51-6; Barnes to TJ, 14 Feb. 1801).

From Stephen Cathalan, Jr.

SIR   Marseilles the 10th. april 1801.

I take the Liberty of handing you a Copy of my Respects of the 8th. Inst.

I will only add now, that I have, and am Still acknowledged by the Govert. of France, as Consul of the united States, that tho' I have deffended with Constancy & energy, the American Vessels Captured Since the arreté of the 12th. Ventose, and obtained in the most Critical Periods the restitution of Some of them, I have been protected, & acted in a manner of not displeasing to the French autorities.

The American Ministers Plenipotentiary who made the Convention with France, with whom I had the honour of being acquainted during three Months at Paris, have granted me their Esteem, & have been Witnessess of the Consideration, I obtained from Citizen Joseph Bonaparte, who by his wife is a Relation to Missess. Cathalan, & the whole Bonaparte's family; Missess. Cathn. and my whole Family begs you, Sir, to accept the assurance of their best Respects & congratulations.

I have the honour to be with Great Respect Sir Your most obedient humble & Devoted Servant   STEPHEN CATHALAN JUNR.

RC (DLC); at foot of text: "the Right honorable Thos. Jefferson Esqr. President of the united States of america City of Washington"; with Dupl of Cathalan's letter of 8 Apr. conjoined; endorsed by TJ. Recorded in SJL as received 17 July.

The French Directory's arrêté of 12 VENTOSE Year 5 (2 Mch. 1797) had made American ships subject to capture as lawful prizes (Duvergier, *Lois*, 9:315-18; Vol. 29:486n; Vol. 31:13n).

The wife of JOSEPH BONAPARTE, née Julie Clary, was from a prosperous commercial family of Marseilles (*Dictionnaire*, 8:1370-1, 1374; Tulard, *Dictionnaire Napoléon*, 425).

To Rufus King

DEAR SIR   April 10. 1801.

The bearer hereof, mr Louis Buchanan Smith, son of Genl. Smith now acting as Secretary of the navy, proposing to visit Europe, I take the liberty of introducing him to your civilities & services. his personal merit will do justice to any attentions you shall be pleased to shew him, & his station & prospects in life render it interesting that he should derive from his travels all the advantages they are capable of yielding. the state of my acquaintance in England not enabling me to give him any other letter, I will ask the favor of you to supply for him that deficiency. Accept assurances of my high consideration & respect   TH: JEFFERSON

RC (NHi); addressed: "Rufus King esq. M.P. of the US. at London"; endorsed as received 25 Mch. 1802. PrC (DLC); in ink at foot of text TJ wrote the names William Short and Fulwar Skipwith and the notation "mutat. mutans.," that is, "mutatis mutandis," or, "the necessary changes having been made"; in SJL, at this date, TJ entered the names of King, Short, and Skipwith, connecting them with a brace and adding the notation: "recomg. mr Smith."

From Meriwether Lewis

DEAR SIR   City of Washington, Apl. 10th. 1801

Enclosed[1] is a letter which was this morning handed me by the Secretary at War. Genl. Smith arrived last evening, his election has succeeded without opposition.

There not being any thing material to detain me longer at this place, I shal set out for Virginia the 12th. inst.: my horse from his lameness is unable to travel, I shall therefore take the advantage of the stage as far as Richmond; perhaps my journey may not be extended further, in which case, I shall leave that place the 23d. on my return hither. Should it be in my power to visit my friends in Albemarle, I shall be at Monticello by the 20th. inst.

Accept assurances of the sinceer regard & attatchment of—Your Most Obt. & very Humble Sert.   MERIWETHER LEWIS

RC (DLC); at foot of text: "Thos. Jefferson. President of the U States"; endorsed by TJ as received 16 Apr. and so recorded in SJL. Enclosure not identified; according to SJL, TJ received 28 letters on 16 Apr. in addition to the one above, none of them directly from Henry Dearborn.

[1] MS: "Enclclosed."

To Levi Lincoln

DEAR SIR   Monticello Apr. 10. 1801.

I reached this place on the 4th. having passed an evening with mr Madison who is in as good health as for some time past, but that is very indifferent. he will set out for the seat of government about the time I shall. I did not percieve till I got here, that I had brought away the inclosed commissions before they were sealed. I therefore return them. if sealed and returned to me in Thursday evening's mail (the 16th.) they will still find me [here?], & by that time I shall probably have information how to fill them up. [the] district is within 20. miles of me.—I have recieved the inclosed petition from a sufferer under the Sedition law. if my memory is faithful it is from the person to whom we remitted the fine, & consequently [provided] for. if not, it should be done. with respect to Callender's fine, [I find] it to be the opinion &[1] practice here (founded on the principles of the Common law, and not on any law peculiar to this State) for the Executive to act on any fine till it gets into the treasury of the state, when his power to remit it ceases. but as long as it is in the hands of any officer whatever, it is considered as in the hands of the Executive, & remissible by him. will you think of this and consider whether Callender's can be repaid, & order it if you approve? mr Kerby of Connecticut would accept of the Supervisor's place if vacant. but I would rather consider him as a Candidate for the Collector's place for his own sake, as well as ours. he would compare with E. Goodrich to advantage. I inclose a letter for mr Short to be forwarded whenever letters go from [. . .] the post which leaves this a week hence, will reach you a week before I shall and will be the last I shall write by, if any thing occurs. Accept assurances of my sincere & affectionate esteem & high consideration   TH: JEFFERSON

PrC (DLC); faint and blurred; at foot of text: "Levi Lincoln. Actg. Secy. of State." Enclosures: (1) Petition of David Brown to TJ, 23 Mch. (see note to Pardon for David Brown, 12 Mch. 1801). (2) TJ to William Short, 10 Apr. (not found but recorded in SJL with notation "recomg. mr Smith"; see TJ to Rufus King, 10 Apr.). Commissions not found, but possibly those for the attorney and marshal of the western district of Virginia (see TJ to John Monroe and to Archibald Stuart, both of 25 Apr. 1801).

[1] Preceding word and ampersand interlined.

From Joseph Priestley

DEAR SIR   Philadelphia Apl 10. 1801.

Your kind letter, which, considering the numerous engagements incident to your situation, I had no right to expect, was highly gratifying to
me, and I take the first opportunity of acknowledging it. For tho I believe
I am completely recovered from my late illness, I am advised to write as little as possible. Your invitation to pay you a visit is flattering to me in the
highest degree, and I shall not wholly despair of some time or other availing myself of it, but for the present I must take the nearest way home.

Your resentment of the treatment I have met with in this country is
truly generous, but I must have been but little impressed with the principles of the religion you so justly commend, if they had not enabled me
to bear much more than I have yet suffered. Do not suppose that, after
the much worse treatment to which I was for many years exposed in
England (of which the pamphlet I take the liberty to inclose will give you
some idea) I was much affected by this. My *Letters to the Inhabitants of
Northumberland* were not occasioned by any such thing, tho it served me
as a pretence for writing them, but the threatnings of Mr Pickering,
whose purpose to send me out of the country Mr Adams (as I conclude
from a circuitous attempt that he made to prevent it) would not, in the
circumstances in which he then was, have been able directly to oppose.
My publication was of service to me in that and other respects, and I
hope, in some measure to the common cause. But had it not been for the
extreme absurdity and violence of the late administration, I do not know
how far these measures might have been carried. Much, however, must
be ascribed to the successes of the French and something also, perhaps,
to the seasonable death of Genl Washington. I rejoice more than I can express in the glorious reverse that has taken place, and which has secured
your election. This I flatter myself will be the permanent establishment of
truly republican principles in this country, and also contribute to the
same desirable event in more distant ones.

I beg you would not trouble yourself with any answer to this. The
knowledge of your good opinion and good wishes is quite sufficient
for me. I feel for the difficulties of your situation, but your spirit and
prudence will carry you thro them, tho not without paying the tax
which the wise laws of nature have imposed upon predominance and
celebrity of every kind, a tax which, for want of true greatness of mind,
neither of your predecessors, if I estimate their characters aright, paid
without much reluctance.

With every good wish, I am, Dear Sir, yours sincerely

                                                    J PRIESTLEY

P.S. As I trust that *Politics* will not make you forget what is due to *science*, I shall send you a copy of some articles that are just printed for the *Transactions of the Philosophical society* in this place. No 5 p 36 is the most deserving of your notice I should have sent you my *Defence of Phlogistin*, but that I presume you have seen it.

RC (DLC); addressed: "Thomas Jefferson President of the United States"; endorsed by TJ as received 24 Apr. and so recorded in SJL. Enclosure not identified.

YOUR KIND LETTER: TJ to Priestley, 21 Mch.

I SHALL SEND YOU: six brief papers by Priestley appeared in Volume 5 of the American Philosophical Society's *Transactions*. Number 5 was entitled "Experiments on the Production of Air by the Freezing of Water" (APS, *Transactions*, 5 [1802], 1-50). SHOULD HAVE SENT YOU: in 1800, Priestley published *The Doctrine of Phlogiston Established, and that of the Composition of Water refuted* (Sowerby, No. 3771) and gave a copy of the second edition as a gift to TJ in 1803 (Sowerby, No. 836). Priestley's fourth article for *Transactions* had to do with experiments relating to phlogiston (APS, *Transactions*, 5 [1802], 28-35).

From Stephen Sayre

SIR   Point Breeze, New Jersey. Apl. 10th 1801—

I am now at my house, in the country—have neither map, or any thing else, but memory, to aid me, as to the eastern, or western positions, of the powers, on the continent of Europe.

In my former letter, I gave some outlines, by which, it might be practicable to acquire an Island in the west Indies—if obtain'd—supposing it that of Porto Rico—& supposing the Island 175 miles long, & about 70 in breadth—more or less—I sho'ld propose to divide it, as inclosed, into 17 parts, that Europe & America might hold a valuable interest, by its possession—giving Russia the east, & the united states the west ends—by placing the Capital, at the west end, the rest of the lands, in this, would be more valuable, than any other proportion of the same extent—& of still more value, because the leward end is always a harbour. I would also divide the capital into proportionate parts, like the Island, to prevent disputes, as to situation.

As to the plan of the city, I leave that for consideration, after the Island may be so acquired—Also the princeples, & form of government

The first object is, to impress the european powers, with the importance of the proposition, as to solid & universal benefits, political, & commercial—you must want no information as to the extensive effects such an establishment must have, on the affairs of the world—the commercial advantages are, perhaps, far beyond any thing you may have thought of—I will state some of them. Guaranteed by such powers—

under a constitution, forbiding port duties—or if permitted, not to be augmented—every port & harbour open to the universe—the lands would be purchased with eagerness—they would be cultivated with rapidity—the richness of its soil, under the hand of industry would, in a short space of time, render it productive beyond all example—always supply'd by the manufactures of Europe & Asia—ever open to the markets of north & south America—it would—it must—by a forced trade, supply all the other Islands. I am so far convinced, that this, or any other Island, under such advantages, would be of more worth than all the rest in its vicinity, that were I at the head of the government of France, I would place St Domingo under this system, as the most profitable, & most desirable—for the variety of nations, & languages, & the multitudes of white people, as settlers would, if possible, to be done, give safety to the inhabitants against revolt—France would receive more benefit, from the sale of her wines, & manufactures, than she will ever obtain by subduing the negroes, or holding its exclusive trade—It would be good policy in Bonaparte, to propose the cession of St Domingo, & Porto Rico—Spain could not decently refuse—*What a prospect would thereby be open'd to these states*— while we risque nothing by the attempt.

I entertain hopes, that if this measure is adopted, we might, after some time, send a considerable part of our negroes, & render them happy & useful under such establishment.

My reasons for supposing such an Island would be settled by numerous whites, are. That when the influence, & wishes of the governments in Europe, are turn'd to this object, many leading characters will take an interest in those settlements, bringing, or sending out, their friends & dependents—At this moment, the immense armies which must be disbanded, would, in part be employ'd usefully—the emigrants, & the dissatisfied, under recent changes, would universally flock to such an asylum—in all the other Islands there is danger of revolt from the negroes—in this, there would be none—presuming when I say this—that the principles of government shall be wise, liberal & protective to all men, & all opinions—

If you do me the honor of writing to me, on this, or any other subject— Please to direct to my House, No 31. north 8th Street, Philaa—

I am most respectfully   STEPHEN SAYRE

RC (DLC); at foot of text: "Thomas Jefferson Esqr. President of the United States—"; endorsed by TJ as received 24 Apr. and so recorded in SJL. Enclosure: Plat of a "supposed survey of an Island" divided among the United States, Russia, France, Great Britain, and 13 other nations, with a capital "to be placed farther north, or south, as nature may be found to favour it" (same).

MY FORMER LETTER: Sayre to TJ, 12 Jan.

To Mary Jefferson Eppes

MY DEAR MARIA   Monticello Apr. 11. 1801.

I wrote to mr Eppes on the 8th. instant by post, to inform him I should on the 12th. send off a messenger to the Hundred for the horses he may have bought for me. Davy Bowles will accordingly set out tomorrow, & will be the bearer of this. he leaves us all well, and wanting nothing but your's & mr Eppes's company to make us compleatly happy. let me know by his return when you expect to be here, that I may accomodate to that my orders as to executing the interior work of the different parts of the house. John being at work under Lilly, Goliah is our gardener, & with his veteran aids, will be directed to make what preparation he can for you. it is probable I shall come home myself about the last week of July or first of August to stay two months, and then be absent again at least six months. in fact I expect only to make [a] short visit to this place[1] of a fortnight or three weeks in April & two months during the sickly season in autumn every year. these terms I shall hope to pass with you here, and that either in spring or fall you will be able to pass some time with me in Washington. had it been possible, I would have made a tour now on my return to see you. but I am tied to a day for my return to Washington to assemble our new administration, & begin our work systematically. I hope, when you come up, you will make very short stages, drive slow & safely, which may well be done if you do not permit yourselves to be hurried. surely the sooner you come the better. the servants will be here under your commands and such supplies as the house affords. before that time our bacon will be here from Bedford. continue to love me, my dear Maria, as affectionately as I do you. I have no object as near my heart as your's & your sister's happiness. present me affectionately to mr Eppes & be assured yourself of my unchangeable & tenderest attachment to you.   TH: JEFFERSON

RC (photostat in ViU); torn at seal; addressed: "Mrs. Maria Eppes Bermuda Hundred."

[1] Preceding three words interlined.

From Joseph Fay

DR SIR   New York 11h. April 1801

Your obliging favour of the 22d. Ulto. has been duly recd. The sentiments it contained are Characteristic of Geneuine Republican principles, they are such as I have ever supported invariably since we assumed our Independence; I hope never to have occasion to change.

I have just recd. the enclosed letter from my Father in Law Mr. Broome, whose Zeal for the cause of his Country has proved unfavourable to his private fortune, he has paid a heavy Tax for the attainment of our happy Government which has left him but barely a Support, which occasions his applying for some Public employment.

Should the office of Collector for the Port of New Haven become Vacant it would be very acceptable to him & his friends to obtain the appointment to that place, and as he has been regularly Bread a Merchant no Doubt but he could discharge the duties to Satisfaction, Permit me therefore to recommend him to your favourable Notice. it would be an act of justice from the Public, and of benevolence in you, and the favour would be ever gratefully acknowledged by Dear Sir

Your friend & Servant   JOSEPH FAY

RC (DNA: RG 59, LAR); at head of text: "Thomas Jefferson President of the U States"; endorsed by TJ as received 24 Apr. and so recorded in SJL with notation "Off."

ENCLOSURE

From Samuel Broome

New Haven State of Connecticut
SIR   April 8th. 1801.

permit me to Congratulate you Sir, and our Country, on your late appointment, under a full belief that different measures will be pursued, that we may hear no more of Eight ℔ Cents &c &c &c. I had the honor, of your acquaintance ten years past in Paris, but the lapse of time, no doubt, has effaced every Idea of me.—Being a Native Citizen of the United States of America, I take the liberty to recapitulate my Conduct and misfortunes during the late American War—I lent the United States, Two hundred Thousand Dollars, in Consequence of Debts I owed and being Severely pressed, by my british Creditors on account of my political Principles, I was Necessitated to sell them at Two Shillings and Nine pence on the Pound, besides Gen'l Gray in Bedford, Massachusetts, and the Traitor Arnold at New London in this State. Burnt property belonging to me, to the Amount of Twelve or fifteen Thousand Pounds, together with other losses, has reduced me from a state of afluence to a pittance, therefore am Necessitated to make application, to my Country through your good Self Sir for any office which may afford my family a Comfortable support—As I am fixed in this City an appointment here, or in this State, would be preferable, if this cannot be done I would remove hence to any other, in the Union, I have it in my power to give ample security for the faithful discharge of office, My eldest daughter has the happiness to be allied by Marriage to Joseph Fay [Snr?] Merchant in New York late of Bennington in the State of Vermont. This Gentleman I am informd has the honor of your Acquaintance, I have requested him to forward this letter. his honor the Vice President is also, well acquainted with me and has been so ever since the summer of one thousand seven hundred and seventy five, when we were at Cambridge previously to his departure from there to Canada under Arnold. Any Communication to myself, or through Mr Fay, will be gratefully received, by your Sincere friend and well wisher

SAMUEL BROOME

RC (DNA: RG 59, LAR); at foot of text: "His Excellency President of the United States"; endorsed by TJ as received 24 Apr. and so recorded in SJL with notation "Off."

Samuel Broome (d. 1810) was a long-time merchant of New York City and New Haven, Connecticut, primarily in partnership with his brother, John Broome, and his brother-in-law, Jeremiah Platt.

Samuel Broome made TJ's acquaintance in Paris in 1789 and Fay married his EL-DEST DAUGHTER Betsey in 1793. He did not receive an appointment during TJ's administration (Joseph A. Scoville, *The Old Merchants of New York City*, 3d ser. [New York, 1865], 208-16; *Vermont Gazette*, 16 Aug. 1793; Syrett, *Hamilton*, 3:661, 675; *Providence Gazette*, 14 July 1810; Vol. 14:560; Vol. 15:92, 486).

From Solomon Southwick

SIR,   Albany, April 11, 1801.

I have received a letter from my friend, Col. Matthew Lyon, informing me of your intention to give me the appointment of Marshal of the District of Albany. Relying on the correctness of Col. Lyon's information, and wishing to save you the trouble of transmitting a Commission—a Commission which, as coming from a Republican Executive, I should think highly honourable—I inform you, that having lately commenced the study of Law, I am prevented by a rule of Court which applies to Students in general, from pursuing openly any other avocation whatsoever during my term of Clerkship.

I am convinced, Sir, that Mr. John Barber, my brother-in-law, would fill the office of Marshal with propriety. I wish him to have it, even if it should not be lucrative. It would perhaps increase his influence in Society, tend to his advantage as printer of the Albany Register (in which I shall not dissemble that I am privately concerned)—and aid the Republican cause. I can assure you, Sir, that Mr. Barber and myself have made very considerable pecuniary sacrifices in consequence of our attachment to and support of republican principles.

The annexed Certificate of Jeremiah Van Rensselaer, Esq. the Republican Candidate for the office of Lieutenant-Governor of this State, I trust will satisfy you, that my recommendation of Mr. Barber is well founded.

I am, Sir, with sentiments of respect and veneration, founded on eight years attentive observation of your public character, Your obedient Servt.   SOLN. SOUTHWICK

RC (CSmH); at foot of text: "Thomas Jefferson, President of the U.S."; with subjoined certificate in Southwick's hand, signed by Jeremiah Van Rensselaer, Albany, 11 Apr., recommending John Barber "as a proper person" for the office of marshal at Albany and noting that the appointment would be considered "by those who know him, as the merited reward of integrity and patriotism"; endorsed by TJ as received 6 May and so recorded in SJL with notation "Off."

Born in Newport, Rhode Island, the son of a newspaper editor, Solomon Southwick (1773-1839) arrived in Albany as a journeyman printer in 1791 and began working at the *Albany Register*, a newspaper owned by John and Robert Barber. Southwick became John Barber's partner in 1792, shortly after Robert Barber withdrew from the newspaper. Due to financial constraints, caused partly by persecutions under the Sedition Act, Southwick withdrew from management of the *Register* in 1800 to study law, but he continued to contribute political essays. He became a prominent Jeffersonian Republican in state and local politics. Upon the death of John Barber in 1808, Southwick assumed

ownership of the *Albany Register* and served as state printer from 1810 until 1814. Participation in a bank scheme and land speculation led to Southwick's political and financial decline, beginning in 1812. In 1817 he was forced to suspend publication of the *Register*. Southwick unsuccessfully ran for governor of New York in 1822 as an independent and in 1828 on the Anti-Masonic ticket (ANB; Kline, *Burr*, 1:564-5).

MY BROTHER-IN-LAW: in 1795 Southwick married Jane, sister of John Barber (ANB, 20:396).

TJ had received the semiweekly ALBANY REGISTER at least since 1800. It was one of the newspapers he supported during the crisis of the Republican press under the Sedition Act. In March 1804 he paid $3 for his subscription (see Sowerby, No. 587; MB, 2:1123; TJ to James Monroe, 17 July 1802).

JEREMIAH VAN RENSSELAER and John Tayler of Albany also wrote Aaron Burr letters recommending Barber. Burr communicated Tayler's endorsement to Madison. On 27 July TJ appointed Hermanus H. Wendell marshal for the Albany district (Kline, *Burr*, 564-6, 571).

From James Thomson Callender

SIR,   Richmond 12th. April 1801

I address this letter to you, by the advice of Mr Edmund Randolph. It had been understood that my fine of two hundred dollars was to be remitted. The late Marshall refused to return the money. It would be unnecessary to repeat the particulars of his refusal; because they were communicated some weeks ago, to Mr Lincoln, and because Mr Randolph has undertaken to explain them to you. I should not have intruded upon you with this application, if I had not lost all reasonable hopes of an answer from the secretary. I was the more hurt by this disappointment because I had wrote to Mr Leiper that I would positively send him this money, and because my friends at Philadelphia have contrived to produce a coolness on his part. It would have been fortunate for me, if I had still remained in Jail as from the change of air I have never had a day's health since I came out of it. Some monies had been collected to assist me, and the greater part of it has been *intercepted!* The Governor has engaged to assist me, in discharging my account of boarding with Mr Rose, although he could hardly believe but what it had been discharged by a Democratical collection. During the two years that I have been in Richmond, I was paid ten dollars per week as an Editor for four months and an half; for the half of the rest of that time I received victuals and for what I did in the next nine months I neither received, nor do I ever expect to recieve a single farthing. I mention these particulars as this is probably the close of my correspondence with you, that you may not suppose that *I*, at least, have gained any thing by the victories of Republicanism. Governor Monroe knows much more which I would be ashamed to put upon paper of the unexempled treatment which I have recieved from the party. This was because I had gone farther to serve them than some dastards durst go to serve themselves; and they wished, under all sorts of bad usage, to bury the memory of offensive obligations. By the cause, I have lost five years of labour; have gained five thousand personal enemies; got my name inserted in five hundred Libels, and have ultimately got something very like a quarrel with the only friend I had in Pennsylvania. In a word, I have been equally calumniated, pillaged, and betrayed by all parties. I have only the consolation of reflecting that I acted from principle, and that, with a few individual exceptions, I have never affected to trust either the one, or the other.

I hope, sir, that you will forgive the length and the stile of this letter; and with great respect, I have the honour to be Sir, your most obliged, hum[ble] Servant, JAS. T. CALLENDER

P.S. For some weeks past, the state of my nerves does not permit of my writing in my own hand.

RC (DLC); in Robert Richardson's hand, with signature and postscript in Callender's hand; torn at seal; addressed: "The President of The United States"; endorsed by TJ as received 15 Apr. and so recorded in SJL.

According to Callender, Edmund RANDOLPH conversed with the president in Charlottesville about the remittance of the fine and later delivered the letter above to TJ "with his own hand." Callender noted of this letter: "I took unusual pains to make it both guarded and explicit. It had not a syllable which could give ground for offence; and while I described the treatment which I had received in Richmond, and the situation into which my exertions in the Cause had brought me, I think the story should have reached the heart of a millstone. I might as well have addressed a letter to Lot's wife" (Madison, *Papers, Sec. of State Ser.*, 1:117).

For David Meade Randolph's refusal to RETURN THE MONEY, see TJ to George Jefferson, 4 Mch.

On 27 Apr. Callender informed James Madison that he had written "an explanatory card" to Thomas LEIPER that read:

"'Mr. Jefferson has not returned one shilling of my fine. I now begin to know what Ingratitude is'" (Madison, *Papers, Sec. of State Ser.*, 1:117).

From Thomas Law

SIR.   Washington April 12. 1801.

The enclosed Letter having met with the approbation of some sensible impartial characters, I have been induced reluctantly to intrude with it upon your retirement.

The measures you have already adopted have extorted an acknowledgement from those persons who persued a conduct diametrically opposite "that General Washington was the founder[1] but that you Sir will be the maker of the City."

On the exertions of less than eight months the fate of Washington City depends, the shortness of the time allowed for creating prosperity & harmony, will therefore plead my excuse I trust for the liberty I now take which shall not be repeated.

I remain with unfeigned respect & esteem yr most obedient & most humble St   THOMAS LAW.

RC (DLC); endorsed by TJ as received 6 May and so recorded in SJL. Enclosure: an eight-page, undated statement, recording the role and expense of Congress in selecting a permanent seat of government at a central location and in building the Federal City, while noting that few "persons of fortune" chose to reside there; acknowledging that George Washington placed the President's House too far from the Capitol and that John Adams and his commissioners favored the West End of the city, thereby creating a bias toward Georgetown; and noting that after surveying the city map and reading TJ's notes, he was convinced of the need for a large commercial metropolis near the Navy Yard so that Georgetown would not be favored over Alexandria (MS in same, TJ Papers, 111:19119-22; unsigned; in same hand as Washington, D.C., Inhabitants to TJ, printed at 21 Mch.; with additions in margin in Law's hand).

[1] Law here canceled: "of the City."

From Salimbeni

MONSIEUR   Paris 22 Germinal An 9

Permettez que je Vous adresse des lettres que ma femme Ecrit a Mesdames Vos filles. En prenant cette Liberté Je Saisis L'occasion de renouveller a Votre Excellence L'hommage de ma profonde reconnoissance et de Joindre ma voix à celle de tous les francais pour la congratuler Sur le poste Eminent auquel la porté la confiance et L'estime de Ses concitoyens.

Rentré dans mon pays par les bienfaits et les recommandations aupres du consul general Létombe, de Votre Excellence Je Viens aujourdhui conjurer Ses bontés pour m'en faire Sortir. Je suis dans ce moment Employé par M. de talleyrand ministre des Relations Exterieures et Jai Sa promesse d'être nommé avant peu a un poste de Commissaire des Relations Commerciales aux états unis de L'amerique. Je Suis Sur qu'un mot de Votre Excellence a M. de talleyrand le mettroit a même de Suivre pour moi toute L'impulsion de Sa bonne Volonté. Il ne me la pas même laissé ignorer. M. Volney qui a beaucoup contribué a me faire avoir la place que Joccupe ma donné le conseil d'en prier V.E.

tout me porte a croire que Je Serai bientot a même de presenter ma profonde reconnoissance de Vive Voix au president des Etats unis de L'amerique. Ma femme Se fait un fêste de pouvoir y revoir Ses anciennes compagnes de Couvent qui lui ont temoigné un si vif interest a Son dernier Voyage d'Amerique.

Je prie Votre Excellence d'agreer Le respect tres humble avec Lequel Jai L'honneur d'etre Son tres humble & Obeissant Serviteur

SALIMBENI

EDITORS' TRANSLATION

SIR   Paris, 22 Germinal Year 9 [12 Apr. 1801]

Allow me to address to you some letters that my wife wrote to my ladies, your daughters. While taking that liberty, I seize the occasion to renew to Your Excellency the homage of my deepest gratitude and to join my voice together with all Frenchmen to congratulate you on the eminent post to which the confidence and esteem of your fellow citizens has borne you.

Having returned to my country through your excellency's kind deeds and recommendations to Consul General Létombe, today I come to implore your kind deeds to make me leave it. I am at this moment employed by Monsieur Talleyrand, minister of foreign relations, and I have his promise to be named soon to a post of commissary for commercial relations in the United States of America. I am certain that a word from Your Excellency to Monsieur Talleyrand would place him in a position to fulfill for me the impulse of his good will. He has not left even me in ignorance of this. Monsieur Volney, who greatly contributed to my obtaining the position I occupy, advised me to beg this of Your Excellency.

Everything leads me to believe that I shall soon be able to present my deep gratitude in person to the president of the United States of America. My wife rejoices at being able to see there again her former convent companions who showed such a lively interest on her last voyage to America.

I beg Your Excellency to accept the very humble respect with which I have the honor to be your very humble and obedient servant   SALIMBENI

RC (MoSHi: Jefferson Papers); endorsed by TJ as a letter from "Salimberi" recorded in SJL. of 22 Germinal received 16 July and so recorded in SJL.

Salimbeni was married to the former Mademoiselle de Bruni (Bruny), who was the same age as TJ's daughter Martha and had been her friend at the Abbey of Pentemont in Paris, where Martha attended school from 1784 to 1789. TJ's younger daughter also attended the school. "Bruni," as she was called by TJ and his daughters, was on the island of Guadeloupe in 1791 and in the United States in 1797, and from the letter above it appears that Salimbeni was also in America in the 1790s. Madame Salimbeni was again in the West Indies, in Trinidad, in 1804. Her husband wrote to TJ again from Paris in 1806, giving as an address the residence of the Comte de Rémusat, who was at that time the first chamberlain and master of the wardrobe of Napoleon's court. TJ habitually recorded the Salimbenis' name as "Salimberi" (*Report of the Curator to the Board of Directors of the Thomas Jefferson Memorial Foundation, April 13, 1960* [Charlottesville, 1961], illus. facing 11, 17; Charles-Otto Zieseniss, *Napoléon et la Cour Impériale* [Paris, 1980], 245-6, 410; Tulard, *Dictionnaire Napoléon*, 1450-1; Vol. 7:411; Vol. 14:xl-xli, 356n; Vol. 18:500, 580n; Vol. 20:377; Vol. 29:314-15; Salimbeni to TJ, 17 Feb. 1806; Madame Salimbeni to TJ, 26 Nov. 1804).

From Benjamin W. Stuart

MOST HOND. SIR   Bale. April 12th. 1801

I presumtively address your fealing soul; although elivated on lifes highest perogative. I daine to request what in my Country's cause, and for my Country's glory, and for the perminant establishment of that liberty, for which my father shed his blood. you will not, you can not, refuse. although a Destitute young man of Eighteen. I reste asured of genirous patronage, in your patriottic soul.

Then Hond. Sir. to one who pants to shed his blood. and to one, whose soul Burnes to raise a monument of heroisem to his Country's faime. grante him Kinde Sir. but Small the means, & he presumes to raise them to as yet unheard of glory. no hills. no Dailes. no Vallies. shall impeed his course.

With the Greatest respect I am Hond. Sir Yr. Very Obe: Hbe. Servent
BENJ W STUART

RC (DNA: RG 59, LAR); at head of text: "Thomas Jefferson Esqr."; endorsed by TJ as received 24 Apr. from Baltimore and so recorded in SJL with notation "Off."

The Editors have been unable to identify the author of this letter, but he is probably the same Benjamin Stuart who wrote TJ an undated letter received on 22 Dec. 1808. By then, suffering from blindness that created "incalculable difficulties for the delivery of my Orations, Political, Phylosophical, and Physical, intended for public benefit as well as my own good," Stuart again sought TJ's "bounty for an elevation of my destitute dustress'd situation" (RC in MoSHi: Jefferson Papers; at head of text: "To the President of the United States"; endorsed by TJ as received 22 Dec. 1808 and so recorded in SJL).

From John West Butler

Sir,   Annapolis, April 13th. 1801.

Having issued proposals for printing the enclosed work, and intending shortly to commence a tour through many of the States, particularly Virginia, for the purpose of obtaining Subscribers, I have ventured to solicit the early patronage of a Character so well known, and justly respected, both on account of his high office, and the brilliant talents which have placed him in it; conscious, that a name so celebrated and beloved, will not only add a pleasing lustre and respectibility to the Proposals, but insure a large increase of Subscribers to a work that is approved by, and graced with, the illustrious name of *Jefferson*. And, believe me, Sir, your name will by no means be dishonoured by patronizing the "*Abbess*"; a work, allowed by the highest judges, to bear the strongest marks of worth and genius. What better proof, Sir, can be produced or required, of the truth of this assertion, than, that it was written by the author of "Shakespeare's Papers," a work, the spirit and genius of which, bore so near an alliance and close imitation of the British Homer, that the greatest literary judges and warmest admirers of the English Bard, not only gave it their decided voice in favour of its originating in Shakespeare's fertile brain, but even the Reviewers, those literary dictators, passed on it a long Eulogium, and congratulated the lovers of wit, taste, and genius, on the restoration of those unlooked for, those valuable, inimitable, and long lost "*Papers*" of the immortal Shakespeare!

My esteem for your Character, and my firm belief that it is your sincere intention, to act up, in every respect, even the most minute, to that wise, virtuous, and liberal conduct, which your "Address" promises in such clear, nervous, and elegant language, can not be better shewn, than by informing you, that I am a Federalist; In despight of party prejudice, and of flimsy evasions, to obtain a favour by renouncing my principles, I make this declaration; and, when I consider to whom I address it, every fear that you will treat me with neglect on that account, vanishes, as that noble sentiment immediately occurs to my mind, that "*We are all Republicans; we are all Federalists*;" a sentiment well worthy of its Author, as it is the vital principle of political tolerance and liberality.

Excuse me, Sir, for detaining you thus long; impelled as I was by the impulse of my mind to let you know the truth, which is far superior, though in a homely garb, to falsehood decked in purple robes.— The favor I ask, Sir, would be particularly grateful, as I am a young

man, just setting out in life; a situation in which a small encouragement is received with gratitude, and remembered with pleasure; and
to whom, on the other hand, the frowns of Fortune or of Friends, are
felt with keenness and cutting severity; as a youth, when embarking
on the troubled and fluctuating ocean of the world, must ever have the
innate sensibilities of his nature, wound up to a peculiar tone of delicacy, consequently the sun-shine of Fortune, or the clouds of disappointment, make a strong & lasting impression on his mind.—Should
you grant this favor, Sir, it will ever be remembered with gratitude,
but, should you do more, & send me a line annexed, it would confer an
obligation that the sweeping hand of time would be unable to erase
from the mind of, Sir, your most grateful, sincere, and obedient humble Servant, JOHN WEST BUTLER.

Easton, April 22.
P.S. Should you Sir, grant my request, you will greatly oblige me, by
directing it to me at Baltimore, whither I shall be at the time of your
sending it, as I shall set off for that City in a few days.

I send this letter from Easton, having had it by me these ten days,
waiting an opportunity of coming hither, as well for the purpose of
obtaining subscribers, as to request Mr. G. Duvall's opinion of the propriety of sending it; and, having obtained his judgment thereon, which
is flattering to my wishes, I now take the liberty of forwarding it.

RC (DLC); addressed: "Thomas Je-
fferson Esq. President of the United
States. Monticello"; franked; endorsed by
TJ as received 30 Apr. and so recorded in
SJL. Enclosure: see below.

John West Butler was a printer in Baltimore, Maryland, at the corner of Water
and South Gay Streets in 1801-2. Eight
years later, he asked TJ to subscribe to another of his printing ventures, the *Maryland Republican*, an Annapolis newspaper
(Stafford, *Baltimore Directory, for 1802*,
19; Brigham, *American Newspapers*
1:223; RS, 1:303-4).

ENCLOSED WORK: Butler was the
American publisher of the English gothic
novel *The Abbess, A Romance* (London,
1799; Baltimore, 1801). The book's AU-
THOR, William Henry Ireland, was better
known for his sensational forgeries of
SHAKESPEARE'S PAPERS that were published in 1795-96 (DNB).

TJ's reply to Butler of 8 May 1801 included his subscription to the book. "Tho'

a stranger to the work I have not hesitated
to give this mark of my personal respect
for yourself as well as of my desire to encourage the art of p[rint]ing in this country generally." TJ wished Butler success in
his endeavor "from the more solid circumstances of the merit of the work & the desires of the editor to the patronage of the
public" (PrC in DLC; faint and blurred;
at foot of text: "Mr. John West Butler";
endorsed by TJ in ink on verso). On 29
May 1801, Baltimore postmaster Charles
Burrall notified TJ that his 8 May letter to
Butler was undelivered (RC in MHi; at
foot of text: "The President of the United
States"; endorsed by TJ as received 30
May and so recorded in SJL). TJ's reply
to Burrall of 1 June communicated Butler's instructions of 13 Apr., "expressly desiring me to address the answer to Baltimore through which he expected to pass"
(PrC in MHi; faint; at foot of text: "Mr.
Charles Burrall"; endorsed by TJ in ink
on verso).

From Andrew Ellicott

DEAR SIR   Philadelphia April 13th 1801

I have accompanied this by a few sheets of my observations, they contain an account of the work on the boundary as far as to Pearl, or half-way river. The manner of describing the prime vertical as mentioned at the beginning of the line, I have not found noticed by any writer, but should think it too obvious to be new.—I am sorry the plate containing the references is not yet engraved.—

Whilst I was engaged in the City of Washington some years ago I made a number of observations to determine its longitude, but all of them with some papers relative to the plan of the City were lost, when the office was pillaged: But fortunately two very important observations had been communicated to our late worthy friend Mr. Rittenhouse, and published in the 4th. volume of the Transactions of our Society.—The *first* is on an annular eclipse of the Sun, and the *second* an occultation of (α ♉) Aldebaran by the moon.—Observations of this kind answer very well for the determination of the longitude, but the calculations are critical, and labourious, owing to the moon's parallax in altitude, latitude, and longitude, and therefore not in common use:—However for want of other materials, and having little to do besides correcting the press, I have gone thro' the calculations.—

The observation on the eclipse stands as below

		D	h	'	"				
1791	Annulas completed at	2	18	35	45	} Apparent time		Observed at George Town
April	Annulas broken	2	18	39	57			
	End of the eclipse	2	19	52	20			Lat. N. 38° 55'

	h	'	"	
The Longitude by the completion of the Annulas is	5	7	53	} West from Greenwich
do by the breaking of the Annulas	5	8	14	
do by the end of the eclipse	5	8	5	

The second observation was made near the meridian of the Capitol in latitude 38° 52' 40" N. and as follows.

		D	h	'	"	
1793	α ♉ immersed at	21	7	55	49.5	} apparent time
January	α ♉ emerged at	21	9	25	21.5	

	h	'	"	
Longitude by the immersion	5	7	13	} West from Greenwich
do by the emersion	5	7	47	

The observation on the eclipse was made about 10" west from where the occultation was observed, which when deducted from the eclipse, the results will stand as below for the meridian of the Capitol.

	h	'	"	
Longitude by the completion of the annulas	5	7	43	
do by the breaking of the annulas	5	8	4	
do by the end of the eclipse	5	7	55	West from Greenwich
do by the immersion of α ♉	5	7	13	
do by the emersion of α ♉	5	7	47	

Mean   5 7 44.4 = 76° 56' 6"

From which it appears, (in the language Americans ought to use), that Greenwich is 5^h 7' 44.4" or 76° 56' 6" east from the City of Washington.—

I have been long wanting our longitudes to be reckoned, or counted, from our own Capitol, and not from a place within another country; and for this purpose calculated, and published an Almanac with the sun's declination, eclipses of ♃trs. Satellites &c. adapted to the meridian of the City of Washington, which I had estimated at 5^h 8' west from Greenwich, but the plan fell thro when I left the City.—

We appear yet to be connected to Great Britain by a number of small ligaments, which tho apparently unimportant, are nevertheless a drawback upon that absolute independence we ought as a nation to maintain.—It would be very well when the longitude of the City of Washington is more accurately settled by a sufficient course of observations, consisting both of the eclipses of ♃trs. Satellites, and lunar distances, to have an American gazetteer published, in which the longitudes should be reckoned east, and west from the Capitol.—Wishing you health and happiness in discharging the important duties of your appointment, I am with sincere respect, and friendship, your Hbl. Servt.

ANDW; ELLICOTT.

RC (DLC); at foot of text: "Thomas Jefferson President of U.S. and of the American Philosophical Society"; Ellicott used the astronomical symbols "α ♉" ("alpha Tauri," which identifies the star as the brightest in the constellation Taurus) for the star Aldebaran and "♃" for the planet Jupiter; endorsed by TJ as received 24 Apr. and so recorded in SJL. Dft (DLC: Ellicott Papers). Enclosure not found; see Ellicott to TJ, 20 Mch.

Ellicott's assertion that his OFFICE WAS PILLAGED referred to his acrimonious relationship with the commissioners of the Federal District before his departure from the surveying department in 1793. Elsewhere he stated that his information on eclipses of the moons of Jupiter had been "privately taken from my lodgings in Georgetown" along with some other notes. His figures on the 1791 solar eclipse observed at Georgetown and the 1793 occultation of Aldebaran by the moon appeared in the TRANSACTIONS of the American Philosophical Society in 1799 with data from several other astronomical observations (APS, *Transactions*, 4 [1799], 48-9; Bryan, *National Capital*, 1:209-10; note to James Reed Dermott to TJ, 7 Mch. 1801).

PUBLISHED AN ALMANAC: early in his career Ellicott was associated with the *United States Almanack*, and in the 1780s and early 1790s John Hayes of Baltimore issued *Ellicott's Maryland and Virginia Almanac* (for examples, see Evans, Nos. 19619, 23347, 22482; DAB).

From Silas Hubbell

SIR   Stratford April 13th 1801

you will be Pleased to Except the Pettion of A Poor Mekanick in Behalf of my Son in Law John Selby Junr. Who on the 20th of Sept. 1795 Did With the Influence of his owners Ellcitly Land 16 Hogsets of Rum and it Was Seased By Mr Smedly the Custom hous officer and he Was Prosicuted By Mr Edwards Destrict Atarny as Well as his owners But by there Influence they Purswaded him to keep out of the Way and they Would git him Cleair But Alas Sir they took good Care of them Selvs and Left him to Suffer two Jugments of A thousand Dolars Each With A Bill of Cost of 424 Dollar 60 Cents Which Sum he is Not Abel to pay the Grand Jury Found A Bill of Inditement Against him and he Was Obliged to quit his Cuntry and Reside in the West Indes for Some time he then Returnd and Was taken Put into gole Lay there one Winter and maide his Escape and Again Resides in the West Indes he has Left A Wife and one Child A Burden on my hands for 5 years and I am A man in Low Surcomstances as to Property they have Become A Large Burden I Now Sir in Behalf of him have Dared to take my Pen and Ask your Excellency this question Wheither you will be Pleased to Pardon the Bill of Inditement Against him that he may Return and be A Citterson once more and Whether the Secatary of treasure Will Pleas to Metigate Some part of the Judgment against him as he is Willing to Contribute his Littill all about 1000 Dolars if this Should Meat your Approbation and the Secatarys I Will Secure to Mr Edwards that Sum untill I Can Inform him that he may Come and pay the Money had I thought Neasarey I Could have got Large Numbers of Gentelmen of the First Carackter to Subscribe in his Behalf and think that he has Sufferd Addiquate to his Crime But as the Law Was then in its Infant State and Attending to you Speach to Both Houses of Congres I thought it Not Neasary But Shall Leave it to your kind Benovalance But if this Should Not Meat your approbation I Should be glad to know wheither any thing Short of the Severity of the Law Can be obtained in his Favour as he is Constanly Writing me to know Whither any thing Can Dun for him I am your Faithfull Cittercon and Most Obident Humbel Servant

SILAS HUBBELL

RC (DNA: RG 59, GPR); at head of text: "to his Excellency Thomas Jefferson Esqr. President of the Eunited States."

JOHN SELBY was a young mariner from Stratford, Connecticut, who by 1795 was captain of a brig in the West Indian trade. He married Hubbell's daughter Betsey that same year. A copy of a pardon has not been found by the Editors. A local historian asserted that Selby, through intermediaries,

was able to secure a pardon after agreeing to pay a fine of $9,000. He returned to Stratford "a dissipated, wretched man" (Frederic W. Bailey, ed., *Early Connecticut Marriages as Found on Ancient Church Records Prior to 1800*, 7 vols. [New Haven, 1896-1906; repr. Baltimore, 1982], 7:13; Samuel Orcutt, *A History of the Old Town of Stratford and the City of Bridgeport, Connecticut*, 2 vols. [New Haven, 1886], 1:435).

From Montgomery County, Kentucky, Citizens

SIR   [13 April 1801]

We most sincerely concur in sentiments with the many addresses of Congratulation you have been daily receiving upon your being elected to the first office of your Country. Since the death of our first illustrious president, whose great and essential services rendered to his Country Justly gave him a title to the first place in the esteem and Confidence of his Country, you are the first of our fellow Citizens in whom we wish to repose our rights, the most important of all trusts, and most sincerely Congratulate you on that appointment: From your past Conduct both in public and private life, since the declaration of independence to the present time, from your patriotism and wisdom, from the political sentiments which you have uniformly expressed, and from the measures you have endeavoured to carry into effect, we doubt not but your chief object will be to preserve the Constitution inviolate, to defeat the measures of all those who may have an interest seperate from the Good of their Country, or may act under any improper influence whether foreign or domestic. We have strong hopes, Sir, from your conciliating sentiments and Conduct, that, under your administration every different party in the united states will cordially unite under the banners of republicanism.

We assure you that our feelings were much agitated upon hearing that a party in Congress were endeavoring to defeat the choice and wishes of the people in your election, and greatly dreaded the Confusion such an event might have occasioned, such schemes—appeared to us the product of principles—diamitrically opposite to true republicanism.

As far as depends on us we promise you our support in your arduous task and may that infinite power who presides over the Councils of the universe so guide your administration that it may tend to the prosperity of your Country and your own Honour and happiness. Done by unanimous Consent JOHN ROBERTS Chairman
Attest
WILL. B. ELAM Secretary

RC (DLC); in an unidentified hand, signed by Roberts and Elam; at head of text: "The address of the first Battalion of the 31st regiment of the state of Kentucky and a number of the citizens of Montgomery County Assembled at Nicholas Anderson's in said County on the 13th day of April 1801" and "To Thomas Jefferson President of the United States of America"; endorsed by TJ as received 29 May 1801 and so recorded in SJL.

From Thomas Newton

DR SIR   Norfolk 14 Apl. 1801
Inclosed is a bill of parcels & Lading for a pipe of old Brasil Madeira wine, which I have hopes will meet your Approbation— Mr. Cocke the purser of the Cheasepeak frigate has been so good as to take this letter, has promised me, he will see the wine taken care of from Alexandria to Washington, he is a worthy young man & conducts himself with great propriety (I have heard) in his office. I am very respectfully
Yr Obt. Servt   THOS NEWTON

RC (DLC); endorsed by TJ as received 1 May and so recorded in SJL. Enclosure: Invoice, Norfolk, 14 Apr., for one pipe of old Brazil Madeira wine for the president of the U.S., purchased of James Taylor, Jr., for $350 plus 12.5 cents for drayage, taken aboard the sloop commanded by Abel Willis for delivery to the president or his agent upon payment of the freight "as customary" (MS in same; signed by Willis).

From Jonas Simonds

SIR   Philadel April 14th 1801
Near Nine years the period of my life the most Active and the most Valuable when Consumed in the Contest to Establish the liberty and Independence of this My Native Country, which the inclosed Certificate will Explain, Since that period Sir, and since the adoption of the Constitution of the united States I have held a Subordinate Station in the Custom House department of this district, But my political Opinions & Sentiments not Harmonising with those who

called themselves Federal, left me no room to hope or Expect any preferment, and in that humble Station I have been left with no other Consolation then having performed my part with fidelity to my Country, amidst all the changes that have taken place, I have lately learnt sir, that Applications have been made to you in my favour for the Marshals Office of this district, but in that effort I have been unsuccessful not withstanding that, may I not yet hope sir, that if other Changes should take place that you will look Over those papers Once more, which have been handed to you, And if the Surveyors Office of this district should be vacated, that you will think of me, I have taken the liberty of naming that Office because I am som what Connected with It at present, & am acquainted with the duties of It, you will be plesed to pardon the liberty I have taken and

Believe me Respectfully   J SIMONDS

RC (DNA: RG 59, LAR); at foot of text: "Thomas Jefferson President of the United States"; endorsed by TJ as received 24 Apr. and so recorded in SJL with notation "Off." Enclosure not found.

Jonas Simonds (d. 1816) was an inspector in the Philadelphia Custom House. He achieved the rank of captain in the Continental artillery during the Revolutionary War and later accepted the appointment of major in the Philadelphia militia, which earned him the enmity of his Federalist supervisors in the customhouse. On 8 July 1808, TJ appointed him colonel of infantry, a position he held until honorably discharged in June 1815. He died in St. Louis, on 13 July 1816 (James Robinson, *The Philadelphia Directory, City and County Register, for 1802* [Philadelphia, 1801], 221; Heitman, *Dictionary*, 887; Heitman, *Register*, 497-8; JEP, 2:100; *Daily National Intelligencer*, 6 Aug. 1816; Thomas Leiper to TJ, 26 Jan. 1806).

From John Broadbent

SIR   Messina 15 April 1801—

Thy fellow Cityzens assembled in this Port (whose names appear in the inclosed Document) having done me the honor to appoint me Agent of Commerce for the United States of America in the Island of Sicily, I avail myself of the first Oppertunity for informing thee thereof, in order that, if my Services should be thought useful to thy Country Men in this Part of the World thou shouldst confirm the appointment—

I introduced the American Flag into this Island for the first time about two years ago and I have lately had the pleasure of seeing eight or ten Vessels at a time in this Port—

With best wishes for thy Happyness and the Prosperity of the Nation of which thou art now placed at the Head I remain a Cityzen of the World—   JOHN BROADBENT

RC (DNA: RG 59, LAR); at foot of text: "To the Hble Mr. Jefferson President of the U:S. of America. Washington town"; endorsed by TJ as received 29 June and so recorded in SJL; also endorsed by TJ: "to be consul of Messina. see Caveat by Jos. Barnes." Dupl (same); enclosed in Broadbent to TJ, 23 Sep. 1803 (see below). Enclosure: Statement signed at Messina, 27 Feb. 1801, by Robert H. Rose, Joseph Barnes, and ten other American citizens, noting "the great increase of Commerce between our Country and this Island" and appointing "our friend John Broadbent (a man equally recommended to us by his affection for the United States, and his honesty and activity)" as commercial agent for the United States for the island of Sicily (MS in same, in Rose's hand, signed by him and eleven others, signed additionally in attestation by seven other people with notations in Italian; Dupl in same, in an unidentified hand, omitting the additional names in attestation, at head of text: "Copy," enclosed in Broadbent to TJ, 23 Sep. 1803).

John Broadbent was an English merchant residing at Messina, Sicily. In 1805 TJ named him U.S. consul at Messina,

and Broadbent remained in the position for more than 20 years (JEP, 2:7, 13; 3:573; Joseph Barnes to TJ, 14 Feb., 18 May 1801).

In May 1801, Joseph Barnes, who sought a consular appointment for himself, intimated to TJ that the enclosure to the letter above "purporting" to make Broadbent an American AGENT OF COMMERCE had been intended merely as a device to allow the Englishman to remain in Sicily after the eviction of the British from the island. Broadbent's use of the certificate signed by Rose, Barnes, and the others to seek an actual appointment was, according to Barnes, "a violation of our confidence" (Barnes to TJ, 7, 18 May 1801).

Broadbent wrote to TJ again from Messina on 23 Sep. 1803. In that brief letter Broadbent renewed his offer of services as commercial agent or consul general, enclosed the duplicates of the letter printed above and its enclosure, and concluded: "Being hitherto deprived of the honour of a reply, and as no one has made his appearance here in the above capacity I renew the offer of my services and have the honor to be thy friend" (RC in same; endorsed by TJ as received 26 Dec. 1803 and so recorded in SJL; also endorsed by TJ: "to be Consul at Messina").

From James Currie

DR SIR   Richmond April 15th. 1801

I take this opportunity to inform you that I have never been able to see the gentlemen, arbitrators between yourself & Mr Ross to be at leisure to have the matter settled. but have this day seen all three of them Who have pledged themselves to, act upon it Efficiently the moment the pressure of the Court of appeals (now sitting) shall be over, permit me with great truth & sincerity to congratulate you, on your well merited Elevation to the highest honors—of your Country & that you may enjoy good health & undisturbed tranquillity while you administer the Goverment, with honor to yourself & the benefit of our common country: (& of which I am fully impressd)—is the fervent wish of

Dr Sir Your very Respectfull & most Obed Hble. Serv.

JAMES CURRIE

RC (MHi); endorsed by TJ as received 24 Apr. and so recorded in SJL.

For the settlement of TJ's dispute with David ROSS, see note to TJ to George

Jefferson, 14 Oct. 1799. Currie last wrote TJ regarding the arbitration on 8 Jan. 1801.

From Gideon Granger

DEAR SIR,   Suffield April 15th; 1801

Yours of the 29th. ult. has been received. While I feel delighted with the high confidence you have been pleased to repose in me, its charms cannot lead me to forget that the interests of our Country may suffer through my defect of judgment or ignorance of characters. I can give but one assurance; my intentions will be right. The firm support of the true principles of the Constitution and Republicanism will be my sole object;—to that all other considerations will be secondary.

My opinions and information have been desired respecting offices generally, and particularly respecting Post-offices. As to the conduct of Post-Masters, I can only say that the Republicans have suffered many embarrassments owing to a failure of regular communications. the loss of letters and papers &c. and that the evil has extended itself so far that confidence is at an end. It is extremely difficult to bring home a clear charge of designed neglect or violation of Duty. Excuses of accident, error and the like are always at hand, and from the nature of the office many such instances will actually occur—I have spoken to several Gentlemen to give me the desired information, and as far as it can be correctly obtained it shall be forwarded.

The rules suggested in your last letter will be clearly agreed to by most people as perfectly proper to regulate the Executive in deciding upon questions of removals from office. I believe both federalists and republicans will acquiesce in them.—There is however great difficulty in the application of these rules to particular Cases. The federalists will rally round each federal officer, whether attorney, Marshall, Collector, or whatever, and deny the application of either of the rules to which I have refered. Their sensations are already extreme. They deify Harrison and Watson, but say nothing against their successors. They boldly attack the appointment of Willard to the office of Marshall in Vermont; they charge that he is totally destitute of moral character, or any thing like a fair reputation; that he is detested by his neighbors, and the people in the neighboring towns who agree with us in politics: And they delight themselves with the expectation that it will injure the Cause in that part of the State.—What foundation there is for these suggestions I know not—I thought it my duty to give this information.

As to the case of Mr. Goodrich and the general questions respecting removals from office in this State, I have had a full consultation with Messs. Edwards, Kirby and Wolcott and a few other tried friends. They are all agreed that the cause requires the removal of Mr. Goodrich immediately, and of various other principal officers as soon and in such manner as the Exccecutive should deem proper; for my own part I have yielded to the same opinion so far as respects the principal offices in Newhaven, Hartford, Middletown and Litchfield though reluctantly and with some apprehension. I had always till last winter fondly cherished the hope that when the public will should declare in favor of the friends of equal liberty, the foes to the Constitution would attempt a reconcilliation, and the Country be happy and quiet; nor was this hope abandoned untill I became acquainted with the scandalous scenes acted on the floor of Congress, with a clear view of destroying every thing dear and valuable at a single blow. I am now fully convinced of this truth, that though defeated our foes are not conquered, though they crouch it is but to secure their prey;—that their exertions are and will be encreased; and that finally the Republic must expire at the feet of Aristocracy, or the faction be fully prostrated.

Our labors are commenced, but not perfected. We are yet to experience the most violent and severe contest every where East of Pennsylvania. In many of the States our friends are safe, and have a fair prospect of success: but with us in Connecticut the prospect is not pleasing, the exertions of Our Clergy and Aristocracy at yesterdays election have exceeded every thing before known. The torrents of abuse from the pulpits were incredible, and this State whose representatives have the damning credit of planning the ruin of our happy Constitution, design to make themselves terrible in the opposition. The precise modes of their attacks cannot be known; but that attacks will be made is certain. They may attempt the insideous policy of assumed confidence, and ostensibly yield before the Storm while they secretly take every measure to destroy all confidence. I should not be astonished at such an appearance.— We are not deficient in Jesuits—.But Sir, let it assume what appearance it may, rest perfectly assured of this truth, "that the most rancorous and deadly hatred & revenge are the sole passions of all the leaders of the party."

Premising that I am fully sensible of the agitations which will be produced by removals from office, that I have no connextions for whom

I wish office, and that I sincerely lament the existence of a state of things which require acts calculated to affect individuals, and to give pain to the feelings of the Executive.—I proceed to state the reasons upon which I have founded my opinion—

First,—the principle cannot be controvereted, that it is just, fair and honorable that the friends of the Government should have at least as great a proportion of the honors and Offices of the Government as they are of the whole people.—It is true this has been denied by the former administration, and scarcely a republican exists in office. But the abuse of power never creates right;—those who have been injured have a right to justice;—and those who by exertions of party friends, or shameful abandonment of principle have gained or rather usurped office cannot farly claim to hold that which was unfairly acquired. At least reasonable men cannot complain, untill after the favors of the Executive have raised the Republicans to their just and true standing;—when that has taken place, in my opinion it will be best to select for office a due proportion of Moderate federalists for various reasons which will naturally present themselves.

Secondly, The general depression of the Republicans in this State, who have suffered everything, combatting a Phalanx vastly superior to what can be found in any other part of the union forms a strong reason. Nothing can be lost here, and something may be gained: How far this applies to other parts of the union is not for me to judge.—A knowledge that we had the real confidence of the Executive I think would have a happy effect, for already it is used as an argument to affect our elections that the President used the Democrats to ride into office, that now seated there he has evinced his contempt of them, and will rely solely on the federalists for support.

Thirdly, If changes are not made it will be attributed to what is just stated, or to fear, for already threats are united with their other suggestions.

Fourthly, Our people are ambitious and Aspiring, and will presently court the Influence which springs from office:—but while those offices are kept in the hand of our Enemies, the whole patronage of Government exists as a weapon against its sole friends;—and that which has generally been employed to preserve Government, will be employed solely to destroy it; for it will be noticed that no one friend of the present administration, has ever been employed by the past.

Fifthly, If dismissions are made in the early part of administration, it will have sufficient opportunity to explain its motives and views by a regular series of wise and beneficent acts calculated to promote the Interests of the people, and conciliate their feelings. Under the late administration officers of Government were generally insolent, abusive and intolerant, totally destitute of all that politeness, affability and condescention which should always mark the conduct of public agents, particularly in Republics, and which I feel confident will be experienced together with the most prompt discharge of all trusts, under the present Administration. Our final and complete success, in my opinion, depends so much upon the conduct of the various Officers in the Country, that I shall take the liberty of giving you the earliest information, should any defect of duty or impropriety of conduct occur within my knowledge.

Lastly, The sacred rule that no man shall be persecuted for his opinions decently and reasonaly maintained will not apply to any of our oficial Characters. I believe without a single exception All, and I know most have been bitter persecutors—You well know Sir, what has taken place in Connecticut.

I have withheld this letter for some time as I understood the President was not at the seat of Government; in the mean time I have had an opportunity to consult with most of the principal Republicans in this State—WE unanimously recommended the following Gentlemen to the offices hereafter mentioned if the same should in any manner become vacant.

Ephraim Kirby Esquire to be Supervisor of the internal revenue.

The honorable Samuel Bishop, Mayor of the City of Newhaven an old and experienced Officer under the State Govt. of long standing and of unblemished Character the father of Abram Bishop, Collector of the Customs at Newhaven;—Alexander Wolcott Esquire, Collector of the customs at Middletown;—and Enoch Parsons Esqr. to be Marshall of Connecticut. John Welch Esqr. has been much much thought of for the last mentioned office, but local considerations require that Mr. Parsons should have the office.

I cannot close this Letter without congratulating you, Sir, upon the complete success of republicanism in Rhodeisland—

With the highest Esteem & Respect I have the Honor to subscribe myself Your real friend   GIDN. GRANGER

RC (DNA: RG 59, LAR); in an unidentified hand, signed by Granger; closing quotation marks supplied; at foot of text: "Thos. Jefferson Esq Presidt of U States"; endorsed by TJ as received 4 May and so recorded in SJL; also endorsed by TJ: "Goodrich Bishop Saml. Wolcott Parsons."

TJ followed the recommendations of Granger and the Connecticut Republicans in his appointments for the state. Joseph

Willcox, not ENOCH PARSONS, became U.S. marshal, but only after Connecticut Republicans warned TJ against appointing Parsons and recommended Willcox instead (JEP, 1:397, 399, 402-3; Pierpont Edwards and Ephraim Kirby to TJ, 22 Oct. 1801).

From Hammuda Pasha, Bey of Tunis

Mr. President

At Bardo of Tunis the 2d. of the moon Haggia, of the year Egira 1215, and the 15 April 1801

Altho' I have charged the worthy and zealous Consul of your nation, the Sieur William Eaton, to acquaint you with a proposition, which I have found myself under the absolute necessity of making to him, I have nevertheless determined to apply directly to you about it by these presents, in order that I might at the same time procure for myself the pleasure of reiterating to you[1] the assurance of the continuance of my esteem and my friendship.

After the request I formerly made for forty cannon of different calibres, the present circumstances in which I find myself require that I should procure 24 pounders, of which I have the most pressing need. I should therefore wish that you would cause them to be sent to me as soon as possible, in case you should not, on the receipt of the present, have sent the first to me. If finally they should have been already sent away, I expect, Mr. President, as a real proof of your friendship, for which I shall be infinitely obliged to you, that you will furnish and convey to me forty other pieces, all of the calibre above mentioned.

This request will not appear in the least extraordinary to you, when you consider the very moderate and very friendly manner in which, differently from others, I have conducted myself towards the United States and their flag, not withstanding that the douceurs and presents, stipulated four years ago for my making peace with the United States have not all arrived, and that not the smallest part of those which were intended for me individually have been sent. I make no doubt on this subject, that your Consul will have forwarded the letter I addressed to you about two years past relative to it, and that you will thereby have seen, that I consented to wait the space of a year, in consequence of the representation which the same Consul made to me, that several of the articles composing the present, due to me, and which I constantly expect, could neither be had or manufactured in the United States, and that they were to be procured from foreign countries.

Wishing on my part to return you a reciprocity (whenever an occasion of urgency in your nation happens) in my country, and hoping to see that good harmony which happily subsists between us continued

[591]

and remain undisturbed, I pray Almighty God to preserve you, and I assure you, Mr. President, of all the extent of my esteem and my most distinguished consideration

(signature & seal of HAMOUDA Pacha Bey of Tunis)

Tr (DNA: RG 233, President's Messages, 7th Cong.); in Jacob Wagner's hand; at head of text: "The Bashaw Bey of Tunis To Mr. John Adams, President of the United States of America"; also at head of text: "Translation" (possibly translated from French, judging from the bey's communication of 8 Sep. 1802); transmitted to Congress among the papers supplementing TJ's 8 Dec. 1801 message (ASP, *Foreign Relations*, 2:358; JHR, 4:24). RC, not found, enclosed in William Eaton to secretary of state, 10 Apr. 1801, which Eaton held open for the bey's letter (DNA: RG 59, CD). Recorded in SJL as received 27 Aug. 1801.

Hammuda (1759-1814) became bey of Tunis, and received the title of pasha, on his father's retirement in 1777. He was educated for the role and trained as his father's deputy before assuming power with the sanction of the Ottoman Empire. The BARDO was the royal palace in Tunis (Asma Moalla, *The Regency of Tunis and the Ottoman Porte, 1777-1814: Army and Government of a North-African Ottoman Eyalet at the End of the Eighteenth Century* [London, 2004], 44-6, 67, 70-76, 141; Kenneth J. Perkins, *Historical Dictionary of Tunisia*, 2d ed. [Lanham, Md., 1997], 30, 77).

The bey had attempted to convey his desire for 24-pounder cannons, which he wanted for shore batteries, through WILLIAM EATON, the U.S. consul at Tunis. Eaton refused to transmit the request, believing that Hammuda might treat his acceptance of the application as a guarantee of its fulfillment. Eaton suggested that the United States might be willing to substitute 24-pounders for other cannons it had already agreed to send (see below). Once Hammuda decided to write directly to the president, Eaton advised the secretary of state that a failure by the president to answer the bey might give offense and create a pretext for hostile action by the Tunisians (Madison, *Papers, Sec. of State Series*, 1:79-82).

FORTY CANNON: in 1797 Hammuda's terms for negotiating with the U.S. had included 26 12-pounder naval guns and 14 8-pounders. Those cannons, along with ammunition and quantities of ship-building supplies, formed a category of goods called the "regalia," which was in addition to other payments and gifts to Tunis. Hammuda agreed to a treaty of PEACE WITH THE UNITED STATES in August of that year. The U.S. Senate approved the treaty in March 1798 but withheld consent from one article that concerned customs duties and most favored nation status. The Adams administration initiated a renegotiation of that article and requested alterations in two other sections. As a result, in 1799 new wording was substituted for three articles of the treaty. The Senate approved those changes, which did not affect the regalia or other principal gifts. In his previous LETTER to the president of the United States, dated 30 Apr. 1799, Hammuda threatened to void the pact if he did not receive the weapons he had demanded for negotiating the treaty. John Adams replied to that letter from the bey in January 1800 when he sent notice of the treaty's ratification (ASP, *Foreign Relations*, 2:125-6, 281-2; Miller, *Treaties*, 2:386-426).

[1] Preceding two words interlined, possibly by TJ.

From Matthew McAllister

Sir,   Savannah April 15 1801.

I am informed Mr. Clay has declined the office of Circuit Judge for this District, to which he had been appointed under the New Arrangement.

Should you, Sir, feel at a loss for a person to fill the vacancy, I take the liberty of suggesting my readiness to take a part under your Administration so far as I may be deemed capable.

Some time since, I received a commission as one of the Judges of our Superior Court. The great labor attached to the office—the duties of it requiring half the years absence from my family, will not permit me to continue long in the appointment; for this reason, Sir, I must beg your indulgence for the trouble I now give you.

I acted as Atty Genl. of this State three years and was about seven years Atty for the District.

That you may enjoy every degree of, happiness in the exalted & arduous station to which your Country has called you is the sincere wish of

Sir Yours with the highest consideration

MATT. MC.ALLISTER

P.S. As it is probable the Gentn. from this State may have left the Seat of Governmt. ere this—for your satisfaction, I inclose a small extract from a Sava. paper, merely to show that out of 20 odd Gentn. of the Law residing in this City there was unanimity on that occasion—This I am persuaded comes with an ill grace from me, yet there may be a propriety in indeavoring to satisfy your mind on a point where the responsibility attaches in a great measure to the first Executive Majestrate.—

With great respect   MATT MCALLISTER

Dupl (DNA: RG 59, LAR); at head of text: "(Duplicate)"; at foot of first page: "The President of the United States &c."; endorsed by TJ as received 4 May and so recorded in SJL with notation "Off." RC (same); dated 13 Apr.; torn, with minor variations and lacking postscript; endorsed by TJ as received 1 May and so recorded in SJL with notation "Off"; also endorsed by TJ: "to be Circuit judge vice Clay." Enclosure not found.

Matthew McAllister (1758-1823) was a native of York County, Pennsylvania, and a graduate of the College of New Jersey at Princeton. He moved to Savannah, Georgia, around 1784, where he established a lucrative legal practice. He was appointed federal attorney for the district of Georgia in 1789, but was replaced by Charles Jackson in 1797. McAllister also served in the Georgia legislature. In the late 1790s, however, he became linked with the Yazoo Land Fraud of 1795 and was the target of scathing public attacks by James Jackson, Georgia's leading Republican. McAllister's subsequent political ambitions were seriously handicapped by the allegations; he did not receive an appointment during TJ's administration (Harrison, *Princetonians,*

1776-1783, 269-72; George R. Lamplugh, *Politics on the Periphery: Factions and Parties in Georgia, 1783-1806* [Newark, Del., 1986], 108, 175, 182-4; Paul M. Pressly, "The Northern Roots of Savannah's Antebellum Elite, 1780s-1850s," *Georgia Historical Quarterly*, 87 [2003], 157-99; JEP, 1:29, 228).

Joseph CLAY, Jr., had served as judge of the federal district of Georgia since 1796. On 23 Feb. 1801, John Adams appointed him to be a judge of the Fifth U.S. Circuit Court (JEP, 1:217, 383; DAB).

From Joseph Léonard Poirey

MONSIEUR   Paris Ce 25. Germinal an 9.

Permettez moi de vous adresser le mémoire d'une demande que des Circonstances impérieuses me portent à présenter au Congrès des Etats-unis d'Amerique. Je vous Supplie de le lire avec intéret: et S'il est en votre pouvoir de la faire accueillir, que votre humanité aussi forte sans doute que toutes les Vertus qui vous Caracterisent devienne l'appui d'un homme qui a Servi l'amerique avec désintéressement et que vous avez honoré de votre Estime en france.

Je vous Supplie, Monsieur, d'agréer avec bonté l'homage de ma reconnoissance et de mon tres profond Respect   POIREY

EDITORS' TRANSLATION

SIR   Paris this 25 Germinal Year 9 [15 Apr. 1801]

Permit me to address to you the statement of a request that pressing circumstances bring me to present to the Congress of the United States of America. I beg you to take an interest in reading it: and if it is in your power to present it for approval, may your humanity—no doubt as strong as all the virtues that characterize you—become the support of a man who has served America disinterestedly and whom you have honored with your esteem in France.

I beg you, Sir, to accept with kindness the homage of my gratitude and my very deep respect,   POIREY

RC (DLC); at head of text: "A Monsieur Thomas Jefferson President des Etats-unis d'Amérique"; at foot of text: "Rue Mézieres No 900"; endorsed by TJ as received 20 Aug. and so recorded in SJL. Enclosure not found.

À PRÉSENTER AU CONGRÈS: in 1796 Poirey, who had been an aide and secretary to the Marquis de Lafayette during the American Revolution, petitioned for permission to file a claim for compensation from the United States for that service. Poirey, like Lafayette, had initially refused any payment, but changed his mind when he found himself in need of money. By then the statute of limitations for such claims had expired, and although James Madison, then a member of the House of Representatives, urged the approval of Poirey's request, some other congressmen, including Henry Dearborn, were reluctant to allow special exemptions to the time limits on claims.

The House did pass a bill in 1797, but the measure failed in the Senate. In 1819 Congress passed an act allowing the settlement of Poirey's claim. Poirey and TJ had corresponded in 1788, when Poirey continued to act as Lafayette's secretary (ASP, *Claims*, 1:183; JHR, 2:436, 640, 643-4, 645; 11:393; JS, 2:309-11; *Annals*, 6:1817, 1828-30, 1839-40; U.S. Statutes at Large, 6:225; Vol. 12:529).

From John Barnes

SIR   George Town 16th. April 1801.

I was last Evening honred: with your favr: Monticello 11th. Inst: with Memdm: for, 250 square feet sheet Copper, for covering, part, of your house—

The exact particulars—I have by this post, transmitted to my Correspondt: Mr Richards Philada. who I have no doubt, will Attend Minutely to your instructions—and shipp it, with the files and Chissills—by very first Vessel, with Bill Lading, to Messrs. Gibson & Jeffersons, Address, at Richmond. Invoice of particulars, I have Ordered to be charged to my a/c & sent—to me here—nothing of consequence transpires—at Washington for Noticing—all is—peace & quiet.

I am sir, Your mst Obedt: H st   JOHN BARNES

I was informed Yesterday—Mr Marshalls late dwelling House— (6 buildings) was to let. If Mr Madison—wanted One, it would I presume be a most elegible situation—but I dare not, do any thing in it—without Order—

RC (ViU); addressed: "Thomas Jefferson Esqr. President, US—at Monticello"; franked; postmarked 17 Apr.; added notation in unidentified hand: "Milton"; endorsed by TJ as received 24 Apr. and so recorded in SJL.

TJ's letter to Barnes of the 11TH, recorded in SJL with the notation "(copper, tools, &c.)," has not been found.

6 BUILDINGS: on Pennsylvania Avenue at 22d Street were the "Six Buildings," one of the few clusters of buildings standing in the new capital city when the national government moved there from Philadelphia. In the last months of the Adams administration the structures housed, in addition to some residences, the offices of the State Department and the Navy Department. John Marshall left Washington for Virginia on 6 Mch., and when he returned in August he and his colleagues on the Supreme Court all took up residence at Conrad & McMunn's. James and Dolley Madison, after their stay with TJ at the President's House, apparently lived in one of the Six Buildings temporarily before taking up residence near William Thornton's house (Evelyn Levow Greenberg, "Isaac Polock: Early Settler in Washington, D.C.," *Publication of the American Jewish Historical Society*, 48 [1958], 1, 9-10; Bryan, *National Capital*, 1:233n; Jean Edward Smith, *John Marshall: Definer of a Nation* [New York, 1996], 286; Madison, *Papers, Sec. of State Ser.*, 1:113n, 165, 166n).

From Joseph Fenwick

SIR   Norfolk 16 April 1801.

Having complained to you of my removal from office, without sufficient cause—it becomes me to endeavor to repel anything advanced to support the contrary. With this view, I have the honor to send you the inclosed strictures, on what has been published concerning my Consular Conduct, in a Washington paper of the 1 & 7th. Inst.

The desire of preserving the good opinion of those who thought well of me, as a man, is the primary object of this printed letter. I shall therefore be gratifyed if your important occupations permit you to read it. Few men, very few indeed like yourself, can boast of being out of the reach of calumny.

I have the honour to be with the greatest respect Sir your most obedient & humble Servant   JOSEPH FENWICK

RC (DLC); at head of text: "Thomas Jefferson Esquire President of the United States Monticello"; endorsed by TJ as a letter of 18 Apr. received on the 24th, and so recorded in SJL. Enclosure: response by Fenwick to charges of improprieties in his office as consul at Bordeaux that appeared against him in the *Washington Federalist* of 1 and 7 Apr. (printed copy in DLC; dated Norfolk, 14 Apr. 1801, altered by hand to 16 Apr.).

COMPLAINED TO YOU: Fenwick to TJ, 22 Mch.

Also in TJ's papers is a letter from Fenwick to Madison of 16 Apr. in regard to the charges against him (RC in DLC; Madison, *Papers, Sec. of State Ser*, 1:94-6).

From Levi Lincoln

SIR   Washington April 16. 1801

I had the honor of recg. yours of the 10th, this morning. It is much to be regreted, that Mr Madison indisposition continues. The public have much to expect from his abilities, and his Patriotism. The two returned Commissions are recorded, with blanks left for the *names* and *dates*—These will be necessary to complete the record. Joseph Clay jr. declines accepting his commission, as judge of the circuit court of the fifth district. Judge Sullivan refuses to accept of the office of district attorney. His assigned reasons are, an unsuitableness from age and standing, to engage in new professional business. Jones has accepted & recd his commission. Brown, whose petition you inclosed, has already been discharged. This information I have, by a letter, from Bradford the Marshal, recd some days since. The officer having the custody of Callendar's fine shall be instructed on the subject. Edwards has been written to, respecting the removal of Goodrich, as yet no answer has been received.

Nothing worthy of particular notice has occurred in this city, since you left it. Genl. Smith set off for Baltimore this morning, he will return in the course of the next week. By some means, a report has spread, and found its way into several newspapers, that the preparing frigates, were destined to the coast of Barbary. It is to be hoped, the rumor, will not preceed the arrival of the ships, at the place of their destination. I have caused a paragraph to be inserted, in the intelligencer, to counteract its effects—

The political intelligence from Massachusetts is rather favorable. This is the general complexion of my private letters. The inclosed is a state of the poll in Boston & Charlestown. There can be but little doubt of the three first named Senators being chosen. Tudor & Bowdoin are republicans. B. Zealous—Wendell an accomodating man, & will act with the Government—I have strong hopes in favour of Gerry. By the papers, I find both parties have been pushing, with their utmost strength.

I forward a pamphlet, on the agriculture of the U.S. The Author is said by some Gents. here, who have been acquainted with him to be a man of sense, and observation. He may be, it is probably that you are acquainted with him—Sure I am, neither his facts, his principles or his observations apply to any part of America with which, I am conversant. the policy of the publication may be, to discourage emigration. Mr. Williams, by the direction of Mr King, has sent 200 copies to the office.

Mr. Pichon is desirous you should see a copy of a circular letter, which he has addressed to the officers of his Government in the west Indies. At his particular request I forward it. Mr Kings dispatches have been received as late as the 25th of Feby He states generally that the situation of that Country is critical & full of difficulties. that the King had been attacked with a violent fever, and a delirium, and was not able to attend to business. That no overture had been made to France. That England must and would resist the claims of the northern powers. That his, Mr Kings negotiations, with the british Govt. had been deranged by the change of the ministry. That however Ld. Hawksbury, who is secretary of State for the foreign department, had assured him that an early and an impartial attention should be given to the objects of that negotiation. Mr. King hopes also that Ld. St Vincent will be inclined to attend to the reiterated remonstances against the impressment of our Seamen, and the vexations of our trade.

The dispatches from Tripoli are similar to those heretofore sent, on the subject of abuses, and a demand of presents by the Bashaw. Our

Consuls want ships of war. The inclosed letter from Smith, from the variety of matter it contains I have thought proper to forward—

With sentiments of the highest esteem I have the honor to be most respectfully your obedient Sevt   LEVI LINCOLN

RC (DLC); at head of text: "The President of the United States"; endorsed by TJ as received 24 Apr. and so recorded in SJL. Enclosures not found, but see below.

A REPORT HAS SPREAD: the mission and destination of the U.S. naval squadron assembling at Hampton Roads was a subject of speculation both in the public papers and among navy officers. On 13 Apr. the *National Intelligencer* reported an understanding that the squadron was destined for the Mediterranean, and would not, "as has been stated in several prints, proceed with convoys to the West Indies." Four days later, the same newspaper sought to quell rumors of a "*secret expedition*" by pointing out that under the Peace Establishment Act it was intended that navy vessels remaining in service would be employed in convoy duty and periodically "exercise and discipline the officers and seamen." Gathering vessels at Norfolk was merely a convenient location for them to prepare for sea and "to await ulterior orders" regarding their appointed destination. The squadron's mission was also unclear to its appointed commander, Thomas Truxtun. On 2 Apr., Truxtun informed the secretary of the navy that he would not accept command of the squadron "unless It should be intended to act decisively Against the Algerines." Samuel Smith replied on the 10th that the squadron's object was to train young officers and to carry out the terms of the Peace Establishment Act. He added, however, that "such a squadron Cruizing in view of the Barbary Powers will have a tendency to prevent them from seizing on our Commerce, whenever Passion or a Desire of Plunder might Incite them thereto." Dissatisfied with Smith's response, Truxtun declined the command. On 28 Apr., Smith appointed Richard Dale the squadron's commanding officer (NDBW, 1:428-9, 432, 435, 438-40).

Favorable Republican POLITICAL INTELLIGENCE FROM MASSACHUSETTS of the 6 Apr. senators' and governor's election appeared in local newspapers, including the *Boston Mercury and New-England Palladium* of 7 Apr. In a letter to Madison of 16 Apr., Lincoln reported on the governor's race indicating Elbridge Gerry's sizable lead over Caleb Strong in Boston (2,078 to 1,851) and Charlestown (288 to 170). Although titular head of the Massachusetts Republican party and an oft-run gubernatorial candidate, Gerry ultimately lost the 1801 election (George Athan Billias, *Elbridge Gerry: Founding Father and Republican Statesman* [New York, 1976], 304; Madison, *Papers, Sec. of State Ser.*, 1:101).

Lincoln probably forwarded a PAMPHLET by William Strickland, *Observations on the Agriculture of the United States of America* (London, 1801; Sowerby, No. 819). Samuel WILLIAMS, at Rufus KING's direction, sent numerous copies of the pamphlet to the State Department. According to a handwritten note on a copy of the pamphlet from the Kress Collection at the Baker Library, Harvard University, King requested permission from Strickland and the Board of Agriculture, which first published the tract, to publish and distribute it in the U.S. For Strickland's tour of the United States, which included a visit with TJ at Monticello in May 1795, see Vol. 28:371-3.

On 14 Apr., Louis André PICHON sent Lincoln a copy of a circular letter addressed to officials at the Île de France, Cayenne, Guadeloupe, and Saint-Domingue. In the circular, which Pichon asked Lincoln to bring to the president's attention, the diplomat informed the colonial officials of his recognition by the United States as France's commissary general and chargé d'affaires. Reminding the officials on the French islands that they should implement the terms of the Convention of 1800, Pichon stated that he was ready to receive claims related to government ships captured since the conclusion of hostilities or private vessels that had not yet been condemned when the convention was signed.

Declaring that the Baltic Sea nations of the league of armed neutrality were on the brink of war with Great Britain, Pichon stressed the importance to France of a resumption of good relations and said that commerce under American colors ("le Pavillon americain") would be the only neutral shipping available to France (RC and enclosure in DNA: RG 59, NL).

MR KINGS DISPATCHES: as Rufus King reported to the secretary of state from London on 25 Feb., George III had been incapacitated by illness (since attributed to porphyria). While the monarch's condition delayed some of the CHANGE OF THE MINISTRY, Lord Hawkesbury was the new secretary of state for foreign affairs and Lord St. Vincent was the new first lord of the admiralty (Dupl in DNA: RG 59, DD; Ehrman, *Pitt*, 500n, 525-8, 553; Delamotte to TJ, 27 Feb.).

From William C. C. Claiborne

DEAR SIR,   Nashville April 17th. 1801.

By an Act of the late Congress, the District of Palmira, in this State, being discontinued, and all the Waters, Shores and Inlets lying within Tennessee, being annexed (from and after the 30th day of June next) to the *District of Massac' on the Ohio*, it has become an Object of much Importance, to the Merchants & Traders of this State, that a deserving and judicious Citizen should be appointed Collector at this *latter place*—which Office (I learn) is, at this time vacant.—

Several Merchants of *Nashville*, who are engaged in the Mississippi Commerce, have spoken to me, in very exalted terms, of a Mr. James Irwin of that Town, and requested, that I would name that Gentleman to you, as a Candidate for the Office of Collector & Inspector at Massac':—To the good opinion, which the Merchants have expressed of Mr. Irwin; permit me to add my own, and to say, that he is a young Man of good moral Character, handsome Talents, and great prudence.

I pray you, to accept of my best Wishes for your private & public happiness.—

I have the honor to be Sir, With sincere Esteem & Respect Yo: Mo: Obt, hbl servt.   WILLIAM C. C. CLAIBORNE

RC (DLC); endorsed by TJ as received 21 May and so recorded in SJL; also endorsed by TJ: "refd. to the Secy of the Treasury Th:J."

William Charles Coles Claiborne (1775-1817) had recently completed his second term in the U.S. House of Representatives. Before moving to Tennessee as a young man, Claiborne, a native of Virginia, had been an assistant to John Beck-ley. In Tennessee he began the practice of law and was appointed to a judgeship before succeeding Andrew Jackson as the state's sole congressman in 1797. TJ named him governor of Mississippi Territory in 1801, a commissioner to bring Louisiana under U.S. control in 1803, and governor of the Territory of Orleans in 1804. In 1812 he was elected governor of the new state of Louisiana (ANB; *Biog. Dir. Cong.*).

An ACT of 2 Mch. 1801 modified a statute passed two years earlier "to regulate the collection of duties on imports and tonnage." Under the new law the DISTRICT OF MASSAC, which included territory on the north side of the lower Ohio River, would also encompass the state of Tennessee. Petitioners to the House of Representatives from Tennessee in December 1800 had contended that Palmyra was not a convenient port of entry for them (U.S. Statutes at Large, 1:637-8; 2:108; JHR, 3:747).

On 4 June TJ appointed JAMES IRWIN collector of the district and inspector of the port of Massac, but Irwin declined the position and TJ named another person to fill the vacancy (Appendix I, Lists 3 and 4; JEP, 1:401; Albert Gallatin to TJ, 6 Oct. 1801).

To Thomas Cooper

DEAR SIR   Monticello Apr. 17. 1801.

Your favor of the 2d. inst. is just now recieved. your former one had also come duly to hand, and was properly disposed of to produce it's effect at it's just season. it was not therefore from inattention that I had not acknoleged it, but from the absolute impossibility of doing this in the immense number of those I daily recieve. it reduces me to the painful necessity of leaving those who are so kind as to write to me on matters of business to see the answers to their letters in what is *done* in consequence of them. be assured that your's shall not fail of it's effect in due time. your disinterested anxiety on this subject adds to the just estimation in which your character is held by the wise and the good. the apostles of human improvement may inspire with the neophobia those who are fattening on the labour & ignorance of their fellowmen. darkness is their delight, & the harbingers of day their dread: but the world will do justice to both. I have not yet heard whether Dr. Priestley is perfectly recovered: but hope he is. accept assurances of my perfect esteem & respect.   TH: JEFFERSON

PrC (DLC); at foot of text: "Thomas Cooper esq."

YOUR FORMER ONE: Cooper to TJ, 17 Mch., received 20 Mch.

From Enoch Edwards

DEAR SIR   Frankford 17 April 1801

I wrote to you on the 3rd Inst. informing you of your favor of the 30th. of March. I have since contracted with Mr: Hanse for the making of your Chariot. he is by Reputation, & by Experience I have found him to be, one of the best Workmen in Philadelphia—

The inclosed paper contains what I demanded the price of—which after taking time to make his Estimate was 1290 Dollars—I afterwards gave a Copy of the same to Mr: Fielding another excellent Workman. whose price was upwards of 1500 Dollars. I am better satisfied on every account that I deal't with the former, I think better of his magazine of seasoned Timber than any other in the City. You will have an excellent & an elegant Chariot—In the list you will see I have put down probably[1] more than we want—but have contracted with him to be allowed for all I strike off—this is the best way, allowances afterwards always come heavy—that is with Reluctance but by making them part of the Contract the Thing is setled—

The semicircular Light—all Coach Makers object to—& think oval Lights must have been mean't. they complain they are so totally out of fashion & indeed I lean to their Opinion. but you are the best Judge of what suits your Climate. or any other Reasons you may have—

I myself now decide against Caps to the Hubs—on Enquiry I find they are easily knocked out of Shape & Order. & never can be repaired in a Countrey where plating is not understood—the same Objection lays in some Degree against plated harnes, & they are less fashionable than formerly.

I would wish your Directions about Cloth, as I do not know whether you desire[2] to have that as well as the calico lining—

On the whole I think I have now put it under your Command as to particulars—& I will thank you for your Orders as soon as you can make it convenient, especially about the back light—as the workman can spare Me only about ten Days for that—

If you wish for any Extra's not yet thought of, you see what may be thrown off from my inclosed List will pay for them—I will manage that for you.

With the greatest & most perfect Respect I have the honor to be with sincere wishes for your prosperity & Happiness—your obedt St

ENO. EDWARDS

RC (DLC); addressed: "Thomas Jefferson—President of the United States—Monticello Virginia"; franked; postmarked Washington, 24 Apr.; endorsed by TJ as received 6 May and so recorded in SJL. Enclosure not found.

Coachmaker Conrad HANSE conducted business at 86 South Fourth Street, Philadelphia (Stafford, *Philadelphia Directory, for 1801*; MB, 2:1067-8).

[1] Word interlined.
[2] Interlined in place of canceled "wish."

To John Hoomes

DEAR SIR   Monticello Apr. 17. 1801.

I came here on the 4th. & shall leave it on the 25th. inst. for Washington after compleating some arrangements previous to my final removal there. but for fear any accident of health or weather should detain me here longer, I forward you the inclosed order for paiment for the horse, which mr Barnes will pay to your order in Washington, Philadelphia, or Richmond, or remit to your own house in *bank bills* if they will suit you & you shall so direct. the first view of the horse did not impress me equal to his merit. I soon however became sensible of it, am extremely pleased with him, & attached to him as a riding horse, & am thankful to you for having thought on me on the occasion & furnished the opportunity of procuring so fine a creature. I was offered the same money very soon after recieving him: but had already become too much pleased with him to part with him. accept assurances of my sincere esteem & respect.   TH: JEFFERSON

PrC (MHi); at foot of text: "Colo. John Hoomes"; endorsed by TJ in ink on verso.

In his financial account book, TJ recorded on this date an ORDER for payment FOR THE HORSE: "Drew on J. Barnes in favr. Colo. John Hoomes for 300 D. payable the 1st. week of May" (MB, 2:1037). TJ again requested direction for the preferred place and method of payment in a letter to Hoomes of 7 May (PrC in MHi; at foot of text: "Colo. John Hoomes"; endorsed by TJ in ink on verso).

To George Jefferson

DEAR SIR   Monticello. Apr. 17. 1801.

Yours of Apr. 6 is recieved; so is the syrop of punch forwarded by you. I must ask the favor of you to call on Colo. Carrington & pay him 30. Dollars on account of Matthew Rhodes collector of the direct tax of this county. also to pay mr Jones & mr Pleasants, a year's subscription for their papers, and notify them that they may annually apply to you for the paiment without awaiting the ordinary course of collection. I presume you recieved from J. Barnes 920.26 D. on my account about the 4th or 5th. inst. on which I drew on you for 600. D. in favr. of John Watson, to which some smaller draughts will be added here, & have been added. I will further strengthen you immediately on my return to Washington, for which place I depart hence on the 25th. inst.—I will take the 7. Dolls. pr. Cwt. offered you for my last year's tobo. payable in 4. months. on this subject I must inform you that mr Clarke by a late letter apprises me that tho' the mass of the Bedford tobo. is as good as usual, yet there are a few hogsheads of inferior quality, which he would not advise to submit to reinspection. he could not specify the particular hogsheads, having kept no note of them. on the other hand, the crop from this place is declared by the Milton inspectors to be the *very best* crop ever passed at that inspection. you will use this information as you shall judge best. Accept assurances of my affectionate esteem

TH: JEFFERSON

P.S. draughts made—
April 13.   in favr. Rob. Hemings 22. D.
      15.   Wm. & Julius Clarkson £ 9-8-4

PrC (MHi); at foot of text: "Mr. George Jefferson"; endorsed by TJ in ink on verso.

TJ paid Edward CARRINGTON, supervisor of federal internal revenue collection for Virginia, the direct tax owed on William Short's land for 1800. SUBSCRIPTION FOR THEIR PAPERS: Meriwether Jones published the Richmond *Examiner* and Samuel Pleasants the *Virginia Argus.* In October 1800, TJ purchased 300

barrels of corn from JOHN WATSON of Milton, with a March delivery date and payment due in mid-April at $2 per barrel (MB, 2:915, 958, 1028, 1036-7).

LATE LETTER: probably Bowling Clark to TJ of 9 Apr., recorded in SJL as received on the 13th, but not found.

According to TJ's financial records the payment to Robert HEMINGS was for James Oldham's moving expenses. Oldham began working as a house joiner at Monticello on 14 Apr. (MB, 2:1035, 1037).

To George Jefferson

DR. SIR   Monticello Apr. 17. 1801.

I this moment recieve your favor on the subject of my bonds, [the] possession of mr Hanson, and now inclose you an authority to recieve them, of which I notify him by this post. I am Dear Sir
   Your's affectionately   TH: JEFFERSON

PrC (MHi); faint; letterpressed at head of same sheet as TJ to Richard Hanson, 17 Apr.; at foot of sheet below Hanson letter: "Mr. George Jefferson"; endorsed by TJ in ink on verso. Enclosure not found.

George Jefferson's FAVOR regarding the BONDS is printed at 7 Apr.

I NOTIFY HIM BY THIS POST: in his brief letter to Richard Hanson of this date, TJ requested that the bonds "given to the representative of Farrell & Jones for the debt of John Wayles" be delivered to Gibson & Jefferson (PrC in same; blurred; letterpressed on same sheet as letter above; at foot of text: "Mr Richard Hanson Petersburg").

To Levi Lincoln

DEAR SIR   Monticello Apr. 17. 1801.

Yesterday I recieved your favors of the 8th. & 9th. and as the delay of the post here is short, I can only acknolege their reciepts. before the next post (a week hence) reaches you I shall be with you myself; that is to say on the 28th. health & weather permitting. till then I can say nothing on Priestman's case: & the rather, as having been already the subject of a deliberate decision, it should be reconsidered with deliberation. I do not see why he has addressed his petition to mr Madison, as it seems to have been before properly in the hands of the Secy. of the Treasury.—we must unquestionably act on the case referred to us by Govr. Sinclair. if any thing preparatory can be done before my return, it will be well, because it is one of those cases which require promptness & pressing.—On the subject of mr Yznardi I think with you that Pintard's suit is our's, & Israel's his own. while I was Secretary of state, the Consuls in each country of Europe where we had a minister was under the ordinary direction & controul of that minister; and with him he was instructed to settle all his accounts. his vouchers are easily produced to him, & the minister can better watch over & controul his expenditures. I imagine this has been changed but, I think, not for the better. I should propose the referring the settlement of mr Yznardi's accounts, so far as vouchers are wanting, to Humphries or Pinckney.—As to mr Greene he is no protegé of mine. If his patron has made a false catch at an office for him, and has missed it, I feel no obligation to mend it. I think it my duty to take up the subject de novo, & see whether we may not begin here the reformation of the judiciary federalism. the forwarding his commission when in my power to withold it was enough.—as I cannot act here on the papers you inclosed me, I think it better to return them by post, to be resumed when with you. accept assurances of my high & affectionate consideration & esteem   TH: JEFFERSON

PrC (DLC); at foot of text: "Levi Lincoln acting Secy. of State."

To James Madison

TH:J. TO J. MADISON   Monticello Apr. 17. 1801.

I shall be with you on the 25th. unless health or weather prevent. but if you propose leaving home sooner for Washington, do not let my coming prevent you. only, in that case, if convenient, lodge word at Gordon's, or write me by next post, that you will be gone; as I should then wish to lengthen my day's journey. I have not been able to look yet into my newspapers, but I presume yours contain all mine do. my respectful compliments to mrs Madison, & affectionate attachment to yourself. Th: Jefferson

PrC (DLC); endorsed by TJ in ink on verso.

To Joseph Rapin

Sir   Monticello Apr. 17. 1801.

I duly recieved your letter under cover of Capt. Lewis's. what you propose as to the arranging the apartments is very right.   of Edward I know very little, as he has been but a short time in my service. it is yet to be seen therefore how far he may be fit for his present station. the negro whom he thinks so little of, is a most valuable servant.   I propose to leave this place on the 25th. instant, and if health & weather permits, I shall be with you on the 28th. I shall have with me two gentlemen, travelling companions, who will possibly take beds with us. I would wish you therefore to have rooms & beds prepared for them. I hope I shall find Julien with you, and every thing ready mounted for the entertainment of company. accept assurances of my friendly attachment. Th: Jefferson

PrC (MHi); at foot of text: "M. Rapin"; endorsed by TJ in ink on verso.   your letter: Rapin to TJ, 3 Apr.

To Samuel Smith

Dear Sir   Monticello Apr. 17. 1801:

On the 9th. inst. I recieved your's of the 2d. and acknoleged it by return of post. yesterday your favor of the 6th. came to hand. the orders for the sale of the vessels which are to be sold, for the equipping three others for sea, & the laying up others are all right. I shall really be chagrined if the water into the Eastern branch will not admit our laying up the whole seven there in time of peace, because they would be under the immediate eye of the department, and would require but one set of plunderers to take care of them. as to what is to be done, when every thing shall be disposed of according to law, it shall be the subject of conversation when I return. it oppresses me by night & by day: for I do not see my way out of the difficulty. it is the department I understand the least, & therefore need a person whose compleat competence will justify the most entire confidence &

resignation. I was in hopes you could aid us till Congress, when mr Jones would be on, & between you we might hope for a regular Secretary.—I inclose you mr Nicholson's letter on the subject of his namesake. I am a stranger to the merits of the several captains. I recieve some information very much to the disadvantage of a Capt. Cowper of this state. if he be one you had meditated to retain, look to a letter from St. George Tucker to mr Stoddart, & another to the late President. both probably in the navy office.—I inclose you a letter from mr Sayre, stating a purchase in Long island of very ill aspect. if we have any power over it, suspend it: and if any thing can be done to arrest Watson from clenching it, it should be done instantly. be so good as to return me Sayre's letter when I come on to Washington as it relates to other subjects. I inclose you also a letter from Genl Spotswood of this state. some acknolegement from yourself to these gentlemen that their letters are referred to you & shall be attended to, will be proper, & generally in similar cases. to mr Sayre we should express thankfulness, in order to encourage gentlemen to apprise us of what may be doing amiss without our knolege. not a word to be said as to his application for office, as I find the necessity of ab-solute silence on all such applications; & to leave the party to see his answer in what we do. it would be impossible to say any thing in answer to these applications without either giving offence, or com-mitting ourselves. to my most intimate friends therefore I observe entire silence on these applications. yet I am glad to recieve them because it is well to know who will accept of office.—I shall leave this on the 25th. & be in Washington on the 28th. health & weather permitting. I hope mr Madison will come on with me. accept assur-ances of my respectful & affectionate esteem.

TH: JEFFERSON

RC (Mrs. Leonard Hewett, Louisville, Kentucky, 1944); at foot of first page: "Genl. Smith." PrC (DLC). Enclosures: (1) Joseph H. Nicholson to TJ, 27 Mch. 1801. (2) Stephen Sayre to TJ, 21 Mch. 1801. (3) Probably Alexander Spotswood to TJ, 2 Apr. 1801 (recorded in SJL as re-ceived 16 Apr. but not found).

William COWPER of Virginia was the former master commandant of the ship *Baltimore*. He was discharged in April under the terms of the Peace Establish-ment Act, which contained no provi-sion for retaining masters commandant (NDQW, Dec. 1800-Dec. 1801, 177, 324; VMHB, 6 [1899], 421).

From Thomas Sumter, Sr.

My Dear Sir   Stateburgh—17th Apl. 1801

I am now prepaired to acknowledge the receipt of your favor of the 24th. of March Last & my obligations for the Honor you propose my son—Next to his own happiness—my highest wish has been to see him useful to his Country—or at least prepaired to be so. Whenever there Should be a real occasion for his Service—& from his dispositions I have had no reason to dout of his readiness to devote his exertions to his duty on Such an occasion—But my Public engagements, for many years past, have confined his attention almost wholy, to Private concerns, & those of such a nature as were rather inimical to his preparation for other pursuits—however present arrangments will enable me to dispense with his farther Application—& therefore leaving the Proposition you have made, entierly to his Own determination. I only suggested that I was convinced, if he ever should enter on Public life he would meet with no oppertunity of doing it, under auspicies more consonant to his own feelings or more Gratifying to mine—I was highly Pleased to See, he made a Proper istimate of the appointment as well as of the Polite & friendly Terms in which you offered it—& I found that he was, from various considerations more pleased with this perticuler one than he would have been with any other as affording Greater advantages for his improvement, & as it might be acepted without incuring the prevalent Suspicions of having Mercenary enducements either for his Past or future conduct—I am convinced he woud not have accepted one of a difrent nature. he was not without Scruples in this case—He has been much engaged from home Since the arival of your letter, Which I plead as an excuse for not returning the immediate answer it required—at length he has determined to accept the appointment in the form you Seem to wish, if it should not be inconsistent with the Public Service for him to remain here untill the latter Part of May, in which time, Perhaps rather Sooner, with exertions he may adjust his own affairs & mine so as to go away without much inconvenience—& will be at Washington or wherever you may be Pleased to direct him, at the latest between the 10th. & 15th. June—I have desired him to make his own answer to you on this Subject—Which he will take the Liberty of doing—I am persuaded Sir you are fully acquainted with my Views, & wishes as to Public affairs—& you can readely enter into my feelings as a Parent—If my Son should be imployed—I will only answer for his zeal & integrity—as to his quallifications you will judge of them— if they are deficient, I hope & trust, he will endeavor to remedy that inconvenience & that he may be able to do so by the advice & instruction your Goodness may Procoure him—for which I am sure he will be Gratefull, & by which I Shall be more obliged than I can express—

Since my return nothing Important of a Public nature has occurred other then what is every day heard from Various parts of the Continent—Perhaps that Calm & yeilding disposition we hear much of, ought not to be Considered as Grounded on Principles of Sincerity & affection. Since upon every occasion, where the republicans have met to Testify their Satisfaction & Joy, they feel on the result of their late exertions, none, no not one of the Supporters of the Views of the late administration can be enduced to mingle, or in any way participate in the pleasure we feel by anticipation—

Therefore I think there are Strong reason to Suspect, that if this Discription of men be not Troublesom, & formidable it will happen by the inabillity of a foreign nation to promote their Veiws, & not from a deriliction of their origenal Designs—

I am Dear Sir, With the highest respect & Sincerest friendship your Most Hble Servt   Thos. Sumter

RC (MoSHi: Jefferson Papers); endorsed by TJ as received 1 May 1801 and so recorded in SJL.

From Peter Delabigarre

Sir,   Washington April 18th 1801.

The great object of my Journey here was to pay my personal respects to the first magistrate of this my adopted country and to express you my heart felt satisfaction on the auspicious day which promises so many blessings under your government. as a lover of sciences and of our republican constitution I must beg your leave to say, without any adulatory meaning, That I feel myself proud to contemplate now a true philosopher at the head of a nation so happily circumstanced as this is.

I sincerely regret to have it not in my power either to go to monticello or to wait here for your return, Thus I leave in the hands of mr. pichon my friend *trois dents de lait d'un mamoth* and a letter which the chancellor Livingston my Neighbour desired me to deliver you. may I intreat you to honor me with your commands for the state of N. york during the absence of the chancellor, I would offer you my Zealous care in the collection of the Mamoth bones lately discovered and such as remain to be dugd. up on the walkill?

[608]

with respectful sentiments I remain Sir one of Your warmest admirers & most obedient Servt.   PETER DELABIGARRE

RC (DLC); at foot of text: "Ths. Jefferson esqr."; endorsed by TJ as received 6 May and so recorded in SJL.

PERSONAL RESPECTS: Delabigarre, originally of France, had lived in the United States for more than a decade. In October 1790 he had written to TJ to request a passport for travel to England and France on business. A neighbor of Robert R. Livingston in the Hudson Valley, Delabigarre was an enthusiastic supporter of his friend's experiments in science and technology (George Dangerfield, *Chancellor Robert R. Livingston of New York, 1746-1813* [New York, 1960], 284-6; Vol. 17:601).

TROIS DENTS DE LAIT D'UN MAMOTH: that is, three milk teeth of a mammoth. The LETTER from Livingston was that of 29 Mch.

To Enoch Edwards

DEAR SIR   Monticello Apr. 18. 1801.

Your favor of Apr. 3 finds me on a short visit to this [place] for the purpose of making some [. . .] arrangements preparatory to my removal to Washington, which will be in one [week] from this time. a thousand of the ordinary formulas of compliment would not have [pro]ved the sincerity & kindness with which you undertake my commission so strongly as the [detailed views] you have given of it, which prove you have already contemplated it with [. . .] attention. your views so perfectly coincide with mine, that I shall only note the few particulars in which you seem doubtful.—the calico is to be over a cloth lining [. . .] because it can easily be taken out, [. . .] & kept clean. it has a [cooler] look too in summer.—a large & strong [hub] you are perfectly right in the opinion that the outer half inch gives more strength than all the rest. I agree with you too that the beauty of the body depends mainly on the sweep of the stern, & that being too square is the worst extreme. the other extreme is more [tolerable] as it leads to lightness.— collars are greatly preferable to breastplates. the latter [gall] the horse immediately & then by [. . .] the motion of his breast under [these] they cha[fe?] [. . .] the gall & set the best horse to [kick]ing. I have had [. . .] experiences travelling with collars, and never yet had a [horse] [galled?] by them. [. . .] they would lie so dead on it, as (after the [. . .] out) to press only like a tight [harness?]. I saw lately a very simple [. . .]ing off and on the driver's seat, by only 2. [. . .].

I have made some attem[pt in] the margin to sketch it but only exempli[. . .]. you [may think] of something better. the last of June or beginning of July will [be] perfectly in time. my best respects to Mrs. Edwards and a thousand [grateful]

acknolegements to you [. . .] and assurances of my high esteem & attachment.   TH: JEFFERSON

PrC (DLC); faint and blurred; at foot of text: "Doctr. Edwards"; endorsed by TJ in ink on verso.

From John Wayles Eppes

DEAR SIR,   Eppington April 18th. 1801.

Previous to receiving your last letters, I had engaged Mr. Bells Horse and his match for you at 600 dollars—I had never seen the match and relied solely on Mr. Bells representation of him as a fine match—On going to Petersburg however after Davy came down I found the Horse called a match so far inferior to Mr. Bells that I refused him altogether—Not wishing to send a single Horse I bought Doctr. Shores pair at $800 dollars as a case of necessity & after making the purchase received your last letter of the 1st. of April which from some accident or rather had taken the near route of Williamsburg—This letter contained instructions for the immediate purchase of Haxhalls Horse, with which I complied—So that you receive four horses instead of three—

My Bills for the Horses are all drawn at 90 days from the time of the respective purchases—Bells was bought on the 15th. of March—Shores on 1[2]th.[1] of april—Haxhalls on the 16th.—So that the payments become due

Bells on the 16th. of June	$300
Shores on the 1st. of July.	800
Haxhalls on the 16 of Do.	500
	$1600

These prices are excessively high and such as I can scarcely justify myself for having given—They are all however horses of fine form gentle well broke and steady—You will find Shores a first rate pair for Service—They match well both in appearance and spirit and carry themselves finely in Harness—They are not equal I think in form to Haxhalls or Bells tho' they appear at present under every disadvantage having returned from a long journey the day before I got them— Haxhalls and Bells also are gentle and perform well in harness & Bells tho' different in colour would appear well in harness with Shores being of the same height & having the same marks—

That they may please you is my sincere wish—In selecting them I have regarded qualities only as perhaps horses of equal figure might have been purchased much lower—As they were intended for your own use I thought a few hundred dollars more than the real value would be well bestowed upon such as were gentle & steady.

Accept for your health & happiness the affectionate wishes of yours

JNO: W: EPPES

RC (MHi); endorsed by TJ as received 20 Apr. and so recorded in SJL.

recorded in SJL under 1 Apr. See 8 Apr. for TJ's last letter to Eppes.

TJ's LAST LETTERS regarding the purchase of the horses were dated 27 and 28 Mch. In that of 28 Mch., TJ requested the IMMEDIATE PURCHASE of William Haxall's horse. No letters by TJ are

[1] Eppes may have canceled the second digit here, but TJ interpreted the date as the 12th when he informed George Jefferson in his letter of 21 Apr., that Shore's note was due on 12 July.

From Mary Jefferson Eppes

Eppington April 18th [1801]

I recieved your letter only yesterday My Dear Papa nor did I know 'till a few days before that you were at Monticello, as we have been here for some time past which has prevented our hearing from you, the prospect of seeing you so much sooner than I expected has in some degree consoled me for not being able to join you at this time, tho' I am afraid I shall lament more than ever the distance which seperates me from Monticello as I fear it will be an obstacle not allways to be surmounted & that I shall not have the satisfaction even of allways spending with you the short time that you will now remain there. it will not be in our power to go up before the 20th of july Mr Eppes says, & from that time My dear Papa till you return it will not be necessary to make any difference in your arrangements for us, the servants we shall carry up will be more than sufficient for ourselves & you would perhaps prefer yours being employed in some way or other.   I send you the lettuce seed which Mr Bolling promis'd you last year. Adieu My dear Papa I shall be much obliged to you if you will take the trouble of keeping that small sum which is at present in Mr Jeffersons hands for the tobacco, for me as I should prefer laying it out in Washington Adieu once more my dear Papa pardon this scrawl for I have had scarcely time to write it & believe me with tenderest affection yours   M EPPES

RC (MHi); partially dated; endorsed by TJ as received 20 Apr. 1801 and so recorded in SJL.

YOUR LETTER: see 11 Apr.

From Tench Coxe

Sir   Lancaster Pa. April 19th. 1801.

The gentleman to whom you wrote on the 26th. of March arrived here a few days ago from Philadelphia, and, during a stay of six days, mentioned to me a passage you did me the honor to write in relation to myself. You will permit me to repeat that I never knew of his writing either of his letters about me 'till they were sent, that I never asked such an act of friendship of him, and that I regret the solicitations, with which you have been incommoded. I am sure that no one can add to your knowledge & information in regard to me, and you are master of the subject of services to be rendered by those you may appoint.

It may not be useless however, Sir, to communicate to you some ideas, which will enable you to regard my interests and situation, as far as public circumstances may render convenient & proper. Those circumstances are next to sacred.

Three aged relations, and considerable landed affairs in Pennsa. New York, and Delaware, with the education of my children, and experience of this climate will render it highly desireable to me to remain in Pennsylvania. My interests call me *strongly* to Philadelphia, where alone there are federal offices adequate to the decent maintenance of my large family. It was therefore my wish to take the Situation No. 1., which I supposed would be vacated. You are possessed of the circumstances, which have prepared me for it more than any other person. It is an office of *great intrinsic difficulty*, and which from its patronage should be in the hands of *a true and energetic friend* of our government and administration. If that office be properly attended to, your administration can, in no respect, bear hard on Pennsylvania, without a timely knowledge of the facts by the possessor, who should be a faithful and judicious *videt*. If N. 2 or N. 3[1] cannot be given to and accepted by[2] the person for whom you proposed N. 1, then, *on thorough knowledge*, I am convinced it will be to be *much* regretted. The execution of the office is one important cause for this regret, but another is that all those wholesome uses of its great opportunities, to which I allude, will be turned, by an attendant character, to personal ends, and not to public. The principal for whom the office has been designed, I acquit of any such views or practices, but the attendant character is *extremely* exceptionable on that score.

Should however N. 1. go as you have intended, then if N. 3 should be intended to be vacated, or can be vacated by a change of the incumbent to some other, consistently with public good, I should prefer N. 3 next to N. 1., before either N. 2, or any office at the seat of

Government of the U.S. I am not fond of the pecuniary responsibilities of No. 2. even tho the Bank will hold the money.

If N. 1. & N. 3, are not likely to be at your disposal, Sir, and N. 2 should be so, then I would submit my pretensions for that office, tho I greatly prefer N. 3 & N. 1.

N. 4. would be less acceptable to me than any other—here. I hope I do not estimate myself and my conduct & sufferings too highly, when I say that I fear my appointment to N. 4 or N. 5 would be of ill impression upon the Administration.

If I am not favored with N. 1 or N. 3. nor N. 2, then although I trust I am not ambitious and have proved it by my letter, I would respectfully submit my pretensions to N. 6, for which, *on cautious reflexion*, I do not feel myself incompetent. On the reduction of the Salaries in 1802, it will barely maintain such a family as mine at Washington. No. 7 will not maintain them & me there after the reduction in 1802.

I hope, Sir, you will not consider me as too importunate, or as running into prescribing, when I may not reasonably expect any consideration. When the Government was first placed in republican hands, I will confess my long and earnest exertions in the amelioration of our affairs and in the defence of our republican institutions drew me imperceptibly into ideas, in regard to my future situation, connected with the public councils of my country. It appeared to me, at the Moment, that I might be passed through the public mind for two situations of that nature, tho I would have accepted with real regret of that which is to be filled on the first of May. The other (N. 6) was, from the beginning a preferable object in my mind. I observe it has been offered to a person of this state, whose *knowledge* of all the objects it comprehends I cannot prefer to my own. I return however, with sincerity Sir, to N. 1. N. 3 and N. 2 in the order I have mentioned; and if I consider my own wishes, without any regard to the public interests, *I earnestly desire the modest irresponsible station N. 3. before any office in your gift—either in Washington or Philadelphia.* I should in that, have considerable leisure to pursue those investigations of the public interests, which are so pleasing to myself, and which may be rendered eminently useful to my country. Such, Sir are all my views.—

I remain, with perfect respect, Sir, your most faithful friend and most obedient servant   T. C.

RC (DNA: RG 59, LAR); endorsed by TJ as received 30 Apr. but recorded in SJL under the 29th.

GENTLEMAN TO WHOM YOU WROTE: Thomas McKean. For the governor's comments regarding an appointment for Coxe, see McKean to TJ, 21 Mch.

For the key to SITUATION NO. 1, Pennsylvania supervisor of the internal revenue, and to the other positions Coxe referred to by number, see the enclosure below.

VIDET: vedette, a sentinel or advance watch.

REDUCTION OF THE SALARIES: the pay of the secretary of the navy remained at $4,500, with the appropriations for his salary and that of his office staff varying from $9,055 to $9,671 between 1799 and 1803. The office of revenue commissioner, with a $3,000 salary, was the last post on Coxe's list—"N. 7"—and the one he had previously held. It was eliminated in April 1802 by the passage of the "Act to repeal the Internal Taxes" (U.S. Statutes at Large, 1:719; 2:64, 119, 148-9, 186, 212; ASP, *Miscellaneous*, 1:304; Coxe to TJ, 23 Mch. 1801).

THAT WHICH IS TO BE FILLED ON THE FIRST OF MAY: fearing that the Senate, which met in a special session on 5 Mch.,

would reject the nomination of Albert Gallatin as secretary of the Treasury, TJ deferred his appointment until May. Gallatin left Washington after 14 Mch. to settle his affairs at New Geneva, Pennsylvania, and bring his family to the capital. He arrived back in Washington on 13 May. The next day Judge William Cranch administered the oath of office to him. On 26 Jan. 1802, Gallatin was confirmed by the Senate along with numerous other interim appointments (JEP, 1:400, 405; Raymond Walters, Jr., *Albert Gallatin: Jeffersonian Financier and Diplomat* [New York, 1957], 141-3; Gallatin to TJ, 14 Mch., 23 Apr. 1801).

[1] Coxe interlined the "or N. 3."
[2] Preceding three words interlined.

ENCLOSURE

Tench Coxe's Key to Federal Positions, with Jefferson's Notes

H. Miller. Muhlbg	No. 1.	H. M. Supervisor of the Reve.
Latimer	No. 2.	The collector of the Customs, Phila.
Mc.pherson	N. 3.	The naval officer, Philada.
Jackson	N. 4.	The Surveyor of the port of Phila.
T. Ross ⎫ ⎬ *Coxe* *Ashe* ⎭	N. 5	The Inspector of the Revenue of the *first* survey,[1] with the genl. Collectorship of the internal Revenues Philada. City & County, annexed—[2]
	N. 6	The Secretary of the Navy—Washn.
W. Miller	N. 7	The Commissioner of the Revenue, Washington

MS (DNA: RG 59, LAR, 2:0614); undated; in Coxe's hand, with names in italics on left side of numbered list added by TJ on or before 17 June 1801; for other additions by TJ, see notes below.

On 16 June Gallatin evaluated the offices described by Coxe above, referring to them as the "seven Offices applied for by T. Coxe." He recommended that TJ offer Coxe the combined positions of INSPECTOR and collector of INTERNAL

REVENUES in Philadelphia—"N. 5." See TJ to Coxe, 17 June, and Coxe to TJ, 24 June 1801, for TJ's offer and Coxe's refusal of the office. At the urging of Peter Muhlenberg, Coxe accepted the position of internal revenue collector in place of James Ash in the fall of 1801 (Cooke, *Coxe*, 399-400).

[1] TJ here interlined "abt <5 or> 600."
[2] TJ here added "about 2000. D."

From William Short

Dear Sir   Paris April 19th. 1801.

Since my last of the 9th. of Decr. written from La Rocheguyon & sent by the French Chargé des affaires, I have remained silent; first because no good conveyance presented itself, & secondly because we have been for some time past expecting intelligence from America, which I wished to recieve before writing. Although I have as yet recieved no letter & nothing official has as yet arrived here, I cannot longer delay writing because the cartel is to sail in a few days from Havre. This vessel is the Benjamin Franklin which left New-York in the beginning of Jany. last. Since it, no vessel has arrived in the ports of this country from the U.S. until within a few days, when two or three came into the port of Bordeaux, having sailed after the expiration of the prohibition law. One of them wch. left Philadelphia the 9th. of March, brings a letter from the late Consul at Bordeaux to his wife here, mentioning that I am named Minister near the French Republic. She recieved this letter the day before yesterday & immediately sent to communicate this intelligence to me. I recieved several notes from different persons yesterday & today complimenting me on this occasion. Whether they all get their intelligence from the same source I know not—but one of the Paris papers of this morning mentions among a variety of articles under the London head that the Chancellor Livingston is designated to come here—this article is without any American date of time or place—Mr. Fenwick's letter I think is written from Philadelphia. This is all we know upon the subject. In general, a private letter from a person known would seem to carry with it a greater degree of authenticity than a vague article in a gazette—but as I am at all times far from being disposed to flatter myself, I cannot help giving greater weight in this instance than perhaps it deserves, to the article of the gazette—I percieve that I have by this expression betrayed myself & discovered that the appointment would be flattering to me. You know by old experience my dear Sir, that I am not accustomed to dissemble with you—I will not therefore at present withdraw the expression.—I have until now abstained from entering on this subject, from the time of its being supposed that you would be at the head of the Government, because I have chosen that you should remain entirely free & unembarassed by any thing previous on my part.—But at present I am free to own that an appointment under you would give me real pleasure & satisfaction. It would doubly so, because the contrary would be a subject of so much surprize to all those who know me here, whether French or Americans, that I feel it would somewhat embarass me. From their knowlege of the long habits of friendship & favor in which you have been towards me, & from my long employment in the diplomatic line & acquaintance with this country, they have laid it down as certain that I should be appointed here, & complimented me on it from the time of the first reports having circulated here that you would be President. I have always of course replied by those *lieux communs*, used in such cases, & avoided as far as possible giving any ground to suppose I expected it.—A very short time will of course elucidate this matter, & in the mean time I will not occupy more of your attention respecting it. Should you think my services useful to my country I feel that I should be happy to devote them again, under your administration—Should you think others more able & more adequate to the task, I will not say that I shall feel no pain from this circumstance, but it is certain that I desire to see employed those whom you concieve most proper & most able to second your views.—If however the conditional ratification of the treaty is to bring on a new negotiation, I should prefer much to have at least one other person joined with me for that particular purpose—In such a delicate matter & which touches so nearly such a variety of interests & in such a variety of ways, I should feel the responsability too heavy on me alone.—There is one circumstance of which you will be probably apprized before you recieve this letter.—You will recollect the plan which Dumoustier had in view & about which he wrote a good deal to his Court as you informed me in the time—It is now reduced to a certainty that that plan is resumed & will be carried into execution.—I mentioned to you in my last the favorable crisis which had taken place in the North, relative to neutral rights. I see nothing to change as to what I then said,—Events have rather confirmed the propriety of the subject being well examined & nearly to the centre of action—I still think it to be regretted that the U.S. had not an Envoy at Copenhagen—& it seems to me that it would at this moment be one of the most desirable missions of the U.S. because I concieve it might be made one of the most useful, on account of the circumstances mentioned in my last. Whatever may be the issue at the present time it is to be desired that the whole matter should be well observed so as to form a proper opinion of what plan should be adopted by the U.S. for the future.—The King of Prussia has taken possession of Hanover—& Hamburgh & Lubeck are possessed by the Danes, provisionally—We only know as yet the death of Paul I.—& the attack made by the English on the Danes, the 2d. of this month—We know not what will be the immediate consequences of these two events.—I have not had the pleasure of hearing from you since my letters of

Aug. 6th. & Sep. 18th.—As those who carried them arrived safe in the U.S. in October & Decr. last I take it for granted you recieved them in due time—I had counted that the cartel which sailed in Jany. last would have brought me a letter from you. I wrote to Mr Barnes by the same conveyances—He has acknowleged the reciept of one of them by a letter of the 25th. of October—I am surprized at not having heard from him since, as I pressed him in my letters, notwithstanding my intention of returning to America, not to delay writing to me—The cartel was so public a conveyance that he must have known of it I should imagine.—I have for some time past suspended my preparations for my vernal voyage—but I shall still persevere & return ere long, if I am not detained on this side of the Atlantic by any thing from you.—A letter for my brother will accompany this—I shall put them under cover to Mr Barnes—they will be forwarded by post from the port where the vessel may arrive. I beg you my dear Sir, to accept my earnest wishes for your health, happiness & success in the thorny path in which the public voice of our country has placed you—May you long enjoy that recompense which I know will be most satisfactory to you—the seeing of Liberty & Tranquillity united by your efforts—& the furnishing this proof to the world of the superiority of the knowlege, virtue & enlightened character of the American people.—Such is the full persuasion at this time as it has long been of your friend & servant

W: SHORT

RC (PHi); at foot of first page: "Thomas Jefferson President of the U.S."; endorsed by TJ as received 25 July 1801 and so recorded in SJL. Enclosed in William Short to John Barnes, 19 Apr. (summary in Short's epistolary record, DLC: Short Papers).

EXPIRATION OF THE PROHIBITION LAW: the "Act further to suspend the commercial intercourse between the United States and France, and the dependencies thereof," approved 27 Feb. 1800, expired on 3 Mch. 1801 (U.S. Statutes at Large, 2:7-11).

Joseph Fenwick was the former U.S. CONSUL AT BORDEAUX.

PARIS PAPERS: the Moniteur of 19 Apr. contained no direct news from the United States later than 28 Feb., but did print items from London dated 15 Apr. that included news of TJ's inauguration, his appointment of Madison as secretary of state, and the selection of Robert R. LIVINGSTON as minis-

ter plenipotentiary to France (Gazette Nationale ou le Moniteur Universel, 29 Germinal Year 9).

LIEUX COMMUNS: commonplace language.

PLAN WHICH DUMOUSTIER HAD IN VIEW: the Comte de Moustier was minister plenipotentiary from France to the United States from 1787 to 1791, but returned to France in 1789 on a leave of absence that was effectively a recall prompted by American complaints. In August 1790, when Short was U.S. chargé d'affaires in Paris and TJ was secretary of state, TJ reported suspicions that Moustier had advocated establishing a French colony on the Mississippi River (Shackelford, Jefferson's Adoptive Son, 44; Vol. 14:520-2; Vol. 15:555; Vol. 17:122-3; Vol. 26:479).

A coup planned by several months resulted in the DEATH OF PAUL I by assassination on 24 Mch. 1801 and the installation of his son Alexander as emperor (Roderick E.

McGrew, *Paul I of Russia, 1754-1801* [Oxford, 1992], 1, 322-54).

Lord Nelson commanded the British ATTACK on the Danish fleet at Copenhagen on 2 Apr., forcing Denmark to accede to an immediate truce. On 9 Apr. the Danes agreed to an armistice of 14 weeks that included a moratorium on any action in behalf of the league of armed neutrality (William Laird Clowes, *The Royal Navy: A History from the Earliest Times to the Present*, 7 vols. [London, 1897-1903; repr. 1996-97], 4:427, 432-40).

WROTE TO MR BARNES: according to Short's summary record of his correspondence, he had written to John Barnes on 5 Aug., 11 Aug., and 1 Oct. 1800. Short wrote to his BROTHER Peyton on 15 Apr. 1801, enclosing that letter and the one to TJ printed above in a letter to Barnes of 19 Apr. (epistolary record in DLC: Short Papers).

From Elizabeth Barnet

SIR. New Germantown April 20th. 1801.

As differences are happily terminated between France & America, I am induced to hope, that I may take advantage of the present favorable season, to accept the solicitations of an affectinate & dutiful Son, who is the only prop of my declinining years, and who at present resides in Bordeaux as Consul for the United States—Well acquainted with his difficulties during the last four Years, prudence has hitherto prevented me from gratifying his wishes, and the desire of my heart—to spend the remnant of my days with him My pecuniary resources will not justify a Voyage to France, unless I shou'd be so happy to learn that his conduct merits your approbation, & that it is probable he will be continued, as on this circumstance alone his stay in France depends— Maternal anxiety is the only apology I can offer for the liberty of thus addressing You.

I have the honor to be With the highest respect Sir, Your most obedient humble Servant— ELIZABETH BARNET

RC (DNA: RG 59, LAR); at foot of text: "His Excellency Thomas Jefferson, President of the United States"; endorsed by TJ as received 2 May and so recorded in SJL with notation "Off."; also endorsed by TJ: "Barnet to be contind Consul at Bordeaux."

DUTIFUL SON: Isaac Cox Barnet.

From John Browne Cutting

SIR, Antigua 20 April 1801

The elevation of their fellow citizen to preside among millions of intelligent freemen—over a cluster of genuine republics, obedient, members of one great, durable, and growing Empire—is doubtless a dignified and dignifying Spectacle. The philosophic contemplate it with hope, and it is an object that fills a wide space in the eye of mankind

But to the Individual (like myself) an equal lover of order and liberty, who can appreciate the advantages resulting from the periodical election of a powerful yet responsible first Magistrate to the great body of our Nation (a people who from reflection and habit cherish in their hearts a love for republican systems of government)—this event becomes yet more interesting. And, if in addition to patriotic motives of joy and congratulation, the Individual notices such an event under an aspect of partiality for the character and predilection for the politics of the eminent Magistrate thus chosen: if he soberly believes too that a crisis in the Mind and affairs of Man approaches, involving forms and indeed the essence of government through out the Globe; and shou'd also be of opinion that a faithful administration of the Constitution of our western portion of it by an upright and truly republican President at this juncture may establish the happy condition of his own Country, and have no small influence upon the future freedom and welfare of other Republics—impress'd by such feelings and opinions he will fervently rejoice, as I do, Sir, that You are President of the United States of America.

I have long had the pleasure to be with sentiments of public veneration & private esteem

Your faithful and obedient Servant

JOHN BROWNE CUTTING

RC (DLC); at foot of text: "Thomas Jefferson President of the U. States"; endorsed by TJ as received 19 Jan. 1802 and so recorded in SJL.

John Browne Cutting (ca. 1755-1831), a native of Boston, met TJ in 1787, when Cutting was in London studying law, and the two corresponded for several years. As secretary of state, TJ had supported Cutting's claim against the government for monies spent for the relief of Americans impressed by the British navy. Cutting received only $2,000 of the more than $7,000 he claimed. He would continue to press his claim, however, and wrote TJ again in 1824 for his assistance (Heitman, *Register*, 183; *National Intelligencer*, 4 Feb. 1831; Cutting to TJ, 22 June 1824 in DLC; Vol. 12:321-2; Vol. 18:313-17; Vol. 23:104-6).

To George Jefferson

DEAR SIR   Monticello Apr. 20. 1801.

I did not know till this moment that the manifests for my tobo. [passed] at Milton the last winter had not been sent to you. I am now sending off a messenger to Milton for them. if they arrive before the departure of this letter they shall be inclosed. if not, some other private conveyance from our [court] shall be sought, so at farthest they shall go by the next post. I hope it will be no obstacle to the sale of the tobo. as directed in mine by the last post. accept assurances of my sincere esteem.   TH: JEFFERSON

PrC (MHi); blurred; at foot of text: "Mr George Jefferson"; endorsed by TJ in ink on verso.

MINE BY THE LAST POST: TJ to George Jefferson, 17 Apr. (first letter).

From Nathaniel Macon

SIR   Warrenton 20 April 1801

Since my return it has not been in my power to see General Davie. He is now at his plantation on the Catawba. I will endeavor to see him as soon as he gets home, which will probably be about the 10. of May; If you should wish to appoint more than one Commissioner from this state to treat with the Indians, I do not think a second could be found that would do better than Major Absalom Tatom of Hillsborough; but it seems to me, two, if not one, could do every thing that is to be done, and if only two it might be well to appoint one from Tennessee or if there should be preferred, one from this state, one from Tennessee & the third from some other state—We wish no change of any of the federal officers, unless they are delinquent, and then the delinquency to be made public—I have understood that Sitgreaves did not accept his new appointment, if this be the fact, and you determine to make a new appointment, permit me to name you, Henry Potter of Raleigh for the place, As a Judge I am sure he would be acceptable to every Democrat in the state. He is a sound one himself and has always been so

Suffer me to say to you, that the people expect,—

That Levees will be done way—

That the communication to the next Congress will be by letter not a speech—

That we have too many Ministers in Europe—

That some of the Collectors, perhaps all, had better recieve a fixed salary, than commissions—

That the army might safely be reduced—

That the navy might also be reduced—

That the Agents to the War & navy might be reduced—In fact that a system of œconomy is to be adopted and pursued with energy—

[620]

As soon as I see Davie I will inform you, and If he does not incline to be a commissioner to treat with Indians, I will then name some other to you

I am with perfect respect & esteem Sir yr. most obt. sert.

NATHL MACON

RC (DLC); endorsed by TJ as received 29 Apr. and so recorded in SJL with notation "Off."

Nathaniel Macon (1758-1837) of North Carolina had served in the U.S. House of Representatives since 1791. His political career was marked by his fervent devotion to the principles of states' rights, limited government, a strict construction of the Constitution, and democratic simplicity. In December 1801 he was elected Speaker of the House of Representatives, remaining in the position until 1807. Although a strong supporter of TJ early in his presidency, Macon broke with the administration in 1806. He remained in the House until 1815, when he was elected to the Senate. He retired from Congress in 1828 (ANB; *Biog. Dir. Cong.*).

In a brief letter to TJ dated 1 May, Macon again recommended HENRY POTTER in place of John Sitgreaves, a judge of the District Court for North Carolina who had declined an appointment to the U.S. Fifth Circuit Court. "I am well informed," wrote Macon, "that he would be acceptable, he has been uniformly a sound Republican" (RC in DLC; endorsed by TJ as received 9 May and so recorded in SJL with notation "Off."). On 30 Nov., TJ appointed Potter to the circuit judgeship. Following Sitgreaves's death in March 1802, TJ in April named Potter to be his replacement as judge of the District Court for North Carolina (Appendix I, List 3; JEP, 1:401, 418; William S. Powell, ed., *Dictionary of North Carolina Biography*, 6 vols. [Chapel Hill, 1979-96], 5:131-2, 353-4; Levi Lincoln to TJ, 21 Mch.).

From Charles Pinckney

DEAR SIR   Near Columbia April 20: 1801

I wrote you on the road respecting the Chief Judge of this circuit— as I am necessarily detained in visiting my plantations in the country I do not expect to be in Town before the 20th May after which I shall be enabled to write you from Charleston on that subject & to recommend to you some gentleman who will probably accept. I find our citizens in this neighbourhood extremely pleased & am glad to hear they sent you an address as the opinion of Columbia & its Vicinity always has great Weight in our State—

I have impressed on many gentlemen of Consequence in this District the necessity of having a proper Successor to myself chosen & if either of the Gentlemen here spoken of consents to be a Candidate, scarcely any opposition will be attempted. I am arranging my affairs to enable me to embark in June & if You will give me leave I will take the liberty of suggesting that should opposition be intended to my nomination it may be proper to state to you some facts which probably I ought to have stated to you before—one is, that so long agoe as 1786 it became peculiarly my duty in Congress to investigate & attend to the situation of the Western Country— it's boundaries & rights & the differences then existing between the United States & Spain. it was on the Treaty proposed by M Gardoqui, which treaty I have reason to believe, Spain herself is since glad was not entered into—one article of it proposed to shut the Misissipi against the Citizens of the Union for 25 Years & this extraordinary proposal was supported by Mr Jay, then Secretary for foreign affairs in a written report of great length—at the request of the southern members I answered this report in writing & submitted it to Congress & had a very principal share in preventing the Treaty being adopted & in keeping the river open—my reasoning was printed & if I have a copy left I will look for it when I go to Town & send it to you—Mr: Madison was not in Congress then but happened to be in New York & perfectly remembers it & so do Governour Monroe & all the Members then present—

Mr King & General St Clair were amongst the most strong & persevering supporters of Mr Jay's opinions & in favour of the Occlusion— the rejection of this Measure opened the way to the favourable treaty since made with Spain—the laborious & accurate investigation I was obliged to give M Gardoqui's proposition at that time, has impressed the subject of our boundaries & intercourse with Spain so strongly on my mind that I am hopeful with the instructions I shall recieve from yourself & Mr Madison I shall be tolerably able to discharge the duties of my appointment—I think I posess at least the quality of patient & persevering Industry, where the subject is interesting & where I am convinced the rights or welfare of our country & my own honour & character in attending to them are involved—it will be my determination as I know it is my duty to add to this Industry, moderation & calm attention—If any objection should be made to my appointment on the ground of my not being acquainted with the Duties expected from a Minister to Spain I should suppose a knowledge of the facts I had mentioned will remove it, & I trust upon trial I shall not be found very greatly inferior to those who have preceded me at that court.—

I trust we shall have such a decided majority in the Senate as not to make the confirmation doubtful or that none of our *own friends* will join, or contribute by their absence to prevent it—I am not without my apprehensions that my conduct in this state on the Election[1] will not be easily forgotten by the federal party & therefore should not be surprised at their Wish to mortify me— the best mode of my escape from it I must leave to your superior discernment & knowledge of the state of things at the next session, & to what I consider as among the greatest comforts of my life, your friendship for me. it is in Your Power to protract the nomination to the End of the Session, & if you find they are then determined to reject it, by doing so & recalling me at the End or nearly at the End of the Session You will enable me to avoid the affront of a rejection & at the same time give me until the ensuing fall twelvemonth to remain in Europe.—if at nearly the End of the Session, you find the federal party or others, are determined not to confirm me & that it is unavoidable to appoint a successor to me, out of those who have more friends amongst the federalists, or have been less strenuous or decisive in their opposition to them, I suppose it will be easily in your power to do so in a manner that will give me sufficient time to return without inconvenience or hurry & in a manner reputable to myself. I have however every reason to believe that if our own friends are as true to me as I have been & am to them & the republican interest that my nomination will be confirmed. I must however my dear Sir rely on your friendship under all Events to prevent the disgrace of a rejection by protracting it to nearly the End of the Session & then, if you find it impracticable to obtain a confirmation, by recalling me. Independent of my own wish to avoid the affront, I fear the rejection of me will be injurious to the republican Interest in South Carolina, as nothing can convince of the People here of the least[2] Difficulty of my confirmation if the republican interest in your cabinet & the Senate prove true to me—I shall hope favourable things from Mr. Madison, Mr Gallatin & General Smith—the other gentlemen I but slightly know but much value & respect.—

I have written you a long letter which I am to request your goodness will excuse, I conclude it with praying that you may long continue to hold the executive power of our Government & that I may be always able so to conduct myself as to be deserving of the Esteem & friendship with which you have been pleased to honour me.—

With great respect & regard & profound attachment I am dear Sir yours truly   CHARLES PINCKNEY

RC (DLC); endorsed by TJ as received 11 June and so recorded in SJL.

I WROTE YOU ON THE ROAD: letter not found, but probably one from Pinckney to TJ recorded in SJL as written on 6 Apr.

THEY SENT YOU AN ADDRESS: Columbia, South Carolina, Citizens to TJ, 6 Mch.

A PROPER SUCCESSOR: Thomas Sumter, Sr., would succeed Pinckney in the U.S. Senate in December 1801.

In 1786 Pinckney had joined James Monroe and other southern congressmen to block a TREATY under negotiation between the Spanish minister to the U.S., Don Diego de GARDOQUI, and the secretary for foreign affairs, John JAY, in which the U.S. would forbear free navigation of the Mississippi River for 30 years in exchange for trade concessions from Spain (Marty D. Matthews, *Forgotten Founder: The Life and Times of Charles Pinckney* [Columbia, 2004], 34-7; Ammon, *Monroe*, 53-9).

[1] Preceding three words interlined.
[2] MS: "lest."

From Thomas Sumter, Jr.

Sir   Stateburgh 20th. April 1801

My Father has desired me to determine for myself & communicate to you my answer on the subject of the appointment, you have done me the honor of offering me—

I must confess Sir, that had I expected or wished for a public employment, no appointment would have been so agreeable to me as one of this nature; & no one so acceptable, for several reasons, as this particular one.—

I am therefore not only indebted to you for the flattering manner in which you have proposed it, but also for selecting the one which is most grateful to me—& I must beg your pardon for hesitating so long in making up my mind on the acceptance of it—

I am not insensible to the honor of serving the public, when a mans circumstances & qualifications authorize him to undertake it—On the contrary, I think it his duty—but I really feel great diffidence in my abilities to discharge the duties which may occur in one of the stations, to which this appointment may introduce me—I concieve the functions of a private Secretary, to be simple & easy, under the direction of an able man, & the situation an excellent one for attaining political ac-quirement, & not unfavorable to improvement of any other kind; And in truth, my desire to obtain an opportunity for these purposes, which private concerns have hitherto denied me, renders this one verry inviting especially in the scene where I should be placed & at the present crisis of affairs in Europe—such an occasion indeed, might well deserve some sacrifices of time and interest, & I should be perfectly satisfied with the allowance even were it less—as I am not under the necessity of making that an object of consideration—I am well aware of the advantages which the rank of Secretary of legation, would add to the situation of a private Secretary, & of the difference between those & the grade of Chargè des affaires; but as I cannot dis-tinctly foresee what objects may arise under the latter character—I cannot help being timid in undertaking it—If, as I believe, the oper-ations of such an officer, are left verry little to his own discretion & are guided by specific instructions from Government; his duty is much simplified & I might hope with the favor of your friendship & explicit directions, to be enabled to give satisfaction—at least so much, as fidelity & zeal could insure—Thus Sir, have I ventured to lay before you my wishes & my fears as an appology for, the delay I have already made—& were I to proceed to France before Mr. Liv-ingston, the disposition of my Father's affairs & my own, would oblige me to extend the delay probably[1] untill the middle of June, which would be as early as I should be able to arrive at the seat of Government; where I presume you design to have my instructions delivered & where I should be pleased to recieve them—as it would afford me an opportunity of being made acquainted with some of the officers of government & perhaps with Mr. Livingston which would be verry desireable to me before my departure—

Should it be convenient Sir, to admit this arrangement, in point of time, I have determined to accept the appointment—in the mode you are pleased to recommend—& I shall be proud & happy If I can aquit myself so as to merit the approbation of an Administration, under which I promise myself it will be an honor to serve—

However If the public service should risk any prejudice from this postponement—I beg you will not make my appointment a matter of any consideration—I should be inexcuseable to wish it—I shall therefore be prepared to recieve your commands—whatever the descision may be.

I am Sir, with the highest respect & esteem your mt. obt. Hu St

Tho. Sumter Jr.

RC (MoSHi: Jefferson Papers); endorsed by TJ as received 1 May and so recorded in SJL.

Thomas Sumter, Jr. (1768-1840), was the only son of Congressman Thomas Sumter, Sr., of South Carolina. His term as secretary of the U.S. legation in Paris was brief, ending with his resignation in May 1802 following a dispute with Robert R. Livingston over the duties of the office. He served briefly as James Monroe's private secretary in London before returning to South Carolina in November 1803. Shortly before he left office, TJ appointed

Sumter a lieutenant colonel in the light artillery on 7 Jan. 1809. On 6 Mch. 1809, President James Madison appointed him minister plenipotentiary to the Portuguese court at Rio de Janeiro, where he remained until 1821 (*S.C. Biographical Directory, House of Representatives*, 4:546-7; Madison, *Papers, Sec. of State Ser.*, 3:220n, 228, 5:564; JEP, 2:93, 119; Thomas Tisdale, *A Lady of the High Hills: Natalie Delage Sumter* [Columbia, S.C., 2001], 31, 49-57).

[1] Word interlined.

Petition from Colin C. Wills

His Excellency Thomas Jefferson Esqr President of the United States of America

The petition of Colin C. Wills (a native of Virginia) humbly sheweth, That your petitioner hath by his assiduity & genius attained the art of making brushes, but is in such indigent circumstances that he is utterly unable to carry on his trade, for the want of materials to work on, Your petitioner has a wife & two small female children who

look to him for support; is a further inducement to Your petitioner to make this application to your Clemency, hoping you will devise some way or means by which your petitioner might be enabled to lay in a sufficent stock to enable him to carry on his Trade with advantage to society with credit & profit to himself, so as to enable him to make provision against the arival of old Age, which he sees most glaringly approaching with all its concomitant evils—& which your petitioner is utterly unable to evade unless by the interposition of some Benevolent & Charitable hand. Your Petitioner more particularly chose to make application to your Excellency because he ever understood you lov'd to encourage our own manufactures—Your Excellency may greatly accellerate this business without affecting your own resources, Your petitioner feels himself adequate to the discharge of the duties of many of the pecuniary offices which you as President have in your gift—if your Excellency thought proper to bestow one of those on your petitioner he might by his Economy & frugality amply provide for the establishing his trade on an eligible basis—shou'd no such office be vacant or shou'd any impediment lay in the way that your petitioner is[1] unable to foresee, your petitioner wou'd most willingly be employed in any domestic employment of your own, which you might conceive him adequate to—Your petitioner earnestly solicits your serious attention & consideration of his case, and hopes your known Clemency will induce you to form & lay some plan to extricate him from his present calamity—and as in duty bound Your petitioner for your Temporal & Eternal felicity & hapiness will ever ardently pray—   COLIN C. WILLS
Alexandria District of Columbia 20th April 1801

RC (MoSHi: Jefferson Papers); endorsed by TJ as received 10 May.

In a letter dated Alexandria, 11 May 1801, Wills offered TJ a bound volume of one year of issues of the newspaper Baltimore *American*, with the suggestion that TJ could give it to an "acquaintance" in the "back part" of Virginia who might "be glad of such an acquisition" (RC in same; endorsed by TJ as received on 11 May and so recorded in SJL).

[1] Preceding three words interlined in place of "I am."

From Aaron Burr

DEAR SIR   NYork 21 Ap. 1801
    I have written to Mr. Madison respecting the Consul of Madeira, the Marshall of Massts. Bay and the Marshall of N Jersey—To Mr. Gallatin respecting the Supervisor of N, Jersey and something of

Bailey, Davis and Willett, and to Genl Smith something further of [Bailey]: to all which I take the liberty to refer you.

Upon my arrival in this City I found it noised about that [Bailey] was destined for the office, either of Supervisor or Naval Officer, and it is with regret I declare that I have not been so fortunate as to meet the cold approbation of any one of our friends to either appointment—We talk of placing him on the bench of our S. Court; but of this we can better determine a few Weeks hence—after the Election.

Edwards, Kirby, A, Wollcott and Bishop have aseperately been with me since my return and We have talked over Connecticut—They all urge the Necessity of a pretty speedy change in the offices of Collector of N Haven, Collector of Middletown & Supervisor—As to the first of these offices, they Yielded to the reasons which opposed [Munson]— A. [Bishop] Junr. would not do for a reason of which you and I were ignorant—They unite however in recommending Abraham[1] Bishop father of the Orator—a pretty Vigorous & active Man of about sixty five; always used to business—has been some twenty or thirty times "deputy"—now enjoying two or more offices of trust—besides being a Deacon of long standing—this appointment, will not only be unexceptionable; but, will appear to accord with the fashion of that Country.

Kirby mentioned to me Judge Bull as Supervisor; but the other gentlemen think that office, in point of influence, much the most important in that State, and that the Superior energy and activity of Kirby are necessary to it's due & effectual execution—In this Case, and when Bradley shall resign, John Welch of Litch[field] is the Man they unanimously recommend for Marshall—Judge Bull, they say, will be as well satisfied & better suited, with the Post office at Hartford—A. Wollcott is recommended to succed the Collector in Middletown.

Mr. Swan has written me from Paris and *Mrs. Swan* from Boston, that he has setled his accounts with the french Govt. to their entire Satisfaction &, proposing to remain in Paris, would be gratified by the appointment of Consul General: all which I promised to communicate to you—I have often met Mr Swan in Society: he appears to be a sensible well informed man and to be entitled to respect as a gentleman; but there must be persons about you who know more than I do of Mr Swan—I cannot pretend to give an opinion of the preference due to him above others who may de[serve] the office & of whose Names even I am ignorant.

Hamilton seems to be literally Mad with spleen and envy and disappointment—as far as I can yet judge, his efforts are perfectly impotent.

respectfully & affecy   A. BURR

RC (NHi: Gilder Lehrman Collection at the Gilder Lehrman Institute of American History); effaced or cut, removing almost entirely some names and causing damage also to verso of page; at foot of text: "[Th. Jefferson]"; endorsed by TJ as received 29 Apr. and so recorded in SJL.

Burr wrote to James MADISON, Albert GALLATIN, and Samuel SMITH on 21 Apr. Theodorus Bailey, Matthew L. Davis, and Marinus Willett were under consideration for the position of naval officer at New York. Burr's letter to Madison, which was in regard to the federal marshal for Massachusetts, did not touch on the positions in Madeira and New Jersey (Kline, *Burr*, 1:566-9; Madison, *Papers, Sec. of State Ser.*, 1:107).

The results of the New York State ELECTION for the assembly and governor became known beginning 2 May (Kline, *Burr*, 1:572-7).

[1] Word canceled by TJ, who interlined "Samuel."

To George Jefferson

DEAR SIR   Monticello Apr. 21. 1801.

I now inclose you the manifests for my tobo. of the Milton inspection & growth of the last year, being 7. hhds weighing 10,028 th total. Mr. Eppes's draughts on you on my account are now fixed

to mr Bell	300. D. paiable June 16.
Doctr. Shore	800. D. paiable July 12.
mr. Haxhall	500. D. paiable July 16.

for all of which I will make provision in your hands in time to prevent the inconvenience of advances. I am Dear Sir

Your's affectionately   TH: JEFFERSON

PrC (MHi); at foot of text: "Mr. George Jefferson"; endorsed by TJ in ink on verso. Enclosed manifests not found, but for a list of the hogsheads and their weights, see MB, 2:1038.

From Caesar A. Rodney

HONORED & DEAR SIR,   Wilmington April 21st. 1801.

The ardent wishes of the friends of the revolution have been realized in the exaltation of yourself who laid the corner stone & who has ever been a firm & uniform supporter of its principles to the Presidential chair. The universal joy diffused over the whole face of the Country on this happy event is better felt than described. I believe among all who rejoiced none experienced more heartfelt satisfaction than myself. Already has the curtain dropped over a system of political persecution more hard & more intolerable than that of the Roman See or the inquisition of Spain. Those who were wasps yesterday have been deprived of their stings. Like a Talisman in the Arabian Mythology you have paralyzed all the creatures of the plan of *Espionage*, all the actors in the cruel drama or rather tragedy[1] of political intolerance. Under the mild rays of your administration I flatter myself that all those clouds which have so long overcast our political horizon will be dissipated, that the vessel of State with her helm under your guidance will sail down the current of time blest with a favouring breeze & a clear serene skye. I hope to see the hatchet of party oppression & proscription buried & the calumet of reconciliation resumed. I wish in the honest sincerity of my heart in your own language to see equal justice done to all men. Of your speech delivered at your installation & which may be considered as the index to the system you mean to pursue as the chart by which the bark of government is to be directed, it is impossible to speak in terms of panegyric[2] too lofty. It will be recurred to hereafter as a *Magna Carta* in politics. I must confess myself not less pleased with the comment given by the acts of administration on the text.

We are about to support Mr. Dickenson as Governor of this State. He has at lenth consented to be a candidate & the prospect of carrying him daily brightens. On mentioning the name of this venerable patriot excuse me for suggesting that altho' I know he would decline the acceptance of any office under the Genl. Government on account of his inferiority, yet I have it from him & communicate it confidentially that he would be pleased at having some dignified station offered to him. I suggested this to Col: Burr as he passed thro' to Washington who approved the idea. A mark of confidence of this kind known before the election which is in Octobr. would add to his popularity.

In the County of Kent we are very sanguine of success this year & if so shall send you a good whig as a senator next winter, as that County holds the ballance & its weight will turn the scale. A single senator being so important at this juncture to give strenth to your administration you may rest assured that every nerve will be exerted with a veiw to that object—With sentiments a great regard & esteem I remain Hond & Dr. Sir

Your Most Obt Sevt & Friend   Caesar A Rodney

RC (DLC); endorsed by TJ as received 29 Apr. and so recorded in SJL.

In the end John Dickinson declined to run for GOVERNOR in 1801, although Delaware Republicans had Aaron BURR intercede for them. David Hall won the election in October by a slim margin and became the state's first Republican governor. The opposition, however, continued to control the state legislature and Samuel White, a Federalist, was elected to serve in the U.S. Senate (Milton E. Flower, *John Dickinson, Conservative Revolutionary* [Charlottesville, 1983], 297; John A. Munroe, *Federalist Delaware, 1775-1815* [New Brunswick, N.J., 1954], 209-11, 268).

[1] Preceding three words interlined.
[2] MS: "panegric."

From James Madison

DEAR SIR   [22 Apr. 1801]

Your favor of the 17th. came to hand by the last mail. You will find us at home on saturday. It would have been expedient on some accounts to have set out before that day, but it has been rendered impossible by several circumstances, particularly by an attack on my health which kept me in bed 3 or 4 days, and which has not yet permitted me to leave the House. I hope to be able to begin the journey by sunday or monday at farthest and to get as far as Capt. Winston's the first day. I should have been glad to have taken a ride to Monticello during the Court especially as it would have given me an interview with Mr E. Randolph whom I wished to consult on some law points, but it was first inconvenient & then impossible.

RC (DLC: Madison Papers); date supplied from TJ's endorsement; endorsed by TJ as a letter of 22 Apr. received 24 Apr. and so recorded in SJL.

From Thomas Oben

                                        Dublin, April the 22nd, 1801
SIR,   N. 49 Marlborough St.

It is with peculiar satisfaction, that I address this letter to you, as President of the Congress of the U.S. and in order that it may more speedily & safely arrive to your hands, I enclose it in one to the Min. Plenip. of America in London. At present I shall wave those elaborate & vain appologies often made use of in writing to people in high stations: the exalted ideas of the Person, whom I now have the honour to address, do not want such a tribute. I shall therefore proceed singly to state, that (after having passed in Italy upwards of twenty years of my life in the pursuit particularly of mathematical knowledge, in the study of Architecture, & in the observation of the ancient & modern buildings in that fine country) the situation of affairs in this part of the globe, & the alarm at approaching hostile armies made me quit that ground, with great propriety called by Addisson, classick. Among the effects I brought from thence were some capital paintings; at present I need only to mention two: the one (in high preservation) by Guercino, & the other by Caravaggio. These two I should wish to present to the American Government: they will, I am sure, be of great utility, & ornament to an Accademy of the fine Arts. At present I desire no recompense, & only *wish to have a commodious passage, & free from all expences whatever*, in the vessel that should carry them from hence to Washington; as I should not like to undertake, in these troublesome times, so long a voyage without being perfectly informed of the persons I went with. If upon occular inspection any other recompense will be assigned by Government, well & good; but I shall claim none. My only ambition will be to contribute with my efforts to the embellishment of a City, which there is every reason to think, will be the finest on the face of the earth, & worthy of being the seat of the Goverment of a Great Nation. How far my abilities may extend in this point, I shall not take upon me to say: this I can aver, that my productions have met with the approbation of the principal Accademies of Italy. It will suffice to mention among others that of Florence, of which I have the honour to be a member, & see my name in the same list with those of the immortal Michael Angelo Buonarotti, of a Bruneleschi, a Peruzzi, a Vasari &c. If this my proposal shall meet with your approbation, & my undertakings with your Patronage, I should then be glad to embark in the summer season either here, in Bristol, or in Liverpool: this last place being nearer, would be more convenient to me. But I should hope the Captain of the vessel should receive due instructions to write to me 3 weeks or a month beforehand, that I might have time to settle my affairs, & to get my books &c packed up, among which there are some rare editions of the Classicks, besides all the interesting works, that have been published on Architecture. In expectation of being favoured with your answer, & in the anticipated satisfaction of admiring the virtuous & grand pursuits of the American Nation under your Government, I feel none greater than that of subscribing myself with the greatest attachment & esteem

Sir Your most humble & most obedient Sert.

THOMAS OBEN LL.D.

RC (DLC); addressed: "Thomas Jefferson Esqr. President of the Congress of the United States of America Washington"; franked; postmarked New York, 16 July; endorsed by TJ as received 18 July and so recorded in SJL.

MIN. PLENIP.: Rufus King.

SOME CAPITAL PAINTINGS: more likely than not, the paintings that Oben offered were copies of seventeenth-century Italian Baroque works. Michelangelo Merisi da Caravaggio was a widely copied artist in the seventeenth and eighteenth centuries. Guercino's art reached the height of its popularity in England in the later eighteenth century. British—and in Oben's case, Irish—tourists on their Grand Tour of Europe purchased fine art to take home as souvenirs. Some were unwittingly deceived into buying fakes or variants of original paintings, as Oben may have been (Alfred Moir, *Caravaggio and His Copyists* [New York, 1976], 6, 17, 47; Jane Turner, ed., *The Dictionary of Art*, 34 vols. [New York, 1996], 13:789; Jeremy Black, *The British Abroad: The Grand Tour in the Eighteenth Century* [New York, 1992], 261, 266).

1.° Un quadro perfettamente ben conservato; alto, piedi 3: pollici 8. largo, pi. 2: pol. 6½

Rappresenta S. Gerolamo nel deserto: ed è una figura itieramente ignuda, avendo solamente i lombi coperti d'un panno di porpora; siede legendo un libro posto dalla banda sinistra, dove si vede parimente un teschio, ed un leone sdrajato: tiene la mano sinistra quasi sul cuore, e colla drita accenna ad un crocifisso, ch'è legato al tronco d'un arboscello. Una bellissima barba gli scende sul petto; gli estremi, cioè le mani ed i piedi sono eccellenti, e le muscolature così espresse che indicando un corpo robusto insieme ed asciuto fanno vedere il gran valore del Pittore, Francesco Barbieri da Cento, detto il Guercino.

2.° Un quadro assai ben conservato; alto pi. 4: pol. 1½. largo pi. 5: pol. 9.

Rappresentante la cena in Emaus. Sono mezze figure grandi *al naturale* che sedono a tavola. A mano destra del Salvatore vi è un pelegrino, ed a mano sinistra un altro un poco più vecchio, vicino a cui vi è un servitore, che porta un piatto di frutta. Si vede, per così dire, la divinità nel volto del Salvatore, e la meraviglia e lo stupore negli atteggiamenti, e nei volti degli attoniti discepoli quando "cognovernut eum in fractione panis" il colorito è di una robustezza ed armonia singolare. Di Michel-Angelo Merisi da Caravaggio.

EDITORS' TRANSLATION

1st A perfectly preserved painting, 3' 8" long and 2' 6½" wide.

It portrays St. Jerome in the desert; it is a fully disrobed figure with only a red cloth covering the loins; it is seated and reading a book placed on the left side, where one can see also a skull and a reclined lion; the left hand rests almost on the heart and the right hand gestures toward a crucifix which hangs from the trunk of a small tree. A beautiful beard flows down his breast; the extremities—that is, his hands and feet—are excellently portrayed and the muscles are so well expressed that, by presenting a body at once strong and lean, the figure manifests the great artistry of the painter, Francesco Barbieri da Cento, called il Guercino.

2d A very well preserved painting, 4' 1½" long and 5' 9" wide.

It depicts the dinner at Emmaus. *Life-size* half-figures are sitting around a table. On the right-hand side of the Savior there is a pilgrim and on the left-hand side another pilgrim, a slightly older one; close to the latter a servant is carrying a plate of fruit. One can see, so to speak, the divinity on the face of the Savior, and the marvel and stupor in the gestures and faces of the bewildered disciples when "cognoverunt eum in fractione panis"; the tone is of remarkable strength and harmony. By Michel-Angelo Merisi of Caravaggio.

MS (DLC); in Oben's hand.

COGNOVERUNT EUM IN FRACTIONE PANIS: they recognized him in the breaking of the bread (Luke 24:35).

From Tench Coxe

Sir   Lancaster April 23d. 1801.

It is only by candid representations of the disinterested, or the applications of the concerned, that you can add to that stock of information, which your own and your ministers knowledge afford. I trust therefore that in doing myself the honor to communicate these remarks, I shall contribute to your accommodation.

The question of alterations in the list of officers, civil, and all others, may be under your consideration. I take the liberty to presume, that you will not deem it necessary to remove men from office, merely because they are of sentiments different from the chief Magistrate. If that Idea was formerly adopted and pursued in practice by some too zealous persons, it might justify their misconduct to act similarly to what we blamed. It is true that innocent men are often dangerous from an undue attachment to and support of men of pernicious principles & designs. But, 'tho' prudence may require some respect to be paid to that idea, it cannot have more than a limited influence, where peculiar abilities, opportunities or other circumstances occasion such an innocent man to continue dangerous to state.

It is however really true, that the idea of employing none but what were of a particular way of thinking has incorporated a bias, and I believe a wrong bias, in the governmental machinery.

The judiciary incumbents,

The law incumbents,

The external revenue incumbents,

The internal revenue incumbents,

The Army incumbents &

The Navy incumbents

may perhaps be usefully passed under review, with an eye to this consideration. It seems to have been considered, that the joint system, which combines the two first, might be brought to an equilibrium, might have the bias counterbalanced by attention to the second. This and time are the only remedies considering all circumstances—but time must do a part ere all will be right.

The external revenues are very large, & drawn, in the first instance, from the body of Merchants, shipowners, and sea Captains. These, in our largest ports, are but a very few thousand persons. Of course large contributions and other transactions in those offices must often place those contributors in a situation to be oppressed, retarded, forced, or in some manner incommoded, if prejudice takes possession of the breasts of the external revenue officers. This reflexion suggests the

propriety of considering, whether it may not be[1] prudent and necessary to change one of the two great *indoor* officers of this Revenue,
wherever there are two, in order that men, who have been placed
under the ban of society & office may find one unprejudiced person in
the principal or checking officer. This idea the better merits consideration from the facts which have occured in some instances. It is no
indifferent circumstance, in relation to this point, that too many of the
monied corporations, Banks, Insurance companies, Chambers of
Commerce &ca. are of an uniform cast, and are deeply tinctured with
foreign ingredients. Nor is it of small importance, that both the principal and check officer should not be prejudiced in favor of a commercial preference for one foreign Nation & against another. If therefore
merit or an absence of demerit were to persuade to the continuance of
each of two incumbents, (of one sentiment) in office, the public service may require that one of them be placed in another situation, and
that his place be so filled, that all the citizens, all transient or resident
foreigners, all foreign interests & nations shall be sure to find a freedom from prejudice within the combined offices. Some important remarks might be added, touching the consideration of maintaining the
commercial rights & interests of the middle & southern states; and of
the states in general from partial domestic, or foreign influences.[2]—

Many of the same considerations apply, tho with less force to the internal revenue system. But it is highly important, *that this touches the
people every where,*—No State, County, Township, or vicinity is without
an internal revenue officer. The sums to be contributed are, it is true,
much smaller, but there are no Banks at hand to aid the Country payer
of revenue. There are seasons of irremediable scarcity, & years of failing
crops and unfavorable markets. It is therefore as easy to oppress, for a
small internal duty, or for an erroneous conduct under an internal revenue law, as for a large custom house due or an unintential breach of a
trade law—Hence it is necessary to consider the policy of counterbal-
ancing any existing bias in the body of internal revenue officers.

More serious and more impressive reasons persuade to a consideration of these ideas in relation to the navy, and particularly the army—
The two classes, who immediately and at all times hold a large part of
the public force. In those situations innocent men attached to dangerous and pernicious men, are themselves dangerous and may be pernicious. Persons distinguished for unfriendliness to the Militia, or
violations of the peace of families, or the order of society call for particular consideration.

There are two descriptions of men, it is said in our country. By the
last test, it would seem that one is larger than the other. If the executive

is to be representative throughout, that larger part should not be kept out of office; it should not have less than half, since it is more than half; and it seems to be a sound & moderate point, towards which to progress, to give to it, the manifested proportion. With less than half the equilibrium will continue to be destroyed. With less than the full proportion the executive power will not be a true representation. The unalterable quality of the Judiciary power seems to demand a counter-balance, & it is a ponderous weight.

I have never known a calm, ingenuous appeal, *upon facts*, to the public understanding, to fail of success. I cannot therefore doubt that the rational part of those, who may have differed from the present Majority, would admit the justice of a moiety, nay even of the indicated Majority of offices. *It is an exhibition of the subject which the Senate would yield to*—for they must admit, in private, that the ground of equality would be a very honorable moderation. It is substituting an equal distribution in the place of a total exclusion. It is giving to the two parties what has been confined to one. If the Government of the Country cannot be conducted to that utmost advantage without employing the wise & good of both parties, then may a President hasten to call into service the 73 (in 138), whose virtues and talents have been so rigidly held at a distance. It is to be a President of a nation, and not a President of a party. To suffer things to remain as they are, would be not unlike being the President for an adverse party.

Too many who go out will do so from incompetency, neglect, impunctuality, defaulting and other justifying causes. Some were incapable by the constitution of receiving the offices, with which they were intended to be invested. The Constitution did not allow it. These things admit of decent and just explanations and will receive them. If these gentlemen ring the changes upon a conciliating expression, they must be led to remember that those who have been for years placed under an antisocial ban, have claims too to the character of *"federal republicans,"* from the rights of which they stand partially deprived.

It is not a pretence, that there exists in the United states an interest unfriendly to representative government, and that it has formed a local American alliance, and a foreign anti-republican Alliance. How far it has influenced the appointments of many incumbents in office will not escape consideration on the present occasion. Representative Government stands upon unsatisfactory not to say alarming ground in Europe. If there are in three or four places *intelligent attachments* to it in Majorities of the nations, their dispositions are prevented from operating by obvious and uncomfortable causes. It is so important therefore that we cherish an enlightend attachment to republicanism, that its enemies here must consider it as their most desireable object to frustrate the employment of its Friends. If we survey the channels thro which the persons alluded to have worked upon the public mind we shall find them filled with arguments against any changes, to cover those, which they most desire to maintain in office & promote the introduction of other persons of like principles and opinions. Under such circumstances it becomes *deeply* interesting, that sincere, vigilant, energetic, firm and able friends to our form of government should be employed. Such persons, whether at the seat of government or in the states, besides the impartial & faithful performance of their proper official duties, ought "to support the Constitution of the U.S." Such is their oath; such is their high duty. This is not to introduce party into office. I will venture to challenge an imputation of party in the execution of my office. But I never was allowed by circumstances to refrain from exertion on that point. *The dangers to our form of government, at home and abroad yet exist.* Prejudices have been conjured up in many bosoms, which will be carried to the graves of those, who have imbibed them. Yet these things need not either alarm or discourage, for every industrious, well intentioned & upright officer will acquire the confidence of his opponents in politics. I know it to be a truth, that Mr. Hamilton has paid me the tribute of Justice for my conduct in office, and great pains were taken about seven or eight months ago to convince me that a gentleman, superior to him, was disposed "to take me by the hand." I am aware of the considerations of policy which led to such declarations, but I do not believe that they would have been made to one, who had been culpable in office. I always felt myself invulnerable while there was no complaint unanswered: and much more so while I had the happiness to know that no citizen of the U.S had ever prefered a complaint against me. Therefore tho removed, I was not wounded.

The people, who are friendly to the constitution look for some relief from such as have oppressed them. The government is certainly disposed to afford that relief. It is sir my intention in this letter to offer some views, which may contribute to effect it with comfort and honor to the chief Magistrate, without dissatisfaction to the people, and without ill impression upon the Senate.

I have the honor to be with perfect respect, sir, your faithful h. Servant   TENCH COXE

RC (DNA: RG 59, LAR); endorsed by TJ as received 30 Apr. and so recorded in SJL.

[1] Word supplied.

[2] Preceding sentence interlined by Coxe.

From Albert Gallatin

SIR   Fayette County 23d April 1801

I have not lost any time since my return here, & have succeeded, in arranging my business, complex as it was, in this part of the Country.

We have had another deep fall of snow in the mountains last Tuesday, 20th instt., which will render the roads extremely bad across the Allegheny. I have, however, very strong horses, & expect to leave home the day after to morrow, and to be in the city of Washington within ten days after, if no accident shall happen on the road to my family or carriage.

With great respect I have the honor to be Your most obt. Servt.

ALBERT GALLATIN

RC (DLC); endorsed by TJ. Recorded in SJL as received 8 May.

From Nathaniel Macon

SIR   Buck Spring 23 April 1801

In my letter to you dated a few days past at Warrenton, I forgot to mention a subject, which may of itself appear triffling, but when considered as a general regulation may have importance enough to deserve consideration. It is this, that no person concerned in a printing office, especially where news papers are printed, should hold any appointment in the post office. This would have so much fair play in it, that none could with reason complain; Things of this small kind are mentioned, on a supposition, that while you are attending to the great interest of the nation, they may possibly escape your attention

I have not made any apoligy for this or my other letter, because I am confident they are always useless, and not expected by you from your freinds.

I am with great respect Sir yr. most obt. Sevt.

NATHL MACON

RC (DLC); endorsed by TJ as received 1 May and so recorded in SJL.   MY LETTER TO YOU: Macon to TJ, 20 Apr.

From Samuel Adams

MY VERY DEAR FRIEND   Boston April 24th: 1801
Your Letter of the 29th. of March came duly to my hand. I sincerely congratulate our Country on the arrival of the day of Glory, which has called *you* to the first office in the administration of our federal Government. Your warm feelings of friendship must certainly have carried you to a higher tone of expression, than my utmost merrits will bear: If I have at any time been avoided, or frowned upon, your kind ejaculation in the language of the most perfect friend of Man, surpasses every injury. The Storm is now over, and we are in port, and I dare say, the ship will be rigged for her proper service; she must also be well man'd and very carefully officered. No man can be fit to sustain an office, who cannot consent to the principles, by which he must be governed. With you, I hope, we shall once more see harmony restored; but after so severe and long a storm, it will take a proportionate time to still the raging of the waves. The World has been governed by prejudice and passion, which never can be friendly to truth; and while you nobly resolve to retain the principles of candour and of justice resulting from a free elective Representative Government, such as they have been taught to hate and despise; you must depend upon being hated yourself, because they hate your principles, not a man of them dare openly to despise you, your inaugural speech, to say nothing of your eminent services to the acceptance of our Country, will secure you from contempt. It may require some time before the great body of our fellow citizens will settle in harmony, good humour and peace: When deep prejudices shall be removed in some, the self interestedness of others shall cease, and many honest Men, whose minds for want of better information have been clouded[1] shall return to the use of their own understanding, the happy and wished for time will come. The Eyes of the people have too generally been fast closed from the view of their own happiness; such Alass has been always the lot of Man! but Providence, who rules the World, seems now to be rapidly changing the sentiments of Mankind in Europe, and America: May Heaven grant, that the principles of Liberty and virtue, truth and justice may pervade the whole Earth. I have a small circle of intimate friends, among whom Doctr. Charles Jarvis is one; he is a man of much information and great integrity: I heartily wish, there may be an epistolary correspondence between him and you.—I should have written this Letter before, had not my faithfull friend and amanuensis John Avery; who is your friend as well as mine, been occupied in the business of his office of Secretary of this Commonwealth, which he attends with great punctuallity and

integrity.—It is not in my power my dear friend, to give you council, an Old Man is apt to flatter himself, that he stands upon an equal footing with younger Men, he indeed cannot help feeling, that the powers of his Mind, as well as his body are weakened; but he relies upon his memory, and fondly wishes his young friends to think, that he can instruct them by his Experience, when in all probability, he has forgot every trace of it, that was worth his memory. Be assured, that my esteem for you is as cordial, if possible, as yours is to me:—Though an Old Man cannot advise you, he can give you his Blessing: You have devoutly my Blessing and my Prayers.—

My dear Mrs. Adams will not suffer me to close this Letter, 'till I let you know, that she recollects the pleasure and entertainment, you afforded us, when you was about to embark for France, and hopes that your administration may be happy to yourself, and prosperous to our Country.— SAML ADAMS

RC (DLC); in John Avery's hand, signed by Adams; at foot of text: "Thomas Jefferson Presidt. of the United States"; endorsed by TJ as received 6 May and so recorded in SJL. Tr (NN).

[1] Preceding three words interlined in Adams's hand.

Statement of Account with Gibson & Jefferson

Gibson & Jefferson with Th: Jefferson	Dr.	Cr.
1800.		£ s d
Dec. 11. By balance Dec. 11. 1800.		60–10– 6
14. By ord. in favr. James Lyon		15– 0– 0
1801.		
Jan. 7. By ord. in favr. Rogers		17– 7– 0
Lilly		9– 7–10
Walker		14– 3– 9
Dyer		53– 0– 0
Richardson		165– 1– 0
15. To remittance from J. Barnes 920.26	276– 1–7	
By pd Callendar Nov. 7		15– 0– 0
Mar. 31. To remittance from J. Barnes 950. D.	285– 0–0	
Apr. 1. To amt. of my tobo. of 99. sold		
Mc.Murdo & Fisher	813–19–9	
By my ord. in favr. James Lyle now payable		300– 0– 0

	By do. in favr. Litt. W. Tazewell 1000. D.	300– 0–0
	By do. in favr. TM Randolph 450. D.	135– 0–0
6.	By do. in favr. John Watson 600. D.	180– 0–0
13.	Rob. Hemings 22. D.	6–12–0
15.	Wm. & Julius Clarkson	9– 8–4
17.	Carrington for Rhodes 30 D.	9– 0–0
	Jones & Pleasants	
24.	Richd. Richardson	16– 11–1
	Joseph Brand	31– 5–9
	By Syrop of punch	4– 4–0[1]
	balance due Th:J	33–10–1
		1375.1.4 1375– 1–4
	To balance due Th:J	33–10–1

MS (MHi); entirely in TJ's hand.

For TJ's loan of $50 to JAMES LYON, see Lyon's letter to TJ of 14 Dec. TJ explained his 7 Jan. payments to John ROGERS and others in his financial accounts of that date (MB, 2:1032) and in letters to George Jefferson, 5 Jan., Francis WALKER, 7 Jan., and Richard RICHARDSON, 8 Jan. 1801. For the remittance from John BARNES of 15 Jan., see Barnes's letter to TJ of that date.

[1] Remainder of statement in pencil.

From Haden Edwards

HOND. SIR   Kentuckey April 25th 1801

It being the first time I ever applyed for an office either under the State or United States government, I have no other appology to offer but a desire to live and support a growing family—I suppose you may recollect me when I inform you that during a short residence in Philidephia with my father John Edwards, who acted at that time as Senator in Congress from this State, I received instructions from you in the law—Cloase application has proved so injurious to my health that I have been compelled to refrain from the practice of the law and being informed that there would be a vacancy in the Marshalls office of this state sometime the ensueing fall which requires an active life has induced me to solicit the office, which if it meets with your approbation will ever be greatfully acknowledged by your unfeigned friend   HADEN EDWARDS

RC (DNA: RG 59, LAR); endorsed by TJ as received 21 May and so recorded in SJL with notation "Off."

Haden Edwards (1771-1849), a native of Stafford County, Virginia, was the son of the U.S. and state senator from Kentucky,

JOHN EDWARDS. Although trained as a lawyer, Haden was active in land speculation and, with his brother, became involved in Texas colonization plans and separatist movements, especially the Fredonia Rebellion (Ron Tyler, ed., *The New Handbook of Texas*, 6 vols. [Austin, Tex., 1996], 2:798-9).

For the VACANCY in the marshal's office in Kentucky, see Appendix 1, Lists 1 and 2, and Vol. 32:592.

To John Wayles Eppes

DEAR SIR   Monticello Apr. 25. 1801.

Martin & Davy arrived on the 20th. with the horses. I am perfectly satisfied with them all, & they completely answer my expectations. they are dear certainly, but horses, less perfect, however cheaper, would not have answered my purpose at all, so that I think the extra prices better submitted to. your draughts will be duly honored & provided for at maturity. the horses being tried in the Phaeton which is probably new to them, with the reins, in a new place, and handled by new hands, have given us a good deal of trouble, under every circumstance of gentle & cautious management which could be practised. I have kept Martin two days to help me break them, as I have nobody used to drive horses. it is still questionable whether, considering the dreadful state of the roads, I can venture with them in the Phaeton. if not, I shall go on in a chair, have them led, hire a waggoner to carry on the Phaeton & have them broke at Washington under more favorable circumstances. Martin had been detained two days by the weather, which is still rainy insomuch that neither he nor myself may perhaps be able to set out tomorrow. mr Randolph, Patsy & the family are all well here. Peter Carr is elected by a majority of 110. Mr. Trist's family is removed, to their farm. mr Randolph has compleated his part of the road. no more small news. we count on Maria's taking up her quarters here with yourself as soon as you can come. the servants will be in place to recieve you; the resources of the smoke house & garden are all you will find. I shall join you the last of July. my tenderest affections ever rest with my dear Maria, and affectionate esteem to yourself.

TH: JEFFERSON

P.S. my affectionate respects to mr & mrs Eppes & the family. I hope they will come up during the months of August or September, while I shall be here.

RC (ViU); postscript written in left margin; addressed: "John W. Eppes Eppington," with notation "by Martin."

On this day TJ paid three dollars to MARTIN, one of the slaves TJ transferred to his daughter and her husband when

they married (MB, 2:1039; Vol. 29:550).
YOUR DRAUGHTS: see Eppes to TJ, 18
Apr., and TJ to George Jefferson, 21 Apr.
PETER CARR represented Albemarle
County in the Virginia House of Delegates
for four terms from 1801 to 1804 and 1807
to 1808 (Leonard, *General Assembly*, 223,
227, 231, 247).

To Levi Lincoln

DEAR SIR   Monticello Apr. 25. 1801.

I should have set out for Washington this morning, but that it has now
been raining upwards of a week, with some intermissions, is still raining
& the wind at North East. of eight rivers between this & Washington,
5 have neither bridges nor boats. as soon as the one on which I live is ford-
able, it will be a signal that the others are so. this may be tomorrow; and
in that case, if it has ceased to rain, I shall set out & be with you on the 4th.
day, which will be before you get this. otherwise as soon as the weather &
watercourses permit, for as to the roads they are to be knee-deep the whole
way for some time yet.—mr Madison has been so ill as to be confined to
his bed some days; but so far recovered as to propose to set out when the
weather permits. the post arrived yesterday with your letter of the 16th.
after being retarded 36. hours.   accept assurances of my affectionate esteem & respect.   TH: JEFFERSON

RC (MHi); at foot of text: "Levi Lincoln esq. Secretary of state." PrC (DLC).

To James Madison

TH:J. TO J.M.   Monticello Apr. 25. 1801

I received yesterday your's of the 22d. & learn with regret that you
have been so unwell. this & the state of the [country, the river &]
roads should delay your departure, at least till the weather is better.
I should have set out this morning, but it is still raining, and the
rivers all but [swimm]ing at the last ford. if these circumstances are
more favorable tomorrow I shall then set out, or whenever they become so, as I do not like to begin a journey in a settled rain. contrive,
if you can, to let it be known at Gordon's if you shall be gone, as I
would then continue on the direct road, which is better as well as
shorter. my best respects to mrs Madison & affectionate esteem & attachment to yourself.   TH: JEFFERSON

PrC (DLC); blurred; endorsed by TJ in ink on verso.

To John Monroe

DEAR SIR   Monticello Apr. 25. 1801.

Having to dispose of the inclosed commission I cannot better do it
than by inserting your name. I am told you will not leave your present
residence till the fall, or perhaps not at all. if in the fall, we can but
then supply it, and indeed I think it highly probable the law will be repealed at the meeting of Congress. I set out tomorrow to take up my
abode in Washington. accept assurances of my esteem & respect

TH: JEFFERSON

PrC (DLC); at foot of text: "John
Monroe esq." Enclosure: Commission, not
found, for Monroe as U.S. attorney for the
western district of Virginia (see below).

John Monroe (1749-1837) was a
Staunton, Virginia, lawyer and a member,
in 1800, of the Republican committee for
Augusta County. He had kinship ties to
James Monroe and was acquainted with
John Marshall and Bushrod Washington.
In 1800 he sought, unsuccessfully, an
appointment as the U.S. attorney for Kentucky. On 25 Apr. 1801, TJ named him
the attorney for the western district of Virginia in place of Samuel Blackburn, one of
John Adams's late-term appointments.
The Senate confirmed TJ's appointment
of Monroe in January 1802. Later Monroe did relocate to Kentucky, where by
1807 he was presiding judge of the circuit
court (Madison, *Papers, Pres. Ser.*,
1:326n; Marshall, *Papers*, 4:217; JEP,
1:402, 405; Vol. 32:38-9, 41; Appendix I,
Lists 3 and 4).

LAW: the Judiciary Act of 1801.

To Archibald Stuart

DEAR SIR   Monticello Apr. 25. 1801.

I wrote on the 8th. inst. to ask your recommendation of an Attorney
& Marshall for the Western district of this state, but I learn you were
absent on your circuit. on the enquiry I have been able to make, I have
appointed mr John Monroe Attorney. but I cannot decide between
Andrew Alexander, John Alexander, & John Caruthers, recommended by different persons for the Marshall's office. pray write me
your opinion, which appointment would be most respected by the
public, for that circumstance is not only generally the best criterion of
what is best, but the public respect can alone give strength to the government. I set out tomorrow to take up my residence in Washington
where I shall hope to recieve a letter from you. accept assurances of my
sincere esteem & respect.   TH: JEFFERSON

RC (ViHi); at foot of text: "Honble
Arch. Stuart." PrC (DLC).

ON YOUR CIRCUIT: Stuart was a judge
of the General Court of Virginia (DAB).

In June TJ selected John CARUTHERS
for the marshal's position, but Caruthers
turned down the appointment (Appendix I,
List 4; TJ to Andrew Moore, 5 Aug. 1801).

From William Barton

Sir,   Lancaster (Penns.) Apl. 26. 1801

Jacob Mayer, Esquire, late Consul of the United States at St. Domingo, will have the honor to present to you this Letter. With Mr. Mayer's name, in his Official capacity, you cannot be unacquainted: But, being personally unknown to you, he is desirous of an introduction.—This desire, being prompted as well by his high veneration for your character, as by motives which concern the dignity of the Government and his own reputation,—having been expressed to me,—I have presumed, Sir, to afford him this opportunity of gratifying his earnest wish—

I have known this gentleman, almost from his childhood; and, from the confidence I feel in his probity and honor, as well as talents and zeal for his Country's service, I humbly beg leave to recommend him to the notice of the President.—

With the most respectful attachment And highest personal consideration, I have the Honor to be, Sir, Your most obedt. Servt.

W. Barton

RC (DNA: RG 59, LAR); at foot of text: "The President of the United States"; endorsed by TJ as a letter of 24 Apr. received 20 May and so recorded in SJL, with a brace connecting it with two other letters received on the same date, one from Thomas McKean of 6 May (not found), and the other from George Logan of 10 May, with notations "for Myers" and "Off."; also endorsed by TJ: "Mayer to be Consul St. Domingo."

JACOB MAYER, who was named U.S. consul to the port of Cap-Français in May 1796, was removed from office in May 1800 after criticizing the conduct of the consul general, Dr. Edward Stevens, whom Mayer accused of exploiting his office to benefit himself and Timothy Pickering. Mayer was replaced by Henry Hammond in December 1800 (JEP, 1:213, 356; Madison, *Papers, Sec. of State Ser.*, 1:127-9, 221-2).

From Thomas Mendenhall

Dear Sir,   Wilmington April the 27th. 1801

At a time when I have no doubt but that you are much intruded on by useless and unnecessary applications from different quarters, it is extremely painful to me, to risque adding to thier number; but how to avoid this, and comply with the wishes of many of my friends, and a laudable impulse, which probably I ought not to resist, I am totally at a loss.

Beleiving as I do, that changes will be made, from the necessity of organizing the subordnate departments of the Government so as to harmonize with its Principal, more especially, where it is evident, that men in Office have betray'd a want of Integrity & rectitude in the discharge of official duties.

Beleiving also, that it will be of the first consideration with you, not only to make the change for the better, but to select proper characters, and such as are the best qualified for the Office, from the number, out of which, such choice is to be made.

Under these impressions, it is with extreme defidence I present myself to you Among those who have, or may, come forward as applicants for the Collectors office of this port & district in case it should be Vacated; having but little to presume upon, and on that little itself, from motives to which you are no stranger constrain'd to be silent.

But in obedience to the earnest request of a number of my friends & fellow Citizens, and a regard for the progressive welfare of my family, I have endeavoured to overcome the restraints of personal delicacy, & submit my claim to your unbiased Judgment.

I am pursuaded, that there are, or shortly will be, several applications for this office with various pretentions, some perhaps predicated on exclusive qualifications; others on specific services render'd during the glorious struggle for American Independence, aided by the relative Circumstances of the parties; and if a man be Justifiable in becomeing his own historian in any case, it probably is in cases of personal competition.

My progenitors emigrated from England Shortly after the establishment of the Proprietory government, and Settled in Pennsylvania, from whom has sprang a numerous and extensive family connection, many of them living in this place, but principaly in Pennsylvania, where I gained my birthright in the year 1759.

Having been, by my own desire, put apprentice to the Sea in early life (and before the revolution) it was my misfortune to be five times a prisoner of war with the British, and to suffer all the rigours of their inhuman tyrany usualy inflicted on American *rebels* on board their Prison ships and Men of war; besides once escaping in the dreadful Catastrophe of our Vessel's being blown up, in an engagement with a British sloop of War on our own shores.

From the commencment of my career, I follow'd the sea constantly for about Twenty one years; then embarked in Mercantile pursuits till the year 97. when I deem'd it prudent to close an extensive buisness; & transfer my attention to the care of a rising family;—to relax my mind a little from its habitual rigidity;—and to regard more attentively the progress and decline of Political Intoxecation & delusion.

We are now hapily rescued from the pestilence of Anglo-federalism, and it is proper & necessary, that I should turn my attention to some kind of buisness again; as I find by experience, that my present income of Eight or Nine hundred dollars a year, will be insufficient to satisfy the encreasing claims of a growing family of seven Children.

It would be truly grateful to my feelings to remain with my family; but however much, I may be impressed with those Extraneous circumstances, they can have but little influence on your decision; and to avoid the imputation of egotism or insincerity, I must embrace the privilege of refering you to John Dickenson Esqr. of this place,— Govr. McKean of Pennsa. & John Mason Esqr. Mercht. George Town, for those more solid recommendations which you will doubtless require of every successful candidate.

This reference is founded on a beleif, that disinterested evidence [must] be most satisfactory to you especialy, if obtained without solicitation on my part; Those Gentlemen, with whom I have the honour of some acquaintance are more competent to Judge of my fitness for Office than I can posibly be; and I will cheerfully rest the merits of my pretentions on their representations; and my official destiny on the Justice of Your decision.

Should I be so fortunate as to obtain the appointment, I will endeavour to execute the duties of the office, with Justice to others, & credit to myself:—If I am not the successful applicant, I shall be content with filling the humble but honourable Station of a private Citizen.

With sincere regard for Your Political & personal welfare, I am very respectfully your devoted friend, & Humble Servant.

THOMAS MENDENHALL

RC (DLC); damaged; at head of text: "Thomas Jefferson Esqr. President of the United States"; endorsed by TJ as received 12 May and so recorded in SJL with notation "Off."; also endorsed by TJ: "to be Collector of Wilmington."

On 25 Feb. Mendenhall had written TJ a short congratulatory letter from Wilmington noting that "every true Republican" was rejoicing "in the Triumph of virtuous and patriotic principles, over an Organized System of persecution & proscription." Mendenhall stated that his object had always been the public good, and under TJ's direction he "could not err" (RC in DLC; at head of text: "The Honourable Thomas Jefferson. President Elect of the United States"; endorsed by TJ as received 1 Mch. 1801 and so recorded in SJL).

From James Woodhouse

RESPECTED SIR,   Philadelphia April 27th, 1801.

In the month of June 1799, my brother Samuel Woodhouse, a well educated lad, about seventeen years of age, sailed as Midshipman, on board of the Constillation, and was present during the ever memorable action between that frigate and the Vengeance, and has since continued in the service of the United States. Owing to some cause, of which I am ignorant, he never recieved his warrant, from the Navy Office.

As one hundred and fifty Midshipmen are to continue in service according to a late act of Congress, the object of this letter is to request, that he be placed among them, and should this be granted, you will confer an obligation on me, which shall be remembered with gratitude.

My anxiety for the wellfare of a brother, is my only apology, for troubling you upon a business to you of a trifling nature, but I am fearfull he may be neglected, unless I apply to the fountain head.

I have just recieved from a French Gentleman, an extract from a work, on the species of Quadrupeds, whose bones have been found in the interior of the earth. As it is probable, you may not have seen this work, I inclose it in my letter.

May science become *fashionable*, during your administration of the Fœderal Government. I say *fashionable*, for I believe there is no other method of making it attended to, by the generality of mankind.

It will never do to establish Seminaries of learning, in which the Professors are to enjoy handsome salaries, for whereever this is the case, they become drones.

Swift and Gibbon speak with contempt, of the University of Oxford, and to this we may add that of Pennsylvania, which has degenerated so much, that it is now merely a nursery for children.

That health and happiness may ever attend you, and that your administration may unite the people of the United States, is the fervent wish of

Respected Sir, your most obedient, & most humble servant

JAMES WOODHOUSE

RC (CSmH); addressed: "Thomas Jefferson Esqr. President of the United States"; endorsed by TJ as received 1 May and so recorded in SJL. Enclosure: "Extrait d'un ouvrage sur les espèces de quadrupèdes dont on a trouvé les ossemens dans l'intérieur de la terre, adressé aux savans et aux amateurs des sciences," a paper given by Georges Cuvier to the French National Institute of Arts and Sciences in 1800 and printed in Paris; see Martin J. S. Rudwick, ed., *Georges*

Cuvier, Fossil Bones, and Geological Catastrophes: New Translations & Interpretations of the Primary Texts (Chicago, 1997), 42-58.

A midshipman's warrant for Woodhouse's BROTHER was issued on 2 May, the day after TJ received the letter above (NDBW, *Register of Officer Personnel*, 61).

Thirty-year-old James Woodhouse had been professor of chemistry at the University of PENNSYLVANIA since 1795. He held B.A., M.A., and M.D. degrees from the university. In 1792 he gave TJ a copy of his doctoral dissertation on the chemistry and medical properties of the persimmon tree, to which TJ responded with interest (ANB; Vol. 23:621).

From Walter Boyd

SIR   London 28th April 1801

If I were not convinced that your mind is still more elevated above the ordinary motives of human action than your high and important situation is above the common lot of humanity, I should not venture to address you, on the strength of the acquaintance which I had the honour to form with your Excellency upwards of Twelve years ago at Paris.—Presuming upon that acquaintance, I beg leave to recommend to the notice of Your Excellency, the Bearer of this letter, my Nephew, Mr George Boyd, who has, for these last three years been employed in the office of Mr Dundas, one of His Majesty's Principal Secretaries of State. The Change which has recently taken place in the Ministry, joined to the desire which my Nephew has long had to revisit his Native Country, has led him to leave this country—He is a young Man of good abilities and of the very best disposition. The experience he has acquired in this Country must be of service to him in any line of Business in which he may be placed in America. It would be highly flattering to him, and agreeable to me, if his abilities were found deserving of Your Excellency's patronage and protection. Having just hinted this wish, I shall leave it with your Excellency, with the single assurance that if he shall be so fortunate as to merit Your Excellency's favour, I am persuaded you will never have occasion to regret any mark of that favour which you may bestow upon him.

I have taken the liberty to send by this conveyance a few Copies of a Pamphlet which I published lately on the present state of the Circulation of this Country. Believing that Your Excellency must be particularly acquainted with such subjects, and that in the Country under Your administration all such subjects must be particularly well understood, I trust you will find leisure from the high duties of your elevated situation, to peruse this little tract which has given rise to much more animadversion than any thing of the same kind I ever remember to have seen.

Your Excellency will, I am persuaded, not hear without some portion of concern, that the very flattering and splendid prospects which attended the first years of my arrival in this Country, have been succeeded by a reverse of fortune as unparalleled as my partial friends think it has been unmerited. I am however now indulging once more the hope, which has so often deceived me, that by the return of peace, I may be enabled to resume my situation at Paris, and recover the considerable property which has so long been under sequestration in France. I ought to apologise for intruding upon your attention the particular concerns of an individual, while it ought to be directed to the welfare of so many thousands who, I trust, will every day of their lives bless Your Excellencys enlightened and beneficent Administration.

I have the honour to be, with the most profound veneration and respect,

Sir, Your Excellency's Most obedient and devoted humble Servant
WALTER BOYD

RC (MHi); at foot of text: "His Excellency, The Honourable Thomas Jefferson Esqr. President of the United States of America"; endorsed by TJ as received 27 July and so recorded in SJL.

STRENGTH OF THE ACQUAINTANCE: when TJ left France in the fall of 1789, he agreed to deliver correspondence and miniatures for Boyd to his brother, Archibald Boyd, at Bladensburg, Maryland. TJ also promised to suggest ways that Walter Boyd, of the banking firm of Boyd, Ker & Company, could aid his brother financially. In 1790, TJ provided the banker with detailed information about his brother's circumstances. TJ also noted that the family wanted Walter to take his talented NEPHEW George, ten years old at the time, and educate him. In 1793, Boyd established a banking firm in London when he had to flee France dur-

ing the revolution (S. R. Cope, *Walter Boyd: A Merchant Banker in the Age of Napoleon* [London, 1983], 11-13, 30-41; Vol. 13:149; Vol. 15:487-8, 503; Vol. 16:311-12, 489-90).

COPIES OF A PAMPHLET: *A Letter to the Right Honourable William Pitt, On the Influence of the Stoppage of Issues in Specie at the Bank of England, on the Prices of Provisions, and other Commodities,* written by Boyd and published in London in 1801 (see Sowerby, No. 2808). According to a short letter from George Boyd, dated 27 July 1801 at Georgetown, he had that morning delivered the correspondence from his uncle to the president and was now transmitting the pamphlets (RC in MHi; at foot of text: "To His Excellency The Honble Thomas Jefferson Esq &c—&c—&c"; endorsed by TJ as received 27 July and so recorded in SJL).

From Theodore Foster

DEAR SIR, Providence April 28th: 1801

When I last had the Honor of being in your Company, you was pleased to say a Letter from Me would be acceptable, at any Time.— I hope not to abuse your Goodness in permitting Me to enjoy what I esteem, not only a great Honor, but, a particular Favour, that of direct epistolary Communications, relative to the Business and Police of the State, as it may be connected with the supreme executive Power of the Nation.—

I now have the *sincere* Pleasure to inform you that there is every Appearance of your having the firm and effectual support of the Legislature of this State in your Administration of the Government, on the genuine Principles of *true* Federal Republicanism.—This is the more pleasing because it tends to destroy and remove the *pernicious Opinion* that the People of New England are *alienated* from the national Government, on those Principles, and are disposed to support Politics, materially different from those of the Southern States.— I hope and expect an Address to the President of the United States from the Legislature of this State, at their session next Week will be carried by a great Majority—expressive of Sentiments discountenancing *that* Opinion, and harmonizing perfectly with those you was pleased to express, on the 4th of March, and promising you such support as will tend to discomfit the vain though wicked Attempts to keep up a Phalanx of Politicks in New England in Oposition to the General Government under Your Administration—Mr. David L. Barnes who is the Attorney of the District of Rhode Island and who is one of the Representatives for this large Town, in the State Legislature and is esteemed for his Moderation and Integrity by both Parties mentioned to Me the other day that he intends to move an Address from the Legislature to yourself which I expect will be carried, perhaps, unanimously and which must be productive of Good in the present State of things in New England. He had some Doubts on accepting his Appointment of Representative for this Town, in the State Legislature lest it might be thought a Reason against his being continued in the office of District Attorney, choosing rather not to serve as representative in the State Legislature, if *that* would be considered as an objection to his being continued in the Office of district Attorney. Knowing him to be *favorably disposed to an Union of Parties* and thinking that he could do much in breaking down the Opposition which some wish to keep up against the new Order of things I advised him to accept the Appointment, and promised that I would mention the Circumstances to you, in my First Letter, supposing however, (as I informed him), that it would not be considered, on the Part of the Executive, as any objection to his holding the other Office—

Yesterday my late Colleague Mr. Greene was at my House, and informed Me that a Mistake had been made in filling the Commission intended for him as Judge of the District of Rhode Island, instead of which it constituted him Judge of the Circuit Court—That having recd. the Commission from the Office of Secretary of State he returned it and had since heard nothing of the Matter. I conclude it must have been a mere *clerical* Mistake, and, with your Permission, that it might be rectified accordingly, as you should direct. I understand there is *Business of Consequence now pending* delayed, until the Commission shall arrive—Under all the Circumstances of this Appointment, I am disposed to think that Mr. Greene's *Continuance* in Office, will be as Satisfactory as any which can now be made, taking into Veiw the Feelings and wishes of all People of the State collectively and the Probability of Legislative Alterations at the next session of Congress of the Judiciary System.—

I enclose the Seventh Number of a *new Publication* in this Town which bids fair to the good. You will find in it an Account of the late Election to the State Legislature &c. in Newport—a Specimen of the public Opinion of the People there

I have the Honor to be with every Sentiment of most sincere Esteem and Regard, and with the warmest Wishes for your Happiness in every form in public and private Life very respectfully

Your Friend and Obedient Servt.   THEODORE FOSTER

RC (DLC); at foot of text: "To the President of the United States"; endorsed by TJ as received 4 May and so recorded in SJL with notation "Off." For enclosure, see below.

On 12 May Arthur Fenner sent TJ AN ADDRESS TO THE PRESIDENT by the General Assembly of Rhode Island.

DAVID LEONARD BARNES had been the U.S. attorney for the district of Rhode Island since November 1797. He was appointed to the district judgeship on 30 Apr. (JEP, 1:252, 381, 395, 401; *Biog. Dir. Cong.*, 1091; TJ to Foster, 9 May; Appendix I, List 4). For the commission of Ray GREENE, see Levi Lincoln to TJ, 8 Apr.

A NEW PUBLICATION IN THIS TOWN: probably the Providence *Impartial Observer*, which, after a brief suspension, resumed publication on 14 Mch. with new volume numbering (Brigham, *American Newspapers*, 2:1011-12).

From Caleb Haskell

To the Honorable Thomas Jefferson Esqr President of the United States

I congratulate you upon your arival into the first seat of the Nation; after receiving a heavy Cannonadeing from the Prisses of the four N England states and many Popgun squibs from Individuals to stigmatize you as a Jackobin or an enemy to your Country, that many thousands of us was duped. into a Jealousy to believe that it possibly might be so—untill you arivd. into that seat of Honour to take the Helm of the Nation and there made Proclamation of your sentiments which has done Honour to yourself and to the Sons of Columbia; It has struck us all with admiration and I presume to say the major part of us in the N England states feel agreeable disappointed that you are at the head of the Nation hopeing you will ever feel Interested in a Republican Government; that the bassis of all Constitutions is the Sovereignty of the People and that from the People alone Kings Judges and Magistrates derive all theire authority

That Providence of God which builds up a Nation pulls down another and makes its appearance into Families

Amonge the Vicisitudes of this transatory state I have ben calld. of late to part with my Companion which has brought me to a determination to leave this place of my Residence; hopeing you will Remember me as Joseph of Old wishd. to be to the Chief Magistrate of Egypt and give me some lucrative Post in the United States; or to some foreign Port as your Honor shall see fit; in so doing you will much Oblige your humble Servt   CALEB HASKELL

N.B Columbia the place of my residence is about 300 Miles east of Portsmouth the Metropolis of the State of N Hampshire which brings me not far from the division line that seperates us from the English Dominions, which Obliges me to present you with a recommendation from the selectmen of said Town not *being* able at such an extream part of the United states to furnish me with a Queen Easter to bear my message

Any post that will hansomly maintain me with my Industry I shall not refuse

April 28th 1801 Columbia in the County of Washinton district of Main State of Massachusetts

RC (DNA: RG 59, LAR); addressed: "To the Honl. Thomas Jefferson esq President of the United States At his Place of Residence"; postmarked Narraguagus, 29 Apr.; endorsed by TJ as received 16 May and so recorded in SJL with notation "Off." Enclosure: Certificate signed by William Patten and Elisha Coffin, selectmen of Columbia, undated, stating "that Doctr Caleb Haskell since our acquaintence with him which is a number of years has behaved him self in an upright Judicious way both in Practice of Physick and Post of Office" in the town (MS in same, in Patten's hand).

From Samuel Fulton

Paris le 9 florial an 9m.

<small>Citizen President.</small>　　de La Republic français [i.e., 29 Apr. 1801]

Haveing served the cause of Liberty during the american war, in the Defence of My native Country, Could not see France strugling Against all the Tyrants of Europe without offering her my service, for which purpose I Came to Paris in 1794. I was amediately appointed Chef d'Escadron, Lieutenant Colonel of Cavalry, in which quallity I served untill (1797) when it was thought that a war would inivitably brake out betwen the two Sister Repulicks, I then give my dismission, and Remained a Silent Spectator, untill the arival of the three Last envoys at Paris, seeing then there was hopes of Reconsiliation, and france press'd on evry side by her enenimys, I againe offered my Service, in the army which the first Consul (Buonaparte) was to Command in person, which was Excepted, the Extroirdinary success of that army has been so well announc'd to the world that Leaves me only roome to say that I have the honour of being one of the vanquers of Marango. Peace being now made betwen france & Germany, I have returnd into the Interior, whare I have just heard of the happy Changement which has takein place in The government of my native & beloved Country now would I fondly fly to it to ask service under her Banners, if my situation permitted me, but haveing sacrefised the principle part of my fortune during the seven years I have been in france and being now the father of a famely cannot quit my present imploy untill I am certaine of an other,

Knowing well your attachment to all True Republicans, I am imboldend to address myself To you to ask some imploy under your auspecious. Be it Sivill or Military, in the United States, or in any foreign Country, it will be eaqually aceptable for it is a pleasing thing for a man to serve his Native Country, particularly when the principalls of her government are those of his owne—

from my long Stay in france I have acquired a Considerable Share of her Language & art of war—

Perhaps I might be usefully imploy'd on the bords of the Mississipi haveing a perfect Knowledge of that vast region & the Diffrent nations of Indians who inhabit the Country bordering thereon—

your answer to the present, Citizen President will be ever gratefully acknowledged by a true Republicain & a reil friend to his native Country

I refer you to Citizen James Munroe for information Relitive to my moral & political Charecter,

Salut et Respect　　　　　　　　　　　　　　　S. Fulton

RC (DNA: RG 59, LAR); English date supplied; addressed: "Au Citoyen Gefferson President, des États unis de L'amerique á Washington"; endorsed by TJ as received 24 July and so recorded in SJL with notation "for an office." Dupl (same); endorsed by TJ as received 26 Aug., but recorded in SJL under 25 Aug. with notation "Off."

REFER YOU TO CITIZEN JAMES MUNROE: TJ received the letter above with a hastily drafted statement by James Monroe, who reported that James Madison had sent him Fulton's letter by way of Milton, Virginia. Noting that Joel Barlow had referred to Fulton "as one having some skill in mechanics," Monroe reported that he had become acquainted with Fulton in Paris in the winter of 1794-95, when Monroe was U.S. minister to France. Monroe learned at that time that Fulton was in France with General "Chaise" (Auguste Lachaise), who in 1793 played a leading role in an intended scheme by Edmond Charles Genet to restore the Mississippi Valley to French control. Monroe met with Fulton and used information from him to discredit Lachaise's attempt to gain the ear of the French government. A faction within the Washington administration, Monroe believed, was using Lachaise "with a view to involve us in a war with France." In support of that argument, Monroe discussed a forged letter, purportedly by Fulton, that was published in American newspapers. Monroe had also caught a rumor of something said by Rufus King in London that indicated the "attention" that the Federalists were giving to Fulton. The only letter that Fulton had written from France about the western intrigue was one that he composed for John Breckinridge at Monroe's suggestion and with his guidance "to tranquilize the western people on the subject of the missisippi." On Monroe's advice, Fulton wrote a refutation of the fraudulent letter. That rebuttal, which intimated that Timothy Pickering was involved in the publication of the forgery, never appeared in the United States even though two copies were sent by separate ships from France. Monroe thought that Fulton's refutation of the forgery may have been "laid hold of in the post office & suppressed" and that "the postmaster Habersham must have some knowledge" of what had transpired. Believing that members of the Washington administration were involved in manipulating the separatist plots of Lachaise, Monroe did not report his contact with Fulton to the U.S. government—nor, lacking concrete evidence, did he discuss the affair in the book he wrote after his recall from France (*View of the Conduct of the Executive*). In 1793 the Spanish envoys in the United States, Josef de Jaudenes and Josef Ignacio de Viar, had warned TJ, who was then secretary of state, of the intentions of Lachaise, a native of Louisiana. TJ then advised President Washington, Secretary of War Henry Knox, and Isaac Shelby, the governor of Kentucky, of the situation. Fulton was in New Orleans by August 1802 and spent the next several years seeking a commission from the American government. Following the sale of Louisiana to the United States, Fulton entered the service of Spain and commanded the Spanish militia in West Florida. He subsequently became active in efforts to annex the territory to the U.S. (MS in DNA: RG 59, LAR, in Monroe's hand with emendations, undated, unaddressed, and unsigned, endorsed by TJ "Fulton for office" and as received 26 Aug. 1801, but recorded in SJL under 25 Aug. in association with Fulton's letter printed above; Madison, *Papers*, 16:304n, 397-8, 401; Madison, *Papers, Sec. of State Ser.*, 3:247, 470; Madison, *Papers, Pres. Ser.*, 2:305, 320-1, 5:390; Vol. 27:176-80, 311-14).

From Elbridge Gerry

Cambridge 29th April 1801

My Dear Sir   put into the office this day.

On the 22d instant I received your friendly letter of the 29th of march, twenty three days after it was put into the post office. the seal is enclosed, having no impression; but the appearance of having been wet, for the purpose of opening the letter. you can determine whether this was the case, or whether there is a probability[1] of it: be this as it may, the seals of the letters which I have received for a number of years, have been so often & so manifestly violated, as to have destroyed my confidence in such institutions; which in most if not in all countries, are mere political traps. among such a number of officers, as are in the department of a post office, it would be an extraordinary case, if every one was proof against the corrupt arts of faction; & one prostituted officer on each line, is sufficient, to betray all the secrets of the chief magistrate; conveyed thro this channel. indeed it will be no difficult thing to make arrangements for discovering the culprits; but these must be constantly operative, before they can cure the evil. I have tho't it necessary to be thus explicit to yourself, as I was to your predecessor; because the success of an administration, perfectly just, mild, & honorable, as I am sure yours will be, in its veiws & measures, depends much on it's preserving an impenetrable cabinet. the discovery of the political opinions of a private individual, can be of no great consequence, altho directed to the supreme executive; because before they can be adopted by the latter, they must be well examined, modified, & digested, & in a crude state can only expose him to the calumnies & malice of party; but those of the prime agent of politicks, if even expressed with caution & precision, have a tendency, in many cases in the present state of society, to excite jealousies & apprehensions in honest minds of a different persuasion, & [. . .] are always abused by mal-contents, & even tortured, as your religious opinions have been, for the purposes of slander & vengeance. but you will think, as well as myself, that eno' has been said on this subject.

The Gazettes, eer this, have announced the disappointment of your expectations in regard to my election. it has terminated as I supposed it would; for those who were disaffected to our revolution & are now pining for monarchy, conceived, that a compleat overthrow of their anterepublican projects, would be the result of my administration, & have made the most incredible exertions to prevent it. their insolence has kept pace with their triumph, altho it is well known, that the office was not the object of my wishes. indeed the emolument is not above two thirds of the sum, which, in addition to present expences, I must have furnished, to have appeared decent: so that the office would have operated as a tax. as to titles, annual, or perennial, they are in my mind mere baubles; for I am well convinced that

"Honour & shame from no condition rise;
act well your part, there all the honor lies."

but I could not have withdrawn myself from the nomination, without an injury, which I shall always endeavour to avoid, to the cause of republicanism; altho the office was manifestly at variance with the greatest of all blessings, domestic happiness.

The principles which you have adopted, cannot fail, as I conceive, to render your administration successful. official gifts & bereavements, always have had, & always will have their effects; but it is not probable that the public will be so lost to its own interest, as to oppose its own government, for having removed from office, such as it conceived had malconducted, or for not appointing every expectant. it may nevertheless be expedient, to be guarded at all points; because great injury may result from the want of exertion, none from the adoption of it.

Your inaugural speech, was in my mind, the best I had ever met with. no reasonable mind, however, could have supposed that you was pledged by it, to a disgraceful inattention to demerit; & yet by the *friends of order*, you are not allowed to judge of this, altho obliged to do it, by the obligations of law, of an oath, & of honor. does this manifest a love of order, or of disorganization.

The change of political principles amongst the people, has principally arisen from the engrossment of the press. porcupine urged this very justly, as a sure mean of governing the public opinion: & his patrons rendered thereby, the term *republicanism*, for a while, odious & disgraceful. but the whigs, in nearly all the states, have rallied under republican presses, which are continually multiplying, & must eradicate feudalism.

I propose soon to accompany Mrs Gerry, & my eldest daughter to New York, & to write you from thence. they present their best respects to you, & be assured my dear Sir that I remain with the most sincere & respectful attachment, Your constant friend   E GERRY

RC (DLC); at foot of text: "His Excellency Mr Jefferson"; endorsed by TJ as received 7 May and so recorded in SJL.

HONOUR & SHAME: from Alexander Pope's *An Essay on Man*, Epistle IV, lines 193-4.

PORCUPINE: William Cobbett.

[1] MS: "probabity."

From James Monroe

DEAR SIR   Richmond 29. April 1801

I am inclined to think the mode by which a certain end is to be accomplished, refering to a subject in discussion when I last saw you, is
of less importance than I then thought it. A gradual operation will not
offend republicans, nor will an off-hand entire one, make friends of the
tories. Sooner or later that party will rally and make another effort.
That course which best preserves, at the height the spirits of the republicans, and gives the tories least hold, is the soundest. The point in
question is a subaltern one of no great importance any way. There is
another object to which I found the attention of the republicans here,
comprizing many from the country who are attending our ct. of appls. &
the federal ct., drawn with much more anxiety; that is the propriety of
continuing Mr. K. at the British ct. I will endeavor to communicate
some thing on that head in my next. I am at present too much indisposed with the consequences resulting from my late journey. Your
friend & servt   JAS. MONROE

RC (DLC); endorsed by TJ as received 4 May 1801 and so recorded in SJL.

WILL ENDEAVOR TO COMMUNICATE: Monroe drafted a letter to TJ dated Richmond, 30 Apr., but did not send it. In it, Monroe reported that John Taylor and others strongly advocated the recall of Rufus King from London: "They think nothing is done unless that is done." Monroe, deeming the subject "an important question difficult to be decided," contrasted the possible consequences of retaining King, and thereby attempting to make the Federalists responsible for good relations with Britain, with the effects of sending a new minister to demonstrate that the new Republican administration had confidence "in its strength & the purity of its views" (Dft in DLC: Monroe Papers; in Monroe's hand, including note at head of text: "This letter was not sent"; on the final page Monroe also drafted a version of the opening portion of his letter to TJ of 4 May).

From Charles Goodwin

                           Silver Bluff, Barnewell District So Carolina,
SIR   April 30th 1801.

The conversations of Mr Allston who has lately returned from the
northward, & of Mr Charles Pinckney who has since him returned,
seem to render it certain that Mr Cochran the present Marshall is to
be removed. The circumstance of his being an eastern man, & the dupe
of eastern policy, made us hope, as soon as we should be blessed by
your exhaltation to the dignified office which is now dignified by you
Sir, that a factious wrong headed youngster would no longer be continued in the important office of Marshall, where he has unremittingly

checked the free course of justice by his partial selection of jurymen—our hopes are to be realized as we learn from Mr Pinckney; & many of my partial friends having expressed a wish that I would offer myself for the office of Marshall, I take the liberty of notifying to you that my services are at your disposal. If however, Sir, any other gentleman has been thought of by yourself, I entreat that I may not interfere with him, & that you will be assured that the prefference of any other gentleman will not occasion the least abatement of the homage I owe you, & of the veneration inspired by your virtues. As my friend Judge Ramsay is going down the country to preside in the circuit spring court, I shall solicit him to take charge of this letter, & as there are strong reasons for believing that a letter addressed to yourself would be opened at the Charleston post office, by Mr Bacoat the post Master, I shall request Judge Ramsay to deposit this at the Savannah post office (as he will return by Savannah) & will also take the precaution of putting it under cover to the postmaster general. I have the pleasure to inform you, good & great Sir, that your being called to preside over the people of America has given infinite delight in this district, & we all rely with confidence on a republican & at the same time energetic administration of the government. That you may live long, & throughout life enjoy all those blessings which we are permitted to enjoy here is the fervent prayer of

Yr devoted fellow Citizen   CHARLES GOODWIN

RC (DNA: RG 59, LAR); endorsed by TJ as received 26 May and so recorded in SJL with notation "Off."

London native Charles Goodwin emigrated to South Carolina in 1780 and became a naturalized citizen in 1783. A lawyer, major

of militia, and planter at Silver Bluff on the Savannah River near Augusta, Georgia, he represented Winton (later Barnwell) District in the South Carolina General Assembly from 1800 to 1805 (*S.C. Biographical Directory, Senate*, 1:583; Ephraim Ramsay to TJ, 2 May 1801).

To James Madison

TH:J. TO J.M.   Washington Apr. 30. 1801

I hasten the return of the bearer that he may meet you at Brown's and convey you information as to the road. from Songster's I tried the road by Ravensworth, which comes into the turnpike road $4\frac{1}{2}$ miles below Fairfax courthouse. there are about 2 miles of it which I think cannot be passed by your carriage without oversetting; and consulting with Colo. Wren who knows both roads, he says there is no comparison; that you must absolutely come by Fairfax courthouse, all that road being practicable till you come to Little's lane, which you have to encounter whatever way you come. I passed it yesterday, a waggon being then stuck fast in it, nor do I suppose any four wheeled carriage could then have got through the spot where the waggon was without stalling. but two days of wind & sun will by tomorrow make immense odds in it; so that I hope you will be able to pass it.—I met with mr Gaines & a mr Brawner at Brown's. they live near. I spoke of the difficulty of your getting up the Bull run hill. they agreed together to take each a horse & draw your carriage up. accept their offer by all means: as however steady your horses, they will be in the utmost peril of baulking; and should they once begin there are other bad hills sufficient to make them give you a great deal of vexation. the Bull run hill is really the worst I ever saw on a public road. still let nothing tempt you to go by Centerville as on that rout the whole is cut by waggons into Mudholes. from Brown's to Fairfax court house you have 14. miles of very firm road, only hilly in the beginning. you had better start as soon as you can see to drive, breakfast at Colo. Wren's, and come on here to dinner. we shall wait for you till 4. aclock. my respects to mrs Madison & affectionate esteem to yourself.

RC (DLC: Madison Papers); at foot of text: "Mr. Madison." PrC (DLC); endorsed by TJ in ink on verso.

From John Monroe

Sir.   Staunton April 30th. 1801.

My friends Col. Monroe, Mr. Coalter have mentioned to me a conversation, which lately took place between your self & those Gentlemen, relative to your appointing me Attorney for the Western District of Virginia. And they also hinted the propriety of my communicating with you on the subject.

My attatchment to, and confidence in your public & private character, have been sufficiently evinced by my open and public conduct; I will not therefore excite a suspicion of the sincerity of my professions, by any declaration to your self, for this your friendly attention to me.

It may however be proper, here, to mention a resolution which I formed, instantly on the success of your election, to wit, That I never would, by a solicitation for an Office, embarrass you: But that I would await the call of the Administration; conscious that the best men would be selected to fill all offices; and determining to support such appointments, if in my Judgement they tend to promote the common weal.

Whilst governed by this resolution, you Sir, never would have recieved a letter from me on the Subject of an Office for my self; had not the above communication made it necessary to declare the postponement, for a while, of my removal to Kentuckey.

In my present situation, any office of profit will be a great convenience to me. But my character is little known, & my principles less understood; if it is supposed, that, either the imposing influence of confidential friendship, or the more imperative demands of necessaty can induce me to accept of an office, for the discharge of the duties of which, I do not think myself qualified.

I love my country, and wish its happiness. Public good is my great object, personal benefit my second: and believe me, Sir, when I say, I had rather remain for ever in the back ground, than take the place of any man who is more capable of rendering service to his country than my self. Accept, Sir, my sincere wishes for your health & happiness both here and hereafter.   J, MONROE

RC (DLC); endorsed by TJ as received 6 May 1801 and so recorded in SJL.

From Henry Brinkerhoff

Hackensack New Jersey April 1801

Mr Jeforson you High President of North America that in the year 180   than I Left Hackensack New Jersey and than I Moved up for Me to go to Live Me than With one Abraham Ackerman Hue than him Lived than in the County of Montggomery in Broad Albin in New york state Above Shenackady in North America their and Mr Jeforson I Must tell you Now that verry same Man Abraham Ackerman he Stolid bonds all of Me of Me of A Hundred and fifteen Pounds of all My upright Money all of Me and he Stolid My Deed of All fifty Ackers Lot of all My Land Which I have bought all tham fifty Ackers I of one Archabel Mackentire hue Lives Now in in broad Albin in New york state Now Above Shenanactadey in North America their and Mr Jeferson I Must tell you Now that all My Deed that was that he Abraham Ackerman that he stolid all from Me Was Seven Hundred Dollars out of My Chest of Mine in the inside of all My Lock and I Asked Abraham Ackerman three or four times or five times for spend Money for Me for to Me to go down into the Jersey state at Hackensack in North America their and he Abraham Ackerman he Would Not Give Me Henry Brinkerhoff all tham four five times that I Asked I him Abraham Ackerman for spend Money and he would Not

Give all this Last year 1800 and this Last year 1801 all tham times he would Not Give Me Not one Penny of No Pasage Money all that time he to Me None at all None because I thaught I that Abraham Ackerman that he Meant to kill Me all that time with Every bodys on Lasterd Heaveness Persecution [. . .] Me unupright as A Devil unupright as he is and he thaght that he would get all My Estate [than] as Dam unupright Devil unupright as he is and the one and twenteath Day of february in the year 1801 than I Left Abraham Ackerman in [. . .] in New york state Above [. . .] in North America their and I had Me to spend on the Boat two Raisors and A Raisor box and two Jackets and two Coats and My Hat I [kept] and My traveling was two hundred Miles what I traveled All for that Dam unupright Raskel he all he is all unupright and Mr Jeferson as soon as you Receive this all My Letter all from Me than I wish that you Mr Jeferson Will indite Abraham Ackerman than Write Away Quick for he stealing My bonds all and he stealing My Deed of My Land and he kept Me their under and unupright Persecution and I that he Meant he than to kill Me than that time when I Lived with him he Bought A half Barrel of Rum for Me and I think that he bought the half Barrel of Rum than Porpose to kill Me if he Could than he thaught that he would Got all My Money all and as soon as you Mr Jeferson Receive all this My Letter all from Me than I wish that you will Quick Pas A Law for to have Abraham Ackermans Land all sold for his stealing My bonds and My Deed of all My Land and Mr Jeferson I advise you than Quick that you Must tare all Abraham Ackerman Cloaths of all his back all Clean all of him and Put him in the undermost Lowest Dungeons their and Chain him with three Chains of iron one Chain over the Middle of his Neck and the other Chain Middle over his Heart and the other Chain Middle over his breach Band and he Must be Chained on his back and he Must have three Crums of bread A Day but and Not A No More and the first Court he fetch up in and before the Court of People that before the Lawyers and the high Gudge of the Court and the Grand the Grand Jury of the Court too and Mr Jeferson I will advise you for to do that because he is A Devil of A theef unupright and A unupright wrong Murderer he is Against Me wrong unupright and than if you do that than than you will do than upright Mr Jeferson for all My Love   HENRY BRINKERHOFF

RC (MHi); faint; addressed: "To Mr Jeferson high President of the united states of North America"; endorsed by TJ as received 4 May and so recorded in SJL.

Appendix I

Lists of Appointments and Removals

1. LIST OF CANDIDATES [CA. 23 DEC. 1800-31 MCH. 1801]

2. LIST OF APPOINTMENTS AND REMOVALS [CA. MAY 1802]

3. LIST OF APPOINTMENTS AND REMOVALS [AFTER 10 MAY 1803]

4. LIST OF APPOINTMENTS AND REMOVALS [5 MCH. 1801-14 MAY 1802]

EDITORIAL NOTE

Appointments and removals demanded and received Jefferson's attention during the first months of his presidency. He confided to John Dickinson on 21 June 1801, "it is the business of removal & appointment which presents the serious difficulties; all others compared with these are as nothing." To another correspondent Jefferson noted: "there is nothing I am so anxious about as good nominations, conscious that the merit as well as reputation of an administration depends as much on that as on it's measures" (TJ to Archibald Stuart, 8 Apr. 1801).

While the dates of these documents extend from December 1800 to May 1803, they all concern the appointments Jefferson began to make following his inauguration. Lists 2, 3, and 4 reveal the disdain Jefferson had for the appointments made after 12 Dec., when John Adams knew he had lost the election. They underscore Jefferson's policy of removing Federalist marshals and district attorneys and appointing Republicans to give some balance to the judicial process. "The only shield for our Republican citizens against the federalism of the courts," Jefferson contended in his correspondence, "is to have the Attornies & Marshals republicans." But in compiling these documents, especially Lists 2 and 3, Jefferson sought to justify removals on other than purely political grounds, as the various classifications and explanations indicate. In his early correspondence as president, Jefferson maintained that removals were based on "fixed rules, applied to every case without passion or partiality. the rule may be disapproved, but the application shall be beyond reproach." He described the dilemma removals presented: "no one will say that all should be removed, or that none should, yet no two scarcely draw the same line." As to appointments, Jefferson maintained that since Federalists had been "in the exclusive possession of all offices from the very first origin of party among us to the 3d. of March at 9 aclock in the night," it was "perfectly just" that Republicans only be appointed "until something like an equilibrium in office be restored" (Cunningham, *Jeffersonian Republicans in Power*, 61; Malone, *Jefferson*, 4:72-5; TJ to Benjamin Rush, 24 Mch. 1801; TJ to John Wayles Eppes, 27 Mch. 1801; TJ to Gideon Granger, 29 Mch. 1801; TJ to Archibald Stuart, 8 Apr. 1801).

It is clear that Jefferson compiled the names of candidates included in List 1 over several months. The entries are not in strict chronological order, but most of the recommendations for candidates included in the first part of the document—those entries appearing above the first appearance of John

Caldwell in the "candidate" column—were received in Washington between 23 Dec. 1800 and 1 Mch. 1801. Perhaps the great number of applications and recommendations after this date discouraged Jefferson from continuing the list. He compiled the second part of this record, which is confined to recommendations for candidates seeking consular appointments, from letters received primarily in March 1801. In both parts of the list Jefferson also recorded recommendations gained through conversations with congressmen, cabinet members, and others in Washington. For example, Congressman Joseph B. Varnum's recommendation of Boston printers on 20 Jan. and Senator John Langdon's endorsement of James Sullivan in February were undoubtedly done through conversations, as no correspondence with either legislator is recorded in SJL during this period. Some candidates received both written and oral testimonials. Matthew Lyon recommended candidates for marshal in his letter to TJ of 1 Mch. In another letter written two days later, he recalled the pleasure of speaking twice with the president-elect "on the Subject of appointments in Vermont." In a letter for Thomas Aborn, dated 19 May 1801, Rhode Island Senator Theodore Foster reminded Jefferson "I mentioned him to you the day before I left the city."

The earliest Jefferson could have compiled List 2 is at the close of the first session of the Seventh Congress, and since the list includes three appointments that Jefferson later dated at 14 May 1802, although the Senate approved them before the close of the session, the later dating probably indicates that he did not compile List 2 until after 14 May. Excluded from this list are John Adams's midnight appointments, which the new president considered as "nullities." All of the appointments entered on this document also appear in Lists 3 and 4. List 4 extends in its entirety to February 1809. The first installment of this document, as printed below, extends from Jefferson's first appointments on 5 Mch. 1801 to 14 May 1802, where he entered the last of his nominations presented during the first session of the Seventh Congress. It appears to be one of Jefferson's working lists and certainly is the most complete. All of the entries in List 3 are found under the same dates in List 4 (the one exception is Peter Dobell, who appears under 3 June in List 3 and 4 June in List 4). The dates for the eight entries in List 4 inserted with the notation "omitted by me at their proper dates" can be supplied from List 3 (JEP, 1:422-5).

While the dates in Lists 3 and 4 are consistent, it is unclear how Jefferson derived many of them. The interim appointments of William Gardner, Edward Livingston, John Smith, and John Swartwout, recorded in List 4 on 28 Mch., were reported in the biweekly *National Intelligencer*—the newspaper Jefferson saw as the authority on appointments—on 30 Mch. 1801, and thus appear to be accurate. But the appointments of John Shee, Alexander J. Dallas, Presley Carr Lane, James Hamilton, David Fay, John Willard, and the justices of the peace for the District of Columbia and Alexandria County, recorded in List 4 under 5 Mch., were not officially noticed in the *National Intelligencer* until 18 Mch. The appointments of Daniel Carroll Brent and John Thomson Mason, also recorded under 5 Mch., did not appear in the *National Intelligencer* until 25 Mch. Correspondence and other notes by Jefferson confirm that those appointees recorded in Lists 3 and 4 at 5 Mch. 1801 were actually decided upon after that date but most likely before 24 Mch., the next dated entry in List 4. In List 4, TJ recorded Delamotte's commission as vice commercial agent at Havre at 30 June 1801, but his commission was dated 1 June. The dates recorded with appointments in early 1802, when Congress was in session, are also difficult to explain. Nominations for all of the entries in List 4 appearing between 22 and 25 Feb. 1802 were presented to the Senate on 2 Feb. and approved between the 4th and 10th. In the case of Joseph Barnes, the Senate consented to his appointment as consul at Sicily on 10 Feb., the date that appears on his commission. Commissions for John Appleton, William Jarvis, and William Riggin are dated 4 Feb. 1802, but the executive journal indicates the Senate did not confirm the nominations until 9 Feb. The president presented the last five nominations appearing on the list at 20 Apr. to the Senate on 10 Mch. The Senate approved the appointments on 11-12 Mch., along with that of William P. Gardner, who appears on the list at 11 Mch. Commissions for Edward Croft and Gardner are dated 11 Mch. 1802 (JEP, 1:406-7, 409-10; FCs of commissions in DNA: RG 59, PTCC, MPTPC; Notes on a Cabinet Meeting, 8 Mch. 1801).

1. List of Candidates

[ca. 23 Dec. 1800-31 Mch. 1801]

Candidate	Residence	Office	by whom recommended	Date.
Munson William.	New haven.		Pierpt Edwards	1800. Dec. 16.
Meade Everard				
Cranch Wm. nephew mrs. A.	Washington	Commr. vice Scott.	William Thornton	Dec. 31.
Barnes Joseph.	Hamburg	Consul Genl. of 2. Sicilies.		
Paine Thomas.	Paris	Commr. of indemnificns		Oct. 4
Thomas Cooper	161. Chesnt. street or Nthmbld	Supervisor of Distr. of Pensva. loco Genl. Miller.		
Hamilton	Northmbld. Pensva.	Collector of Excise. loco Buyers who was put loco Hamilton unjustly	Thomas Cooper.	
Doctr. Thos. J. Vandyke		Superintendt. of Cherokee nation loco Majr. Thos. Lewis	David Campbell	Dec. 28.
William Brent	clk to Commrs. of Washington	my private Secretary	Richd. Brent	1801. Jan. 14
Stephen Sayre	Philada	foreign mission	himself. & Govr. Mc.kean	Jan. 10. 12. Feb. 20[1]
		or in the revenue	himself	Feb. 5
Genl. Wm. Irvine	Carlisle	Supervisor of the excise	Govr Mc.kean	Jan. 10.

Robert Mc.kean	Philada	in the customs	Govr. Mc.kean	Jan. 10.
Zantzinger Paul.	Lancaster	in the revenue &c	Benj. S. Barton	Jan. 18.
Sullivan.	Boston	district judge	J. Langdon	Feb.
Genl. Muhlenbg		Supervisor of revenue	delegates of Pensva.	Feb. 20.
Genl Irvine			mr. Brown.	
J. Beckley		Comptroller vice Steele	do.	
Claiborne		Govr. Missi territory	Gregg. Davis	Feb. 23.
Charles Wilkins	Kentucky	marshal Vice Mc.Dowell	Innes. Short. S. Brown. J. Brown	
John Jouett	do.	do.	Innes. Todd. Breckinr. Hopkins	
Muhlenburg F. A.	Phila	Collector Phila. vice Latimer	himself	Feb. 11
Adams & Rhoades	Boston	Printing	Genl. Varnum	Jan. 20.
Dr. John Willard ⎫ Genl. Isaac Clarke ⎬ Dr. James Witherill ⎭	Vermont	Marshal Vermont v. Fitch	M. Lyon	Mar. 1.
Lane. George.	Dumfries	Marshal of Columbia.	Richd. Brent	Feb. 24.
John Page	Roswell	Director of Mint ⎫	John Page	Feb. 1.
Thos. Tudor Tucker	S. Cara.	Treasr. of Mint ⎭		
John Caldwell. bkr.	N. Jersey	Consul in W.I.	Boudinot. Rush.	21.
Brown	English. S.C.	Consul Algiers	Pierce Butler[2]	
Joseph Fenwick				
Lewis Searle Pintard		Consul Madeira.	J. M. Pintard. Burr	
Schuyler Livingston		do.	Burr	
Marien Lamar	Madeira	do.	Fitzsimmons. Stoddart.	
Barnet	Bordeaux	Consul at Bordeaux	mr A.	
Orr Wm. Grayson. bkrpt.	Washington	do.	Walt Jones	
√ Lee Wm.	Boston	do.	mr A. Monroe. Genl. Lincoln. Tudor. J. C. Jones. Russell. Dexter. Minot. Gerry. Marshal. Pinckney.	
Jno. W. Forbes.	R.I.	do. or Havre	T. Foster. Monro? Dexter.	
√ Peter Dobel Phila do.		Dr. Wistar.		
Theodore Peters	Bordeaux	do.		
Thorn Stephen		Consul at Havre.		
√ La Motte Havre do.				
John Mitchell		do.		
√ Skipwith Paris		Consul Genl. France.		
Mountflorence do.		do.		
Jas. Swan bkrpt. do.		do.		
John Leach		Dunkirk	Jas. Monroe[3]	

Anderson Nathanl.		Consul in France	
Wm. E. Hulings	N. Orleans	Consul at N. Orleans	Wm. Jones Phila
Lewis Jacob		do. Isle of France	
Stacy George		do.	appd by mr A. recent.
Wm. Buchanan	Baltimore	do.	Genl. Smith.
Henry Preble	Boston	do. Cadiz	namd by mr A.
Blake James.	Phila	W.I.	Dr. Stevens.
Prevost.			
John Caldwell	N.J.	do.	Boudinot. Rush.
bkrpt			J. R. Smith
Jacob Mayer	Pensva	St. Domingo	Mc.kean. W. Barton.
			Duane.
George A. Cushing	Massachusets	Havanna[4]	
Benjn. Rawlins	Baltimore	Span. islds.	
Edwd. Jones	Geo. T.	Guadeloupe	the Masons. Stoddert.
Anthony Van	Phila	Antwerp.	baron de Beelen
Mannierck			Bertholf. Wm. Jones &c
John J. Murray	N.Y.	Glasgow	Burr. C. Pinckney.
Thomas Aborne	Warwick	Cayenne	Theodore Foster

MS (DLC: TJ Papers, 108:18557); undated; entirely in TJ's hand; check marks added by TJ indicate candidates who received consular appointments in June 1801.

A letter from Everard MEADE of 19 Dec. 1800, recorded in SJL as received from "Hermitage. Amelia" on 30 Dec., has not been found. The letter from DAVID CAMPBELL dated 28 Dec., recorded in SJL as received from Tennessee on 16 Jan. 1801, is also missing.

For the recommendations TJ received for CHARLES WILKINS, see Samuel Brown to TJ, 14 Jan. 1801. TJ received another recommendation for Wilkins from Kentucky congressman John Fowler, dated 15 Mch. at Washington. Fowler forwarded applications from Wilkins and Gwyn R. Tompkins and letters from Joseph Crockett and Thomas January, all candidates for marshal of Kentucky in place of Samuel McDowell, Jr., who it was assumed would be replaced "on Grounds of Complaint against him." Fowler described Wilkins as "an Amiable Man well qualified to fill the office" who "has been a Moderate Federalist." Fowler closed by wishing TJ "a prosperous Administration" (RC in DNA: RG 59, LAR, endorsed by TJ: "Kentucky. Marshall Fowler's lre," TJ later adding "Wilkins

to be Marshal of Kentucky" in place of "Kentucky. Marshall"; Dauer, Adams Federalists, 318). TJ received the application from Wilkins, consisting of a letter from Wilkins to Fowler, dated Lexington, 14 Jan. 1801. Wilkins noted that several friends had encouraged him to become a candidate for the office. He had already enclosed "a very warm & friendly letter from Judge Innes to Mr Jefferson" in correspondence with Kentucky Senator John Brown. But believing there would be "a number of applicants for this office," Wilkins desired that Fowler also "make known to the President your sentiments as to my Character & capacity to fill the office" (RC in DNA: RG 59, LAR, endorsed by TJ: "Wilkins to be Marshal of Kentucky"; Biog. Dir. Cong.).

Recommendations for JOHN JOUETT, Jr., are noted at his letter to TJ of 12 Jan. 1801.

LEWIS SEARLE PINTARD: on 18 Mch. John M. Pintard, consul at Madeira since 1790, wrote Burr from New York and enclosed recommendations in favor of his cousin from Madeira merchants (Kline, Burr, 1:546-8).

MARIEN LAMAR: on 7 May 1801 Thomas FitzSimons wrote Madison recommending the Maryland native as consul at Madeira. TJ endorsed a copy of a letter from Lamar at Madeira to Benjamin Stoddert dated 28

Jan. 1801 and postmarked at Baltimore, 20 Apr.: "Lamar Marien to mr Stoddart to be consul at Madeira." A navy department clerk also endorsed the letter: "Marien Lamar—wants the Consulate at Madeira." Philadelphia merchant Robert Waln wrote Samuel Smith and Albert Gallatin on 23 Mch. and 6 June 1801, respectively, recommending Lamar (all in DNA: RG 59, LAR).

ORR WM. GRAYSON: that is, Benjamin Grayson Orr.

Boston merchants, including Joseph RUSSELL, Aaron DEXTER, and George R. MINOT, signed a letter to President Adams, dated 11 Dec. 1799, which William Lee cited in his letter to TJ of [before 9 Mch. 1801] (Tr in DNA: RG 59, LAR).

TJ endorsed a 2 Mch. letter from ANTHONY VAN MANNIERCK to the secretary of state, noting that he sought to be "consul at Antwerp" (RC in DNA: RG 59, LAR). Van Mannierck perhaps enclosed the letter from Baron de Beelen Bertholf to TJ of 2 Mch., that, according to SJL, TJ received on the 24th (now missing).

[1] TJ interlined remainder of entry for Stephen Sayre.
[2] Entry interlined.
[3] Entry interlined.
[4] Entry interlined.

2. List of Appointments and Removals

[ca. May 1802]

Officers *commissioned* by the President. those not commissioned are appointed & removed without his knolege. Midnight nominations, to wit, those made after Dec. 12. when the Charleston election became known at Washington, will not be included: most of them had not[1] recieved commissions.

		appointed.
4. Attornies.	Davies of Maine	Silas Lee
	Marsh of Vermont the oppressor[2] of Lyon.	Fay
	Harrison of New York: a revolutionary refugee	Edw. Livingston
	Woodruff of Georgia	Mitchell
9. Marshals.	Fitch of Vermont. the oppressor of Lyon.	Willard
	Cilley of New Hampshire. commission expired & not renewed.	Mc.Clary
	Giles of New York	Swartwout
	Lowry of New Jersey	Herd.
	Hall of Pensylvania[3]	Smith.
	Hamilton of Delaware. commission expired & not renewed	Lewis
	Hopkins of Maryland	Etting
	Randolph of Virginia[4]	Scott
	Gordon of Georgia	Wall.

2. restorations. Pierce Commr. of loans N. Hampsh. removd. & the place restored
   to Gardner[5] deprivd. for not signg. address to J.A
   Martin Collectr. N. Hampshire removed & the place restord. to
   Whipple deprived for not signing address to J.A

9. removals[6]	Lee Collector of Penobscot	Hook
	Livermore Naval officer of New Hampshire	Folsome
	Chester Supervisor of Connecticut	Kirby
	Whittlesey Collector of Connecticut	Wolcott
	Lyman Surveyor in Rhode isld.	Slocum
	Fish Supervisor of New York	Osgood
	Sands Collector of New York	Gelston
	Miller Supervisor of Pensylvania	Muhlenburg
	Bell. Collector of New Jersey. a revolutionary tory, aid to Genl. Carlton.	Marsh.

The above 24. cases are the whole of the removals which have been made in order to give some participation in office to the Republicans, previous to the close of the session of Congress.
the following removals have been made for malversation.[7]

8. Malconduct.	Stillman Surveyor R.I. for non residence & drink	Cross
	Watson Collector of New Jersey for non-attendance on duty	Crane
	Mc.Dowell Marshal of Kentucky. for extortion in office.	Crockett
	Dunham Supervisor of N. Jersey for drunkenness & profligacy	Lynn
	Kirby Collector of Hampton Virginia. for delinquency in accounts	Chisman
	Wilkins Collector of Cherrystone's Virginia for do.	Smith.
	Powell Collector of Savanna for do.	Johnson
	Serjeant Govr. of Missisipi. commission expired & not renewed for malconduct, & his brutal & odious deportment generally	Claiborne

MS (DLC: TJ Papers, 119:20542); entirely in TJ's hand; undated, but see below. PrC (same, 119:20543-4). Dft (same, 120:20568; entirely in TJ's hand; undated; list only, with significant variations noted below; at head of list: "officers commissioned by the President Midnight appmts, to wit, all after Dec. 12."

Michael McCleary (MC.CLARY), John Heard (HERD), and Silas CRANE are entered in List 4 under 14 May 1802, but TJ presented the nominations of Mc-Cleary and Crane to the Senate on 27 Apr. and they were approved two days later. The Senate received and approved Heard's nomination on 3 May, the closing day of the session (JEP, 1:422-3, 425).

[1] TJ first wrote after colon "only some of them had" before altering the clause to read as above.

² In Dft TJ wrote "ill treatmt" not "oppressor" here and when it appears again at "Fitch of Vermont."
³ TJ here partially erased "who packed." Dft: "packing juries."
⁴ In Dft TJ here wrote "packg. juries. delinqy."
⁵ Dft lacks remainder of passage here and in next entry.
⁶ In Dft TJ here wrote "federalism" instead of "9. removals."
⁷ Dft lacks preceding two sentences.

3. List of Appointments And Removals

[after 10 May 1803]

A correct view of certain appointments arranged in classes.

I. in place of those resigned, declined, promoted or dead.
1801. Mar. 5. Wm. Kelty Ch. judge of Circuit court of Columbia vice Thos. Johnson declined.
May. 12. Tobias Lear Coml. Agt St. Domingo vice Dr. Stevens resigned
14. Albert Gallatin. Pensva. Secy. Treasy. vice S.   Dexter resigned
25. David Howell R.I. Atty v. D. L. Barnes promoted to judge.
July 15. Robt Smith. Maryld. Secy. Navy v. Benj. Stoddart. resd.
27. Silas Lee. Maine. Atty v.   Davies made a state judge.
Oct. 7. John Oakley Collectr. &c Geo.Town v. Jas. M. Lingan resd.
22. Wm. Stephens. judge of the district court of Georgia.¹
Nov. 18. Jas. Alger. Commr. loans Georgia v. Thomas Wylly decd.
19. Jas. Nicholson. Comr. loans N. York v.   Clarkson resd.
28. Gideon Granger. Conn. P. M. Genl. v.   Habersham resd.
30. Thos. Tudor Tucker. S.C. Treasurer v.   Meredith resd.
Henry Potter N.C. judge 5th. Circuit v. John Sitgreaves declined
Wm. Chribbs. Indiana. Collectr. Massac v.   Irvin declined.
Feb. 19. Timothy Bloodworth N.C. Collector Wilmington v. Griffith Mc.rae. dead.²
1802. Apr. 20. Andrew Lyle. N.J. Surveyr. New Brunswic v. Anthy. W. White resd.
May 14. Walter Nichols. R.I. Navl. offr. Newport v. Robert Crooke decd.
John Heard N.J. Collectr. Perth Amboy v. Danl Marsh drowned.
July 28. Peter Muhlenberg Pensv. Collectr. Pensva v. George Latimer resd.
Tenche Coxe. Pensva. Supervisor of Pensva v. P. Muhlenberg promotd.
31. Wm. R. Lee. Mass. Collectr. Salem & Beverley v. Joseph Hiller resd.
Aug. 25. George Wentworth Surveyr. Portsmouth N.H. v. Saml. Adams decd.
28. Abraham Bloodgood v. Henry Bogert. resd.³
Dec. 10. Gabriel Duval. Maryld. Comptroller Treasy. v. John Steele resd.
1803. Apr. 11. J L. Cathcart. Consul Tunis v. Wm. Eaton resd.

APPENDIX I

IId. Vacancies left unfilled when I came into office.
1801. Mar. 5. James Madison of Virginia. Secy. of state vice John Marshall
            appointed Chief justice
            Henry Dearborn. Mass. Secy. at War.
            Robt. R. Livingston M.P. to France vice Bayard declined
      Apr. 1. Jonathan Russel R.I. Collectr. Bristol. nomind by mr Adams.
            approvd Senate
          30. David Leonard Barnes. Judge R.I. vice Benjamin Bourne
            promoted
      June 4. Jas. Irwin of Tenn. Collectr. Massac.
      July 15. Malachi Jones. Surveyor of Curratuck
      Aug. 4. Jonas Clarke Inspector Kennebunk.
      Oct. 3. Wm. Goforth & John Reiley Commrs. for Symmes's
            contracts.
            Walter Jones jnr. Columbia. Atty of district of Ptomak.
            David Duncan of N.W.T. collector Michillimackinac. new.
1802. Jan. 21. Wm. Foster jr. Comml. Agt Morlaix nomd by mr Ad. apprvd.
            by Senate.

III. Offices expired & not renewed.
1801. May 25. Wm. C. C. Claiborne. Tennessee. Govr. Missipi v. Winthrop
            Serjeant.
      June 7. Chas. Pinckney S.C. M. Plen. to Spain v. David Humphreys.
            11. years
      July 1. Joel Lewis. Marshl. Del. v.   Hamilton
      Dec.   Joseph Wilcox Marshl. Conn. v.
1802. May 14. Michl. Mc.lary. Marshl N.H. v. Bradbury Cilley.
1803. Mar. 3. Cato West Secretary Missipi v. John Steele

IV. Midnight appointments. that is to say appointments made by mr Adams after Dec.
    12. 1800. when the event of the S.C. election which decided the Presidential election
    was known at Washington and until Midnight of Mar. 3. 1801. these were consid-
    ered as Null
1801. Mar. 5. Levi Lincoln. Mass. Atty Genl. v. Parsons.
            Alexr Jas. Dallas. Pensva. Atty West. distr. Pensva. v. John
            Wilkes Kittera.[4]
            Jas. Hamilton Atty Westn. distr. Pensva. vice Thos. Duncan
            Presley Carr Lane Marshl. Westn. distr. Pensva v. Hugh
            Barclay.
            Danl. C. Brent. Virga. Marsh. Columbia v. Jas. M.Lingan.
            John T. Mason. Columbia. Atty of Col. v. Thos. Swan.
      Apr. 25. John Monroe. Virga. Atty West. distr. Virga. vice Saml.
            Blackburn
      May 23. Saml. Bishop. Collectr. New haven vice Elizur Goodrich.
      June 3. Wm. Lee. Mass. Coml. Agt. Bordeaux v. Isaac Coxe Barnet
            Peter Dobell Pensva. do. Havre v. John M. Forbes
          26. George Maxwell Atty N. Jersey v. Fred. Frelinghuysen.
          27. Hermannus H. Windell Marsh. Albany v. James Dole.
      July 8. Stephen Cathalan Coml. Agt Marseilles *restored* v. Wm. Lee

July 9. Wm. Buchanan Maryld. Coml. Agt. I. France & Bourbon v. George Stacey

Joseph Yznardi Consul Cadiz. restord v. Henry Preble.[5]

John S. Sherbourne. Atty N. Hamp. v. Edwd St. Loe Livermore.

16. Andrew Moore Virga Marshl West. distr. Virga. v. Robt. Grattan.

21. Lewis F. Taney. Coml. Agt. Ostend v. John Mitchel.

27. George Blake Mass. Atty Mass. v. Harrison Gray Otis.

Oct. 16. Wm. Patterson N.Y. Coml. Agt. Lorient v. Turell Tufts

17. Chas. D. Coxe. Pensva. Coml Agt Dunkirk v. James H. Hooe.

Nov. 7. Thos. Gantt. Col. Coml. Agt. Nantz v. John Jones Waldo.

V. restorations to office of those who had been removed on principles not justifiable

1801. Mar. 28. Wm. Gardner N. Hamp. Comr. loans N.H. v. John Pierce

30. Joseph Whipple N. Hamp. Collectr. Portsmth. v. Thomas Martin

June 4. Fulwar Skipwith Coml. Agt Paris. v. J. C. Mountflorence.

30. La Motte. Vice Coml. Agt Havre.

VI. Attornies & Marshals removed for high federalism, & republicans appointed as a protection to republican suitors in courts entirely federal & going all lengths in party spirit.

1801. Mar. 5. David Fay Verm. vice Charles Marsh. Atty for Vermont

28. Edwd. Livingston Atty N.Y. v. Richd. Harrison

John Heard Marsh. N. Jersey v. Thos. Lowry.[6]

1802. Apr. 20. Benjamin Wall. Georgia. Marshl. Georgia. v. Ambrose Gordon.

David Brydie Mitchell Atty Georgia v. Woodruff.

VII. removals on the principle of giving some participation in office to republicans, & also to disarm those who were using the weight of their official influence to oppose the order of things established.

1801. June 5. Danl. Marsh N.J. Collectr. N.J. v. Andrew Bell a revolutionary tory

July 2. Ephraim Kirby. Con. Supervisor Connectt. v. J. Chester.

9. David Gelstone N.Y. Collectr. N.Y. v. Joshua Sands.[7]

Nov. 14. Alexr Wolcott. Con. Collectr. Middleton v. Chauncey Whittlesea.[8]

1802. Feb. 23. John Cross jr. R.I. Surveyor Pawcatuc v. George Stillman.

John Slocum R.I. Surveyor Newport v. Daniel Lyman.

Apr. 20. Nathanl. Folsome N.H. Navl. officer Portsmth. v. Edwd St. Loe Livermore

Aug. 25. John Gibaut. Mass. Collectr. Gloster v. Wm. Tuck

Ralph Cross. Mass. Collectr. Newbury port. v. Dudley A. Tyng.

Sep. 6. John Shore Virga Collectr. Petsbg v. Wm. Heath.

1803. Feb. 8. Jabez Pennyman Verm. Collectr. Alburg. v. David Russell.

Mar. 1. Zachariah Stevens. Mass. Survr. Gloster v. Saml.
Whittermore.

May 10. Saml. Osgood N.Y. Navl. Officr. N.Y. v. Richd. Rogers.
revoly. tory
Saml. Ward Mass. Navl Off. Salem & Beverley. v.
Wm. Pickman

VIII. removals on mixed grounds including[9] delinquency or misconduct.

1801. Mar. 5. John Willard. Vermt. Marshl. of Vermt v. Jabel Fitch for cruel
conduct

28. John Swartwout N.Y. Marshl. of N.Y. v. Aquila Giles. money
delinquency

June. 27. Peter Muhlenberg Supervisor Pensva v. Henry Miller. money
delinquency.

May 25. Reuben Etting. Marshl. Maryld. v. Hopkins. money
delinquency.

June 27. Saml. Osgood Supervisor N.Y. v. Nichs. Fish. delinquent.

Nov. 14. Josiah Hook Collectr. Penobscot v. John Lee a revoluty. tory &
delinquent.

1802. Aug. 25. Joseph Farley Collectr. Waldsbro. v. Joshua Head. delinquent.

1803. Mar. 1. Isaac Illsley jr. Collectr. Portland v. Nathl. F. Fosdyck.
delinquent money.

VIIII. Removals for Misconduct or delinquency.

1801. Mar. 24. Joseph Scott Marshl. Virga v. Dav. M. Randolph. packing
juries.

28. John Smith Marshl. Pensva v. Hall. packing juries.

June 6. James Linn. Supervisr. N.J. v. A. Dunham. habitl.
drunkenness.

27. Joseph Crockett. Marshl. Kentucky v. Mc.Dowell. extortion.

July 3. George W. Erving. Mass. Consul London v. Williams. not
rend[g. acct]

Aug. 31. Mount Edwd Chisman Collectr. Hampton v. Wm. Kirby.
delinquency. money.

Sep. 15. Thos. de Mattos Johnson. Collectr. Savanna v. not
renderg [acct]

Nov. 18. Isaac Smith Collectr. Cherrystone v. Nathl. Powell. Wilkins.
delinquent.

1802. May 14. Silas Crane Collectr. Little egg harbr. v. Wm. Watson. absence
& neglect.

Oct. 11. Robt. Anderson New Collectr. Louisville v. Jas. Mc.Connel
delinquent

1803. Mar. 3. Isaac Dayton Surveyor Hudson v. J. C. Tenbroeck delinqt of old.
Henry Warren Collectr. Plymouth v. Wm. Watson. malpractice.
Turner Collectr. Brunswic Georgia v. Claud Thompson insane.

May 10. Jeremiah Bennet jr. Collectr. Bridgetown N.J. v. Eli Elmer.
delinqt money
George House mastr of Cutter. N. Lond. v. Hindman
malpractice.

MS (DLC: TJ Papers, 119:20545-6); undated; entirely in TJ's hand; words obscured by binding.

WILCOX MARSHL. CONN. V.: Joseph Willcox became marshal of the district of Connecticut in place of Philip B. Bradley (JEP, 1:397).

THOMAS WYLLY: that is, Richard Wylly.

[1] Entry interlined.
[2] Entry interlined and preceded by mark to indicate "1802."

[3] Entry interlined.
[4] Entry interlined.
[5] Entry interlined.
[6] TJ here canceled a 28 Mch. entry for John Swartout and entered it under "VIII."
[7] TJ here canceled a 14 Nov. entry for Josiah Hook and interlined it under "VIII."
[8] TJ here canceled two entries for 27 June, one for Peter Muhlenberg and the other for Samuel Osgood, and interlined them under "VIII."
[9] Interlined in place of "of participation."

4. List of Appointments and Removals

[5 Mch. 1801-14 May 1802]

1801.

Mar. 5. James Madison. Secy. of state. Virga. vice John Marshal appointed Ch. Justice

Henry Dearborn. Mass. Sec. at war. vacant

Levi Lincoln. Mass. Atty Genl. vacant by resignation of Charles Lee to mr Adams. Parsons named at midnight Mar. 3.

Rob. R. Livingston. M.P. to French republic. Commn. Oct. 2. long vacant. Bayard named in last days of mr A's admin

Alexr. James Dallas. Atty for Eastern district Pensva. new. Kittera one of the midnight appointments not being confirmed.

* David Fay. Atty for distr. of Vermont. vice Charles Marsh Atty. removd on the genl. necessity of havg. republicn. officers where the court is federal

* John Willard. Marshal for do. vice Jabel Fitch removed for cruelty, as well as on the genl. necessity of repb. off. in a fedl court

James Hamilton. Atty W. distr. Pensva. new. vice Thos. Duncan a midnight appointment

Pressley Carr Lane Marshl do. new. vice Hugh Barclay a midnight appointment.

[John Shea. Marshl. E. distr. Pensv. refused

Geo. Gilpin. Wm. Fitzhugh. Francs. Peyton. Richd. Conway. Elisha Cullen Dick. Chas. Alexander. Geo. Taylor. Jonah Thompson. Abram Faw. John Herbert. Alexander Smith. Cuthbert Powell. Pet. Wise junr. Jac. Houghman. Thos. Darne. Just. cnty Alexandr.

Thos. S. Lee Danl. Reintzel. Thos. Corcoran. Danl. Carrol. Cornels. Cuningham. Thos. Peter.—Rob. Brent. Thos. Addison. Abram. Boyd. Benjam Moore. J. Mason.

Wm. Thornton. Benj. Stoddart. Wm. Hammond Dorsey.
Jos. Sprigg Bell. Justices of Washington county.
Danl. Carrol Brent Marsh. distr. Columbia. new. vice
James M. Lingan a midnight appmt
Wm. Kelty. Chief judge of the Circuit ct. for the distr. of
Columbia vice Thos. Johnson who declined acceptg.
J. T. Mason Atty distr. Columbia. new. Thos. Swan. a
midnight appmt. rejected.

Mar. 24.   * Joseph Scott. Marshl. E. distr. Virga. vice D. M. Randolph
removed for misconduct to wit packg. juries. holds back
money also

    26.   Wm. Hammond Dorsey. Judge Orphan's ct. Washn. John Hewitt.

    27.   Register of wills for Washn. county. v. John Peter a
midnight appmt

    28.   * John Smith. Marsh. E. distr. Pensva. vice Hall removed for
misconduct, to wit packing juries & severity in office

           [Jas. Sullivan. Atty distr. Mass.   refused

      * Edwd. Livingston. Atty distr. N.Y. vice Richd. Harrison
removed on genl. principle of havg. republicn. officers
where the court is federal

      * John Swartwout. Marsh. do. vice Aquila Giles one of the
midnight renewals.¹ delinquent in money largely

      * Wm. Gardner. Commr. loans N.H. vice John Pierce removed
to restore Gardner who had been removd. for not signg
address to mr A.

    30.   * Joseph Whipple. Collectr. distr. Portsmouth. vice Thomas
Martin removed to restore Whipple. same case as
Gardner

           Cleon Moore. Register of wills Alexandria county.

Apr. 1.   Jonathan Russell. Collectr. of customs for Bristol in R.I.
named by mr Adams & approvd by Senate

    25.   John Monroe. Atty W. distr. Virga. new. vice Saml. Black-
burn a midnight appointment

    30.   David Leonard Barnes. Judge distr. R.I. vacant. Greene had
been nominated & approved, but the commn. not issued.

May. 12.   Tobias Lear. Genl. Commercl. agent St. Domingo. v. Doctr.
Stevens resigned.

           Thos. Sumpter S.C. Sec. legn. Fr. rep. new

    14.   Albert Gallatin. Pensva. Secy. treasy. vice   Dexter
resigned

           Geo. Gilpin. Judge Orphan's ct. county of Alexa. v.
John Herbert a midnight appmt

    23.   Saml. Bishop. Collectr. distr. New Haven. vice Elizur
Goodrich. one of the midnight appmts

    25.   Wm. C. C. Claiborne Govr. Missi. territy. vice Winthrop
Serjeant whose time is expired.

      * Reuben Etting. Marsh. distr. Maryld. vice Hopkins removed
for delinquency as well as general principle.

           David Howell. Atty distr. R. I. vice D. L. Barnes² made a
judge

June   3.   Wm. Lee. Commercl. agent Bourdeaux. vice Barnet. a
               midnight appmt

        4.   Fulwar Skipwith virga. Commercl. agent Paris vice
               J. C. Mountflorence a midnight appmt

           Peter Dobell. Pensva. do. Havre. v. John M. Forbes a
               midnight appointmt.

           De la Motte. France. Vice agent do.

           Edwd. Jones. Com. Agt. Guadaloupe.

           Thos. Aborne. R. I. do. Cayenne.

           John C. Murray.   Consul Glasgow.

           [John Neufville Commr. direct tax. S.C.

           Wm. Baker. Columb. Marsh. distr. Patomac. new

           Jas. Irwin. Ten. Collectr. Massac. & Inspector of revenue.
               vacant

        5. * Danl. Marsh. N.J. Collectr. & Inspector rev. N.J. vice Andrew
               Bell a revoluty. tory

June   6. * James Linn. Supervisor N.J. vice A. Dunham. removd for
               habitual drunkenness

        7. * Charles Pinckney M. P. Spain vice Humphries recalled because
               of long absence

      11.   [John Caruthers. Marsh. W. distr. Virga.

      17.   Wm. R. Davie, Jas. Wilkinson. Benj. Hawkins Commrs. for
               Choctaws, Chickasaws, Creeks, Cherokees.

      19.   Jas. Blake. Com. Agt. Antwerp. new

      25.   John Caldwell. Com. agt. Sto. Domingo.[3]

      26.   George Maxwell. Atty distr. N.J. vice L. H. Stockdon
               resigned & Fred. Frelinghuysen a midnight appmt

      27.   James Findlaye. Marsh. distr. Ohio. new

           Wm. Mc.Millan Atty do. new

           Harmannus H. Wendell. Marsh. distr. Albany. new. vice
               James Dole a midnight appmt.

          * Joseph Crockett. Marsh. Kentucky. vice Mc.Dowell removed
               for delinquency, to wit extortion & other malpractices

          * Peter Muhlenburg. Supervisor distr. Pensva. v. Henry Miller,
               removed, a great delinquent.

      30.   La Motte. vice Agent Havre.

July   1.   Dominic Augustus Hall. Ch. judge of 5th. Circuit.

           Joseph Pulis. Consul Malta

           Joel Lewis. Marshal. Del. vice   Hamilton time expired &
               he has taken a state office

      2. * Ephraim Kirby. Supervisor Con. vice J. Chester. removed

      3.   George W. Erving. Consul Lond. vice   Williams,
               delinquent in havg never rendd any acct.

      8.   Stephen Cathalan. Com. Agt. Marseilles a restoration, vice
               Wm. Lee a midnight appmt

      9.   Wm. Buchanan. Maryld. Com. Agt. I. of France & Bourbon.
               vice George Stacey a midnight appmt

          * David Gelstone. Collectr. N.Y. vice Joshua Sands.

           John S. Sherbourne. Atty distr. N.H. vice Edwd. St. Loe
               Livermore a midnight appointment

13. Edward Darrell. Commr. direct tax S.C. vacant
15. Malachi Jones. Surveyor of Curratuck. vacant
    Robert Smith. Maryld. Sec. Navy vice Benjamin Stoddart resigned.
16. Danl. Clarke. Consul N. Orleans.
    Andrew Pickens Commr. cum aliis for Chocktaws &c
    Andrew Moore. Marshal. W. distr. Virga. qu. commn. dated. Aug. 8. vice Robt. Grattan a midnight appmt
21.⁴ Theodore Peters. Vice Com. Agt. Bordeaux. new.
    Lewis F. Taney. Com. Agt. Ostend. vice John Mitchel a midnight appmt
27. * Enoch Parsons Marsh. Conn vice⁵
    George Blake. Atty distr. Mass. vice Harrison Gray Otis a midnight appmt
   * Silas Lee. Atty distr. Maine vice Davis. made a state judge.
29. Jacob Lewis. Consul Calcutta. Bengal
         Forbes. Consul Hambg vice   Pitcairn⁶
Aug. 4. Jonas Clarke. Inspector port of Kennebunk. left vacant
31. Mount Edwd. Chisman. Collector & Inspector port of Hampton vice Wm. Kirby   removd. for delinqency in money matters
    John Graham. Kentucky. Sec. legn. Madrid. new
Sep. 10. Thos. Worthington. Inspector of rev. for the survey formg. the N.W. distr. new.
15. Thos. de Mattos Johnson. Collectr. distr. Savanna vice Powell delinquent as havg never rendd an account.
Oct. 3. Wm. Goforth & John Reiley Commrs. for Symmes's contracts. left vacant
7. John Oakley. Collectr. & Inspectr. Geo. T. vice Jas M. Lingan resigned
16. William Patterson. N.Y. Com. Agent Lorient vice Turell Tufts a midnight appmt.
17. Charles D. Coxe. Comml. Agent. Dunkirk. vice James H. Hooe a midnight appmt
22. William Stephens. Judge of the district court of Georgia
Nov. 4. William R. Davie Commr. with Tuscaroras on treaty with N. Carolina.
7. Thos. T. Gantt. Coml. agent. Nantz. vice John Jones Waldo. a midnight appmt.
9. Bartholomew Dandridge. Comml. Agent Port Republicain.
14. Josiah Hook Collector of Penobscot vice Jarvis vice Lee antirevolutionary tory & delinquent
18. Isaac Smith Collector for Cherrystone vice Nathaniel Wilkins removed for delinquency
    James Alger. Commr. loans for Georgia vice Thomas Wylly decd.
19. James Nicholson. Commr. loans N. York vice   Clarkson resigned
24. Thomas Hewes. Consul for port of Batavia in isld. of Java.
28. Gideon Granger P. M. Genl. vice   Habersham resigned

30. Thomas Tudor Tucker. Treasurer vice   Meredith resigned
         Commr. of the direct tax for S.C.

Dec. 22. Joseph Wilcox. Marshl. Connect. vice   time expired
         omitted by me at their proper dates[7]
         Walter Jones junr. of Columbia. Atty. of district of Potomac.
         left vacant
         Henry Potter of N.C. judge of 5th. circuit vice John
         Sitgreaves declined.
         John Heard Marshal of N. Jersey. vice Thomas Lowry.
         removed on general principle
         Samuel Osgood Supervisor of New York. vice Nichs. Fish.
         removed. delinquent in accnt
         David Duncan of N.W.T. collector for district of Michilli-
         makinac. new. left vacant
         Alexander Wolcott. Collector for the district of Middleton
         vice Chauncey Whittlesey removed
         Joseph Yznardi Consul at Cadiz. restored vice Henry Preble
         a midnight nomination.
         William Chribbs of Indiana Inspector & Collector for
         district of Massac. vice Irwin declined.

1802.
Jan.   8. James Madison, A. Gallatin, Levi Lincoln Commrs. to treat
         with those of Georgia.
     21. Wm. Foster junr.   Commercl. agent. Morlaix nominated by
         mr Adams & approved by Senate
     29. John Beckley librarian. new
Feb. 19. Timothy Bloodworth Collector for the district of
         Wilmington vice Griffith Mc.rae dead
     22. Bartholomew Dandridge. Com. Agent at Port republ. in St.
         Domingo.
     23. Joseph Barnes. Consul in the island of Sicily. new
         George Washington Mc.elroy. Consul for Oratava in
         Teneriffe. of Pensva. new
         John M. Forbes of Mass. Consul at Hamburg vice   Pitcairn
         Robert Young of Columbia. Consul for Havana in Cuba.
         John Appleton of Massachusetts. Com. Agent at Calais. new
         William Jarvis of Massachusetts. Consul at Lisbon vice John
         Bulkeley
         William Riggin of Maryld. Consul at Trieste. new
         John Cross junr. of R.I. Surveyor for the port of
         Pawcatuck in R.I. vice George Stillman removd.
         John Slocum of R.I. Surveyor for the port of Newport in R.I.
         vice Daniel Lyman removd.
         Henry Molier of Maryld. Consul at Corunna. new
     25. James Leander Cathcart Consul Genl. at Algiers vice
         Obrien resigned[8]
     15. John Taylor Commr. to hold convention between N.Y. &
         St. Regis Indians

11.   Wm. P. Gardner Consul at Essequibo & Demarara

Mar. 11.   John Taylor Commr. to hold convention between N.Y. &
          6 nations

Apr.   8.   Henry Potter of N. Carola judge of District court of N.C.

     20.   Nathaniel Folsome of N.H. Naval officer for the
          district of Portsmouth v E. S. L. Livermore. removd.

          Andrew Lyle of N.J. surveyor for the port of
            New Brunswick v. Anth. W. White resigned

          Benjamin Wall marshal of Georgia. vice Ambrose
            Gordon. removd. on the genl principle respectg.
            marshals & Attornies

          David Brydie Mitchell Atty for district of Georgia.
            vice   Woodruff removed on same genl. principle

          Edward Croft. Commr. of direct tax in S. Carola.

end of session

May   14.   Michael Mc.lary N.H. marshal of New Hampshire district.
            vice Bradbury Cilley. time expired

          Walter Nichols of R.I. Naval officer for district of Newport.
            vice Robert Crook decd.

          Silas Crane of N. Jersey Collector for district of Little egg
            harbour N.J. vice Wm. Watson removd for absence &
            neglect of his office

          John Heard of N.J. Collector for district of Perth Amboy. vice
            Daniel Marsh drowned

          Benjamin Cheney N.C. Surveyor of the port of Beaufort. new

          James L. Shannonhouse N.C. Surveyor for the port of New-
            begun creek. v Frederic B. Sawyer removd from his
            residence

          Edward Harris N.C. judge of circuit court of US. for
            5th. circuit.

          David Duncan of Indiana territy. Inspector of revenue
            for port of Michillimakinac. new

          Thomas Worthington of N.W. territory. Supervisor
            in the N.W. district. new

MS (DLC: TJ Papers, 186:33095-6); entirely in TJ's hand; first section of a list that continues at 3 June 1802 and extends to 23 Feb. 1809; with notation "refused" and opening brackets added by TJ at a later date; asterisks also added at later sitting, probably when compiling other lists; TJ also added, while compiling another list, numbers and check marks in pencil in the left margin, which have not been reproduced here.

[1] Preceding five words interlined in place of "removed."

[2] TJ here canceled "promoted" and then "appd judge."

[3] Entry interlined.

[4] TJ here canceled "Gantt. Com. Agt. Nantes" and entered it at 7 Nov.

[5] Entry later canceled.

[6] Entry interlined.

[7] TJ wrote this phrase in left margin perpendicular to the entries from "Walter Jones" to the rule below.

[8] Entry interlined.

Appendix II

Notations by Jefferson on Senate Documents

E D I T O R I A L   N O T E

As vice president of the United States, Jefferson's primary responsibility was to preside over the Senate (see Vol. 29:633) and rule on procedural issues. Jefferson did not take an active legislative role in the Senate's proceedings, but he often did make notes on documents that came before that body. These markings, which reflect less his own thought or opinion than his recording of the deliberations of the senators, give some indication of Jefferson's involvement in day-to-day proceedings of the Senate. Some documents are entirely in Jefferson's hand, as in the case of the order of 20 Feb. "for return of sundry Papers to the President of the U.S. relative to the late negotiation with France" (MS in DNA: RG 46, Senate Records, 6th Cong., 2d sess.).

Between 17 Feb., when Jefferson learned of his election as president, and 28 Feb., when he delivered his farewell address to the Senate, that body considered bills pertaining mostly to the transition from one administration to another, including military, naval, and government appropriations for the year, relief bills, and such housekeeping matters as procuring a clock for their chamber. The Senate also had for its consideration the nominations for appointments submitted by John Adams in the final days of his administration. Because these nominations were made after Adams had learned that he would no longer be president, they were of particular interest to Jefferson. For this reason, the Editors record Jefferson's notations on them.

The Senate also resolved on 18 Feb. that Aaron Burr be notified of the results of the election and his status as vice president elect. Jefferson canceled the original wording that the candidates had "each 73 votes" and revised it to state more precisely that the candidates had "a majority of the votes of the electors & an equal number of votes," in consequence of which, the House of Representatives selected the president (MS in DNA: RG 46, Senate Records, 6th Cong., 2d sess.).

As he did in 1798 (Vol. 30:121), Jefferson occasionally recorded an emendation to the Rough Journal of the Senate. On 26 Feb. 1801 he drafted an emendation regarding the report of the committee on House amendments to the bill on the District of Columbia: "to insert between 13th & [14th] sect. as numbd in amdmt. of H. of R. disagree by Y. & N." (in Jefferson's hand with his emendation and notation; printed in JS, 3:132). Jefferson's emendation appears on the verso of a page in the journal that included a motion that Georgetown and Alexandria flour and tobacco inspectors continue to discharge their duties governed by the same compensation, rules, and penalties as in their respective states. The entire motion, which included three additional jurisdictional matters about the District of Columbia, was defeated with a 16 to 12 vote.

The following list enumerates bills, motions, committee reports, petitions, and nominations that came before the Sixth Congress during the second session and received some written comment by the vice president, who took his seat as presiding officer on 28 Nov. 1800 (JS, 3:110). The Editors have grouped Jefferson's markings on the documents into three categories: (1) "emendation" indicates that Jefferson recorded changes to a bill or motion, from a word or two to several sentences, often incorporating amendments passed; (2) "notation" means that information on action taken by the Senate appears in Jefferson's hand, most often in a brief entry such as "disagreed," "agreed," or "consent" in the margin of the text of the document; (3) "endorsement" indicates that Jefferson provided one or more entries in the docketing or clerical record of the history of the document. On the documents listed below, Jefferson often provided the title as well as all of the entries on the panel. This was the case with the bill concerning the relief of Arnold Henry Dohrman or his legal representatives, where Jefferson recorded the action taken by the Senate between 24 and 26 Feb. 1801, three entries in all.

The endorsement panel provides inclusive dates for a document; in the absence of such endorsements we have derived the dates from the printed *Journal of the Senate* and they are supplied in brackets. If the document marked by Jefferson was a motion or bill printed for the Senate's consideration, that fact is also noted in the description below. Motions are rendered as they appear on the endorsement panel unless clarification requires substituting the language of the motion itself.

All the documents listed below are from Senate Records, DNA: RG 46, 6th Cong., 2d sess., from 17 to 28 Feb. 1801.

Motion, for a joint committee to report further accommodation of President of the United States, 18 Feb. 1801; endorsement by TJ. Printed in JS, 3:127.

Notification to the Vice President elect, of his election, 18 Feb. 1801; notation and emendations by TJ. Printed in JS, 3:127-8.

Message of the President nominating Elizur Goodrich to office, 18-19 Feb. 1801; endorsement by TJ. Printed in JEP, 1:382.

Message of the President nominating John Lowell and others to office, 18-19 Feb. 1801; notations and endorsement by TJ. Printed in JEP, 1:381.

Message of the President nominating Henry Prebble and others to office, 18-23 Feb. 1801; notations and endorsement by TJ. Printed in JEP, 1:381-2.

Bill Making appropriations for the support of Government for the year One Thousand Eight Hundred and One, 20 Feb. 1801; printed; notation in pencil and endorsement by TJ.

Ordered, that the bill, entitled "An Act to amend the act, intituled, 'An Act to provide for the valuation of lands and dwelling houses, and the enumeration of Slaves within the United States,' and to repeal the Act, intituled 'An Act to enlarge the powers of the Surveyors of the revenue,'["] be referred to Mr. Ross, Mr. Hillhouse and Mr. Nicholas, to consider and report thereon, [20 Feb. 1801]; notation by TJ.

Order of Senate for return of sundry Papers to the President of the U.S. relative to the late negotiation with France, 20 Feb. 1801; entirely in TJ's hand; notation by TJ. Variant text printed in JEP, 1:383.

Bill for the relief of Nathaniel Holmes, 20-24 Feb. 1801; printed; endorsement by TJ.

Bill To amend the act, entitled "An act to provide for the valuation of lands and dwelling-houses, and the enumeration of slaves within the United States," and to repeal the act, entitled "An act to enlarge the powers of the surveyors of the revenue," 20-25 Feb. 1801; printed; emendation and endorsement by TJ.

Bill Making appropriations for the Military Establishment of the United States, for the year One Thousand Eight Hundred and One, 20-27 Feb. 1801; printed; endorsement by TJ.

Amendments reported by the Committee to whom was referred the Bill, entitled "An Act giving a right of pre-emption to certain persons who have contracted with John C. Symmes, or his associates, for lands lying between the Miami rivers, in the territory of the United States, north-west of the Ohio," 23 Feb. 1801; printed; notations and emendation by TJ.

Bill for the relief of William Arnold, 23 Feb. 1801; endorsement by TJ. Printed copy, 23-24 Feb. 1801; endorsement by TJ.

Message of the President nominating Thomas Bee and others to office, 23 Feb. 1801; notations and endorsement by TJ. Printed in JEP, 1:383-4.

Bill Directing the mode of estimating certain foreign coins and currencies, and of making out invoices in certain cases, 23-27 Feb. 1801; printed; emendation and endorsement by TJ.

Message of the President nominating Elijah Paine and others to office, 24 Feb. 1801; notations and endorsement by TJ. Printed in JEP, 1:384-5.

Mr Wells's motion respecting State ballances, 24 Feb. 1801; notation and emendation by TJ. Printed in JS, 3:130.

House consideration of the bill, sent from the Senate, entitled "An Act concerning the district of Columbia," 24 Feb. 1801; printed; notations by TJ.

Bill For the relief of Arnold Henry Dohrman, or his legal representatives, 24-26 Feb. 1801; printed; endorsement by TJ.

Bill Making appropriations for the Navy of the United States, for the year one thousand eight hundred and one, 24-28 Feb. 1801; printed; endorsement by TJ.

Motion, to procure a clock for the use of the Senate, 25 Feb. 1801; notation by TJ. Printed in JS, 3:131.

Committee Report on amendments to a bill, entitled "An act to add to the district of Massac on the Ohio, and to discontinue the districts of Louisville in the state of Kentucky, and Palmyra in the state of Tennessee, and therein to amend the act, entitled "An act to regulate the collection of duties on imports and tonnage," 25 Feb. 1801; printed; notations and emendation by TJ.

Bill Declaring the consent of Congress to an act of the state of Maryland, passed the twenty-eighth of December, one thousand seven hundred and ninety-three, for the appointment of a health officer, 25-26 Feb. 1801; printed; endorsement by TJ.

Message of the President nominating Louis C. Baily and others to office, 25-26 Feb. 1801, notations and endorsement by TJ. Printed in JEP, 1:385, 386.

Message of the President nominating Philip Barton Key and Chas. Magill, to office, 25-26 Feb. 1801; notations and endorsement by TJ. Printed in JEP, 1:385, 386.

Bill Further to alter and to establish certain Post-roads, 25-27 Feb. 1801; printed; emendation and endorsement by TJ.

Bill Supplementary to an act, entitled, "An act to divide the territory of the United States north-west of the Ohio, into two separate governments," 25-27 Feb. 1801; printed; emendation and endorsement by TJ.

Bill to prohibit the Secretary of the Navy from carrying on the business of Trade Commerce or Navigation, 25 Feb. 1801; endorsement by TJ. Printed copy, 25 Feb.-3 Mch. 1801; endorsement by TJ.

APPENDIX II

Message of the President nominating Wm. Tilghman to office, 26-27 Feb. 1801; endorsement by TJ. Printed in JEP, 1:386, 389.

Memorial of Philip Sloan, 27 Feb. 1801; endorsement by TJ.

Memorial of Thos. Claxton and Thos. Dunn, 27 Feb. 1801; endorsement by TJ.

Report of the Committee to whom was referred the bill, further to alter and to establish certain post roads, 27 Feb. 1801; printed; notations and emendations in pencil by TJ.

Appendix III

Letters Not Printed In Full

EDITORIAL NOTE

In keeping with the editorial method established for this edition, the chronological series includes "in one form or another every available letter known to have been written by or to Thomas Jefferson" (Vol. 1:xv). Beginning with Volume 33, when Jefferson's substantial presidential correspondence necessitates greater selectivity, the Editors will summarize or briefly describe in annotation a larger proportion of letters than has been their practice in recent volumes. The situation is like that which our predecessors faced as they edited Jefferson's papers from his tenure as governor of Virginia or secretary of state. The present Editors will follow their methods, but will also present in an appendix a list of the letters falling within the period covered by the volume that are not printed in full. Arranged in chronological order, the list provides for each letter the correspondent, date, and location in the volume where it is noted. Among the letters to Jefferson that will not be printed in full are brief letters of transmittal, multiple testimonials recommending a particular candidate for office, repetitive letters from a candidate seeking a post, and official correspondence that he saw in only a cursory way. While letters written by Jefferson typically are printed in full, in some instances the brevity and routine nature of his reply or the near illegibility of an especially blurred press copy, when it is the only extant text, suggest the advantages of noting the letter in annotation.

Using the list in this appendix, the table of contents, and Appendix IV (correspondence not found but recorded in Jefferson's Summary Journal of Letters), readers will be able to reconstruct Jefferson's chronological epistolary record for 17 Feb.-30 Apr. 1801. Letters that fall outside of this chronological span but are most usefully discussed in annotation here, will be listed in their chronological place in an appendix to a future volume.

To George Jefferson, 19 Feb. Noted at TJ to Jefferson, 21 Feb.
From Samuel Maclay, 24 Feb. Noted at Samuel Bryan to TJ, 26 Feb.
From Thomas Mendenhall, 25 Feb. Noted at Mendenhall to TJ, 27 Apr.
From William Reed, 26 Feb. Noted at Samuel Bryan to TJ, 26 Feb.
From Aaron Kitchell and John Condit, 28 Feb. Noted at James Linn to TJ, 24 Mch.
From Thomas Whitelaw, 28 Feb. Noted at TJ to Whitelaw, 19 Feb.
From Walter Bowie, 2 Mch. Noted at John W. Pratt to TJ, 6 Mch.
From Gabriel Duvall, 2 Mch. Noted at John W. Pratt to TJ, 6 Mch.
To Theodore Sedgwick, 2 Mch. Noted at TJ to James Hillhouse, 2 Mch.
From Richard Sprigg, Jr., 2 Mch. Noted at John W. Pratt to TJ, 6 Mch.
From Thomas Duckett, 3 Mch. Noted at John W. Pratt to TJ, 6 Mch.
From Thomas Law and others, 3 Mch. Noted at TJ to Samuel Hanson, 17 Mch.
To John Marshall, 4 Mch. Noted at Marshall to TJ, 2 Mch.
From John Marshall, 4 Mch. Noted at Marshall to TJ, 2 Mch.

From Robert H. Rose and others, 4 Mch. Noted at Joseph Barnes to TJ, 10 Apr.

From William Jernigan and others, 5 Mch. Noted at William Rose to TJ, 16 June.

From John T. Mason, 5 Mch. Noted at John W. Pratt to TJ, 6 Mch.

From Commissioned Officers of the Militia Legion of Philadelphia, 5 Mch. Noted at John Smith to TJ, 11 Mch.

From Philadelphia Committee of Arrangements and Correspondence, 5 Mch. Noted at John Smith to TJ, 11 Mch.

From Osborn Sprigg, 5 Mch. Noted at John W. Pratt to TJ, 6 Mch.

From Tarleton Bates, 6 Mch. Noted at TJ to Bates, [ca. 28 Feb.].

From William Coats and others, 7 Mch. Noted at John Smith to TJ, 11 Mch.

From John Dawson, 7 Mch. Noted at TJ to Dawson, 12 Mch.

To William Heath, 8 Mch. Noted at Heath to TJ, 25 Feb.

From Samuel J. Cabell, [ca. 10 Mch.]. Noted at Edmund Custis to TJ, 15 Mch.

From David Austin, 11 Mch. Noted at Austin to TJ, 9 Mch.

To Charles Copland, 11 Mch. Noted at Copland to TJ, 15 Mch.

From John Fleming, 11 Mch. Noted at John Gardiner to TJ, 25 Feb.

From Gabriel Duvall, 12 Mch. Noted at John F. Mercer to TJ, 8 Mch.

To Francis Peyton, 12 Mch. Noted at Peyton to TJ, 13 Mch.

From Nathaniel W. Price, 12 Mch. Noted at John Gardiner to TJ, 25 Feb.

From Edward Gantt and others, 14 Mch. Noted at Richard Parrott to TJ, 14 Mch.

From Reading, Pennsylvania, Citizens, 14 Mch. Noted at John Smith to TJ, 11 Mch.

To Jonathan Williams, 14 Mch. Noted at Williams to TJ, 7 Mch.

From John Fowler, 15 Mch. Noted at Appendix I, List 1.

From David Austin, 16 Mch. Noted at Austin to TJ, 15 Mch.

From Amariah Frost, 16 Mch. Noted at TJ to Samuel Hanson, 17 Mch.

From William Rhodes and others, [ca. 16 Mch.]. Noted at TJ to Samuel Hanson, 17 Mch.

From William Brent, 17 Mch. Noted at Brent to TJ, 11 Mch.

To Peyton Short, 18 Mch. Noted at TJ to William Short, 17 Mch.

To Carlos Martinez de Irujo, 19 Mch. Noted at TJ to Irujo, 24 Mch.

From Ralph Bennet Forbes, 20 Mch. Noted at Theodore Foster to TJ, 23 Mch.

To William Kilty, 20 Mch. Noted at Kilty to TJ, 23 Mch.

From Samuel L. Mitchill, 21 Mch. Noted at Providence Citizens to TJ, 5 Mch.

From David Brown, 23 Mch. Noted at Pardon for Brown, 12 Mch.

From Peter Legaux, 25 Mch. Noted at TJ to Legaux, 24 Mch.

From James C. Mountflorence, 26 Mch. Noted at Joseph Allen Smith to TJ, 22 Mch.

To Samuel L. Mitchill, 27 Mch. Noted at TJ to Providence Citizens, 27 Mch.

To the District of Columbia Commissioners, 30 Mch. Noted at Commissioners to TJ, 28 Mch.

From Samuel Bootes, 1 Apr. Noted at John Gardiner to TJ, 25 Feb.

From Benjamin Rawlings, 3 Apr. Noted at Nathaniel Anderson to TJ, 13 Mch.

From Ira Allen, 4 Apr. Noted at Matthew Lyon to TJ, 4 Apr.

From Francis Hoskins, 6 Apr. Noted at John Gardiner to TJ, 25 Feb.

From George Helmbold, 7 Apr. Noted at Helmbold to TJ, 3 Apr.
From Ralph Mather, 7 Apr. Noted at Mather to TJ, 27 Mch.
From Pierce Butler, 8 Apr. Noted at John Hall to TJ, 7 Mch.
From Thomas Newton, 8 Apr. Noted at Newton to TJ, 8 Apr.
From Thomas Newton, 8 Apr. Noted at Newton to TJ, 8 Apr.
To William Short, 10 Apr. Noted at TJ to Rufus King, 10 Apr.
To Fulwar Skipwith, 10 Apr. Noted at TJ to Rufus King, 10 Apr.
From Peter Legaux, 12 Apr. Noted at TJ to Legaux to TJ, 24 Mch.
From Charles Webb, 12 Apr. Noted at Webb to TJ, 16 June.
From John Minor, 13 Apr. Noted at John F. Gaullier, 14 May.
To Richard Hanson, 17 Apr. Noted at TJ to George Jefferson, 17 Apr.
From Edward Dowse, 28 Apr. Noted at Dowse to TJ, 12 May.
From Daniel Trump, 28 Apr. Noted at Trump to TJ, 6 May.
From James Monroe, 30 Apr. Noted at Monroe to TJ, 29 Apr.
From Samuel Smith, 30 Apr. Noted at Amos Windship to TJ, 2 May.
From Northumberland County, Pennsylvania, Citizens, undated. Noted at
    John Smith to TJ, 11 Mch.

Appendix IV

Letters Not Found

EDITORIAL NOTE

This appendix lists chronologically letters written by and to Jefferson during the period covered by this volume for which no text is known to survive. Jefferson's Summary Journal of Letters and other sources provide a record of the missing documents. For incoming letters, Jefferson typically recorded in SJL the date that the letter was sent and the date on which he received it. He sometimes included the location from which it was dispatched and an abbreviated notation indicating the government department to which it pertained: "N" for Navy, "P" for the Postmaster General's Office, "S" for State, "T" for Treasury, and "W" for War. "Off." designated a person seeking office.

From John Barnes, 18 Feb.; received 18 Feb.
To James Dinsmore, 18 Feb.
To Gabriel Lilly, 18 Feb.
From John Barnes, 20 Feb.; received 20 Feb.
From Edmund Jenings, 21 Feb.; received 6 May from London.
From John H. Craven, 22 Feb.; received 6 Mch.
From James Monroe, 22 Feb.; received 25 Mch.; notation: "Forbes."
From Gerard Banks, 24 Feb.; received 4 Mch. from Louisa County, Virginia.
From Richard Brent, 24 Feb.; received 26 Feb. from Dumfries.
To Bowling Clark, 24 Feb.
From Andrew Torborn, 24 Feb.; received 6 Mch. from City Point.
From William Barton, 27 Feb.; received 7 Mch. from Lancaster.
From Edward Jones, 28 Feb.; received 28 Feb.
From George Wythe, Mch.; received 16 Apr.
From Pierre Samuel Du Pont de Nemours, 1 Mch.; received 6 Mch. from New York; notation: "W."
From Baron de Bertholf de Beelen, 2 Mch.; received 24 Mch. from Philadelphia.
From George Thatcher, Henry Dearborn, and Joseph B. Varnum, 4 Mch.; received 8 Mch. from Washington.
From Andrew Ellicott, 5 Mch.; received 7 Mch. from Philadephia; notation: "T."
From Matthew Lyon, 5 Mch.; received 6 Mch. from Washington.
From Hezekiah Richardson, 5 Mch.; received 18 Mch. from Townsend, Massachusetts.
From Gabriel Lilly; received 6 Mch.
From Anonymous; received 7 Mch.; notation: "[arms Harp's ferry.] W."
To Elizabeth House Trist, 7 Mch.
From Joseph Fenwick, 8 Mch.; received 9 Mch. from Georgetown.
From Thomas Nelson, 8 Mch.; received 14 Mch. from "York."
From Alexandre Charles Louis d'Ambrugeac, 9 Mch.; received 9 Mch.; notation: "Memoire."
From Matthew Lyon, 11 Mch.; received 15 Mch. from Washington.
From John Divine, 12 Mch.; received 25 Mch. from New York.

From George Franck, 12 Mch.; received 16 Mch. from Philadelphia.
From Long Kennedy, 12 Mch.; received 13 Mch. from Baltimore.
To William Brent, 13 Mch.
From William Thornton, 13 Mch.; received 18 Mch. from Washington.
From John Hilts, 16 Mch.; received 20 Mch. from Philadelphia; notation: "W."
From Thomas Tudor Tucker, 18 Mch.; received 21 Mch. from Philadelphia.
To Madame de Corny, 19 Mch.
From William Lambert, 20 Mch.; received 25 Mch. from Richmond.
To Elizabeth House Trist, 24 Mch.
From Philip Wilson, 25 Mch.; received 28 Mch. from Philadelphia.
From Jones & Leib, 28 Mch.; received 9 Apr.; notation: "Off."
To Henry Sheaff, 29 Mch.
From Antonio Dugnani, 30 Mch.; received 3 Sep. from Milan.
To Edmund Randolph, 30 Mch.; notation: "Johnson's examn."
To Francis Peyton, 31 Mch.
From William Gardner, 1 Apr.; received 24 Apr. from Portsmouth.
From Nathaniel Irish, 2 Apr.; received 16 Apr. from Pittsburg; notation: "Off. P."
From Alexander Spotswood, 2 Apr.; received 16 Apr. from Fredericksburg; notation: "Off. N."
From James Bringhurst, 3 Apr.; received 16 Apr. from Philadelphia; notation: "Off. P."
From John Moody, 5 Apr.; received 16 Apr. from Richmond; notation: "Off."
From Charles Pinckney, 6 Apr.; received 6 May; notation: "Off."
To Joseph Moran, 8 Apr.
From John Bowyer, 9 Apr.; received 24 Apr. from Rockbridge; notation: "Off."
From Bowling Clark, 9 Apr.; received 13 Apr.
From Edmund Randolph, 9 Apr.; received 17 Apr.
From Ard Welton, 9 Apr.; received 24 Apr. from Waterbury.
From William Wirt, 9 Apr.; received 15 Apr. from Staunton; notation: "Off."
From Elisha Babcock, 10 Apr.; received 24 Apr.
From Edward Livingston, 10 Apr.; received 24 Apr. from New York.; notation: "Off."
To General Samuel Smith, 10 Apr.
To James Traquair, 10 Apr.
To John Barnes, 11 Apr.; notation: "copper, tools &c."
From Henry Duke, 12 Apr.; received 24 Apr. from Hanover.
From John Mullowny, 12 Apr.; received 2 May from the ship *Ganges* at Basse Terre; notation: "N." Recorded in SJL as a letter from "Thos." Mullowny.
From Joseph Yznardi, Sr., 14 Apr.; received 24 Apr. from Georgetown; notation: "S."
From Samuel Lewis, Sr., 15 Apr.; received 6 May from Philadelphia; notation: "W." TJ drew a brace connecting this letter's entry with that of a letter by Thomas Procter of 18 Apr. received the same day.
To Bowling Clark, 18 Apr.
From Thomas Procter, 18 Apr.; received 6 May from Philadelphia; notation: "W." TJ drew a brace connecting this letter's entry with that of a letter by Samuel Lewis, Sr., of 15 Apr. received the same day.
From James Traquair, 18 Apr.; received 6 May.

From Bishop James Madison, 19 Apr.; received 6 May from Williamsburg.
From Everard Meade, 20 Apr.; received 24 Apr. from Amelia; notation: "Off."
From Henry Sheaff, 20 Apr.; received 6 May.
From Comte de Grandcour, 21 Apr.; received 29 June 1801 from Grandcour near Bern, Switzerland.
From William Bache; received 22 Apr.
From Elisha Brown, 24 Apr.; received 2 May; notation: "Foster R.I.   W."
From Aaron Burr, 24 Apr.; received 29 Apr. from New York; notation: "Off."
From Uriah M. Gregory, 24 Apr.; received 11 May from Derby.
From George Mitchel, 24 Apr.; received 6 May from Staunton.
To Joseph Moran, 24 Apr.
From John Strode, 25 Apr.; received 4 May; notation: "N."
From Elijah Boardman, 28 Apr.; received 8 May from New Milford; notation: "W."
From Andrew Ellicott, 28 Apr.; received 30 Apr.
From Charles Louis Clérisseau, 29 Apr.; received 10 Sep. from Paris.
From Robert Rives, 29 Apr.; received 6 May from Warminster.
From James Traquair, 30 Apr.; received 2 May from Philadelphia.

INDEX

"A.B." (pseudonym): letter from, 522-3; recommends Tucker, 522-3

Abbess, A Romance (William Henry Ireland), 578, 579n

Abbeville, France, 468

Aborn, Thomas, 173n, 664, 667, 676

Academy of Natural Sciences of Philadelphia, 327n

Ackerman, Abraham, 660-1

Adams, Abigail, xi, 665

Adams, Abijah, 666

Adams, Charles, 426

Adams, Elizabeth Wells, 639

ADAMS, JOHN: letters to, 12, 213; letters from, 23-4, 426

Minister to Great Britain
receives visitors, 83n

Personal Affairs
name respected across Europe, 359; death of son, 426

President
late-term appointments, ix, 100, 127, 167, 172-3, 230n, 231n, 235n, 245, 250n, 271n, 367, 368n, 411, 412-13n, 413-14, 428, 436-7, 452n, 461, 489, 491, 493, 555, 643n, 663, 668, 671-2, 674-8, 681-4; leaves Washington, xi, 153, 367; makes appointments, 3n, 15, 16, 46n, 52, 120n, 124n, 165n, 169-70, 171-2, 196, 203n, 206n, 210, 211n, 226n, 239-40, 268n, 376, 378, 380n, 390, 419, 420n, 447n, 448n, 481n, 521, 553n, 556, 593n, 604, 664, 667, 671, 675, 678; criticism of, 8, 47, 69n, 367, 392; reelection of, supported, 11n, 313; informed of election results, 12, 25n; calls Senate into session, 16, 29; leaves horses and carriages for TJ, 23; and President's House accounts, 23-4n, 153n; and forged letter to Cushing, 48n; addresses to, from state legislatures, 69n, 558; and Indian affairs, 70, 176; bullied by Federalists, 74; pro-British, anti-French, 84-5; threat to Constitutional rights, 130, 138; accused of nepotism, 159, 465; wants Americans in consular posts, 169-70, 171; removals by, 183, 184n, 437, 461, 669, 675; patent

applications to, 214n; applications to, for appointments, 225n, 434, 462, 668n; petitions to, for pardons, 252n, 318; and Spain, 269n, 384; removal from office an act of God, 295; instructions to envoys to France, 349n; and Tripoli, 364n; replies to addresses on XYZ affair, 393, 394n; and S. Nicholson, 472-4; and D.C. development, 480, 575n; *Olive Branch* affair, 534-5, 536n; and Priestley, 567; treaty with Tunis, 592n; and Cowper, 606; and postal service abuses, 655; recommends aspirants to office, 666

Relations with Jefferson
confusion of mail, xi, 213, 303; TJ's views toward Adams, 16, 115, 393; renewal of friendship, 395n

Adams, Samuel: letter to, 487-8; letter from, 638-9; influence on TJ's inaugural address, viii, 138, 486-7; admiration for, 60, 213; congratulates TJ, 638-9

Adams, Samuel (N.H.), 670

Adams, Thomas, 27

Addington, Henry, 90n

Addison, Alexander, 5

Addison, Joseph, 630

Addison, Thomas, 674

"Address and Reasons of Dissent of the Minority of the Convention of the State of Pennsylvania to their Constituents" (Samuel Bryan), 71, 73n

adultery, 11, 12n

Aeneid (Virgil), 269n

agriculture: straw-cutting machines, 31; encouraged by repeal of taxes, 85; societies for promoting, 200; improvements to, 214; Mazzei's interest in, 328; viticulture, 431n; pamphlets on, 597, 598n. *See also* tobacco

Albany, N.Y.: marshal for, 52, 331-2n, 572, 573n, 671, 676; U.S. attorney for, 52; postmaster, 192, 194n; R. R. Livingston at, 255; newspapers, 572; surveyor and inspector at, 672

Albany Register, 572, 573n

Albemarle Co., Va.: plantations in, 51n, 241n; schools, 51n; TJ's election celebrated at, 273; legislators, 642n

INDEX

Clarke, Caleb: letter from, 194-5; congratulates TJ, 194; identified, 195n
Clarkson, Matthew, 670, 677
Clarkson, William & Julius, 603, 640
Claxton, Thomas: letter from, 153; takes possession of President's House, 153; identified, 153n; memorial of, 684
Clay, Joseph (Pa.), 358n
Clay, Joseph, Jr. (Ga.), 52, 593, 596
Clay, Matthew, 49
Clérisseau, Charles Louis: letter from cited, 691
clerks: applications for clerkships, 64, 342-3, 356n; duties of, in State Department, 512-13
Clinton, George, 11, 64n, 212n, 419
clocks: manufacture of, 337n, 374-5; for Senate chamber, 681, 683
cloth: for military, 467-8, 469n; linen, 468; sail, 468; cassimere, 503; prices, 503
clover seed, 158, 203
Clymer, George, 261
Coalter, John, 555, 556n, 659
Coats, William: recommends J. Smith, 246n, 247n; letter from cited, 247n, 686
Cobbett, William: as P. Porcupine, 262, 656
Cochran, Charles Burnham: removal of, sought, 331, 332n, 333, 513, 657
Cochran, Robert (N.C.), 157, 319n
Cochran, Robert E. (S.C.), 332n
Cocke, Buller, 584
Cocke, William: letters from, 69-70, 174-5; seeks Cherokee cessions, x, 69-70, 174-5; as reference, 341
Coffin, Elisha, 652n
Cogswell, Thomas: letter from, 365-6; congratulates TJ, 365-6; identified, 366n
Colaud, Claude Sylvestre, 406n
Cole, Levy P., 559n
Coles, Mr., 290
Coligni family, 285
Colle (Mazzei's Va. estate), 329
Collot, Georges Henri Victor, 404, 406n
Colonna, Fabio, 497, 498n
Columbia, Bank of (Georgetown), 478
Columbia, S.C.: congratulatory address from, 194-5, 621; thanked by TJ, 409
Columbia Manufacturing Company (Washington, D.C.), 242n
Columbian Advertiser (Alexandria), 362n

Columbian Inn (Georgetown), 415n
Columbianum, 105n
Columbus, Christopher, 397
Commercial Advertiser (New York), 204n
Committee of Correspondence (New York), 212n
Common Sense (Thomas Paine), 185
Compact Maritime (Thomas Paine), 185, 241
Comte, Benjamin, 318
Condit, John: recommends aspirants for office, 183, 432; letter from cited, 432n, 685
Congregational Church, 228n, 353n

Congress, U.S.

Confederation
proposed treaty with Spain, 622, 623n

Continental
treatment of prisoners of war, 127-8n; naval affairs, 256n; supplies purchased by, 538n

House of Representatives
letter to, 25-6; elects TJ president, xlv, 3, 12n, 16-17, 20, 54, 134, 241, 383, 391, 414, 432n, 442, 681; meets in Senate chamber, xlvi; conduct of Federalists in, criticized, 16, 21, 37-8, 100, 185, 194, 442, 583-4, 588; thanked by TJ, 25, 54; clerks, 25n; committees, 25n, 54, 100, 427n; journal of, 54; speaker, 91, 118n, 321n; chaplains, 104n; and TJ's inauguration, 118n, 128-9, 134-5; doorkeeper, 153n

Legislation
Mine and Metal Company, 9-10; president's household, 23-4n, 153n; Indian cessions, 70, 174, 175-8; monument for Washington, 91; oaths of office, 120; salt springs, 123, 124n; doorkeepers, 153n; establishment of customs districts, 164, 165n, 599, 600n; fortification of ports and harbors, 164, 309n; cabinet vacancies, 181-2; Ga. boundary, 183n; postal service, 191-2; taxes, 194n, 614n; public lands, 197-8, 373-4; agricultural societies, 200; jurisdiction of D.C., 239; appropriations for army, navy, 276-7, 280-1; marines, 277n, 308n; construction of frigates, 496n; De Grasse's pension, 519n;

INDEX

INDEX

INDEX

INDEX

INDEX

with Fenwick, 402, 402n; appointed justice of the peace, 674
Mason, John Thomson: letters from, 380, 508-11; recommends aspirants for office, 202, 380, 667; letter from cited, 203n, 686; as reference, 231, 341, 446, 540; appointed U.S. attorney, 238n, 312, 380n, 664, 671, 675; identified, 380n; sale of D.C. lots, 508-11
Mason, Jonathan, 102n, 118n
Mason, Stevens Thomson: as reference, 231n, 341, 446; relation to J. T. Mason, 238, 380n; recommends E. Jones, 667
Massac: customs district, 599, 600n, 670, 671, 676, 678, 683
Massachusetts: U.S. attorney for, 15, 16, 219, 245-6, 596, 672, 675, 677; lieutenant governor, 48n, 66n, 182n; governors, 56n, 182n, 520, 655; legislature, 56n, 66n, 520, 558; emigration from, 133; influence in Vt., 133; Federalists in, 167, 338, 442, 597, 655-6; midnight appointments in, 167; governor's council, 168n, 182n; presidential electors, 168n; Dedham, 252n; justices of the peace, 320n; Republicans in, 338, 442, 519-21, 558, 597, 598n, 655-6; and American Revolution, 366n, 377n, 571; elections in, 379, 520, 558, 597, 598n, 655-6; attorneys, 411-12; election of 1800, 442; prejudice against southerners, 473; marshal for, 596, 626, 628n; secretary of, 638; Salem and Beverly collection district, 670, 673; Gloucester customs district, 672; Newburyport collectorship, 672; Plymouth collectorship, 673. See also Boston
Massachusetts (ship), 474n
mastodon: skeleton sought for APS, 19-20, 511; remains discovered in Hudson Valley, 20n, 325, 327n, 511, 557, 608; called "mammoth," 199, 323-7, 608; distinct from the elephant, 199, 327n; teeth of, 199, 323-5, 497, 608, 609n; appearance of, 325; believed extinct, 325-6; TJ on, 326, 327n
Mather, Ralph: letter from, 467-9; seeks appointment, 467-9, 469n; letter from cited, 469n, 687
Mathers, James, 153n
Matlack, Timothy, 73n
Mattawoman Creek, 545-6

Matthieu, John S. M., 364, 365n
Mattoon, Ebenezer, 320n
Mauritius. *See* Île de France (Mauritius)
Maury, Fontaine, 3n
Maury, James, 266, 267n
Maxwell, George: appointed U.S. attorney, 183, 184n, 196n, 671, 676
Mayer, Jacob, 644, 667
Mazzei, Philip: letter to, 328-9; prints Italian version of inaugural address, 138; TJ's letter of 24 Apr. 1796, 229n; exchanges seeds, plants with TJ, 328; marriage of, 328; finances of, 328-9; TJ's correspondence with, 328-9
Meade, David, 311-12
Meade, Elizabeth Randolph, 311, 312n
Meade, Everard: candidate for office, 665; letters from cited, 667n, 691
Meade, George: letters from, 8-9, 367-8; supports TJ's election, 8-9; advises on appointments, 367-8
"Meal Tub Plot" (1679), 208, 209n
Mease, James, 381n
Mease, Sarah Butler: letter to, 454; letter from, 380-2; opposes Hall's removal, 381, 454; identified, 381-2n
Medical Repository (New York), 20n, 200n
medicine: physicians, 13n, 111, 288n, 381n, 395n, 407, 543n; pleurisy, 41; plague, 172n; medical schools, education, 288n. *See also* fever; yellow fever
Mediterranean Sea: navy squadron sent to, xi, 233, 298n, 597; vessels warned to stay out of, 365n
megalonyx, 200, 325-6, 327n
Memoirs of the Late Reverend Theophilus Lindsey (Thomas Belsham), 395n
Mendenhall, Thomas: letter from, 644-6; seeks appointment, 644-6; congratulates TJ, 646n; letter from cited, 646n, 685
Mennonites, 233n, 498n
Mentges, Francis: letter from, 161-2; accused of Federalist sympathies, 124; seeks appointment, 161-2; identified, 162n
Mercer, John F.: letter from, 217-19; family of, 10, 11n; advises on appointments, military affairs, 217-19
Meredith, Mr. (Philadelphia), 377
Meredith, Margaret Cadwalader (Mrs. Samuel Meredith), 547-8
Meredith, Samuel, 547-8, 670, 678
Merry, Anthony, 191n

insolence, 184-6; letters to, from cited, 186n; as congressman, 423n

Page, Margaret Lowther (Mrs. John Page), 423

Paine, Elijah, 15n, 113, 683

Paine, Thomas: letter to, 358-9; TJ sends news of personal and public affairs, viii, 358-9; sends packet to TJ, 21; *Common Sense,* 185; *Compact Maritime,* 185, 240-1, 358; "On the Jacobinism of the English at Sea," 185; offered passage in the *Maryland,* 358-9; seeks employment, 665

Palermo, Sicily, 363

Palfrey, William, 57, 226n

paper: from cornstalks, 104n; ruling machine, 104n; manufacture of, 195n, 497, 498n, 529n

Papin, Denis, 224n

Paradise Lost (John Milton), 185-6, 186n

pardons: granted by TJ, x-xi, 251-2, 309-10, 318n, 558-9n; petitions for, x-xi, 252n, 582-3; refused, 79, 80n

Paris: commercial agent at, 52, 173n, 420n, 672, 676; publishing in, 77n, 341n, 420n; building regulations in, 155n; Catholic Church in, 189-90n; schools, universities, 189-90n; booksellers, 339n; education, 408; post office, 469n; chargé d'affaires at, 617n; consul general at, 627, 667; banks, 649n

Parker, Isaac, 219, 377n

Parker, Thomas, 513, 514n

Parrott, Richard: letter from, 289-90; seeks appointment, 289-90; identified, 290n

Parsons, Enoch, 590, 591n, 677

Parsons, Theophilus, 15, 16, 671, 674

parties, political: criticism of, 8, 19, 201, 286, 289, 337-8, 341, 442; newspapers carry away party rage, 262

patents: on saddles, 104; on papermaking, 104n, 497; on steam engines, 166n; applications for, 214; on shipbuilding, 214n; on fireplaces and stoves, 222-4; on nailmaking machine, 435

Paterson, Cornelia Bell, 183, 184n

Paterson, William (N.J.), 183, 184n

Patriot (French schooner), 60n

Patten, William, 652n

Patterson, William (N.Y.), 672, 677

Patton, Robert, 78, 80n, 192, 194n

Paul I, Emperor of Russia: character of, 93; seeks compact with France, 561, 563n; death of, 616, 617n

Peace Establishment Act (1801): implementation of, vii, 292n, 527; officers retained, discharged under, 250n, 340n, 469, 475n, 545, 555n, 605, 606n, 647, 648n; terms of, 250n, 340, 598n, 606n; vessels sold under, 250n, 340n, 545, 605

peaches, 328

Peale, Charles Willson: letter to, 34-5; letter from, 221-4; forwards music to TJ, xlvii, 98n; sends lecture to TJ, 34; *Discourse,* 35n, 221; recommends Eckstein, 91n; plan for improving fireplaces, 221-4; lectures on natural history, 224n; receives premium from APS, 224n

Peale, Raphaelle, 224n

Peale, Rembrandt: letters from, 114, 433-4; portraits of TJ, x, xlvii, 34-5, 114, 433-4; seeks aid to study abroad, x, 433-4; writes lyrics, xlvii, 223, 224n; recommends Eckstein, 91n; *Apotheosis of Washington,* 245n

Peale, Titian Ramsey (1780-1798), 224n

Pearl River, 580

Peck, Henry, 91, 92n

Peck, William, 291

Penniman, Jabez, 125n, 672

Pennsylvania: western, 5; U.S. attorneys, 15, 207n, 219, 230, 392, 671, 674; legislature, 26, 28-9, 42n, 69n, 73n, 93, 94, 337n, 391, 431n; usurpation feared in, 26, 28, 391; election for U.S. Senate, 28-9; Federalists in, 28-9, 41, 71, 78-80, 106n, 207n, 523-4; Republicans in, 29, 69n, 73-4, 78, 95n, 105, 247n, 248, 317, 352n, 391, 539, 543n; supervisor for, 29n, 78, 179, 219, 237, 344n, 387n, 392, 410, 453, 523-4, 543, 612-13, 614, 665, 669, 670, 673, 676; Democratic Republican Society of Pennsylvania, 42n, 358n, 543n; treasurer, 69n, 72n; gubernatorial elections in, 71, 72n, 105, 247n; Lancaster Co., 71, 72-3n; and ratification of U.S. Constitution, 71, 73-4n, 80n; relocation of state government in, 71; Adams Co., 73n; comptroller-general, 73n, 212n; constitution of 1776, 73n; and election of 1800, 73n, 364, 391; Irish in, 73n, 80n; militia, 73n, 80n, 162n, 337n, 391; Presbyterians in, 73n, 80n;

INDEX

Treatise of Artillery (Heinrich Otto von Scheel), 211n
Trieste, 678
Trimble, James, 212n
Trinidad, 577n
Tripoli: threatens war against U.S., vii, 364, 551, 597-8; consul at, 364n, 551, 597-8; treaty with U.S., 364n; tribute paid to, 365n. *See also* Qaramanli, Yusuf, Pasha and Bey of Tripoli
Trist, Elizabeth House: letters from, 115-16, 273-4; congratulates TJ, 115-16, 273-4; letters to cited, 116n, 209n, 689, 690
Trist, Hore Browse, 641
Trist, Mary Brown, 116
Trojans, 268, 269n, 437, 438n
Trumbull, John: paintings of Warren and Montgomery, 244, 245n; advises Hadfield, 462, 463
Trump, Daniel: letter to, 35-6; letter from, 265; as reference, 18; asked to recommend housejoiner, 35-6; recommends Oldham, 265, 377; letter from cited, 687
Truth its own test and God its only judge (Stanley Griswold), 106
Truxtun, Thomas, 132n, 545, 546n, 598n
Tuck, William, 672
Tuckabatchee: U.S. Indian agency at, 110n
Tucker, St. George, 606
Tucker, Thomas Tudor: seeks appointment, 100, 186n, 422, 522-3, 666; appointed treasurer of the U.S., 423n, 670, 678; letter from cited, 690
Tudor, William, 225n, 597, 666
Tufts, Turell, 173n, 672, 677
Tunis: and Tripoli, 364n; dispatches from, forwarded, 551; treaty with U.S., 591, 592n; payments to, by U.S., 591-2; royal palace at, 592n; consul at, 670. *See also* Hammuda Bey (of Tunis)
Tunnicliff, William, 320n
Turner, Joseph, 673
turnpikes, 395n, 658-9
Tuscany: kingdom of, created, 406n
Tuscarora Indians, 677
Tyler, Samuel, 37, 126
Tyng, Dudley Atkins, 672
Tyrians, 268, 269n, 437, 438n

Union Hotel (Philadelphia), 227
Unitarian Church, 381n

UNITED STATES

Economy
trade with W. Indies, 60n, 68n, 467-8, 583n; encouragement of manufacturing, 85, 93, 168, 247n, 431n; as market for British manufactures, 93, 467-8; speculation in lands, 107n, 122n, 353n, 373-4, 480-2, 508-11, 521, 573n, 641n; imprisonment for debt, 121, 122n, 255-6, 377n; smuggling in, 164, 261, 582-3; trade with E. Indies, 248-9; baneful effects of commerce, 287-8; resumption of trade with France, 347, 615, 617n; trade with Sicily, 364, 586; promotion of viticulture, 431n; cloth market, 467-8; regulation of imports, 559n

Foreign Relations
Sayre proposes multinational agreement, 30-1; avoidance of entangling alliances, 85, 347-8, 390-1, 469n; defensive system to protect commerce, 85; protective duties, 85; should seek commercial reciprocity, 85; potential alliance with neutrality league, 88, 89, 94, 348, 390-1, 616; with Denmark, 93, 406n; need to promote free trade, 93; with Russia, 93; with Sweden, 93-4; with Batavian Republic, 94; with Prussia, 94; boundaries, 175-6, 372n, 622, 652; reduction of diplomatic establishment, 276; with Spain, 294, 295, 321-2, 382, 622, 623n; with Tunis, 591-2; regulation of foreign coins and currency, 683. *See also* Convention of 1800; France: U.S. Relations with; Great Britain: U.S. Relations with; State, U.S. Department of; Tripoli

Government
estimated cost of, 276; appropriations for, 682. *See also* Congress, U.S.; Courts, U.S.; Navy, U.S.; postal service; Treasury, U.S. Department of the; War, U.S. Department of

Public Finance
Gallatin's sketch of public finances, x, 275-81; repeal of internal taxes, x, 275, 276, 279; strict economy called for, x, 85, 280; opposition to liquor excise, 179; Dutch loan, 275; national public debt, 277-9; revenue

INDEX

UNITED STATES (*cont'd*)
estimates for 1801, 278; revenues
for 1800, 278; foreign debt, 279;
collection of duties interrupted by
war, 280; $5 million loan, 288,
289n; six percent stocks, 480, 510n.
See also Treasury, U.S. Department
of the

Public Opinion
asylum for oppressed people, 42

United States (U.S. frigate), 132n, 397
United States Almanack (Andrew
Ellicott), 582n
Upper Louisiana Territory, 51-2n
Urquijo, Mariano Luis de, 295n, 351

Vandegrift, Leonard, Sr.: letter from,
315-16; seeks appointment, 315-16
Van der Kemp, Francis Adrian,
497, 498n
Vandyke, Thomas J., 665
Van Mannierck, Anthony, 667, 668n
Vanmetre, John: letter from, 102-3;
letter from TJ published, 47-8,
102-3, 534n
Van Rensselaer, Jeremiah, 572, 573n
Van Staphorst & Hubbard, 329
Varden, Charles, 503-4n
Vardle, Susannah, 12n
Varnum, Joseph: and appropriations
for president's household, 23n;
carries letter to TJ, 320n; recommends Adams & Rhoades, 664, 666;
letter from cited, 689
Vasari, 631
Vaughan, Benjamin: letter to, 511; letter
from, 303-5; advises TJ on religion
and humility, 303-5, 511
Vaughan, John (Philadelphia): letter
from, 482-3; commissioner of
viticulture company, 431n; forwards
brother's letters, 482-3, 511n
Vengeance (French frigate), 647
Vermont: and election of 1800, 3, 4n,
16, 17n, 20, 130; U.S. district court,
15n; newspapers, 27; Middlebury,
111; physicians, 111; Republicans in,
111, 113, 125, 130, 442, 532-3; marshal for, 111-12, 219, 532-4, 587, 664,
666, 668, 673, 674; Royalton, 112;
Windsor Co., 112; Federalists in,
112-13, 125, 130, 533; gubernatorial
elections in, 112-13; legislature,
112-13, 130; Castleton, 113; Alburg
collectorship, 125, 672; supervisor,

125; U.S. attorney, 125, 219, 532-4,
668, 672, 674; churches, 131n;
militia, 131n, 536n; emigration from,
133. *See also* Bennington, Vt.
"Vermont Republican" (pseudonym):
letter from, 532-4; opposes appointments of Fay and Willard, 533-4
vetch, 328
Viar, Josef Ignacio de: letter from, 26;
congratulates TJ, 26; as Spanish
envoy, 654n
View of the Conduct of the Executive
(James Monroe), 335n, 412,
413n, 654n
Vincennes, 127n
Virgil: *Aeneid,* 269n

VIRGINIA

Constitution of U.S.
ratification of, 253n, 301n

Council of State
treatment of prisoners of war, 127n

Courts
meet at Rockbridge, 555; General
Court, 556n, 643n; state district,
556n; Court of Appeals, 586. *See
also* Potomac District

Description
poplar trees, 370, 370n

Economy
river transportation, 36, 50; taverns,
inns, 203, 204n, 256, 259-60, 315,
369, 445, 508n, 658, 659; merchants, 303n; turnpikes, 395n,
658-9; roads, 507-8, 642, 658-9. *See
also* Alexandria, Va.; Milton, Va.;
Norfolk, Va.; Richmond, Va.

Education and Science
academies, 205n

House of Delegates
members, 117n, 253n, 301n, 345n,
395n, 556n, 642n; speaker, 556n

Laws
land law of 1778, 373-4

Military
Continental regiments, 116, 117n;
and outstanding claims for supplying, 538n

Politics
TJ avoids appointing Virginians to
office, ix, 439; and election of 1800,

A comprehensive index of Volumes 1-20 of the
First Series has been issued as Volume 21.
Each subsequent volume has its own index,
as does each volume or set of volumes
in the Second Series.

THE PAPERS OF THOMAS JEFFERSON are composed in Monticello, a font based on the "Pica No. 1" created in the early 1800s by Binny & Ronaldson, the first successful typefounding company in America. The face is considered historically appropriate for The Papers of Thomas Jefferson because it was used extensively in American printing during the last quarter-century of Jefferson's life, and because Jefferson himself expressed cordial approval of Binny & Ronaldson types. It was revived and rechristened Monticello in the late 1940's by the Mergenthaler Linotype company, under the direction of C. H. Griffith and in close consultation with P. J. Conkwright, specifically for the publication of the Jefferson Papers. The font suffered some losses in its first translation to digital format in the 1980s to accommodate computerized typesetting. Matthew Carter's reinterpretation in 2002 restores the spirit and style of Binny & Ronaldson's original design of two centuries earlier.

✧